THE Sīrah OF THE Prophet

A Contemporary and Original Analysis

صلى الله عليه وسلم

DR YASIR QADHI

ADAPTED & EDITED BY: Dr Salah Sharief

THE ISLAMIC FOUNDATION

KUBE PUBLISHING

The Sīrah of the Prophet ﷺ:
A Contemporary and Original Analysis

Published by:
The Islamic Foundation
Markfield Conference Centre
Ratby Lane, Markfield, Leicestershire
L67 9SY, United Kingdom

Quran House, P.O. Box 30611, Nairobi, Kenya

PMB 3193, Kano, Nigeria

Exclusively Distributed by:
Kube Publishing Ltd.
Tel: +44 (0)1530 249230
e-mail: info@kubepublishing.com

3rd impression, 2024.

British Library Cataloguing-in-Publication Data

ISBN: 978-0-86037-873-0 Paperback
ISBN 978-0-86037-878-5 Hardback
ISBN 978-0-86037-883-9 Ebook

Cover Design: Jannah Haque
Proofreading and Editing: Wordsmiths (www.wordsmiths.org.uk)
Internal Concept Design and Layout: Jannah Haque
Typesetting: LiteBook Prepress Services
Internal Illustrations: Rakaiya Azzouz
Printed in Turkey by Elma Basim

Transliteration Key

Arabic Letter	Transliteration	Arabic Letter	Transliteration	Arabic Letter	Transliteration
ء	'	ز	z	ق	q
ب	b	س	s	ك	k
ت	t	ش	sh	ل	l
ث	th	ص	ṣ	م	m
ج	j	ض	ḍ	ن	n
ح	ḥ	ط	ṭ	ه	h
خ	kh	ظ	ẓ	و	ū
د	d	ع	ʿ	ي	ī
ذ	dh	غ	gh	ا	ā
ر	r	ف	f	ة	ah

Symbol	Arabic	English
ﷺ	صلى الله عليه وسلم	May peace and blessings be upon him.
﷾	سبحانه وتعالى	Hallowed and exalted.
	جل وعلا	Majestic and exalted.
﷿	عز وجل	Mighty and majestic.
﵁	رضي الله عنه	May Allah be pleased with him.
﵄	رضي الله عنهما	May Allah be pleased with them both.
﵃	رضي الله عنهم	May Allah be pleased with them (masculine).
﵂	رضي الله عنها	May Allah be pleased with her.
﵅	رضي الله عنهن	May Allah be pleased with them (feminine).
﵇	عليه السلام	Peace be upon him.
﵈	عليهم السلام	Peace be upon them (masculine).
﵍	عليها السلام	Peace be upon her.
﵀	رحمه الله	May Allah have mercy on him.

Contents

Part I: Introduction

Part II: Early Life

Part III: The Meccan Era

Part IV: The Medinan Era

Foreword

All praise be to Allah,
Who knows what the hearts conceal,
and what the tongues shall not reveal.
The One before Whom the believers kneel,
and on Judgement Day to Whom all shall appeal.
And may ṣalāh and salām be upon the one
to whom the Qur'an was revealed,
And whose Message and teachings cause
the hearts and souls to heal.

I began my studies at the Islamic University of Madinah in August of 1995. During my first semester of the Arabic programme, a teacher whose name I cannot recall—but whose face and manners are forever etched in my memory—first taught me the very basic outline of the *sīrah*. Although at this level of the Arabic Institute (or the "*Shuʿbah*" as we used to call it), the goal was not the academic study of the subject as much as learning the language. However, I will never forget one point that this teacher made, which forever resonated with me. "I was born and raised an orphan", he said, "...and only Allah knows how difficult life was for me, but hearing that the Prophet ﷺ was an orphan always gave me much comfort and courage to face the challenges of life."

I was twenty years old when I heard that phrase, and up until that point had never really *connected* with the Prophet ﷺ. Of course, there was immense love and reverence, but if I look back at that phase, my perception of him ﷺ was like a highly respected ancestor of whom you hear legends but have never met. Seeing this teacher feel a direct connection with him, and find inspiration for his life, stirred feelings in me that planted the seed to a life-long study, and which I am continuing to this day. I wanted to have that direct connection, and I wanted to be inspired by him in my daily life!

When I entered the Faculty of Hadith Studies at the University, we had the opportunity to take far more advanced classes on the *sīrah*, and I had the privilege of studying with erudite professors, many of whom were trained by, and had written dissertations under, the world-famous *sīrah* specialist from Iraq, Dr. Akram Ḍiyā' al-'Umarī. Sadly, he was no longer teaching in Medina when I arrived, but I did have the honor of meeting him at some conferences. That same year, Allah blessed me to make the acquaintance of someone who was to have a profound impact on my life: none other than Shaykh Ṣafī al-Raḥmān al-Mubarakpūrī (d. 2006), the author of *al-Raḥīq al-Makhtūm* (*The Sealed Nectar*), which was awarded the top prize in a global competition for the best modern book on *sīrah* organised in the late 1970s by the Muslim World League.

The Shaykh was a quiet and humble man living in Medina, and did not have many students. Somehow, and for a wisdom Allah knows, he agreed to give me private lessons in the Masjid of the Prophet ﷺ daily, and teach me *Ṣaḥīḥ al-Bukhārī*. He was my first Hadith teacher, and the first from whom I received *ijazah* (license to teach), but it is not because of my lessons in the *Ṣaḥīḥ* that I remember him. He was an encyclopedia of information, and he had a silent charisma and wry sense of humor of an elderly grandfather—you would know he was about to crack a joke by that peculiar smile and a twinkle in his eye! Frequently, our discussion over Imam al-Bukhārī's *Ṣaḥīḥ* would turn over to aspects of the *sīrah*.

Those were magical moments in my life that I cherish to this day. At the time, I had no idea of how blessed I was, sitting in al-Masjid al-Nabawī, with the greatest scholar of *sīrah* alive, reflecting over aspects of the Prophet's life that took place barely a few feet from where I was listening to them! Even as I write these lines, my eyes fill with tears recalling those joyous years and bygone memories...

One evening, as he was narrating some aspects of the *sīrah*, on the spur of the moment I begged him for one favour. I asked him if he could spend a morning with me (our lessons were between Maghrib and 'Ishā'), and take me around the city to see the sites of Medina where incidents of the *sīrah* took place. It was a bold request, for who was I to take up such valuable time of someone so esteemed as he!? But he readily agreed, and so one early morning on a beautiful spring day in the city of the Prophet ﷺ, I picked him up outside of al-Masjid al-Nabawī and we went around the city of Medina, to its outskirts to see Mt. ʿAyr and Thawr, to the site of the Battle of Uḥud and the Battle of the Trench, some famous wells that are mentioned in our books, and some other sites. What a wonderful day it was! Every single time I lead a *ziyārah* trip during the sightseeing tours of Medina that I frequently do with my Hajj and ʿUmrah groups—and especially as I climb on Jabal al-Rumāh where the archers stood with their backs to Mt. Uḥud—I recall that beautiful morning I spent with the Shaykh as I literally trace his footsteps and narrate to my audience the stories he told me. Sadly, that morning was one of the last times I would spend with him, for shortly afterwards, the Shaykh informed me that he had cancer and would not be able to teach anymore. He returned to his home in India, and after battling with the disease for a few years, passed away in December of 2006. Allah have mercy on Sh. Ṣafī al-Raḥmān for all that he taught me, and for the love of the *sīrah* he instilled in me.

My studies at the Islamic University lasted an entire decade, and I specialised at the undergraduate level in Hadith and its science, and at the graduate level in the development of early Islamic theology. Whilst my actual courses of study were not historical or *sīrah*-based, the passion and desire to study the *sīrah* afresh, and to analyse it from different angles and sources, remained in me throughout. Every time I would find a book on the topic, I purchased it, and my personal library of references on the *sīrah* slowly continued to grow. But alas…my studies did not allow me time to peruse them and benefit from them!

When I returned to America in early 2005, one of the masjids in my hometown of Houston, TX, approached me and asked if I wanted to start a regular weekly class in their masjid. The masjid (Synott Masjid) was one I had grown up praying *tarāwīḥ* in as a teenager. I readily agreed, and immediately told them that I wanted to start a class on the *sīrah*, but that I would only be in Houston for six months, as I would start my studies for my doctoral degree in Connecticut later that year. Thus, within days of returning from Medina, I found an excuse to start researching the *sīrah* again, and began my first actual class on the subject.

Within a few weeks, word spread across the city, and the attendance continued to grow, until the masjid became packed, and the parking lot full. One particularly amusing incident that I recall was when an elderly family friend, who had known me as a child, came up to me with a look of pride in his eyes, and referring to the crowd in the masjid, said: 'Your *ḥalaqah* has made this night like Ramadan!' But it was not I who brought such a crowd, rather it was the love of the *sīrah* in the hearts of the people that caused so many of them to come. This series was recorded on audio cassettes, and for a few years distributed in Houston, but unfortunately, I only managed to finish most of the Meccan timeframe before my studies forced me to discontinue and move away from Texas. Then, in New Haven, CT, I was again asked to start a series for the local masjid (Masjid al-Islam, where a few months before me Imam Zaid Shakir had been the Imam). And so once again I started teaching the *sīrah*, and this time made it to early Medina before I had to move away from Connecticut, on to my first job, as professor of religious studies at Rhodes College, in Memphis, TN. Hence, twice I started and stopped the *sīrah* because of my life's circumstances.

It was in Memphis where I also joined the newly formed masjid, the Memphis Islamic Center (MIC), as its resident scholar. It was a very beautiful phase of my life; my young children were growing up, and my jobs kept me busy, whilst I was surrounded by a vibrant and close-knit community of Muslims. At MIC, I had the opportunity to finally teach the *sīrah* from beginning to end, and it was with MIC's support and help that the series was recorded and uploaded onto YouTube.

My first lesson of the *sīrah* began on the last Wednesday of April, in 2011. Whilst I had already prepared notes from my previous two times of having taught the *sīrah*, I wanted to make this series even more comprehensive and analytical than any previous class I had taught. Hence, every Wednesday, from morning until Maghrib, I began my weekly routine. I would first read the original sources, starting with Ibn Hishām's *Sīrah*, and then peruse Ibn Saʿd's *Ṭabaqāt* and al-Wāqidī's

Maghāzī and other primary texts, then turn to the books of Hadith (and of course due to my studies in Hadith I had an extensive personal library). I would also consult the tidbits of the biographies found in such works like Ibn Ḥajar's *al-Iṣābah fī Tamyīz al-Ṣaḥābāh*, before moving on to the modern works of *sīrah* to see if they had any insights I could cull. Throughout all this research, I put on myself a few conditions:

Firstly, I would go wherever my own curiosity wandered. If I needed to explain why a certain practice was being done, or whether a particular Companion had other notable incidents, I would let my mind wander and research whatever I did not know. Time, for this series, was not important, and I did not care how many lessons it would take. I wanted to benefit *myself* before benefitting anyone else.

Secondly, I decided to teach at what I call an "intermediate-advance" level. A basic level, for me, would be something like *The Sealed Nectar*: a simple, chronological narrative from the beginning to end, with few references, and hardly any benefits extracted. That is ideal for a beginning student. An intermediate level would begin to discuss where the sources of each incident are found, and extract some practical benefits from every episode of the *sīrah*. And an extremely advanced level would require an encyclopedic effort of extracting each and every source of an incident, with an analysis of its chains of narrators, and then mentioning any controversies, and misunderstandings, along with an exhaustive extraction of its benefits. Such an "advanced level" project has not been done in any language, and frankly is a never-ending project (rather, it can be done for specific incidents, and an entire monograph can be written, for example, just about one particular incident).

By "intermediate-advance", therefore, I mean to indicate that my *sīrah* should reference all incidents to their primary sources, and derive benefits from every episode of the *sīrah*. It should also bring in more advanced nuances and discussion where applicable, such as the authenticity of narrations where required, and differences within the primary sources.

Thirdly, I put a strict condition on myself to *never* shy away from any controversial or easily misunderstood topic. When I was first taught the *sīrah* as an undergraduate, even I found some incidents difficult to comprehend. I felt a sense of frustration in how one could grapple with ethical or moral issues found in that time frame that we, in our generation, understand in a different way. It took me a while to come to terms with some easily misunderstood aspects, and when I did, my love for Islam and admiration for the Prophet ﷺ only increased. Upon returning to America and seeing how often Islamophobes misused incidents or brought up awkward narrations from our own sources, I decided that it made absolutely no sense to sugarcoat the truth. We have nothing to be ashamed about in the *sīrah*, and *if* something happened, it is our job to explain, contextualise, and understand the wisdom of it. If, of course, it did not happen, then our job is to explain why such narrations might be found in some works. It is far better for our youth to hear everything they need to hear from me, in the proper context, rather than having it presented to them in a cut-and-paste job out of context. There is no reason to censor our tradition and history.

Hence, I do feel a sense of fulfillment that my *sīrah* lectures—in contrast to almost all other works of a similar nature I have come across—actually delved into issues that are typically never discussed, or are glossed over or presented in a skewed manner.

This time, my circumstances allowed me to continue fairly uninterrupted for many years (except for Hajj, Ramadan, and summers), and so, after four years, and 104 lessons, the last episode was finally completed at MIC in March of 2015.

Since then, the series has gone viral online, and a number of people have transcribed it and even summarised it in other languages. I am humbled to see the feedback I receive wherever I travel around the globe, and I ask Allah to accept this modest effort, which is without a doubt tainted with faults and imperfections of my own.

Whilst the idea of converting my classes into book form was always in my mind, my other time commitments simply did not allow me the luxury of dedicating the amount of effort needed to undertake such a task. It was at this stage that Kube Publishing, with whom I had already published a few works, introduced me to the ever-capable Dr. Salah Sharief. Together, we brainstormed a vision of an editorial process that would be needed to convert my series into book form. The result of these efforts is now what is in your hands—may Allah reward the publisher and editor for their hard work in producing the printed form!

On a very personal and private note, I am writing these lines almost three decades after my first published book, and at a time when I am about to enter my fifth decade on this planet. In this duration, I have obtained multiple degrees, published over a dozen books, changed houses (and cities) around half a dozen times, started a family and raised four children, and have had the honour of seeing my parents grow wiser and eventually move in with me in my home. Whilst much has changed, it has been my family who has throughout all of this been my constant bedrock of support. I would not be here today had Allah not blessed me with the parents that He did, my patient and supportive life-partner whom He gifted me, and my children who are no longer children but have become young men and women who continue to instill in me a source of happiness and pride every day. It is to them that I dedicate this work.

I pray that Allah accepts this humble effort from me, and that He grants me the honour of the intercession of the Prophet ﷺ on Judgement Day!

O Allah! For a wisdom known to You, You have chosen for us
to be amongst those who never interacted with the Prophet ﷺ in this life.
Yā Rabb! We testify that we love Your Prophet ﷺ with our hearts and souls,
and so we pray and beg You that You not deprive us
of his companionship in the Afterlife!
O Allah! Allow us to be with Your Ḥabīb and
Muṣṭafā Muhammad ﷺ in Jannāt al-Firdaws.

Dr. Yasir Qadhi
Plano, Texas
1st Ramadan, 1444
(March 22, 2023)

Editor's Preface

This book provides an in-depth examination of the *sīrah,* delicately combining a chronological account of the life of the Prophet ﷺ with a contemporary analysis. Almost every page includes a reflection on the actions of the Prophet ﷺ and how they are relevant to our lives. The book is also unique in intertwining the Qur'an and *sīrah,* drawing out verses of the Qur'an and its relevance to the *sīrah*. After reading this book, the reader will have a deeper understanding of the Qur'an and, most importantly, the context upon which it was revealed.

With 1,184 references, this book is by far the most academically sound and thoroughly referenced work of *sīrah* in the English language. Most references are primary sources, consisting of Hadiths and Qur'anic verses, and the supplementary sources are almost all classical, relied-upon works on *sīrah*. It is, however, accessible to every anglophone Muslim; the style is easy to understand and the content flows naturally. I ask Allah ﷻ to make this book a reference point for every Muslim family to draw closer to Allah and His Messenger ﷺ.

Editor's Acknowledgements

It has been the greatest honour to dedicate a year of my life under the shade of the Prophet ﷺ. I would like to extend my heartfelt thanks to Shaykh Dr. Yasir Qadhi for producing such groundbreaking content in the English language, and I would like to thank Haris Ahmad and the team at Kube Publishing for facilitating its publication and allowing the wider Muslim community to benefit from this special work. I would also like to thank the Wordsmiths team for their stellar efforts in upholding the utmost standard of work. Finally, I would like to thank my beloved wife, Rakaiya Azzouz, for her endless patience and support.

Dr. Salah Sharief
Director, Wordsmiths

Style Guide

The Wordsmiths style guide has been used in this book, which employs British English. Foreign words that appear in the English dictionary (namely, Collins English Dictionary) are considered English words, such as Allah, Muhammad, Hajj, Hadith, hijab, and so on. As such, they are not italicised or transliterated. All other foreign words are italicised and transliterated with full diacritics, such as *dunyā, ākhirah, ḥamd, shukr, fiqh, sīrah,* and so on. Foreign names are transliterated with diacritics but are not italicised, such as ʿAlī ibn Abī Ṭālib and Abū Bakr al-Ṣiddīq. Transliterated words are not capitalised except if the grammar rule dictates e.g., a proper noun or the start of a sentence. Foreign words are defined in the first instance—either in parantheses or as a footnote—and the transliteration is used thereafter. Explanatory notes are marked with Roman numerals (i.e., i, ii, iii, iv) and are displayed via footnotes whereas references are marked with Western Arabic numerals (i.e., 1, 2, 3, 4) and are displayed via endnotes.

صلى الله عليه وسلم

May the peace and
blessings of Allah
be upon him.

PART

I

Introduction

About the Prophet ﷺ 1

Shamā'il

To truly delve into the life of our noble Prophet ﷺ, it is appropriate to first outline and discuss his unique characteristics, known as the *shamā'il*. Learning about the characteristics of the Prophet ﷺ provides motivation and builds desire to learn more about him; his teachings and morals, the incidents that occurred in his life, and the lessons therein.

It is impossible to do justice in describing the Prophet ﷺ when Allah ﷻ Himself said, "And We raised your remembrance."[1] Allah indeed raised up his remembrance such that whenever Allah ﷻ is mentioned, the Prophet ﷺ is mentioned immediately after. This is evidenced in the *shahādah*[i], the *adhān*[ii], the prayer, and the Qur'an itself.[2] Allah ﷻ Himself describes the Prophet ﷺ as a "mercy to all people"[3]. The Prophet ﷺ is the embodiment of mercy; he is the channel of Allah's

i The testimony of faith, which is: "I bear witness that there is no god except Allah, and I bear witness that Muhammad is the Messenger of Allah."

ii The call to prayer.

mercy, his sending is mercy, his Message is mercy, his teachings are mercy, believing in him is mercy, and implementing what he teaches is mercy. He is unequivocally everything associated with the word mercy. We therefore inevitably falter in our attempts to describe the noble Messenger ﷺ when Allah ﷻ praised him so highly.

The Prophet ﷺ had many names, some given to him by Allah ﷻ and some by his Companions. While names given by human beings are of benefit, the names given by Allah ﷻ provide the primary base upon which we can learn about him ﷺ. The Prophet ﷺ said, "I have a number of names: I am Muhammad; I am Aḥmad; I am al-Māḥī—the one by whom Allah erases disbelief; I am al-Ḥāshir—the one after whom people will be resurrected; I am al-ʿĀqib—the one after whom there will be no Prophet; I am The Prophet of Mercy; I am The Prophet of Repentance; I am al-Muqaffā—the one who completes a long chain [of Prophets]; and I am the Prophet of Malāḥim (Trials)."[4]

The name "al-Māḥī" is derived from the word *maḥā* which means "to wipe out". Al-Māḥī therefore means The Eraser [of Disbelief], and it is evidenced by the Prophet's impact on reducing disbelief in such a short frame of time. The name "al-Ḥāshir" refers to the Prophet's existence signalling the Day of Judgement. Indeed, the Prophet's coming is the first sign of the coming of the Day of Reckoning.[5] The name "al-ʿĀqib" is the Prophet's confirmation as the Final Messenger. The title "Prophet of Repentance" describes the Prophet ﷺ as being the source of repentance and the one whose teachings will result in people's repentance. The name "al-Muqaffā" describes the Prophet ﷺ sufficing the world of any other prophet. The statement, "I am The Prophet of Malāḥim (Trials)" is a warning for both believers as well as disbelievers who oppose him.

The above list of names given to the Prophet ﷺ are descriptive in nature, functioning more as adjectives. The only two proper nouns by which Allah ﷻ names the Prophet ﷺ are: Muhammad and Aḥmad. The name "Muhammad" is mentioned in the Qur'an four times,[6] and the name "Aḥmad" is mentioned once, which was via the tongue of Jesus Christ ﷺ.[7] Both "Aḥmad" and "Muhammad" are derived from the root word *ḥamd*. The closest English equivalent to the word *ḥamd* is "praise".

There is, however, a distinction to be made between *ḥamd* and "praise". *Ḥamd* is more accurately defined as a combination of "thanks" (*shukr*) and "praise" (*madḥ*). Being thankful to someone does not necessitate praise, and vice versa. For example, if somebody lends you money, you thank them, but may not necessarily praise them. Likewise, you may praise a talented athlete, but you are not thanking them *per se*. *Ḥamd* is given to an entity irrespective of what has been done to you. When we say *"alḥamdulillāh"*, it is because Allah is inherently worthy of being praised; even if we did not exist, He would still be worthy of praise ﷻ.

Both of his names ﷺ revolve around the word "praise"[iii] because Allah has praised him, the Angels have praised him, the Prophets have all praised him, and everyone on Earth has praised him. The Prophet ﷺ is praised in the Heavens and on the Earth; he was praised by previous nations and our current Ummah (nation); and he is praised in this life as well as the Hereafter. No human will exist who has been, is being, or will ever be praised more than our Prophet ﷺ. A single second does not pass without hundreds of millions of tongues and hearts praising him ﷺ. At any given moment throughout the 24 hours of a day, people around the globe are praying to Allah ﷻ and are thus praising the Prophet ﷺ and sending peace and salutations upon him. This is in addition to the millions of believers voluntarily sending peace and blessings upon him and giving lectures and reminders about him ﷺ.

The Prophet's ultimate praise is given by Allah. As for humanity's praise, it will culminate on the Day of Judgement. When all of humanity are desperate for Allah ﷻ to begin the Reckoning, they will rush to Adam ؑ and say, "O Adam, you are our father. Allah created you with His Hand and blew the *rūḥ* (soul) into you."[8] They will then beg him to ask Allah ﷻ on their behalf. Adam ؑ will excuse himself and say "Myself, myself" after explaining that he had lapsed[iv] and that he is not worthy for the task. He instead will instruct, "Go to someone else." The whole of humanity will go to Nūḥ ؑ and beg him to ask Allah ﷻ to begin the Reckoning. Nūḥ ؑ will also excuse himself, saying,

---

iii To be used synonymously with *ḥamd* in light of the preceding explanation.

iv Referring to eating from the forbidden tree in Paradise.

"I made a mistake which I should not have done. Allah instructed me not to ask anyone to be saved, but I asked Allah to save my son." He will then say, "Myself, myself. Go to someone else." Humanity will go to Ibrāhīm ﷺ with the same request, and Ibrāhīm ﷺ will respond, "I told three lies[v] and so I need to worry about myself. Go to someone else." Mūsā ﷺ will similarly excuse himself and cite that he killed[vi] someone. Humanity will flee to ʿĪsā ﷺ, who will in turn excuse himself and state, "I am not worthy." Eventually, the entirety of mankind will go to Muhammad ﷺ and beg him to intercede on their behalf to Allah ﷻ. As humanity's representative to Allah ﷻ, the Prophet ﷺ will respond, "This is my responsibility."[9] Mankind in its entirety—Muslims and non-Muslims alike—will praise him, and he will thus be raised to al-Maqām al-Maḥmūd: The Station of Praise.

The word "Muhammad" means "to be given continuous praise", and "Aḥmad" means "to be given the best type of praise". The former indicates quantity of praise while the latter indicates quality. They are both combined in our blessed Prophet ﷺ. This also explains why previous Prophets referred to our noble Prophet in different ways. Mūsā ﷺ refers to our Prophet as "Muhammad" because the Banū Isrāʾīl (The Children of Israel) were the largest nation before the Ummah of Muhammad ﷺ. As for ʿĪsā ﷺ, he refers to our Prophet as "Aḥmad" because his true followers were few in number but of the highest calibre of quality.

Khaṣāʾiṣ

The *khaṣāʾiṣ* are the unique and distinctive traits of the Prophet ﷺ. They include, but are not limited to, the following:

v All three "lies" are explained by the scholars of Islam as not being lies. The first instance refers to his claim that the big idol smashed the other idols. This statement was a rhetorical device designed to force the idolaters to introspect, and thus not a lie. The second instance was when he ﷺ claimed to be "sick" in order to avoid a trip, when in fact he was "sick" of the state of his people. Finally, the third instance was when he claimed that Sārah was his sister, and this too was not a lie, as she was his sister in Islam.

vi This incident was an accident and therefore not a sin.

1. He is the final Prophet. Allah ﷻ Himself states, "Muhammad is not the father of any of your men but is the Messenger of Allah and the Seal of the Prophets." [10]
2. The Prophethood of Muhammad ﷺ was decreed before Allah even blew the *rūḥ* into Adam ﷺ.
3. He ﷺ is the only human being upon which Allah ﷻ swore an oath (*qasam*).[vii]
4. He ﷺ is the only Prophet sent to the whole of humanity.[viii]
5. He ﷺ is the only Prophet sent directly to the jinn.[ix]
6. He ﷺ was granted the largest Ummah of all the Prophets.
7. He ﷺ was given the most powerful miracle—the Qur'an. It is the only scripture that is a miracle in and of itself.
8. He ﷺ was the only one raised up to the presence of Allah ﷻ via the Night Journey and Ascension (al-Isrā' wa al-Miʿrāj).
9. He ﷺ is the leader and master of all of humanity.
10. His grave ﷺ will be the first to be opened on the Day of Judgement.
11. He ﷺ will be the first to be resurrected on the Day of Judgement.
12. He ﷺ will be given the largest *ḥawḍ* (pool) in Paradise.
13. He ﷺ will be the first to cross over the Ṣirāṭ[x].
14. He ﷺ will be the first to knock on the doors of Paradise.
15. He ﷺ will be the first to enter Paradise.

---

vii Allah ﷻ states, "[I swear] by your life, they certainly wandered blindly, intoxicated [by lust]." (*al-Ḥijr*, 72).

viii It may be said: Adam ﷺ and Nūḥ ﷺ were also technically sent to the whole of humanity. The response is that this is a coincidence, i.e., they were sent to their people who just so happened to be the entirety of humanity. Muhammad ﷺ, on the other hand, was specifically sent to the entirety of humankind.

ix The jinn have believed in previous Prophets, such as Mūsā ﷺ. However, Mūsā ﷺ was not sent to the jinn—they believed in him after hearing his Message, but he was not sent to guide them. The Prophet ﷺ is the only Prophet sent directly to the jinn, which means there are jinn Companions. He ﷺ gave them *daʿwah* and taught them their religion.

x A bridge that every human must pass on the Day of Judgement before entering Paradise. Those who fall will enter the Hellfire, and people's ability to cross will be determined by their deeds in this life.

16. His name ﷺ is the only name for whom the gates of Paradise will be opened.

17. He ﷺ will receive the highest level of Paradise—an entire level in its own right.

His Physical Appearance

It is from the Sunnah—the custom—of Allah ﷻ to send down Prophets and Messengers with the most perfect characteristics, both inner and outer. The Prophets ﷺ not only had beautiful characteristics and mannerisms, but they were all handsome in nature. Yūsuf ﷺ alone was said to have had "half of all beauty".[11] The predominant view amongst scholarship is that this refers to half of the beauty of mankind in its entirety. There is, however, another scholarly opinion that states that this refers to half of the beauty of our Prophet Muhammad ﷺ.[12]

Al-Rubayyiʿ bint Muʿawwidh ﵂ was asked about the appearance of the Prophet ﷺ, and all she could say was, "My son, if you could have seen him, you would have thought that the Sun had risen up."[13] In a perfect juxtaposition, Kaʿb ibn Mālik ﵁ described him ﷺ as the Moon, "Whenever the Prophet ﷺ was happy, his face would light up as if it were the full Moon."[14] Likewise, Jābir ibn Samurah ﵁ said, "I saw the Prophet ﷺ walking one night and beside him was a full Moon. By Allah, he was more beautiful in my eyes than the full Moon."[15] ʿAmr ibn al-ʿĀṣ ﵁—once a staunch opposer[xi] of Islam—said, "There was nothing more beloved to me than to stare at the face of the Prophet ﷺ, and I would never suffice myself from looking at him. However, were you to ask me how to describe him, I could not, as I would lower my gaze out of awe."[16]

---

xi   A noteworthy point can be made here about different types of opposition within the Quraysh. Some opposed the Prophet ﷺ and did so by employing dirty and unsavoury tactics. There were others, however, that were in opposition but within limits and with dignity. Allah ﷻ eventually guided all of the latter, which included Khālid ibn al-Walīd, ʿIkrimah ibn Abī Jahl, ʿAmr ibn al-ʿĀṣ, and Abū Sufyān, amongst other notable figures in Islam ﵏.

Anas ibn Mālik 🙵 was introduced to the Prophet 🙵 at the age of seven after his mother gifted him to the Prophet 🙵 as a helper. Through this blessing of a relationship, we are relayed the most explicit description of our noble Prophet 🙵, "The Prophet 🙵 was neither very tall such that he stood above a crowd, nor was he short such that he would be overlooked. He 🙵 was not extremely yellow [xii] nor dark brown. His hair was not in curls nor was it completely straight. I have not felt any velvet or silk softer than his hair, nor have I smelled musk or perfume more fragrant than the Prophet 🙵." [17]

ʿAlī ibn Abī Ṭālib 🙵 said, "The Prophet 🙵 did not have a very fleshy face, nor was it completely round. He had a white face with a red tinge (i.e., tanned). His eyes were large with jet-black pupils, and his lashes were long. His joints were large, as was his upper back. He was not hairy all over his body, but he did have a fine line of hair extending from his chest to his navel. When he walked, he did so briskly, as if he were descending a slope. When he turned to face you, he would turn with his whole body. Between his two shoulders was the Seal of Prophethood. [xiii] Whoever unexpectedly saw him would stand in awe of him. Whoever accompanied him and befriended him, loved him. I have never seen anyone before him or after him, like him." [18]

His Character

ʿUmar ibn al-Khaṭṭāb 🙵 once walked in on the Prophet 🙵 in his room adjoined to The Prophet's Mosque (Masjid Nabawī). There was nothing inside except a jug of water and a bed made from date palm branches. The Prophet 🙵 had been lying down when ʿUmar 🙵 walked in and so

---

xii   The Arabs in the 7ᵗʰ century AD would describe someone as "yellow" whom a 21ˢᵗ century audience would describe as "white". They referred to the Romans as "Banū al-Aṣfar (The Yellow People)". Likewise, what the Arabs would refer to as "white" a 21ˢᵗ century audience would refer to as "tanned". The tone of the Prophet 🙵, like that of most of his tribe, was a wheatish-brown complexion.

xiii   A physical mark on his body that was given as a sign of his Prophethood. It is described as an outgrowth of hair of a different colour shaped like a small oval (akin to a pigeon's egg).

he got up to greet him, revealing the marks on his back ﷺ from the harsh material. ʿUmar wept at the sight of these marks and exclaimed, "O Messenger of Allah, look at the Roman and Persian leaders and how they live; don't you deserve better as the Messenger of Allah?" The Prophet ﷺ rebuked ʿUmar, "Aren't you happy that they have the *dunyā* (this life) and we have the *ākhirah* (the Hereafter)?"[19] When his wife ʿĀ'ishah once softened his bed, the Prophet ﷺ slept longer than usual and missed *tahajjud* (the night prayer) as a result. When he woke up, he asked what happened and requested that it be changed back.[20]

ʿĀ'ishah would recall that the Prophet ﷺ would, at times, not taste meat for up to six weeks. Upon hearing this, a young Successor (Tābiʿī)[xiv] enquired curiously, "How did you live?" To which she replied, "We sufficed on the two black things (i.e., dates and murky water)."[21] Many years later, ʿAbdurraḥmān ibn ʿAwf was offered a platter of meat and bread, to which he cried and said, "Until his death, the Prophet ﷺ never ate wheat bread to his fill. And I worry that Allah allowed us to remain [on this Earth] to witness these blessings whereas the Prophet ﷺ has returned to something greater (i.e., he is being rewarded in the Hereafter instead)."[22]

One day, ʿUmar was walking and saw the Prophet ﷺ sitting outside in the middle of the day. ʿUmar asked, "O Messenger of Allah, what are you doing outside at this time of day?"[xv] The Prophet ﷺ replied, "I am here for the same reason as you: I have nothing to eat at home." Abū Bakr then walked by, asked the same question, and received the same answer. Another Companion, Abū al-Haytham, was rushing home from work and saw the blessed trio and asked them the same question. ʿUmar replied that they did not have any food at home, so they went for a walk instead. Abū al-Haytham protested at the noblest three people standing in the heat out of hunger, so he invited them to eat. He returned home and saw that he had an old goat, so he said to

xiv The generation after the Companions (Ṣaḥābah) of the Prophet ﷺ, referred to as the Successors (Tābiʿūn).

xv Due to the extreme heat, it was very abnormal to be outside in the middle of the day. It was thus custom (and Sunnah) to take a midday siesta.

his wife, "By Allah, we must sacrifice this goat."[23] Abū al-Haytham ؓ then served the three of them meat and bread, and the Prophet ﷺ reminded Abū Bakr and ʿUmar ؓ that they left their houses hungry only to be fed by Allah ﷻ. He then quoted the verse of the Qur'an, "Then, on that Day, you will definitely be questioned about [your worldly] pleasures."[24]

His humility in character was also narrated by those closest to him. As the timeless maxim states: a person is known by how they treat their family. Anas ibn Mālik ؓ said, "I served the Prophet ﷺ for ten years, and not once did he ﷺ say as much as *'uff'*[xvi] to me."[25] Anas ؓ narrates that on one occasion, the Prophet ﷺ sent him to run an errand. Anas, being a young boy at the time, got distracted on the way and began playing with children on the street. After a while, the Prophet ﷺ noticed the delay and searched for Anas, finding him in play. Anas ؓ recalled, "I felt someone behind me picking me up by my ears. I turned around and saw the Prophet ﷺ smiling at me."[26]

His humility and dignity extended to his enemies. Once, a Jewish leader visited the Prophet ﷺ and said, *"al-sāmmu ʿalaykum"*. It was a play on words with the Islamic greeting of *"al-salāmu ʿalaykum"* except the former means "may death be upon you" as opposed to "may peace be upon you". The Prophet ﷺ maintained his composure and simply said, *"wa ʿalaykum"* (and to you too). ʿĀ'ishah ؓ was so furious that she shouted, "May Allah curse you, and may He cause you to perish! How dare you say that to the Prophet?!" The Prophet ﷺ reprimanded her and said, "Calm down, O ʿĀ'ishah. Don't you know that whatever is gentle is beautiful, and whenever gentleness is in something, it makes it beautiful, and whenever harshness is in something, it makes it ugly?"[27]

The Prophet ﷺ was a man of the people. A female Companion said, "It was possible for any little girl to grab the hand of the Prophet ﷺ and ask him to do any chore for her."[28] He ﷺ would also joke with his Ummah, but only with innocent jokes free from lies. When an elderly

---

xvi An expression of discontent.

lady asked the Prophet ﷺ about Paradise, he ﷺ replied, "Haven't you been informed that old ladies cannot enter Paradise?" As she began to cry and wail, the Prophet ﷺ interrupted her and clarified, "Don't cry. By Allah, old ladies cannot enter Paradise because Allah will first make them into young maidens and *then* enter them into Paradise."[29] He was sincere, approachable, and compassionate; yet strong, courageous, and dependable ﷺ.

Setting the Scene

2

Benefits of Studying the *Sīrah*

The word *sīrah* stems from the verb *sāra—yasīru,* which means "to traverse". It is commonly translated as "biography" because the reader travels the path of that person, following in their footsteps. The word *sīrah,* linguistically speaking, may be used for the biography of any person, but since the passing of the Prophet Muhammad ﷺ, the word—when used in Islamic literature—is understood to be exclusively for him ﷺ.

Allah ﷻ commands us throughout the Qur'an to take the Prophet ﷺ as our example and model. The Qur'an states, "Indeed, in the Messenger of Allah you have a perfect example for whoever has hope in Allah and the Last Day, and remembers Allah often."[30] The study of the life and times of the Prophet ﷺ is therefore not only an obligation but a source of benefit and guidance in every facet of our lives. This is not limited to ritualistic aspects of religion but extends to our work, marriage, family life, and social life. Allah ﷻ states, "Had Allah willed, He could have easily sent down Angels instead."[31] Instead, in His infinite wisdom, He sent human beings—our own flesh and blood—as carriers of His Message for us to relate to and aspire to emulate.

Studying the *sīrah* is a marker for one's relationship with the Prophet ﷺ as well as the primary way to increase one's love for him ﷺ. We cannot claim to love someone or something yet know very little about them. A sign of loving someone is to yearn to know more about them. Neglecting the *sīrah* of our beloved Prophet ﷺ is therefore a strong indication of an absence of love for him. Studying the life of the Prophet ﷺ in turn increases one's love for him, producing a cycle of love and learning; the more we study, the more we love.

The *sīrah* provides the context upon which the Qur'an was revealed. Familiarity with the *sīrah* is therefore a prerequisite to understanding the Qur'an. It also outlines the methodology and blueprint for any nation's revival. Allah ﷻ even mentions in the Qur'an that He relays the stories of the previous Prophets to Prophet Muhammad ﷺ to strengthen his resolve. "And We relate to you [O Prophet] the stories of the Messengers to reassure your heart."[32] The Prophet's *īmān* (faith) would only increase upon hearing about the previous Messengers and Prophets ﷺ. It is only befitting for us to increase our *īmān* by learning about the life of the Prophet ﷺ—we are surely in greater need.

An oft-overlooked aspect of the *sīrah* is that it is a *bona fide* miracle. There is no particular event that grants the *sīrah* its miracle status; the entire *sīrah*, start to finish, is a miracle. The context by which the Prophet ﷺ emerged from a largely illiterate and disorganised tribal setting to conquer large swathes of the world in such an impossibly short space of time is nothing short of a miracle. Imam Ibn Ḥazm ﷺ aptly states, "By Allah, if the Prophet ﷺ wasn't given any miracle other than his life and times, it would have been sufficient to prove that he was a Prophet from God."[33]

The earliest generations in Islam would teach the *sīrah* just as they would the other Islamic sciences. ʿAlī ibn al-Ḥusayn—the great grandson of the Prophet ﷺ said, "We would teach our children the *maghāzī* (expeditions of the Prophet ﷺ) just like we would teach them the Qur'an."[34] The *sīrah* provides an insight into the lives and conduct of the best generation to ever live: the Ṣaḥābah (Companions) of the Prophet ﷺ. It is set in the most blessed locations in the world,

Mecca and Medina. It can therefore be said to be the best of the best of the best: the best man ﷺ amongst the best nation in the best location.

Primary Sources of the *Sīrah*

The foremost source when researching the *sīrah* is the Qur'an. The Qur'an was revealed during the *sīrah* and thus addresses the events that occurred within the Prophet's life. It references every major incident that occurred during his Prophethood. The Qur'an is the speech of Allah ﷻ which guarantees its veracity. Moreover, its divine nature grants the additional benefit of disclosing the Unseen. The Qur'an and *sīrah* comprise a perfect partnership; the *sīrah* is required to understand and contextualise the Qur'an, and the Qur'an is needed to reference the *sīrah*.

The second prominent source of the *sīrah* is Hadith. A Hadith is a narration reporting the speech, action, or tacit approval of the Prophet ﷺ, and so individual Hadiths can be viewed as snapshots of the *sīrah*. Most relied-upon Hadiths are located in the Six Canonical Books of Hadith (al-Kutub al-Sittah).[i] The third source of the *sīrah* is books written specifically for the *sīrah*, the first of which were written by the children of the Companions, starting with ʿUrwah ibn al-Zubayr. ʿUrwah's father was a Companion; his mother was a Companion; his grandfather and grandmother were both Companions; his brother was a Companion, and his aunt was a Companion—none other than ʿĀ'ishah ؓ, the daughter of Abū Bakr al-Ṣiddīq ؓ, wife of the Prophet ﷺ and Mother of the Believers[ii]. As a result of this blessed heritage, he was one of the primary narrators of Hadith, *fiqh* (jurisprudence), *tafsīr* (exegesis), and *sīrah*. This was largely due to his familial relation to ʿĀ'ishah ؓ, which gave him unrestricted access to the wife of the Prophet ﷺ and thus a plethora of information on the household of the Prophet ﷺ.

i They are: Ṣaḥīḥ al-Bukhārī, Ṣaḥīḥ Muslim, Sunan al-Tirmidhī, Sunan Abū Dāwūd, Sunan al-Nasā'ī, and Sunan Ibn Mājah.

ii An honorific title given to the wives of the Prophet ﷺ.

Abbān, the son of ʿUthmān ibn ʿAffān[iii] ﷺ, also wrote a booklet on the *sīrah*. Other children of the Companions also wrote their own booklets. Ibn Shihāb al-Zuhrī then wrote one of the first treatises of *sīrah*. The aforementioned books no longer exist because they were absorbed by the books written in the following generation, who compiled multiple texts to create a comprehensive account of the Prophet's life ﷺ.

Muhammad ibn Isḥāq (d.150 AH[iv]) then authored the greatest and most comprehensive work in *sīrah*, producing a chronological account of the Prophet's life ﷺ. Ibn Isḥāq lived in Medina alongside the children and grandchildren of the Companions ﷺ. He travelled to other major cities such as Basra and Kufa to compile the narrations of other significant Companions such as that of Ibn Masʿūd ﷺ. Ibn Isḥāq's *sīrah* was also significant because it included the *isnād* (chain of narrators) for each narration.

The concept of *isnād* is a phenomenon unique to Islamic history; it is the practice of compiling each and every person who retold a story up until the individual from whom it was first narrated. This practice adds a level of authenticity and veracity that cannot be found in any other culture, which leaves the historiography of Islamic history incomparable. Ibn Isḥāq's *sīrah* was so extensive that it was difficult for people to copy and duplicate by hand, so another scholar named ʿAbd al-Malik ibn Hishām (d.213 AH) summarised the text into one half, or one third of the size. While Ibn Isḥāq began from the time of Prophet Adam ﷺ, Ibn Hishām began his abridged version from the time of the Prophet ﷺ.

Other primary sources of the *sīrah* include books written about the characteristics of the Prophet ﷺ (*shamā'il*); books written about proofs of his Prophethood ﷺ (*dalā'il*); and general history books of Mecca and Medina.

iii The third Caliph of Islam and close confidant of the Prophet ﷺ.

iv From the Latin "Anno Hegirae" i.e., "In the year of the Hijrah (Emigration of the Prophet ﷺ)".

Origins of Arabia

Every book of *sīrah* must begin from the pre-Islamic era in order to properly set the scene for the Prophethood of Muhammad ﷺ. In the 21st century, the "Arab world" is vast, spanning over 22 countries throughout Western Asia, Northern Africa, Western Africa, and Eastern Africa. However, most modern Arabs have been "Arabised" over time through migration, assimilation, and language. At the time of the Prophet ﷺ, the Arabs could trace their lineage back to specific names. There are two categories of classical Arabs: al-ʿArab al-Bāʾidah (The Perished Arabs) and al-ʿArab al-Bāqiyah (The Remaining Arabs).

Al-ʿArab al-Bāʾidah are extinct. They are the earliest civilisation of humanity in the Arabian Peninsula. They existed before the land was even referred to as "Arabia". The Qurʾan references them when relaying the stories of ʿĀd and Thamūd.[35] Modern archaeological evidence suggests that Thamūd flourished circa 3,000–5,000 BC. The historian Ibn Khaldūn stated that these peoples fled from the ancient city of Babylonia and settled in the area now known as Arabia.[36]

Al-ʿArab al-Bāqiyah are still in existence. They are comprised of two subgroups: Qaḥṭān and ʿAdnān. Qaḥṭān is considered the father of the Arabs. The word Arab is linguistically derived from his son, Yaʿrab (or Yaʿrib). Most scholars opine that Qaḥṭān's lineage extends to Nūḥ ﵇ through his son, Sām, father of the Semites.[37] A second minority opinion is that Qaḥṭān is also a direct descendent of Ibrāhīm ﵇,[38] and a third opinion is that Qaḥṭān is descended from Hūd ﵇.[39] The Qaḥṭānīs are known as al-ʿArab al-ʿĀribah (The Original Arabs).

ʿAdnān is the ancestor of our Prophet Muhammad ﷺ. He is the descendent of Ismāʿīl ﵇, son of Ibrāhīm ﵇, who originated from Iraq. Ismāʿīl ﵇ married into the Qaḥṭānīs and began speaking their language, which began the integration of his bloodline with the Arabs. ʿAdnān then emerged a few generations later, and the Arab tribes flowed from ʿAdnān. ʿAdnānī Arabs are thus known as al-ʿArab al-Mustaʿribah (The Arabised Arabs) because they acquired Arabic from the Qaḥṭānīs via Ismāʿīl ﵇. The Arabised Arabs settled in central Arabia and as a result interacted the most with nearby Arabian tribes, thus becoming more proficient in Arabic than the Original Arabs. The scholars of genealogy unanimously agree that the Prophet Muhammad ﷺ is the 20th grandson of ʿAdnān.[40]

Pre-Islamic Arabia

Concepts are often understood and appreciated by analysing their opposites. Light is appreciated after experiencing darkness, heat after cold, and so on. Delving into Jāhiliyyah (Pre-Islamic Arabia, referred to as The Age of Ignorance) allows us to further appreciate and internalise the blessing of Islam.

The Qur'an affirms that a Prophet has been sent to every nation, "There is no community that has not had a warner."[41] The Prophets sent to the Arabs were Ibrāhīm ﷺ and Ismāʿīl ﷺ. Ibrāhīm ﷺ sanctioned many practices that have continued until our time. He ruled Mecca to be Ḥaram (Sacred), which shares the same root as the word haram (*ḥarām*—forbidden). It is a sanctuary where some ordinarily halal (*ḥalāl*—permissible) acts are deemed haram, such as hunting game, cutting down trees, and so on. Ibrāhīm ﷺ built and venerated the Kaʿbah. He instituted the four sacred months[v] where all hostilities are ceased, and he instituted the Hajj pilgrimage with all its rituals.

The person who first altered the religion of Ibrāhīm ﷺ and introduced Paganism was ʿAmr ibn Luḥayy al-Khuzāʿī. The Prophet ﷺ said, "I saw ʿAmr ibn Luḥayy al-Khuzāʿī wandering around in the fire of Hell with his entrails cut open behind him. He was the first to alter the religion of Ismāʿīl."[42] ʿAmr ibn Luḥayy travelled to the Pagan Amalekites in Syria and returned to Mecca with an idol named Hubal, and thus Paganism was born in Mecca.

Vital lessons can be derived from this deeply consequential event. The Amalekites were notoriously powerful, and they attributed their power

v They are: Dhū al-Qaʿdah, Dhū al-Ḥijjah, Muḥarram, and Rajab.

and dominance to their idols and their Paganism. ʿAmr ibn Luḥayy's inferiority complex led him to yearn to emulate their apparent success and in turn destroyed his nation's faith. The lesson here is that technological or infrastructural advancements do not necessarily equate to moral or ethical correctness. Secondly, ʿAmr ibn Luḥayy was the Chieftain of the tribe of Khuzāʿah, one of the most respected Chieftains of Arabia. It demonstrates how scholars and influential figures can have a profound impact on their community, whether positive or negative.

After the introduction of the idol Hubal, idol worship began to proliferate. Pieces of stone from the Kaʿbah would be taken as mini-idols and worshipped when travelling. It is pertinent to note that Muslims do not believe in the sanctity of the materials used for the Kaʿbah; they are merely bricks and clay. Rather, Muslims believe in the sanctity of the location. Neither the marble floor nor the clay structure or silk cloth of the Kaʿbah hold any sacred value in Islam. Abū Rajā' al-ʿUṭāridī ﵁ narrated, "Before the advent of Islam, we used to worship rocks and stones, and if we found a rock more beautiful than the other rock we were worshipping, we would throw the first rock and replace it with the new one. If we were travelling and did not have a rock, we would collect a pile of sand, use milk from a goat to make the sand firm, and perform *ṭawāf* (circumambulation) around the structure."[43] When the Prophet ﷺ conquered Mecca, there were around 360 idols in and around the Kaʿbah.[44] Some were in the shape of humans, some were in the shape of animals, but most were half-human, half-animal structures. The Quraysh also had the theology that Allah had Angel daughters, so they also worshipped Angels as the daughters of God.

It is worth noting that the Pagans of Arabia believed in Allah ﷻ and did not have an idol for Him. While some forms of Paganism worship an idol as their ultimate god, Arab Paganism did not depict Allah, as they knew that He ﷻ could not be represented by an idol. The Qur'an notes, "If you ask them who created the Heavens and the Earth and subjected the Sun and the Moon [for your benefit], they will certainly say, 'Allah!' So how can they be deluded [from the truth]?"[45] However, when asked why they worship idols when they believe in Allah, they say, "We worship them only so they may bring us closer to Allah."[46]

The Qur'an further states, "They worship besides Allah others who can neither harm nor benefit them, and say, 'These are our intercessors with Allah.'"[47] They did, however, attribute a level of divinity to these idols, believing them to be lesser gods in comparison to Allah ﷻ. They believed in the divinity of Allah ﷻ but viewed Him as "too holy" thus requiring intermediaries.

There were, however, a group of people referred to as the Ḥunafā', meaning "those who turn away" i.e., turning away from *shirk* (polytheism) and towards *tawḥīd* (Oneness of Allah). Four prominent Ḥunafā' were: Waraqah ibn Nawfal, 'Ubaydullāh ibn Jaḥsh, 'Uthmān ibn al-Ḥuwayrith, and Zayd ibn 'Amr. They made a pact to search for the true religion of Ibrāhīm ﷺ in the form of Ḥanīfiyyah. Another significant Ḥanīf (singular of Ḥunafā') was Quss ibn Sāʿidah al-Iyādī, who used to preach against idolatry. Ḥanīfiyyah was the closest thing to Islam during those times.

Prophetic Lineage ﷺ

There is no verified information about the lineage between Adam ﷺ and Ismāʿīl ﷺ. There are a handful of opinions regarding the lineage between Ismāʿīl ﷺ and 'Adnān, but none of them have authentic sources to verify their claims. Modern archaeology dictates that homo sapiens have existed for tens of thousands of years at least. Credible scientific evidence even suggests over one hundred thousand years. Islamic creed need not reject this, as we do not have textual basis to argue the contrary. A Hadith states that Allah ﷻ created the children of Adam, and Adam ﷺ saw a bright light amongst his children. He ﷺ asked, "Who is this, O Allah?" and Allah responded, "This is your son, Dāwūd, who shall live towards the end of times."[48] If Dāwūd ﷺ, who lived thousands of years before the time of Muhammad ﷺ, is considered to have lived towards the end of time, then it is reasonable to assume that humanity has lived for much longer than a few thousand years.

The lineage of the Prophet Muhammad ﷺ to 'Adnān is, in contrast, well documented and without controversy. It is as follows:

Muhammad ibn ʿAbdullāh ibn ʿAbd al-Muṭṭalib ibn Hāshim ibn ʿAbd Manāf ibn Quṣayy ibn Kilāb ibn Murrah ibn Kaʿb ibn Luʾayy ibn Ghālib ibn Fihr[vi] ibn Mālik ibn al-Naḍr ibn Kinānah ibn Khuzaymah ibn Mudrikah ibn Ilyās ibn Muḍar ibn Nizār ibn Maʿd ibn ʿAdnān.

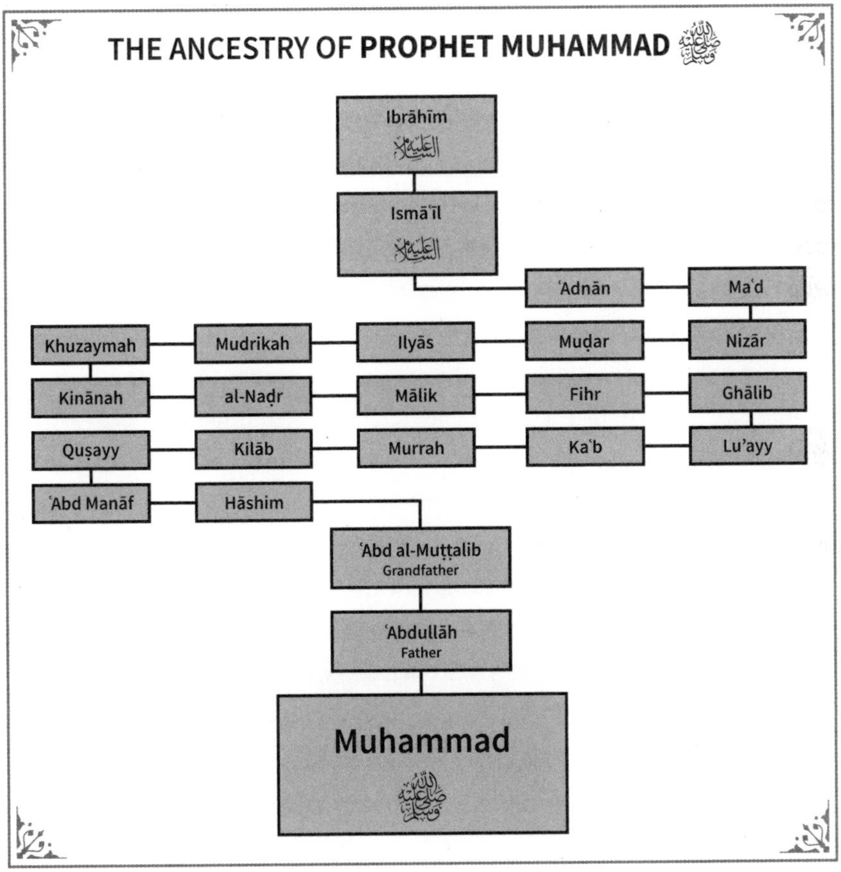

The Prophet ﷺ stated, "Allah chose Kinānah from all of the descendants of Ismāʿīl, and He chose the Quraysh from Kinānah, and He chose Banū Hāshim from the Quraysh, and He chose me from Banū Hāshim."[49] The Prophet's lineage ﷺ is therefore the most noble lineage to exist.

vi Fihr is the founder of "the Quraysh".

Quṣayy propelled the success of the Quraysh and is thus referred to as "The Small Quraysh". He wrestled back power in Mecca from the tribe of Khuzāʿah into the lineage of the Quraysh. Quṣayy married the daughter of the Chieftain of Khuzāʿah and demonstrated his prowess above the sons of Khuzāʿah, which gained him notoriety and respect. He leveraged this position to gain internal support and claimed Mecca for the Quraysh. He also founded the Dār al-Nadwah (parliament) of Mecca as well as the tradition of caring for and accommodating the pilgrims of Hajj.

Hāshim's name was ʿAmr, but he would grind (*hashama*) barley for the Hajj pilgrims and thus became known as Hāshim (The Grinder) due to his generosity. After a deadly drought, he was responsible for the economic success of the Quraysh after founding the idea of the bi-yearly trade routes to Rome in the summer, and Yemen in the winter. The Qur'an references this in Sūrah Quraysh, "For [the favour of] making the Quraysh secure—secure in their trading caravan [to Yemen] in the winter and [Syria] in the summer—let them worship the Lord of this Sacred House, Who fed them against hunger and made them secure against fear." [50]

ʿAbd al-Muṭṭalib's name was Shaybah al-Ḥamd. *Shaybah* means "grey hair" and *ḥamd* means "praise". He was born with some grey hair and thus he was called "grey hair of praise". As his father died when ʿAbd al-Muṭṭalib was a child, he was raised amongst his mother's tribe in Yathrib (later to be renamed "Medina"). When he was brought into Mecca as a young boy riding with his uncle, Muṭṭalib, people assumed he was his slave and said, "There is ʿAbd al-Muṭṭalib (the slave of Muṭṭalib)" and the name stuck. ʿAbd al-Muṭṭalib was famous for a number of reasons, one of which was his rediscovering of the well of Zamzam[vii]. Hundreds of years prior, the well of Zamzam was buried, and it was lost ever since. ʿAbd al-Muṭṭalib had a recurring dream

---

vii   A miraculous well situated in Mecca which appeared after Hājar was left with her son Ismāʿīl 🕮 in a scorching and desolate desert. The water began to spout forth from the ground and continued to pour, marking the beginning of a civilisation in the previously barren Mecca. (Bukhārī, *Ṣaḥīḥ al-Bukhārī*, pp. 828–830).

about its location and would not stop receiving the dream until he took his son and began digging until he struck water.[51] He grew to be a source of pride and joy for the Quraysh.

ʿAbdullāh was the son of ʿAbd al-Muṭṭalib, the Chieftain of Banū Hāshim, and he married the daughter of the Chieftain of Banū Zuhrah, Āminah bint Wahb. They married a few days before the trade caravans would leave for Syria, and ʿAbdullāh passed away on that journey. This meant that they only spent a few days together, though it was enough for the conception of the blessed Prophet ﷺ.[52]

Why Arabia?

Arabia was located right in between two large empires: the Byzantines and the Sassanids. It was connected, but distinct, to these two mighty nations. The Arabs were perfectly placed—with some Prophetic guidance—to conquer these two superpowers within 30 short years. They also had no colonial history, which meant that the infrastructure, or lack thereof, was perfectly placed for Prophethood to flourish. The civilisational vacuum was filled by Prophetic teachings, culture, and ethos.

The Arabs also had certain qualities that made them receptive to a Prophetic Message. They were a simple people, and while simplicity has its own limitations, one of its benefits is its lack of resistance to accepting the truth. They did not have deep-seated ideologies that would oppose the innate Oneness of God. They also lived in a harsh environment, which made them chiselled instruments for combat, both physically and mentally. This was a vital attribute required in the early battles in Islam. The Arabs also nurtured praiseworthy characteristics such as bravery, honesty, and honour. They were known to uphold their oaths as a matter of principle, honour, and integrity.

Mecca was the site of the first House built for Allah's worship. It was the home of Ibrāhīm ﷺ and Ismāʿīl ﷺ, and so it was appropriate to host the world's first universal religion. Above all, Ibrāhīm ﷺ made a *duʿā’* (supplication) to Allah ﷻ, "Our Lord, raise from among them a Messenger who will recite to them Your revelations, teach them the Book and wisdom, and purify them. Indeed, You [alone] are Almighty, All-Wise."[53] Ibrāhīm ﷺ asked Allah to grant a Prophet from his progeny. All Prophets after Ibrāhīm ﷺ came from the progeny of his son Isḥāq ﷺ except for Muhammad ﷺ who descended from Ismāʿīl ﷺ due to this *duʿā’*. The Prophet stated, "I am the response of the *duʿā’* of my father, Ibrāhīm, and I am the glad tiding that Jesus foretold."[54]

وإنك لعلى خلق عظيم

Truly, you (Muhammad ﷺ)
are of a magnificent
standard of character.
al-Qalam, 4

PART

II

Early Life

The Prophet's Birth and Childhood ﷺ

3

His Date of Birth

The commonly cited birth date of the Prophet ﷺ is the 12th of Rabīʿ al-Awwal, however the earliest sources mention a number of potential dates with no unanimous agreement on any date in particular.[55] When asked why he fasted on Mondays, the Prophet ﷺ replied, "This was the day that I was born, and it was the day that Revelation first came to me."[56] The Prophet ﷺ was born in the Year of the Elephant[i].[57]

Ibn Hishām posits that the Prophet's date of birth is 12th of Rabīʿ al-Awwal. However, he mentions this with no chain of narration or source, and Ibn Hishām was writing almost 200 years after the birth of the Prophet ﷺ. Ibn Saʿd states, "The Prophet ﷺ was born on a Monday.

i In pre-Islamic Arabia—similar to other cultures at the time—exact years and dates were not recorded. Instead, momentous events would be referenced, and any particular event would be quoted in reference to that major event. The Year of the Elephant (ʿĀm al-Fīl) is in reference to Abraha's attempted destruction of the Holy Kaʿbah using African elephants.

Some state that he was born on the 10th of Rabīʿ al-Awwal, and others say he was born on the 2nd of Rabīʿ al-Awwal." [58] Ibn Kathīr ﷺ said:

> "Most scholars agree that the Prophet ﷺ was born in Rabīʿ al-Awwal. Some said that he ﷺ was born on the 2nd of Rabīʿ al-Awwal. This opinion is mentioned by Ibn ʿAbd al-Barr in *al-Istiʿāb,* and al-Wāqidī narrates it from Abū Maʿshar Najīḥ ibn ʿAbdurraḥmān al-Sindī al-Madanī. Another opinion was that he ﷺ was born on the 8th of Rabīʿ al-Awwal. Al-Ḥumaydī relates this from Ibn Ḥazm; and [Imams] Mālik, ʿAqīl, Yūnus ibn Yazīd, and others all narrate this view from Muhammad ibn Jubayr ibn Muṭʿim via al-Zuhrī. Ibn ʿAbd al-Barr adds that there are historians who bolster this proposed date. Further, the preservers [of knowledge] Muhammad ibn Mūsā al-Khwārizmī and Abū al-Khaṭṭāb ibn Diḥyah both preferred this date, the latter mentioning it in *al-Tanwīr fī Mawlid al-Bashīr al-Nadhīr.* A third opinion was that he ﷺ was born on the 10th of Rabīʿ al-Awwal. Ibn Diḥyah also mentioned this opinion, and Ibn ʿAsākir related it from Abū Jaʿfar al-Bāqir while Mujālid reported it from al-Shaʿbī. The fourth opinion is that he ﷺ was born on the 12th of Rabīʿ al-Awwal, and this is the opinion of Ibn Isḥāq. This is the most popular opinion in our time, and Allah knows best." [59]

Other scholarly opinions include: 9th of Rabīʿ al-Awwal; 17th of Rabīʿ al-Awwal; 22nd of Rabīʿ al-Awwal; and that he ﷺ was born in Ramadan. There are over ten opinions within the earliest sources of Islam regarding the exact day the Prophet ﷺ was born, with no clear cut, indisputable certainty.

When the Prophet ﷺ was named "Muhammad"—which was not the most common name—the people asked ʿAbd al-Muṭṭalib why he chose such a unique name, to which he replied, "I want him to be praised amongst the people as I want him to be praised by Allah in the Heavens." [60]

His Childhood

It was custom amongst the nobility of the Quraysh to send some of their newborn children to the desert for the first few years of their life. This was done to protect the children by raising them in a purer environment at a time when infant mortality was extremely common. It also conditioned the infants' bodies to withstand an austere environment and equipped them with a purer, unadulterated form of the Arabic language. The Prophet ﷺ was one of these children, and he was sent as a newborn to the Banū Saʿd ibn Bakr tribe, who were known for their eloquence and proficiency in the Arabic language.

Ḥalīmah bint Saʿdiyyah recalled the annual custom of travelling to Mecca to choose infants for care. No-one wanted to choose the Prophet ﷺ because he was an orphan, and payment for this service would usually come from the father. By the end of her stay, Ḥalīmah found herself without a child to take back and so chose the Prophet ﷺ. As soon as she took the Prophet ﷺ, miracles began to occur. She said, "When I was unable to take any other child, I took him and brought him back to my camp and I was able to feed him all the milk he wanted with ease. He drank until he was full, as did his milk-brother[ii]. My husband then went to our old she-camel, and to our surprise her udder was full of milk. He was able to milk so much that my husband and I both drank until we were full. My husband said, 'Ḥalīmah, by Allah, I think that you have brought a blessed soul.'"[61] Her donkey was the oldest and slowest, yet when it would carry her with the Prophet ﷺ it overtook the rest. Ḥalīmah continued to experience many miracles of this nature throughout the two-year tenure. It reached the extent that Ḥalīmah would desperately persuade the mother of the Prophet ﷺ, Āminah, to extend the period of care so that she could continue enjoying these blessings and benefits.

When the Prophet ﷺ was four years old, the Archangel Jibrīl ﷺ came to the Prophet ﷺ. The other children ran away while the Prophet ﷺ stood his ground. Jibrīl ﷺ overpowered him ﷺ and forced him onto

ii Milk-kinship is formed when children are nursed by a non-biological mother.

the ground. He opened up the Prophet's chest ﷺ, took out his heart, and removed a black slither from his heart. Jibrīl ﷺ then said, "This is Shayṭān's portion[iii] in you." He then washed his heart in a golden cup of Zamzam, put it back, and sealed his chest.[62] Many decades later, Anas ibn Mālik ﷺ remarked, "I used to notice the mark left on his chest."[63] This incident worried Ḥalīmah and she decided to return him ﷺ in case anything else happened. It is the Sunnah of Allah ﷻ that the Prophets are infallible with perfect character. This event was Allah's preparing the Prophet ﷺ for a life of exemplary conduct. Some scholars of *tafsīr* (Qur'anic exegesis) note that the verse, "Did we not expand your heart for you?"[64] refers to this event.

As previously mentioned, the Prophet's father passed away while Āminah was pregnant with the Messenger of Allah ﷺ. Āminah also passed away when the Prophet ﷺ was six years old. Despite their short time together, he ﷺ still had a deep love for her. This was made apparent on a journey some 50 years later when he ﷺ took a detour into a village. His Companions ﷺ followed him without uttering a word until he reached a grave and began to cry. He wept until his beard was wet. The Companions only ever witnessed the Prophet ﷺ cry a handful of times in his life, and this moving event collectively brought everyone to tears. Eventually, the Prophet ﷺ said, "I used to forbid you from visiting graveyards, but you may visit them now.[iv]"[65] Another report states that the Prophet ﷺ was granted permission to visit his mother's grave.[66] Note how the Prophet ﷺ did not take a single step without being granted permission, including visiting his mother. The mercy of this abrogation has been extended to the Ummah, and the permissibility of visiting graves was sanctioned, serving as a reminder of the transience of this life.

iii Shayṭān (Satan; the devil) pricks the heart of every baby as soon as they are born, which is why babies immediately cry as they emerge. (Al-Bukhārī, *Ṣaḥīḥ al-Bukhārī*, p. 850). This event signified Jibrīl ﷺ removing this foreign element, purifying the Prophet ﷺ from any of Shayṭān's whispers.

iv Visiting the graves was forbidden in early Islamic law but this ruling was later abrogated.

When both his parents passed away, the Prophet ﷺ was taken into the custody of his grandfather, ʿAbd al-Muṭṭalib, who also had a special affinity to the Prophet ﷺ. However, two years later at the tender age of eight, the Prophet ﷺ once again became an orphan as ʿAbd al-Muṭṭalib passed away. The Prophet ﷺ was then entrusted to his uncle, Abū Ṭālib, who raised the Prophet ﷺ and lived a long life, passing away when the Prophet ﷺ was over 50 years old.

Allah ﷻ said to Mūsā ﵇, who was expelled from his hometown both as a child and adult, "And I have chosen you for Myself."[67] Similarly, our Prophet ﷺ was left in Allah's care and nurture. Growing up in such a harsh environment develops one's maturity, forbearance, patience, and humility. When the Prophet ﷺ said, "I, and the one who takes care of an orphan, will be like this (gesturing to his index and middle fingers being pressed together) in Paradise"[68], he ﷺ was speaking from a place of true empathy and understanding.

The Prophet's Early Adulthood ﷺ

His Role as a Shepherd

The Prophet ﷺ said, "Allah did not send any Prophet except that he was a shepherd of sheep." The Companions ◈ replied, "What about you, O Messenger of Allah?" and the Prophet ﷺ replied, "Yes, I was a shepherd; I used to tend to the flock of the people of Mecca in return for some pennies." [69] The wisdoms of mandating this profession on the Prophets of Allah ﷺ are many. Being a shepherd offers the opportunity of solitude, which encourages reflection and introspection. There is a clear correlation between godlessness and affluence in urban surroundings, especially when compared to the faith of farmers and shepherds largely surrounded by nature and solitude. Constantly observing the miraculous nature of God's creation impacts one's faith and sense of being.

The Prophet ﷺ also specified shepherds of sheep, because sheep are known for their heedlessness, as humans are. They require constant attention lest they be led astray. Sheep also vary considerably in personality, and each sheep must be managed in a particular way according to their tendencies. Being a shepherd of sheep requires one to be simultaneously soft and tender as well as brave and courageous; tenderness is needed for one's own flock, and bravery is essential when defending the flock against wolves and other predatory animals. Being a shepherd necessitates humility and contentment. It is hard, menial labour with minimal remuneration. It is thus difficult to develop arrogance and pride as a shepherd of sheep. The mandating of Prophets in this role provides an important lesson in our understanding of honour and nobility; it teaches that we should be proud and happy to earn money with our own hands to feed our families and communities, just as the Prophets before us did ﷺ.

The Fijār Wars & Ḥilf al-Fuḍūl

When the Prophet ﷺ was around 15 years old, a series of small battles broke out between two large tribes. A tribe member from the branch of Kinānah[i]—to whom the Quraysh belonged—killed a man from the branch of Hawāzin. The killer escaped and fled into the precinct of the Ḥaram because no-one can be harmed in the sacred grounds. Hawāzin, in their rage, entered the Ḥaram and attacked the man. The Quraysh were so incensed that the sanctity of the Ḥaram was violated that they declared all-out war. The Prophet ﷺ recalled these events at a later date and said, "I remember participating in the Fijār Wars[ii]. I would collect and return arrows for my uncles…I do not regret participating in that war."[70]

A few years later, when the Prophet ﷺ was 20 years old, another incident occurred. A Yemeni man came to Mecca to perform Hajj. To fund his travels, he sold a few items to al-ʿĀṣ ibn al-Wā'il, a Chieftain and influential politician. Al-ʿĀṣ evaded payment and continued to stall. The man sought assistance from different tribe leaders of the Quraysh but was met with a variety of excuses, as no-one wanted to create

i A collection of many tribes, referred to as a "branch".

ii They were termed "Fijār Wars" because *fijār* means evil, and both sides had committed evil acts. Moreover, it pertained to the violation of the Ḥaram, which was considered a major evil.

tensions with a powerful diplomat on behalf of a lone traveller. As a last resort, the man took to a public platform. The closest equivalent to 21st century contemporary media platforms at the time was public speeches through the medium of poetry. The man headed to the Kaʿbah, which was a popular gathering place, and began to recite:

O Fihr's[iii] folk, attend to me,
A man aggrieved and robbed of wares
In Mecca's valley by a Chief
Whose clan attends to pilgrims' care.

In pilgrim's robes[iv], I come to you,
A man alone and far from home
And hearth and tribe, and ask my due
As guest between the *ḥijr*[v] and Stone[vi].

The true Ḥaram's for noble ones,
Not those who cheat its sanctity
And on its guests they set upon;
While wearing thobes[vii] but being thieves.[71]

The poem proliferated rapidly until the likes of al-Zubayr ibn ʿAbd al-Muṭṭalib, the Prophet's uncle, heard about it. He convened a meeting between the senior tribesmen of the Quraysh in the house of ʿAbdullāh ibn Judʿān, a widely respected and revered Chieftain who passed away before the Prophethood of Muhammad ﷺ. A pact was made, and a treaty was formed whereby the Quraysh vowed to support the

---

iii Fihr ibn Mālik, who is said to be the progenitor of all the clans of the Quraysh.

iv i.e., *iḥrām*. One performs Hajj or ʿUmrah in a state of *iḥrām* (sanctity). It is forbidden to perfume oneself, comb one's hair, cut one's nails, or wear any threaded clothes until the Hajj or ʿUmrah is complete.

v The Maqām (Station) of Ibrāhīm, denoting where Ibrāhīm and Ismāʿīl ﷺ built the Kaʿbah

vi Al-Ḥajar al-Aswad (The Black Stone), a sacred stone attached to the Kaʿbah.

vii An ankle-length dress commonly worn in the Arabian Peninsula.

oppressed over the oppressor regardless of the tribal standing of either party. They gathered in front of the Kaʿbah and made a collective vow, signing a treaty by dipping their hands in perfume and imprinting it onto the document. It was thus called Ḥilf al-Muṭayyibīn (Treaty of the Perfumed), or Ḥilf al-Fuḍūl, because al-ʿĀṣ ibn al-Wāʾil bemoaned the pact, claiming the matter was *fuḍūlī* i.e., none of their business. The pact was made to proclaim that matters of oppression are a societal concern and therefore everyone's business.

The pact was unprecedented, remembered as a momentous event in the face of injustice. The Prophet ﷺ stated, "I witnessed in the house of ʿAbdullāh ibn Judʿān a treaty that, were I asked to uphold it even in Islam, I would do so. And I would not give up my place even if offered a large amount of money."[72]

These two events are noteworthy because they occurred before Prophethood, but the Prophet ﷺ approved and affirmed them after Prophethood. He ﷺ did not regret participating in the Fijār Wars; rather, he was proud. This shows us that it is permissible to fight for causes that do not necessarily pertain to religion but are for a good cause. There is a scholarly debate as to the extent to which we may participate in such disputes and battles, but there is precedent to involve oneself in such disputes. Similarly, the Prophet's comments ﷺ on Ḥilf al-Fuḍūl demonstrate how he was involved in his society, even though it was a non-Muslim society. He ﷺ was involved in the betterment of his society and stood up against injustices of any kind.

Oftentimes, the best *daʿwah* (calling to Islam) is through calling to neutral matters of goodness, truth, and justice. Being a spokesperson against racism, or calling on others to give blood, for example, is extremely effective in enhancing the image of Islam simply due to the fact that it is a visibly Muslim person fighting for these causes. Moreover, when somebody is known to care for their community, they are valued and respected. When the time comes for more direct proselytising, they will be listened to and taken more seriously, and Islam is then depicted as a sincere faith. This is the Prophetic method.

His Marriage to Khadījah ﷺ

Khadījah bint Khuwaylid was a noblewoman of the Quraysh. She shared a common ancestor with the Prophet ﷺ via Quṣayy on her father's side, and ʿĀmir ibn Lu'ayy on her mother's side. Her lineage is as follows:

> Khadījah bint Khuwaylid ibn Asad ibn ʿAbd al-ʿUzzā ibn Quṣayy.

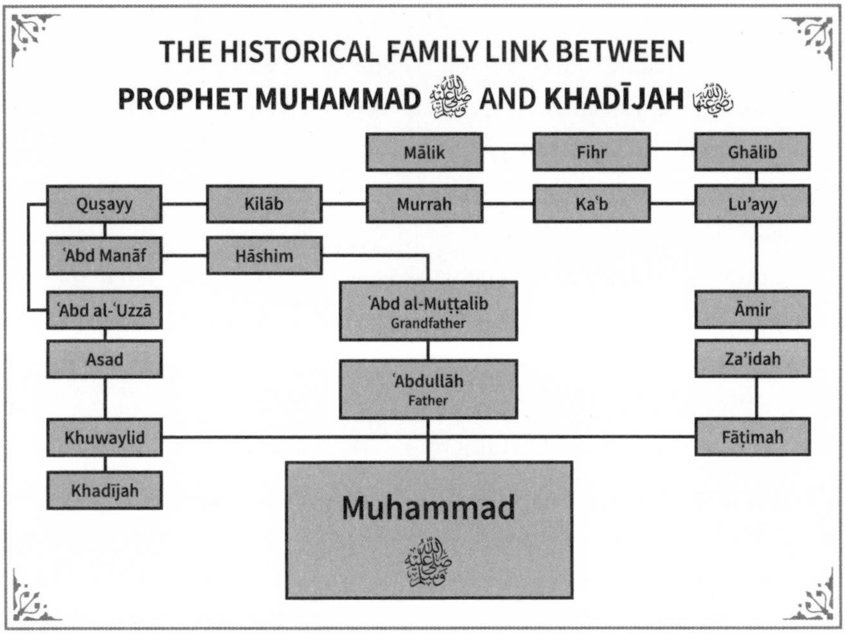

Khadījah was twice married before marrying the Prophet ﷺ. She married Abū Hālah ibn Zurārah and bore two children: a son, Hālah, and a daughter, Hind. Following Abū Hālah's demise, she married ʿUtayq ibn ʿĀbid al-Makhzūmī and bore a third child, also named Hind. ʿUtayq also died, leaving her a handsome inheritance.[viii] As might be expected following the consecutive deaths of two husbands, the Mother of the Believers led a somewhat secluded life before meeting the Prophet. She was proposed to on multiple occasions by the

viii In Jāhiliyyah, women did not ordinarily inherit. However, her ex-husband had no siblings and was not survived by any children, and so in this rare circumstance, she inherited all his wealth.

noblemen of Quraysh, but as a widow remained aloof and contented herself with solitude.

She continued to reinvest her money and grew her profits through trade as a businesswoman in her own right. She would primarily buy goods at Hajj season, but as a woman in Jāhilī society, she relied on men to travel and sell the goods for her in Syria and beyond in exchange for profit-share agreements. Due to her reliance on the honesty and transparency of her business partners, she would often be short-changed or scammed.

As aforementioned, the Prophet ﷺ would tend to people's flocks for a living. Khadījah's sister had a herd of camels and hired the Prophet ﷺ alongside another young man to graze them outside Mecca. When it was time to collect their remuneration, the Prophet ﷺ told the second shepherd to ask for his wages on his behalf, as he ﷺ was too shy to ask directly. Khadījah's sister said, "I have not seen a man more bashful, noble, and honourable than him."[73] She continued to praise him in such a manner that Khadījah—it being the first time she heard about him ﷺ—felt something enter her heart. After hearing her sister's extravagant praise of the Prophet ﷺ, Khadījah ؓ decided to extend an offer of a business partnership to him despite his lack of entrepreneurial experience.

As per his respectful nature, the Prophet ﷺ sought counsel from his uncle, Abū Ṭālib, who strongly encouraged him to accept the offer. He ﷺ agreed, and Khadījah ؓ gave a generous offer of an even split, which was above average for such a partnership. The Prophet ﷺ embarked on the first business trip to Syria, and successfully returned with multiplied profits. Not only was the Prophet ﷺ inherently blessed in all his actions, but his honesty and integrity undoubtedly contributed to his successes.

One day, an elderly friend of Khadījah ؓ asked, "O Muhammad, why don't you get married?" The Prophet ﷺ—who was yet to be a Prophet—smiled and replied, "And who would marry me? I am a poor orphan of the Quraysh." She responded, "And what if Khadījah wanted to marry you?" After a short pause, he ﷺ replied, "Why would she want to marry me?"[74] The conversation ended there but developments continued until they did indeed marry.

Abū Ṭālib gave the sermon, praising Allah and recalling the lineage of the Quraysh. He then said, "My nephew Muhammad ibn ʿAbdullāh ibn ʿAbd al-Muṭṭalib—to whom there is no equal amongst the youth in the Quraysh in manners, nobility, and lineage—has proposed to your noble daughter. Should he be lacking in wealth then let it be known that wealth is a temporary provision akin to a fleeting shadow. He desires to marry Khadījah, and she shares the same sentiment in the matter."[75] A dowry of 12 *ūqiyyah*[ix] of silver was then offered.[76] Her uncle, ʿAmr ibn Asad, said, "This is a young man that cannot be refused" and gave her away.

There is a difference of opinion regarding Khadījah's age when she married the Prophet ﷺ. The most widespread view is that she was 40 years old[77] when she married the Prophet ﷺ and that she died at the age of 65.[78] However, the likes of al-Bayhaqī and Ibn Kathīr opine that she died in her fifties.[79] There is a consensus that they were married for 25 years, and if she died in her fifties, she would have married the Prophet ﷺ in her late twenties or early thirties. An early authority, Hishām al-Kalbī, states that she married at 28 years old.[80] Likewise, al-Ḥākim narrates from Ibn Isḥāq that she was 28 years old.[81] The latter opinion—that she was 28—holds more weight; the narrations are more in quantity, and the narrators, such as the likes of Ibn Isḥāq, are more authoritative. Moreover, the Prophet ﷺ and Khadījah had at least six children. It is much more plausible for a woman in her twenties to have six children than someone in their forties through their fifties.

The Prophet's transition from a shepherd to a businessman demonstrates the value of good character and conduct. His honesty, integrity, hard work, and modesty led directly to multiple opportunities. It also paved the way for a perfect marriage. This blessed event also confirms

ix An *ūqiyyah* is a historical unit of weight worth 40 dirhams. In 2022, 12 *ūqiyyah* is worth roughly £860 GBP or $1,200 USD.

the permissibility of falling in love and even pursuing that feeling in a legitimate way. Khadījah ؓ proved to be a vital asset in the Prophet's mission ﷺ, as is evidenced throughout this book.

Khadījah ؓ provided our beloved Messenger ﷺ with invaluable emotional support and was a source of tranquillity and peace. The Prophet once said, "O Khadījah, here is Jibrīl ؉. He is sending Allah's *salām* (peace) on you, and he is giving you glad tidings of a house in Paradise with no noise or struggle." Khadījah, displaying her intelligence and understanding of the religion by not returning peace back to Allah, responded, "Indeed, Allah is al-Salām (The Giver of Peace), and may peace be upon Jibrīl, and upon you, O Messenger of Allah."[82]

His Wives and Children ﷺ

The Prophet ﷺ married 11 women in his lifetime. In chronological order, they are as follows: Khadījah bint Khuwaylid, Sawdah bint Zamʿah, ʿĀʾishah bint Abī Bakr, Ḥafṣah bint ʿUmar, Zaynab bint Khuzaymah, Umm Salamah bint Abī Umayyah (Hind), Juwayriyyah bint al-Ḥārith, Zaynab bint Jaḥsh, Umm Ḥabībah bint Abī Sufyān, Maymūnah bint al-Ḥārith, and Ṣafiyyah bint Ḥuyayy ؓ. The Prophet ﷺ married Khadījah ؓ at the age of 25 and remained in a monogamous relationship for 25 years. After the death of Khadījah ؓ, the Prophet ﷺ remarried and practiced polygyny for the remainder of his life ﷺ, marrying for a variety of reasons; his wives varied in status, age, and previous marital experience.

The Prophet's ﷺ first child, al-Qāsim, was born before his Prophethood. The Prophet's title was Abū al-Qāsim (The Father of al-Qāsim), as it was—and is still—tradition in Arab culture to be named in relation to one's first-born child. He passed away at the age of six or seven. He then had Zaynab, Ruqayyah, Umm Kulthūm, Fāṭimah, ʿAbdullāh, and Ibrāhīm. Some suggest that he ﷺ had two more children: al-Ṭāhir and al-Ṭayyib, however it is more likely that they were two nicknames for ʿAbdullāh, both meaning "The Pure". ʿAbdullāh and Ibrāhīm died in their infancy. His four daughters lived until they reached maturity, however three of them died in his lifetime, leaving only Fāṭimah to outlive him.

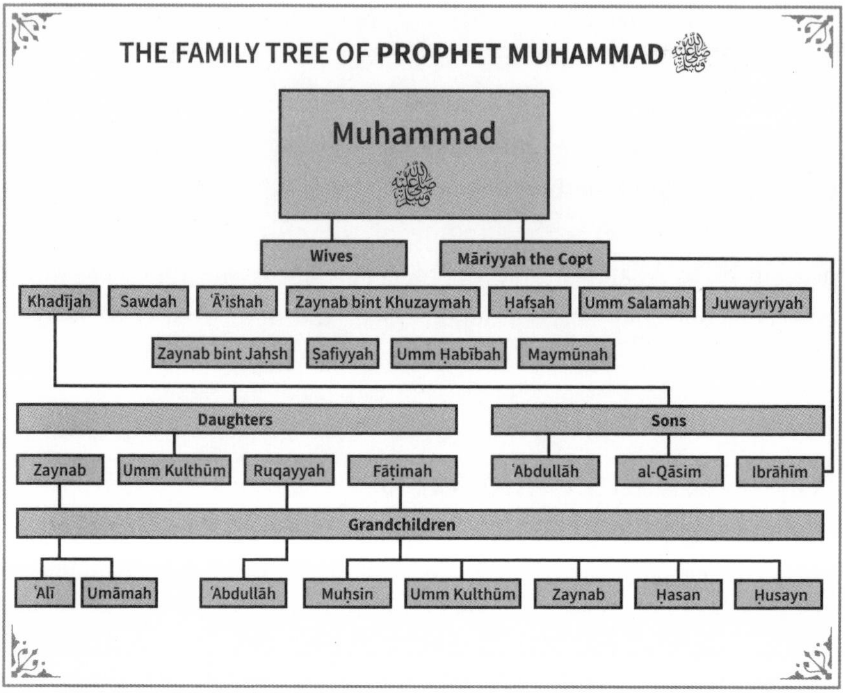

It is pertinent to highlight the unrelenting calamities and tests our Prophet faced. Humanity is unified in the notion that losing a child is the worst calamity that can befall a person, and we find the Prophet burying six out of his seven children. This is after growing up as an orphan, with his mother, father, and grandfather all passing away in his own childhood. Allah is cementing his role as a Prophet, because perseverance through trials breeds firmness in belief and *tawakkul* (reliance on Allah). The Prophet is therefore tested far more than the rest of humanity. Hardship softens the heart, just as heedlessness hardens it, because it forces us to turn to the only One Who can relieve us.

Upon the passing of his son ʿAbdullāh, the Prophet's enemy, Abū Jahl, ran through the streets of Mecca shouting, "Muhammad's progeny is cut off! Muhammad's progeny is cut off!"[83] In Jāhilī culture, male offspring was of the most important aspects of social prestige. Not only did the Prophet ﷺ have to mourn the death of his child, but he also bore his enemy's gleeful boast, adding salt to an already raw wound. Allah ﷻ replied on his behalf, "Indeed, We have granted you abundant goodness. So pray and sacrifice to your Lord alone. Only the one who hates you is truly cut off." [84] Indeed, the Prophet's followers, through his Ummah, amassed billions, each of whom sends peace and blessings upon him multiple times a day. Meanwhile, the likes of Abū Jahl—which literally translates as "Father of Ignorance"—is only ever spoken about negatively and will continue to be so until the end of time. Allah's promise is undoubtedly true, and He is sufficient as a defender.

The Rebuilding of the Kaʿbah

The Kaʿbah was damaged by both a fire and a flood. At the time, the closest houses to the Kaʿbah were a mere few metres away. A woman's cooking pot caught on fire and spread to the cloth of the Kaʿbah. The Kaʿbah was damaged but not completely destroyed. Later that year, a big flood occurred. Because Mecca is located in the basin of numerous mountains, massive floods occur approximately every decade. The flood destroyed the roof of the Kaʿbah as well as parts of the walls, especially because it was already damaged from the fire. The Quraysh decided that it must be rebuilt.

Meanwhile, the Christian Romans and Zoroastrian Persians continued to war. A church in Yemen was destroyed in the war, and the Caesar financed the rebuilding of the church with the highest quality marble and wood. Allah ﷻ decreed that a powerful storm damaged the ship containing the materials, forcing it to dock at Jeddah. The Romans were forced to sell their materials at Jeddah and return home. The Quraysh caught wind of this rare sale and pooled their funds to buy the materials as well as the services of the expert Roman carpenter onboard the ship.

After initial hesitations to knock down the sacred House of Allah, al-Walīd ibn al-Mughīrah finally stepped up and swung the first blow. The next day, everybody else joined, and the Kaʿbah was torn down and rebuilt. The Banū ʿAbd Manāf were the most prestigious tribe and thus claimed the honour of rebuilding the side of the Kaʿbah with the door. Their rivals, the Banū Makhzūm, claimed the side from the Yemeni corner to the Black Stone. As both walls meet at the Black Stone, both tribes demanded the right to place the Black Stone in the Kaʿbah. The quarrelling escalated to the point that construction was halted for five days while they were in deadlock.

The Banū Makhzūm made a secret pledge that they would fight to the death before backing down, and even dipped their hands in blood to sign this pledge. On the fifth day, Abū Umayyah ibn al-Mughīrah, the oldest person alive in Mecca, put a stop to the madness and forbade any further fighting. He suggested that they simply allocate the honour to the first person who enters through the door, thus leaving the matter to "chance". The person that walked in next was none other than our Prophet Muhammad ﷺ. Both tribes cheered upon seeing the Prophet ﷺ walk in, as he was loved by all. His integrity was recognised so much that it did not matter to them which tribe he belonged to. The Prophet ﷺ placed the Black Stone in a garment and ordered every tribe to send a representative to place the Black Stone in the Kaʿbah in unison.

When rebuilding the Kaʿbah, a number of changes were made to its structure. First, the original Kaʿbah was a rectangle, not a square. However, the expensive material they purchased from the Romans was not enough for the entire rectangle, so they decided to build it as a square, signposting the original format of the rectangle. Perhaps they intended that it be rebuilt again in the future to the original specification. However, Allah ﷻ willed that it be a permanent change. Second, the Kaʿbah was doubled[x] in height. Third, they adapted the door of the Kaʿbah to begin from an elevated position, as it previously began from the ground. This was done to limit access inside the Kaʿbah out of prestige. Finally, they built a waterspout to limit future water damage.

x The Kaʿbah of the 21st century is considerably taller at 15 metres high. At the time of the Prophet's childhood ﷺ, it was as tall as someone riding a camel. This is the height that was doubled.

When the Prophet ﷺ conquered Mecca 20 years later, he said to ʿĀ'ishah ؓ, "Were it not for the fact that your people are still new to Islam, I would have rebuilt the Kaʿbah on the original specification of Ibrāhīm ؑ and made the door accessible to everyone."[85] During the early Umayyad Dynasty (661–750 AD) under the governorship of the infamous al-Ḥajjāj ibn Yūsuf, a group led by the Companion ʿAbdullāh ibn al-Zubayr ؓ broke away from the Umayyad Empire and founded a mini-Caliphate in Mecca. When he heard of the above Hadith, he destroyed the Kaʿbah and rebuilt it as a rectangle and extended the door back down to the floor, as per the Prophet's description.[86]

Eventually, al-Ḥajjāj reclaimed Mecca by throwing catapults into the Kaʿbah, destroying the Kaʿbah itself. Not wanting to rebuild the Kaʿbah according to ʿAbdullāh ibn al-Zubayr's plan, al-Ḥajjāj decided to rebuild it as a square according to how the Jāhilī Arabs did. Sometime later, in the era of Imam Mālik ؒ, the then-Caliph asked the Imam if the Kaʿbah should be rebuilt according to the Prophet's description, to which the noble Imam replied, "No, I do not want the Kaʿbah to become a plaything of the rulers."[87] The Kaʿbah has thus remained upon this structure until our current time.

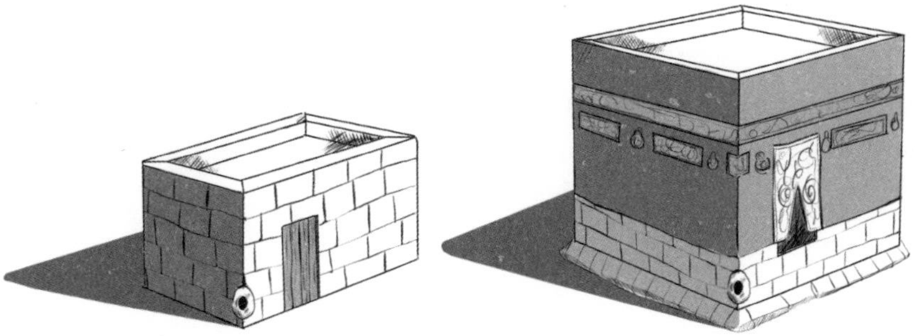

There is a great wisdom in Allah ﷻ decreeing that the Kaʿbah remain upon this structure. Praying inside the Kaʿbah is a great honour which holds great reward. Praying inside the Kaʿbah with the raised door is practically impossible for the vast majority of people, as entry is controlled. However, praying where the old structure would have been holds the same reward as praying inside the Kaʿbah; as mentioned, the location of the Kaʿbah is holy, not the bricks themselves.

There is clear symbolism in the Kaʿbah being destroyed and rebuilt five years before the Prophethood of Muhammad ﷺ; the religion of Ibrāhīm ﷺ had been destroyed, and Muhammad ﷺ is coming to rebuild it again. The Kaʿbah represents the religion of Ibrāhīm ﷺ, as well as the first House of Allah. The foundation (the ground) remains the same, i.e., "There is no god but Allah", but the dressing (the bricks) is renewed. The Prophet ﷺ being chosen to save the tribes from civil war and bloodshed symbolises him being chosen by Allah ﷻ to save them from misguidance and Hellfire.

Adopting Zayd ibn Ḥārithah ﷺ

Zayd ibn Ḥārithah was from a Yemeni tribe, descending from the Qahṭānī branch of the Arabs, not the ʿAdnānī branch. Zayd's parents were from two different tribes in Yemen who would sometimes be in conflict. In one particular skirmish, his relatives from his father's tribe kidnapped him and sold him into slavery. He was sold in the Souk of ʿUkkāẓ, the largest marketplace in pre-Islamic Arabia, to Ḥakīm ibn Ḥizām, Khadījah's nephew, on her behalf. When Khadījah married the Prophet ﷺ, she gifted Zayd to him, and he became the Prophet's servant.

Over a decade had passed, and Zayd's father, Ḥārithah, was still frantically looking for his son. One day, a man recognised Zayd's Yemeni features and word eventually reached Ḥārithah, who made his way to Mecca. He found the Prophet ﷺ (though this was before his Prophethood) and said, "O Muhammad, [grand]son of ʿAbd al-Muṭṭalib, you are a noble man of noble lineage, and you are from a people of trustworthiness." He continued to praise the Prophet before requesting that he return his son. The Prophet ﷺ replied, "I will let Zayd decide. If he chooses you, I will return him without any ransom. But if he chooses me, then I can never turn away someone who has turned to me." His father was overjoyed and praised the Prophet ﷺ for going above and beyond what was asked. The Prophet ﷺ had genuine love and affinity for Zayd, and the laws of Jāhiliyyah allowed him to refuse, but the Prophet's morality was above the laws of Jāhiliyyah, even prior to his Prophethood.

He called Zayd, who by now was in his twenties, to decide. Zayd instantaneously chose the Prophet ﷺ, saying, "I can never choose anyone over you, for you are more than a father and uncle combined."[88] This astonishing response could only ever occur with a Prophet, for the bond of a Prophet is the only bond stronger than that of parenthood. Ḥārithah grew exasperated, "Zayd, have you lost your mind? You prefer to remain a slave to a man who is not your kin rather than return with your own father to your own tribe?!" Zayd responded, "I stick to my choice, for I have seen from this man that which prevents me from choosing anyone over him."

Upon hearing his response, the Prophet ﷺ took Zayd to the Kaʿbah and announced, "O people of Mecca, I want you all to testify that Zayd is a free man, and I have adopted him as my son. He will inherit from me, and I will inherit from him."[89] He became known henceforth as Zayd ibn Muhammad. Over 30 years later, ʿAbdullāh ibn ʿUmar, the son of ʿUmar ibn al-Khaṭṭāb ؓ, recalled, "I never knew of any other name for Zayd other than Zayd ibn Muhammad until Allah ﷻ revealed verse five of Sūrah al-Aḥzāb."[90] The verse in question states, "Let your adopted children keep their family names. That is more just in the sight of Allah."[91] The Prophet ﷺ then changed his name back to Zayd ibn Ḥārithah.

Zayd was married to Umm Ayman, the servant of the Prophet's mother, Āminah. Their child was born in the house of the Prophet ﷺ—the famous Usāmah ibn Zayd ؓ. Usāmah was so beloved to the Prophet ﷺ that whenever the Companions ؓ wanted something from the Prophet ﷺ, they would ask Usāmah to ask on their behalf, as the Prophet ﷺ could not resist Usāmah's requests. He was nicknamed "The Prophet's beloved, son of the Prophet's beloved".[92] When ʿAbdullāh ibn ʿUmar ؓ asked his then-Caliph father, ʿUmar ibn al-Khaṭṭāb, why his salary was lower than that of Usāmah ibn Zayd ؓ, ʿUmar responded, "Because he was more beloved to the Messenger of Allah ﷺ than you, and his father (i.e., Zayd) was more beloved to the Messenger of Allah ﷺ than yours (i.e., ʿUmar himself)."[93]

The biggest blessing attributed to Zayd ibn Ḥārithah ؓ is that he is the only Companion ever to be mentioned in the Qur'an by name.[xi] The Prophet's best friend, Abū Bakr ؓ, was only ever mentioned by inference.[xii] The Prophet ﷺ sent Zayd on at least ten expeditions, and he was the commander in each of them. No-one ever commanded Zayd, regardless of age, which demonstrates the high status given to him by the Prophet ﷺ. He was eventually martyred in the Battle of Mu'tah, a fierce battle against the Romans. ʿĀ'ishah ؓ declared, "If Zayd had been alive when the Prophet ﷺ died, he would have been chosen [as Caliph]."[94]

xi A reference to *al-Aḥzāb*, 37.

xii A reference to *al-Tawbah*, 40.

صلى الله عليه وسلم

May the peace and
blessings of Allah
be upon him.

PART

III

The Meccan Era

The Revelation

5

Prior to the Revelation, the Prophet ﷺ would frequently seclude himself in Cave Hira, a crevice within a mountain on the outskirts of Mecca. He would remain for increasingly long periods, only returning to tend to his duties and collect food and water. The crevice is perfectly carved out in the mountain for one person to reflect and contemplate with a view overlooking the Kaʿbah. During this period, miraculous things would begin to occur. He ﷺ would hear *salām* but not see anyone, only to realise it was coming from the rocks and stones. He ﷺ recalled to the Companions, "I know of a stone in Mecca which would give me *salām*."[95] The Prophet ﷺ would also receive premonitions in his dreams that would come true the following day. These dreams continued daily for six whole months. We know that the Revelation began in Ramadan. The Qur'an states, "Indeed, We sent the Qur'an down during the Night of Decree."[96] This means that the visions began in Rabīʿ al-Awwal and continued for six months. During this time, the Prophet ﷺ grew worried and informed Khadījah ﵂ about his dreams, but his closest confidant duly reassured him ﷺ that these visions were glad tidings.

The Appearance of Jibrīl ﷺ

On a Saturday during Ramadan in Cave Hira, the Prophet ﷺ saw a light and heard a sound, but nothing came of it. The same thing occurred the next day; he saw a light and heard a sound. The following day, on a Monday, Jibrīl ﷺ appeared. When the Prophet ﷺ was later asked why he fasts on Mondays, he ﷺ said, "I was born on Monday, and the Revelation began on Monday."[97] The Angel Jibrīl ﷺ came to him and said, "Read! (*Iqra'*!)" The Prophet ﷺ replied, "I cannot read." Jibrīl ﷺ then grabbed him and squeezed him so tightly that the Prophet ﷺ lost all energy. Jibrīl ﷺ again demanded, "Read!" And the Prophet ﷺ again replied, "I cannot read." Jibrīl ﷺ squeezed him again a second time with the same vigour. The third time, Jibrīl ﷺ said, "Read!" This time, he continued with the first verses of the Qur'an ever to be revealed, "Read in the name of your Lord Who created; [He] created humans from a clinging clot. Read! And your Lord is the Most Generous, Who taught by the pen; [He] taught humanity what they knew not."[98]

Scholars have discussed why Jibrīl ﷺ squeezed the Prophet ﷺ, and why he did it so tightly. There is no definitive answer, but some assert that it was done to show the Prophet ﷺ that he was not dreaming, and that this was indeed a reality.[99] Others suggest that Jibrīl ﷺ was indicating to the Prophet ﷺ that he was about to receive a weighty inspiration;[100] Sūrah al-Muzzammil states, "We will soon send upon you a weighty Revelation."[101] Some scholars opt for a more symbolic explanation, stating that the three squeezes refer to three major trials the Prophet ﷺ would experience but ultimately survive.[102] They are: the Meccan Boycott, the assassination attempt and hijrah (migration), and the Battle of Uḥud—all three events will be explained in detail throughout this book.

The word *iqra'* has two linguistic meanings: to read, and to recite from memory.[i] When Jibrīl ﷺ commanded "*Iqra'*!", the Prophet ﷺ understood the former i.e., to read, so he responded, "I cannot read" because he ﷺ

i Some scholars, such as Shaykh Dr Akram Nadwi, argue that *iqra'* here means "pray". The notion is that each component of the prayer represents the entirety of the prayer, so *qum* (stand), *usjud* (prostrate), *irkaʿ* (bow), and *iqra'* (read) all mean "pray". Therefore, Jibrīl ﷺ was commanding the Prophet ﷺ to pray i.e., read the Qur'an in prayer.

was unlettered. Jibrīl ﷺ intended the latter, as the recitation will be in the Name of Allah ﷻ. Jibrīl ﷺ responded, *"Iqra' bi ismi Rabbika al-ladhī khalaq"*. The *bi* is commonly translated as "in" i.e., in the Name of your Lord, however it can also mean "by", so, "Read by the name of your Lord", i.e., by Allah's help and permission. Allah ﷻ then ends the first sentence with "created" because He created everything.

He ﷻ specifies that the Creator of everything created mankind. This magnificent Creator is commanding you to recite. *Iqra'* is then repeated intentionally, as it means "keep reciting" i.e., keep spreading the Message no matter what. Some scholars add that the first *iqra'* is for knowledge of the Qur'an, and the second is for knowledge of this world,[103] which is why the verse following the second instance is "Who taught by the pen; taught humanity what they knew not."[104]

After this event, the Prophet ﷺ raced back to Khadījah ﷺ with a palpitating heart. As he entered the door he exclaimed, "Cover me up, cover me up!" This clearly shows how unexpected the whole event was for the Prophet ﷺ. Moreover, it demonstrates his sincerity and humanity; he did not know what had just occurred and returned to his wife terrified. This was clearly not a premeditated ploy to claim Prophethood for worldly gain. Khadījah ﷺ calmed him down and asked him what was wrong. The Prophet ﷺ revealed, "I am worried for myself."[105] This sentence has led to strange interpretations about what the noble Messenger ﷺ intended, such as him doubting his sanity ﷺ. The much more credible and sensible explanations are that either he feared for his safety due to the intensity of the squeezes, or that he ﷺ was scared about seeing things other humans could not. Solidifying her role as his emotional rock, Khadījah ﷺ responded, "No, by Allah, Allah will never cause you harm; you are good to your kin, take on the burdens of others, give charity to the needy, are hospitable to guests, and you carry out all types of good." Khadījah ﷺ eloquently encapsulated the character of the Prophet ﷺ and then espoused the unequivocal principle that whoever does good by Allah ﷻ will have Allah ﷻ do good by them.

After this event, Khadījah ﷺ went to ʿAddās, her uncle's Christian slave. After hearing what happened, he exclaimed, "What?! An Angel of Allah in this heathen place of idols?" Khadījah 🌸 then went to Waraqah ibn Nawfal, her cousin and one of the only Ḥunafā' remaining in Mecca. Waraqah replied, "By Allah this is the Keeper of Secrets who came down to Mūsā." [106] Mūsā 🌸 was mentioned rather than 'Īsā 🌸 because Waraqah correctly predicted that his Prophethood would resemble that of Mūsā 🌸 more, as they both had political power and established laws, while the Message of 'Īsā 🌸 was spiritual. Waraqah continued, "How I wish I were a young man so I could help you when your nation ridicules, persecutes, and expels you." The Prophet 🌸 asked in disbelief, "My nation will expel me?" Waraqah replied in the affirmative, "Yes. Never has a Prophet been sent except that his people ridicule, persecute, and expel him." Waraqah then passed away a short while after this conversation.

It may sound peculiar for a Prophet to ask a non-Prophet for guidance, but at this moment the Prophet had not yet digested and internalised the implications of what had occurred. The Arabs of Mecca were not familiar with the concept of Prophethood whereas the Jews and Christians had a long history of Prophethood. Years later, Waraqah's relatives would ask the Prophet 🌸 about his fate in the Hereafter, to which the Prophet 🌸 said, "I saw him wearing white robes, blessed with gardens in Paradise." [107] Some are thus of the opinion that Waraqah was the first person to accept Islam, even though he did not utter the *shahādah* (declaration of faith), because the declaration did not even exist at the time.

A few months passed without Revelation or Jibrīl's presence at all. The Prophet 🌸 would wander around the valleys of Mecca and revisit Cave Hira expecting to see him but to no avail. This continued until one day, the Prophet 🌸 suddenly saw him again. His name was called but he could not see anyone. The Prophet 🌸 looked left and right but not see anyone until he finally looked up and saw Jibrīl 🌸. The Prophet 🌸 said, "I saw the same Angel I saw in Cave Hira. He was sitting on a throne that was both in the Heavens and the Earth. I began to tremble and palpitate and rushed back to Khadījah again, saying 'Cover me, cover me.'" [108]

That is when Jibrīl ﷺ came with the second Revelation in the form of Sūrah al-Muddaththir, "O you covered up, arise and warn. Revere your Lord [alone]. Purify your garments. [Continue to] shun all idols. Do not do a favour expecting more [in return]. And persevere for the sake of your Lord."[109] The symbolism is clear: O you wrapped up in comfort, discard the cloak; stand up and be active. Purify your garments physically, but more importantly spiritually. Do not put your hopes and expectations in the hands of men, but rather rely on Allah ﷻ.

Some scholars note that with the first Revelation—"Read"—he became a Prophet, and with the second Revelation—"Arise and warn"—he became a Messenger.[110] As for the difference between a Prophet and a Messenger, there are numerous scholarly opinions. Some state that they are synonymous, however Allah ﷻ states, "Whenever We sent a Messenger or Prophet before you..."[111] which clearly indicates a difference. Moreover, another Hadith states that there have been 313 Messengers as opposed to 124,000 Prophets.[112] Another scholarly opinion is that a Messenger has a new Shariah—a code of Allah—whereas a Prophet follows the Shariah of a previous Messenger. However, Dāwūd and Sulaymān ﷺ are examples of Messengers that followed a previous Messenger's Shariah (that of Mūsā ﷺ). Imam Ibn Taymiyyah ﷺ submits the opinion that a Prophet is sent to a believing nation to renew and correct their faith, whereas a Messenger is sent to an unbelieving nation. Linguistically, the word Nabiyy (Prophet) is derived from the word *naba'a—yanba'u* (to inform), and Rasūl (Messenger) is from *arsala—yursilu* (to send). This definition is most plausible and correlates with all the Qur'anic verses describing the previous Prophets and Messengers.

Forms of Revelation

Waḥy (Revelation) is direct communication from Allah ﷻ to mankind. Imam Ibn Qayyim ﷺ mentions that our Prophet ﷺ was inspired through *waḥy* in seven different ways. The lowest form of Revelation is true dreams. Dreams can be categorised in three ways: regular dreams resulting from daily activity or thinking; dreams from the Shayṭān; and dreams from Allah.[113] The third type is characterised through its content as well as being able to vividly remember them.

The second form of Revelation is *ilhām*, whisperings from an Angel other than The Archangel Jibrīl ﷺ. An example of this form of Revelation is the mother of Mūsā ﷺ being inspired by Allah ﷻ to part with her baby. The Qur'an states, "We inspired the mother of Mūsā, 'Nurse him, but when you fear for him, put him into the river, and do not fear or grieve. We will certainly return him to you and make him one of the Messengers.'"[114]

The third form of Revelation is to speak to an Angel directly but in human form. When Jibrīl ﷺ would usually reveal himself to the Prophet ﷺ, he would do so in the form of a human. In Medina, Jibrīl ﷺ would often take the form of Diḥyah al-Kalbī ﷺ, a Companion known for his beauty. Sometimes he would appear in the form of an unknown man. ʿUmar ﷺ once recalled, "We were sitting with the Messenger of Allah when a man walked towards us with extremely white clothes, extremely black hair, and no dust on him from travelling. We all looked at each other [as if to say] we do not know this man and he does not look like a traveller..."[115] The Prophet ﷺ then informed ʿUmar that it was indeed Jibrīl ﷺ.

The fourth form is for Jibrīl ﷺ to communicate the Revelation through an intense noise. When this would happen, the Prophet ﷺ would enter some sort of trance. Jibrīl ﷺ would not be seen by anybody else, but in this trance the Prophet ﷺ would somehow communicate with Jibrīl ﷺ and remember the words upon his waking. ʿĀ'ishah ﷺ stated multiple times that when Jibrīl ﷺ would visit the Prophet ﷺ and bring Revelation, the Prophet ﷺ would break into a sweat even on the coldest day.[116] When Sūrah al-Mā'idah was revealed, the Prophet ﷺ was on a camel. The Revelation was so heavy that the camel was forced to sit down due to the pressure. Al-Ḥārith ibn Hishām ﷺ asked the Prophet how he received Revelation. The Prophet ﷺ replied, "Sometimes, Jibrīl communicates with me in a form resembling the ringing of a bell, and this is the most difficult state for me. After it ends, I become aware of what was said. Sometimes he would come in the form of a man, and I would understand what he says." [117]

The fifth form is to communicate with Jibrīl 🕊 in his original form. This is what occurred in the two abovementioned cases of verses from Sūrah al-ʿAlaq and Sūrah al-Muddaththir being revealed. Jibrīl 🕊 was in his true Angel form on both occasions, which overwhelmed the Prophet ﷺ. The sixth form is when Allah ﷻ inspires the Prophet ﷺ without an intermediary Angel. Ibn Qayyim 🕊 recalls this, referring to Mūsā 🕊 speaking to Allah ﷻ on Mount Sinai from behind a barrier. [118]

The seventh form—the highest form of Revelation—is Allah's direct Speech ﷻ. This has only ever occurred once, namely in al-Isrāʾ wa al-Miʿrāj i.e., the Night Journey and Ascension. The Prophet ﷺ journeyed to the Heavens and spoke to Allah ﷻ directly, without the presence of Jibrīl 🕊 or anyone else. The Prophet ﷺ is the only person to be granted the highest honour of speaking to Allah ﷻ without any barrier. This will be expounded upon in Chapter 10.

Early Islam

6

The First Converts

In the earliest days of Prophethood, immediately following the Revelation of "Arise and warn"[119], the Prophet ﷺ would preach to his family and closest friends. An argument can be made for Khadījah being the first convert to Islam, as she believed in the Prophet ﷺ before even knowing what had truly happened, demonstrating her unwavering faith. As such, Waraqah ibn Nawfal would be the second to convert despite never uttering the *shahādah*. Scholars differ over the third convert to Islam; some say Abū Bakr al-Ṣiddīq, some say ʿAlī ibn Abī Ṭālib, and some say Zayd ibn Ḥārithah. The way some scholars reconcile all these opinions is to say: Khadījah was the first woman to accept Islam, Abū Bakr was the first free man to accept Islam, ʿAlī was the first child to accept Islam, and Zayd was the first freed slave to accept Islam.

There is, however, no dispute regarding the status of Abū Bakr al-Ṣiddīq. The Ummah of Islam is unanimous in championing Abū Bakr as the best of all Companions. The Prophet ﷺ said, "Allah has chosen me as a *khalīl* (close friend), so I am not allowed to choose a *khalīl*, but if I were allowed, I would choose Abū Bakr." [120] Once, when Abū Bakr and 'Umar 🙵 had an argument, the Prophet 🙵 said to 'Umar 🙵, "When Allah sent me with the Truth, all of you accused me of being a liar, and it was only Abū Bakr who believed me. So won't you leave my Companion alone?!" [121] On another occasion, he 🙵 said, "There was not a single man whom I invited to Islam except that he had some doubts before converting, except for Abū Bakr, for as soon as I presented [Islam to him], he did not hesitate before accepting." [122] Abū Bakr 🙵 was directly referenced in the Qur'an, "[It does not matter] if you do not support him, for Allah did in fact support him when the disbelievers drove him out [of Mecca] and he was only one of two." [123] This is in reference to the Prophet 🙵 and Abū Bakr 🙵 hiding in the cave, moments away from capture and death. The verse continues, "While they were both in the cave, he reassured his Companion, 'Do not worry, for Allah is certainly with us.'" [124] Allah 🙵 refers to Abū Bakr as the Prophet's Companion, which is indeed sufficient a praise.

The next batch of converts all accepted Islam at the hand of Abū Bakr 🙵, further reinforcing his status in Islam and his integral role as the Prophet's helper. They were Sa'd ibn Abī Waqqāṣ, 'Uthmān ibn 'Affān, Zubayr ibn al-'Awwām, and 'Abdurraḥmān ibn 'Awf 🙵. Sa'd ibn Abī Waqqāṣ was the youngest at around 16 years of age. His faith was so strong that he remained steadfast despite his mother's severe emotional blackmail. She went on a hunger strike, not eating or drinking until he renounced his faith and returned to idol worship; her health deteriorated until she began withering away. Sa'd finally said, "O my mother, I will never renounce Islam. Even if you had one thousand lives, I would let you lose them one after the other before renouncing my faith." [125] Only upon witnessing such unwavering faith did she realise her efforts were futile and so began eating and drinking again. Allah 🙵 revealed verses of Qur'an in response to this event, "But if they pressure you to associate with Me what you have no knowledge of, do not obey them. But keep their company in this world courteously, and follow the way of those who turn to Me [in devotion]." [126]

'Uthmān ibn 'Affān 🙵 was one of the Prophet's closest friends. The Prophet 🙵 said, "Even the Angels are shy in his presence." [127]

He went on to become the third Caliph in Islam and will be mentioned frequently throughout this book. Zubayr ibn al-ʿAwwām ؓ is a direct cousin of the Prophet ﷺ, his mother being Ṣafiyyah bint ʿAbd al-Muṭṭalib. The Prophet ﷺ once said, "Every Prophet has his disciples, and my disciple is Zubayr ibn al-ʿAwwām."[128] ʿAbdurraḥmān ibn ʿAwf ؓ was the oldest of these four converts. When he emigrated to Medina, he left behind all his possessions and did so with no money or belongings. One of the Anṣār (Helpers) in Medina famously said, "I have two wives and two gardens. I will divorce one wife for you and give you one garden." ʿAbdurraḥmān ibn ʿAwf replied, "May Allah bless you. Just direct me towards the marketplace."[129] In no time, his entrepreneurial nature led him to be of the wealthiest businessmen in Medina, serving the Prophet ﷺ in every way he could. Each of these early converts became giants in the Muslim Ummah, leading prominent lives in Islam and playing pivotal roles in the growth and development of Islamic society.

The next to convert was ʿAbdullāh ibn Masʿūd ؓ. He was the first prominent figure not from a noble class to convert. He was not a slave but was of the servant class. He was hired as a shepherd for ʿUqbah ibn Abī Muʿayṭ, a severe enemy of Islam. One day, the Prophet ﷺ was travelling with Abū Bakr ؓ and as they passed by a farm, they said to Ibn Masʿūd, "O young man, we are thirsty. Can you give us some milk?" Ibn Masʿūd, demonstrating his honesty and integrity early on, replied, "I cannot because it is not mine to give." The Prophet said, "Very well. Show us one of the elderly she-goats that has stopped giving milk." Ibn Masʿūd pointed to one and the Prophet ﷺ went to the goat, made *duʿā'*, and its udder filled until it was full, so the two of them drank. In his astonishment, Ibn Masʿūd asked who he was talking to, and after introducing himself as a Prophet, Ibn Masʿūd converted on the spot, becoming the sixth convert to Islam.[130] The Prophet ﷺ once said about Ibn Masʿūd, "Whoever would like to know how to recite the Qur'an properly as it was originally revealed should read according to the recitation of Ibn Umm ʿAbd (i.e., Ibn Masʿūd)."[131] Ibn Masʿūd once said, "I learned more than 70 *sūrahs* (chapters) directly from the mouth of the Prophet ﷺ."[132]

The next batch of converts primarily comprised the slave class of Mecca. The most famous of them were Bilal ibn Rabāḥ, Khabbāb ibn al-Aratt, and Yāsir ibn ʿĀmir alongside his wife Sumayyah bint Khayyāṭ and their son ʿAmmār ibn Yāsir. Later, when the Prophet ﷺ wrote to the Byzantine Emperor, Heraclius, the Emperor quizzed Abū Sufyān, the Prophet's enemy. One of his questions were, "Who are his followers? Are they the rich and powerful or the weak and downtrodden?" Abū Sufyan replied that the latter was true, and Heraclius responded, "This is the sign of a true faith; that the first people who accept are the weak and downtrodden." [133] The rich and powerful have more to lose by the changing of the status quo. They are also more embedded in their own philosophies and traditions. The poor, on the other hand, have less attachment to the world.

The first non-Meccan convert to Islam was ʿAmr ibn ʿAbasa, a Yemeni Arab. He recalled, "I always knew that idolatry was wrong. One day, news came to me that someone in Mecca was preaching the same, so I travelled all the way from Yemen to Mecca to meet him." ʿAmr found the Prophet ﷺ who had not yet publicly disclosed his Prophethood. After conversing, ʿAmr asked, "What are you?" To which the Prophet ﷺ replied, "I am a Messenger." ʿAmr asked to join the Prophet ﷺ but the Prophet ﷺ did not allow it, for the *daʿwah* was too weak and ʿAmr would have no protection. The Prophet ﷺ then said, "Return home, and when news reaches you that I am victorious, come back." [134] The Prophet ﷺ demonstrated his firm belief at the earliest stage of his Prophethood. Over 15 years later when the Muslims entered Medina, ʿAmr delivered on his promise and reunited with the Prophet ﷺ.

Stages of *Daʿwah*

The above event shows that the Message was preached in stages. When ʿAmr ibn ʿAbasa asked the Messenger of Allah ﷺ about his Message, he ﷺ replied, "To fulfil the ties of kinship, to be good to one's family, and to break all idols so that only Allah ﷻ be worshipped." [135] At this stage, neither prayer nor fasting nor the Hajj pilgrimage were prescribed.

As the *daʿwah* did not have any political implications at this point, it did not cause major tensions with the Quraysh, even when they heard rumours.

This continued for three years, and the *daʿwah* did not result in any significant confrontation between the Muslims and the rest of the Quraysh, as it did not impact their trade or politics. The Prophet's teachings focused solely on matters of personal religion. As a result, the strength and resolve of these early Companions was unparalleled. Note that there were eventually over 100,000 Companions, but we only know the names of around 5,000. The first few hundred, many of whom experienced this intimate period with the Prophet ﷺ, were equal to entire nations in status and influence. Their training with the Prophet ﷺ in close quarters prepared them for the lofty duties to come as well as the gruelling tests they had to endure. They went on to lead entire cities and countries even after the Prophet ﷺ.

Prayer and ablution were then revealed; prayer was voluntary but was practiced regularly. When the Prophet ﷺ traversed the Night Journey and Ascension, prayer was mandated, and the units of prayer (*rakʿāt*) were upgraded from a uniform two units for all prayers to: two units for Fajr, four for Ẓuhr, four for ʿAṣr, three for Maghrib, and four for ʿIshā'. When Allah ﷻ obligated the prayer, He ﷻ did not need to teach the Prophet ﷺ how to pray, as the Muslims were already praying.

Three years on, the second stage was public *daʿwah* with no military combat. The Muslims were persecuted but did not retaliate. The first three to four years of this phase were difficult, but the following six to seven years were of extreme hardship. The Muslims were boycotted, tortured, and persecuted, and they were forced to endure it all. This hardship lasted for ten years and intensified until it reached boiling point, after which the Muslims migrated to Abyssinia, the details of which will be explained in detail in Chapter Seven.

The third stage was public *daʿwah* with selective military combat. In this phase, the Muslims fought the Quraysh but did not fight anyone else, as the conflict was strictly limited to the Quraysh's persecution and pressure. This occurred for the first six years after the Hijrah. The fourth stage was open *daʿwah* to all with self-defence. The Message was extended to the whole world, but fighting was not prescribed except in instances of self-defence. In this stage, the Muslims had political power, but it was not utilised for *daʿwah*. This stage occurred from the Treaty of Ḥudaybiyyah (Chapter 20) until the Conquest of Mecca (Chapter 25). The Treaty stipulated no fighting, even though the Prophet ﷺ had an army, political power, and resources. While the Muslims were disheartened at the time, it transpired to be one of Islam's biggest successes. Allah ﷻ said, "Indeed, We have granted you a clear triumph."[136]

The fifth and final stage was *daʿwah* with full military combat to anyone who opposes Islam. The Prophet ﷺ passed away in this stage, as he was sending armies alongside delegates to surrounding nations. The Caliphs after him continued this stage, conquering the Persian and Roman empires. The Umayyad Dynasty sustained this, conquering the lands of modern-day Tajikistan, Uzbekistan, Afghanistan, and more, all the way to China. By the era of the Abbasid Dynasty, the Muslims reverted to the fourth stage, whereby global *daʿwah* took place but without military conquest. This stage continued for most of Islamic history.

The stages of *daʿwah* were thus five:

1. Private *daʿwah*.
2. Public *daʿwah* with no military combat.
3. Public *daʿwah* with selective military combat.
4. Open *daʿwah* with self-defence.
5. Open *daʿwah* with full military combat.

It is pertinent to distinguish private *daʿwah* with "secret" *daʿwah*, as secrecy means to keep something to oneself, which is contrary to the principle of *daʿwah*. It also implies a degree of deceit whereas the Muslim is proud and firm in their belief. Private *daʿwah* is simply to limit the call to Islam insofar as the Ummah can be protected and sustained. The Prophetic method also demonstrates that in some cases it may be more appropriate to give *daʿwah* privately if the political climate is that of fear and danger. *Daʿwah* can never be secret, and so seekers of truth must always be taught the truth. However, some circumstances may require a private approach be utilised.

Declaration of Prophethood

Three years after the initial Revelation of "Read", Allah ﷻ revealed a number of verses commanding the Prophet ﷺ to preach publicly. Two of those Revelations were especially pivotal in taking the Message public. The first was Sūrah al-Ḥijr, "So proclaim what you have been commanded, and turn away from the polytheists." [137] The other explicit verse is in Sūrah al-Shuʿarāʾ, "And warn your closest relatives." [138] The verse was not limited to the Prophet's close relatives; the command extended to all of the Quraysh, but with particular emphasis on those closest.

First, the Prophet ﷺ went to his immediate tribe, the Banū Hāshim, which included his immediate uncles and aunts. He instructed ʿAlī ibn Abī Ṭālib ؓ, who was a young boy at the time, to prepare some food. He invited around 40 of his relatives and tribesmen. It was a blessed broth, as it was reported that everyone ate from one plate yet ate until their fill.[139] Abū Lahab, who had already heard the rumours, suspected that the Prophet ﷺ may make an announcement and declare publicly what he had been preaching privately. He then strategically excused himself, citing some business he needed to take care of. A number of other tribesmen followed suit and left. The Prophet ﷺ recognised this tactic and organised a similar gathering a few days later. This time, he ﷺ made the announcement before anyone could leave.

The Prophet ﷺ stood up and began by praising Allah ﷻ. He gave the Khuṭbah al-Ḥājjah, now recited in most Friday sermons around the world, though it was not known to the Quraysh at the time. It is as follows:

> All praise is due to Allah. I praise Him and seek His help. I believe in Him and rely upon Him alone. I testify that there is no God but Allah alone, without any partners.[140]

The Prophet ﷺ then continued, "O Banū ʿAbd al-Muṭṭalib, I do not know of any Arab before me who has come to his people with a message that is better than that which I am coming to you with." He ﷺ then continued to preach his Prophethood. This was the first time that the Prophethood was publicly announced in such a manner. Abū Lahab grew irritated and stood up, remarking to those around him, "O Banū ʿAbd al-Muṭṭalib, by Allah this call is reprehensible, so obstruct him before others do so. If you don't, you'll either accept Islam, which will be your disgrace, or you'll later oppose him and be killed." [141] The other relatives were not as harsh, though they did not take the Message that seriously.

A short time later, the Prophet ﷺ announced his Prophethood publicly to the whole city. He climbed Mount Safa (which is now much smaller than it was due to erosion). A man would only climb Mount Safa in such a manner if he had an elaborate announcement. The Prophet ﷺ exclaimed, "O *sabāḥāh*!", an exclamation specifically used to gather people's attention in sudden and dramatic fashion. He then called out to each tribe, "O Banū Fihr! O Banū ʿAdiyy!" and so on. People began to gather in throngs, and those who could not attend sent a representative in their place, until the Prophet ﷺ asked, "If I told you that horsemen were advancing to attack you from the valley on the other side of this mountain, would you believe me?" They replied, "Yes of course! We have never known you to lie." The Prophet ﷺ then said, "Then [know that] I am a warner of an impending severe punishment." He ﷺ then called them to Islam and to the worship of Allah ﷻ alone.

He continued to call them, starting from the furthest tribe from him and working inwards, "O Banū Kaʿb ibn Lu'ayy, save yourselves from the fire of Hell, for I will not be able to help you [on the Day of Judgement]. O Banū Murrah ibn Kaʿb, save yourselves from the fire of Hell...O Banū ʿAbd Manāf..." and so on. When he ﷺ arrived at Banū Hāshim, he began naming his family members one by one, "O Ḥamzah ibn ʿAbd al-Muṭṭalib...O Ṣafiyyah bint ʿAbd al-Muṭṭalib, aunt of the Prophet...O Fāṭimah bint Muhammad" and after each name was said, the same sentence was uttered, "...save yourselves from the fire of Hell, for I will not be able to help you [on the Day of Judgement]."

Abū Lahab stood up, picked up some sand, and threw it in the direction of the Prophet ﷺ in a display of disgust, saying "May your hands perish! Is this the reason you have gathered us here today?" Allah ﷻ revealed the verses in response, "May the hands of Abū Lahab perish, and may he [himself] perish! Neither his wealth nor his [worldly] gains will benefit him. He will burn in a flaming Fire, and [so will] his wife, the carrier of [thorny] kindling. Around her neck will be a rope of palm-fire[i]." [142] Proving his own demise, Abū Lahab would indeed go on to display the most animosity and cruelty to the Prophet ﷺ and his Companions ‎رضي الله عنهم.

The Prophet's methodology in calling out the tribes in order of closeness to him is particularly striking. It clearly outlines how each person is responsible first and foremost to their immediate family followed by society at large. Indeed, Allah ﷻ revealed "And warn your closest relatives." [143] The Prophet ﷺ first called Banū Hāshim, then he made a public call to the people of Mecca, and a few years later he extended his call to the whole of humanity. After this event, the Prophet ﷺ began preaching publicly throughout Mecca. He would preach at the Kaʿbah, at public venues, and at the marketplace. He ﷺ would even wait outside Mecca for Pilgrims of Hajj to preach to them too. The Prophet's *daʿwah* became public, and opposition inevitably began.

Dār al-Arqam

As the number of believers grew over a dozen, they needed a place to congregate. They did not have a mosque and could not meet in public without compromising their safety. A few months after the *daʿwah* became public, the Prophet ﷺ chose the house of al-Asad ibn ʿAbd al-ʿUzzā, more famously known as al-Arqam ibn Abī al-Arqam.

i It is reported that the wife of Abū Lahab wore a valuable necklace and would say, "By al-Lāt and al-ʿUzzā, I will sell this necklace and spend the money to satisfy my enmity against Muhammad." (Al-Qurṭubī, *al-Jāmiʿ li-Aḥkām al-Qur'ān*, vol. 22, p. 554.) Allah ﷻ therefore promised her a necklace in the Hellfire.

He was one of the first ten people to accept Islam but was from the Banū Makhzūm clan, not the Banū Hāshim. This situated him perfectly to be the host of this gathering, as no-one would suspect a Makhzūmī to harbour a Hāshimī. Moreover, al-Arqam's house was situated in the centre of Mecca, which was always busy. It was therefore an ideal location for regular meetings, as attendees could seamlessly enter and exit without suspicion. Dār al-Arqam (The House of al-Arqam) thus became the hub of the Muslims—a centre for teaching, prayer, and strategy.

Opposition from the Quraysh

The people of Mecca did not have one ruler. Instead, they deferred to a council of senior figures. Their rule can be described as a form of aristocracy. Each tribe had a leader, and each leader held a seat on this senior council. The leader of the Banū Hāshim was Abū Ṭālib, so the Quraysh tried to appeal to him. Abū Ṭālib calmed their moods and briefly stalled them. A few weeks later, as the *daʿwah* continued to spread, they returned to him, this time with intensified efforts. They tried to cajole him, bribe him, and even threatened him.

The Prophet ﷺ condemned idolatry. The Quraysh took this as a personal attack and equated it to a condemnation of their culture, way of life, and honour. They gave Abū Ṭālib an ultimatum: either stop him from preaching or hand him over. This ultimatum was significant, as Abū Ṭālib had never been confronted in such a manner before. Tribal law dictates that they cannot do anything to the Prophet ﷺ without the tribe leader's consent lest they be subject to dishonour and ridicule.

Abū Ṭālib returned to the Prophet ﷺ and said, "O my nephew, my people have approached me and told me such-and-such. So, be merciful to yourself and be merciful to me; do not place me in a situation that I cannot bear." The Prophet ﷺ responded in the most profound manner, "O my uncle, by Allah if they were to give me the Sun in my right hand

and the Moon in my left, I cannot give up this Message until I succeed or I am martyred."[144] In another narration, he ﷺ said, "Do you see the Sun in the sky, O uncle? By Allah I have no more power to stop preaching than you have to light your [walking] stick with the Sun."[145] When Abū Ṭālib saw the Prophet's persistence in his actions, passion in his eyes, and sincerity in his speech, he replied, "Do as you wish, my nephew, for by Allah I will never approach you again asking you to stop."[146] Indeed, Abū Ṭālib fulfilled his word until his death, even when ridiculed, boycotted, and expelled.

The Quraysh then gathered and approached Abū Ṭālib once more, this time in their entirety, not just Banū Hāshim. They proposed an offer, "We have chosen the most noble young man in Mecca, al-ʿUmārah ibn al-Walīd (the son of al-Walīd ibn al-Mughīrah, the Chieftain of the Banū Makhzūm clan). Our offer is to exchange one son for the other; you adopt al-ʿUmārah in exchange for your nephew." Abū Ṭālib was livid with this proposition, "What an evil bargain! You want me to fatten up your son in exchange for you to kill mine?" Muṭʿim ibn ʿAdiyy then spoke out, "Your people have done all they can and exhausted all their means. You must choose an option."[147] This was a weighty remark, as this senior figure was the last person to remain neutral, and his decision to side with the Quraysh meant that the entirety of Mecca was against one single man.

Abū Ṭālib's bravery in this regard is unparalleled, as the next step would be to overthrow a tribe leader—an unprecedented move. Abū Ṭālib stood firm in his brave support. He said, "O Muṭʿim, this is a plot you have hatched! Do as you please, for I will not stand down."[148] Abū Ṭālib then composed a series of poems of the highest calibre of eloquence chastising the Quraysh, accusing them of treachery. Abū Ṭālib's poetry was so powerful and moving that it caused the Quraysh to momentarily back down and de-escalate. Abū Ṭālib's strength and dignity in his sincerity saved the Prophet ﷺ by the will of Allah when there was no other way out.

The Prophet ﷺ did not love anyone more than he did Abū Ṭālib. He served as his father and mother in one, raising, supporting, and nurturing him his whole life. Abū Ṭālib was so beloved to the Prophet ﷺ and the Companions that years later at the conquest of Mecca, when Abū Bakr's father, Abū Quḥāfah, accepted Islam near the end of his life, Abū Bakr ؓ wept and said to the Prophet ﷺ, "O Messenger of Allah, how I wish that this hand was the hand of your uncle, Abū Ṭālib, rather than the hand of my own father." [149] Alas, Abū Ṭālib never converted to Islam, despite the Prophet's most desperate pleas. Indeed, Allah's wisdom reigns supreme; had Abū Ṭālib converted, he would have been deposed as Chieftain, and the *daʿwah* would have been crushed. Moreover, it clearly demonstrates both the sincerity and limitation of our Prophet ﷺ. Only a sincere Messenger would accept this fate despite the emotional impact. Moreover, he ﷺ is a slave of Allah, not a god; only Allah ﷻ Himself can guide.

Tensions Rise in Mecca

The Quraysh tried to ban the recitation of the Qur'an. Not only did they try to physically stop any recitation, but they would also drown it out with abuse and profanity. Ibn ʿAbbās ؓ narrated that whenever the Prophet ﷺ would raise his voice to recite the Qur'an in front of the Kaʿbah, they would curse both Allah ﷻ and His Messenger ﷺ.[150] The Prophet ﷺ would then raise his voice to overcome their insults, but Allah ﷻ revealed, "Do not recite your prayers too loudly nor silently but seek a way between." [151] Allah ﷻ here is instilling the methodology of focusing on one's own mission without being distracted by the actions of others.

The Companions gathered at Dar al-Arqam. No-one had publicly recited the Qur'an except the Prophet ﷺ, so they discussed who would be the first. ʿAbdullāh ibn Masʿūd ؓ volunteered to take on the task. The Companions refused because Ibn Masʿūd had no Qurashī family to protect him (i.e., someone from the Quraysh). Tribal custom dictated that tribe members protected each other, thus the bigger and more powerful the tribe, the more protection one had. Not only did Ibn Masʿūd not belong to a tribe, but he was not even from Mecca. He therefore had no-one to protect him in the event of an attack.

Nevertheless, Ibn Masʿūd 🙵 persisted and again volunteered himself, saying "I put my trust in Allah." [152]

Ibn Masʿūd went to the Kaʿbah at the peak time of gathering. As the qāriʾ (reciter) of the Companions, he had a beautiful voice, and he began reciting in an exquisitely melodious tone. He recited Sūrah al-Raḥmān, and it was so captivating that people started to gather. Moreover, the style of Qurʾanic recitation was a unique phenomenon to the Quraysh; it did not emulate poetry nor prose. It was equally fascinating as it was captivating. When they eventually realised what he was reciting, they pounced on him, physically beating him. He could not even finish two pages of the sūrah before being driven out, battered and bruised. The Companions bemoaned, "This is exactly what we were worried about!" Ibn Masʿūd boasted, "By Allah, nothing changed today except that my contempt for the Quraysh has only increased, and I am willing to do the same tomorrow." [153]

Three of the senior leaders of the Quraysh—Abū Jahl, Abū Sufyān, and al-Akhnas—were mesmerised by the parts of the Qurʾan they had heard. Their reputation did not allow them to listen in public, so they waited until the dead of the night to listen. The Prophet 🙵 would pray tahajjud every night, which was the perfect opportunity. Each of them had set out to listen in secret, not knowing that the other two did the same. When they bumped into each other at Fajr time, they realised what had just happened. Each of them made their own excuse as to why they were there, but the reality was clear to all. The next night, the same thing happened. The third night, it happened once more, and their embarrassment grew. They admitted what they were doing and made a pact not to come again lest they be exposed by anyone else. For a person to wake up at three-o-clock in the morning, leave their bed and home, and stand in an alleyway in the dead of the night just to listen to a recitation truly demonstrates the mesmerising nature of the Qurʾan. One can only imagine the tranquillity, charisma, and exquisiteness of the Prophet's own recitation 🙵.

Al-Akhnas then approached Abū Sufyān and asked, "What do you think about what we heard?" Embarrassed, Abū Sufyān said, "You tell me your opinion first." After al-Akhnas insisted, Abū Sufyān, not wanting to compromise his reputation, replied diplomatically, "Some parts were beyond my comprehension and other parts I understood." [154] Al-Akhnas then approached Abū Jahl, asking the same question. Abū Jahl responded frankly, "We (i.e., the Banū Makhzūm) and the Banū ʿAbd Manāf have always been in competition; when they began giving food to the pilgrims, we did too. When they began giving out water, we did too. We are like two horses about to reach the finish line, and they now come and say they have a Prophet who Allah inspires from the Heavens. How can we compete with that? By Allah, for as long as I live, I will never accept it." [155]

Another tactic used by the Quraysh was to disparage the Prophet ﷺ and the believers, spreading rumours and hurling insults and mockery. For example, when a period of time passed without the Prophet ﷺ receiving Revelation, a Qurashī woman mocked, "I see that your Shayṭān has abandoned you!" [156] This remark deeply hurt the Prophet ﷺ, and Allah ﷻ revealed the famous verses of Sūrah al-Ḍuḥā, "By the morning sunlight, and the night when it falls still. Your Lord has not abandoned you, nor has He become hateful [of you]. And the next life is certainly far better for you than this one. And surely your Lord will give so much to you that you will be pleased. Did He not find you as an orphan then shelter you? Did He not find you unguided then guide you? And did He not find you needy then suffice you? So do not suppress an orphan, nor repulse the beggar. And proclaim the blessings of your Lord." [157]

Abū Jahl would especially go out of his way to denigrate the believers. If they were a slave or *mawlā*[ii] he would physically abuse them and instruct their owners to do the same. If they were noblemen of a prestigious clan, he could not physically attack them but would instead verbally abuse them at any given opportunity. He would play on their notion of honour and tribal sensibilities, asking, "Are you better than your father and grandfather?" He would mention their names to evoke

ii A *mawlā* is a client of manumission who would oftentimes still hold a sense of loyalty and allegiance to the person that freed them.

a response. If they were businessmen, he would boycott their business and pressure others to do so too. The Prophet ﷺ described Abū Jahl as "The Pharoah of my Ummah".[158]

Once, someone bought something from Abū Jahl but did not receive his payment. In a bid to prank the Prophet ﷺ, Abū Jahl remarked mockingly, "Go to Muhammad, he will pay you!" The man, who was not from Mecca, assumed that the Prophet ﷺ perhaps owed Abū Jahl, and so went to the Prophet ﷺ and asked for the money. The Prophet ﷺ took him by the hand to Abū Jahl's house and knocked on his door. He ﷺ said, "O Abū Jahl, give the man his money right now." Abū Jahl's face turned pale and he began trembling. He scrambled for some money and thrust a bag of money at the man. Later, a friend of Abū Jahl said, "How could you give the man his money after Muhammad demanded it?" Abū Jahl replied, "I saw something terrifying that you did not see."[159] In another narration, he said, "I saw a herd of angry camels behind him waiting to pounce!"[160]

The Quraysh then stooped to an unprecedented level and began to slander and lie about the Prophet ﷺ and the believers. They would regurgitate the same lies: he is crazy; he is a fortune teller; he is a magician; he is bewitched. It is of course impossible for madness to be compartmentalised; one cannot be crazy in one aspect yet be perfectly sane in every other aspect of their life. The Prophet ﷺ was not only sane in every other regard, but he was exceptional in his role as a leader, a family man, and a warrior. The reality is that the Prophet's sincerity could not be doubted, even by his staunchest enemies, which left madness and sorcery as the only conceivable explanations.

Abū Jahl and Abū Lahab would stand on the outskirts of Mecca and warn travellers that the Prophet ﷺ was a magician "O people, be careful! Do not be mesmerised into turning away from the gods of your forefathers!"[161] These tactics ironically led to some people's conversion. Ḍimād al-Azdī, a leader of a Yemeni tribe, literally put cotton in his ears until he eventually questioned his actions as an intelligent man. He said to himself, "I am a doctor, so I will cure him." He approached the Prophet ﷺ, "I heard you are a madman, and I am here to cure you." The Prophet ﷺ replied, "I am not a madman, but listen to my Message." He ﷺ then began with the Khuṭbah al-Ḥājjah, and before the Prophet ﷺ could even start reciting Qur'an, the man said, "Stop! Repeat what you just said." The Prophet ﷺ repeated the Khuṭbah al-Ḥājjah and the man said, "By Allah I have not heard anything more beautiful than this. What are you?" The Prophet ﷺ declared himself as a Prophet and Ḍimād accepted Islam.[162]

They also called him a poet, even though it was well-known that the Prophet ﷺ could not even read or write. Allah ﷻ revealed, "You could not read any writing [even] before this Revelation, nor could you write at all. Otherwise, the people of falsehood would have been suspicious."[163]

The Unlettered Prophet

Pre-Islamic Arabia was at the pinnacle of linguistic prowess. The poets of Mecca were masters of the Arabic language, and their reputations preceded them. Society revolved around the use of language and poetry, from media and politics to entertainment and leisure. The most eloquent poets were the most influential and respected figures. The greatest poet of them all was al-Walīd ibn al-Mughīrah, the Chieftain of the Banū Makhzūm and father of Khālid ibn al-Walīd ؓ. On one occasion, the Prophet ﷺ was reciting the Qur'an in front of the Kaʿbah and al-Walīd ibn al-Mughīrah finally had a chance to listen properly. He was mesmerised and stopped in his tracks until the Prophet ﷺ finished. He muttered a statement of prose which then spread like wildfire:

> "By Allah, there is no-one amongst you more knowledgeable in poetry than me, neither the [metre of] *rajaz*, nor the [form of] the *qaṣīdah*, or the poetry of the jinn. By Allah, what he is saying does not resemble any of these, and by Allah, the speech he utters has a certain sweetness and charm. The upper part is fruitful and the lower part is well-watered and abundant. It supersedes and nothing supersedes it, and it crushes whatever is beneath it."[164]

The people of Mecca began to panic. The greatest poet of Mecca—as a Pagan—admitted defeat after hearing a single recitation of Qur'an. When the news reached Abū Jahl, he sought to rectify the situation. He said to al-Walīd, "Your people have heard that you have praised the Qur'an, and they will not be satisfied with you until you disassociate with Muhammad and speak out against the Qur'an." [165] Unlike Abū Ṭālib, who was the embodiment of integrity and leadership, standing his ground and sticking to his principles, al-Walīd was a more typical politician, acquiescing to external pressure. He replied, "Tell me what to say." Abū Jahl said, "Call him a madman." Al-Mughīrah responded, "But everyone knows he's not a madman, and he does not exhibit any symptoms of a crazy person." Abū Jahl said, "Okay, so call him a fortune teller." Al-Mughīrah again responded, "But he is not a fortune teller; he doesn't have their vernacular nor their style." Abū Jahl then said, "Call him a magician." Once again, al-Mughīrah said, "But he is not a magician; he does not have their invocations or tricks." Abū Jahl finally said, "Call him a poet." Al-Mughīrah responded, "By Allah I am the best poet amongst you; none of you can compete with me, and I am saying that this is not poetry." Abū Jahl persisted, demanding, "You must say something, and we will not be satisfied with you until you do." Al-Mughīrah then asked to be left alone for a few days to think of a solution.

He grew increasingly exasperated thinking of a solution until he finally came up with an idea. However, before he even had the chance to vocalise it, Allah ﷻ sent down verses of Qur'an articulating—with striking accuracy—his ideas, thoughts, feelings, and even facial expressions. "And leave to me the one I created all by Myself, and granted him abundant wealth and children always by his side, and made life very easy for him. Yet he is hungry for more. But no, he has truly been stubborn with Our Revelations. I will make his fate unbearable, for he contemplated and determined [a degrading label for the Qur'an]. May he be condemned! How evil was his determination! May he be condemned even more! How evil was his determination! Then he re-contemplated [in frustration], then frowned and scowled, then turned his back [on the truth] and acted arrogantly, saying 'This [Qur'an] is nothing but magic from the ancients. This is no more than the word of man.'

Soon I will burn him in Hell! And what will make you realise what Hell is? It does not let anyone live or die, scorching the skin."[166] It is only befitting for Allah ﷻ to send down some of the most powerful verses in the entire Qur'an in response to al-Walīd, who inevitably died a Pagan despite both his children eventually accepting Islam.

The Quraysh would also challenge the Prophet ﷺ to produce a miracle. This occurs in many instances, one of which is narrated in Sūrah al-Isrā', "They challenge, 'We will never believe you until you cause a spring to gush forth from the Earth for us, or until you [miraculously] produce a garden of palm trees and vineyards, and cause rivers to flow abundantly in it, or cause the sky to fall upon us in pieces, as you have claimed, or bring Allah and the Angels before us, face to face, or until you have a house of gold, or you ascend into the Heaven—and even then we will not believe in your ascension until you bring down to us a Book that we can read.' Say, 'Glory be to my Lord! Am I not only a human Messenger?'"

As to why Allah ﷻ did not reveal the miracles they asked for, it is because He revealed the biggest miracle of all: the Qur'an. Moreover, it is clear that they were demanding miracles out of arrogance, not sincerity. Allah ﷻ says, "Even if We had sent them Angels, made the dead speak to them, and assembled before their own eyes every sign [they demanded], they still would not have believed—unless Allah so willed. But most of them are ignorant."[167] The previous nations—such as the likes of 'Ād and Thamūd—indeed refused to accept the Truth even after being shown miracles. "Nothing keeps Us from sending the signs except that they had [already] been denied by earlier nations."[168]

Between Bribery and Torture

The Quraysh then began bargaining and exploring other solutions. They began negotiating with the Prophet ﷺ directly, offering a compromise. One such attempt was the offer to share religions; they proposed that Allah alone be worshipped one day, and the idols be worshipped the next day, alternating between the two. There is of course no compromise in the Oneness of Allah ﷻ, and Allah revealed Sūrah al-Kāfirūn, "Say, 'O you disbelievers! I do not worship what you worship, nor do you worship what I worship. I will never worship what you worship, nor will you ever worship what I worship. You have your way, and I have my Way.'"[169] As previously mentioned, the Quraysh did worship Allah, and yet Allah ﷻ instructs the Prophet ﷺ to say "I do not worship what you worship" because worshipping Allah ﷻ through intermediaries is *shirk* (polytheism), nullifying the worship in its entirety. The Quraysh then asked what the Prophet ﷺ wanted in order to cease. The Prophet ﷺ replied that he wanted one statement from them, to which Abū Jahl replied ecstatically, "We will give you ten!"[170] The Prophet ﷺ revealed the statement to be the Islamic declaration of faith: There is no god but Allah. They responded as described by Allah in the Qur'an, "'Has he reduced [all] the gods to One God? Indeed, this is something totally astonishing.'"[171]

When offers of compromise failed, the Quraysh resorted to outright bribery. ʿUtbah ibn Rabīʿah, a distant uncle of the Prophet ﷺ, approached him on behalf of the Quraysh. He said, "O my nephew, you know your lineage and status; you are the grandson of ʿAbd al-Muṭṭalib and the son of ʿAbdullāh. You have come forward with a matter that has wreaked havoc on our people. O Muhammad, are you better than ʿAbd al-Muṭṭalib? Are you better than ʿAbdullāh?"[172] The Prophet ﷺ did not respond, as there is no wisdom in replying to a loaded, rhetorical question. ʿUtbah continued, "We have never seen a young man as promising as you flip around so suddenly and bring so much harm to our people. The Arabs are mocking us, you are creating disunity, and we are on the precipice of civil war. We have a number of suggestions that may interest you. If you are interested in money, I have the power of the Quraysh vested in me to offer you more money than any of us have, and you shall be the richest Arab. If you want power, we will make you our king. And if you want women, choose any woman that you want, and we will ensure that she marries you. If you think you are ill, we will hire doctors to cure you."[173] Embodying true wisdom and respect, the Prophet ﷺ waited until he finished and replied, "Are you done, O Abū al-Walīd?" ʿUtbah replied in the affirmative, and the Prophet ﷺ said, "Now listen to me." He ﷺ then began reciting,

"I seek refuge in Allah from the accursed devil.[iii] In the Name of Allah, the Most Compassionate, Most Merciful.[iv] *Ḥā-Mīm.* [This is] a Revelation from the Most Compassionate, Most Merciful. [It is] a Book Whose verses are perfectly explained—a Qur'an in Arabic for people who know, delivering good news and warning. Yet most of them turn away, so they do not hear. They say, 'Our hearts are veiled against what you are calling us to; there is deafness in our ears, and there is a barrier between us and you. So do [whatever you want] and so shall we!' Say, 'I am only a man like you, but it has been revealed to me that your God is only One God. So take the Straight Path towards Him, and seek His forgiveness.' And woe to the polytheists—those who do not pay *zakāh* (alms-tax) and are in denial of the Hereafter. [But] those who believe and do good will certainly have a never-ending reward. Ask them, 'How can you disbelieve in the One Who created the Earth in two Days[v]? How can you set up equals with Him? That is the Lord of the worlds. He placed on the Earth firm mountains, standing high, showered His blessings upon it, and ordained [all] its means of sustenance—completing four Days exactly—for all who ask. Then He turned towards the Heaven when it was [still like] smoke, saying to it and to the Earth, "Submit, willingly or unwillingly." They both responded, "We submit willingly." So he formed the Heaven into Seven Heavens in two Days, assigning to each its mandate.' And We adorned the lowest Heaven with [stars like] lamps [for beauty] and protection.

iii Refuge is sought from Allah before one recites the Qur'an, referred to as the *isti'ādhah.*

iv One begins every *sūrah* in the Name of Allah, referred to as the *basmalah.*

v The word "Days" is capitalised as it does not refer to 24-hour periods of time, but rather unspecified periods of time unknown to mankind. (Muhammad Jamāl al-Dīn al-Qāsimī, *Tafsīr al-Qāsimī*, Dār al-Kutub al-'Ilmiyyah, Beirut (1424/2003), vol. 5, pp. 67–68.)

> That is the design of the Almighty, All-Knowing. If they turn away, then say, 'I warn you of a [mighty] blast like the one that befell 'Ād and Thamūd.'"[174]

Prior to this conversation, and like most of the Quraysh, 'Utbah had not actually listened to the Qur'an with intent. As the Prophet ﷺ continued reciting, 'Utbah's expression began to change, and as the power of the recitation and tempo began to intensify, he started palpitating. It continued to increase in power and intensity until it rose to a crescendo with the verse, "If they turn away, then say, 'I warn you of a [mighty] blast like the one that befell 'Ād and Thamūd.'"[175] At which point 'Utbah could not take it any longer and jumped up, forcibly putting his hand over the blessed mouth of the Prophet ﷺ, pleading, "I beg you by Allah—and by the rights I have over you as a blood relative—stop, and not to send this punishment." He then turned and ran back to the Quraysh from whom he came, and said, "Listen to me: leave this man alone because I have heard a speech from him which I have never heard before. I could not comprehend all of it,[vi] but he will hold importance [in the world]. If the Arabs get rid of him for us, our hands are clean; but if he is victorious over the Arabs, then by Allah his victory is our victory, and his power is our power."[176] The Quraysh dismissed his advice, remarking, "He has bewitched you like he bewitched everybody else."

The Quraysh then turned to a nation more experienced in dealing with Prophethood. Although remnants of the religion of Ibrāhīm ﷺ were present in Mecca, most notably through the presence of the Ka'bah, his Prophetic teachings were largely forgotten, and the concept of Prophethood was now foreign to them. The Jews and Christians, on the other hand, retained their history of Prophethood. Their teachings had been distorted and corrupted, but the "People of the Book" i.e., Abrahamic religions, were still familiar with the idea of Prophethood and the role of a Prophet or Messenger.

---

vi This is not the first time that the Quraysh made such a statement about not comprehending all of the Qur'an. Some scholars explain that this was due to some complicated words, but in truth, the words were not particularly complicated. Rather, it was due to their entrenchment in *shirk* clouding their comprehension of pure, unadulterated Truth.

Two of the worst of the Quraysh—ʿUqbah ibn Abī Muʿayṭ and al-Naḍr ibn Ḥārith—approached the Jews in Medina and asked for ways to quiz and catch out the Prophet ﷺ. One instruction was to ask the Prophet ﷺ about Prophets Isḥāq, Yaʿqūb, and Yūsuf ﷺ, particularly about what happened to the family of Yaʿqūb ﷺ. The Quraysh asked the Prophet ﷺ and Allah ﷻ revealed the entirety of Sūrah Yūsuf as a response. On another occasion, they instructed the Quraysh to ask the Prophet ﷺ three questions, adding, "No-one would know the answers to these three questions except a true Prophet."[177] The three instructions were:

1. Ask him about the young men who slept in the cave and slept a long time.
2. Ask him about the man who travelled the world from the east to the west whose experiences are now legends.
3. Ask him about the *rūḥ* (spirit; soul)—where does it come from?

The Prophet ﷺ responded confidently, "I will inform you of what you have asked about tomorrow."[178] However, because the Prophet ﷺ was confident that Allah ﷻ would respond, he ﷺ forgot to say *inshāAllāh* (if Allah wills). As a result, Revelation did not descend the next day, but rather after two long weeks. The Quraysh began to mock the Prophet ﷺ after Revelation did not descend the following day as promised. They would provoke him, "Muhammad promised us that he would inform us the next day. Two weeks have passed and he has not informed us of anything!"[179] Allah ﷻ reminded the Prophet—and the believers at large—as to the relationship between the Lord and His slave. Allah is the One Who plans in His infinite wisdom.

It should be noted that being referred to as a slave of Allah is the highest praise, not a derogatory remark. Allah ﷻ refers to the Prophet ﷺ as His slave five times: "Yet when the slave of Allah stood up calling upon Him [alone], the Pagans almost swarmed over him"[180]; "Glory be to the One Who took His slave by night..."[181]; "Blessed is the One Who sent down the Standard to His slave so that he may be a warner to the whole world."[182]; "All praise is for Allah Who has revealed the Book to His slave, allowing no crookedness in it."[183];

"He is the One Who sends down clear Revelations to His servant to bring you out of darkness and into light." [184] Indeed, there is no honour higher than being a worshipper and slave of Allah ﷻ.

Allah ﷻ revealed verses of the Qur'an as a response to the three aforementioned questions. Details were provided about the people of the cave that even the Jews did not know. Similarly, Allah ﷻ identified the man with famous expeditions as Dhū al-Qarnayn.[vii] As for the *rūḥ*, Allah ﷻ maintained that it is of the mysteries of knowledge that human beings on Earth will never know. "They ask you about the *rūḥ*. Say, 'Its nature is known only to my Lord, and you [O humanity] have been given but little knowledge.'" [185] The Jews indeed knew that no-one has knowledge of the *rūḥ*, and so it was a trick question placed alongside two genuine questions in a bid to expose the Prophet ﷺ.

Undeterred, the Quraysh escalated their persecution and began to physically torture the Companions. Saʿīd ibn Jubayr ؓ asked Ibn ʿAbbās ؓ about the extent of the torture, to which Ibn ʿAbbās said, "The believers were tortured in the early days of Islam so severely that they were deprived of food and water to the extent that they could not even sit upright. They were tortured until they were asked 'Is al-Lāt[viii] your god? Is al-ʿUzzā your god?' and answered in the affirmative." [186]

The Struggles of the First Muslims

ʿAbdullāh ibn Masʿūd mentioned that the first group of seven that embraced Islam were himself, Abū Bakr, ʿAmmār, Sumayyah, Ṣuhayb, Bilāl, and al-Miqdād ؓ. He continued,

vii Some people believe that Alexander the Great was Dhū al-Qarnayn. However that is patently false, as Alexander the Great was a Pagan under the tutelage of the Pagan philosopher, Aristotle. It seems that he was not identified in Western sources, and there is a difference of opinion amongst the scholars as to whether he was a Prophet or just a king.

viii Al-Lāt, al-ʿUzzā, and Manāt were the three chief goddesses worshipped by the Quraysh. They were also referred to as "god's daughters".

> "As for the Prophet ﷺ, Allah ﷻ protected him through his uncle; as for Abū Bakr ﷺ, Allah protected him through his own tribe, the Banū Quḥāfah; and as for the remainder, then the Quraysh rounded them up and began torturing them. They would take burning iron and place it on their bodies until they complied. Every one of them gave up and said out of duress whatever the Quraysh wanted them to say—except for Bilāl ibn Rabāḥ. He did not consider his soul worth anything in front of Allah ﷻ (i.e., he was willing to give up his soul), and he refused to budge in the slightest. As a result, they concentrated all their efforts in torturing him. I saw Bilāl handed over to the thugs of Mecca who proceeded to tie a rope around his neck and drag him across the streets of Mecca, all the while he shouted 'One; One!' (proclaiming the Oneness of Allah ﷻ)." [187]

Bilāl's master was one of the worst culprits of the Quraysh, Umayyah ibn Khalaf, who participated in his torture. It is worth noting that slaves were expensive to acquire and own. It was therefore counter-intuitive to harm one's own slave, further demonstrating the extent of their animosity to Islam and Muslims. Umayyah would personally take Bilāl ﷺ into the desert and place a massive rock on his chest and leave him in the Sun for the entirety of the day.[188]

Ḥassān ibn Thābit ﷺ once recalled that when he performed Hajj from Medina, he noticed how badly Bilāl ﷺ was being punished, wondering how he remained alive. ʿAmr ibn al-ʿĀṣ similarly recalled that the rocks placed on Bilāl ﷺ were so hot that meat could be cooked on them. ʿAmr ﷺ continued, "I heard Bilāl repeatedly say, 'I reject al-Lāt and al-ʿUzzā and I believe in Allah!'" [189] Many years later, ʿUrwah ibn Zubayr, the nephew of the Mother of the Believers ʿĀ'ishah ﷺ, narrated, "Bilāl was tortured by the people of Mecca, and by Umayyah ibn Khalaf in particular, but he never gave them a single word to please them." [190]

Bilāl's honour and reward matched his struggles, as the Prophet ﷺ eventually appointed him as the *mu'adhdhin* (caller to prayer) of the Ummah. The same voice that roared "One; One!" would echo throughout the city of Mecca five times a day calling the Muslims to prayer. Bilāl's reputation and prestige withstood 1,400 years of Islamic history, as he is still most known for his bravery, forbearance, and unwavering belief in Allah ﷻ. The Qur'an states, "Is there any reward for goodness except goodness?"[191] The Prophet ﷺ said, "Give the *adhān* even if you are alone because no jinn or human will hear your voice except that they will testify to what you said on the Day of Judgement."[192] Bilāl ؓ, having the honour of being the Prophet's *mu'adhdhin,* will therefore have the Prophet's testimony in front of Allah ﷻ on the Day of Judgement.

Khabbāb ibn al-Aratt ؓ was of the first ten people to embrace Islam. He was an Arab slave of Yemeni origin and had a female master, Umm Anmār. When she found out that he embraced Islam, she hired a mob to beat him so badly that he lost consciousness, waking up in a pool of his own blood. She would even partake in his torture, holding a piece of burning iron against his back. The Prophet ﷺ was pained by Khabbāb's state so he made a heartfelt *duʿā'* to Allah ﷻ, "O Allah, please help Khabbāb against his enemy." A few days later, Umm Anmār woke up in a rabid state of psychosis. The doctors of Mecca prescribed her with a treatment of cauterisation, which led to her death. The Prophet ﷺ once commanded, "No-one may punish with fire except the Lord of fire."[193] Allah ﷻ then decreed poetic justice that her demise was via a painful bout of cauterisation.

Many years later, when ʿUmar ibn al-Khaṭṭāb ؓ was Caliph, he asked Khabbāb about Umm Anmār. Without saying a word, Khabbāb simply lifted his shirt and exposed his back. ʿUmar exclaimed, "By Allah, I have not seen anything like this before!"[194] He then placed Khabbāb on the seat beside him as a show of honour. When Abū Bakr ؓ was Caliph, he ruled that all government representatives receive the same salary, however when ʿUmar took charge he ruled that the earliest converts receive the highest salaries. Khabbāb therefore received a very generous salary as one of the earliest to embrace Islam. He built a modest house in Kufa and used the remainder of the money to create a charitable trust in the form of a treasure box in his house. The box was unlocked and open for anybody to take whatever they wanted without needing to request permission.

On his deathbed, he began to cry. The people around him said, "Why are you crying? You have suffered so much to reach the highest level and meet the Prophet ﷺ." He replied, "I am not crying out of pain or fear of meeting Allah; I am crying because of what you see around you (i.e., the house). How will I answer Allah about this luxury? Indeed, I was with a group of people who were all tortured on equal footing, but every one of them has departed without tasting the sweetness of this world, and Allah has left me to enjoy the fruits of this world. I am scared that because I have enjoyed the fruits of this world, my share of the Hereafter will be less than that of my companions." As they prepared his *kafan* (cloth for shrouding), he began to cry once more, and said, "By Allah, I remember Ḥamzah, the uncle of the Prophet ﷺ. He did not even have enough cloth for his own *kafan*, yet here I have this luxurious *kafan* in front of me. With what will I meet Allah?" [195]

The stories of Yāsir, Sumayyah, and their son 'Ammār ؓ have captured the hearts of Muslims for over a millennium due to their unified struggle in the face of unrelenting, merciless torture. They were tortured in front of each other, a fate far worse than the physical pain itself. Their torture was so severe that the Prophet ﷺ made a special *du'ā*, "Be patient O family of Yāsir, indeed your place is in Paradise." [196] Yāsir ؓ was then brutally killed and became the first martyr in Islam. Sumayyah grew enraged and bravely rebuked Abū Jahl despite her slave status, to which Abū Jahl murdered her in the most brutal and inhumane manner. He then killed Muhammad, 'Ammār's older brother, and turned to 15-year-old 'Ammār, the youngest of them all. At this point, 'Ammār could not bear the pain any longer and succumbed to Abū Jahl's demands, outwardly renouncing his faith.

'Ammār was so distraught about what he uttered that his worry about potentially committing disbelief was at the forefront of his mind despite the horrific events that just occurred. He ran to the Prophet ﷺ in despair and said, "O Messenger of Allah, I have uttered words of *kufr* (disbelief)." The Prophet ﷺ asked, "How do you find your [faith in your] heart?" He replied, "As it always was" i.e., his faith is as strong as it always was, and his words did not depict what was in his heart. The Prophet ﷺ reassured him that he had no blame, and he was permitted to repeat those words if they tortured him again. Allah ﷻ then revealed Sūrah al-Naḥl, "Whoever disbelieves in Allah after their belief—not those who are forced while their hearts are firm in faith, but those who embrace disbelief wholeheartedly—they will be condemned by Allah and suffer a tremendous punishment." [197] The Prophet ﷺ said about ʿAmmār, "His *īmān* has been filled in his heart all the way to his neck" [198] i.e., his faith is overflowing; and, "Whenever the son of Sumayyah is faced with two options, he always chooses the most correct of the two." [199]

Ṣuhayb al-Rūmī (the Roman) ﷺ was not actually Roman; he was of Iraqi descent but was captured by a Byzantine force as a child and was enslaved in Rome. He escaped, recalling his Arab heritage, and fled to Arabia. Eventually, he was bought by ʿAbdullāh ibn Judʿān in Mecca. While Ibn Judʿān did not torture him, he did not prevent the likes of Abū Jahl from doing so. However, compared to the likes of Abū Jahl and his ilk, Ibn Judʿān was more lenient as a master. He granted Ṣuhayb responsibilities in trade and granted him freedom in his will. Upon Ibn Judʿān's death, Ṣuhayb emigrated to Medina but was stopped by the Quraysh on the outskirts. Ṣuhayb took out his bow and arrow, saying, "You know I am the most accurate shooter, and I promise that none of you will be able to touch me until every arrow in my quiver will touch human flesh. And I promise that none of you will be able to touch me until my sword is bent and broken upon your bones and blood." [200]

They did not approach any further but demanded that he leave his money behind if he wanted to continue his journey. Not only did they demand his wealth, but they insisted that he leave his horse behind and continue on foot. Ṣuhayb was faced with a choice: turn back with his wealth or continue to the Prophet ﷺ penniless and on foot. Ṣuhayb thus became the only Companion ever to perform hijrah on foot, leaving with nothing but the clothes on his back. He reached the Prophet ﷺ in

Masjid Qubā' dishevelled, dehydrated, malnourished, and crawling on his hands and knees. The Prophet ﷺ personally received him and wiped the dust off him. He ﷺ smiled and repeated three times, "Your trade was profitable, O Ṣuhayb." Astonished, Ṣuhayb replied, "No-one could have told you about that, O Messenger of Allah, except Jibrīl ﷺ."[201] Allah ﷻ then revealed a beautiful verse regarding Ṣuhayb al-Rūmī, "And there are those who would sell themselves for Allah's pleasure. And Allah is Ever Gracious to [His] servants."[202]

Once, the leaders of the Quraysh were conversing with the Prophet ﷺ in a promising manner. Abū Jahl intervened, pointing to Ṣuhayb, Bilāl, and ʿAmmār ﷺ, saying, "We cannot accept being the subordinates of such people, so expel them."[203] Allah ﷻ then revealed, "Do not dismiss those [poor believers] who invoke their Lord morning and evening, seeking his pleasure. You are not accountable for them whatsoever, nor are they accountable for you. So do not dismiss them, or you will be one of the wrongdoers."[204] Allah ﷻ honoured them so much that He instructed the Prophet himself that leaving them would be ruinous.

Emigration to Abyssinia

7

Attacks on the Prophet ﷺ

The Prophet ﷺ himself was harassed and even physically attacked. The abuse escalated into assassination attempts which culminated in the eventual Hijrah. The Prophet ﷺ was one of the few who prayed publicly in front of the Kaʿbah, which particularly infuriated Abū Jahl and his ilk. Abū Jahl said, "I swear by al-Lāt and al-ʿUzzā, if I see that man again I will put my foot on his neck and throw sand on him."[205] Later that day the Prophet ﷺ began praying in front of the Kaʿbah and Abū Jahl marched towards him. However, as he approached, he suddenly stopped and began walking backwards, pushing the air in front of him frantically. When asked about this, he said, "I was about to step on him until I saw a pit of fire, above which there were massive wings." The Prophet ﷺ later explained that those wings belonged to Angels, and had he taken one more step, they would have ripped him to shreds.[206]

Allah ﷻ then revealed the remainder of Sūrah al-ʿAlaq, "Most certainly, one exceeds all bounds once they think they are self-sufficient. But surely to your Lord is the return [of all]. Have you seen the man who prevents a servant [of Ours] from praying? What if this [servant] is [rightly] guided or encourages righteousness? What if that [man] persists in denial and turns away? Does he not know that Allah sees [all]? But no! If he does not desist, We will certainly drag him by the forelock—a lying, sinful forelock. So let him call his associates. We will call the wardens of Hell. Again, no! Never obey him! Rather, prostrate and draw near [to Allah]." [207]

As previously mentioned, the Prophet's enemies were of two types: the first type were the likes of 'Umar ibn al-Khaṭṭāb and 'Amr ibn al-'Āṣ ؓ who initially opposed the Prophet ﷺ but did so with dignity, not resorting to lowly and distasteful tactics. Allah ﷻ decreed that all of these adversaries eventually accept Islam. The second type were the likes of Abū Jahl and Abū Lahab who not only opposed the Prophet ﷺ but did so shamelessly, knowing no bounds of disgrace and dishonour. 'Uqbah ibn Abī Mu'ayṭ was one of these figures who opposed the Prophet ﷺ in this lowly manner.

'Urwah ibn Zubayr asked 'Abdullāh ibn 'Amr, "What was the worst thing you saw happen to the Prophet?" 'Abdullāh said, "One day, the Prophet ﷺ was praying in front of the Ka'bah and 'Uqbah ibn Abī Mu'ayṭ approached him from behind, took off his outer garment, threw it over the Prophet's neck, and began to choke him. The Prophet ﷺ was struggling to breathe, and no-one was intervening until Abū Bakr ؓ was informed. Abū Bakr ran over and pushed 'Uqbah over and shouted, 'Are you going to kill a man just because he says "My Lord is Allah"?'" [208] Allah ﷻ honoured Abū Bakr ؓ by revealing verses of Qur'an about Mūsā ؑ with the exact same phrasing, "A believing man from the Pharoah's people, who was hiding his faith, argued, 'Are you going to kill a man just because he says "My Lord is Allah", while he has in fact come to you with clear proofs from your Lord?'" [209]

Assassination Attempts

As time passed, the intensity grew and acts of violence and aggression escalated. News eventually spread that the Quraysh planned to assassinate the Prophet ﷺ. A neighbour warned Fāṭimah ؈ and she informed the Prophet ﷺ, to which he responded, "My dear daughter, fetch me some water." The Prophet ﷺ then performed ablution, made *duʿāʾ* to Allah, and walked to the mosque. His enemies were in the mosque, armed and ready to kill him, but were all suddenly paralysed. The Prophet ﷺ threw dust in their faces and said, "May their faces be cursed." [210] Just like the abovementioned narration of Ibn Masʿūd ؈, every one of these people were killed in the Battle of Badr.

Pondering upon these extreme hardships, one may wonder why Allah's foremost Messenger ﷺ was tested in such a manner. Why was the greatest generation on Earth subjugated to such dire tribulations? Allah ﷻ is reminding the believers that we were not created to live in comfort on Earth; the purpose of our creation is to be tested in preparation for the Hereafter. Allah ﷻ states, "He is the One Who created the Heavens and the Earth in six Days—and His Throne was upon the waters—in order to test which of you is best in deeds." [211] Allah reminds the Prophet ﷺ and Companions ؈, and through them He reminds us, that we were not created to merely live; we were created for something greater.

While we do not—and cannot—truly earn Paradise, we can earn Allah's Mercy which in turn enters us into Paradise. Allah ﷻ states, "*Alif-Lām-Mīm.* Do people think once they say 'We believe' that they will be left without being put to the test? We certainly tested those before them. And Allah will clearly distinguish between those who are truthful and those who are liars." [212] He ﷻ further states, "Do you think you will enter Paradise without Allah proving which of you [truly] struggled [for His cause] and patiently endured?" [213] And, "Do you think you will be admitted into Paradise without being tested like those before you?" [214]

Even Khabbāb ؈, who remained steadfast and undeterred in the face of severe torture, momentarily felt deflated and asked the Prophet ﷺ, "For how long, O Messenger of Allah? For how long will we be tortured like this? You are the Messenger of Allah; why don't you ask Allah ﷻ to help us?" The Prophet ﷺ was leaning against the Kaʿbah but leaned forward and sat straight, responding, "Indeed the people before you were tortured worse than this; one of them would have their flesh stripped from their bones by a comb of iron, and another would be cut in half by a sword, but that would still not turn them away from the worship of Allah. Indeed, I swear to you by the One Who sent me, that Allah will perfect this matter until you will see a day when a shepherdess will take her flock from Hadramout to Sanaa fearing no-one except Allah and the wolf against her sheep. However, you are a hasty people."[215] The Prophet ﷺ did not relent in his belief and faith in Allah ﷻ; indeed, the earliest followers of Christ suffered a similar fate, enduring equally severe torture and persecution. The Prophets and righteous believers of the past were tested by Allah ﷻ according to their calibre and piety. Even the Messengers of Allah were required to prove their devotion to the Almighty.

A Muslim's level and status in the sight of Allah can be measured according to their struggles and subsequent patience in those struggles. Allah ﷻ states, "Surely the most noble of you in the sight of Allah is the most righteous among you."[216] The Companions hold the highest status in Islam due to their unparalleled struggle in the cause of Allah, and even among the Companions there are levels; those who accepted Islam in Mecca and endured those struggles have their own station above those who accepted later. Allah ﷻ states, "Those of you who donated and fought before the Conquest [of Mecca] are unparalleled. They are far greater in rank than those who donated and fought afterwards."[217]

The First Emigration

Eventually, in the fifth year of the *daʿwah*, the Prophet ﷺ suggested that the Companions head to the Negus[i] in Abyssinia. "This land has become too constricted for you. For those who want to, why don't you emigrate to the neighbouring land of Abyssinia? There is a Christian

i Contrary to popular belief, Negus (Najāshī) was a title, not a name. His name was Aṣḥamah, and the title of Negus is akin to King, Khosrow (of Persia), Caesar (of Rome), and so on.

king there who is a just king, and he will allow you to worship Allah without interfering."[218] The *daʿwah* became public in the third year of Prophethood, signifying that the aforementioned torture and struggle all occurred in an 18-month window, which ultimately became unbearable.

In our current age of globalisation and transcendent technology, it may be difficult to fathom the true significance of what hijrah entails in seventh century Arabia. In an age where tribal backing, familial prestige, and community ties dictate one's stature and esteem, uprooting oneself to a nearby city instantaneously and dramatically demotes one's quality of life. Suddenly moving to another land entirely is therefore a truly drastic measure. With no passports or bank transfers, an impromptu hijrah compromises one's safety and wealth; rich Companions became poor overnight, as the secretive nature of their departure meant that they could not sell their property or even carry their money with them. This all indicates the extent of the difficulty they endured in Mecca to even consider such a move.

The first to emigrate were 12 men and four women. The great ʿUthmān ibn ʿAffān ﵁ was amongst them alongside his wife, Ruqayyah, daughter of the Prophet ﷺ. The rest were ʿUthmān ibn Maẓʿūn, ʿAbdurraḥmān ibn ʿAwf, Zubayr ibn al-ʿAwwām, Muṣʿab ibn ʿUmayr, Jaʿfar ibn Abī Ṭālib, Abū Salamah and Umm Salamah, Jaḥsh ibn Ri'āb, ʿAbdullāh ibn Jaḥsh, Abū Ḥudhayfah ibn ʿUtbah, Sahlah bint Suhayl, ʿĀmir ibn Rabīʿah, and Laylā bint Abī Ḥathmah ﵃. It may be observed that they were all noblemen and women of the Quraysh, with the notable absence of the servant class Muslims; as slaves, they did not have the freedom to emigrate despite needing it the most.

Abū Bakr ﵁ made intention to join them, but as he embarked, the Chieftain of a neighbouring tribe, Ibn al-Daghinah, saw them leaving and asked why. Ibn al-Daghinah had a good working relationship with Abū Bakr, and after hearing the story, he said, "Someone like you does not deserve to leave the land of Mecca. If your people have persecuted you, let me go and speak on your behalf and grant you my protection."[219] Abū Bakr's tribe had relinquished their tribal protection so Ibn al-Daghinah offered his own. As he was not from the Quraysh, he was required to seek permission from the Quraysh. As a trade partner and neighbouring tribe leader, the Quraysh accepted, but on one condition: Abū Bakr must not pray publicly. Other than the Prophet ﷺ, Abū Bakr ؓ was one of the only people fearless enough to pray in front of the Kaʿbah, and the Quraysh complained that it was impacting the people. Abū Bakr agreed and instead made an extension to his house as a makeshift mosque.

Abū Bakr ؓ then continued to pray but from within his house. However, Abū Bakr's recitation was very moving and emotional; Ibn Isḥāq narrates that the women and children of the Quraysh would gather outside his house in amazement and marvel at his recitation.[220] ʿĀ'ishah ؓ mentioned about her father, "He was a man who would be easily brought to tears [out of emotion]."[221] Abū Bakr abided by the condition and prayed in his house, but due to his impact even from within his own home, the Quraysh sent a message to Ibn al-Daghinah notifying him that they had updated their condition to ban his recitation even from within his own home. Ibn al-Daghinah then requested that Abū Bakr ؓ stop praying aloud or else he would be forced to rescind his protection. Abū Bakr resolutely replied, "I return your protection and accept the protection of Allah."[222] Abū Bakr ؓ remained in Mecca relying solely on his unwavering trust in Allah.

The Prophet's suggestion of hijrah demonstrates that not all non-Muslim lands are the same. Abyssinia and Mecca were both non-Muslim, but the former allowed freedom of religion while the latter was hostile. Further, it validates the notion of living in such a land. The Companions who emigrated did not immediately return once Medina was established as a Muslim land; in fact, they remained in Abyssinia for 14 years and the Prophet ﷺ only recalled them after the Battle of Khaybar. The Prophet ﷺ chose Abyssinia for a number of reasons. As mentioned, their Negus was a man of justice and integrity. Abyssinia was also familiar to them as they had previously established some trade, and it was relatively practical to reach albeit via the Red Sea. In addition to this, they were Christians, who were much more cordial due to the shared notion of Prophethood. Within Christian theology, they were closer to the teachings of Christ compared to the now-mainstream teachings of Christianity. Upon hearing about the Prophet's teachings, the Negus said, "This comes from the same well as that of [Prophet] Mūsā."[223]

The 'Satanic Verses'

The first batch of emigrants initially returned to Mecca after a mere three months due to a misunderstanding. An infamous event occurred which led to widescale rumours that the Quraysh had finally accepted Islam, prompting the Muslims to hastily return. Despite their safety and freedom to practice their faith, the early emigrants had an extremely difficult time adjusting to life in a foreign country with a new language, culture, norms, and even climate. They were still beginning to adjust when they heard the rumours that the Quraysh accepted Islam, and so they pounced on the idea of returning home.

The famous incident is the Prophet ﷺ reciting Sūrah al-Najm in public. He ﷺ recited the *sūrah* in its entirety, and as the verses compounded, an audience gathered. The *sūrah* is particularly powerful, full of rhetorical devices captivating the listeners. It then builds up to its climax and ends with, "Prostrate to Allah and worship Him!"[224] Not only did all the Muslims immediately prostrate, but the Pagans of the Quraysh were so overwhelmed and captivated that they could not help but to fall into prostration too. Other than al-Walīd ibn al-Mughīrah—who was too arrogant and was instead sufficed with wiping dust onto his forehead—the entirety of Mecca was in prostration.[225] This unprecedented event inevitably led to rumours that the Quraysh had accepted Islam, prompting the Muslims in Abyssinia to return.

This event is not controversial enough to be infamous, however there are versions of this narration in very weak reports that have caused much controversy. It must be noted that the abovementioned version is located in the most authentic work in Islamic history, Ṣaḥīḥ al-Bukhārī. The remaining versions are not only absent in the Six Canonical Books of Hadith, but they are also not present in the primary sources of

Ibn Hishām and Ibn Isḥāq. They only appear in the most obscure of references, or in the major exegesis (*tafsīr*) of al-Ṭabarī. However, it must be made clear that unlike al-Bukhārī, whose aim was to compile the most authentic of narrations, Tafsīr al-Ṭabarī was written as an encyclopaedia of knowledge. Imam al-Ṭabarī distinctly clarified that this text is a compilation of all the reports, not solely the authentic ones. Relying on a narration's existence in al-Ṭabarī to bolster its authenticity is therefore not only incorrect but disingenuous.

In a second, inauthentic version of this report, it was narrated by ʿUrwah ibn al-Zubayr—who was a Successor and thus did not meet the Prophet ﷺ directly—that Shayṭān cried out, adding two verses, heard only by the polytheists. The Qur'an states, "Have you considered al-Lāt and al-ʿUzzā, and the third of them, Manāt?"[226] According to this report, Shayṭān added, "They are the mighty Pelicans (Gharānīq), and their requests will be granted."[227] These "verses" are clearly praising the idols, and the Quraysh had assumed that the Prophet ﷺ had finally compromised and so were happy to prostrate. There is a third, even more problematic version of the same narration whereby Shayṭān impersonated Jibrīl ﷺ, and the Prophet ﷺ could not distinguish between the two, leading to the Prophet ﷺ himself repeating the "verses".[228] This led to the 20th century orientalist, William Muir, coining the term "Satanic Verses". In Islamic tradition, it is referred to as The Story of the Pelicans (Qiṣṣah al-Gharānīq). However, as mentioned, the second and third versions of this story are inauthentic without the presence of a single *ṣaḥīḥ* (authentic) narration.

The emigrants journeyed to Mecca, and as they were on the outskirts of the city, they asked passersby about the Quraysh accepting Islam, to which they were informed that the rumour was false. Deflated and disappointed, they considered returning to Abyssinia, but their beloved hometown of Mecca was in their sights, and they yearned to reunite with the Prophet ﷺ. When they left Mecca, they effectively reneged on their tribal protection, and so upon their return they needed to seek new protection agreements. ʿUthmān ibn Maẓʿūn ﷺ reached out to his long-time friend al-Walīd ibn al-Mughīrah for protection. As one of the most powerful men in Mecca, al-Walīd's protection ensured that ʿUthmān was completely safe. Meanwhile, he saw the rest of the Muslims being persecuted while he was safe, and he was consumed by guilt. His feelings of guilt grew to be unbearable and eventually asked for his protection to be revoked. He did not do anything wrong and had every right to seek out his own protection, but his conscience would not allow him to continue in peace while his companions were suffering.

Shortly after having his protection revoked, ʿUthmān passed by a gathering which included one of Arabia's most talented poets, Labīd, who had been invited to Mecca. Labīd recited a line of poetry that the Prophet ﷺ would later describe as "the most truthful statement that any poet has ever said"[229] which was, "For truly everything except Allah is naught." ʿUthmān was truly impressed, and exclaimed, "You have spoken the truth!" Labīd continued, "And every pleasure will undoubtedly cease." ʿUthmān retorted, "You have lied!" because Paradise will never disappear. Labīd was incensed—not being privy to the Meccan context of the Islamic struggle—saying, "Since when have you people treated your guests in this manner?"[230] Somebody stood up in anger and punched ʿUthmān in the face, giving him a black eye. When al-Walīd heard, he said, "My nephew (a term of endearment), why did you rescind my protection? Please allow me to reinstate it." ʿUthmān replied, "No! Indeed, my other eye is in need of the blessings incurred by this eye."[231]

A Meeting with the Negus

After a short while in Mecca, the initial emigrants conferred and decided it was better to return to Abyssinia. Despite Mecca being their homeland, Abyssinia provided safety and security. Health and sustenance are indeed the cornerstone of human need. Allah ﷻ affirms these priorities in Sūrah Quraysh, "...let them worship the Lord of this [Sacred] House, Who has fed them against hunger and made them secure against fear."[232] After reuniting with the Muslims in Mecca, word spread about the peaceful existence in Abyssinia. More than 80 Muslims decided to emigrate, which was around half of the Muslims in Mecca, and more than 10% of the entire population.

Losing such a significant portion of the population was humiliating for the Quraysh, especially considering the way in which they voluntarily left their own families and tribes. They could not tolerate such shame, and so sent ʿAmr ibn al-ʿĀṣ, who had not yet converted to Islam, to lobby the Negus to order their return. ʿAmr ibn al-ʿĀṣ was an extremely intelligent and shrewd politician who was the ideal tactician to disrupt the Muslims. He eventually used these talents for the betterment of Islam, but for now he was an asset to the Quraysh. He, alongside another delegate, presented to the Negus' council gifts from Mecca. They gave each of his ministers expensive gifts, saying, "You have in your midst a group of renegades and rebels. We will speak to the Negus tomorrow about their case, and we want you to hand them back to us and support us in this cause. When we give the Negus his gifts, remember our gifts to you."[233]

The next day, they approached the Negus, saying, "Some foolish youth in our nation have emigrated to your country. They have left our faith but have not embraced yours. The leaders of our community have sent us to you in order that you send these young foolish people back to us so that we can deal with them." ʿAmr was appealing to their shared values and customs, such as religion, politics, and respect. The ministers, as promised, stood up and agreed with the Quraysh, recommending that the Muslims be returned. Confirming the Prophet's description as a just king, the Negus then spoke, "No, by Allah, I cannot turn them back after they chose my land. The least I can do is listen to them."[234]

The Negus summoned the Companions, led by Jaʿfar ibn Abī Ṭālib ﵁. It was customary for everyone to prostrate to the king, but Jaʿfar entered with a firm chest. Outraged, the ministers yelled, "How dare you walk in without prostrating?" It was a defining moment where their lives hung in the balance, yet Jaʿfar and the Muslims stuck to their principles, saying, "Our Prophet has told us that we can only prostrate to our Lord."[235] The Negus asked, "What is this new religion that you have invented, and what is the matter that you have forsaken your people yet you have not embraced my religion nor any of the other religions on Earth?" Jaʿfar ﵁ responded, embodying the pinnacle of eloquence,

"We used to be a nation steeped in ignorance; we would worship idols, eat dead meat, and perform promiscuous acts. We would break ties of kinship and treat our neighbours with contempt. The strong amongst us would devour the weak, and we remained in this state until Allah ﷻ sent a Messenger to us. He was known in the community; he never told a lie in his life, and he invited us to worship One God, alone, and to leave idol worship. He told us to abandon the way of our forefathers in the worship of stones and statues. He commanded us to be true when we speak, to fulfil our promises, and to fulfil ties of kinship. He told us to be good to our neighbours and avoid all evil. He told us not to spill blood and to give true testimony. He forbade us from stealing the property of orphans and accusing others of adultery, and commanded us to worship Allah ﷻ alone without associating anything with him. He told us to pray, fast, and give charity, so we believed in him, followed him, and had faith in him. He worshipped Allah alone and did not worship idols. We forbade upon ourselves everything he prohibited, and we made permissible all that he allowed for us. But our people opposed us, showed hatred towards us, and tortured us. They punished us and tried to force us back to idol worship. They were unjust to us, made life miserable, and prevented us from being who we were. So we emigrated to your land, and we chose you above all other rulers, and we wish to come under your generosity and hospitality; we put our trust in you that we would not be shown injustice in your land, O exalted highness."[236]

Jaʿfar ibn Abī Ṭālib ﷺ vindicated the Prophet's decision in choosing him as the leader of the group, as he showed wisdom, eloquence, and integrity. He appealed to the Negus' honour, magnanimity, and values, all without compromising his own dignity or beliefs as a Muslim. The Negus was duly moved by the beautiful speech. He asked,

"Do you have any Revelation sent to your Prophet?" Jaʿfar replied in the affirmative, and the Negus asked to hear some of it. Jaʿfar recited the first few pages of Sūrah Maryam, as it pertained to Jesus Christ and the Virgin Birth. The Negus alongside all his ministers began to weep, and he said, "By God, this recitation and the Message of Moses have sprung from the same fountain."[237] He then resolutely denied the Quraysh and told them to leave. As they were leaving, ʿAmr said to his companion, "Do not give up just yet; I have one more trick up my sleeve."

The next morning, they returned to the Negus, saying, "O Holy Emperor, we forgot to mention one more thing: these people say something blasphemous about your Lord, Jesus Christ." The Negus immediately recalled the Companions, demanding their prompt attendance. The Companions were anxious about how they would explain their stance, but Jaʿfar reassured them, "We will say exactly what the Prophet ﷺ told us to say: Jesus Christ is a Prophet of Allah, servant of Allah, and the spirit born of the Virgin Mary." They approached the Negus once more, who irritably asked, "What is this that I have heard about your blasphemous views on Jesus Christ?" Jaʿfar responded, "Your Royal Highness, we say exactly what our Prophet teaches, namely that Jesus Christ is the Prophet of Allah, servant of Allah, and spirit born of Mary, the chaste virgin." The Negus picked up a twig and said, "By God, what you have just said does not exceed what Jesus Christ said by this branch."[238] He then turned to ʿAmr ibn al-ʿĀṣ, and said, "Be gone from here, and take your gifts with you, for I have no need for them."

This story highlights the pragmatism and practicality of the Companions in using the system available to them to exact change and fight for justice. They did not dismiss themselves out of the Negus' court because he was not Muslim; rather, they maintained their beliefs but used his system to fight for their cause. Without violating Islamic creed, they praised him for his good and appealed to his good nature while remaining steadfast upon the tenets of their faith. Without lying or hiding the truth, Jaʿfar ؓ remained wise, emphasising the similarities between the two religions without insulting the Negus as to the differences.

The Negus' profound response indicates that his belief represented the Oneness of Allah, similar to the early followers of Christ. This could explain why he was so tolerant of the Muslims and why he was so moved by the Qur'an. It also explains his response when the Prophet ﷺ eventually emigrated to Medina and wrote the Negus a letter, inviting him to Islam. The Negus wrote back, affirming that he was a Muslim, and that he believes in Islam, saying, "If you command me, O Messenger of Allah, I will come to Medina and serve you." [239]

However, the Negus' firm acceptance of the Muslim emigrants earned the suspicion of a group of his ministers who began to plot a coup. The Negus set out to address this matter; he wrote on a parchment, "I bear witness that there is no god except Allah, and that Jesus is the spirit of Allah, the Word of Allah, and the slave of Allah." [240] He placed this parchment inside his robe next to his chest. He then called the problematic ministers and asked, "What is the matter? Have I not been a good king to you?" They responded, "Yes, but you have abandoned our religion, and you have heretical beliefs." The Negus asked, "What do you believe?" To which they replied, "We believe that Jesus Christ is the son of God, our Lord and Saviour, and the third of the trinity." The Negus responded, "I swear by God that this is exactly what I believe." However, the Negus was pointing to his chest—or, more accurately, the parchment within his chest—when he said "this" is what he believed. The Negus utilised *tawriyah*[ii] to preserve his beliefs while safeguarding his position. Prior to this meeting, the Negus sent a message to the Muslims, explaining that he was experiencing tension within his ranks, and that his assassination was possible. He instructed that if they were to hear news about his death, he had organised for one of his ships to be in a certain location for the Muslims to use and escape.

The Negus overcame the ministers, but at a later date faced another threat to his throne. Tensions rose from another faction within the government, and civil war was on the horizon. Umm Salamah ﵂ narrated,

ii *Tawriyah* can be translated as "equivocation" or "double meaning" whereby vague language is utilised to deceive without explicitly lying.

"We were scared that the Negus would be defeated and that somebody else would be installed in his place. We began making *du'ā'* to Allah ﷻ to help the Negus win and remain in power." Civil war did indeed take place, and the Muslims in Abyssinia grew increasingly anxious. Zubayr ibn al-'Awwām ؓ decided to observe the battle in order to warn the Muslims if the Negus was defeated so that they could flee. In the meantime, Umm Salamah recalls, "We were praying to Allah the most serious prayer, 'O Allah, allow the Negus to remain in power and grant him authority in the land.'" [241] Zubayr returned to the city a few days later, yelling, "Rejoice, for the Negus has won!" The Negus and his contemporaries were fighting a purely political battle which did not directly pertain to Islam, yet the Muslims were making *du'ā'* fervently for his success.

A number of years later, the Negus died. The Prophet ﷺ explained that Jibrīl ؑ informed him, "Your brother Aṣḥamah the Negus has died, so pray for him." [242] News from Abyssinia would usually take a number of days to reach Medina, but the Prophet ﷺ was provided the information instantaneously. He ﷺ gathered the Companions and prayed the Absentee Funeral Prayer (Ṣalāh al-Ghā'ib) for the Negus—the only time the Prophet ﷺ ever prayed such a prayer.[iii] The Muslims in Abyssinia remained for over ten more years despite the Prophet ﷺ emigrating to Medina and establishing an Islamic state. They did not participate in the famous battles of Badr, Uḥud, and Khandaq. It was only after the Battle of Khaybar that the Prophet ﷺ recalled the Companions to Medina. This perhaps indicates that the Prophet ﷺ was preparing for all contingencies until his authority in Medina was solidified. The Prophet ﷺ undoubtedly had *tawakkul* but nevertheless showed the importance of planning ahead.

---

iii   There is a difference of opinion as to when the Absentee Prayer should be prayed. One view is that the Absentee Prayer is conducted when no-one else prays over a person in their land. No-one had prayed for the Negus in Abyssinia, and so the Prophet ﷺ prayed for him in Medina. The Prophet ﷺ did not pray the Absentee Prayer for anybody else despite many Companions passing away in distant lands.

PART III • THE MECCAN ERA

Mecca Reaches Boiling Point

8

Conversion of Ḥamzah and ʿUmar ﵄

After the mass emigration to Abyssinia, the number of Muslims in Mecca dwindled, leaving around 37 or 38 Muslim men. However, Allah ﷻ blessed two figures to accept Islam which in turn strengthened the Ummah exponentially. The two figures were, of course, ʿUmar ibn al-Khaṭṭāb and Ḥamzah ibn ʿAbd al-Muṭṭalib.

The first of them to convert was Ḥamzah, and his conversion story was truly unique. He was the only major figure in Islam to convert out of anger but then have it develop into sincere faith. One day, Abū Jahl was in a particularly foul mood and began hurling insults at the Prophet ﷺ. He continued to verbally abuse him ﷺ, increasing in vulgarity and profanity, cursing him like he had never done before. The Prophet remained silent despite the relentless tirade. Eventually, Abū Jahl grew tired of his own insults and stormed off home. The women of the Banū Hāshim were enraged; while they were not necessarily Muslim, their own kin was being insulted, and they were infuriated as a matter of tribal pride.

Incensed, the women began to goad Ḥamzah. They narrated everything that happened and Ḥamzah's blood began to boil. When they relayed that this was a public incident in front of the whole of Mecca, he flew into a rage and marched towards the Kaʿbah. As soon as he approached Abū Jahl, he struck him violently with his hunting bow, causing a gush of blood to spurt out, yelling "How dare you abuse my own nephew..." and without realising what he was saying, he blurted out, "...and I too am a follower of his religion!"[243] The surrounding Banū Makhzūm members were ready to pounce, but Abū Jahl stopped them, saying, "Leave him be, for by Allah today I cursed his nephew like I never cursed him before."

Ḥamzah returned home, confused by his own actions. He was truly in a conundrum: he had to save face but had now committed to this religion merely out of familial pride. He made a *duʿā'* to Allah, "O Allah, you know that I am one of the leaders of the Quraysh, and I have now said something too embarrassing to retract. So, if this matter is true, then cause my heart to be guided to it, and if it is not true, then cause to me to die right now."[244] He spent the rest of the night sleepless, tossing and turning, until he went to the Prophet ﷺ the following morning. He explained what happened, and the Prophet ﷺ spent the entire morning preaching to him the tenets of Islam until Ḥamzah ؓ said, "I testify that you are truthful, and now I do not ever want to return to the Paganism of my forefathers."[245] As the son of ʿAbd al-Muṭṭalib and brother of Abū Ṭālib, Ḥamzah, thus became the most senior convert to Islam. That day, the Quraysh conceded that they had to tone down their animosity.[246]

Within a few short days, the Ummah was blessed with another huge boost through the conversion of ʿUmar ibn al-Khaṭṭāb. ʿUmar's conversion was a pleasant surprise for the Ummah, and a shocking blow for the Quraysh. When the Companions were previously preparing for the second emigration to Abyssinia, Laylā bint Abī Ḥathmān was begrudgingly packing her things when ʿUmar saw her and asked why she was packing. She replied in frustration, "You dare ask? It is because of you and your animosity that we are leaving our land and belongings!"[247] ʿUmar was taken aback, replying, "Has it really reached this level?" He then made *duʿā'* for her, "May Allah grant you protection." Laylā excitedly relayed the story to her husband, who scoffed and said, "Do you really think he is going to accept Islam? By Allah, his father's donkey will accept Islam before he does!" [248] This was the impression that the Companions had about ʿUmar due to his tough exterior. However, unbeknownst to him, the Prophet ﷺ had made a special *duʿā*', "O Allah, bring glory to Islam through the more beloved to you of these two men (referring to Abū Jahl and ʿUmar)." [249] Allah answered the Prophet's *duʿā*' and guided ʿUmar. His conversion was a shock, but in retrospect, it was a culmination of a number of events. The above narration of Laylā bint Abī Ḥathmān was one example of his heart softening towards the Muslims. After all, ʿUmar's famous tough exterior was matched by his equally famous soft and sensitive interior.

One day, he decided to go for a late-night drink with some friends but did not find any. After searching for a while with no success, he changed his mind and decided to go to the Ḥaram instead. He found the Prophet ﷺ alone, praying in front of the Kaʿbah, as would often be the case. ʿUmar thought to himself: this is the perfect time to attack, as he ﷺ was completely alone without any witnesses. He crept up behind him but was taken aback by the beauty of the recitation and instead began to listen. ʿUmar was hiding, and the Prophet ﷺ was oblivious to his presence. ʿUmar narrates, "I stood behind him and he began reciting Sūrah al-Ḥāqqah, and I was amazed at its rhythm and composition. I thought to myself: 'By Allah, this is the speech of a poet.' As soon as I thought this, the Prophet ﷺ read the verse, 'It is not the word of a poet, little do you believe!' [250] So I thought: 'It must be a soothsayer.' And the next verse was, 'Nor is it the word of a soothsayer, little do you reflect.' [251] I then thought: 'Where is this from then?!' And the next verse was, 'It is a Revelation from the Lord of the worlds.' [252] I thought: 'What if he is inventing it?' And the next verses were, 'Had the Messenger made something up in Our Name, We would have certainly seized him by his right hand, then severed his aorta.' [253] And that was the first time Islam entered my heart." [254] ʿUmar then quietly left without harming the Prophet ﷺ.

Nothing immediately transpired from the above event. A short while later, the Quraysh were gathered, and Abū Jahl was once again spouting hatred. He said, "This man (i.e., the Prophet ﷺ) has done more to insult our fathers and gods than anyone else. He has cursed our religion and said that anyone who worships idols will go to Hell, which means he is damning our forefathers to Hell. Who will finally rid us of this man? By Allah, I promise 100 of the best camels (an extraordinary amount of wealth) to anyone who succeeds in doing this, and I will add 1,000 pouches of silver."[255] 'Umar became greedy and decided to take Abū Jahl up on his offer. He left and began walking with an unsheathed sword—an unspoken declaration of war. He heard voices from afar telling him to stop but he ignored them and continued forth.

He was finally stopped by Nu'aym ibn 'Abdillāh al-Naḥḥām ◈ who had recently accepted Islam but had not yet publicised it. He asked him where he was going, and 'Umar replied, "Enough is enough. We have been cursed for too long and our ancestors have been ridiculed. I am now going to kill this man."[256] Nu'aym panicked, "Have you lost your mind, O 'Umar? Do you really think the Banū 'Abd Manāf will let you live after this?" He then had to think on his feet, "If you really want to do something, go and fix your own family!" 'Umar was perplexed and demanded an explanation. Nu'aym responded, "Haven't you heard? Your own sister and brother-in-law have accepted Islam!"[257] In a bid to protect the Prophet ◈, Nu'aym sent 'Umar to his sister in the hopes that he would not harm his own family.

Enraged, 'Umar changed course and marched to his sister's house. As he approached the door, he heard the Qur'an being recited aloud. Khabbāb ibn al-Aratt ◈ was teaching Fāṭimah bint al-Khaṭṭāb ◈ and her husband, Sa'īd ibn Zayd ◈. Even in times of persecution and tension, education was paramount; the Companions did not stop learning and teaching, demonstrating the central importance of seeking knowledge. 'Umar's rage grew once more and he banged on the door, demanding to be let in. Khabbāb scurried into a hiding place, and Fāṭimah covered the Qur'an parchment with her garment. 'Umar entered and demanded to know what he heard. Fāṭimah denied that anything was said, but 'Umar dismissed her, insisting, "I know what I heard. And it has reached me that you have both accepted Islam." They continued denying it until 'Umar stepped forward to punch Sa'īd. Fāṭimah stepped in to stop it and 'Umar accidentally punched her instead, causing blood to gush out from her lip. Both Fāṭimah and Saʿīd both grew angry and yelled defiantly, "Do as you please! We have indeed accepted Islam, and we believe in the Prophet ﷺ."[258] When ʿUmar saw his sister bleeding coupled with the courage it took for them to stand firm, his heart once again softened, and he calmed down. He then asked to see what she was reading. Fāṭimah hesitated but ʿUmar assured her that he would not disrespect the Qur'an. She said that only the pure could touch the Qur'an. While she was referring to spiritual purity, he still offered to do *ghusl*[i] and did so. He then took the parchment and read from Sūrah Ṭā-Hā. Finally, Islam wholly entered his heart.

He then asked Saʿīd where the Prophet ﷺ was, and Saʿīd, seeing that ʿUmar's demeanour and intentions had changed, directed him to al-Arqam's house. ʿUmar set off to Dār al-Arqam, and perhaps unknowingly, he was still holding on to his unsheathed sword. He knocked on the door, and a Companion peaked through and saw ʿUmar holding a sword. He returned to the Prophet ﷺ, trembling, "O Messenger of Allah, ʿUmar is at the door with a sword in his hand!" Ḥamzah ؓ, who had been Muslim for a mere few days, said, "Let him in! If Allah wants good, he will accept Islam, and if Allah wants other than this, the very sword he is holding will be the end of him!"[259] The Companions then opened the door and pounced on ʿUmar, grabbing his arms and pulling him in. They escorted him to the Prophet ﷺ and he sat down. The Prophet ﷺ grabbed ʿUmar by the collar and said, "O Ibn al-Khaṭṭāb! What are you doing here? By Allah, if you continue on this path, Allah will destroy you with a punishment!" ʿUmar shocked the room and replied, "I came to accept Islam and believe in Allah." The Prophet ﷺ shouted *"Allāhu Akbar*! (Allah is the Greatest!)" so loudly that everyone in the house immediately knew that ʿUmar accepted Islam.

ʿUmar's conversion was a watershed moment. On ʿUmar's deathbed, Ibn Masʿūd said, "We have ever remained in glory since the day ʿUmar accepted Islam."[260] Ibn ʿAbbās ؓ once asked ʿUmar how he acquired the title "al-Fārūq" (The Distinguisher). ʿUmar ؓ replied, "The Prophet ﷺ gave me this title when I converted, and we marched to

i Ritual purification consisting of washing the entire body and rinsing the mouth and nose.

the Kaʿbah and prayed in public for the first time. The Prophet ﷺ then said, 'You are ʿUmar al-Fārūq.'"[261] Immediately after his conversion, the Muslims indeed marched to the Kaʿbah in unison under this newfound protection. They marched in two rows: one led by Ḥamzah, and the other led by ʿUmar.

Excited by this momentous occasion, ʿUmar insisted on personally informing Abū Jahl of his conversion. He knocked on his door, and Abū Jahl opened the door with a smile, "Welcome! What has brought you here?" ʿUmar replied, "I have come to personally inform you that I believe in Allah and His Messenger, and I am now a follower of the religion of Muhammad ﷺ." Abū Jahl slammed the door in his face, shouting, "May Allah curse you for what you have come with!"[262] ʿUmar then continued walking, asking the people, "Who is the biggest gossip among you?" Somebody directed him to Jamīl ibn Maʿmar, so ʿUmar brought him close and said, "I have a secret to tell you. I have just accepted Islam and I am now a follower of Muhammad ﷺ." Jamīl jumped up, barely grabbing a garment to clothe himself, and rushed outside to spread the news. He began shouting down the streets, "O people of the Quraysh! ʿUmar ibn al-Khaṭṭāb became a Sabian[ii]!" ʿUmar then gently corrected him in that he did not become a Sabian, but rather became a Muslim. As soon as he converted, ʿUmar would be attacked, though ʿUmar was unparalleled in his strength and power, and so he would fight them off each time. Eventually, the influential Chieftain al-ʿĀṣ ibn al-Wā'il intervened, saying, "What is the matter with you people? Let this man be. If he chose a different path to you, it is none of your business."[263] Al-ʿĀṣ ibn al-Wā'il then officially gave ʿUmar protection.

Boycott and Exile

Months passed and the Quraysh were still reeling from the multiple blows they suffered. After the shame of losing a huge portion of their

ii The Sabians were an ancient nation of historical prominence. Whenever somebody changed religion, the Quraysh would often describe them as "becoming a Sabian" (*ṣabaʾa*). When the early Muslims left idolatry for Islam, the Quraysh would erroneously call them Sabians.

population to self-imposed exile, they lost two of their most prominent figures in Ḥamzah and ʿUmar. Things were going from bad to worse, and they had gathered to finally put a stop to it. The only way to do that would be to kill the Prophet ﷺ. All the tribes agreed that the Banū Hāshim, led by Abū Ṭālib, must hand the Prophet over, and they would be paid any amount of blood money. They even agreed to allow a third party to kill him ﷺ to avoid revenge attacks. They once again approached Abū Ṭālib, but this time did not give him a choice in the matter: either you hand him over, or we will cut you off from the Quraysh. In a truly unprecedented move, they threatened to disown the Banū Hāshim. Abū Ṭālib was furious and immediately refused.

The boycott was comprehensive: businesses no longer traded with the Banū Hāshim; shops no longer sold to them; bachelors no longer married into them; social gatherings with them were banned; and they were even denied access to food and water. It was an economic, political, and social boycott. They even formalised the boycott with a treaty, which was hung inside the Kaʿbah. It was said that Buʿayd ibn ʿĀmir wrote the treaty, so the Prophet ﷺ made a specific *duʿāʾ* against him and his hand became paralysed until his demise.[264] Abū Ṭālib then decided to undergo a self-imposed exile and the Banū Hāshim relocated to a nearby valley, eking out an existence. Relying on shrubbery and rainwater for food and water, they managed to barely survive by the grace of Allah ﷻ. Due to the scarcity of nutrients in their diet, their droppings became "like that of sheep".[265] As they teetered on the brink of death, sympathisers from the Quraysh, such as the likes of Muṭʿim ibn ʿAdiyy and Ḥakīm ibn Ḥizām, secretly sent in food and water. Tribal kinship was so strong that non-Muslims from the Banū Hāshim also subjugated themselves to this exile with the exception of Abū Lahab, who was too cowardly to join. Instead, he revoked his allegiance to the Banū Hāshim in exchange for remaining in Mecca. During this time, the Prophet ﷺ would continue to give *daʿwah* to travellers and pilgrims.

The boycott lasted for two or three years, and the matter was so dire that the Prophet ﷺ began to make severe *duʿāʾ* against them, "O Allah, send upon them a famine like the famine of [Prophet] Yūsuf ﵇."[266]

The Prophet's *duʿā'* was accepted, and the Quraysh experienced a famine so bad that they were forced to eat dead carcasses and animal skin. The Quraysh knew that this must be due to the Prophet ﷺ so they sent some messengers to the valley to ease tensions. Meanwhile, some senior tribesmen of the Quraysh began to sympathise with the Banū Hāshim, feeling guilty about the anguish their kith and kin were suffering. Hishām ibn ʿAmr, a cousin of the Prophet ﷺ, was one such advocate, and he sought a way to bring an end to the boycott. He called Zuhayr ibn Abī Umaymah alongside other sympathisers, such as Muṭʿim ibn ʿAdiyy and Ḥakīm ibn Ḥizām, mentioned above. Zuhayr concocted a plan: they gathered for the regular council meeting and Zuhayr stood up, saying, "For how long shall we to starve our own kith and kin to death?" Abū Jahl responded adamantly, "Who do you think you are? We all agreed to the treaty!" Hishām then stood up, "No, I didn't agree! It was all your idea!" Abū Jahl began to defend himself when Muṭʿim also stood up, "You forced this upon us!" One by one, each person stood up and added to the argument until Abū Jahl grew privy to what was happening, "By Allah this is a plan you have all hatched up!"[267] However, the plan was successful in shifting public opinion.

One day, the Prophet ﷺ approached Abū Ṭālib, saying, "O my uncle, Allah has informed me that the treaty they wrote has been consumed by termites except for the phrase 'In the Name of Allah'." Abū Ṭālib decided to stake his entire bid on the word of the Prophet ﷺ and marched into Mecca with a group of non-Muslims from the Banū Hāshim. He said, "Let's revisit this treaty and negotiate." The Quraysh were obviously happy, as they understood that Abū Ṭālib was ready to hand over the Prophet ﷺ. As they entered the Kaʿbah to retrieve the treaty, which was secured in a pouch and locked inside the Kaʿbah inaccessible to the public, Abū Ṭālib said, "My nephew has informed me that his Lord has told him that the treaty is no longer in existence except for the phrase 'In the Name of Allah'. So my challenge to you is: if that is the case, then let us be and we will return to Mecca; and if it is not, then I will hand him over to you, and you can do as you please."[268] They of course agreed and opened the pouch only to find the scroll devoured except for the phrase 'In the Name of Allah'. They begrudgingly stuck to the agreement and lifted the boycott.

9 The Year of Sorrow

Not long after the reintegration of the Banū Hāshim, Allah ﷻ willed for two great calamities to afflict the Prophet ﷺ consecutively: the death of his uncle, Abū Ṭālib, and the death of his wife, Khadījah ﷺ. They occurred within a span of 40 days, but the magnitude of the trials led to the entire year being called The Year of Sorrow.

The Death of Abū Ṭālib

Less than six weeks after the boycott ended, the pangs of death were upon Abū Ṭālib. At his deathbed, the Prophet ﷺ begged, "O uncle, say just one statement ('there is no god but Allah') that I can use to argue [your case] in front of Allah to save you." Abū Ṭālib was on the precipice of conversion, with the words on the tip of his tongue, when Abū Jahl and ʿAbdullāh ibn Abī Umayyah quickly interjected, "Are you going to leave the religion of ʿAbd al-Muṭṭalib?!"[269] Whenever he would be on the verge of uttering the *shahādah*, they would repeat the same question. Abū Ṭālib loved the Prophet ﷺ more than anything, but the only person more beloved to him was his father. The prestige and honour of being ʿAbd al-Muṭṭalib's heir meant everything to him.

He was the son of the most respected, revered, and honoured person of the previous generation whose reputation was at its height. Though he knew the truth deep down in his heart, the prestige of his lineage gripped his heart to a detrimental consequence, as he passed away that moment without uttering the testimony of faith.

The Prophet ﷺ was so overwhelmed by his death that he ﷺ said, "I will ask Allah to forgive you unless I am prohibited."[270] No Prophet can take a step forward in their preaching without permission from Allah ﷻ. The Prophet ﷺ was so overcome with emotion that he acted and then waited for Allah's approval rather than waiting for permission first. The Prophet ﷺ continued to ask for his forgiveness until Allah ﷻ sent down a multitude of verses. One of them was from Sūrah al-Tawbah, where Allah ﷻ gently reprimanded the Prophet ﷺ, "It is not [proper] for the Prophet and the believers to seek forgiveness for the polytheists, even if they were close relatives, after it has become clear to the believers that they are bound for the Hellfire."[271]

Al-ʿAbbās ؓ, the brother of Abū Ṭālib, asked the Prophet ﷺ, "O Messenger of Allah, have you benefitted your uncle at all? He used to protect you and become angry on your behalf." The Prophet ﷺ replied, "Yes, I have. He is on the peripheries of the Fire of Hell, and were it not for me, he would be in the depths of Hell."[272] The Prophet ﷺ also said that the person with the least punishment of all [eternal[i]] inhabitants of Hell was Abū Ṭālib. Indeed, all Abū Ṭālib's goodness could not prevent him from escaping the punishment of Hell. Despite the Prophet's love for him and the immense benefit he provided the Muslims, his heart contained the pride and arrogance of being ʿAbd al-Muṭṭalib's heir. This demonstrates the fallibility of mankind and the possibility of good and evil being intertwined within a single soul. The Prophet ﷺ was deeply hurt by Abū Ṭālib's fate, yet he submitted to the decree of the Almighty.

---

i The addition of the word "eternal" has been placed to differentiate between them and Muslims who may face the punishment of Hell to purify their sins but eventually be admitted into Paradise. A core tenet of Islamic creed is that all Muslims will eventually reside in Paradise.

Some find it difficult to accept that a man of Abū Ṭālib's standing could be damned to Hell despite his goodness and the benefit he provided. It also leads some to maintain that he died a Muslim. The historical records are clear that he did not die a Muslim, and our acceptance of this fact is rooted in our inherent belief in Allah ﷻ as our only Lord. Indeed, the case of Abū Ṭālib reaffirms one's belief in the Almighty's supreme decree; despite being the most beloved creation to Allah ﷻ, the Prophet ﷺ could not guide Abū Ṭālib. This unequivocally affirms Prophet Muhammad ﷺ as a slave and Messenger, and Allah ﷻ as the Lord of all the worlds. Allah ﷻ states about Himself, "He cannot be questioned about what He does, but they will [all] be questioned."[273] Mankind will never truly comprehend the unseen, but our loyalty remains with Allah.

As for the wisdoms of Abū Ṭālib's fate, his standing within the Quraysh provided the Prophet ﷺ the protection that he desperately required to survive and spread the Word of God. His conversion would have led to him being disowned by the Quraysh, leaving the Prophet ﷺ exposed and unprotected. However, as a true representative of ʿAbd al-Muṭṭalib, Abū Ṭālib's word was final and the Quraysh never dared to undermine his authority. The Prophet's relationship with Abū Ṭālib also provides vital lessons in navigating our relationship with non-Muslims. Allah ﷻ recognised the Prophet's love for Abū Ṭālib despite his religious affiliation. Allah ﷻ states, "You cannot guide whom you love, but it is Allah Who guides whoever He wills, and He knows best who are [fit to be] guided."[274] The Prophet's love was recognised as a familial love, not that which stems from religious affiliation. Allah ﷻ indeed states, "You will not find a people who believe in Allah and the Last Day truly loving those who defy Allah and His Messenger, even if they were their parents, children, siblings, or extended family."[275] However this is referring to love rooted in shared beliefs and religion, not natural feelings of affection.

The case of Abū Ṭālib also inspires reflection on what it means to be a Muslim. *Īmān*—faith—cannot be accurately defined as just believing in Allah and His Messenger, because Abū Ṭālib admitted his faith in Islam but refused to accept it. Therefore, Islam is defined as submitting to the truth, not just knowing the truth. Even Iblīs—the devil himself—believed in Allah, yet Allah referred to him as a *kāfir* (disbeliever) because he "refused and acted arrogantly"[276]. *Kufr* is therefore understood as rejection, not necessarily disbelief. A pertinent lesson derived from this fact is that theoretical faith does not suffice a Muslim, and an integral part of belief is applying that faith to the best of one's ability.

The Death of Khadījah ﵂

Just over a month after Abū Ṭālib's death, the Prophet ﷺ was struck with another major calamity in Khadījah's passing. The Prophet ﷺ personally shrouded and buried her, and the experience exacted a heavy toll. The trauma compounded for the Prophet as he lost the love of his life and his father figure within 40 days. Abū Ṭālib protected him ﷺ externally while Khadījah ﵂ protected him internally. The Prophet's love for Khadījah was unparalleled; long after her passing, he ﷺ would buy her friends gifts and talk about her with the deepest admiration.

The Prophet ﷺ loved Khadījah ﵂ so much that his wives that never met her were deeply jealous of her existence. 'Ā'ishah ﵂ had later captured the heart of the Prophet ﷺ and was known to be his most beloved wife, and she admitted that she did not feel jealous of any of his wives except for Khadījah ﵂. Once, her jealousy intensified so much that she crossed the line. One day, Khadījah's sister, Hālah, knocked on the door and the Prophet ﷺ was almost asleep, but when he heard her voice, he jumped up in happiness simply to meet Khadījah's relative. 'Ā'ishah ﵂ said, "O Messenger of Allah, for how long are you going to keep on remembering an old, toothless hag of the Quraysh when Allah replaced her with someone better?"[277] In a rare occurrence, the Prophet ﷺ responded angrily, "No, by Allah, Allah did not give me someone better! She supported me when no-one else supported me; she spent upon me when everyone boycotted me; she comforted me when the whole world gave me grief; and Allah gave me children through her when Allah deprived all my other wives of this blessing."[278]

When narrating this Hadith, ʿĀ'ishah recalled, "After that day I never once opened my mouth about Khadījah again."[279]

Loss of Protection

As explained in depth, Abū Ṭālib was the Prophet's protection, both emotionally and politically. After his demise, the Prophet ﷺ was exposed and the Quraysh could intensify their persecution. ʿAbdullāh ibn Masʿūd ؓ narrated a story which grew famous as a defining point in the struggle,

> "Once, the Prophet ﷺ was praying in front of the Kaʿbah when Abū Jahl was sitting with a group. A day prior, a camel had been sacrificed, so Abū Jahl challenged them, 'Who amongst you will go to the carcass of that camel and bring the entrails to dump on Muhammad?' The worst of them, ʿUqbah ibn Abī Muʿayṭ, stood up and went to the carcass and carried the entrails all the way back to the city. He waited until the Prophet ﷺ was in prostration and dumped it all onto the head of the Prophet ﷺ. The weight of the entrails was so heavy that the Prophet ﷺ could not lift himself back up. People began to laugh so hard that some of them were falling onto their sides and others were smacking themselves out of laughter. I was standing from a distance looking, but I had no help or support [due to my servant status] so I could not do anything. The Prophet ﷺ remained in prostration until somebody went to notify Fāṭimah ؓ. She was a little girl at the time, and she began crying and running towards the Prophet ﷺ, lifting the entrails off him. The Prophet ﷺ stood up, turned towards the Quraysh, and raised his finger up towards Allah ﷻ, which silenced the Quraysh. He then began making *duʿā'* against them by name, one by one. He mentioned each of them by name three times until the

> blood drained from their faces. They were Abū Jahl ibn Hishām, ʿUtbah ibn Rabīʿah, Shaybah ibn Rabīʿah, Walīd ibn ʿUqbah, Umayyah ibn Khalaf, ʿUqbah ibn Abī Muʿayṭ, and there was a seventh, but I forgot his name. I swear by the One Who sent Muhammad with the Truth that I myself saw every one of those seven dead in the Battle of Badr."[280]

Consider the vulgarity: a prestigious nobleman of the Quraysh, wearing expensive clothing, volunteered himself into the wasteland to pick up entrails from a carcass and walk from the outskirts of the city all the way into the centre of Mecca, all to humiliate a man of piety. Not a single bystander intervened; the only person who desperately wanted to help, Ibn Masʿūd ﵁, would have been immediately killed for defying noblemen. It was left to a teary-eyed, eight-year-old girl to traumatically help her father. Nevertheless, the Prophet ﷺ kept his composure and faced vulgarity with dignity and honour, turning to his Lord for support, and the support of his Lord did not fail.

After Abū Ṭālib died, Abū Lahab became Chieftain of the Banū Hāshim clan. Under Abū Ṭālib's leadership, Abū Lahab was relentless in his tirades, but as the leader of the tribe, his perspective somewhat changed; the Prophet ﷺ was now his subject, and Abū Lahab felt a sense of responsibility and duty. His demeanour softened, and he approached the Prophet, "O Muhammad, be as you were under Abū Ṭālib." In other words: you have my protection. After this change in stance, rumours spread that Abū Lahab accepted Islam. The Quraysh asked, "Have you become a Sabian?" Abū Lahab responded, "No, but I am protecting my flock."[281]

Abū Jahl and ʿUtbah then hatched a plot to change Abū Lahab's mind. They suggested, "Why don't you ask your nephew about the fate of your father, ʿAbd al-Muṭṭalib?" Abū Lahab asked the Prophet, and he ﷺ responded, "He is with his people."[282] The Prophet's wise response was generic enough to suffice Abū Lahab without lying. However, Abū Lahab returned to Abū Jahl who responded, "You fool!

Where are his people except in the Fire of Hell?!" Abū Lahab was so enraged that their plot was successful and he revoked his protection within a week. The Prophet ﷺ was once again left exposed, relying only on the protection of Allah.

The Incident of Ṭā'if

After a period of time without protection, the Prophet ﷺ began searching for sustainable options outside Mecca. His reluctance to do so for so many years despite the increasing hardships truly demonstrates the Prophetic method of patience and perseverance. The Prophet ﷺ took inspiration from Prophets before him, such as Prophet Nūḥ ؑ who gave *daʿwah* to his people for 950 years. However, without protection, the Prophet's life was in imminent danger, and so hijrah was imperative.

The closest prominent city to Mecca was Ṭā'if. Between tensions and peace treaties, the two competing cities enjoyed a love-hate relationship. The people of Ṭā'if were intimately aware of the people of Mecca, and vice versa. Ṭā'if was therefore an ideal base for the Prophet ﷺ to explore. He took Zayd ibn Ḥārithah ؓ and covertly travelled to Ṭā'if on foot so as not to arouse suspicion. They walked for two days and met with the leaders of Ṭā'if, three brothers who ruled the tribe of Thaqīf in unison: ʿAbd Yālīl, Masʿūd, and Ḥabīb.

The Prophet ﷺ presented the Message of Islam but all three brothers rejected the call with utmost contempt, disrespect, and disdain. One of them replied, "If Allah chose you to be a Prophet, then I might as well tear down the curtains of the Kaʿbah [in remorse]." The other added, "Has Allah not found anyone better than you?" The third mocked, "I cannot speak to you because if you really are a Prophet, you are too holy for me, and if you are a liar, then you are too beneath me to deserve a response."[283] Despite their insults and mockery, the Prophet ﷺ remained dignified and responded, "Very well. If you have rejected my Message, then at least do not inform the Quraysh of my visit." Note that the Prophet ﷺ continued to cover his tracks.

This does not contravene having trust in Allah ﷻ, but rather is an implementation of how to trust Allah; namely, place your trust in Him ﷻ and remain diligent.

Even though the Prophet ﷺ was rejected in the vilest manner, he remained in Ṭā'if for another week, spreading his Message to the common folk. This provides invaluable insight into the Prophetic methodology of *daʿwah*. The Prophet ﷺ would always approach the elite class first, as they have most influence over society. That said, Allah ﷻ made it clear on many occasions that the sincere masses are not to be ignored or neglected. One such example is in Sūrah ʿAbasa, "He frowned and turned away because the blind man came to him [interrupting]. You never know, perhaps he may be purified, or he may be mindful, benefitting from the reminder. As for the one who was indifferent, you gave him your [undivided] attention, even though you are not to blame if he were not purified."[284] The Prophetic balance is to first approach the elite of the society; if they accept Islam, the masses often follow suit. If they reject, effort is made to preach to the masses.

Despite the Prophet's efforts, the masses also rejected the call, and no-one converted. Eventually, there were some people who were warming to the idea, which worried the Chieftains. In retaliation, they ordered mobs to physically attack the Prophet ﷺ. They viciously pelted the Prophet ﷺ, and although Zayd ؓ tried his best to protect him ﷺ, they were both bloodied and bruised from head to toe. They escaped the city and continued until eventually they sat under a tree for shade and respite.

ʿĀ'ishah ؓ once asked the Prophet ﷺ, "Was there a day more difficult for you than the day of Uḥud?" The Prophet ﷺ immediately replied, "Yes. Indeed, your people hurt me greatly, and the worst of it was on the Day of ʿAqabah[ii]. On that day, I presented to ʿAbd Yālīl, Masʿūd, and Ḥabīb and they did not respond to me in the way I wanted.

ii The Prophet ﷺ is referring to the incident at Ṭā'if. He ﷺ called it the Day of ʿAqabah because it took place on a patch of land called ʿAqabah on the outskirts of Ṭā'if.

I found myself in a state of grief and sadness, and I did not realise where I was until I reached Qarn al-Thaʿālib.[iii]" [285]

Numerous benefits can be derived from the manner in which the Prophet ﷺ answered the question. First, the fact that the Prophet ﷺ described the incident of Ṭā'if as more traumatic than the Battle of Uḥud—where he was physically injured and his life was threatened—indicates the severity of emotional distress. Even the Prophet ﷺ acknowledged emotional pain as a bigger hardship than the ferocity of war. Second, the Prophet ﷺ described what we would now refer to as disassociation: disconnecting from reality as a result of stress or trauma. This humanising moment depicts the Prophet ﷺ as a human in need of Allah's mercy, and great inspiration can be taken from this. Third, the Prophet ﷺ described his situation in a dignified manner, not seeking sympathy. He would not have mentioned it had ʿĀ'ishah not asked, and he did not complain or victimise himself ﷺ. We only learn through Zayd's narration that the reality was much harsher and that the Prophet ﷺ indeed faced a truly traumatic ordeal. Instead, the Prophet ﷺ reserved his complaints to the Almighty.

When the Prophet ﷺ escaped the mobs and finally found some shade to rest under, he began making one of the most profound supplications ever recorded,

> "O Allah, to You I complain of my weakness and my humiliation before men. You are the Most Merciful of all those who have mercy. You are the Lord of the humble, and You are my Lord. To whom do you entrust me? To a stranger who receives me with hostility, or to a close relative You have given power over me? As long as You are not angry with me, I do not care, but Your protection is easier for me. I seek refuge in Your Face by which all darkness is illuminated, and from which all the affairs of this world and the Hereafter are rightly

iii An area around 7-8 km from Ṭā'if.

guided. May it never be that I incur Your wrath or be subject to Your anger. It is Your right to criticise until You are content, and there is no power nor strength except through You."[286]

This beautiful, profound, emotional *duʿāʾ* showcases a masterclass in how to converse with Allah ﷻ. The Prophet ﷺ establishes the etiquettes of complaining to Allah ﷻ, and how it differs from complaining to other people. There are two types of complaint: the former is the essence of *tawḥīd* (monotheism), whereby one complains to Allah, seeking refuge in Him and hoping for His sympathy. As Prophet Yaʿqūb ﷺ complained to Allah ﷻ, "I complain of my anguish and sorrow only to Allah, and I know from Allah what you do not know."[287] The latter is to reject the will or wisdom of Allah, questioning His decree; this form of complaint constitutes *kufr* (disbelief). Iblīs himself is guilty of this, complaining, "My Lord, for allowing me to stray I will surely tempt them on Earth and mislead them all together."[288]

The Prophet ﷺ surrendered himself to Allah, expressing that he had no-one to turn to except Him ﷻ. He had no foreseeable option except his enemies, but then he ﷺ stressed that as long as Allah is happy with him, he has no concerns. However, the Prophet ﷺ then went on to mention that if Allah were to make it easier for him, he ﷺ would prefer that. This clearly shows us that asking Allah ﷻ for ease is permissible and that one should not seek hardship. The Prophet showed that his priority was whether Allah was pleased with him, and his concern was not that he was bloodied and bruised, but whether or not Allah was angry with him ﷺ.

When the Prophet ﷺ sat down for shade, he did not realise that the land belonged to his Qurashī uncles, ʿUtbah and Shaybah ibn Rabīʿah. They had witnessed his brutal expulsion from Ṭāʾif and felt pity on their kin as well as a sense of tribal pride. They decided to gift him some fruits from their orchards. They sent their servant, ʿAddās, who was an Iraqi Christian, with some grapes. The Prophet ﷺ accepted the gift and said "*Bismillāh* (In the Name of Allah)" before eating.

ʿAddās was intrigued, "What is this phrase?" The Prophet ﷺ replied, "This is something my Lord has taught me. Where are you from, O ʿAddās?" ʿAddās replied, "I am from Nineveh (modern-day northern Iraq)." The Prophet ﷺ smiled and said, "From the city of Yūnus ibn Mattā!" (Jonas, son of Matthew). ʿAddās was stunned, "And how do you know Yūnus ibn Mattā?!" ʿAddās was a lone Christian in these lands surrounded by Pagans with no knowledge of Judeo-Christian Prophetic lineage. The Prophet ﷺ replied, "How can I not know Yūnus? He is my brother; we are both Prophets of Allah." As soon as the Prophet ﷺ uttered this statement, ʿAddās immediately began kissing the feet of the Prophet ﷺ in adoration. His two masters, ʿUtbah and Shaybah, looked from afar in bewilderment. When he returned, they shouted, "Woe to you! Why are you kissing his hands and feet?" ʿAddās replied, "O my masters, there is no-one on Earth better than him, for he told me things only a Prophet could know." His masters responded dismissively, "O ʿAddās, he has bewitched you from your religion! Your religion is better than his."[289] Later on, when the Battle of Badr commenced, ʿAddās was asked to fight against the Muslims, to which he responded, "You want me to fight that man who was sitting under the tree? By Allah the mountains could not harm him." In a truly bold move, he refused his masters' command, who both met their death in the Battle of Badr.

The Prophet ﷺ described the following events, "Allah ﷻ sent a cloud to protect me and offer me shade. Jibrīl ﷺ was in that cloud, saying, 'O Muhammad, your Lord has heard what your people have said to you and their rejection of you. He has sent me with the Angel of the Mountains to be at your disposal and do as you please.' I then heard another voice, 'I am the Angel of the Mountains. Peace be upon you. O Muhammad, say as you wish—I am at your disposal. If you want, I can crush this city between these two mountains.' I replied, 'No. Rather, I hope Allah ﷻ will extract from their progeny those who will worship Him without associating partners with Him.'"[290]

The symbolism of these events is clear: O Prophet, even if your kith and kin reject you, those furthest away will accept your Message. Just as the *duʿā'* of Mūsā ﷺ was immediately answered[iv] as he sat under a tree, exasperated and depleted, the Prophet's *duʿā'* was similarly accepted. Allah ﷻ provided physical respite through shade and luscious fruits, and spiritual respite through Jibrīl ﷺ and the Angel of the Mountains at his command. While the Prophet's wounds were still fresh and his shoes were still soaked with blood, he ﷺ had the option of revenge, yet he opted for the higher path, a Prophetic path befitting of true nobility. The true miracle is that the Prophet ﷺ still had the proclivity for mercy after being treated with such cruelty. The Prophet ﷺ once again embodied his famous title of "Mercy for the Whole World"—"We have not sent you except as a mercy for the whole world."[291] Less than ten years later, Ṭā'if was conquered, and most of its inhabitants accepted Islam, including many who were alive at the time the Angel of the Mountains offered to destroy it. The very spot that the Prophet ﷺ was brutally stoned on has now been turned into a mosque wherein Allah is worshipped throughout the day.

A Meeting with the Jinn

On the way back to Mecca, the Prophet ﷺ camped in a small desert grove in the valley of Nakhlah. As per his long-standing habit, he ﷺ stood up to pray *tahajjud*. He had not yet washed his body or clothes of the dried blood but maintained his priority in worshipping Allah ﷻ. A miracle then ensued which was narrated by Allah ﷻ in Sūrah al-Aḥqāf, "[Remember, O Prophet] when We sent a group of jinn your way to listen to the Qur'an. Then, upon hearing it, they said [to one another], 'Listen quietly!' Then when it was over, they returned to their fellow jinn as warners."[292] Allah is making it clear to the Prophet ﷺ that this was no coincidence; rather, He ﷻ planned for their paths to cross. The Prophet's prayer was always long, and his *tahajjud* was for hours on end, which meant that the jinn were basking in the Qur'an for so long that they returned back to their

iv In reference to *al-Qaṣaṣ*, 24, "So he watered [their herd] for them, withdrew to the shade and prayed, 'My Lord! I am truly in desperate need of whatever provision You may have in store for me.'"

people not only as Muslims but as warners, preaching the Message of Islam to the jinn.

Sūrah al-Aḥqāf continues, "They (i.e., the jinn) declared, 'O fellow jinn! We have truly heard a scripture revealed after [Prophet] Mūsā, confirming what came before it. It guides to the truth and the Straight Path. O fellow jinn! Respond to the caller of Allah and believe in him, He will forgive your sins and protect you from a painful punishment."[293] Allah's symbolism to the Prophet ﷺ continues; not only will a distant Iraqi Christian accept your Message, but nations from a different species will accept and spread your Message. Even if the whole of mankind rejects you, a world beyond mankind has accepted you.

When the Prophet ﷺ left Mecca, he did so covertly because he had no political protection. Physically leaving for ten days was yet another confirmation that he had severed all ties with the Quraysh. Zayd ﷺ hence asked, "O Messenger of Allah, how will we enter Mecca after you were expelled?" The Prophet ﷺ replied, "O Zayd, Allah ﷻ will make a way out for us, and Allah ﷻ will help His Prophet and make His Message supreme."[294] After doing all he could, he simply had *tawakkul*. The Prophet ﷺ then began sending emissaries to some of his allies in Mecca in hopes for protection. He sent messages to al-Akhnas ibn Shurayq and Suhayl ibn ʿAmr but was met with apologies and excuses. Finally, he ﷺ sent a message to Muṭʿim ibn ʿAdiyy, Chieftain of the Banū Nawfal subtribe, the same man who broke the boycott and sent aid to the exiled Muslims. Muṭʿim did not only send a message back, but he sent his four sons, instructing them, "Put your armour on and escort Muhammad back to me." He then stood in front of the Kaʿbah and said, "O people of Mecca, I have given my protection to Muhammad."[295] Abū Sufyān stood up and asked, "Are you his follower or are you just giving him protection?" Muṭʿim replied, "I am not a follower; I am just giving protection." Abū Sufyān said, "In that case, we accept." The Prophet ﷺ finally returned to Mecca safely.

The Prophet's Marriage to Sawdah ﵂

After the death of Khadījah ﵂, the Prophet ﷺ was caring for three daughters and was in need of remarrying. One day, Khawlah bint Ḥakīm ﵂ visited the Prophet ﷺ and said, "O Messenger of Allah, you appear to be withdrawn (due to grieving the death of Khadījah ﵂)." The Prophet ﷺ replied, "Yes, she was the mother of my children and the caretaker of my house." After testing the waters, Khawlah asked, "Should I then not make a proposal?" The Prophet ﷺ asked who she had in mind, and she said, "If you want an unmarried lady, then ʿĀ'ishah is ideal, and if you want a widowed lady, then Sawdah is ideal."[296] ʿĀ'ishah ﵂ was too young at this stage, and so the Prophet ﷺ gave Khawlah permission to approach Sawdah and gauge her interest. She approved, as did her father, and the Prophet ﷺ wed Sawdah bint Zamʿah ﵂.

The Prophet's Marriage to ʿĀ'ishah ﵂

The Prophet's marriage to ʿĀ'ishah ﵂ is one of two[v] marriages commanded by Allah ﷻ. ʿĀ'ishah ﵂ narrated that he ﷺ said, "I saw you in a dream twice. Someone was carrying you in a silk cloth and said, 'This will be your wife.' When I lifted the cloth, I saw you. I said to myself, 'If this is from Allah, it will come to pass.'"[297] The dreams of Prophets are Revelation, and the Prophet ﷺ seeing ʿĀ'ishah ﵂ as his bride was a command from Allah ﷻ. The Prophet ﷺ saw the dream after the death of Khadījah ﵂ but did not immediately act upon it, knowing that it will be decreed in time.

When Khawlah bint Ḥakīm ﵂ visited the Prophet ﷺ and suggested both Sawdah and ʿĀ'ishah ﵂, she first approached Sawdah and her family. Later, she also approached Abū Bakr al-Ṣiddīq ﵁ and Umm Rumān ﵂, ʿĀ'ishah's parents. They rejoiced at the news but Abū Bakr ﵁

v The other is his marriage to Zaynab bint Jaḥsh ﵂.

was initially confused. The Prophet ﷺ would always refer to Abū Bakr ؓ as his brother, and Abū Bakr ؓ understood that the rules of kinship would apply to him. The Prophet ﷺ explained that they were brothers in Islam, and Abū Bakr ؓ was pleased to offer his daughter in marriage.[298] They presented the marriage contract but did not consummate[vi] the marriage for another three years.

---

vi In recent times there have been sensitivities regarding ʿĀ'ishah's age of marriage. She was six years of age at the time of the marriage contract (nikah) and nine at the age of consummation. Detractors have levelled criticisms against the Prophet ﷺ for marrying a "child", however these criticisms are underpinned by a postmodern notion of childhood and adulthood. In 7th century Arabia—and throughout most of human history—adulthood was understood as the age of puberty. The fact that the Prophet ﷺ waited three years to consummate the marriage clearly shows that ʿĀ'ishah ؓ reached the age of physical maturity. As for emotional maturity and intelligence, then that differs between each society and era. This is evidenced by the fact that the age of consent varies considerably between countries throughout the world. In Islam, the age of puberty is designated as the age of intelligence and responsibility.

The Prophet's enemies seized with alacrity any opportunity to besmirch his reputation, yet they did not recall his marriage to ʿĀ'ishah ؓ in their list of criticisms. It was understood as a norm, so much so that Khawlah bint Ḥakīm ؓ was the one to suggest ʿĀ'ishah ؓ as a potential bride before the Prophet ﷺ even married Sawdah ؓ. Moreover, ʿĀ'ishah ؓ was already engaged to Muṭʿim ibn ʿAdiyy, which was later called off. In late antiquity, the average lifespan was half that of the 21st century. Naturally, therefore, the ages of marriage, childbirth, and labour were all earlier than the modern era. This was the case across cultures, such as the Queen of England, Isabelle of France, marrying Richard II at the age of seven. This occurred in 1396, over 700 years after the time of the Prophet ﷺ.

There have since been attempts to employ a revisionist interpretation that ʿĀ'ishah was 18 years old at the age of marriage—the age of consent in some Western countries. The year of marriage is indirectly deduced based on other Hadiths such as the age of her sister, Asmā' ؓ. However, it is recorded in both Ṣaḥīḥ al-Bukhārī and Ṣaḥīḥ Muslim—the two most authentic books of Hadith—that ʿĀ'ishah ؓ herself states that the Prophet ﷺ married her when she was six, began living with her at the age of nine, and passed away when she was 18 years old. (Bukhārī, *Ṣaḥīḥ al-Bukhārī*, p. 1309). The evidence is clear and explicit, but as demonstrated above, the subject is only sensitive if modern culture and understandings of adulthood are superimposed onto historical events over 1,400 years ago.

The Night Journey & Ascension (al-Isrā' wa al-Miʿrāj)

10

After the Year of Sorrow, Allah ﷻ gifted the Prophet ﷺ the blessing of al-Isrā' wa al-Miʿrāj. As He ﷻ promises, "So, surely with hardship comes ease. Surely with hardship comes ease."[299] After one of the most difficult periods of his life, the Prophet ﷺ experienced one of the biggest blessings of Allah. The whole journey was a gift and blessing. Al-Isrā' means "The Night Journey", referring to the Prophet's journey from Mecca to Jerusalem, and al-Miʿrāj means "The Ascension", referring to the Prophet ﷺ ascending to the Heavens.

It is worth clarifying the difference between Paradise (*Jannah*) and Heavens (*Samāwāt*). Allah ﷻ states, "[He is the One] Who created seven Heavens, one above the other."[300] Everything in our universe, including all the galaxies and solar systems, are contained within the first Heaven. Allah ﷻ states, "And We adorned the lowest Heaven with [stars like] lamps [for beauty] and protection."[301] Each Heaven above that is bigger in size and grandeur to an incomprehensible scale. Paradise (*Jannah*) occupies the seventh Heaven, and it has many of its own levels, increasing in size, beauty, prestige, and exclusivity until Firdaws, the highest level of Paradise reserved for the best of creation.

Al-Isrāʾ wa al-Miʿrāj has been thoroughly documented, with over 20 Companions narrating this event. The reports of al-Isrāʾ wa al-Miʿrāj alone outweigh the reports of the rest of the Meccan era combined. However, the researcher is tasked with differentiating fact from fiction, as grandiose stories attract storytellers, and al-Isrāʾ wa al-Miʿrāj is the most magnificent story of all. As with any event, reports on the topic are assessed to distinguish the most authentic narrations. The researcher must also compare interpretations; some believe that al-Isrāʾ wa al-Miʿrāj was a dream, or that the Prophet ﷺ travelled in spirit, but that is not the case. As a *bona fide* miracle from Allah, the Prophet ﷺ physically journeyed—in a state of wakefulness—from Mecca to Jerusalem, and then to the Heavens and back, within a single night.

There is a difference of opinion as to when al-Isrāʾ wa al-Miʿrāj took place. However, there are some indications. ʿĀʾishah ﵂ narrated, "Khadījah died before the prayer became obligatory."[302] This is definitive proof that al-Isrāʾ wa al-Miʿrāj took place within the last 18 months of the Meccan era because the prayer was made obligatory in al-Miʿrāj. The day, or even month, of the event is unknown, and any specified date is not authentically narrated. It is yet another indication that the Companions did not place great emphasis on the dates and anniversaries of major events; they focused on the substance of the events rather than commemorating its existence.

The Night Journey (al-Isrāʾ)

Allah ﷻ revealed an entire *sūrah* titled Sūrah al-Isrāʾ, opening with the following verse, "Glory be to the One Who took His slave by night from the Sacred Mosque to al-Aqsa Mosque whose surroundings We have blessed, so that We may show him some of Our signs. Indeed, He alone is the All-Hearing, All-Seeing."[303] Allah ﷻ praises the Prophet ﷺ by referring to him as a slave. The Qurʾan states, "I did not create jinn and humans except to worship Me."[304] The word *ʿabd* means "slave" but also means "worshipper", as it stems from the same root word as *ʿibādah* (worship). Allah ﷻ is therefore praising the Prophet ﷺ as the perfect worshipper and slave. Allah ﷻ mentions the Prophet's name in the

Qur'an four times whereas He refers to him by his title, *ʿabd*, many times. The name ʿAbdullāh (slave of Allah) is a prestigious title and descriptor.

The Prophet ﷺ was sleeping at home when Jibrīl ﷺ arrived and took him to the Ḥaṭīm[i] to pray two units (*rakʿāt*) of prayer. The Prophet ﷺ narrated. "Jibrīl opened up my chest and brought a bowl made of gold filled with Zamzam.[ii] He took out my heart, washed it, and put it back."[305] This is the second time that Jibrīl ﷺ washed the Prophet's heart, however on this occasion he did not need to remove a black spot. Nevertheless, his heart needed to be washed with Zamzam to prepare it for the overwhelmingly awe-inspiring sights to come. As Allah ﷻ stated, "He certainly saw some of his Lord's greatest signs."[306] It was through Allah's divine intervention and special facilitation that the Prophet was able to traverse into the Heavens without being subjected to any of the physical laws of this world.[307]

The Prophet ﷺ continued, "Jibrīl then brought me a beast, smaller than a mule but bigger than a donkey, pure white, called al-Burāq. Each of its strides is as far as the eye can see." The word "*burāq*" stems from the root word "*barq*" which means "lightning", denoting its lightning speed. However, al-Burāq is a physical animal, created of flesh and blood, not a spiritual creature. There are no authentically narrated reports about a winged horse. Al-Burāq had a harness and saddle, and Jibrīl ﷺ held the harness as the Prophet ﷺ mounted. Al-Burāq neighed, and Jibrīl ﷺ tugged the harness, saying, "Woe to you! Are you not shy? By Allah, no-one has ridden you that is more blessed in the eyes of Allah than your current rider!"[308] The Prophet ﷺ continued, "I rode al-Burāq and he took me to al-Aqsa Mosque. I tied al-Burāq to the animal posts used by the Prophets, and I entered and prayed two units of prayer."

The Prophet ﷺ then saw all the Prophets. He saw Mūsā ﷺ and described him as a strong and muscular man of brown colour; he saw ʿĪsā ﷺ and

---

i The Ḥaṭīm is the semi-circular area next to the Kaʿbah denoting the size of the original Kaʿbah built by Ibrāhīm ﷺ.

ii Another narration states, "...filled with *īmān*" however there is no contradiction, as Zamzam is holy water and thus a source of *īmān*.

described him as tanned, shorter than Mūsā 🕊, with flowing, glistening hair. He saw Ibrāhīm 🕊 who looks the most like the Prophet 🕊 himself. The Prophet 🕊 then led all the Prophets and Messengers in prayer, which demonstrates his noble standing amongst the whole of mankind, earning the title, "Master of the Prophets"[309]. Jibrīl 🕊 then approached the Prophet 🕊 with two utensils: one with wine[iii] and one with milk. Jibrīl 🕊 said, "Choose, and choose for your Ummah." The Prophet 🕊 chose the milk, and Jibrīl 🕊 replied, "You have chosen the *fiṭrah* (innate and pure disposition)."[310] The symbolism is clear: milk is pure and unadulterated, whereas wine is fermented and corrupted (from grapes).

The Ascension (al-Mi'rāj)

Allah 🕊 references the Mi'rāj in Sūrah al-Najm, "The [Prophet's] heart did not lie about what he saw. So, will you dispute with him over what he saw? Indeed, he saw him (the Angel) descend a second time at the Lote Tree of the Utmost Boundary [in the Seventh Heaven]—near which is the Garden of Abode—while the Lote Tree was overwhelmed with Heavenly splendours. The [Prophet's] sight never wandered, nor did it overreach. He certainly saw some of his Lord's greatest signs."[311]

From al-Aqsa Mosque, Jibrīl asked permission for the doors of the Heavens to open, and the gatekeeper behind the door asked, "Who is it?" and Jibrīl replied, "It is Jibrīl." The gatekeeper asked, "Do you have anybody with you?" and Jibrīl replied, "I have Muhammad." The gatekeeper asked, "Has he been sent for?" and Jibrīl replied, "Yes." The door opens and the Prophet 🕊 saw a huge man. Jibrīl 🕊 said, "This is your father, Adam 🕊, so give *salām* to him." The Prophet 🕊 did so, and Adam 🕊 replied, "Welcome, O righteous son and righteous Prophet." The Prophet 🕊 then entered the second Heaven and had the same initiation with another gatekeeper, but this time Prophets Yaḥyā and 'Īsā 🕊 were behind the door, who replied, "Welcome, O righteous brother and righteous Prophet." The third Heaven had Yūsuf 🕊 who repeated the same greeting, which prompted the Prophet 🕊 to inform

iii   Note that alcohol had not yet been prohibited in Islam.

the Companions, "Lo and behold, it was as if he were given half of all beauty!"[312] The fourth and fifth Heavens contained Idrīs ﵇ and Hārūn ﵇ respectively. The sixth Heaven had Mūsā ﵇, and as the Prophet ﷺ began to ascend further, Mūsā ﵇ began to cry, saying, "This young man, who was sent after me, shall have a larger following that will enter Paradise than my Ummah." The Prophet ﷺ entered the seventh Heaven and saw Ibrāhīm ﵇ who greeted the Prophet as Adam ﵇ did, "Welcome, O righteous son and righteous Prophet."

It is often thought that the Prophet ﷺ met the Prophets in order of rank, but this is not the case, for Adam ﵇ is certainly not the lowest. All the Prophets will be in Firdaws, the highest level of Paradise. The Prophet ﷺ met Adam ﵇ first, as he is the father of all mankind. Adam ﵇ had to temporarily leave Paradise for Earth—a glad tiding for the Prophet ﷺ who would be forced to leave Mecca but eventually return triumphantly. Yaḥyā and ʿĪsā ﵇ were next and were the closest to the Prophet ﷺ chronologically. They were also persecuted by their people as the Prophet ﷺ was. Next, Yūsuf ﵇ was betrayed by his own family, but they eventually repented and accepted him back, inspiring the Prophet ﷺ to quote him when he eventually conquered Mecca, "There is no blame on you today. May Allah forgive you. He is the Most Merciful of the merciful."[313] Idrīs ﵇ was described by Allah as being lifted into a lofty station, "And We elevated him to an honourable status."[314] Hārūn ﵇ was hated by his people but then was eventually accepted, and Mūsā ﵇ faced the most similar trials to the Prophet ﷺ and had the most similar journey. Whenever the Prophet ﷺ was hurt by his people, he would say, "May Allah have mercy upon Mūsā. He was hurt more than I was yet remained patient."[315]

A challenge for the researcher when analysing major events and long stories is piecing the multitude of narrations into an accurate chronological narrative. It is narrated that during al-Miʿrāj, the Prophet ﷺ had a longer conversation with Ibrāhīm ﵇ who said, "O Muhammad, give my *salām* to your Ummah. Inform them that the soil of Paradise is luscious, but it is empty. Its trees are planted through [uttering] '*Subḥānallah* (Glory be to Allah)'; '*Alḥamdulillāh* (Praise be to Allah)'; '*Lā ilāha il Allāh* (There is no god but Allah)'; and '*Allāhu Akbar*

(Allah is the Greatest)'."[316] It was also narrated that the Prophet ﷺ met the gatekeeper of Hell, Mālik, who was referenced in the Qur'an, "They will cry, 'O Mālik! Let your Lord finish us off.' He will answer, 'You are definitely here to stay.'"[317] The Prophet ﷺ described Mālik as completely sombre, not smiling at all. This was a stark difference to all the other Angels who greeted the Prophet ﷺ with joy. The Prophet ﷺ asked Jibrīl ﷺ why, and Jibrīl ﷺ responded, "He has never smiled or laughed since he was created." After seeing the Hellfire, he never smiled. However, Jibrīl ﷺ added, "Were he to have smiled for anyone, it would be to you."[318] The Prophet ﷺ met the Angels at their appointed stations, but Mālik, whose station is in Hell, was brought to the Prophet ﷺ to convey his *salām*, emphasising the Prophet's distance from the fire of Hell.

The Prophet ﷺ then proceeded above the seventh Heaven, at which point he saw Sidrah al-Muntahā (The Lote Tree of the Utmost Boundary). It is an overarching tree whose branches extend forth over a vast area, bearing delicious fruits with sweet scents. Jibrīl ﷺ then took him ﷺ even higher, and the Prophet ﷺ said that there were "colours that covered the tree which I cannot describe".[319] Other versions of the Hadith mention that the Prophet ﷺ witnessed "beautiful butterflies made of gold".[320] ʿAbdullāh ibn Masʿūd ﷺ narrated that the Prophet ﷺ said, "The Sidrah al-Muntahā is in the sixth Heaven, and anything that rises up from the Earth stops there and is absorbed by it. And everything that descends from above is absorbed by it and is distributed below." In other words, the Sidrah al-Muntahā is the barrier between this world and the next; anything that rises to the Heavens, such as our good deeds, is absorbed by it, and anything that descends, such as Allah's Mercy, is taken in. Another narration states that it is in the seventh Heaven, but this can be reconciled by understanding that it begins in the sixth Heaven and transcends into the seventh Heaven.

The Prophet ﷺ described four rivers flowing at the base of Sidrah al-Muntahā: two hidden and two visible. The Prophet ﷺ asked Jibrīl ﷺ what they were, and Jibrīl ﷺ answered, "The hidden ones are two rivers in Paradise—al-Kawthar[iv] and Salsabīl[v]—and the visible ones

iv Referenced in *al-Kawthar*, 1.

v Referenced in *al-Insān*, 18.

are the River Nile and the Euphrates River. Throughout human history, the tree has been known as a symbol of spirituality, peace, and nourishment. Our innate disposition towards the tree could very well be linked to the blessings of Sidrah al-Muntahā. The Prophet ﷺ then saw al-Bayt al-Maʿmūr (The Frequented House). Al-Bayt al-Maʿmūr is a structure equivalent to the Kaʿbah on Earth, situated directly above the Kaʿbah but in the seventh Heaven. Every single day, 70,000 Angels visit The Frequented House to pray for the first and last time.[321]

At this point, the Prophet ﷺ saw Jibrīl ؑ in his original form, as if he were now unshackled from the limitations of this world. The Prophet ﷺ described his majestic form, "He had 600 wings, blocking the horizon. Pearls and corals were emanating from his feathers." Allah states in the Qur'an, "All praise is for Allah, the Originator of the Heavens and the Earth, Who made Angels as messengers with wings—two, three, or four."[322] However, as the greatest Angel of all, Jibrīl had 600 wings in his true form. ʿAbdullāh ibn Masʿūd ؓ said that the verse, "He certainly saw some of his Lord's greatest signs"[323] refers to seeing Jibrīl ؑ in this form.

A Divine Meeting

The Prophet ﷺ was then blessed with a divine meeting with Allah ﷻ. He ﷺ said, "Then I was caused to ascend forth to a level whereby I could hear the Pen writing." It is noteworthy that the Prophet ﷺ used the singular, passive phrase, "I was caused to ascend" which implies that at this stage, he was alone, because until this point, he explicitly mentioned Jibrīl ؑ taking him. This indicates that the Prophet ﷺ met Allah ﷻ without Jibrīl ؑ, as he did not mention Jibrīl ؑ again after the Sidrah al-Muntahā. As for the Pen, it was the first thing ever to be created, and the first action ever to be initiated was the writing of all of history.[324] It can therefore be said that the Prophet ﷺ was raised to a level that no living creature ever was.

The Prophet ﷺ did not see Allah ﷻ directly, but he ﷺ saw His veil, which is the closest any human has ever gotten to seeing Him. ʿĀ'ishah ؓ said, "Whoever says that the Prophet ﷺ has seen his Lord has told a grave lie against Allah." [325] Masrūq, a student of the Companions, retorted, "O my mother, allow me to ask something, but don't be angry with me. Didn't Allah ﷻ say in the Qur'an, 'And he certainly saw him descend a second time' [326] and 'And he certainly saw him on the clear horizon' [327] and '...he was only two arms-lengths away or even less' [328]?" 'Ā'ishah ﷞ responded, "Glory be to Allah, my hairs are standing on my head from what you are saying. I was the first person to ever ask the Prophet about these verses. The verses are referring to Jibrīl. Have you not read in the Qur'an, 'No vision can encompass Him, but He encompasses all vision.' [329]? And have you not read in the Qur'an, 'It is not [possible] for a human being to have Allah communicate with them, except through inspiration, or from behind a veil, or by sending a Messenger-Angel to reveal whatever He wills by His permission.' [330]?" Abū Dharr asked the Prophet ﷺ directly, "O Messenger of Allah, did you see Allah?" To which the Prophet ﷺ replied, "There was light! How could I see him?" [331] The scholars interpret this light to be the veil of Allah ﷻ. Another Hadith states, "His veil is light. If Allah were to lift this veil, the rays that emanate from His Face would destroy everything." [332] That is exactly what happened when Mūsā ﷺ spoke to Allah ﷻ on Mount Sinai. [333] As for seeing Allah ﷻ in the Hereafter, it is an existence not bound by physical dimensions or limitations in a way that only Allah ﷻ knows.

Despite many legends, there are no authentically narrated reports about the conversation between the Prophet ﷺ and Allah ﷻ. The meeting was so precious and noble that it is exclusive; the Prophet ﷺ did not need, or perhaps want, to relay it. We do know, however, that the Prophet ﷺ was granted three things: the obligation of prayers, the final two verses of Sūrah al-Baqarah, and the promise that every Muslim will eventually reside in Paradise.

As for the last two verses of Sūrah al-Baqarah, they are, "The Messenger believes in what has been revealed to him from his Lord, and so do the believers. They all believe in Allah, His Angels, His Books, and His Messengers. [They proclaim:] 'We make no distinction between any of His Messengers.' And they say, 'We hear and obey. [We seek] Your forgiveness, our Lord! And to You [alone] is the Final Return.'

Allah does not require of any soul more than what it can afford. All good will be for its own benefit, and all evil will be to its own loss. [The believers pray:] 'Our Lord! Do not punish us if we forget or make a mistake. Our Lord! Do not place a burden on us like the one you placed on those before us. Our Lord! Do not burden us with what we cannot bear. Pardon us, forgive us, and have mercy on us. You are our [only] Guardian. So grant us victory over the disbelieving people.'"[334] The Prophet ﷺ said, "Whoever recites these two verses every night will be sufficed." And in another narration, "...will be protected."[335]

As for the prayer, then it had already been taught and practiced, but not obligated. At the divine meeting, Allah ﷻ obligated the prayer upon Muslims 50 times a day. The Prophet ﷺ then left and descended through the Heavens. When he reached Mūsā ﷺ, Mūsā ﷺ asked, "What did your Lord reveal for your Ummah?" The Prophet explained that he was instructed for his Ummah to pray 50 times a day. Mūsā ﷺ responded, "Return to your Lord and request some relief (i.e., lower the number)." The Prophet ﷺ looked at Jibrīl ﷺ, as if to consult his opinion, and Jibrīl ﷺ nodded in approval.[336] The Prophet ﷺ then returned to Allah ﷻ for a reduction and was once again stopped by Mūsā ﷺ with the same advice. There is a difference of opinion as to how many times the Prophet ﷺ returned but he did so at least five times until he was instructed for his Ummah to pray five times a day. Mūsā ﷺ once again advised, "Return to your Lord and request some relief." However, at this point the Prophet ﷺ replied, "I have gone back and forth, and now I am embarrassed [to ask my Lord for more]. But I am content and happy [with Allah's command]." Allah ﷻ then called out, "My obligation is decreed, and I have eased the burden on my slaves; it is five [prayers] but it shall be rewarded with 50."[337]

It is noteworthy that the Prophet ﷺ would have passed Ibrāhīm ﷺ before reaching Mūsā ﷺ yet Ibrāhīm ﷺ did not comment on the 50 prayers. It could be said that Ibrāhīm ﷺ has a higher station and thus accepts Allah's commands without hesitation, or it could equally be said that Mūsā ﷺ has more experience with large Ummahs and knows the challenges that the Prophet ﷺ will face in this matter. Furthermore, Mūsā ﷺ is the only other Prophet with the experience and honour of speaking to Allah ﷻ, so he had the expectation that Revelation would be sent, hence why he asked the Prophet ﷺ about what he received. Indeed, Mūsā ﷺ spoke to Allah ﷻ on Mount Sinai and received the Torah.[338] Nevertheless, the Prophet ﷺ knew exactly when to stop, as Allah ﷻ confirmed that five was the correct number, and the whole exercise was conducted so that the reward of 50 prayers was established for five.

Another reason why Allah ﷻ began with 50 prayers but decreed five was to establish to the Ummah that the primary purpose of life on Earth is prayer, "I did not create jinn and humans except to worship Me."[339] The reduction is Allah's Mercy and Compassion towards his deficient slaves, "And it is Allah's Will to lighten your burdens, for humankind was created weak."[340] Nevertheless, the origin is continuous worship, just as the Angels do, "They glorify Him day and night, never wavering."[341] In his excellence as a Prophet and slave, the Prophet ﷺ regularly prayed 50 units of prayer a day.[vi]

This event truly honours the five daily prayers, emphasising their importance and gravity. They are so important in the sight of Allah ﷻ that, unlike any other command, the Prophet ﷺ had to be summoned to the Heavens in the presence of the Divine to receive the blessing of prayer. Allah ﷻ equally commanded Mūsā ﷺ of the significance of prayer when He spoke to him, "It is truly I. I am Allah! There is no god except Me. So worship Me [alone], and establish the prayer for My remembrance."[342] The Qur'an mirrors this emphasis throughout, such as "Establish the prayer at both ends of the day and in the early part of the night. Surely good deeds wipe out evil deeds. That is a reminder for the mindful."[343] Many other verses corroborate this significance.[344]

After dissecting this Divine meeting, the opening verses of Sūrah al-Najm can be understood from a more accurate and profound perspective,

vi The five daily prayers comprise 17 units. The Prophet ﷺ prayed 13 units of the night prayer (two brief units of initiation, eight long units, and three units for Witr). He ﷺ prayed 12 units a day for Sunan al-Rawātib distributed before and after each obligatory prayer, and eight units for the Ḍuḥā prayer, prayed 15–20 minutes after sunrise. This totals 50 regular units a day, and it does not include extra prayers such as two units for entering the mosque, two units after completing ablution, and so on.

"By the stars when they fade away! Your fellow man is neither misguided nor astray. Nor does he speak of his own whims. It is only a Revelation sent down [to him]. He has been taught by the [Angel of] mighty power and great perfection, who once rose to [his] true form while on the highest point above the horizon, then he approached [the Prophet], coming so close that he was only two arms-lengths away or even less. Then Allah revealed to His servant what He revealed. The [Prophet's] heart did not doubt what he saw. How can you then dispute with him regarding what he saw? And he certainly saw [the Angel descend] a second time at the Lote Tree of the Utmost Boundary—near which is the Garden of Abode—while the Lote Tree was overwhelmed with Heavenly splendours. The [Prophet's] sight never wandered, nor did it overreach. He certainly saw some of his Lord's greatest signs."[345]

Informing the Quraysh

When the Prophet ﷺ descended back to Jerusalem, he rode al-Burāq back to Mecca. He ﷺ then narrated firsthand,

"When I woke up the next morning, I felt an anxiety about how I will inform the people about what happened and what they would say, and that they would disbelieve me. As I sat by the Ka'bah, nervous and worried, Allah willed that the enemy of Allah, Abū Jahl, passed by and saw me in that state. He asked mockingly, 'What's the matter?' And I said, 'Last night I was taken to al-Aqsa Mosque.' He was shocked, and asked, 'And you are now here amongst us?' And I replied, 'Yes.' He did not know whether to mock me now or call the Quraysh to listen in before I could retract. He said, 'If I call the Quraysh, will you tell them exactly what you told me?' I said, 'Yes.' And Abū Jahl began shouting,

'O people of Kaʿb ibn Lu'ayy' until everyone gathered, and he said, 'Tell your people what you just told me.' I said, 'Last night I was taken to al-Aqsa Mosque.' They asked, 'And you are now here amongst us?' And I replied, 'Yes.' Some began clapping mockingly, others put their hands on their head, and others began laughing." [346]

Someone from the crowd who had been to al-Aqsa Mosque then said, "Can you describe it for us?" Everyone knew that the Prophet ﷺ had never been to Jerusalem, so this was a clear test. The Prophet ﷺ began describing al-Aqsa Mosque, but the Quraysh began asking about specifics that he ﷺ was not able to recall. The Prophet ﷺ travelled at night, and was on a surreal mission, so he ﷺ did not notice every detail of his surroundings. Demonstrating his humanity, the Prophet ﷺ admitted, "I was more terrified than I had ever been before." This was because he could not answer the people's questions. As the Prophet grew in worry, he suddenly saw al-Aqsa Mosque descend from above until he could see everything clearly. He then answered every single question with precision and accuracy, and the Quraysh admitted that his descriptions were correct.

One of the Quraysh then ran to Abū Bakr ؓ and said, "Do you know what your companion has just said? He claims to have gone all the way to Jerusalem and back in one night!" Abū Bakr ؓ replied most diligently, "If he said that, then it is true." He did not blindly believe it in case the man was lying, yet he did not doubt the Prophet ﷺ for a single second. The man then scoffed, "Do you believe him?! (*atuṣaddiquhu?*)" Abū Bakr ؓ replied, "I believe him in something much more amazing than that. He claims that Revelation descends to him from the seven Heavens!" [347] Thenceforth, he became known as Abū Bakr al-Ṣiddīq ؓ—The Truthful.

In Search of a New Base

11

The Prophet's living arrangements in Mecca grew more precarious as time passed; his protector, Muṭʿim ibn ʿAdiyy, was nearing the end of his life, and his own tribe, Banū Hāshim, had disowned him. After the people of Ṭā'if rejected him and Mecca grew ever more hostile, the Prophet ﷺ accelerated his efforts of finding a base. He began approaching tribes visiting for Hajj. As previously discussed, the Prophet ﷺ did this in the past to preach the Message of Islam, but now he was seeking to join a new tribe. Such a move was not unprecedented but was very rare, and it was clear that this was the Prophet's last resort.

During Hajj season, camps at Mina were allocated according to tribe, and the Prophet ﷺ would utilise this opportunity to approach the tribe leaders separately. Rabīʿah ibn ʿAbbād said, "I remember a young man coming and speaking to my father, telling him to embrace the worship of Allah and leave idolatry, and asking him to accept him into his tribe. I saw an elderly man wearing a Yemeni cloak standing behind him waiting for him to finish. As the first man would go from one tribe to another, the elderly man would approach the same tribes after him, saying, 'O people, this person is telling you to abandon your gods, al-Lāt and al-ʿUzzā, and he is calling you to abandon the way of your forefathers!' I asked my father, 'Who is this young man, and who is the other man?' My father said, 'This is the young man they claim to be a Prophet, and the elderly man is his uncle, ʿAbd al-ʿUzzā ibn ʿAbd al-Muṭṭalib (i.e., Abū Lahab).'"[348]

The Prophet ﷺ would usually visit tribes alongside his confidant, Abū Bakr ؓ. As well as being his most trusted ally, Abū Bakr was the foremost expert in genealogy, having memorised the history and lineage of a wide variety of tribes throughout Arabia. The Prophet ﷺ relied heavily on Abū Bakr ؓ, demonstrating the permissibility and wisdom in accepting help and utilising expertise. The Prophet's perfection and infallibility was in religious knowledge and guidance. As for his capacity as a human, he ﷺ would accept advice and assistance. Before meeting each tribe, Abū Bakr would inform the Prophet ﷺ of the names of the people he was addressing, the strengths and weaknesses of the tribe, and so on.

The Prophet ﷺ approached many major tribes and was faced with varying degrees of apprehension; some politely declined while others replied sarcastically or even aggressively. One of the tribes he approached was Kindah, a historically powerful and imposing Kingdom that had fizzled out over time into a modest tribe. One of their Chieftains listened to the Prophet ﷺ and his interest was piqued. He said, "This is a very interesting message. Come with me and I will grant you an audience with the other Chieftains." The Prophet ﷺ followed him and preached the Message to the Chieftains. The first Chieftain then said, "O my fellow tribesmen, if we were to take this young man from the Quraysh, we will have a message through which we could conquer the other Arabs." He then turned to the Prophet ﷺ and said, "If we were to follow this matter of yours, and Allah grants us victory over all your enemies, will you give us control over this affair after you?" The Prophet ﷺ replied forthrightly, "The lands belong to Allah, and He gives it to whomever He pleases." The Chieftain then said, "So you are asking us to follow you, stick our necks out behind you to have them cut off, and after we have spilled our blood and you have used it to conquer the Arabs, you will take the Kingdom? Go, for we have no need for this."[349] Despite the Prophet's desperate situation, he ﷺ did not compromise; he saw that Kindah were not completely sincere theologically and were instead politically motivated, so he did not push them any further.

The Prophet ﷺ also met with Banū Shaybān ibn Thaʿlabah. Abū Bakr ﷺ advised, "O Messenger of Allah, the Banū Shaybān are of the most noble, illustrious, and intelligent tribes of the Arabs, and they have amongst them So-and-so and So-and-so."[350] After exchanging pleasantries, the Prophet ﷺ said, "We have come to invite you to the worship of Allah ﷻ without any intermediaries, and that you reject the false gods. We ask that you accept us into your tribe, as the Quraysh has arrogantly and unjustly prevented us from spreading the Word of Allah." The Prophet ﷺ then ended by venerating Allah and differentiating his needs from Allah's self-sufficiency, "And Allah is al-Ghaniyy al-Ḥamīd (The Self-Sufficient, Praiseworthy)." They replied, "Do you have anything else?" And the Prophet ﷺ recited from Sūrah al-An'am, Ayah 151

> "Say [O Prophet], 'Come! Let me recite to you what your Lord has forbidden to you: do not associate others with Him [in worship]. [Do not fail to] honour your parents. Do not kill your children for fear of poverty. We provide for you and for them. Do not come near indecencies, openly or secretly. Do not take a life—made sacred by Allah—except with [legal] right.' This is what He has commanded you, so perhaps you will understand."[351]

They replied, "Do you have anything else?" And the Prophet ﷺ recited from Sūrah al-Naḥl in what was to become one of the most famous admonitions in Islam, recited in most Friday Sermons, "Indeed, Allah commands justice, grace, and courtesy to close relatives. He forbids indecency, wickedness, and aggression. He instructs you so perhaps you will be mindful."[352] The Chieftain finally replied, "You have indeed come with goodness. You have come with the best of manners and morals." Proving that the Quraysh went out of their way to approach tribes and slander the Prophet ﷺ, they added, "And the Quraysh has lied against you." He continued, "I refer you to our elder, Hāni' ibn Qays." Hāni' then stood up and said, "I have heard what you have said, O member of the Quraysh. I feel that if we leave our religion and our way for your religion and way after one meeting, it may be a hasty decision that would cause us harm in the long term. We also have people we left behind (i.e., who did not come for Hajj) whose advice we have not sought and whose support is necessary. I therefore think that we should wait, and you should wait, and we shall return, and you shall return (i.e., next Hajj). I also ask the advice of our military leader: al-Muthannā ibn Ḥārithah." Al-Muthannā then stood up and said, "What our elder Hāni' said is true; we will not make any hasty decisions. There is also another matter. We are a group of Arabs who have loyalties and treaties with two groups of people: our neighbouring Arab tribes, and Kisrā (Khosrow, King of the Sassanid Empire). As for the Arabs, we do not fear or worry about them, but as for Kisrā, we have an agreement to be neutral in all affairs of the Arabian Peninsula, and this matter of yours does not seem to be something that Kings approve. If we were to accept your proposal, it would only be on the Arab side."[353]

The Prophet ﷺ once again remained firm on his principles and responded, "Your response has been good and is sincere, but Allah's religion will only be helped by those who embrace it wholeheartedly." Indeed, the Qur'an states, "O believers! Enter into Islam wholeheartedly."[354] As previously discussed, even the Quraysh had offered to accept Islam on the condition that they alternate between Islam and Paganism, and Allah responded, "Say, 'O you disbelievers! I do not worship what you worship, nor do you worship what I worship. I will never worship what you worship, nor will you ever worship what I worship. You have your way, and I have my Way.'"[355] As the Prophet ﷺ was exiting the tent, he turned back to the Chieftains and said, "And what if I were to tell you that Allah ﷻ would grant you victory over Kisrā's Kingdom, and you will enjoy their land, money, and captives—would you then accept?" A younger tribesman replied elatedly, "Yes, of course!" But they did not believe that this would ever happen.

The Persian Sassanid Empire was so colossal that the Roman Empire failed to conquer it despite hundreds of attempts and battles. No-one could ever predict that the meagre tribes of Arabia would slay the goliath. Nevertheless, the Prophet ﷺ had unwavering certitude in his belief (*yaqīn*) and the Persian Empire was brought to its knees after a few short years of Islamic conquest. The Banū Shaybān did eventually accept Islam after Mecca was conquered, but because they did not formally adopt the Prophet ﷺ, they missed out on the reward, status, and honour of being titled al-Anṣār (The Prophet's Helpers).

An Unlikely Saviour in Yathrib

Allah ﷻ willed that the Prophet's attention be turned to the fledgling city of Yathrib (later to be renamed "Medina"). On the 10th year of the *daʿwah*, the year of Abū Ṭālib's death, the Prophet ﷺ approached a small group of Arabs from Yathrib. The demographic in Yathrib was comprised of three main groups: two Arab tribes, al-Aws and al-Khazraj, and the Jews. The two Arab tribes were the majority and were in power, but they enjoyed a love-hate relationship, alternating between war and peace, as was common in intertribal politics. Tensions gradually rose between the tribes over decades, eventually culminating into a fully-fledged civil war. This was known as the Battle of Buʿāth, and it depleted both tribes to an alarming degree; the elders were largely killed, and the youth grew tired and disillusioned of the constant warring.

ʿĀ'ishah ﷺ once said, "The Day of Buʿāth was a gift that Allah granted the Prophet ﷺ. It was due to Buʿāth that their unity (i.e., the Aws and Khazraj) had been fragmented, and their leaders were decimated." [356] The youth that survived were raised in a fruitless war and were thus naturally more open to change. The lone senior figure who survived the war was ʿAbdullāh ibn Ubayy ibn Salūl. As the *de facto* leader, he was opposed to a foreign entity that would jeopardise his leadership. Nevertheless, he was outnumbered by exuberant youth with an openness to change.

There were indications that the Message of Islam had reached Yathrib prior to the Prophet's official contact. Suwayd ibn al-Ṣāmit was the leading poet of the Khazraj who heard that there was a mysterious poet or magician from the Quraysh. When he travelled to Mecca for Hajj, he sought the Prophet ﷺ to observe him. He approached the Prophet ﷺ and said, "I have heard that you have eloquent speech. I have something similar." He then recited extremely eloquent poetry of the utmost calibre. The Prophet ﷺ replied, "What you have is good, but what I have is better. I have Revelation from the Lord of the worlds." The Prophet ﷺ then began reciting the Qur'an, and Suwayd was dumbfounded by its divine eloquence. He returned to Yathrib, and later that year died in the Battle of Buʿāth. Later, his people said, "We are certain that he died a Muslim."[357] Another reference states that a young man from the Khazraj was stabbed in the Battle of Buʿāth, and as he took his last breaths, his last words were, "*SubḥānAllāh* (Glory be to Allah), *Alḥamdulillāh* (Praise be to Allah), *Allāhu Akbar* (Allah is the Greatest)."[358]

Aside from miscellaneous reports, the Message of Islam formally arrived in Yathrib after the Prophet ﷺ spoke to a group of six members of the Khazraj during Hajj. As the Prophet ﷺ was passing between the tents of the major tribes, he saw a small group of young men near the ʿAqabah area in Hajj. Abū Bakr ؓ was not with him, so he ﷺ asked, "Who are you?" They replied, "We are from the Khazraj." The Prophet ﷺ replied, "Which Khazraj? The neighbours of the Jews (i.e., in Yathrib)?" They replied in the affirmative, and the Prophet ﷺ sat down and explained the teachings of Islam, warned against polytheism, and recited the Qur'an. He ﷺ preached to these six youths with the same passion and sincerity as he did with the major tribes of Kindah and its like. They accepted Islam, and the Prophet ﷺ finally made a breakthrough.

Allah ﷻ willed that the Prophet's Helpers (Anṣār[i]) came from a small, obscure tribe from Yathrib. This clearly teaches us not to belittle any

i The Aws and Khazraj will eventually be given the title of al-Anṣār (The Helpers) because they helped the Prophet ﷺ at his time of need. The Meccan Muslims who emigrated to Medina would be called al-Muhājirūn (The Emigrants). Hence, the oft-repeated phrase "al-Muhājirūn wa al-Anṣār (The Emigrants and Helpers)" was born.

action for the sake of Allah, no matter how small. Had the Prophet ﷺ not approached those six young men in favour of a bigger tribe, they would not have accepted Islam and the Prophet ﷺ would not have established a base. Of Allah's many wisdoms in choosing Yathrib as a base was that the Arabs of Yathrib were of the very few people in Arabia who were familiar with monotheistic religions. The Pagan Arabs were generally not familiar with the concept of Prophethood whereas Yathrib was one of only two cities in the whole of the Hijaz region where Jews resided, creating a relatively multi-cultural society. The Aws and Khazraj were therefore acquainted with the notion of Prophethood, Revelation, and Scripture.

In fact, the Jews would often taunt them with the coming of a Prophet who they claimed would be used to destroy them. Allah ﷻ indirectly references this in the Qur'an, "Although they used to pray for victory over the polytheists, when there came to them a Book from Allah which they recognised, confirming the Scripture they had [in their hands], they rejected it. So may Allah's condemnation be upon the disbelievers."[359] Their arrogance backfired, as the Aws and Khazraj were familiar with the idea of a foretold Prophet, which undoubtedly had an impact on their acceptance of the Prophet Muhammad ﷺ.

The First Covenant of ʿAqabah (The Covenant of Women)

The six members of the Khazraj did not make a formal public declaration of conversion, but they welcomed the Prophet's Message and vowed to return the following year. They indeed returned a year later, in the 12th year of Prophethood, with 12 people who formally converted—the largest number of converts outside Mecca. The 12 members were comprised of both the Aws and Khazraj, showing that they were already putting tribal differences behind them for the sake of Islam. Together, they pledged their allegiance to the Prophet ﷺ; each of them placed their hand in the hand of the Prophet ﷺ and converted to Islam. It is called the Covenant of ʿAqabah because it took place on the plains of

ʿAqabah during Hajj. It is also referred to as "The Covenant of Women" because it was an apolitical covenant. When women would convert to Islam, the Prophet ﷺ did not request from them any political or military commitments; rather, he instructed them to worship Allah ﷻ alone and adopt a moral and righteous life.

This oath was a strictly theological commitment to follow the tenets of Islam, hence the name. The Qur'an states, "O Prophet! When the believing women come to you, pledging to you that they will neither associate anything with Allah [in worship], nor steal, nor fornicate, nor kill their children, nor falsely attribute [illegitimate] children to their husbands, nor disobey you in what is right, then accept their pledge, and ask Allah to forgive them. Surely Allah is All-Forgiving, Most Merciful."[360] ʿUbādah ibn al-Ṣāmit ؓ said, "The first covenant we made was akin to the oath of women; we swore our allegiance to worship Allah alone, not fornicate, not steal, not kill our children, not live immoral lives, and obey the Messenger in all good matters."[361] The Prophet ﷺ said about this covenant, "Whoever fulfils this oath will have their reward with Allah. Whoever commits any of these sins and is punished in this world, then that will constitute their expiation. And whoever commits any of those sins and Allah conceals their sins, then the matter will rest with Him: if He wishes, He may punish them, and if He wishes, He may forgive them."[362]

The converts requested that the Prophet ﷺ send a knowledgeable Muslim to accompany them and teach them Islam in Yathrib. The Prophet ﷺ agreed and sent Muṣʿab ibn ʿUmayr ؓ who taught them Qur'an and led them in prayer. It is narrated that within a few weeks of Muṣʿab reaching Yathrib, 40 people converted to Islam. At that point, the Prophet ﷺ instructed them to pray the Friday Prayer, meaning that the first ever Friday Prayer in Islam did not actually include the Prophet ﷺ. Eventually, every single sub-tribe of the Aws and Khazraj had at least one Muslim household. The conversion of two people in particular led to an instantaneous mass conversion: Saʿd ibn Muʿādh and Usayd ibn Huḍayr ؓ. They were the up-and-coming leaders of the Aws and Khazraj following the gap in leadership created by the Battle of Buʿāth, and they would grow to become formidable leaders in Islam.

Muṣʿab was preaching in the house of Asʿad ibn Zurārah. Saʿd said to Usayd, "This new religion has come to our land, and my cousin, Asʿad, is housing the man spreading this faith. I feel awkward expelling him from my own cousin's house, so why don't you go and expel this man from our city?" Usayd immediately went – spear in hand—to Asʿad's house. Asʿad saw him from afar and warned Muṣʿab nervously, "One of our leaders is approaching!" Usayd stormed in angrily, "Why have you come to our lands? Have you come to brainwash those of us with low intellect? To take our women and children away from our ways? Go back to where you came from if you value your life."

Muṣʿab responded with a calmness and confidence that only *īmān* could instil. He said, "Why don't you sit and listen to what I have to say? If you find it agreeable then good, and if not then I will stop." Usayd calmed down and found the request too reasonable to oppose, so he sat down and listened. Muṣʿab then preached the basic teachings of Islam, and Usayd was immediately convinced. His heart opened up to Islam and he said, "What you said makes complete sense to me. How does one embrace your faith?" Usayd came to Muṣʿab with his spear in hand but left after performing *ghusl* and declaring the *shahādah*. Usayd said, "If you convince the person who sent me (i.e., Saʿd ibn Muʿādh), then you will have no opposition left."[363]

When Usayd returned, Saʿd noticed an immediate difference, stating, "This is not the same man who left us." Usayd said, "I tried speaking to them, but you should try." To add an element of urgency to the matter, he added, "I have also heard that a certain tribe has vowed to kill Asʿad for housing this man." Saʿd became alarmed and immediately took off, taking his weapons with him. He marched in to Asʿad's house and said, "O Asʿad, had you not been my cousin, these weapons would not be hanging from my side. It is only because of our blood relationship that I am not taking this matter further. Get rid of your guest and tell him to leave our lands." Before Asʿad even responded, Muṣʿab interjected with the same proposal he gave to Usayd. Saʿd was so taken aback by his bravery and stoic confidence that he acquiesced. This time, Muṣʿab also recited Sūrah Zukhruf. The Qur'an softened Saʿd's heart, and he immediately accepted Islam. After these two major conversions, the entire[ii] tribe of the Banū ʿAbd al-Ashhal converted, one of the biggest tribes in Yathrib.

The Second Covenant of ʿAqabah (The Covenant of War)

Muṣʿab ibn ʿUmayr ﵁ was very successful in his *daʿwah*, and the following year, the 13th year of Prophethood, 75 people pledged to the Prophet ﷺ—a marked increase from the original 12. These 75 were the ones who were able to perform Hajj, and it would be reasonable to imagine that there were many more Muslims willing to pledge who could not make the journey. A minimum of 250–300 people in Yathrib were now Muslims, and Islam continued to spread rapidly.

Jābir ibn ʿAbdillāh ﵁, one of the most famous Companions from the Anṣār, narrates, "The Prophet ﷺ stayed in Mecca for more than ten years, preaching to the people in Hajj, asking, 'Who will support me so that I can spread the Message of my Lord?' And he would not find anyone embracing his faith except a man or two from such-and-such tribe. Finally, Allah guided a group of us from Yathrib to Islam, and we believed in him and recited the Qur'an until not a single sub-tribe amongst the people of Yathrib existed except there were Muslims amongst them. Then Allah ﷻ caused us to come together and we said, 'For how long will we allow the Prophet ﷺ to be repelled from one valley to another outside Mecca and fear for his life?' And Allah ﷻ gave us the idea to invite the Prophet ﷺ to Yathrib."[364]

The Prophet ﷺ instructed the 75 Muslims of Yathrib to meet him on the last day of Hajj in the dead of the night. Kaʿb ibn Mālik ﵁ narrates,

ii The only person in the whole tribe not to convert was a man called Uṣayrīn. He remained the only Pagan in the tribe for the next three years. At the Battle of Uḥud, he accepted Islam and died in battle on the same day. He accepted Islam after the time of Fajr and died before the time of Ẓuhr, becoming the only ever Companion to be admitted into Paradise without ever having prayed a single prayer (after the prayer was established). The Prophet ﷺ commented, "He has done little but has been rewarded with plenty." And, "He is of the people of Paradise." (Bukhārī, *Ṣaḥīḥ al-Bukhārī*, p. 695).

"When we went for Hajj, we hid our Islam from our Pagan relatives. We were instructed to meet a few hours before Fajr, so we sneaked out of our tents so as not to arouse suspicion. The Prophet ﷺ appeared with his uncle, al-ʿAbbās, who said to the Prophet ﷺ, 'O my nephew, I do not recognise any of these men.'"[365] Al-ʿAbbās was not yet Muslim, but he still accompanied the Prophet ﷺ out of familial love. Thinking tribally, he was searching for the elders that he recognised and traded with, but found none. As aforementioned, the Battle of Buʿāth wiped out the leadership of the Aws and Khazraj. With so much at stake, al-ʿAbbās was uneasy trusting these fresh, unrecognised faces; though, unbeknownst to him, Allah ﷻ recognised and trusted them.

Al-ʿAbbās ؓ then stood up and spoke on behalf of the Prophet ﷺ, "O Khazraj[iii], you know the status of this man amongst us, and we have protected him from his own people even though we agree with our people (i.e., the Banū Hāshim are amongst the same religion as the rest of the Quraysh). He has dignity and honour amongst us, and he has protection, but he has decided to leave us to join you. So, if you are sure that you can live up to your conditions, and protect him from those who oppose him, then you shall bear the responsibility. Otherwise, let him go from now, and realise that he is honoured amongst his people."[366] Al-ʿAbbās was clearly hesitant and cautious. He was also embarrassed at the measures his nephew ﷺ was forced to take, overemphasising the honourable status the Prophet ﷺ had amongst the Quraysh. The reality, at this stage, was the contrary; the Quraysh had all but expelled him ﷺ and did not show honour nor respect.

The Muslims replied, "O ʿAbbās, you have spoken, so let the Prophet ﷺ speak. O Messenger of Allah, tell us your conditions." The Prophet ﷺ then stood up and began reciting Qur'an and preaching to them, advising them to fear Allah ﷻ. He then said, "I shall give you [permission of giving] allegiance in return for protection. You shall protect me as one of your own." Al-Barāʾ ibn Maʿrūr ؓ stood up and said,

---

iii Members of both al-Aws and al-Khazraj were in attendance, although most of them were from the Khazraj. It is a norm in classical Arabic to address a group by its majority.

"We are a people experienced in the art of war; we have inherited it from our forefathers (i.e., this is an easy condition). Stretch forth your hand and we will give you allegiance." Abū al-Haytham ibn Tayyahān then stood up and added his wise perspective, "O Messenger of Allah, we have treaties with the Jews in Yathrib. Once we accept you, we will have broken them. Once you come over to our side, and Allah gives us victory, will you then leave us and return to your people?" Ponder upon the resounding *īmān* of a man asking what will happen *after* victory will be given despite Islam being in its infancy. Moreover, his foremost worry was losing the Prophet ﷺ. Contrast this worry to the Chieftains of Kindah who were worried about who will rule the Kingdom. The Prophet ﷺ replied resolutely, "My blood is your blood, and my destruction is your destruction (i.e., we are now one)."[367]

The Anṣār were thoroughly sufficed and asked the Prophet ﷺ how exactly to pledge allegiance. The Prophet ﷺ instructed, "Pledge that you hear and obey, in ease and in difficulty, and that you spend from your money in the way of Allah ﷻ, and that you command the good and forbid the evil, and that you speak the truth no matter what the consequence, and that you help me when I come to Yathrib just like you help your own family." The Anṣār replied, "And what is in it for us?" And the Prophet ﷺ replied with the one word they were desperate to hear, "Paradise."

They all stood up to pledge their allegiance officially, but Asʿad ibn Zurārah ﵁ stood up and pushed the Prophet's blessed hand down. He said, "Wait! O people of Yathrib, we did not travel all this way except that we know that this is the Messenger of Allah. Once his people expel him, you will be asking for war. If you are ready for your necks to meet swords, then give your oaths. Know that the best of you will be killed, and fathers will lose their sons and sons will lose their fathers. If you realise this, then go ahead, but if not, then stop now; perhaps Allah will forgive you." They responded, "O Asʿad, you have spoken enough. Get your hand off the hand of the Prophet, we want to pledge our allegiance." One by one, they pledged to the Prophet ﷺ and officially became the Anṣār.

There were 73 men who pledged by hand and two women, Asmā' bint ʿAmr and Nusaybah bint Kaʿb, who would pledge by raising their hand towards the Prophet ﷺ, as he never physically touched a non-*maḥram*[iv] woman. Despite the first covenant being termed, "The Covenant of Women", these women participated in this second covenant, "The Covenant of War", in equal standing to the men. Nusaybah ؓ lived the rest of her life on the battlefield, suffering 12 wounds in the Battle of Uḥud but continuing to fight for decades to the extent that her hand was amputated in the Battle of Yarmūk against the Romans.[368]

It is narrated that everybody then heard a loud voice cry out, "O people sleeping in the tents, do you not know that a group of rebels have gathered with the Sabian to wage war against you?"[369] This took place in the dead of the night, so it caused a major disturbance and the pilgrims were awoken. The Prophet ﷺ said to the Muslims, "This is ʿAzab ibn ʿUzayb, the Shayṭān of ʿAqabah." He ﷺ then addressed him directly, "I swear by Allah, O enemy of Allah, I will deal with you!"[370] This Shayṭān was so overwhelmed by the positive impact of this meeting that he took the drastic measure of crying out into the physical realm. The Anṣār proposed to the Prophet ﷺ, "O Messenger of Allah, shouldn't we attack everyone now? We are 70 strong and they are unarmed and asleep." The Prophet ﷺ responded definitively, "I have not been commanded to do that."[371] Contrary to historical slander that the Prophet ﷺ was eager to war, he did not take this easy option. The Prophet ﷺ was simply a slave of the Almighty and never took a step without His instruction. The Muslims then quickly dispersed and quietly returned to their respective tents. The following morning, rumours had already spread, and the Quraysh sent delegations to every camp, asking if anyone had met with the Prophet ﷺ. When they approached the Khazraj, the unsuspecting Pagans amongst them strongly denied the claims while the Muslims remained silent.

iv A *maḥram* is a member of the opposite gender to whom marriage would be impermissible i.e., a family member such as a parent, sibling, and so on. Physical contact is forbidden with a non-*maḥram* except through marriage.

The Anṣār would hold a very special place in the Prophet's heart for the remainder of his life. He ﷺ would frequently praise them, and even went as far as to say, "Were it not for the Hijrah (i.e., were I not from Mecca) I would have been a member of the Anṣār. And if the Anṣār went in one direction, and all of mankind went in another direction, I would go with the Anṣār."[372] He ﷺ also said, "Love for the Anṣār is a sign of *īmān*, and hating the Anṣār is a part of hypocrisy."[373] He ﷺ would often make *duʿā'* for them, "O Allah, forgive the Anṣār and the sons of the Anṣār."[374]

PART III • THE MECCAN ERA

12 The Hijrah

Upon his return, the Prophet ﷺ granted the Muslims permission to emigrate and they began doing so individually and in secret. Tensions in Mecca were at an all-time high, and the Quraysh would not allow anyone to openly emigrate without facing aggression and abuse. The first to emigrate was Abū Salamah ibn ʿAbd al-Asad ﷺ. Abū Salamah was not from the Quraysh, but in a rare occurrence, he switched tribes to marry Umm Salamah, who was from the Quraysh. Abū Salamah and Umm Salamah had previously emigrated to Abyssinia, but when the rumours spread about the Quraysh accepting Islam and the Muslims returned to Mecca, they remained in Mecca whereas most of the emigrants returned to Abyssinia once more. They were of the few Muslims to have made two emigrations for the sake of Allah, and were known as "The People of Two Emigrations".

As the first to emigrate, Abū Salamah packed his things openly, and as he began to leave, the Quraysh confronted him with unsheathed weapons. They said, "As for you, we have no right to stop you (as a non-Qurashī), but as for your wife, she is ours. We will not let you take her or her son, as he is our son now." Abū Salamah's original tribe heard of this oppressive event, and their tribal pride made them march over to the Quraysh. They said, "The lady may be yours, but this boy is ours." They physically took the boy by his arm, and the Quraysh held on to his other arm; they both began pulling until the young boy's arm dislocated, and Umm Salamah cried out and pleaded that the Quraysh let them take the boy. In a most unfortunate turn of events, Abū Salamah was in Medina, Umm Salamah was in Mecca, and their four-year-old son was elsewhere with a foreign tribe. Umm Salamah narrates, "For one year, I would go to al-Abṭaḥ (the furthest part of Mecca) every day, crying, until finally some of my cousins had sympathy with me and pleaded to the Quraysh to let me go."[375]

She was finally allowed to leave, so she took her son and marched into the desert on foot, alone, and without any belongings. By the time she got to Tanʿīm, she saw ʿUthmān ibn Ṭalḥah—who was not yet a Muslim—returning from an expedition. Shocked to see a woman and child alone in such a dangerous environment, susceptible to attacks from wild animals, foreign entities, or even starvation, ʿUthmān asked what she was doing alone. Umm Salamah declared that she was sufficed with Allah ﷻ, but ʿUthmān replied, "By Allah, this will not be. I will take you." Although he was not yet a Muslim, his innate chivalry and honour did not allow him to tolerate such injustice without intervening. Recalling this event, Umm Salamah said, "I do not think there is a more honourable gentleman than ʿUthmān. He walked the entire way from Mecca to Medina while I rode his camel, and he did not talk except that when he stopped, he would gesture to the camel to stop and would turn around (so she could disembark in privacy). He would let me sleep under a tree while he slept next to the camel. He did so all the way home until when I could finally see the houses of Yathrib, he said 'Your husband lives there.'"[376]

The journey was over two weeks, and he would have returned to Mecca on foot. Allah ﷻ undoubtedly recompenses such noble acts, and ʿUthmān was gifted the blessing of Islam. He converted before the Conquest of Mecca, granting him the honour of being amongst the upper echelon of Companions. Allah ﷻ states, "Those of you who donated and fought before the victory [over Mecca] are unparalleled. They are far greater in rank than those who donated and fought afterwards."[377]

Moreover, Allah ﷻ granted him the supreme honour of retaining the keys of the Kaʿbah. Allah ﷻ revealed in the Qur'an, "Indeed, Allah commands you to return trusts to their rightful owners..."[378] This verse was referring to the keys of the Kaʿbah being given to ʿUthmān ؓ, so ʿAlī ؓ gave ʿUthmān the keys and said, "Allah ﷻ revealed something about you." He then recited the aforementioned verse.[379] To this day, almost fifteen centuries later, the keys to the Kaʿbah belong to the descendants of ʿUthmān ibn Ṭalḥah ؓ, and indeed Allah's rewards are never lost.

ʿAlī ibn Abī Ṭālib ؓ narrates, "I don't know of anyone who made the Hijrah publicly except ʿUmar ibn al-Khaṭṭāb." ʿUmar ؓ packed his bags, wore his armour, and performed *ṭawāf* (circumambulation of the Kaʿbah) armed with weapons. He then made an announcement, "O people of Mecca, whoever amongst you wishes that his mother lose him tonight, or that his children become orphans, or that his wife becomes a widow, know that I am performing the Hijrah and you can meet me outside Mecca."[380]

The Prophet's Hijrah ﷺ

On the 27th of Ṣafar, the Prophet ﷺ became the last male adult to officially perform the Hijrah.[381] There were a handful of women and children who emigrated after him but the Prophet ﷺ ensured that he was of the last to depart. ʿĀ'ishah ؓ narrated, "We were sitting in our house in the peak of the afternoon heat (i.e., midday) and we saw a man walking with his face covered. As he approached, we realised that it was the Prophet ﷺ. We said to ourselves that the only reason he would be coming would be for an emergency (due to the extreme midday heat)." The Prophet ﷺ said, "Remove everyone from the room." Abū Bakr replied, "O Messenger of Allah, they are but your family." The Prophet ﷺ then said, "Allah has given me permission to emigrate." Abū Bakr ؓ replied yearningly, "[And my] companionship? I beg you, by my mother and father!" The Prophet ﷺ replied, "Yes." ʿĀ'ishah ؓ then narrated, "I saw Abū Bakr cry, and I had never believed that people could cry out of happiness until I saw him cry out of happiness that day."[382] Abū Bakr ﵁ then said, "O Messenger of Allah, I have prepared[i] two camels, and one of them is yours." The Prophet ﷺ replied, "Only if I pay you." Even the Prophet ﷺ was keen on receiving the full reward for his emigration and thus did not want to rely on any gifts.

Abū Bakr ﵁ had 40,000 dirhams before he accepted Islam, but only 5,000 dirhams at the time of emigration, as he spent most of it freeing slaves and spending it in the path of Allah.[383] When he emigrated, he took the entire amount with him and left nothing behind for his family. His father, Abū Quḥāfah, had not yet accepted Islam and at this time was a stern opposer of Islam. He was a blind, bitter, elderly man armed with a sharp tongue. He approached his granddaughter, Asmā' bint Abī Bakr ﵄, mocking his son, Abū Bakr ﵁, for supposedly abandoning his family with no financial support. Asmā', in her quick-wittedness inherited from her father, quietly filled a pouch with pebbles, tied it up, and handed it to Abū Quḥāfah, saying, "No, my grandfather. He has left us this."[384] As a blind man, he picked up the bag and felt its weight and was taken aback, so he recanted his criticism. Asmā' ﵄ recalled that indeed her father did not leave them a single penny; he knew they would be safe in Mecca and so he put his trust in Allah, whereas he was accompanying the Prophet ﷺ in the wilderness and would need extra money for safety.

Imam Aḥmad ﵀ states that Allah ﷻ revealed a verse in the Qur'an describing the night of the Hijrah, "And when the disbelievers conspired to capture, kill, or exile you. They planned, but Allah also planned. And Allah is the best of planners."[385] Allah ﷻ described the Quraysh gathering in the Dār al-Nadwah of Mecca—their parliamentary meeting place—to find a final solution to deal with the Prophet ﷺ and the religion of Islam. The Quraysh gathered with the exception of

i Preparing a camel for emigration is a laborious task which consists of feeding the camel salt for it to overdrink water, feeding it a special diet, and withholding it from exercise so it stores its fat. This is done for a considerable time until an extra hump appears. On this occasion, Abū Bakr ﵁ stated that he prepared the camels for four months, although historians state that it was three-and-a-half months and that Abū Bakr ﵁ rounded it up to four in his narration.

Banū Hāshim; while the likes of Abū Lahab had no issue with plotting against the Prophet ﷺ, it would have been a public disgrace according to tribal politics if he were to allow such an event to occur regarding his own tribesman. He was therefore not invited so that he could claim ignorance of the matter and save face.

The entirety of the Quraysh—except for Abū Lahab and Muṭʿim ibn ʿAdiyy (because the Prophet ﷺ was living under his protection)—gathered to finally put a stop to the Prophet ﷺ. The first suggestion was to imprison him ﷺ, but imprisonment was an alien concept to the Arabs, considered inhumane and impractical. Shayṭān physically placed himself amongst the crowd and said, "If you imprison him, his words will still reach his followers." The second suggestion was to exile him, but Shayṭān responded, "Sending him into exile is to send him back to his followers." Abū Jahl, the worst of them, then said, "You still haven't said what everyone is thinking: why don't we kill him? We will do it in a way where no single tribe can be blamed; each tribe will nominate a young man and they will all attack him in unison so that no single person is to blame. The Banū Hāshim won't be able to declare war and will be forced to accept blood money." Shayṭān then said, "This is the right decision." The Quraysh agreed, nominated their tribe members, and sent them immediately to the Prophet's house. Jibrīl ﷺ descended and informed the Prophet ﷺ that he must leave for the Hijrah immediately.[386]

The Prophet ﷺ instructed ʿAlī ﷺ to lie in his bed and cover himself as a decoy as he ﷺ slipped out in the dead of the night with Abū Bakr ﷺ. As they left Mecca, he turned around and addressed his hometown, "You are the most blessed land on Earth, and the most beloved to me; were it not for the fact that my own people expelled me, I would not have left you."[387] The Prophet ﷺ used the exact same wording that Waraqah ibn Nawfal did over 13 years ago which transpired exactly as forewarned. The Prophet ﷺ could not comprehend Waraqah's words at the time, but 13 years later, he lived them.

The Prophet ﷺ and Abū Bakr ﷺ headed straight to Cave Thawr and remained there for three days and three nights in a bid to throw the Quraysh off their scent. It is worth noting that Cave Thawr is a three-hour walk southward of Mecca, the exact opposite direction to Medina, which is northbound. This demonstrates the extent to which they planned their trip in such meticulous detail. This provides an invaluable lesson in the implementation of *tawakkul*: it is not blind faith in Allah ﷻ without planning; rather, *tawakkul* is to plan to the best of our ability and leave the rest to Allah ﷻ with full belief and confidence.

Abū Bakr ؓ had even arranged for his household to carry out tasks after they left. He instructed his son, ʿAbdullāh, to bring food and water to the cave. He was also instructed to listen in on the Quraysh's gatherings, as he was a young boy and they did not take much notice of him. ʿĀmir ibn Fuhayrah was Abū Bakr's freed slave who felt a strong sense of loyalty and allegiance to him, so he was tasked with erasing the footprints of ʿAbdullāh as he went out every morning. ʿĀmir was a shepherd, so he would take out his flock and wipe out ʿĀbdullah's footprints without arousing suspicion.

After eventually realising that they took a detour, the Quraysh began to look in all directions. They entered upon Cave Thawr, which was an extremely small crevice barely big enough for two men. The Prophet ﷺ and Abū Bakr ؓ were hiding below the cave when they heard footsteps above them. Abū Bakr whispered to the Prophet ﷺ, "If they just look down to their feet, they will see us." The Prophet ﷺ said, "O Abū Bakr, what do you think about two men whose third is Allah?"[388] There are numerous famous stories surrounding this event which lack authenticity, such as spiders making webs, trees leaning forward, and pigeons setting up nests to block the Quraysh from seeing them. The authentic reports simply state that the Prophet ﷺ reassured Abū Bakr ؓ, and Allah ﷻ protected them.

After three days and three nights in Cave Thawr, they met with an expert guide, ʿAbdullāh ibn Urayqiṭ, to decipher the best hidden route to Medina without leaving themselves exposed in the open. A bounty of 100 camels was offered to find the Prophet ﷺ—dead or alive. A man named Surāqah ibn Mālik, the leader of a Juʿshum tribe outside Mecca, heard someone talking about three men riding in a particular direction. Surāqah became greedy and wanted the full bounty for himself, so he said, "No, that is So-and-so who said they are going on an expedition." Afterwards, Surāqah slipped away, took his warhorse, and galloped away in that direction. Eventually, he saw them from a distance, describing one rider as very agitated, alternating between the front and the back, constantly looking around, and a second rider completely serene, reciting something, not once turning left or right. The first rider was Abū Bakr, worried about the Prophet ﷺ, and the second rider was the Prophet ﷺ, reciting the Qur'an, steadfast on his mission.

As soon as he saw them, his horse sunk into the ground, and flipped him over—something that had never happened before. He then pulled out his *azlām*, an ancient, Pagan version of tarot cards used to predict the future. He threw them onto the sand, and they instructed him not to proceed. In his greed, he ignored the message and proceeded, and his horse flipped him over once more. It then occurred a third time, and Surāqah narrated, "I knew that this was a force beyond me." He then called out to the Prophet ﷺ clarifying that he wanted to approach in peace. Surāqah narrated that he knew that the Prophet's Message would spread successfully, and so he asked the Prophet ﷺ for written protection that he could use when the Muslims come to power. Almost instantaneously, Surāqah went from hunting the Prophet ﷺ to requesting his protection. Afterwards, Surāqah informed the Quraysh of what happened, to which Abū Jahl wrote a scathing poem, criticising him in the harshest terms. Surāqah replied, "If you had been there that day, and you saw what I saw, you would not say what you are saying."[389]

When Surāqah turned to leave, the Prophet ﷺ said, "O Surāqah, how will you be on the day that you put on the bracelets of Kisrā?" Taken aback, Surāqah replied, "Kisrā, the son of Hurmuz?" There was only one infamous Kisrā, but Surāqah could not fathom the idea. The Prophet ﷺ turned away without responding, leaving Surāqah to ponder. Many years later, after the Battle of Ḥunayn, Surāqah approached the Prophet ﷺ with the piece of cloth promising his protection, asking for safe passage and permission to accept Islam. Years after that, following the Battle of Qādisiyyah, the Islamic caliphate under the rule of ʿUmar ibn al-Khaṭṭāb conquered the Persian Empire. ʿUmar called for Surāqah, placed him on Kisrā's throne, and placed Kisrā's bracelets on his wrists, thus fulfilling the prophecy. The Companions broke into a euphoric chant of "*Allāhu Akbar*! (Allah is the Greatest!)" and Surāqah was paraded around the city of Medina wearing Kisrā's jewellery.[390]

The Commandment of Hijrah

Allah commanded the remaining believers to make Hijrah. This was primarily addressing the new converts to Islam in Mecca as well as any secret Muslims who were yet to disclose their conversion publicly. Over the course of a number of verses, gradually increasing in encouragement and warning, Allah's counsel became a stern legal order. The first of these verses was in Sūrah al-Ḥajj, "As for those who emigrate in the cause of Allah and then are martyred or die, Allah will indeed grant them a good provision. Surely Allah is the Best Provider."[391] This is contrasted to the verses of Sūrah al-Nisā' revealed two to three years later, "When the Angels seize the souls of those who have wronged themselves, scolding them, 'What is wrong with you?' They will reply, 'We were oppressed in the land.' The Angels will respond, 'Was Allah's Earth not vast enough for you to emigrate?' It is they who will have Hell as their home—what an evil destination!"[392]

It is the Sunnah of Allah to implement laws gradually for the believers to digest and reflect. For example, the prohibition of consuming alcohol was implemented over a number of years. First, Allah revealed, "They ask you about intoxicants and gambling. Say, 'There is great evil in both, as well as some benefit for people, but the evil outweighs the benefit.'"[393] Then, He revealed, "O believers! Do not approach prayer while intoxicated until you are aware of what you say..."[394] Finally, the prohibition was absolute after the verse, "O believers! Intoxicants, gambling, idols, and drawing lots for decisions are all evil of Shayṭān's handiwork, so shun them so you may be successful."[395] This example perfectly encapsulates Islam's approach to reform, giving people time to digest as well as instilling long-term change.

The stern verses of Sūrah al-Nisā' regarding the Hijrah were revealed after some Muslims died on the battlefield in the Battle of Badr on the side of the Quraysh. There were Muslims who did not yet feel ready to disclose their faith, and they continued to live amongst the Quraysh. When the Battle of Badr ensued, they were forced to participate on behalf of the Quraysh, and while they did not actively fight or kill any Muslims, some of them died from arrows or in the commotion of war. Allah ﷻ then revealed the abovementioned verses detailing their conversations with the Angels—years after being initially instructed to partake in the Hijrah. Ibn ʿAbbās ؓ explains that they were told by Allah that they have no excuse not to emigrate, and that they were sent this verse.[396] Some Muslims then tried to emigrate, and the Quraysh dissuaded them. Allah ﷻ then revealed verses of Sūrah al-ʿAnkabūt, "There are some who say, 'We believe in Allah', but when they are irritated in the cause of Allah, they equate persecution at the hands of people to the punishment of Allah. But when victory comes from your Lord, they surely say, 'We have always been with you.' Does Allah not know best what is in the hearts of all beings?"[397] Allah ﷻ uses the verb *"ūdhiya"* which can be translated as "irritated" or "hurt", denoting the minuscule nature of their test in comparison to the cause.

Jundaʿ ibn Ḍamrah ؓ was a Muslim in Mecca when this verse was revealed. However, he was blind and decrepit; he was so old that he could not physically walk. Nevertheless, when he heard this verse, he said, "I am not of those who have an excuse. I will not spend another night in Mecca." He then ordered his servants to lift him up from his bed and carry him outside the city. He had no feasible plan of getting to Medina, so he put his trust in Allah, and Allah ﷻ bestowed His Mercy and caused him to pass away in Tanʿīm, just outside Mecca. As he was dying, he put his right hand onto his left hand and said, "O Allah, this is my pledge of allegiance to the Prophet ﷺ."[398] When the Muslims in Medina heard, they bemoaned his case, citing that he "almost" made it. Allah ﷻ then revealed the next two verses of Sūrah al-Nisā', "...except helpless men, women, and children who cannot afford a way out. It is right to hope that Allah will pardon them. For Allah is Ever-Pardoning, All-Forgiving."[399]

After the Battle of Khandaq in 5 AH, the rules surrounding Hijrah became more relaxed. After the Conquest of Mecca in 8 AH, the ruling was abrogated. The Prophet ﷺ said, "There is no Hijrah after the Conquest [of Mecca]." [400] The Prophet ﷺ was referring to "Hijrah" with a capital "H", referring to the divinely ordained Emigration from Mecca to Medina. The Prophet ﷺ did not forbid emigrating for the sake of Allah thereafter, but the special status, as well as the legal obligation of the Emigration ceased. After Mecca was liberated, the official phase of Emigration was over, as Mecca was finally under Islamic rule. Fudayk ﵁, a new Muslim in a Pagan land, once approached the Prophet ﷺ, "O Messenger of Allah, the people are saying, 'Whoever does not do hijrah will be destroyed.' And my people are upon *shirk*." The Prophet ﷺ replied, "O Fudayk, establish the prayer, avoid evil deeds, and live with your people wherever you like." [401]

وإنك لعلى خلق عظيم

Truly, you (Muhammad ﷺ)
are of a magnificent
standard of character.
al-Qalam, 4

PART

IV

The Medinan Era

The Blessings of Medina

Medina's original name was Yathrib, but the Prophet ﷺ renamed the city Medina (Madīnah), discouraging use of the name Yathrib. The official name then became "Madīnah Rasūl Allah (City of the Messenger of Allah)". It is also referred to as al-Madīnah al-Munawwarah (The Enlightened City). The Prophet ﷺ also called it "Ṭābah" and "Ṭaybah", both meaning "pure". The word *"yathrib"* means "to criticise", and the Prophet ﷺ disallowed names with bad meanings; he said, "Whoever says 'Yathrib' should seek forgiveness from Allah, for it is Ṭābah (Pure), for it is Ṭābah, for it is Ṭābah."[402]

The Prophet ﷺ would always make *duʿā'* for Medina. He ﷺ said about Mount Uḥud in Medina, "This is a mountain that we love, and it loves us."[403] And, "Uḥud is a mountain in Paradise."[404] The Prophet ﷺ also spoke of the protection of Medina, "The Dajjāl (Antichrist) will not be able to enter Medina. On that day it will have seven gates, each one guarded by two Angels."[405] And, "Neither the Dajjāl nor plagues[i] will ever infest it."[406] He ﷺ said, "No-one shall plot to harm Medina except that Allah will dissolve him like salt is dissolved in water."[407] The Prophet ﷺ made *duʿā'* that Medina be blessed, "O Allah, give us blessings in this City of ours." And, "O Allah, your servant and friend, Ibrāhīm, declared Mecca sacred. I too am your servant and Messenger, and I declare Medina sacred."[408]

Medina is a safe haven for the believer, as he ﷺ said, "*Īmān* returns to Medina just as a desert animal returns to its hole in the desert."[409] And, "No-one leaves Medina not wanting to live there except that Allah ﷻ will replace them with someone better."[410] The Prophet ﷺ will even offer intercession on the Day of Judgement for those who die

i This book is being written amidst the COVID-19 coronavirus pandemic. However, a distinction is to be made between the type of plague referred to in the Hadith, and pandemics such as COVID-19. The word used in the Hadith is "*ṭāʿūn*", which can be translated as "pestilence", a fatal epidemic plague. This is distinct to more general infectious diseases which would be translated as "*wabā'*". A *ṭāʿūn* is more deadly and severe than *wabā'*.

in Medina, "Whoever amongst you is able to die in Medina, do so, because I will intercede on behalf of anyone who dies there."[411]

When the Companions first moved to Medina, they had a very difficult time acclimating to their new surroundings; the climate was different to Mecca, the terrains were new, but most importantly, they were simply feeling homesick. Many of the Companions were both emotionally and physically sick in the first few weeks of life in Medina, so the Prophet ﷺ made a very special *duʿā'*, "O Allah, cause us to love Medina as much as we love Mecca or even more."[412] Ever since that *duʿā'*, Medina held a special place in the heart of the believers, and this remains true to this day.

Establishing a Muslim Nation 13

The First Mosque in Islam

The City of Medina was comprised of a collection of subtribes, each of which occupied their own area, usually separated by areas of desert or date palm plantations. The Prophet ﷺ arrived in the settlement of Qubā' and waited for ʿAlī ؓ as well as Abū Bakr's two daughters, ʿĀ'ishah and Asmā' ؓ. ʿAlī remained in Mecca for a short while to attend to the Prophet's remaining affairs, such as returning valuable items to their owners. Without a centralised banking system, the Quraysh had a custom of entrusting valuable items to one another, especially when embarking on travel. Despite their tensions with the Prophet ﷺ, most people left their belongings with the Prophet ﷺ, as he was known as the most trustworthy, hence his title "al-Amīn (The Trustworthy)". Once again, this is a testament to his standing amongst his peers, and even his enemies.

There were makeshift mosques in Medina, as the Muslims had been praying openly in peace unlike the persecuted Muslims in Mecca. However, the first purpose-built mosque was built by the Prophet ﷺ in Qubā' when he first arrived. The Prophet ﷺ laid down the first stone, followed by Abū Bakr ﵁, and then the Anṣār ﵃. The Prophet ﷺ then set off for Medina to reunite with the Muslims. He continued to pray in Masjid Qubā' every week; 'Alī ibn Abī Ṭālib ﵁ narrates that he ﷺ would either walk or ride his camel every single week, usually on Mondays, and that he ﷺ said, "Whoever does ablution in his house and prays in Masjid Qubā' will receive the reward of a full 'Umrah."[413] Allah ﷻ even revealed a verse in the Qur'an in praise of Masjid Qubā', "Certainly, a mosque founded on righteousness from the first day is more worthy of your prayers. In it are men who love to be purified. And Allah loves those who purify themselves."[414]

The Prophet's First Friday Sermon ﷺ

The Prophet ﷺ continued towards Medina. As he was mid-journey, it was time for the Friday Prayer, so he stopped at the tribe of the Banū Salamah. The Prophet's first Friday Sermon, therefore, was neither in Masjid Qubā' nor the yet-to-be-built Prophet's Mosque. The Companions were already praying the Friday Prayer in Medina, as it was commanded by the Prophet ﷺ for Muslims living in freedom, and so the Friday Prayer is a rare instance whereby the Companions implemented an act of worship before the Prophet ﷺ.

The Prophet ﷺ stood up and gave a very brief sermon. In fact, every one of the Prophet's recorded sermons were three to five minutes long, and the prayers were much longer. He ﷺ said, "It is a sign of understanding that a person shortens the sermon and lengthens the prayer."[415] This is contrary to modern customs of giving long sermons and brief prayers. The Prophet ﷺ then gave the following sermon,

> "All praise is for Allah. I praise Him, ask for His Assistance, seek His Forgiveness, and request His Guidance. I believe in Him and I do not deny Him, and I oppose those who disbelieve in Him. I bear witness that there is no deity worthy of worship except Allah, alone and without partners, and that Muhammad is His slave and Messenger sent with guidance, light, and sincere

advice, at a point when no Messengers had arrived for some time, knowledge had decreased, people were misguided, time stood still, the Hour (i.e., the Day of Judgement) had drawn close, and the [appointed] term was imminent.

Whoever obeys Allah and His Messenger is on the right path, and whoever disobeys them has been negligent, gone astray, and is greatly misguided. I advise you to be conscious of Allah, for the best advice one Muslim can give another is to prepare for their Hereafter and to be conscious of Allah. So, take heed of that which Allah has warned you about Himself. That is the best advice and the best reminder. Whoever embodies consciousness (*taqwā*) out of fear and trepidation, and sincerely seeks assistance, will attain whatever they desire in the Hereafter. Whoever rectifies his relationship with Allah in private and public, purely for the sake of His Face (i.e., seeking His Pleasure), will be remembered and honoured in this life and [his good deeds] will be stored for after his death, when a person will be in need of what they sent forward and will find nothing else. Then, he 'will wish that [his] misdeeds were far off. And Allah warns you about Himself. And Allah is Ever Gracious to [His] servants.'[416] Allah is the One Who spoke the truth and fulfilled His Promise. It is a Promise that can never be abandoned, for Allah Exalted says, 'My Word cannot be changed, nor am I unjust to [My] creation.'[417]

Be conscious of Allah in your affairs of this world and of the Hereafter, in private and in public, for 'whoever is mindful of Allah, He will absolve them of their sins and reward them immensely'[418], and whoever is mindful of Allah 'has truly achieved a great triumph'[419]. Consciousness of Allah repels His anger, punishment, and wrath. Consciousness of Allah brightens one's face, pleases one's Lord, and raises one's rank. So, take your blessings, and do not neglect your relationship with Allah. Allah has taught you His Book and explained His Way, so that He can 'clearly distinguish between those who are truthful and those who are liars'[420]. So, be good, just as Allah was good to you, oppose His enemies, and 'strive for [the cause of] Allah in the way He deserves, for [it is] He [Who] has chosen you...[and] named you "the ones who submit"'[421], so that 'those who were to perish and those who were to survive might do so after the truth had been made clear to both.'[422] There is no strength except with Allah, so increase in your remembrance of Him, and work for what comes after death. Whoever rectifies his relationship with Allah will be sufficed in his relationship with the people, because Allah judges over [the affairs of] the people, but the people do not judge Allah; and Allah owns the possessions of the people, but the people do not own the possessions of Allah. Allah is greater, and there is no strength except with Allah, the Most High, the Almighty."[423]

Another source states that he ﷺ also said:

"To proceed: O people, send forward [good deeds] for yourselves, and know with certainty, by Allah, that one of you will be struck unconscious and will leave his sheep without a shepherd. Then his Lord will say to him, without any intermediary or barrier, 'Did my Messenger not come and convey [My Message] to you? Did I not give you wealth and bless you? So, what have you sent forward for yourself?' The person will look to his right and his left, but he will not see anything. Then he will look forwards, but he will only see the Hellfire. So, whoever is able to protect his face from the Fire, even with half a date, then let him do so. And whoever cannot find even that, then let him say a good word, for the reward of a good action is multiplied by at least ten times, and up to seven hundred times."[424]

The Prophet ﷺ then stood up for the second time and said the Khuṭbah al-Ḥājjah:

> "All praise is for Allah. I praise Him and ask for His assistance. We seek refuge with Allah from the wrong-doing of our souls and the evil of our actions. Whoever Allah guides, no-one can misguide, and whoever Allah misguides, no-one can guide, and I bear witness that there is no deity worthy of worship except Allah."[425]

He ﷺ then continued:

> "The best of speech is the Book of Allah. If Allah beautifies His Book in a person's heart, then he has succeeded. [On account of the Book] he enters Islam after disbelief, and chooses it above all other speech. Certainly, it is the best speech and the most eloquent. Love those whom Allah loves, and love Allah with all your hearts. Do not tire of the Speech of Allah or His Remembrance, and do not allow your hearts to harden. From everything Allah creates, He chooses and prefers [something], then names it the best of His works, the best of His servants, and the best of speech. From everything halal and haram He has given humankind, you should worship Allah, not associate anything with Him, and be conscious of Him in the way He deserves. Be sincere to Allah with the righteous words that leave your tongue, and love one another with the Spirit of Allah between you. Allah hates that you break His Covenant. May peace be upon you, and the Mercy and Blessings of Allah."[426]

The Prophet's speech was profoundly concise and impactful. As mentioned earlier, the Khuṭbah al-Ḥājjah alone led to the likes of Ḍimād al-Azdī to convert to Islam. The Prophet ﷺ urged the Companions to donate; if there were ever a time where funds were most vital, it was the start of the Islamic civilisation. He ﷺ reminded them of the reality of life and certainty of death. He gave them hope of Paradise while reminding them of the consequences of their actions and the punishment of Allah ﷻ. The Prophet's sermons were perfectly balanced between spirituality and practical application. He ﷺ rallied the Companions to purify their hearts and love Allah ﷻ with the entirety of their heart. He ﷺ instructed them to never tire of two acts of worship: reading the Qur'an, and *dhikr* (remembrance) of Allah, lest their hearts harden. He then concluded by instructing the Companions to love one another for the sake of Allah ﷻ and then swiftly reminded them that they have a promise to Allah to fulfil.

Building The Prophet's Mosque (al-Masjid al-Nabawī)

The Prophet ﷺ continued to Medina, and the Anṣār heard of his imminent arrival and rushed to greet him. The children of Medina were running in the streets, yelling, "The Messenger of Allah has arrived!"[427] Even the young women ascended to the top of their houses, asking, "Which one of them is he? Which one of them is he?"[428] The arrival of the Prophet ﷺ in Medina signified a new era in Islamic history—that of strength, growth, and excitement.

The Prophet's arrival was an event that engulfed the entirety of Medina. In anticipation, the Anṣār would head to the outskirts of the city every morning and wait until the midday heat was too strong to remain outside. When the Prophet ﷺ did arrive, a Jewish worker plucking dates from the top of a tree was the first to notice, and in his excitement, he yelled, "O Arabs, your King has arrived!" The fact that even the Jews of Medina were excited was a testament to the atmosphere at the time. However, it is also noteworthy that he said "your King" and not "our King", indicating that the Jews were under the impression that the Prophet ﷺ would only be ruling the Aws and Khazraj. This misunderstanding would resurface, which will be addressed as it occurs in the *sīrah*.

'Abdullāh ibn Salām ☙, one of the most senior Rabbis in Medina who converted to Islam, narrated the first Hadith reported in Medina, "When the Prophet ﷺ entered Medina, the people rushed to see him, and I was of the first to arrive. As soon as I saw his face clearly, I knew that this was not the face of a liar. The first thing I heard him say was, 'Spread peace, feed the people, be good to your relatives, and pray at night when the people are sleeping—you will enter Paradise with peace.'" [429] This Hadith was famously known as the "Hadith of *Salām* (Peace) by 'Abdullāh ibn Salām".

When the Prophet ﷺ entered the city, the Anṣār would all plead with him to stay in their home, pulling his camel in every direction. The Prophet ﷺ let go of his camel and said, "Let the camel be, as Allah has taken care of it (i.e., Allah will decide)." [430] The camel stopped in a particular place, and the Prophet ﷺ understood that this is where his mosque would be built. The Prophet's concern and priority was to build a mosque before he had even thought about his own house. The Prophet ﷺ then said, "Whose house from our family members is closest?" He had distant cousins in Medina (from the Banū Najjār tribe), another indication that Medina was planned by Allah ﷻ to be his safe haven, as ties of familiarity were already built. Khālid ibn Zayd—known famously as Abū Ayyūb al-Anṣārī ☙ rose up and proclaimed his lineage to the Banū Najjār and ecstatically claimed his right to host the Prophet ﷺ.

The Prophet ﷺ lived with Abū Ayyūb ☙ for six months while the mosque was being built. Allah ﷻ blessed Abū Ayyūb with a two-story house, which allowed him to accommodate the Prophet ﷺ. Abū Ayyūb and his wife occupied the top floor while the Prophet ﷺ and Abū Bakr ☙ occupied the ground floor. One night, Abū Ayyūb knocked over some water, and they began to panic that a single drop of water may fall onto the Prophet ﷺ, so they stayed up the whole night soaking their blankets to dry the water. [431] On another occasion, Abū Ayyūb said, "It suddenly occurred to me that we were walking above the head of the Prophet ﷺ." Abū Ayyūb and his wife ☙ then spent the remainder of the night cramped in the corner of the room to ensure that they did not walk or stand over the Prophet ﷺ. The next morning, they requested that the Prophet ﷺ move to the top floor. The Prophet ﷺ said that the ground floor was easier, as he would frequently receive guests and conduct meetings. Abū Ayyūb did not relent, insisting, "Never, O Messenger of Allah, can we be above a roof that is above you."[432] It was also the habit of Abū Ayyūb and his wife to cook food, send it to the Prophet ﷺ to eat, and finish the leftovers. Whenever the plate was returned, Abū Ayyūb asked, "From which place did the Prophet ﷺ eat?" He would then ensure that he ate from the exact same place.

Before the Prophet ﷺ began building on the plot of land where the camel stopped, he asked, "Who does this land belong to?" It belonged to two orphans, Sahl and Suhayl, who had inherited the land from their late father but did not yet put it to use. They said, "O Messenger of Allah, this is a gift from us." But the Prophet ﷺ, in a manner befitting a Messenger of God, refused to accept it as a gift and instead purchased it.[433] The Companions began building the mosque, and the Prophet ﷺ ordered that the old tree stumps in the ground be repurposed as the front and back walls of the mosque. The remaining two sides of the mosque were built with clay bricks, and the roof was made of date palm leaves. The roof only covered half the mosque, and this remained the case for a few years.

Eventually, the Prophet ﷺ ordered that a full roof be built, however even that roof was only purposed to protect the worshippers from the heat of the Sun; it was not sufficient a cover to protect from the rain or cold. In the eighth year of Hijrah, for example, Abū Saʿīd al-Khudrī ﵁ narrated that the entire mosque was flooded due to rainwater, and the ground became extremely muddy. The Companions wondered how they would prostrate in the heavy mud until Abū Saʿīd al-Khudrī said, "For by Allah I saw the Prophet ﷺ prostrate into the mud, and the mud was on his forehead and nose."[434] The Prophet's Mosque remained in this state for the entirety of his life ﷺ as well as the reign of Abū Bakr al-Ṣiddīq ﵁. ʿUmar's Caliphate saw some reinforcements to the mosque, but the first major expansion was under the rule of ʿUthmān ﵁ many years later.

The Companions formed a line to carry out the work, and the Prophet ﷺ was a part of the line. The Companions then recited a line of poetry, "For us to sit as the Prophet works, how misguided our actions would be!" They continued to recite lines of poetry while they worked, and the Prophet ﷺ joined them, "O Allah, there is no good except the good of the Hereafter, so have mercy on the Anṣār and the Muhājirah." [435] It took two weeks to build the mosque, and it was a very large mosque for its time, spanning 100 by 130 feet. It had three main public entrances: The Door of Mercy on the southside, The Door of Jibrīl on the westside, and The Door of Women on the eastside. There were also a number of private entrances for those whose houses connected directly to the mosque. On his deathbed, the Prophet ﷺ said, "Every single [private] door to the mosque shall be locked and sealed except the door of Abū Bakr." [436] Scholars interpret this statement as one of the Prophet's implicit instructions that Abū Bakr ؓ succeed him in leadership, for all doors (i.e., paths) are to close except that of Abū Bakr.

Formalising the Prayer

The five daily prayers were established as an obligation during al-Isrā' wa al-Miʿrāj; however, each prayer comprised of two units (rakʿāt). ʿĀ'ishah ؓ narrated, "When we came to Medina, the prayers were put as you know them (i.e., two units for Fajr, four for Ẓuhr, four for ʿAṣr, three for Maghrib, and four for ʿIshā'), and the two units were kept for the traveller (except Maghrib, which is always three units)." [437]

The Prophet ﷺ also gathered the Companions to decide how to call the people to prayer. Medina was now an open Islamic nation, so the prayer—being the most integral part of Islam—was to be incorporated into everyday life on a public level. The Companions began to discuss, and one said, "Let's use a bell like the Christians" but this was rejected. The Prophet ﷺ did not like bells, and he said, "The Angels do not accompany any caravan with a bell." [438] Another Companion said, "Let's use a shofar [i]" but that was also rejected. The meeting ended without a decision being made. That night, ʿAbdullāh ibn Zayd ؓ had a dream where he encountered a man selling items such as horns and

---

i   An ancient horn, typically made from a Ram's horn, used for Jewish religious purposes.

bells. He tried to buy the items for the Prophet ﷺ but the man said, "Should I not tell you something better? When you call for the prayer, say, 'God is the Greatest, God is the Greatest; I bear witness that there is no god but Allah, I bear witness that there is no god but Allah; I bear witness that Muhammad is the Messenger of Allah, I bear witness that Muhammad is the Messenger of Allah; come to the prayer, come to the prayer; come to success, come to success; God is the Greatest, God is the Greatest; there is no god but Allah.'"

ʿAbdullāh ibn Zayd ؓ woke up and rushed out to the Prophet ﷺ to inform him of the dream. The Prophet ﷺ then said, "Stand up, O Bilāl! You have the loudest voice." The Prophet ﷺ then instructed ʿAbdullāh ibn Zayd ؓ to go with him to the roof and inform him of each phrase for Bilāl to give the *adhān*. As Bilāl ؓ was giving the *adhān*, ʿUmar ibn al-Khaṭṭāb ؓ rushed out from his house and said, "O Messenger of Allah, I heard the same phrases in my dream!" [439] The *adhān* thus became the only act of Islam legislated via the dream of a Companion. However, it is more accurate to state that the legislation was the Prophet's approval, not the Companion's dream itself. There are no narrations regarding the Companion ʿAbdullāh ibn Zayd ؓ except this famous narration of the *adhān*. Suffice to say that he must have had a blessed relationship with Allah and His Messenger to have been bestowed with such a blessing.

A Brotherly Bond

The Prophet ﷺ instated a pact called "*mu'ākhāh*" which bound each Anṣārī to a Muhājir to further instil ties of brotherhood. The Anṣār were already very hospitable and welcoming to their Meccan brothers. The Qur'an states, "As for those who had settled in the City and [embraced] the faith before the arrival of the Emigrants, they love whoever emigrates to them, never having a desire in their hearts for whatever is given to the Emigrants. They give them preference over themselves even though they may be in need. And whoever is saved from the selfishness of their own souls, it is they who are truly successful." [440] It is even reported that when the Muhājirūn arrived in Medina, the Anṣār said to the Prophet ﷺ, "O Messenger of Allah, we shall give half our lands to the Muhājirūn."[441] The Prophet ﷺ made *duʿā'* for them but kindly refused such a generous offer; instead, he ﷺ suggested that the Muhājirūn work for their share of the land.

Despite their generosity, the Prophet ﷺ wanted to impress upon them ties of brotherhood that only the likes of Islam could inspire. A paired Anṣārī and Muhājir were considered brothers by law even in rights of inheritance. The most famous story of *mu'ākhāh* is the bond between the Muhājir ʿAbdurraḥmān ibn ʿAwf and the Anṣārī Saʿd ibn al-Rabīʿ ﷺ. Saʿd, a successful businessman, brought ʿAbdurraḥmān to his house and said, "I am the richest of the Anṣār, and I will give you half of all of my money; I have a two-story house, and one of them is yours; I have two gardens, and one of them is yours; and I have two wives, and one of them is yours." ʿAbdurraḥmān humbly responded, "May Allah bless your wealth and family—just direct me to the marketplace." ʿAbdurraḥmān ibn ʿAwf then bought and sold items day by day until one day the Prophet ﷺ saw him dressed up and perfumed. The Prophet ﷺ asked what the occasion was, and he replied that he just got married and that he paid the dowry with a small amount of gold.[442] The Anṣārī's magnanimity was only matched by the Muhājir's honour and dignity; one genuinely offered out of *īmān* and brotherhood, and the other genuinely declined out of *īmān* and brotherhood.

The Anṣār helped the Muhājirūn so much that the Muhājirūn grew worried and actually complained to the Prophet ﷺ, "O Messenger of Allah, we have never seen a people like this; they share equally with us in times of difficulty, and are generous with us in times of need. They have taken care of our needs and have allowed us to share in times of good, so much so that we are worried that they will take our reward [in the Hereafter]." The Prophet ﷺ replied, "They will not take your reward as long as you praise them and make *duʿā'* for them."[443]

After the Battle of Badr and almost two years of *mu'ākhāh*, Allah ﷻ revealed verses of Sūrah al-Anfāl abrogating the inheritance privileges of the bonded brothers, "And those who later believed, migrated, and struggled alongside you, they are also with you. But only blood relatives are now entitled to inherit from one another, as ordained by Allah. Surely Allah has [full] knowledge of everything."[444] However, the *mu'ākhāh* continued for many more years, even after the Conquest of Mecca. Those who accepted Islam after the Conquest were paired with Anṣār, and the practice did not stop. It can therefore be said that this is a forgotten Sunnah that should be practiced in all times and places, including our own.

The Treaty of Medina

The Prophet ﷺ wrote a constitution for the inhabitants of Medina, which comprised all tribal and religious groups, including the Emigrants, Helpers, Jews, and Pagans. It is recorded in full in the earliest books of *sīrah*, such as Ibn Isḥāq, but without a direct chain of narration.[445] Books of Hadith mention the treaty with a full chain, such as Musnad Imam Aḥmad, which states, "The Prophet ﷺ wrote a book between the Muhājirūn and the Anṣār."[446] However, they only make reference to the treaty or quote one or two clauses therein. The chain of narration for the full treaty stops at Ibn Isḥāq. This has led some to claim that the treaty did not exist. However, the intricate details of the treaty, such as naming every single subtribe, and the archaic language of the treaty, which did not fit with the language of Ibn Isḥāq's era, are strong indications of its authenticity.

The treaty was over five pages long and comprised of four main segments:

1. Matters pertaining to the Muslims.
2. Matters pertaining to the Jews.
3. Matters pertaining to the Pagans.
4. General rules for every inhabitant of Medina.

In the first segment, the treaty stated, "The believers (*mu'minūn*) from the Quraysh and Yathrib[ii] and those who joined them are one

---

ii The usage of "Yathrib" instead of "Medina" is one such indication of the treaty's authenticity, as the Prophet ﷺ later outlawed its usage, but at the time, the city was known primarily as Yathrib.

nation (Ummah). This Ummah is unique to itself to the exclusion of the rest of mankind."[447] The treaty then mentioned 40 subtribes by name and stated that each tribe will carry the responsibilities of its members; they will oversee their own blood-money disputes, prisoners of war, and the poor and needy. Another clause stated, "All Muslims shall unite against those who commit injustice even if it be one of their own."[448] The treaty also made clear that any Muslim, of any social standing, can bring another person into the fold i.e., they can provide protection (the closest equivalent of a modern-day visa).

As for the second segment, the treaty named each Jewish subtribe and stated, "All the Jewish tribes are one nation along with the believers."[449] The treaty clarified that the Jewish nation is responsible for all its internal affairs, such as internal disputes, blood-money, and the poor and needy, as aforementioned. However, if there are disputes between the two nations (i.e., the Jews and Muslims), it will be deferred to the judgement of the Prophet ﷺ. The Jews therefore enjoyed semi-independent statehood within the Islamic state. The treaty added, "Between the two nations shall be mutual support against those who fight the people of the treaty."[450] This included financially and physically supporting one another against any external threats. Moreover, if any Jew wishes to convert to Islam, he is to be supported and no-one shall harm them. Finally, the treaty stated that no Jew can revoke their Medinan citizenship without informing the Prophet ﷺ so that everyone is aware of who is bound by the treaty.

As for the third segment, the treaty stated, "No Pagan shall offer protection to the Quraysh, nor are they to come between the Quraysh and the believers."[451] The Pagans were not forced, or even asked, to convert; the very fact that there was a sizable Pagan population in Medina proves that they were not forcibly converted or coerced.

The fourth and final segment comprised general clauses concerning everyone. First, the treaty outlined the interior of Medina as a *ḥaram* for the subjects of the treaty. Like al-Masjid al-Ḥarām and the Kaʿbah in Mecca, *ḥaram* means that many acts which are ordinarily permissible (halal) are prohibited (haram) in the designated area.

In other words, it is a sacred site. Brandishing unsheathed weapons is forbidden in a *ḥaram*, as well as hunting and even uprooting trees and plucking plants. The treaty also demarcated the borders of Medina as: Mount Ayr, Mount Thawr, the eastern volcanic plain, and the western volcanic plain. The treaty reiterated that any interfaith conflict—i.e., between a Jew and a Pagan, a Pagan and a Muslim, or a Muslim and a Jew—will be resolved by Allah and His Messenger. The final clause stated that whoever leaves Medina is safe except those who commit a crime.

The standing of this treaty has been overstated by some and unduly dismissed by others. Some claim that the treaty was the basis for modern-day constitutions, directly inspiring current conventions around the globe. The treaty was indeed unprecedented for its time; it was the first time in the history of Arabia that relationships were defined based on theology, and that the notion of an Ummah was the backbone upon which society would be governed. That said, it would be an overstatement to claim that the treaty had impacted global governance. In contrast, some claim that the treaty was discriminatory to the Jews, ostracising them. On the contrary, the treaty dealt with the Jews with respect and fairness, identifying them as an Ummah alongside the Muslims. Most of their rules and regulations were equally applied to the Muslims themselves. It could even be said that the treaty signified a bastion of tolerance compared to the religious intolerance rampant throughout the world at the time.

The treaty established the basis and overall philosophy of how an Islamic state is governed. The unification of tribes under the umbrella of Islam was a major step away from tribalism. This was taught from the beginning of Revelation, but it was now codified in a constitution. The Prophet ﷺ did not eradicate tribal identity; the Qur'an states, "O humanity! Indeed, We created you from a male and a female, and we made you into peoples and tribes so that you may know one another."[452] The Prophet ﷺ therefore accepted the legal norms and customs—commonly referred to as *ʿurf*—of every tribe as long as they did not conflict with the laws of Islam. However, rank and status are only derived from piety and closeness to Allah. The same verse continues, "Surely the most noble of you in the sight of Allah is the most righteous among you. Allah is truly All-Knowing, All-Aware."[453] The word "Ummah" shares the same root as the word "*umm*" which means "mother". It is derived from the word "*amma*" which means "to strive for". The object of attention of a child is their "*umm*" i.e., mother. The Ummah is therefore a nation with one common goal—to please Allah. Indeed, ties based on religion—sharing values, ethics, and theology—are far stronger than those derived from sharing a tribe or nationality.

The Changing of the Qiblah

The direction of prayer (qiblah) thus far was Jerusalem, as was the case with previous Abrahamic religions. In Mecca, the Prophet ﷺ would always situate himself in a position where he was facing the Kaʿbah but with Jerusalem behind it. However, in Medina, facing Jerusalem would entail turning one's back towards Mecca and thus the Kaʿbah. The Prophet ﷺ grew increasingly uneasy with turning his back towards the Kaʿbah, so he started making *duʿā'* to Allah ﷻ to change the qiblah to Mecca. It is narrated that the Prophet ﷺ even expressed his hope to Jibrīl ﵇, to which Jibrīl replied, "I am merely a slave like you."[454] The most blessed human asked the most blessed Angel for assistance, yet their subservience was to Allah ﷻ alone.

The Prophet ﷺ then continued to make *duʿā'* earnestly throughout the day. The Sunnah of *duʿā'* is to lower one's head, but in times of extreme distress or desperation, the Prophet ﷺ would raise his hands high and face towards the Heavens. There were no witnesses, as the Prophet ﷺ did so in the dead of the night, but Allah ﷻ attested to it, revealing, "Indeed, We see you turning your face towards the Heaven."[455] Allah ﷻ then gifted the change of qiblah to the Prophet ﷺ, continuing the verse, "Now We will make you turn towards a direction [of prayer] that will please you. So turn your face towards the Sacred Mosque; wherever you are, turn your faces towards it. Those who were given the Scripture certainly know this to be the truth from their Lord. And Allah is never unaware of what they do."[456]

This commandment became a source of confusion for the people of Medina. Allah ﷻ states, "The foolish among the people will ask, 'Why did they turn away from the direction of prayer they used to face?' Say, 'The east and the west belong [only] to Allah. He guides whoever He wills to the Straight Path.'"[457] Some of the Jews would scoff, "Had he truly been a Prophet, he would have prayed towards the direction followed by the Prophets before him."[458] The ruling was a test to the believers to implement a command from Allah ﷻ. However, there was a secondary message to the Jews: this Prophet inherited the tradition of your Prophets (and thus faced the same qiblah) but he shall now supersede it. The qiblah could have been from Mecca from the start, but Allah ﷻ wanted to demonstrate to the Jews the commonality and shared root of the two religions. However, as time passed and they persisted in their arrogance and rejection, guidance was sent instructing the believers to distinguish themselves, and the change of qiblah epitomised this distinction. The Pagans also ridiculed the change in qiblah, but there was a secondary message to them: the Prophet ﷺ was expelled from Mecca, but he honours the Kaʿbah more than you, and he will inherit custodianship of the Kaʿbah.

The Jews insisted on their qiblah being the only avenue of righteousness, and Allah ﷻ clarified the true definition of righteousness, "Righteousness is not in turning your faces towards the east or west. Rather, the righteous are those who believe in Allah, the Last Day, the Angels, the Books, and the Prophets; who give charity out of their cherished wealth to relatives, orphans, the poor, [needy] travellers, beggars, and for freeing captives; who establish prayer, pay *zakāh*, and keep the pledges they make; and who are patient in times of suffering, adversity, and in battle. It is they who are mindful [of Allah]."[459] Allah ﷻ then reassured the Prophet ﷺ, "Even if you were to bring every proof to the People of the Book, they would not accept your direction of prayer, nor would you accept theirs; nor would any of them accept the direction of prayer of another. And if you were to follow their desires after the knowledge that has come to you, then you would certainly be one of the wrongdoers."[460]

There is a common misbelief that the Prophet ﷺ was praying in one direction when Allah ﷻ revealed the verses mid-prayer, and the Prophet ﷺ changed his direction while praying. The authentic reports are clear in that the Prophet ﷺ prayed Fajr facing Jerusalem, and Ẓuhr facing Mecca, which means the commandment was revealed in the morning. After praying Ẓuhr in the new direction, a Companion walked towards his local mosque which was in the tribe of Banū Salamah. When he arrived, the congregation was already praying ʿAṣr, so he announced the change of qiblah while they were praying, which caused them to change their direction mid-prayer. After this event, the mosque was then known as Masjid Qiblatayn (The Mosque of Two Directions).

Ahl al-Ṣuffah (The People of the Ṣuffah)

As the number of Emigrants continued to increase, there were not enough of the Anṣār to continue the *mu'ākhāh* system for everyone. The new arrivals would base in The Prophet's Mosque, and they became known as The People of the Ṣuffah. Their numbers would fluctuate between five and 70, and most of them would stay for a short period of time to learn the fundamentals of Islam and acclimate to life in Medina. However, the Ṣuffah soon became a hub of knowledge and faith, and some members would voluntarily remain to learn from, and interact with, the Prophet ﷺ. Most of them were bachelors, but some family men would opt to stay in the Ṣuffah over their own families in order to be closer to the Prophet ﷺ. The Prophet's Mosque was, in many ways, the first university in Islam.

Ahl al-Ṣuffah were highly respected, as they sacrificed everything for the sake of Allah. Many of them had nothing but the clothes on their backs. It was even narrated that the female Companions would complain to the Prophet ﷺ that the *ʿawrah* (private parts) of some of the young men would be exposed when they prostrated in prayer, as their clothes were not even long enough to cover their whole bodies.[461] Once, the beloved daughter of the Prophet ﷺ, Fāṭimah ﵂, complained of her household chores and asked for a servant to assist her. The Prophet ﷺ

replied emphatically, "How can I give you a servant when the stomachs of Ahl al-Ṣuffah are collapsed from hunger? No, by Allah, I will sell all of them (i.e., the servants) and spend the money on them."[462] Fāṭimah never asked the Prophet for a servant again.

Ahl al-Ṣuffah became the flag-bearers of knowledge and piety. They became memorisers and masters of the Qur'an to the extent that they were known as "The People of the Qur'an". In fact, Ahl al-Ṣuffah were the indirect cause of the compilation of the Qur'an into a single Book. The Qur'an was passed down from Allah to the Prophet via Jibrīl orally, and the Prophet in turn taught the Companions orally. The entirety of the Qur'an was written down on pieces of bone, leather, and parchments, but only as a tool of memorisation. However, many years later during the Caliphate of Abū Bakr al-Ṣiddīq, the Apostasy Wars against Musaylamah the Liar inflicted many casualties amongst the Muslims. The People of the Qur'an, practicing what they preached, were warriors that fought for the Religion of Allah. As a result, many graduates of the Ṣuffah were martyred. ʿUmar ibn al-Khaṭṭāb then pleaded with Abū Bakr to compile the Qur'an before more People of the Qur'an were lost, and Abū Bakr eventually obliged.

The most famous member of the Ṣuffah was Abū Hurayrah. His name was ʿAbd al-Raḥmān ibn Ṣakhr but was more commonly known as Abū Hurayrah (The Father of Kittens) as he would famously carry a small kitten in his sleeve. He came from a middle-class family yet sacrificed his luxuries to accompany the Prophet in the Ṣuffah. He suffered from extended bouts of hunger and fatigue for the sake of this closeness. Later, he would recall, "Many times I would ask Companions questions as they walked home, and by Allah I knew the answer better than them, but I would ask in the hope that the conversation would extend until they reached their house, and they would perhaps invite me in to eat."[463]

Abū Hurayrah was from Yemen and only came to Medina after the seventh year of Hijrah, yet he narrated the most Hadiths of all the Companions. He narrated 1,236 individual Hadiths comprising 5,374 iterations.[464]

The Successors would often ask how Abū Hurayrah knew so much despite accompanying the Prophet ﷺ for a much shorter time than other Companions. He replied, "The people complain that I narrate too many Hadith, but were it not for the fact that Allah ﷻ criticised[iii] those who withhold knowledge, I would not have narrated a single Hadith. As for the Muhājirūn, they were busy buying and selling in the souks of Medina; and as for the Anṣār, they were busy cultivating and harvesting in their fields. As for me, I would stick to the Prophet ﷺ with an empty stomach, and therefore I would memorise what they would not."[465]

Codifying Acts of Worship

As the Prophet ﷺ finally established a base in Medina, a holistic Muslim society began to form. Most major pillars of Islam—except for Hajj which required access to Mecca—were established within the first year of the new state. The basic rulings of prayer were perfected, and the Prophet ﷺ said, "Pray as you have seen me pray."[466] The rulings of purification, including *wuḍū'*[iv], *ghusl*[v], and *istinjā'*[vi], were all revealed. Fasting was gradually introduced; the first obligated fast was the 10th of Muḥarram, nine months after the Hijrah. The Prophet ﷺ decreed, "Whoever ate breakfast in the morning, let him fast for the rest of the day."[467] The following Ramadan was then obligatory to fast. Allah ﷻ revealed, "Ramadan is the month in which the Qur'an was revealed as a guide for humanity with clear proofs of guidance and the standard. So whoever is present this month, let them fast. But whoever is ill or on a journey, then [let them fast] an equal number of days [after Ramadan].

---

iii Abū Hurayrah ؓ was referring to the verse, "Those who hide the clear proofs and guidance that We have revealed—after We made it clear for humanity in the Book—will be condemned by Allah and those who condemn." (*al-Baqarah*, 159).

iv Ablution — which is the washing of one's hands, face, arms, and feet, as well as wiping the head — is an obligatory prerequisite for prayer. The Sunnah of *wuḍū'* is to also rinse the mouth and nose and wipe the ears.

v Ritual washing consisting of washing the entire body and rinsing the mouth and nose. It is required after sexual intercourse or ejaculation.

vi Cleaning one's private parts after urinating or defecating.

Allah intends ease for you, not hardship, so that you may complete the prescribed period and proclaim the greatness of Allah for guiding you, and perhaps you will be grateful."[468] Fasting the 10th of Muḥarram then became Sunnah (i.e., no longer obligatory). In Ramadan, *Zakāh al-Fiṭr*[vii] became obligatory. A few months later, *Zakāh al-Māl*[viii] also became obligatory.

The Prophet ﷺ also began implementing societal reforms, the first of which was to demarcate a new souk to establish financial independence. The Anṣār were historically engaged in agriculture while the marketplaces were run by the Jews. The Prophet ﷺ visited these souks and disapproved of many of the practices such as cheating, deception, and high levies. The Prophet ﷺ then said to the Muslims, "This is not a souk for you." He ﷺ then walked back to the mosque and created lines in the sand with his own blessed feet and said, "This shall be your souk. Let it not be diminished and let no-one tax the people in it."[469] The Prophet ﷺ encouraged a free and open[ix] market for the Muslims so their businesses may thrive.

The Prophet ﷺ linked trade and commerce to religiosity and spirituality rather than secularising the religion or limiting it to personal worship. He ﷺ described the righteous businessmen as blessed on the Day of Judgement, while those who cheat and lie will face their consequences. He ﷺ demanded a certain code of conduct: he forbade cheating and lying, swearing false oaths, and hiding defects. He even monitored the markets himself; it was narrated that he saw a bag of grain which was partly water-soaked and defective. The trader had attempted to conceal

---

vii "Alms-tax of Breaking the Fast", paid after Ramadan. It is one *ṣāʿ* (four double handfuls) of food, grain, or dried fruit for each member of the family. In 2022, it is calculated as roughly £5 GBP or $7 USD.

viii "Alms-tax of Wealth", which is 2.5% of one's wealth, paid once a year. It is obligatory upon every free, sane, Muslim who possesses the minimum amount of wealth required, referred to as the *niṣāb*. The *niṣāb* is the value of 87.48g of gold, or 612.36g of silver, depending on which scholarly opinion is followed.

ix These Hadiths have led some to claim that Islam promotes a capitalist financial system. This is categorically false, especially when compared to unrestricted capitalism. While Islam inevitably shares concepts with capitalism, socialism, and many other "isms", its financial structure transcends any particular economic system.

this defect by placing dry grain over the wet parts. He ﷺ then said, "Whoever cheats is not from me (i.e., my Ummah)."[470] He ﷺ banned the exploitative practice of trading with usury (*ribā*), as commanded by Allah ﷻ. The Prophet ﷺ even forbade Medinan residents from representing Bedouins in the souk, as it was common practice for locals to exploit uninformed Bedouins and travellers.

Tensions Reignite with the Quraysh

The Muslims struggled immeasurably in Mecca and were forced to remain patient. They were abused and oppressed with no respite. The Prophet ﷺ could have ordered someone to kill the likes of Umayyah ibn Khalaf for torturing Bilāl ؓ, but he ﷺ knew that the consequences would be severe and did not want to jeopardise the Ummah of Islam. The Prophet ﷺ always planned many steps ahead, providing vital lessons for Muslims to act with wisdom, long-term planning, and foresight. Some young zealous Companions were eager to fight, and Allah ﷻ revealed about them, "Have you not seen those who had been told, 'Do not fight! Rather, establish the prayer and give charity'? Then when the order came to fight, a group of them feared those [hostile] people as Allah should be feared, or even more. They said, 'Our Lord, why have You ordered us to fight? If only You had delayed [the order for] us a little while!' Say, 'The enjoyment of this world is so little, whereas the Hereafter is far better for those mindful [of Allah]. And none of you will be wronged [even by the width of] the thread of a date stone.'"[471] Allah ﷻ is demonstrating how oftentimes those who talk the loudest intend the least. In Mecca, the command was to remain patient and steadfast, but in Medina, Allah ﷻ allowed the believers to fight back.

The first verse of jihad in the Qur'an underpins the philosophy of jihad and why it was permitted. "Permission [to fight back] is granted to those being fought, for they have been wronged. And Allah is Most Capable of helping them [prevail]."[472] In Mecca, jihad was forbidden, and now it was permitted as a recourse for self-defence. Fighting was permissible for those who have been wronged or oppressed.

Abū Bakr ⁕ commented, "As soon as I heard Sūrah al-Ḥajj, I knew there would be war." [473]

There were four primary stages of jihad in the life of the Prophet ⁕:

1. Military jihad is forbidden, and jihad (to struggle) is limited to *jihād al-nafs* (struggling of the soul i.e., being patient and forbearing).
2. Jihad is permitted—but voluntary—as self-defence.
3. Jihad is obligatory but only against the Quraysh.
4. Jihad is mandated against all the tribes of Arabia.

After the passing of the Prophet ⁕, the Ummah alternated between the different stages. The Ummah continued to expand for around 150 years and then remained relatively settled in its borders for the next 1,000 years.

Military Expeditions

Following Sūrah al-Ḥajj, the Muslims embarked on a series of expeditions. The primary goal of these expeditions was to demonstrate to the Quraysh that the Muslims were not meek and defeated; they were an independent political and military force. The secondary reason was to strangle the Quraysh's imports and exports. Mecca's centrality to Arabia's trade routes made it an economic powerhouse, and compromising those routes was a major blow. A tertiary goal was to expand the Islamic state by forming alliances with nearby tribes.

There were two types of expeditions: *ghazwah* (pl. *ghazawāt*), which is any battle that the Prophet ⁕ attended; and *sariyyah* (pl. *sarāyā*), which is any battle that the Prophet ⁕ commanded but did not attend. Buraydah ⁕ narrates, "The Prophet ⁕ attended 19 *ghazawāt*, and physically fought in eight of them." [474] They were the battles of Badr, Uḥud, al-Muraysī', al-Aḥzāb (i.e., Khandaq), Qadīd, Khaybar, [Conquest of] Mecca, and Ḥunayn. [475] As for the *sarāyā*, there were many; Ibn

Isḥāq lists 30, al-Wāqidī counts 48, Ibn al-Jawzī notes 56, and so on. The discrepancies are due to differences in deciding what constitutes a *sariyyah*. By all accounts, there were at least 30.

The first military expedition was called al-Abwā', which took place on the 12th of Ṣafar in 2 AH, nine months after the Hijrah. The Prophet ﷺ heard that a caravan from the Quraysh was exposed, and the Muslims set off to raid it. They did not catch the caravan, but the Prophet ﷺ made alliances with the tribes surrounding Medina called the Banū Ḍamrah, and the Islamic state expanded for the first time. In the second expedition, they encountered the enemy but there were no casualties, as a third party quashed the conflict. Nonetheless, Saʿd ibn Abī Waqqāṣ ؓ made history by shooting the first arrow for the sake of Allah.

The next expedition was Ghazwah al-ʿUshayrah, which would prove to be a defining moment in Islamic history. The Prophet ﷺ took around 150 Companions to raid the Quraysh's annual caravan heading to Syria. It held over 70% of the wealth in Mecca, including over 70 camels and much more. The Prophet ﷺ had intended to intercept the caravan but they were not able to cross paths. However, a member of the Quraysh had accidentally strayed from the caravan and saw the Muslims approaching, which allowed him to warn Abū Sufyān, the leader of the caravan. The Prophet ﷺ did not know that the Quraysh knew of their approach, and Abū Sufyān used this to his advantage. He sent an envoy to Mecca to mobilise an army. In the meantime, one of the allies of the Quraysh ambushed Medina at night, stole some camels, and killed some camel herders. As soon as the Prophet ﷺ heard, he mobilised 70 Companions, but the men fled. This was referred to as the "First Battle of Badr", or the "Small Battle of Badr", as it took place on the plains of Badr, though no actual fighting took place.

After failing to intercept the Quraysh travelling northbound, the Prophet ﷺ sent eight Muhājirūn southbound to observe the Quraysh travelling to Yemen, nominating his cousin, ʿAbdullāh ibn Jaḥsh ؓ, as the leader. They were all Muhājirūn because the Prophet ﷺ was keen to remind them that Mecca was taken from them, and that their fight was not over. He wrote a letter and told them to travel for two days before opening the letter, which instructed them to abruptly change directions and enter Mecca. The Prophet's secrecy and caution in this regard is a clear indication of the importance of discretion and tactics in warfare. The letter also instructed ʿAbdullāh ibn Jaḥsh not to force any of his seven companions to accompany him into Mecca owing to the extremely high risk of the operation. Assuming certain death, ʿAbdullāh ibn Jaḥsh said, "Whoever of you is eager for martyrdom and wishes to meet Allah ﷻ soon, let him come with me; and whoever does not may return back to Medina."[476] They all accompanied him and continued onwards, and the expedition was called Sariyyah al-Nakhlah.

They had four camels between eight of them—yet another indication of the scarcity of resources in early Islam. One of their camels escaped in the night, so Saʿd ibn Abī Waqqāṣ and ʿUtbah ibn Ghazwān remained in the desert while the remaining six continued to Mecca. As they arrived in the desert grove of Nakhlah, on the outskirts of Mecca, they saw a small business caravan loaded with merchandise. They were faced with a dilemma: this raid would be extremely profitable for the Ummah, but the Prophet ﷺ sent them to gather information, not to fight. Moreover, it was the 30th of Rajab—a sacred month—which means there was one hour left before fighting was permissible. They debated amongst themselves, but the opportunity was so tantalising that they decided to pounce. They attacked, killed one guard, ʿAmr al-Ḥaḍramī, captured two more as prisoners of war, and returned to Medina.

The Prophet ﷺ was displeased with their actions. He reprimanded them and refused to accept any of the war booty, saying, "I did not send you to fight in the Sacred Month."[477] The Quraysh revelled in this mistake; they proliferated the news of this event and spread their criticisms of the Muslims throughout the whole of Arabia, accusing them of violating the sanctity of the sacred months and transgressing the religion of Ibrāhīm ﵇. The Prophet ﷺ felt great stress over these accusations, as they contained elements of truth. Allah ﷻ then revealed, "They ask you about fighting in the sacred months. Say, 'Fighting during these months is a great sin, but preventing [people] from the Path of Allah, rejecting Him, and expelling the worshippers from the Sacred

Mosque is a greater sin in the sight of Allah. And *fitnah* [x] is far worse than killing.'" [478] After this verse was revealed, the Prophet ﷺ accepted the war booty and requested ransoms for the prisoners of war. However, he stipulated that he will not release them until Sa'd ibn Abī Waqqāṣ and 'Utbah ibn Ghazwān ㊌ return safely. The two Companions were not actually captured; they were still in the desert and eventually returned safely. The Prophet ﷺ then released the hostages, and one of them, al-Ḥakam ibn Kaysān, accepted Islam and returned to the Prophet ﷺ on his own accord—but only after the ransom reached the Prophet.

x Ibn 'Abbās ㊌ comments that *fitnah*, linguistically translated as "trial", refers to *kufr*. However, other scholars have added that it may encompass the general persecution of the Muslims. (Fakhr al-Dīn al-Rāzī, *Tafsīr al-Fakhr al-Rāzī*, Dār al-Fikr, Beirut (1401/1981), vol. 5, p. 141).

PART IV • THE MEDINAN ERA

The Battle of Badr

14

A Game of Espionage

The Prophet ﷺ sent several scouts to observe the Quraysh's caravan returning southbound. Ṭalḥah ibn ʿUbaydillāh and Saʿīd ibn Zayd ؓ reported its magnitude, which constituted one of the biggest caravans in the history of Arabia. The reports do not state why the caravan was so spectacularly large, although the recent looting of all the Emigrants' wealth and possessions as they left Mecca is a strong indicator as to why their current trade was particularly vibrant. Intercepting this caravan would therefore be hugely significant, as it would bring the Meccan economy to a screeching halt while simultaneously empowering the Muslims, and the Prophet ﷺ was indeed cognisant of this fact.

After the caravan was located, the Prophet ﷺ made an urgent announcement in the mosque. According to a report in Ṣaḥīḥ Muslim, he ﷺ did not inform the Companions of the details. Instead, he said, "We have a mission to undertake, so whoever has his camel ready shall come with me."[479] Some of the Companions asked to go and retrieve their camels, and the Prophet ﷺ refused, stating that he must leave immediately. The report in Ibn Isḥāq states that he explicitly mentioned that they were heading to the Quraysh's caravan.[480] These reports can be reconciled by placing the first narration in Medina, and the second narration en route to the caravan. This explanation is logical because the Prophet ﷺ may have been wary of spies, as there were Pagans still present in Medina at the time.

As they set up camp, the Prophet ﷺ was finally able to assess his group and plan accordingly. He sent back two people too young to participate: al-Barā' ibn ʿĀzib and ʿAbdullāh ibn ʿUmar ؆, as they were both below the age of 15, which was the cut-off point for combat.[i] There remained 82 Muhājirūn, 61 Aws, and 170 Khazraj, totalling 313.[481] There seems to be divine significance to the number 313, as it is the same number of Messengers sent to Earth [482] and the same number of fighters accompanying Prophet Dāwūd ؈.[483]

The convoy was not prepared for war, as the sole aim was to raid a trade caravan using the element of surprise. The whole group had two riding horses, 100 camels, and minimal armour and weaponry. Each camel was shared by three people, and the Prophet ﷺ shared his camel with ʿAlī ibn Abī Ṭālib and Abū Lubābah ؆. They both insisted that the Prophet ﷺ take the camel for himself and that they walk, but the Prophet ﷺ provided the most eloquent of responses, "The two of you are not any younger or stronger than me, and nor am I any less in need of reward." [484] The Prophet ﷺ could have very easily accepted the offer; from a political standpoint, the leader is expected to receive a higher level of prestige, and from a religious standpoint, a Prophet is not equal to his followers. Nevertheless, he ﷺ displayed the unwavering humility for which he was known. He ﷺ was also setting a Prophetic example for his followers such that the likes of ʿUmar ibn al-Khaṭṭāb ؆ was mistaken for a servant when he was Caliph because he entered Jerusalem on foot while his servant was on horseback.

---

i   In Islam, the age of puberty is designated as the age of intelligence and responsibility. In modern times, 15 is considered very young, however Islam dictates that humans are accountable from the age of puberty. 15-year-olds were considered men and women at the time of the Prophet ﷺ as well as throughout most of human history.

The Prophet ﷺ embodied true leadership and mentorship continued by his successors.

After the close call of Ghazwah al-ʿUshayrah, Abū Sufyān heightened his defence, sending out counterspies to observe the Prophet's spies. One of his scouts spotted two men, and Abū Sufyan began to investigate. He even analysed the camel dung left behind and noticed Medinan date seeds, realising they were Muslim soldiers. Indeed, they were Ṭalḥah ibn ʿUbaydillāh and Saʿīd ibn Zayd ﷺ. As soon as he realised, he ordered the caravan to take an unknown route to avoid an ambush. He then sent his fastest rider, Ḍamḍam ibn ʿAmr al-Ghifārī, to race back to Mecca and call for reinforcements.

A Deadly Dream

While Ḍamḍam was racing back, the inhabitants of Mecca were already sensing tension. The Prophet's aunt, ʿĀtikah bint ʿAbd al-Muṭṭalib, had an explicit dream three days before Ḍamḍam's arrival. She called al-ʿAbbās ﷺ and informed him that she dreamt that a crier would come to Mecca, racing on his camel, shouting, "O traitors! Meet your death in three days!" The crier repeated the same sentence on top of the Kaʿbah, and again on top of Mount Abū Qubays (the highest point in Mecca). The crier then picked up a large boulder and toppled it over the mountain. As the rock reached the base, it splintered into several rocks, hitting every single house in Mecca.[485] The dream worried al-ʿAbbās so he urged her to keep it a secret. However, al-ʿAbbās contradicted his own advice, telling al-Walīd ibn ʿUtbah, who was sworn to secrecy but still told his father, ʿUtbah. Eventually, the entirety of Mecca was gossiping about this dystopian dream.

As al-ʿAbbās was performing *ṭawāf*, Abū Jahl ambushed him, asking sarcastically, "O children of ʿAbd al-Muṭṭalib, since when did you get a female prophetess?"[486] Abū Jahl then threatened that if the prediction does not come true, the Banū Hāshim would be publicly shamed as the liars of Mecca. Caught off-guard, al-ʿAbbās denied everything, but before he even returned to his house, the women of the Banū Hāshim began chastising him, accusing him of failing to defend his own womenfolk. Embarrassed, the next morning al-ʿAbbās headed out to rebuke Abū Jahl to restore his honour, however Abū Jahl turned away in shame and could not even bear to face him. It was the third day after the dream, and the crier had arrived: Ḍamḍam was seen racing into Mecca, screaming. He mutilated his horse for dramatic effect, cutting off its nose as a symbolic cry for help. Blood rushed down its face as Ḍamḍam yelled, "O Quraysh! Your caravan! Your property and wealth with Abū Sufyān are being attacked by Muhammad and his Companions! Help!"[487] He was calling them to their wealth, but as ʿĀtikah predicted, he was calling them to their death.

Ḍamḍam's dramatic plea rallied the Quraysh and they mobilised 1,300 men in a single day. Every single household in Mecca sent at least one fighter, if not more—again corroborating ʿĀtikah's dream. There was an eerie feeling amongst the Quraysh, and the worst of them feared death the most, as they knew how badly they had treated the Prophet ﷺ. Abū Lahab found a way out and did not attend, sending al-ʿĀṣ ibn al-Wā'il in his stead. Al-ʿĀṣ owed Abū Lahab a large sum of money and Abū Lahab offered to forgive the entire loan if he fought on his behalf. It is not explicitly stated why Abū Lahab did not attend, though it is perhaps a combination of cowardice and a conflicted feeling of fighting his own tribe. ʿUtbah ibn Rabīʿah also hesitated in attending for the same reasons, but his brother Shaybah reminded him that if they did not attend, they would be humiliated upon their return. Allah ﷻ decreed that they did not return, as they marched to their deaths.

As described throughout this book, ʿUqbah ibn Abī Muʿayṭ was the worst of them all, and he knew he would not be spared. One day in Mecca, ʿUqbah invited the Prophet ﷺ to eat with him mockingly, to which the Prophet ﷺ said, "I will not eat with you until you testify that there is no god but Allah, and that I am His Messenger." In his fury, ʿUqbah spat in the blessed face of the Prophet ﷺ, and the Prophet ﷺ calmly wiped the spit away and said, "O ʿUqbah, when we meet outside the valleys of Mecca, I will execute you."[488] Deep down, ʿUqbah knew this prediction would come true, hence his hesitation. However, a family member reassured him and offered his fastest camel so he could escape if the Quraysh lost. ʿUqbah then reluctantly agreed to join.

Of those who also desperately tried to avoid attending was Umayyah ibn Khalaf, the wretched abuser of Bilāl . He was obese in stature with no fighting skills whatsoever, so he paid a man to fight in his stead. However, he was of the most senior figures of the Quraysh, and his absence would cause a blow to their morale. Abū Jahl tried to rally him by massaging his ego, but it was not enough, so he went to ʿUqbah and hatched a plot to embarrass Umayyah. ʿUqbah, overcompensating for his own cowardice, approached Umayyah as he was sitting in the Ḥaram and gifted him an incense burner typically used by women, saying, "This is your gift, O Umayyah. Perfume yourself, as you are nothing but a woman."[489] This public humiliation was enough to rile Umayyah to publicly declare his attendance. Indeed, ʿUqbah and Abū Jahl led Umayyah to his death simply to save face.

Marching to War

Before heading to battle, the Quraysh gathered together around the Kaʿbah, held onto its cloth, and made *duʿāʾ*, "O Allah, help whichever of these two tribes is more noble in your eyes, send victory to whichever of these two groups is more honourable, and send your aid upon the better of the two tribes."[490] Allah indeed answered their prayers, and this *duʿāʾ* is referenced in the Qurʾan, "If you sought judgement, now it has come to you. And if you cease, it will be for your own good. But if you persist, We will persist. And your forces—no matter how numerous they might be—will not benefit you whatsoever. For Allah is certainly with the believers."[491]

1,300 men then marched out of Mecca—the largest number ever to march in unison—led by Abū Jahl. As Arabia was tribal, previous battles would typically comprise of dozens of fighters, and bigger wars between multiple tribes may consist of hundreds, but this was the first time in the history of Arabia that an army was marching in the thousands. They had over 100 horses, 600 suits of armour, and hundreds of camels. The Quraysh wanted to make a show of this power, bringing dozens of singing girls and beating drums. The Qur'an references their arrogance, "Do not be like those who left their homes arrogantly, only to be seen by people and to hinder others from Allah's Path. And Allah is fully aware of what they do."[492]

Meanwhile, Abū Sufyān, still in the desert, sent another emissary to Mecca notifying them that the caravan was safe and that they were no longer needed. By this time, the Quraysh were already en route, camped outside Mecca. The message reached them, and the likes of ʿUtbah ibn Rabīʿah argued that there was no longer any need to continue, but Abū Jahl was adamant, "No, we will go to Badr and stay there for three days. We will drink our wine, have women sing for us, and let the Arabs hear that we are a strong and mighty nation."[493] Despite this, some smaller tribes headed back, leaving 950–1,000 of the Quraysh to persist on.

On the Muslim side, the Companions left Medina expecting an easy raid of a relatively unmanned caravan. They did not prepare for—nor expect—a war. As they progressed, rumours began to spread that there was an army leaving Mecca ready for war. The Prophet ﷺ began to quiz the Companions, asking what they thought if the Quraysh were aware of their plan and ready to fight. Some of the Companions expressed their reservations, citing that they were not properly armed. The next day, the Prophet ﷺ asked again, and some Companions again expressed their concerns. The Qur'an cites these doubts, "Similarly, when your Lord brought you out of your home for a just cause, a group of believers were against it. They disputed with you about the truth after it had been made clear, as if they were being driven to death with their eyes wide open. [Remember, O believers,] when Allah promised to give you the upper hand over either target, you wished to capture the unmanned party. But it was Allah's Will to establish the truth by His Words and uproot the disbelievers; to firmly establish the truth and wipe out falsehood—even to the dismay of the wicked."[494] Allah ﷻ gently reprimanded the Companions but still called them believers. They were the best generation to exist but they were still human.

The Prophet ﷺ began scouting for further information alongside his closest confidant, Abū Bakr ؓ. This is the only recorded occasion where the Prophet ﷺ personally scouted, signifying the high stakes of the situation at hand. They eventually came across an elderly Bedouin, and Bedouins were known for carrying information in the desert. The Prophet ﷺ asked, "Do you have any information about the Quraysh, and about Muhammad and his army?" The Prophet ﷺ asked about both parties so as not to arouse suspicion. Replying in kind, the Bedouin said, "First, who are you?" The Prophet ﷺ replied carefully, "I promise to tell you *where* we are from as long as you give us your information." The Bedouin then disclosed: Muhammad left on such-and-such date, and if so, he will be camped at such-and-such place. As for the Quraysh, their army has left Mecca on such-and-such date, and if so, they will be camped at such-and-such location.

The Bedouin's information about the Prophet ﷺ was entirely correct, which indicates that his information about the Quraysh was equally as accurate. The rumours were therefore true: the Quraysh had sent their army in full, and war was on the horizon. The Bedouin then asked the Prophet ﷺ about himself, to which the Prophet ﷺ replied, "We are from water."[495] He ﷺ then immediately left, leaving the Bedouin in a state of bewilderment. The Prophet ﷺ utilised *tawriyah* to protect himself, as he was referring to the Qur'anic verse, "And We created from water every living thing."[496] While excessive or unnecessary *tawriyah* is discouraged in the Shariah, using equivocations in times of need is permissible to avoid lying, as utilised by the Prophet ﷺ and the Prophets prior ؑ.[ii]

The Prophet ﷺ returned to the Muslim camp and prayed to Allah ﷻ before addressing the Companions. Throughout the *sīrah* we note the Prophet's retreat to Allah ﷻ in times of need before resorting to reliance on His creation. As the Prophet ﷺ prayed, the Companions

ii An example of previous Prophets using *tawriyah* is the case of Prophet Ibrāhīm ؑ telling his father that he was "sick" (implying physical sickness) in order to avoid attending a polytheistic festival when in reality he was "sick and tired" of their polytheism. (*al-Ṣāffāt*, 89).

captured two Qurashī slaves. The Companions interrogated them, and they disclosed that they were from the army of the Quraysh, to which the Companions would beat them and say, "Do not lie! You are from Abū Sufyān's caravan!" The captives would relent and agree but only to stop the beating, and the cycle would repeat. The Prophet ﷺ eventually finished his prayer and said, "When they tell you the truth, you beat them; and when they lie, you let them go."[497] The Prophet ﷺ discouraged abuse in interrogation and ordered them to stop. He ﷺ then began to ask the captives, "How many of you are there?" The captives pleaded that they were mere slaves and did not hold such information, so the Prophet ﷺ asked how many camels were slaughtered per day. They said "nine or ten", to which the Prophet ﷺ declared, "They are 900–1,000." The Prophet ﷺ then asked who was amongst them and they began to list every nobleman of the Quraysh.

The Companions felt tense, as they realised the magnitude of the task before them; the presence of the Chieftains necessitates wealth, resources, armour, and more. The Prophet ﷺ, on the other hand, smiled; he ﷺ knew that Allah's promise remained true, "When Allah promised to give you the upper hand over either target, you wished to capture the unmanned party. But it was Allah's Will to establish the truth by His Words and uproot the disbelievers."[498] If the Chieftains of the Quraysh were all present, the victory will be even sweeter. He ﷺ then said to the Companions, "Mecca has presented to you the cream of the crop." When he saw the dejected look on some of their faces, he continued to rile up the troops, "By Allah, So-and-so will be killed over here (pointing), So-and-so will be killed over there, So-and-so will be killed over here, and So-and-so will be killed over there..." He named them one by one, pointing to different locations.[499]

He ﷺ then asked the Companions, "What do you think we should do?" The Prophet did not need to employ consultation (*shūrā*), but the benefit of doing so was twofold: first, his addressees would feel empowered and respected; and second, he was teaching his Ummah the art of leadership. Abū Bakr ﷺ immediately stood up, praised Allah ﷻ, sent blessings upon the Prophet ﷺ, and spoke words of encouragement and support. The Prophet ﷺ thanked him and repeated the same question, "What do you think we should do?" ʿUmar ؓ then stood up and, like Abū Bakr ؓ, uttered words of support.

The Prophet ﷺ thanked him and asked the same question again, and al-Miqdād ibn ʿAmr ؓ, another Muhājir, stood up. He perhaps thought that Abū Bakr and ʿUmar were not convincing enough, so replied emphatically, "O Messenger of Allah, do as Allah commanded you, and we are right behind you; O Messenger of Allah, we will not say to you as the Children of Israel said to Mūsā ؑ, 'So go—both you and your Lord—and fight; we are staying right here!' [500] Rather, we say, 'Go—both you and your Lord—and fight; we are right behind you!'; O Messenger of Allah, take us to all corners of the world, and we will follow you until we meet Allah's decree!" [501] The Prophet ﷺ thanked him and asked for the fourth time, "What do you think we should do?"

Silence ensued, then the great leader of the Anṣār, Saʿd ibn Muʿādh ؓ, stood up, saying, "Perhaps you are intending us, O Messenger of Allah?" At the Covenant of ʿAqabah, the Anṣār pledged to protect the Prophet ﷺ from all aggression, but the Battle of Badr did not constitute defensive jihad, so it was technically outside the fold of the pledge. The Prophet ﷺ did not want to force the Anṣār to continue, as they did not pledge to partake in this type of combat.

The Prophet ﷺ replied in the affirmative—that he was indeed referring to them—and Saʿd said, "O Messenger of Allah, we believed in you and trusted you; we testified that you have come with the Truth; we gave you our promises and oaths that we will listen and obey; so go forth and do as you see fit, for we are with you. I swear by the One Who sent you with the Truth, were you to take us to the ocean and charge, galloping into the sea, we would go right behind you. We are not scared to meet the enemy tomorrow, and we will show you our patience in battle. Perhaps Allah will show you, through us, that which will comfort you. So go forth upon the blessings of Allah—we are right behind you." [502] The Prophet's face was described as a shining moon, overjoyed with Saʿd's response.

Preparations for Battle

The Prophet ﷺ divided the troops into three primary flanks. ʿAlī ibn Abī Ṭālib ؓ was on the left, leading the Muhājirūn, and Saʿd ibn Muʿādh was on the right, leading the Anṣār. He ﷺ also designated a back-up group led by Qays ibn Abī Ṣaʿṣaʿah ؓ. This designation clearly shows that tribal and cultural differences are taken into consideration; the Muhājirūn were together, led by one of their noblest youths, ʿAlī ؓ, just as the Anṣār were led by their leader, Saʿd ؓ. Allah ﷻ states, "O humanity! We created you from a male and a female, and made you into peoples and tribes so that you may know one another."[503] Muṣʿab ibn ʿUmayr ؓ was the flag-bearer, which was a symbolic but revered position. He embodied the unity between the Muhājirūn and Anṣār; he was a Qurashī but converted most of the Anṣār with his own hands and was thus beloved by the Medinans. He was therefore in a perfect position to be a flagbearer, representing both groups.

The Prophet ﷺ and Companions ؓ arrived on the plains of Badr on the 16th of Ramadan, one day before the Quraysh. Before setting up camp, al-Ḥubāb ibn al-Mundhir ؓ, an experienced scout from amongst the Anṣār, asked the Prophet ﷺ, "O Messenger of Allah, is this location for camp ordained by Allah, such that we cannot move it forward or backwards, or is it from your own opinion based on tactics and strategies of war?" The Prophet ﷺ replied that it was his opinion based on strategy, and al-Ḥubāb then suggested that they camp beyond the mid-point of the plains rather than the corner so that the wells of Badr are behind them. This would cut off the Quraysh's access to water, and they would have to suffice with their own limited supply.

The Prophet ﷺ followed al-Ḥubāb's advice and said, "You have directed us to the better opinion."[504] Incidents like this demonstrate a distinction between the Prophet ﷺ acting in his capacity as a Prophet and his capacity as a man ﷺ. Al-Ḥubāb's advice was vindicated because when the Quraysh ran out of water, they began to suffer. Al-Aswad ibn ʿAbd al-Asad al-Makhzūmī volunteered to sneak into Muslim territory to collect some water, and al-ʿAbbās ﷺ spotted him, sliced his leg open, and killed him. He therefore became the first person to be killed in the Battle of Badr before formal battle even began.

The Quraysh were seen approaching the plains of Badr, and the stage was set for battle the following morning. The Prophet ﷺ spent the whole night awake making profuse *duʿā'* and prolonging his prostration. He said, "O Allah, if you destroy this group [of Muslims] You will not be worshipped on this Earth."[505] In other words, failure here will mark the end of Islam on Earth. The stakes were never higher, and the Prophet ﷺ relied on his *duʿā'*. Ibn Masʿūd ﷺ said, "I have never seen anyone pleading more than when I saw the Prophet ﷺ plead to Allah ﷻ on the night of Badr."[506] The Prophet ﷺ lifted his arms into the sky as he made *duʿā'*—an action reserved for the most desperate of prayers and requests. ʿAlī ibn Abī Ṭālib ﷺ said, "If you saw us on the night of Badr, you would have seen every single one of us asleep except for the Prophet ﷺ who was praying behind a tree until the morning."[507]

The very fact that all the Companions fell asleep was a miracle from Allah, as the night before any battle is notoriously tense and nerve-racking. Allah ﷻ states, "[Remember] when He caused drowsiness to overcome you, giving you serenity. And He sent down rain from the sky to purify you, free you from Shayṭān's whispers, strengthen your hearts, and make [your] steps firm."[508] Ibn Kathīr ﷺ reports that the Prophet eventually slept for a few moments.[509] In this brief respite, Allah ﷻ showed him a dream of the Quraysh being few in number. The Qur'an states, "[Remember, O Prophet,] when Allah showed them in your dream as few in number. Had He shown them to you as many, you [believers] would have faltered and disputed in that matter, but Allah spared you. Surely He knows best what is in the hearts."[510]

The Prophet ﷺ then lined up the Companions ready for battle. Historically, the Arabs would charge in batches with intermittent bouts of fighting as they attack and recuperate. The Prophet ﷺ employed an unprecedented tactic—now common in modern warfare—of battalions marching in rows. Allah ﷻ references this tactic, "Surely Allah loves those who fight in His cause in [solid] ranks as if they were one concrete structure."[511] Those with spears were at the front, bows and arrows were at the rear, and those with swords were the bulk in the middle. The Prophet ﷺ did not attend a military school, but Allah ﷻ blessed him with Prophetic intuition to arrange the army. He ﷺ walked between the rows, straightening them as he would straighten the rows in prayer.[iii]

The Prophet ﷺ poked Sawād ibn Ghaziyyah ؓ in the stomach, instructing him to step back in line. Sawād ؓ said, "O Messenger of Allah, you have poked me and caused me pain. Allah sent you with truth and justice, and I demand justice." The Prophet ﷺ immediately dropped his stick, raised his shirt, and said, "Here is your *qiṣāṣ* (equal retaliation)." Sawād then hugged and kissed the Prophet's stomach, to which the Prophet ﷺ said, "What [is this], O Sawād?" Sawād responded, "O Messenger of Allah, if I die, I wish that my last moment was my skin touching yours."[512]

The benefits from this beautiful event are innumerable. First, the audacity of a soldier to question the leader in such a manner could only have been borne out of an atmosphere and culture of trust and equality. Second, the Prophet ﷺ did not dismiss his claim, even though they are standing moments before the biggest fight of their lives and the potential extinction of their religion. Third, Sawād's love for the Prophet ﷺ was so great that he hatched a plot just to kiss him ﷺ. Indeed, the relationship between the Prophet ﷺ and the Companions was truly unique.

The Prophet ﷺ once again turned to his Lord, raising his hands towards the sky, saying, "O Allah, fulfil Your promise to me; O Allah, give me what You have promised; O Allah, if this group is destroyed, You will not be worshipped on Earth…" The Prophet ﷺ continued

iii The Prophet ﷺ would personally straighten the rows in prayer, moving the Companions' feet. (*Ṣaḥīḥ Muslim*, p. 205).

to ask Allah, and continued to raise his hands towards the sky, until his upper garment fell off. He continued, bare-chested, until Abū Bakr ﷺ wrapped the garment around the Prophet ﷺ, hugged him from behind, and said, "Enough, O Messenger of Allah, enough. Your Lord will give you as promised."[513] As soon as he ﷺ lowered his hands, Allah ﷻ sent down Revelation, "When you cried out to your Lord for help, He answered, 'I will reinforce you with a thousand Angels followed by many others.'"[514] Ibn Masʿūd ﷺ said, "He turned around, and his face was like the Moon." Elated, the Prophet ﷺ then said, "Rejoice, O Abū Bakr, for indeed the help of Allah ﷻ has come. This is Jibrīl—turbaned and horseback—riding through the valley." The Prophet ﷺ then began chanting the verse, "Soon their united front will be defeated and forced to flee."[515] ʿUmar later said, "I never truly understood this verse until the Prophet ﷺ recited it on the morning of Badr."[516]

The Prophet ﷺ also made *duʿā'* against the Quraysh. He said, "O Allah, this is the Quraysh; they have come against you with their pride and arrogance, challenging you and rejecting your Messenger. O Allah, [I seek] Your help that has been promised; O Allah, [I seek] Your help that has been promised; O Allah, [I seek] Your help that has been promised. O Allah, cause them to be destroyed today."[517] He then instructed the Companions that certain people should not be killed, such as the youth of the Banū Hāshim, who were forced to attend, the Prophet's uncle, al-ʿAbbās ibn ʿAbd al-Muṭṭalib ﷺ, and Abū al-Bukhtarī, who was integral in lifting the boycott in Mecca.

The Quraysh, still unaware of the size of the Muslim army, sent their most experienced scout, ʿUmayr ibn Wahb al-Jumaḥī, to gather information. He reported, "They are around 300, but I feel that there is an impending catastrophe. Young men of Yathrib are waiting to inflict death; they are a determined people with no help other than their swords (i.e., they have no armour or extra resources and will thus fight valiantly). By Allah, I do not think that you will be able to kill any of them without them killing an equal amount. And if 300 amongst you die, what pleasure will you gain?"[518] Abū Jahl responded with his typical arrogance, "We did not ask for your advice."

Ḥakīm ibn Ḥizām[iv] approached ʿUtbah ibn Rabīʿah, neither of them wanting a war, to try and mediate a truce. Ḥakīm suggested that ʿUtbah volunteer the blood money for ʿAmr al-Ḥaḍramī, the man killed in Sariyyah al-Nakhlah, which was the trigger that led to the current turn of events. ʿUtbah agreed and offered to pay this small fortune to de-escalate the situation. He also preached to the people, "Do not fight, and if anyone accuses you of cowardice, then put the blame on me. Say 'ʿUtbah became cowardly', even though you know that I am not a coward. By Allah, what will you gain by fighting this man? If you are able to defeat him, you will be killing your own father, brother, cousin, and nephew. How would it feel to be amongst the murderers of your own family? Let us return and leave Muhammad and his companions to the rest of the Arabs. If they take care of him, this is what you wanted; and if not, then surely his victory will be ours too (i.e., as a Qurashī). And if he conquers Mecca, then you will have an excuse to be forgiven (by not fighting)."[519] As the Sun was rising, and the two armies were in each other's sight, the Prophet ﷺ saw a man pacing back and forth from afar. He ﷺ said to the Companions, "If there is any good amongst them, it is in the man on the red camel (i.e., ʿUtbah); and if they have any good in them, they will listen to him."[520] The Prophet ﷺ did not know what ʿUtbah was saying, but Allah ﷻ inspired him to know that what he was saying was goodness.

However, when Abū Jahl heard about this, he rushed to the blood-brother of al-Ḥaḍramī and goaded him, "Are you not ashamed of accepting some blood money for your brother while you are able to exact revenge from the killer?"[521] His brother then gave a passionate speech and convinced the troops to remain. Abū Jahl then accused ʿUtbah, "O ʿUtbah, you have become a coward after seeing the ranks of the Muslims!" ʿUtbah—who a moment ago was willing to be labelled a coward to keep the peace—could not tolerate such an accusation directly from Abū Jahl. He lost control, insulted Abū Jahl, and said, "We will see who the coward is!" He then called his brother and son and marched straight towards the Muslim army, volunteering the three of them for the initiation duel.

---

iv Not to be confused with his son, Ḥizām ibn Ḥakīm ibn Ḥizām (رضي الله عنه), who was a Muslim, sharing the same first name as his grandfather.

The initiation duel (*mubārazah*) was a custom in Arabia to commence a war. Three individuals of status from each army would meet at centre stage and fight one-on-one. The idea was to rile up the armies to seek vengeance on behalf of those killed, or build on the momentum of the victors. ʿUtbah and Shaybah ibn Rabīʿah alongside al-Walīd ibn ʿUtbah were the three nominees for the Quraysh. They marched forward, yelling, "Who will come forth and battle us?!" Three of the Anṣār immediately rose: ʿAwf ibn ʿAfrāʾ, Muʿawwidh ibn ʿAfrāʾ, and ʿAbdullāh ibn Rawāḥah. ʿUtbah then said, "We have no issue with you." The Quraysh, thinking through a tribal lens, did not even comprehend the ties of *īmān*. They did not have any desire to fight the Anṣār; they were there solely to fight the Muhājirūn. He then called out, "O Muhammad! Send out equals worthy of us to fight!"

The Prophet ﷺ said, "Stand up, O ʿUbaydah ibn al-Ḥārith; and you, O Ḥamzah; and you, O ʿAlī." ʿUtbah asked them to identify themselves (as they were speaking from afar), and when they did, he said, "Noble adversaries. Come, let us fight!"[522] ʿUbaydah walked towards ʿUtbah, as they were of a similar age; Ḥamzah walked towards Shaybah for the same reason; and ʿAlī walked towards al-Walīd. Both Ḥamzah and ʿAlī instantaneously pounced on their adversaries and killed them without suffering a single injury. ʿUbaydah's leg was cut off by ʿUtbah, but Ḥamzah and ʿAlī came to his support and killed ʿUtbah. ʿUbaydah was carried away to safety but died a few days later from his injuries.

The Battle Begins

Narrating the exact details of a battle with hundreds of people can only be done by compiling individual narrations. The narrations are from surviving Companions as well as those who fought on the side of the Quraysh but later accepted Islam. The difficulty arises when attempting to ascribe a chronological order to each narration. This challenge occurs throughout the *sīrah*, and the researcher is tasked with creating a chronological account from the available resources.

As the Quraysh began charging towards the Muslims, the Prophet ﷺ said to the Companions, "Stand up and charge towards a Paradise whose width is like the Heavens and the Earth."[523] ʿUmayr ibn al-Ḥumām ؓ scoffed, and when the Prophet ﷺ asked him why he scoffed, he said, "If this is true (regarding the width of one level of Paradise equating the entirety of the Heavens and Earth), then what use is it to remain living on this Earth? I want to be of those people!" The Prophet ﷺ replied, "You are of them." ʿUmayr then threw away the dates in his hand and said, "If I live long enough to finish these dates, I would have lived too long of a life!"[524] He charged towards the enemy and met his martyrdom.

As a military commander, the Prophet ﷺ did not usually fight in battles, as he had the responsibility of directing the army, but he fought in Badr. He ﷺ alternated between commanding the army, making *duʿā'*, and physically fighting. ʿAlī ؓ said, "The Prophet ﷺ was the closest to the enemy, fighting most aggressively, and when fighting grew fierce, we would seek protection through him."[525] ʿAlī ؓ also narrated that when he came into the Prophet's tent, he found him ﷺ making profuse *duʿā'* in prostration, "O Ever-Living, O All-Sustaining! O Ever-Living, O All-Sustaining!"[526] ʿAlī ؓ then went out to fight and later returned, finding the Prophet ﷺ in prostration. He again left and later returned and found the Prophet ﷺ still in prostration, and then Allah ﷻ decreed victory for the Muslims. The fact that ʿAlī ؓ narrated both these Hadiths is the strongest indication that the Prophet ﷺ alternated between fighting and making *duʿā'*.

Allah ﷻ sent down 1,000 Angels to reinforce the Muslims. As cited, "When you cried out to your Lord for help, He answered, 'I will reinforce you with a thousand Angels, followed by many others.'"[527] The phrase "reinforce you" is used to translate "*mumiddukum*" because there is a distinction between "help" and "reinforcement". To reinforce is to help an existing effort; the Muslims would raise their swords, while the Angels would lower the enemy's swords—a subtle yet important distinction, and a lesson in *tawakkul* and reliance on Allah. The reinforcement only applies when the initial effort exists.

Allah ﷻ chose specific Angels to attend Badr. Jibrīl ﷺ asked the Prophet ﷺ, "What do you think of those of you (i.e., humans) who participated in Badr?" The Prophet ﷺ said, "We think they are the best of us." Jibrīl ﷺ replied, "We too think the same of those of us (i.e., Angels) who attended Badr."[528] In reality, Allah ﷻ did not need to send 1,000 Angels when one single Angel would have sufficed considering their supernatural existence. When Allah ﷻ destroyed the people of Prophet Lūṭ ﷺ, Archangel Jibrīl ﷺ descended in his true form and slammed the ground with the tip of one of his 600 wings, destroying the entire city.[529]

The sending of 1,000 Angels was a show of force to assure the Muslims of the divine support they had as well as a message that said divine support only appears after the initial effort is made. Allah ﷻ said to Maryam ﷺ, "And shake the trunk of this palm tree towards you; it will drop fresh, ripe dates upon you."[530] The expectation was not that an exhausted, desperate, heavily pregnant lady can shake the firm trunk of a palm tree; rather, the action was necessary—even if symbolic—for Allah ﷻ to cause the fruit to drop. The Angels arrived at Badr in full force but only after the Companions' unsheathed swords were ready to strike.

Ibn ʿAbbās ؓ narrates that a Companion was in pursuit of a Pagan when he heard the sound of a whip and a call, "Go forth, Ḥayzūm!" The Companion then found the Pagan killed before he was even able to strike. The Prophet ﷺ said, "That was an Angel that Allah sent down from the third Heaven."[531] Similarly, when al-ʿAbbās ؓ—a physically imposing warrior—was captured by a shorter, skinnier Anṣārī, he called out defiantly to the Prophet ﷺ, "This man did not capture me!" The Anṣārī insisted, "No, I captured him!" Al-ʿAbbās began looking around searching for the one who captured him, saying, "The man who captured me was the most handsome man on a beautiful, black and white horse, but I cannot find him." The Anṣārī continued to insist until the Prophet ﷺ said, "Be quiet, for Allah helped you with a noble Angel."[532]

ʿAbdurraḥmān ibn ʿAwf ؓ narrated that he was hoping to fight alongside strong soldiers for extra support in battle. He looked to the right and left and was disappointed to see two small-framed adolescents:

Mu'ādh ibn 'Amr ibn al-Jamūḥ and Mu'awwidh ibn al-'Afrā' 🙵. The youth to the right poked him, leaned over, and whispered, "O uncle, do you know Abū Jahl?" 'Abdurraḥmān ibn 'Awf replied that he of course did, and the youth replied, "I heard that he disrespected the Prophet 🙵, and I have made an oath to Allah 🙵 that if I were to see him, we would not part until one of us is dead." [533] The youth to the left then poked him and asked the same question, for they were teenage friends in competition to kill Abū Jahl to avenge the Prophet 🙵. 'Abdurraḥmān ibn 'Awf 🙵 then felt comforted by their valiance and spirit.

When Abū Jahl was in sight, surrounded by his entourage, 'Abdurraḥmān ibn 'Awf 🙵 said to the boys, "There is your man (i.e., your target)." As soon as he spoke, they both darted into the sea of fighting with one target in mind. They navigated through the throngs of people until they were in proximity, and Mu'ādh leaped into the air, sword first, swinging downwards ferociously. The magnitude of the downward force sliced Abū Jahl's leg off completely, but Abū Jahl's son, 'Ikrimah, also swung, chopping off Mu'ādh's entire arm. His arm dangled from his body by a thin piece of skin, and Mu'ādh later remarked that it became burdensome and so he placed the arm under his foot and ripped it off to continue fighting. As 'Ikrimah was turned towards Mu'ādh, Mu'awwidh struck another blow to Abū Jahl.

The two teenage warriors managed to escape the melee and return to the Prophet 🙵 shouting, "O Messenger of Allah, I killed Abū Jahl!" They began arguing with each other, both claiming the fatal blow, until the Prophet 🙵 said, "You both killed Abū Jahl [together]." [534] After the battle ended, the Prophet 🙵 ordered the Companions to find Abū Jahl's body. 'Abdullāh ibn Mas'ūd 🙵, one of Abū Jahl's main victims of torture and humiliation in Mecca, found him on the ground, breathing heavily, resisting the pangs of death. Ibn Mas'ūd 🙵 placed his foot on his chest and said, "Do you finally admit that Allah has disgraced you, O enemy of Allah?" Abū Jahl remained obstinate until his last moment alive, scoffing, "How have I been disgraced? [I am] a person killed by his own people." Likely suffering delirium from blood-loss, he then asked, "Who has won the battle?" And Ibn Mas'ūd 🙵 replied, "Allah and His Messenger!" Referring to Ibn Mas'ūd's foot on his chest, he then said, "You have stepped on a high place, O son of a shepherd." It was to be his last sentence, as Ibn Masʿūd ☙ took Abū Jahl's own sword and sealed his demise.[535] He then returned to the Prophet ﷺ and said that he found the corpse of Abū Jahl. The Prophet ﷺ responded, "You swear by Allah?" And Ibn Masʿūd did so three times. The Prophet ﷺ then uttered the famous Hadith, "He was the Pharoah of this Ummah."[536]

Umayyah ibn Khalaf was another enemy of Allah who met a humiliating demise. As mentioned, Umayyah desperately tried to avoid fighting at every opportunity. His desperate pleas continued until the very end; when he saw that the Quraysh had fled, he tried to bargain for his life. He saw ʿAbdurraḥmān ibn ʿAwf ☙, who was a close friend and business colleague pre-Islam, holding some armour as war booty. He desperately held onto him, pleading, "O ʿAbd al-Ilāh![v] What if I were to give you much more than this? I offer you many milking camels! Take me as a prisoner, and I will give you whatever you want."[537] ʿAbdurraḥmān, a shrewd businessman even on the battlefield, took Umayyah up on his offer. He threw the armour and held Umayyah with one hand and Umayyah's son with the other. However, Allah decreed that justice be served, and Umayyah experienced the timeless truth of "you reap what you sow", for none other than Bilāl ibn Rabāḥ ☙ walked past.

Bilāl saw ʿAbdurraḥmān holding Umayyah's hand and exclaimed, "Umayyah ibn Khalaf, the leader of *kufr*? Over my dead body!" ʿAbdurraḥmān tried to calm Bilāl down and de-escalate, but Bilāl only grew more infuriated with each attempt, repeating, "Umayyah ibn Khalaf, the leader of *kufr*? Over my dead body!" He then called over a group of the Anṣār and said, "This is the man who tortured me!" Bilāl's story was famous, and he represented the epitome of perseverance and unwavering patience in the face of unmitigated evil. Stories of the cries of "One; One!" motivated the Muhājirūn and Anṣār alike to

---

v   ʿAbdurraḥmān's name was originally ʿAbd ʿAmr, and when he converted, he changed it to ʿAbdurraḥmān (Slave of the Most Merciful). Umayyah refused to call him ʿAbdurraḥmān, as the Pagans did not believe in the concept of al-Raḥmān (The Most Merciful). Instead, he offered to call him ʿAbd al-Ilāh (Slave of God), and ʿAbdurraḥmān agreed, as its meaning was still Islamically sound.

keep fighting on. When Bilāl ﷺ identified Umayyah to them, the group of Anṣār surrounded ʿAbdurraḥmān and began poking their swords past him to stab Umayyah and his son. ʿAbdurraḥmān continued to hold them back, trying to negotiate, until his foot was wounded in the commotion, and Umayyah and his son were both killed. When they tried to bury him, they could not lift him, as his flesh was stuck to the rocks and pebbles on the ground. One cannot but help compare his fate to the burning rocks he would place on Bilāl ﷺ in Mecca. ʿAbdurraḥmān recalled in his old age, "May Allah have mercy on Bilāl, not only did he stop me from my ransom, I lost the armour too!"[538]

A tragic incident at Badr was the case of Abū ʿUbaydah ibn al-Jarrāḥ. His father, al-Jarrāḥ, was a staunch Pagan who had a distinct hate for Islam to the extent that he hated his own son for embracing Islam. His hate was so severe that in the Battle of Badr he specifically sought out Abū ʿUbaydah to fight and kill. Abū ʿUbaydah, on the other hand, tried his utmost to avoid his father throughout the day. Eventually, his father cornered him and pounced. Abū ʿUbaydah, in self-defence, held out his sword and killed him. Murmurs spread of Abū ʿUbaydah killing his own father, and deep sadness and shame overcame him. Allah ﷻ then revealed, "You will never find a people who [truly] believe in Allah and the Last Day loyal to those who defy Allah and His Messenger, even if they were their parents, children, siblings, or extended family. For those [believers], Allah has instilled faith in their hearts and strengthened them with a spirit of Him. He will admit them into Gardens under which rivers flow to stay there forever. Allah is pleased with them, and they are pleased with Him. They are the party of Allah. Indeed, Allah's party is bound to succeed."[539]

A Decisive Victory

When victory for the Muslims became clear, the Quraysh fled back to Mecca. 70 of them were killed and 70 were captured, meaning 15% of the Quraysh were either killed or taken as prisoners of war. The Muslims suffered 14 deaths (less than 5%) with no captives. The Prophet ﷺ then informed the Muslims that they would camp at the plains of Badr for a further three days to find and gather the Muslim dead and ensure a proper burial. The *fiqh* (jurisprudence) of martyrs, as well as the dead in general, was revealed at this time. For example, martyrs are not prayed over, shrouded, or even washed[vi]; and the dead are buried as soon as possible and in the location of death, contrary to the common practice of transporting the deceased to their homeland. Maintaining appropriate decorum, the dead of the Quraysh were also placed in an abandoned well and covered from the Sun.

The Prophet ﷺ used this time to allow the Companions to recover and recuperate, but more importantly, to ensure that they were ready for a potential counter-offensive. Above all, the Prophet ﷺ wanted to demonstrate, beyond all reasonable doubt, that the Muslims were emphatically victorious. As they departed on the third day, the Prophet ﷺ diverted the caravan towards the well wherein the Quraysh were buried. He ﷺ stopped and began calling every single leader by name, "O Abū Jahl ibn Hishām! O Umayyah ibn Khalaf! O ʿUtbah ibn Rabīʿah! O Walīd ibn ʿUtbah! (and so on)…have you found the promise of your Lord to be true? As for me, I found the promise of my Lord to be true!" ʿUmar ibn al-Khaṭṭāb ؓ asked, "O Messenger of Allah, how can you speak to corpses with no soul?" The Prophet ﷺ replied, "I swear by the One in Whose Hand is my soul, you cannot hear me more distinctly than them, but they cannot respond."[540] Qatādah, the student of Ibn ʿAbbās ؓ, commented, "Allah ﷻ brought them back to life so that they may hear and be insulted and humiliated as a source of further regret and blame."[541]

Spoils of War

The believing nations of the past, such as The Children of Israel, were forbidden war booty, and so the Muslims did not have religious

vi This is because, as the Prophet ﷺ stated, "There is no wound that the martyr incurs on the path of Allah except that on the Day of Judgement its blood will be flowing; it will have the colour of blood (i.e., red) but the smell of musk." (Bukhārī, *Ṣaḥīḥ al-Bukhārī*, p. 68).

precedent in dealing with their spoils. The Companions began to discuss; in the course of battle, they split up into groups, and each group laid claim to the spoils. One group argued that they collected the war booty and brought it back, another argued that they were the ones to pursue the Quraysh and ensure they did not return, and a third group argued that they were protecting the Prophet ﷺ while the other two groups were busy pursuing or collecting. Allah ﷻ then revealed, "They ask you regarding the spoils of war. Say, 'Their distribution is decided by Allah and His Messenger.' So be mindful of Allah, settle your affairs, and obey Allah and His Messenger if you are believers." [542]

Allah ﷻ then revealed that one-fifth of the spoils are reserved, which is then split into five further categories, "Know that whatever spoils you take, one-fifth is for Allah and the Messenger, his close relatives, orphans, the poor, and [needy] travellers, if you truly believe in Allah and what We revealed to Our servant on that decisive day when two armies met [at Badr]. And Allah is Most Capable of everything." [543] In other words, 4% of the spoils are allocated to each of the five aforementioned categories. The remaining 80% is distributed between the fighters. In the Battle of Badr, every soldier was given an equal share. Later, at the Battle of Khaybar onwards, the Prophet ﷺ gave the cavalry three times more than the infantry.[vii]

Nine people received a full share of spoils despite not attending. 'Uthmān ibn 'Affān ؓ was one of them; he did not attend because Ruqayyah ؓ, his wife and the daughter of the Prophet ﷺ, was severely ill. The Prophet ﷺ instructed him to stay behind and attend to her needs. Allah ﷻ decreed that she would pass away the day of the Prophet's return from Badr.

---

vii These rulings predate the notion of paid armies. None of the fighters were paid a fixed wage and instead received a portion of the spoils of war as well as the armour of the people they killed. They would also use their own personal horses, which is why the cavalry receive triple that of the infantry, as they are responsible for the maintenance costs of the horse as well as the risks incurred.

Prisoners of War

The Prophet ﷺ said, "If Muṭʿim ibn ʿAdiyy were alive, and he uttered a word requesting the release of these filth, I would have freed them all for him."[544] Muṭʿim died a non-Muslim, but the Prophet ﷺ felt indebted to him for his help and compassion in Mecca, particularly for his help in ending the boycott of Banū Hāshim and giving the Prophet ﷺ protection when his own tribe disowned him ﷺ. Their ransoms were to be a fortune—equivalent to millions of dollars or pounds in the 21st century—but the Prophet ﷺ would have released them for free to honour Muṭʿim.

The Muslims were responsible for prisoners of war for the first time. The Prophet ﷺ consulted the Companions and asked for their opinion. He ﷺ particularly asked his two closest confidants: Abū Bakr and ʿUmar ﷺ, referring to them as "The Prophet's Two Ministers".[545] Abū Bakr ﷺ said, "O Messenger of Allah, they are our relatives; they are our blood; they are our kith and kin. Show mercy to them for the sake of brotherhood." ʿUmar ﷺ said, "As for me, O Messenger of Allah, I think you should give ʿAqīl (from the Banū Hāshim) to ʿAlī to execute; give me someone from the Banū al-Khaṭṭāb to execute, and so on. We will not leave any of them."[546] The Prophet's advisors represented both ends of the spectrum, with mercy on one side and retribution on the other.

The Prophet ﷺ said, "Indeed, Allah ﷻ makes some hearts so soft that they are softer than milk, and he makes others so hard that they are harder than stone. As for you, O Abū Bakr, you have the resemblance of [Prophets] Ibrāhīm and ʿĪsā. Ibrāhīm said to Allah ﷻ, 'My Lord! They (i.e., his people) have caused many people to go astray. So whoever follows me is with me, and whoever disobeys me, then surely You are All-Forgiving, Most Merciful.'[547] And ʿĪsā said, 'If You punish them, they belong to You after all. But if You forgive them, You are surely the Almighty, All-Wise.'[548] And you, O ʿUmar, are like [Prophets] Nūḥ and Mūsā. Nūḥ said, 'My Lord! Do not leave a single disbeliever on Earth.'[549] And Mūsā said, 'Our Lord! Destroy their riches and harden their hearts so that they will not believe until they see the painful punishment.'[550]"[551] The Prophet ﷺ then sided with Abū Bakr ﷺ.

The following day, 'Umar ⁂ found the Prophet ﷺ and Abū Bakr ⁂ crying under a tree. He said, "What is causing you to cry, O Messenger of Allah? By Allah, if I understand, I will cry with you; and if I do not understand, I will force myself to cry with you." [552] The Prophet ﷺ then recited the verses of Sūrah al-Anfāl that had just been revealed, "It is not befitting for a Prophet to take captives until he has thoroughly subdued the land. You [believers] settled with the fleeting gains of this world, while Allah's aim [for you] is the Hereafter. Allah is Almighty, All-Wise. Had it not been for a prior decree from Allah, you would have certainly been disciplined with a tremendous punishment for whatever [ransom] you have taken. Now enjoy what you have taken, for it is lawful and good. And be mindful of Allah. Surely Allah is All-Forgiving, Most Merciful." [553]

Taking prisoners was later established in the *sīrah*, but Allah ﷻ conveyed that the most appropriate course of action in this instance was to solidify the Muslims' position first. Clemency from a position of weakness is not considered merciful; rather, gaining strength and then forgiving is true mercy, which occurs throughout the *sīrah* once a position of strength was established. Rather than peddling utopian ideals of unrestricted leniency, Islam teaches a pragmatic code of conduct, carefully balancing the notions of mercy and justice. Indeed, many of the freed captives returned once more to fight, killing Muslims in the Battle of Uḥud.

The Muslims then advanced to Medina, and 70 of the captives were taken as prisoners of war to be released as per their ransoms. However, the Prophet ﷺ insisted that two enemies of Allah be executed: 'Uqbah ibn Abī Mu'ayṭ and al-Naḍr ibn Ḥārith. They were the only two captives that the Prophet ﷺ ever executed in his life, but their crimes against Islam were too severe to ignore. As for 'Uqbah, his crimes have been described throughout this book: he was the one who spat in the blessed face of the Prophet ﷺ; he was the one who strangled the Prophet ﷺ until Abū Bakr ⁂ pled, "Are you going to kill a man for saying, 'My Lord is Allah'?"; he was the one who threw the entrails of a carcass onto the Prophet ﷺ until his young child Fāṭimah ⁂ pulled it off; and so on. As for al-Naḍr, Ibn 'Abbās ⁂ described him as

"A Shayṭān from the Shayṭāns of the Quraysh." [554] He also stated that over eight verses in the Qur'an were revealed about him.[viii] He was one of the few literate residents of the Quraysh, and whenever the Qur'an was revealed, he was the first to make sarcastic and disparaging remarks. He was foremost in trying to derail the *da'wah* of the Prophet ﷺ.

Returning Home

As the Muslims were returning to Medina, rumours already spread that there was a war and that the Muslims were victorious. However, they could not internalise such a shocking event until Zayd ibn Ḥārithah stormed into Medina riding the Prophet's camel, named al-Qaswā'. Zayd galloped in, chanting, *"Allāhu Akbar!"*, listing off the names of the Quraysh's elite that were killed. Medina was thrust into elation and the Muslims celebrated joyfully. In a tragic juxtaposition, 'Uthmān ibn 'Affān heard the celebration as he returned from the cemetery after burying the Prophet's daughter, Ruqayyah. The Battle of Badr was the single most joyous occasion in the history of Islam to date—it was the first moment of relief and pride after 13 years of hardship and sacrifice. Nevertheless, tragedy struck the Prophet's household on the same day; it is as if Allah was reminding the Prophet ﷺ that this world will always be a test, and that pure unadulterated happiness is only for the Hereafter.

The Prophet ﷺ then arrived with the Muslims alongside 70 prisoners of war. Due to the sheer number of captives, the Prophet ﷺ held each Muslim responsible over the person they captured, and he himself hosted the Chieftains of the Quraysh. The Muslims were ordered to personally host their captives and treat them as well as they would their own guests. Never in the history of humankind has a military leader—let alone a Prophet—personally hosted prisoners of war in their own house.

---

viii They are *al-An'ām*, 109; *al-Anfāl*, 32–34; *al-Furqān*, 4–5; *Luqmān*, 6–7; *al-Qalam*, 15; *al-Ma'ārij*, 1–2; and *al-Muṭaffifīn*, 13.

Sawdah ؓ, the wife of the Prophet ﷺ, had a momentary lapse as she entered the house and saw Suhayl ibn ʿAmr, the most senior figure amongst the captives, sitting in the corner. Not realising that the Prophet ﷺ was present, and momentarily forgetting her own Islamic identity, she felt a wave of tribal shame, blurting, "O Abū Yazīd, you surrendered?! Why did you not die an honourable death rather than live as a prisoner?" Sawdah narrated herself, "I did not realise what I even said until I heard the Prophet ﷺ next to me say, 'O Sawdah, are you stoking him to fight against Allah and His Messenger?' I responded to him, 'O Messenger of Allah, I swear by Allah; the One with Whom there is no other god, I did not realise what I said. When I saw him sitting like this, I lost sense of myself and could not control myself.'"[555] The Prophet ﷺ accepted her excuse and forgave her. It was a major blunder—indirectly invoking a fight against the Prophet—but the Prophet ﷺ empathised with the heightened emotions of war and let it go.

The Prophet ordered the Companions regarding their captives, "Treat them with kindness."[556] One captive, Abū ʿAzīz, narrated that he was assigned to a group of the Anṣār, and whenever they ate, they would give him the meat and bread (i.e., luxury food items) while the Anṣār ate dates and water. He felt so embarrassed that he would place the bread back in front of them, but they would insist. This level of kindness towards the enemy was unprecedented, so much so that many of the captives converted to Islam after witnessing such sincere generosity.

The Prophet ﷺ notified the Quraysh that the prisoners would be returned for ransom, and each prisoner's ransom was according to their financial capability to the extent that the poorest of the prisoners were released with no charge. The literate captives were also offered their freedom in exchange for teaching the children of the Anṣār how to read and write. In a largely illiterate society, the Prophet ﷺ truly understood the value of literacy and education. Those who were both poor and illiterate were sent back without a ransom.

When Muṣʿab ibn ʿUmayr's brother, Abū ʿAzīz ibn ʿUmayr, was held captive, he saw Muṣʿab and rejoiced, "O Muṣʿab, help!" Muṣʿab ﷺ then turned to his captor and said, "Make sure he does not escape because his mother is a very wealthy woman who will pay whatever it takes for him." Shocked, Abū ʿAzīz responded, "O brother, is this how you treat me?" Without missing a beat, Muṣʿab pointed to his captor and replied, "He is my brother, not you."[557] The Islamic ties of brotherhood were deeply entrenched in his heart—something a tribal Pagan simply could not fathom.

The Anṣārī that captured al-ʿAbbās—notably with the help of an Angel—approached the Prophet ﷺ and offered to gift al-ʿAbbās to him, but the Prophet ﷺ declined and said, "Do not decrease his ransom by one single coin."[558] The Prophet ﷺ ordered the Companions not to kill al-ʿAbbās because he knew that his heart did not have animosity, but he ﷺ was also sternly against nepotism of any kind and insisted that he be treated the same as the other captives. Al-ʿAbbās approached the Prophet ﷺ and said, "O Messenger of Allah, why is there a ransom on me when I am a Muslim?"[559] The Prophet ﷺ said, "Allah knows best as to whether your Islam is true." In other words, it may be true, but we must judge according to the apparent.

He ﷺ continued, "If what you say is true, Allah will give you something better." Al-ʿAbbās replied, "O Messenger of Allah, you put my ransom as 4,000 dirhams, but I do not have that much money." The Prophet ﷺ replied, "Where is the money that you and Umm al-Faḍl (his wife) hid on such-and-such day? You said to her, 'If I ever die, this money will go to our children.' Where is that money?" Al-ʿAbbās immediately responded, "I swear by the One Who sent you with the Truth that you are the Messenger of Allah. No-one knew about that!"[560] Al-ʿAbbās was a self-proclaimed Muslim, but perhaps certainty did not enter his heart until that moment. He later recalled, "Verse 70 of Sūrah al-Anfāl was revealed about me." In it, Allah ﷻ states, "O Prophet! Tell the captives in your custody, 'If Allah finds goodness in your hearts, He will give you better than what has been taken from you, and forgive you. For Allah is All-Forgiving, Most Merciful.'"[561] Al-ʿAbbās received so many blessings from Allah ﷻ that he would later say, "O Messenger of Allah, I wish you took much more from me so that Allah may multiply His favours upon me."[562]

Another notable incident was the case of ʿAmr, the son of Abū Sufyān. Abū Sufyān, now the *de facto* leader of the Quraysh, was being pressured to pay his son's ransom until he said, "Do they expect me to give up my money along with my blood? They killed Ḥanẓalah (his other son) and now they want to make me penniless to retrieve ʿAmr? Let them keep him!"[563] Abū Sufyān suffered peak humiliation, as all his contemporaries and seniors were wiped out due to his call to arms. The irony, however, is that he would only ever offer to leave his son captive with someone he trusts to protect him. Were it not for his deep-seated respect for the Prophet ﷺ, he would have paid his ransom at the earliest opportunity.

Many months later, Abū Sufyān kidnapped an elderly Muslim by the name of Saʿd ibn Nuʿmān ؓ as he was trading in Mecca. As explained, Mecca is considered a Ḥaram, and this belief was upheld by both the Muslims and the Pagans. Abū Sufyān nevertheless contravened the sanctity of the Ḥaram to gain leverage, demonstrating the hypocrisy of the Pagans when opposing the Muslims. He said that Saʿd ibn Nuʿmān would not be released until his son was returned. Saʿd's tribe pled with the Prophet ﷺ on his behalf, and the Prophet accepted their pleas and released ʿAmr.

Rise of the Hypocrites

When Zayd ؓ arrived in Medina, a group of Pagans still residing in Medina grew increasingly disgruntled. They began murmuring, claiming that perhaps the Prophet ﷺ was killed and Zayd was in denial from his delirium. They were in disbelief and projected their worries onto Zayd ؓ. When the Prophet ﷺ arrived and the victory was confirmed, they realised that a page had turned in the history of Arabia and that the Muslims were here to stay. After Badr, they jumped ship and converted to Islam, thus no Pagans remained in Medina. This group of people who were outwardly Muslim but inwardly resented Islam are known as the Hypocrites[ix] (Munāfiqūn).

The leader of the Hypocrites was ʿAbdullāh ibn Ubayy ibn Salūl, who was the lone senior figure that survived the Buʿāth wars between the Aws and the Khazraj. Were it not for the Prophet's arrival, he would have been the undisputed leader of Yathrib. He would frequently make disrespectful comments about the Muslims. On one occasion, the Prophet ﷺ passed by on a donkey and ʿAbdullāh ibn Ubayy sneered, "Do not pollute us with your dust!"[564] He would also complain about the noise when the Companions would recite the Qur'an. When victory was finally confirmed, he said, "It appears that the matter is now settled (i.e., Islam is here to stay, and he would never be the Chieftain)."[565] He then outwardly converted to Islam, but his resentment did not wane.

ix The term "Hypocrite" as a proper noun is distinguished from the regular adjective "hypocrite", which refers to anyone whose actions and speech contradict. A "Hypocrite" with a capital "H" specifically refers to someone who publicly ascribes to the Islamic faith but does not have true belief of Islam in their heart.

Between Badr and Uḥud

15

The only remaining Chieftain amongst Mecca's sternest opposition was Abū Lahab, and he did not last very long, dying from a crippling illness shortly after. It is not known what caused his death, though it is quite clear that Allah ﷻ wiped the slate clean with the Prophet's foremost adversaries. Granted, the Prophet ﷺ still had enemies, but Abū Lahab equalled the likes of Abū Jahl, ʿUqbah, and al-Naḍr as the Prophet's vilest detractors in Mecca.

Another Assassination Attempt

After the Battle of Badr, the mood in Mecca was sombre. The remaining nobility would reminisce and lament the losses of Badr. ʿUmayr ibn Wahb al-Jumaḥī was one such nobleman of the Quraysh, complaining of his son who was still held captive in Medina. ʿUmayr grew so indignant that he declared, "By Allah, if I did not have a debt to pay and a family to provide for, I would personally go to Medina and execute Muhammad."[566] Ṣafwān ibn Umayyah, the son of Umayyah ibn Khalaf and ʿUmayr's cousin, capitalised on this opportunity and offered to pay ʿUmayr's debts and take care of his family as his own.

ʿUmayr accepted the offer and swore a vow of secrecy. He immediately began preparations: he sharpened his sword, soaked it in poison, and left Mecca immediately.

He entered Medina veiled, as was common amongst desert travellers, but ʿUmar ﷺ recognised him immediately. He said, "This dog is an enemy of Allah. By Allah, he has come with evil intent."[567] ʿUmar then informed the Prophet ﷺ before ʿUmayr entered, and the Prophet ﷺ asked ʿUmar to bring him. ʿUmar instructed an Anṣārī, "Allow him to sit with the Prophet, but watch his every move, as this filth cannot be trusted." ʿUmayr entered the mosque with ʿUmar, hand on sword, beside him. ʿUmayr greeted the Prophet ﷺ by saying, "*Anʿim ṣabāhā* (good morning)" to which the Prophet ﷺ replied, "Allah has given us a greeting better than this—the greeting of the people of Paradise—which is 'peace be upon you (*al-salāmu ʿalaykum*)'"[568] Despite the tense situation, the Prophet ﷺ always had *daʿwah* at the forefront of his mind.

The Prophet ﷺ then got straight to the point, "Why are you here, O ʿUmayr?" ʿUmayr claimed that he came to ransom his son. The Prophet ﷺ then said, "If that is the case, what is this sword around your neck?" ʿUmayr attempted to de-escalate, "Oh, this? What good did our swords do for us [at Badr]?"[569] Undeterred, the Prophet ﷺ said, "Tell me the truth: why did you come, O ʿUmayr?" ʿUmayr maintained his reasoning until the Prophet ﷺ said, "No. Rather, you and Ṣafwān were sitting alone in the Ḥijr [of the Kaʿbah], and you were lamenting your losses at Badr. You said, 'Were it not for my debt and family, I would personally kill Muhammad.' Ṣafwān offered to take care of your debts and family so you could kill me, but Allah ﷻ has come between you and your plans." Astonished, ʿUmayr immediately said, "I bear witness that you are a Messenger of Allah!"[570] ʿUmayr did not tell a soul—not even his wife or servant—and he knew that it was simply impossible for the Prophet ﷺ to have known except if Allah ﷻ informed him.

While the likes of Abū Jahl knew that Islam was the truth but still opposed it out of arrogance and pride, some adversaries of Islam were actually sincere in their opposition. Once the Truth became clear to them, they embraced Islam without hesitation, and ʿUmayr was one such example. He said, "We would reject you when you claimed that Revelation came to you from the Heavens, but no-one knew of this matter except Ṣafwān and I, and there was no way you could have found out except through Allah ﷻ. So, I thank Allah ﷻ for causing me to see the Truth and guiding me to Islam."[571] The Prophet instructed the Companions, "Teach your brother about the religion, assist him in memorising some Qur'an, and free his captive."[572]

ʿUmayr's resentment was so severe that he was willing to leave his family and sacrifice his own life, as well as his captive son's life, to assassinate the Prophet ﷺ. However, as soon as faith entered his heart, he accepted Islam and strived to serve Allah and His Messenger. He continued, "O Messenger of Allah, I used to strive to extinguish the flame of Allah, even torturing those who embraced Islam. I now ask your permission to return to Mecca and call them to Islam just as I would prevent them from embracing Islam."[573]

Meanwhile in Mecca, Ṣafwān was waiting excitedly. He would remark to his companions smugly, "Soon I will bring you glad tidings of an event that will make you forget Badr."[574] When ʿUmayr finally returned, only to disclose his conversion to Islam, Ṣafwān made a vow never to look his cousin in the eye or remain under the same roof for as long as he lived. ʿUmayr preached in Mecca, converting a number of people before emigrating to Medina. Years later, at the Conquest of Mecca, Ṣafwān fled, mistakenly assuming that he would be captured and killed. ʿUmayr still had feelings of brotherly love towards his cousin, and he asked the Prophet ﷺ to grant him amnesty. The Prophet ﷺ duly accepted, and ʿUmayr tracked Ṣafwān down and encouraged him to return, guaranteeing his safety. Eventually, Ṣafwān returned to Mecca and even accepted Islam, declaring his *shahādah* to the Prophet ﷺ directly.

The Banū Qaynuqāʿ

The biggest of the three Jewish tribes in Medina was the Banū Qaynuqāʿ. They comprised 2,000 people, 700 of which were fighting men.

They were displeased with the outcome of Badr and expressed this displeasure on occasion. One day, the Prophet ﷺ went to their souk and gathered them to admonish them for their attitude, reminding them of the agreed treaty of coexistence. One of their leaders stood up and retorted, "O Muhammad, do not be deceived by your recent victory. You fought a group of nobodies; had you really fought men—like us—you would have seen a different result."[575] The Prophet ﷺ did not respond in kind, but tensions continued to fester thereafter.

The final straw that led to breaking point amongst the two groups was an incident wherein an Anṣārī woman was trading in the Jewish souk. A Jewish goldsmith began flirting with the woman, badgering her to expose her body to him. She continued to refuse, and the goldsmith instructed his friend to tie her garment to a post. When she stood up, her entire garment was torn down, exposing her naked body. As they laughed, she screamed for help, and a nearby Anṣārī rushed in and immediately executed the perpetrator. A gang of local residents then surrounded him and killed him. The Prophet ﷺ then made it clear: the treaty has been broken and is no longer valid. The Prophet ﷺ never acted deceptively, so he made it clear to all that the treaty had been violated. As Allah ﷻ revealed, "And if you see signs of betrayal by a people, respond by openly terminating your treaty with them. Surely Allah does not like those who betray."[576]

The Prophet ﷺ marched with the Muslims towards the Banū Qaynuqāʿ, and they fled within their fortresses[i]. The Muslims surrounded them for two weeks until they surrendered. Historically, the Jews had two main allies in Yathrib: ʿAbdullāh ibn Ubayy ibn Salūl and ʿUbādah ibn al-Ṣāmit, so they reached out to them both for assistance. ʿUbādah ؓ went straight to the Prophet ﷺ to relinquish his ties, saying, "O Messenger of Allah, I want to inform you that I am no longer their representative. My ties are with Allah and His Messenger."[577] As for ʿAbdullāh ibn Ubayy ibn Salūl, he marched towards the Jewish captives and said to the Muslims, "I command you to release them!"

i The Jews of Medina were proficient in building lofty fortresses in contrast to the Pagans who had very simple living arrangements.

The Muslims of course refused to breach the Prophet's commands, and ʿAbdullāh ibn Ubayy said, "Either do it or I will!" The Companion in charge, al-Mundhir ibn Qudāmah ﷺ, flatly responded, "If you dare, I will kill you."[578]

ʿAbdullāh ibn Ubayy then marched towards the Prophet ﷺ and said, "O Muhammad! Be generous with my allies!" He would often refer to the Prophet ﷺ as "Muhammad" and rarely "Messenger of Allah", despite Allah ﷻ clearly instructing, "Do not treat the Messenger's summons to you [as lightly] as your summons to one another."[579] ʿAbdullāh ibn Ubayy ibn Salūl was later identified as the leader of the Hypocrites, but at this stage of the *sīrah*, it was not yet confirmed. He was outwardly Muslim, and despite his lack of manners and reverence towards the Prophet ﷺ, he had not yet cemented his reputation as a known Hypocrite.

The Prophet ﷺ remained silent, so he repeated his request, "O Muhammad! Be generous with my allies!" The Prophet ﷺ again remained silent, and this time turned away. In a brazen show of disrespect, ʿAbdullāh grabbed the Prophet's armour, holding onto him ﷺ, repeating, "Be generous with my allies!" With visible signs of irritation, the Prophet ﷺ replied, "Let go of me." ʿAbdullāh refused, and the Prophet ﷺ said, "Woe to you! Let go of me." In an unprecedented display of arrogance, he said, "I swear by Allah, I will not let go until you promise to be generous to my allies. These 700 men protected me from the white and black (i.e., all of mankind), and now you think you will rid them in a single morning? By Allah I fear a turn of fortune will strike us [for not repaying them with good]." The Prophet ﷺ then acquiesced and said, "I give them to you (i.e., I spare them)."[580] It was not clear what the Prophet ﷺ was planning otherwise, but he ensured their safety for the moment. Afterwards, the Prophet ﷺ ordered their expulsion, giving them three days to collect their belongings and leave.

Allah ﷻ then revealed, "O believers! Take neither the Jews nor the Christians as protectors—they are protectors of one another. Whoever does so will be counted as one of them. Surely Allah does not guide the wrongdoing people."[581] Some use this verse to accuse Islam of prejudice, though the context clearly illustrates the meaning; another nation will never serve as an ultimate protector or guardian. The verses continue, "You see those with sickness in their hearts racing for their guardianship, saying, 'We fear a turn of fortune will strike us.' But perhaps Allah will bring about [your] victory or another favour by His command, and they will regret what they have hidden in their hearts."[582]

It must be made abundantly clear that the Prophet ﷺ did not treat the Jews—or any other group—according to their ethnicity or religion; rather, he ﷺ treated them according to their actions. A Jewish criminal was punished, just as a Muslim or Christian criminal was punished. Jews lived under Islamic rule for over a thousand years in peace and harmony. Whenever Jewish communities were persecuted in Christian lands, Muslim leaders provided a safe haven, including the Umayyad, Abbasid, and Ottoman dynasties.

The Battle of Sawīq

Abū Sufyān felt so humiliated from Badr that he took an oath not to bathe until he avenged his people against the Muslims. He remained in a wretched state of impurity for months until he could no longer tolerate it. He gathered around 200 of the Quraysh and launched a surprise attack in the outskirts of Medina. The Banū Naḍīr, the second largest Jewish tribe in Medina, provided him with protection as well as food, water, and supplies—a clear violation of the Treaty of Medina. 20 or so of the Quraysh ambushed a date palm farm, killing two Muslims, burning down the field, and fleeing. Abū Sufyān could finally take a bath, as he shed Muslim blood in retaliation for Badr.

Sariyyah al-Qaradah

In Rabīʿ al-Awwal of the third year of Hijrah, the Quraysh were planning their yearly trade routes. Ṣafwān ibn Umayyah said, "Muhammad and his companions have blocked our passages. If we take the sea route, most of the tribes have given their allegiance to Muhammad and will block us."[583] An elder tribesman suggested that they travel through the

Iraq passage, a major detour, to avoid a Muslim ambush. They agreed, finding a specialised guide to lead them through this unorthodox route. This demonstrates the lasting impact that Badr had on the Quraysh, complicating their most essential decisions. It also shows how Islam continued to spread through *da'wah*; the tribes that had accepted Islam were not threatened with war but rather converted out of their own volition. Historians often focus on detailing the battles throughout the Medinan era, but the conversion of these tribes demonstrates that much more occurred outside the battlefield.

The Quraysh convened with utmost secrecy, but a tribesman amongst them divulged vital information in a state of drunkenness. As he was drinking amongst friends, he was boasting of a secret plan to change their routes to Syria. However, amongst his midst was a Muslim, Salīṭ ibn al-Nuʿmān 🙵, who was still residing in Mecca. Salīṭ immediately sent a message to the Prophet 🙵 informing him of these vital details. The Prophet 🙵 sent Zayd ibn Ḥārithah 🙵 to lead a group of Muslims to intercept the caravan, and they did, successfully raiding over 50,000 dirhams as well as dozens of valuable items and camels. When the Muslims initially intended to intercept the caravan at Badr but were faced with a full-fledged army, Allah 🙵 reassured them that He 🙵 had given them the better of two options. In His generosity, Allah 🙵 actually granted them both, as they defeated the army at Badr and still took the caravan at Qaradah with no casualties. This was a tremendous blow to the Quraysh and a decisive moment that sped up the events leading up to the Battle of Uḥud.

The Killing of Kaʿb ibn al-Ashraf

Kaʿb ibn al-Ashraf was born to an Arab father, and a Jewish mother from the Banū Naḍīr, thereby claiming two prestigious heritages. He was known for his wealth, handsomeness, and eloquent poetry. He was also an adversary of Islam throughout the *sīrah*. Allah 🙵 was referring to Kaʿb when He 🙵 revealed, "The foolish among the people will ask, 'Why did they turn away from the direction of prayer they used to face?'" [584] When the commandment of *zakāh* was revealed, he and his friends would discourage the Anṣār, saying, "Do not give your money away, for I am worried that you will become poor. Do not be hasty, as you do not know what the future will hold."[585] Allah ﷻ again revealed about him, "Surely Allah does not like whoever is arrogant and boastful; those who are stingy and promote stinginess among people, withholding Allah's bounties."[586] When Zayd ؓ returned from Badr announcing victory, Kaʿb responded, "If Muhammad truly did kill all these people, then it is better to be in the ground."[587] There are numerous further instances of Kaʿb's indignation towards Allah and His Messenger.

After Badr, Kaʿb forged a secret alliance with Abū Sufyān, indicating a treacherous plot against the Prophet ﷺ. The details of the plot remain unknown, as Abū Sufyān died shortly after. Upon his return, he began writing erotic poetry about Muslim women, naming and describing specific people. This proved to be the final straw for Kaʿb, as the Prophet ﷺ said to his Companions, "Who will take care of Kaʿb ibn al-Ashraf? For he has transgressed against Allah and His Messenger."[588] Muhammad ibn Maslamah ؓ, a senior member of the Aws, stood up and volunteered himself for the role. The Aws had long-standing ties with the Banū Naḍīr, just as the Khazraj had with the Banū Qaynuqāʿ, so he was well-suited for the job.

Muhammad ibn Maslamah then asked the Prophet ﷺ for permission to speak ill of him ﷺ to get closer to Kaʿb, and the Prophet ﷺ granted permission. He then approached Kaʿb and said, "This man (i.e., the Prophet ﷺ) has come and caused us irritation, and now the Arabs are all against us. Moreover, he is now asking for our money (i.e., *zakāh*) and he has put us through so much hardship."[589] Kaʿb was elated with these comments and began mirroring his sentiments. Muhammad ibn Maslamah then said, "We are now his followers, so we cannot forsake him until the situation changes. Until that time, I need a loan to pay my *zakāh*." Kaʿb was a moneylender and would acquire wealth through usury, so he duly accepted. Muhammad ibn Maslamah required collateral to secure the loan, and his ingenious plan was to offer his weapons as collateral, justifying the presence of weapons in Kaʿb's home. Muhammad ibn Maslamah then suggested that a few of his friends also borrow money using weapons as collateral, and Kaʿb agreed, as it would greatly increase his revenue.

On the 14th of Rabīʿ al-Awwal, they approached Kaʿb's residence in the dead of the night, as it was a secret meeting. Lying in bed with his wife, Kaʿb arose but his wife pulled him back, asking where he was going. When he explained, she said, "You are a man at war, and I am worried for you." Nevertheless, he wore his armour—as was custom when greeting a guest—and went out to receive them. Abū Nā'ilah, who came with Muhammad ibn Maslamah as part of the plan, said, "I smell the nicest perfume on you, can I smell it?" As Kaʿb lowered his head for him to smell, he grabbed him, and they assassinated him. They returned to Medina and informed the Prophet ﷺ that the mission was successful.

This event is often cited as being controversial, as some criticise it as an extrajudicial assassination. In reality, Kaʿb's secret alliance and plot against the Prophet ﷺ was clear grounds for capital punishment, as it was a threat of treason. Moreover, Kaʿb was consistent in inciting hatred towards Allah and His Messenger, going as far as sexually enticing the men of Medina towards the female Companions. The Banū Naḍīr had already violated the Treaty of Medina in the Battle of Sawīq by assisting Abū Sufyān. It is not clear whether Kaʿb physically participated, though it is possible, considering their secret alliance shortly after.

This event is described as extrajudicial because Kaʿb was assassinated without proper proceedings. This requires a broader commentary of the political norms of 7th century Arabia and the danger of imposing contemporary norms onto a society which holds inherently different legal mechanisms and societal understandings. The Prophet's leadership was religious, political, and legal; therefore, his order was inherently judicial. The Prophet ﷺ did not order such attacks in Mecca, but in Medina, he was the ruler with executive power, and thus his commands were given with legal authority. Kaʿb's own wife stated, "You are a man at war", even though he was not in a physical battle, because it was understood as per the norm of the time that his engagements were of a hostile nature.

The Prophet's Marriage to Ḥafṣah ﵂

In Sha'bān 3 AH, Ḥafṣah bint 'Umar ﵂—'Umar ibn al-Khaṭṭāb's daughter—was widowed at a similar time to 'Uthmān ibn 'Affān ﵁. They both lost their partners, and 'Umar ﵁ immediately identified a suitable partnership. He approached 'Uthmān ﵁ and asked if he would be interested in marrying Ḥafṣah. 'Uthmān ﵁ asked for time to deliberate, and a few days later he returned and politely declined the proposal. 'Umar was hurt by the rejection but ultimately moved on and asked Abū Bakr ﵁ if he was interested. Abū Bakr did not even respond; he was too shy to vocalise his rejection and instead turned his head.

'Umar recalled, "Abū Bakr's rejection was even more painful than that of 'Uthmān!" It irked him so much that he expressed his frustration to the Prophet ﷺ. The Prophet ﷺ replied, "Ḥafṣah will marry a person better than 'Uthmān, and 'Uthmān will marry a person better than Ḥafṣah." [590] He ﷺ then conveyed his intention to marry Ḥafṣah. 'Umar of course immediately agreed, and afterwards Abū Bakr approached 'Umar and said, "Perhaps you felt hurt when I rejected your offer." 'Umar replied in the affirmative, so Abū Bakr clarified, "I already heard the Prophet ﷺ mention Ḥafṣah, and I did not want to disclose the Prophet's secret. Had the Messenger of Allah not expressed interest in her, I would have certainly accepted her hand in marriage." [591]

The Prophet's Marriage to Zaynab bint Khuzaymah ﵂

Zaynab bint Khuzaymah ﵂ was married to Ṭufayl ibn-Ḥārith ﵁ who died in the Battle of Badr, becoming the first martyr in Islam. She was not a Qurashī, as she was from the tribe of Hawāzin. As a woman from a foreign tribe widowed to the first martyr in Islam, the Prophet ﷺ offered her hand in marriage, sending a clear message that the families of martyrs will be cared for. The Prophet ﷺ married her a month after his marriage to Ḥafṣah, but she only lived with the Prophet ﷺ for a few months before dying of natural causes. She was known as The Mother of the Poor (Umm al-Masākīn), as she was famous for constantly feeding the poor and orphaned children.

PART IV • THE MEDINAN ERA

The Battle of Uḥud

16

While Badr was an impromptu war, Uḥud was a pre-planned attack. Abū Sufyān, who later converted to Islam, narrated that as soon as the Quraysh returned from Badr, they began to plan Uḥud. Abū Sufyān took ʿIkrimah ibn Abī Jahl and Ṣafwān ibn Umayyah, sons of the two biggest names that died at Badr, and approached every household that contributed to last year's caravan. Abū Sufyān knew how much each participant made, and he demanded the profits back to fund their offensive against the Muslims. Allah ﷻ references this in Sūrah al-Anfāl, "Surely the disbelievers spend their wealth to hinder others from the Path of Allah. They will continue to spend to the point of regret. Then they will be defeated, and the disbelievers will be driven into Hell."[592] As explained, Sūrah al-Anfāl was revealed after the Battle of Badr, and so Allah ﷻ not only exposed the Quraysh's plot as they were planning it, He ﷻ predicted their imminent downfall.

Their motives for the war were threefold: first, their religious animosity towards Islam was increasing; second, they suffered socially and were desperate to save face, yearning for revenge; and third, their economy had capitulated and would continue to suffer greatly without the trade route to Syria. Uḥud was therefore a last gasp attempt to restore the

Quraysh to their pre-Islamic norms. After suffering a major loss in personnel, they required support and thus approached neighbouring tribes who would equally benefit from re-opening the Syrian trade route: the tribes of Kinānah and Tihāmah.

The Battle of Uḥud was a major step in shifting the paradigm from Muslims vs. the Quraysh to Islam vs. *kufr*. Lines were drawn in the sand, and sides were chosen. Recalling the Boycott of Banū Hāshim, there were many non-Muslims included in the self-imposed exile. Now, non-Qurashī tribes are including themselves in a war against the Muslims. On the 7th of Shawwāl 3 AH, the Quraysh and their allies set out from Mecca. The total combined force was 3,000 fighting men, 700 with armour, and 200 on horseback. They even brought two dozen of their women to further incentivise them not to fail in their endeavour. Abū Sufyān led the army and appointed Khālid ibn al-Walīd on the left flank and ʿIkrimah ibn Abī Jahl on the right.

As soon as the Quraysh left, al-ʿAbbās ﷺ sent a trusted servant to inform the Prophet ﷺ. Al-ʿAbbās expressed his *īmān* to the Prophet ﷺ after Badr, but it is theorised that he returned to Mecca as a secret Muslim, formally converting in public at the Conquest of Mecca. The benefits of his clandestine belief in Mecca are clearly demonstrated in this example where he was able to notify the Prophet ﷺ of major developments. The messenger raced to Medina, and as a lone rider was able to overtake the army. He reached the Prophet ﷺ who asked Ubayy ibn Kaʿb ﷺ to read the letter and instructed him to keep the contents top-secret until further notice. The Prophet ﷺ rushed home and met with senior members of the Anṣār then sent out some spies to confirm the news. The Prophet ﷺ did not distrust al-ʿAbbās, but the developments were so significant that wisdom would dictate one act with caution and avoid hastiness. The Prophet's conduct is once again a vital lesson for the believer.

Owing to al-ʿAbbās's forewarning, the Prophet ﷺ had two days to act. He ﷺ convened a general meeting after the Friday Prayer, informing everyone of what was taking place and asking for their input. The Prophet ﷺ suggested that they fight from within the city, as Medina was a naturally protected area; to the east and west were large volcanic plains; to the northwest were the plains of Uḥud; and to the southeast was the area of Qubā' which contained large date palm farms. Fighting within the city would naturally give advantage to the residents of the city who are familiar with its layout. ʿAbdullāh ibn Ubayy ibn Salūl agreed with the Prophet ﷺ. Notwithstanding his resentment of Islam, he was indeed a seasoned warrior and thus understood the benefits of this plan. He said, "Medina has never been successfully attacked when fought within."[593]

However, there were a group of younger zealous Companions who were eager to fight. They said, "Why should we remain in our houses like cowards? Rather, we should go out and fight on the battlefield!"[594] They deeply regretted missing out on Badr and wanted to display their valour. They continued to encourage and push the Prophet ﷺ to go out, and the senior Companions remained silent on the matter, so the Prophet ﷺ sided with the majority vote and proceeded to wear his armour. When the Prophet ﷺ went inside to gather his armour, the senior Companions began reprimanding the youngsters, "The Prophet ﷺ told us his opinion, and yet you persisted in suggesting the opposite until finally he agreed!"[595] The younger Companions felt remorseful and requested Ḥamzah ﷺ to inform the Prophet ﷺ that they changed their mind. The Prophet ﷺ, already dressed in full armour, said, "It is not befitting that a Prophet takes off his armour after wearing it until he fights the enemy."[596]

This incident demonstrates the Prophet's insistence on consulting his Companions. Despite being confident in the plan to remain in Medina, he ﷺ acquiesced to the majority because he understood the importance of a unified force. The incident also reveals the outstanding etiquette of the senior Companions; they did not voice their disapproval until the Prophet ﷺ left out of respect and reverence. Indeed, they had accompanied the Prophet ﷺ for over a decade prior and had learned these soft skills directly from the fountain of Prophethood.

Fitnah on the March to Uḥud

The Prophet ﷺ divided the army into three main groups: the Muhājirūn, under the leadership of Muṣʿab ibn ʿUmayr; the Aws, under the leadership of Usayd ibn Ḥuḍayr; and the Khazraj, under the leadership of al-Ḥubāb ibn al-Mundhir. Every single adult Muslim male—totalling 1,000—marched towards Uḥud with 100 suits of armour and a handful of horses. Contrary to popular belief, Uḥud was not a single mountain, but rather a collection of mountains spanning one whole mile. The Prophet ﷺ chose Uḥud as the battlefield, as it served as a natural shield from multiple directions. Open battle against a much larger enemy would most likely lead to defeat, and so the Prophet ﷺ utilised his surroundings.

A group of 300 Hypocrites, headed by ʿAbdullāh ibn Ubayy ibn Salūl, began lagging behind gradually until they eventually took a complete U-turn. They did not have the decency nor honour to voice their withdrawal but instead opted to sneak away. Some of the Companions saw them and rebuked them, to which ʿAbdullāh ibn Ubayy ibn Salūl said, "He listened to our youth and left my advice. Why should we risk our lives fighting for him when he did not listen to us?" When ʿAbdullāh ibn ʿAmr ibn Ḥarām ؓ saw ʿAbdullāh ibn Ubayy ibn Salūl retreat, he rode towards him and said, "I remind you to fear Allah ﷻ and not leave your Prophet and people at this time when the enemy is about to attack. Did you not promise him that you would protect him and defend him like you would your own families?" ʿAbdullāh ibn ʿAmr ؓ reminded them of their religious duty as well as their tribal honour. ʿAbdullāh ibn Ubayy then meekly responded, "If we thought there would be fighting, we would have definitely gone with you, but we do not think they will attack." [597]

Allah ﷻ quoted him directly in the Qurʾan, "So what you suffered on the day the two armies met was by Allah's Will, so that He may distinguish the [true] believers and expose the Hypocrites. When it was said to them, 'Come fight in the cause of Allah or [at least] defend yourselves', they replied, 'If we had known there was fighting, we would have definitely gone with you.' They were closer to disbelief than belief on that day—for saying with their mouths what was not in their hearts. Allah is All-Knowing of what they hide." [598] One of the benefits of Uḥud was the exposure of the Hypocrites and how sinister and detrimental they truly were. Prior to Uḥud, the Companions were not privy to the extent of their deceit, but their actions at Uḥud made it clear to the Companions, in no uncertain terms, that they were an enemy within. Allah ﷻ described it as "separating the evil from the good"[599]. The only way to distinguish the sincere from the disingenuous is through trying times.

When the Muslims saw such a large group of people turning back, they began debating. A group of Muslims suggested that they turn back and fight the defectors, while another group insisted that they continue forward. Even though this argument was for the sake of Islam, Allah ﷻ still gently reprimanded them, saying, "Why are you [believers] divided into two groups regarding the Hypocrites while Allah allowed them to regress [to disbelief] because of their misdeeds? Do you wish to guide those left by Allah to stray? And whoever Allah leaves to stray, you will never find for them a way."[600] Another consequence of the withdrawal was that some auxiliary tribes began to falter, hesitating in their position. The Banū Ḥārithah from the Aws and the Banū Salamah from the Khazraj almost withdrew but eventually decided to stay. Allah ﷻ references them too, "When two groups among you were about to cower, but Allah was their ally. So in Allah let the believers put their trust."[601] Despite being a moment of weakness, these two tribes would later boast about this event because Allah described Himself ﷻ as "their ally".

700 Muslims marched on, and the Prophet ﷺ ensured that they travelled surreptitiously. He acquired a guide to take them through the valleys and farms, avoiding the open route so as not to reveal their location to the Quraysh. They passed by an elderly blind man who was a friend of ʿAbdullāh ibn Ubayy ibn Salūl and was equally as resentful. He shouted, "Who is that passing by? Is this Muhammad and his companions? I do not give you permission to go through my land!" He then began throwing rocks and pebbles despite his blindness. A Companion raised his sword to attack him but the Prophet ﷺ said, "Leave him. His heart is blind, as is his sight."[602] The Muslims arrived at Uḥud in the afternoon of the 14th of Shawwāl, and the Quraysh then made their way to Uḥud, with both armies prepared to fight the following sunrise.

Preparations for Battle

The Prophet ﷺ began organising his army, assessing each fighter individually. He then sent back a dozen or so Companions for being too young, as the cut-off point was 15 years of age. These adolescents included the likes of ʿAbdullāh ibn ʿUmar, Zayd ibn Thābit, Usāmah ibn Zayd ibn Ḥārithah, Abū Saʿīd al-Khuḍrī, and Zayd ibn Arqam ﷺ.[603] Many of these youngsters tried to argue their way back into the army but the Prophet ﷺ refused with two exceptions. First, 14-year-old Rāfiʿ ibn Khadīj pleaded his case, and his relatives assured the Prophet ﷺ that he was an expert archer despite his age. The Prophet ﷺ accepted his request, and in response, Samurah ibn Jundub began to argue his own case, claiming to be stronger than Rāfiʿ. Some narrations even note that he began wrestling Rāfiʿ to prove his superiority. The Prophet ﷺ duly accepted his plea.[604] These inspiring youths desperate to fight are indeed a far cry from the seasoned veterans who turned their backs in cowardice.

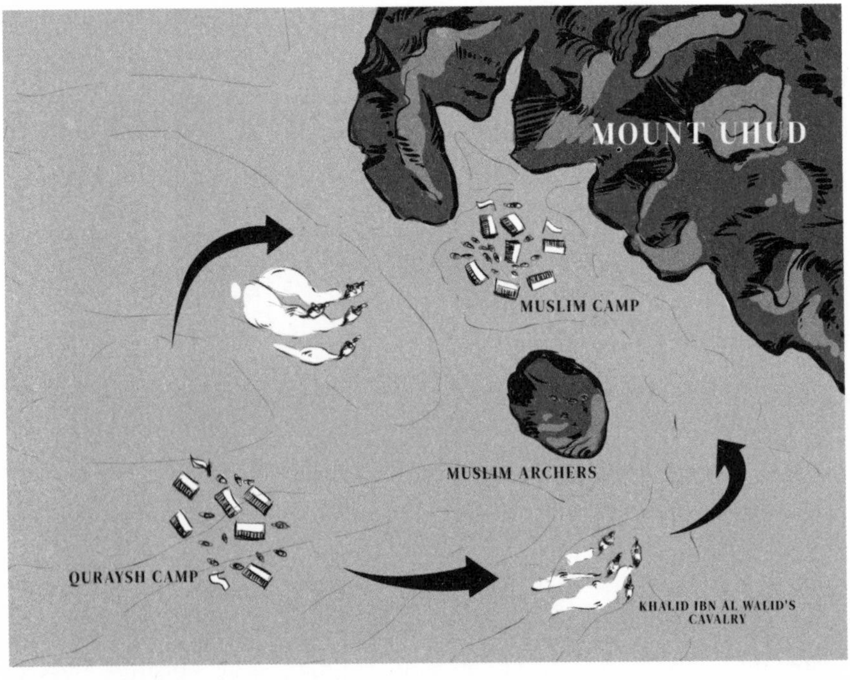

The Muslims were positioned facing Medina. To their backs were the plains of Uḥud and to their left was Jabal ʿAynayn (now called

Jabal al-Rumāh—Archers' Hill). They were situated in a manner whereby they were covered on all sides except for one stretch of land, and in that open area was Jabal ʿAynayn. The Prophet ﷺ quickly identified that area as the only weak link, and so he ordered 50 of the best archers to remain on the hill at all costs. This ingenious tactic ensured that the Muslims were protected from every angle except for a 300-metre opening, which would be utilised for their offensive attack. The beauty of this set-up was in nullifying the Quraysh's massive numerical advantage. By forcing the Quraysh through a 300-metre space, their surplus of 2,300 men was made instantly redundant. The Prophet ﷺ stressed the gravity of the archers' role in this plan, instructing, "Protect us with your arrows for their horses will not charge forth if they see arrows. Even if you see the birds eating our corpses, do not leave your places until I send for you."[605]

As the Sun rose on the 15th of Shawwāl, the Prophet ﷺ began motivating his troops. He unsheathed his sword and asked, "Who will take this sword from me and fight?" Everyone volunteered themselves, especially the Prophet's cousin, Zubayr ibn al-ʿAwwām ؓ. The Prophet ﷺ then asked, "Who will take this sword...with its due right?" Silence ensued, then Abū Dujānah ؓ asked, "And what is its due right, O Messenger of Allah?" The Prophet ﷺ answered, "That you fight with it until it breaks or is no longer usable." Abū Dujānah then confirmed, "I will take it with its due right, O Messenger of Allah."[606]

Abū Dujānah ؓ was a formidable force with a reputation in battle that preceded him. He had a red turban, called "The Turban of Death", reserved for the severest of battles. He donned the turban and began to walk up and down with an arrogant swagger, chest and shoulders puffed out. The Prophet ﷺ remarked, "Allah despises this type of walking except in this time and this place."[607] Years later, Zubayr ؓ mentioned how he felt disappointed that he was passed over for Abū Dujānah, as he was the Prophet's close Companion and cousin, so he followed Abū Dujānah to see what was so special about him. He then observed as Abū Dujānah obliterated every single one of his opponents in quick succession using the utmost skill, strength, and passion. Zubayr conceded that Abū Dujānah indeed stayed true to his vow and gave the blessed sword its due right.

Before the battle even began, the Quraysh attempted to disrupt the Muslim army. A messenger came within shouting distance and said, "I have been sent by Abū Sufyān. He is saying, 'O People of Medina, leave us to our cousins, for we have nothing against you!'"[608] The Anṣār were furious with such an offer and hurled vulgar insults and profanities towards him. Abū Dujānah's haughty strut and the Anṣār's foul language are to be taken in context: each circumstance requires its own behaviour and etiquette, and when faced with life and death in the heat of war, there is no room for courteousness. A man called ʿAbd ʿAmr ibn Ṣayfī, known as Abū ʿĀmir al-Rāhib (The Monk), then stepped forward to Abū Sufyān. Abū ʿĀmir was one of the foremost leaders of the Aws before the Prophet ﷺ arrived, equivalent to ʿAbdullāh ibn Ubayy ibn Salūl amongst the Khazraj. When the Prophet ﷺ migrated to Medina, Abū ʿĀmir could not stomach feigning his Islam, so he left Medina in protest, waiting for a moment such as this to reclaim his city.

Abū ʿĀmir said to Abū Sufyān, "Leave this to me, for my people have always respected and honoured me. You will see the power I hold over them." He then walked out towards the Anṣār, saying, "O Aws! It is me, Abū ʿĀmir..." Before he could continue, the Aws yelled back, "May Allah ﷻ curse you and give you no pleasure. You are not Abū ʿĀmir al-Rāhib (The Monk), you are Abū ʿĀmir al-Fāsiq (The Dissolute)." Abū ʿĀmir was so taken aback that he could not muster a response. He returned to Abū Sufyān and timidly remarked, "My people are afflicted with some sort of disease."[609] As demonstrated throughout the *sīrah*, the bonds of Islam cannot be comprehended by one who has not tasted the sweetness of *īmān*.

A Successful Assault

The *mubārazah* then began. Ṭalḥah ibn Abī Ṭalḥah from the Banū ʿAbd al-Dār stepped forward and exclaimed, "Who will fight me?" The young and ferocious warrior, ʿAlī ibn Abī Ṭālib رضي الله عنه, stepped forward. While Ṭalḥah had full body armour, ʿAlī only had a sword and shield. As soon as they approached each other, Ṭalḥah immediately swung, and ʿAlī—as sharp as he was strong—blocked his strike with his shield in one hand and dealt a counterstrike with the other. Ṭalḥah's body armour covered him from head to thigh, so ʿAlī's meticulous strike was directed below his thigh, slicing his leg off completely. As Ṭalḥah fell backwards, his private parts were exposed, and he pleaded, "I beg you by the rights of kinship[i]!" ʿAlī felt embarrassed to attack an exposed man begging and appealing to family ties, so he lowered his sword and walked back. Ṭalḥah's wound festered and he did not survive the battle, but ʿAlī's decorum and honour in warfare is yet another feather in his cap of manliness.

After ʿAlī's victory, the Muslims charged forward valiantly. As noted, the Quraysh's numerical advantage was neutralised, and so the deciding factor became individual prowess. The Muslims overwhelmed the Quraysh with devastating attacks from every angle, and the Quraysh could not sustain a defence. They fled to the extent that al-Barāʾ ibn ʿĀzib said, "They turned and fled until I saw with my own eyes the ankle-bracelets of the women as they ran up the mountain."[610]

It was the custom of the Quraysh that the Banū ʿAbd al-Dār had the honour of holding the flag. In Badr, the flag-bearers fled, so before the battle began, Abū Sufyān taunted them to rile them up. "O Banū ʿAbd al-Dār, we gave you the flag at Badr, but you turned your backs and fled, and you saw what happened as a result. The flag is the symbol of the army; if it stands, the army stands, and if it falls, the army falls. So, either take the flag with the right that it deserves, or if you cannot, give it back."[611] The Banū ʿAbd al-Dār were incensed by such an insinuation, challenging Abū Sufyān, "You will see what we will do with this flag! As long as one of us remains, the flag will be up!" They remained true to their word and did not flee, but Ḥamzah, alongside ʿAlī and Abū Dujānah ﷺ, killed them off, one by one, until none of them remained. The flag fell and the Quraysh fled.

Ubayy ibn Khalaf, brother of the equally wretched Umayyah ibn Khalaf, was the only Pagan whom the Prophet ﷺ personally killed. In Mecca, he would taunt the Prophet, "I am going to kill you one day."

i They were third cousins.

On another occasion, he said, "I have a special horse which I feed the choicest of barley and grain so that it grows to be strong so that I can kill you while I ride it." In a rare instance, the Prophet ﷺ replied, "No; rather, I will kill you by the will of Allah."[612] On the day of Uḥud, Ubayy was riding that same horse, and he saw the Prophet ﷺ and began charging towards him. The Companions huddled around the Prophet ﷺ to protect him but the Prophet ﷺ refused, saying, "No, he is mine." The Prophet ﷺ then grabbed a spear and lunged forward, dodging Ubayy's sword and thrusting the spear into his neck. It did not kill him, as his armour softened the blow, but it did injure him to the extent that he began screaming. He rushed back and the Quraysh tried to assure him that it was a minor wound which would heal, but Ubayy knew that the Prophet's vow was true, so he continued to panic. Indeed, it was true, and he died before they reached Mecca. The Prophet ﷺ once stated, "Allah's Anger is intensified against anyone whom the Messenger of Allah kills in the path of Allah."[613]

The Calamity of Hastiness

As the Quraysh fled and victory seemed certain, the Companions began celebrating and collecting the lucrative war booty. The exact rulings of distributing the spoils of war were not codified yet, so some Companions were eagerly and hastily collecting valuables not realising that the spoils will be evenly distributed as ordained by Shariah. Meanwhile, the archers watched from above as the spoils were being collected while they waited for their instruction. Up to an hour had passed while they waited for a messenger, and Shayṭān began to instil in them feelings of neglect and impatience. They began to dispute with one another as to their next steps. ʿAbdullāh ibn Jubayr ؓ rebuked the impatient amongst them, "Have you forgotten what the Messenger of Allah instructed?!"[614]

Slowly but surely, the dissenting voices increased, and eventually, 40 archers decided to leave their post, leaving 10 steadfast Companions. Allah ﷻ references this exchange, "Indeed, Allah fulfilled His promise to you when you swept them away by His Will, then your courage weakened and you disputed about the command and disobeyed, after Allah had brought victory within your reach. Some of you were after worldly gain while others desired a Heavenly reward. He denied you victory over them as a test, yet He has pardoned you. And Allah is Gracious to the believers."[615]

Meanwhile, Khālid ibn al-Walīd, a young strategist amongst Abū Sufyān's commanders, continued to scope the area for ideas, even as he retreated. He immediately capitalised on the archers' retreat and pounced, implementing a pincer movement—a military manoeuvre in which forces simultaneously attack both flanks of an enemy formation. Within the blink of an eye, the Muslims found themselves divided into two sections with a formidable foe between them. They lost their advantage, which was their density in numbers, and to add insult to injury, many of them did not have weapons or armour, as they were already collecting the war booty with both hands. The situation was ripe for Khālid to deal a fatal blow, and the Muslims began to panic. Some people began to flee, to which the Prophet ﷺ yelled, "Come to me, O servants of Allah! Come to me, O servants of Allah!"[616] Selflessly, the Prophet exposed his own location to warn the Companions of the surprise attack. Allah ﷻ references this too, "[Remember] when you were running far away—not looking at anyone—while the Messenger was calling you from behind. So Allah recompensed your disobedience with distress upon distress. Now, do not grieve over the victory you were denied or the injury you suffered. And Allah is All-Aware of what you do."[617]

Khālid's surprise attack led to complete disarray and the tables quickly turned. As the Muslims turned around and returned fire, it led to the unfortunate events of Muslims dying at the hands of other Muslims within the chaos of war. The most tragic of these deaths was Ḥusayl ibn Jābir al-Yamān, the father of Ḥudhayfah ibn al-Yamān. He was so old that the Prophet ﷺ exempted him from fighting in Uḥud, but as he and his companion were in Medina alongside the women and children, their dignity could not tolerate it. He said, "How long do we have left to live? Let us go and take our swords to join the Messenger of Allah. Perhaps Allah will bless us with martyrdom."[618]

When they eventually arrived at Uḥud, chaos had already ensued, and Khālid was wreaking havoc. It was narrated that Shayṭān himself cried out, "O Muslims, behind you!"[619] Not recognising al-Yamān, the Muslims charged. Ḥudhayfah screamed out, "Stop! That is my father!" But to no avail, as he could not be heard amidst the commotion of war. After the battle, the Muslims that charged asked Ḥudhayfah for forgiveness for their mistake, to which he responded with the words of Prophet Yūsuf ﷺ, "'May Allah forgive you, He is the Most Merciful of the merciful.'"[620] The Prophet ﷺ then paid Ḥudhayfah ؓ blood money from the government treasury, as it was a communal responsibility. Ḥudhayfah ؓ distributed the money amongst the poor of Medina, and Allah blessed him for the rest of his life.

Muṣʿab ibn ʿUmayr ؓ was another lamentable casualty. He was amongst the most honoured Companions and he held a dear place in the heart of the Prophet ﷺ. In Jāhiliyyah, he was famous for being the most spoilt youth of the Quraysh, wearing new garments every single day and being doted on by his mother to no end. After he accepted Islam, he was equally famous for persevering in brutal torture. The same parents that spoiled him in Jāhiliyyah heartlessly tortured him in Islam. He then became a formidable preacher in Islam, contributing to the conversion of almost every tribe in Medina. He held the Muslim flag in Uḥud valiantly until his right arm was severed, so he took the flag with his left hand until his left arm was severed, then he held the flag between his stumps until he died. He left this world with no possessions except the one garment that he was wearing, which was not even long enough to cover his whole body upon burial.

Ḥanẓalah ؓ was also martyred at Uḥud, and he was famously described as being washed by the Angels. The Prophet ﷺ described how he saw Ḥanẓalah's body being raised and washed by the Angels even though martyrs are not ordinarily washed. He was a newlywed, and on the morning of the battle he was intimate with his wife and did not have any time to bathe before leaving for battle. The Angels then performed *ghusl* as they raised him to the Heavens.

"Master of the Martyrs"

The foremost calamity of Uḥud was the death of the uncle of the Prophet ﷺ, the ferocious warrior, Ḥamzah ibn ʿAbd al-Muṭṭalib ؓ. In the Battle of Badr, Ḥamzah was devastating, as he was in every battle, and one of his victims was Ṭuʿaymah ibn ʿAdiyy, brother of the famous Muṭʿim ibn ʿAdiyy and uncle of Jubayr ibn Muṭʿim. Jubayr, who was not yet Muslim, was deeply aggrieved by the loss of his uncle and was determined to seek revenge. He offered his servant, Waḥshī, his freedom if he killed Ḥamzah ؓ.[621] Hind, the wife of Abū Sufyān, was also enraged, as Ḥamzah killed her father in Badr. She promised Waḥshī many gold coins and jewellery to get the job done.[622] Waḥshī was uninterested in tribal politics or even religious wars, but he was so desperate to gain his long-awaited freedom that he had a singular mission in the Battle of Uḥud to find and kill Ḥamzah ؓ.

Waḥshī narrated this event himself. Decades later, two Successors (Tābiʿūn) from Iraq travelled to visit Waḥshī in his old age to hear the story first-hand. Despite his old age and partial blindness, Waḥshī looked towards the young man's feet and said, "Are you So-and-so, son of So-and-so?" The Successor replied in the affirmative, and Waḥshī said, "I played with your feet in Mecca when you were a baby." The Successors then asked to hear the story and Waḥshī said, "I will tell you verbatim as I told the Prophet ﷺ." Waḥshī then went on to describe the events, "I had no desire to participate in the war but my master, Jubayr, had promised my freedom if I killed Ḥamzah. I took my best spear, and I had no desire to harm anyone except Ḥamzah to gain my freedom. I began following Ḥamzah and edged closer. As soon as he killed So-and-so and his sword was lowered, I stepped out from behind a bush and threw my spear with all my force, so much so that it entered his back and half of it came out from the front. Ḥamzah still turned around to fight me but died before he could swing his sword."[623]

Waḥshī, who later accepted Islam, was mitigating his actions by reiterating that he had no ill will towards the Muslim but was yearning for his freedom. Of course, being attacked from behind is the only way Ḥamzah could have died, as he was successful in every single fight he experienced throughout his life. Ḥamzah was wearing chained armour, but Waḥshī was the best thrower in Arabia, and his precision was such that the spear penetrated Ḥamzah's skin between the individual rings.

After the Conquest of Mecca, Waḥshī fled to Ṭā'if, as he knew how beloved Ḥamzah 🕮 was to the Prophet 🕮. He simply could not envisage ever being forgiven. The following year, Ṭā'if was also liberated, and Waḥshī described how his dread was so severe that he felt the whole world would collapse on him. Eventually, someone said, "Woe to you O Waḥshī, don't you know that this man (i.e., the Prophet 🕮) does not kill anyone from his religion?" Waḥshī decided to accept Islam to preserve his life. He surreptitiously travelled to Medina and did not uncover his face until he was besides the Prophet 🕮 and quickly declared, "I bear witness that there is no god but Allah, and I bear witness that Muhammad is His Messenger." The Prophet 🕮 said, "Is that you, O Waḥshī? Come and tell me how you killed Ḥamzah." Waḥshī described the events until the Prophet 🕮 was crying so much that his beard was soaked. He 🕮 then said, "Hide yourself from me—let me not see your face." [624]

Waḥshī then spent the remainder of his life avoiding the Prophet 🕮, as instructed, and that deprivation of his blessed company was sufficient a worldly punishment. It is also reported that Waḥshī was afflicted with alcoholism, even as he grew older. Under the Caliphate of ʿUmar 🕮 he was lashed numerous times for drinking, and ʿUmar 🕮 lamented, "By Allah, I knew that Allah would not leave the killer of Ḥamzah untouched (i.e., without suffering worldly afflictions)." [625] That being said, Waḥshī repented and managed to atone to an extent. He said, "When the Muslims marched to fight Musaylamah the Liar[ii], I made duʿā' to Allah 🕮 to allow me to kill Musaylamah to atone for [killing] Ḥamzah.

---

ii   Musaylamah the Liar was a false prophet who declared his "prophethood" even in the lifetime of Prophet Muhammad 🕮, who sternly rejected him. Following the death of the Prophet 🕮, he led a rebellion against the Caliphate of Abū Bakr 🕮 termed the "Apostasy Wars" and was eventually killed by Waḥshī 🕮.

I took the same spear with which I killed Ḥamzah, and I struck him just as an Anṣārī wounded him from the other side. Your Lord knows who actually killed him, but if I was the one who dealt the fatal blow, then I have killed the worst of people as I have killed the best of people after the Messenger of Allah (i.e., Ḥamzah)."[626]

Injuring The Messenger of Allah ﷺ

After the Muslims dispersed, the Prophet ﷺ was surrounded by nine Companions: Saʿd ibn Abī Waqqāṣ, Ṭalḥah ibn ʿUbaydillāh, and seven of the Anṣār. They realised that ten people could not withstand the imminent attack, so they fled together up the mountains. They utilised their home advantage, as they were well acquainted with the surrounding mountainous terrains, while the Meccan opposition were not. They sought refuge in a small crevice within a mountain, and as a group of the enemy were nearing, the Prophet ﷺ asked his Companions, "Who will take on these people and will be my Companion in Paradise?" Ṭalḥah immediately offered himself, but the Prophet ﷺ instructed him to remain beside him. An Anṣārī then offered and the Prophet ﷺ allowed him to go forth. The Anṣārī was martyred and another volunteered, and this continued until only the Prophet ﷺ alongside Ṭalḥah and Saʿd remained.

Qatādah ibn al-Nuʿmān al-Awsī narrated that the Prophet ﷺ handed him a bow to use. He used the bow so much that it lost its flexibility, so he used his body to shield the Prophet ﷺ from oncoming arrows. He then said, "I saw an arrow that I could not stop except with my face, so I blocked the Prophet ﷺ with my face and the arrow hit my eye." When the Prophet ﷺ saw this, he began to cry and said, "O Allah, Qatādah has protected your Prophet with his face, so let his eye become the most precise eye."[627] The Prophet ﷺ took the arrow out and Qatādah swore that it instantaneously healed, so much so that it became more precise than his other eye.

Ṭalḥah and Saʿd were expert archers, so they continued to thwart off attacks. As the Prophet ﷺ would look out to try and assess, Ṭalḥah would say, "My chest instead of your chest, O Messenger of Allah." The Prophet ﷺ handed arrows to Sa'd, saying, "May my mother and father be ransomed for you. Fire away, O Sa'd!"[628] The phrase "May my mother and father be ransomed for you" is the highest expression of respect in classical Arabic, meaning, "I would sacrifice my own parents for you." The Companions would frequently address the Prophet ﷺ with this phrase, however this was the first and only time that the Prophet ﷺ ever used the expression to anyone, and Sa'd ؓ would very proudly remember this unique honour.

The situation escalated and the Prophet ﷺ was injured. First, a rock hit the Prophet ﷺ in the face, causing his lip to bleed. Then an arrow hit him ﷺ in his face, penetrating his face guard and knocking out an incisor tooth. Finally, a rider struck the Prophet ﷺ with his sword; Ṭalḥah ؓ partially blocked the strike with his shield, but the sword still made impact on the Prophet's helmet, the force of which formed a gash in the Prophet's face ﷺ which caused blood to gush out. This was perhaps the most critical moment in the entire *sīrah*. The Prophet ﷺ described Ṭā'if as the most distressing event of his life, but that was emotional trauma; the people of Ṭā'if did not try to kill him ﷺ. As for this moment, the Prophet ﷺ was an arrow away from death.

The Prophet ﷺ then bemoaned, "How can Allah forgive them when they wound their Prophet?"[629] Later, Allah ﷻ corrected this statement, "You have no say in the matter. It is up to Allah to turn to them in Mercy or punish them, for indeed they are wrongdoers."[630] Despite being the best of all creation, Allah ﷻ is the only One Who decides who can be forgiven; the Prophet ﷺ may call them wrongdoers, but forgiveness and punishment is in the Hands of the Creator. After this verse was revealed, the Prophet ﷺ said, "O Allah, forgive my people for they do not know."[631] Indeed, many of them were forgiven, namely Khālid ibn al-Walīd ؓ, who led the entire attack but was to eventually become known as "The Sword of Allah"[632] for leading the Muslims to unprecedented military success.

Rumours spread that the Prophet ﷺ was killed, and the Quraysh began to celebrate. Ironically, it perhaps saved the Prophet ﷺ, as the Quraysh began to withdraw after they thought that they killed the Messenger of Allah ﷺ. Some Muslims were in disarray; some walked around aimlessly, and others slumped to the ground. Anas ibn al-Naḍr, the uncle of Anas ibn Mālik ؓ, passed by a group of disillusioned Muslims, berating them for not fighting. They replied, "Haven't you heard? The Prophet ﷺ has been killed." He responded, "Even if the Prophet ﷺ has been killed, the Lord of the Prophet has not been killed. Besides, what will you do with your life after the death of the Prophet? Let us go and die as he died." [633]

Anas marched forth towards the enemy and turned to his friend, Saʿd ibn Muʿādh ؓ, and said, "O Saʿd, I can smell Paradise from behind that mountain." He then walked forward and said, "O Allah, I ask forgiveness for what these men (i.e., the Muslims failing to protect the Prophet ﷺ) have done, and I disassociate from what they (i.e., the Quraysh) have done." [634] He then threw himself into the battle and killed as many of the enemy as he could. Eventually, the Muslims found a body with over 80 wounds from head to toe, and they could not identify the body until Anas's sister recognised him from his fingertips. Allah ﷻ then revealed about him, "Among the believers are men who have proven true to what they pledged to Allah. Some of them have fulfilled their pledge [with their lives], and others are waiting [their turn]. They never changed in the least." [635]

The battle eventually ended, and the Muslims began regrouping. Kaʿb ibn Mālik ؓ was the first to notice the Prophet ﷺ, and he screamed, "O Muslims! Rejoice! The Prophet ﷺ is alive!" The arrow and piece of metal were both still stuck inside the Prophet's face, and as Abū Bakr ؓ went to remove them, Abū ʿUbaydah ibn al-Jarrāḥ ؓ begged Abū Bakr to allow him the honour. He kept begging him until Abū Bakr, soft-hearted as he was, relented. The piece of metal was lodged so deeply in the Prophet's face that it could not be pulled out with one's fingers, so Abū ʿUbaydah then bit down to dislodge it, and he bit so hard that his own tooth fell out in the process. He then repeated the action with the second piece of metal and lost another tooth. [636] Abū ʿUbaydah ؓ would smile proudly knowing that his teeth were sacrificed for the Prophet ﷺ.

The Quraysh still believed that the Prophet ﷺ had died, so Abū Sufyān was seen from a distance standing on one of the mountains of Uḥud. He yelled at the top of his voice, "Is Muhammad alive?" The Prophet ﷺ instructed the Companions, "Do not answer him." He asked again but was met with silence. He then asked, "Is the son of Abū Quḥāfah (i.e., Abū Bakr) alive?" The Prophet ﷺ instructed them not to answer. He then asked, "Is the son of al-Khaṭṭāb (i.e., ʿUmar) alive?" The Prophet ﷺ instructed them not to answer. Note that even Abū Sufyān—leader of the enemy—recognised that Abū Bakr and ʿUmar ﷺ were the Prophet's closest confidants and were first and second in command.

Abū Sufyān then began boasting, "We have killed all of them!" ʿUmar could no longer contain himself and retorted, "You have lied, O enemy of Allah! Indeed, Allah has caused all of them to live, and they will remain to harm you at another date!" Successful in his bait, Abū Sufyān responded, "Today was in response to Badr, and war alternates." He continued, "You shall find amongst the dead mutilated bodies. I did not command this, but I am not angry about it either." ʿUmar responded, "[Badr and Uḥud] are not the same. Our dead are in Paradise and your dead are in Hellfire." Abū Sufyān then yelled, "Hubal be honoured!" The Prophet ﷺ then ordered ʿUmar to respond. ʿUmar asked how to respond, and the Prophet ﷺ instructed, "Allah is Greater and Mightier!" Abū Sufyān again retorted, "We have al-ʿUzzā (the idol) and you have no *ʿuzzā* (honour)." The Prophet ﷺ again instructed ʿUmar to respond, "Allah is our Protector, and you have no protector!"[637] Ibn al-Qayyim ﷺ aptly notes that the Prophet ﷺ instructed the Companions not to respond when they were being insulted, but as soon as Allah ﷻ was insulted and polytheism was being venerated, he ﷺ ordered them to respond. As always, the Prophet ﷺ prioritised the religion of Allah over himself.

The Aftermath

The Prophet ﷺ surveyed the dead as he walked around the field. When he saw Ḥamzah ﷺ he sobbed as he gazed upon his mutilated body.

Hind, Abū Sufyān's wife, brutally cut off his nose and removed his fingers and made a necklace out of them, and there are even reports that she opened up his stomach and took a bite out of his liver as a disgusting show of contempt.[638] The Prophet ﷺ grew so enraged that he proclaimed, "If I catch them, I will show them vengeance." He also said, "I am going to do this to 30 of them because of what they did to Ḥamzah."[639] Allah ﷻ then revealed, "If you retaliate, then let it be equivalent to what you have suffered. But if you patiently endure, it is certainly best for those who are patient."[640] The Prophet ﷺ then announced that mutilation was forbidden in Islam in all circumstances.

The Muslims began burying the dead, and the Prophet ﷺ ordered that those who memorised the most Qur'an be buried first."[641] Indeed, the Qur'an honours its carriers in this life and the next. Allah ﷻ states, "It will debase [some] and elevate [others].[642] The Prophet ﷺ then gave an encouraging reminder to the believers wherein he said, "I will testify for every one of them on the Day of Judgement." The Prophet ﷺ then made *duʿā'* for the martyrs, which has led to some misinterpretations that he ﷺ prayed the funeral prayer (*janāzah*). This is a misunderstanding; as previously stated, there is no funeral prayer for the martyr. He ﷺ praised Allah ﷻ, reminded the believers that everything happens by the will of Allah, asked for security on the Day of Judgement, and asked Allah ﷻ to allow everyone among them to die in the state of *īmān*.[643]

At least 70 Muslims died, most of whom were from the Anṣār.[644] 22 of the Quraysh were killed, and there were no prisoners of war except for one man by the name of Abū ʿAzzah al-Jumaḥī. He was executed on the battlefield due to the treacherous nature of his presence. Abū ʿAzzah was captured at Badr and his ransom was 4,000 dirhams. He begged the Prophet ﷺ to release him, citing that he had no sons and no means of paying the ransom. The Prophet ﷺ was soft-hearted and released him for free on the condition that he never fights the Muslims again. He agreed, but when preparations for Uḥud began, Abū Sufyān persuaded him to join, offering him riches in victory or defeat. If they won, he was offered substantial war booty, and if they lost and he died, Abū Sufyān offered to sponsor his daughters and treat them as his own.

Abū ʿAzzah, unable to resist the offer, betrayed his promise. Allah ﷻ in turn humiliated him by making him the only person amongst 3,000 combatants to be captured and executed.

The Prophet ﷺ then personally visited the families of the dead, especially those who did not have extended family and needed the most consolation. He visited Ḥamnah bint Jaḥsh ؓ, the wife of Muṣʿab ibn ʿUmayr ؓ. The Prophet ﷺ said, "Condolences." She replied, "Who [died]?" The Prophet ﷺ replied, "Your brother." She then said, "To Allah we belong, and to Him we shall return. May Allah accept his martyrdom and forgive him." And she continued making *duʿāʾ* for him. The Prophet ﷺ then said, "Condolences." And she again replied, "Who?" The Prophet ﷺ replied, "Muṣʿab." And she let out the loudest scream, for she could not handle the loss. The Prophet ﷺ later said, "Truly, the husband has a station in the eyes of the wife that no-one else has."[645]

There was also a female Companion whose entire family had been martyred, but she also heard that the Prophet ﷺ died. She grew agitated as she waited for the Muslims to return. When they informed her that her father died, she replied, "And how is the Messenger of Allah?" When they informed her that her brother died, she replied, "And how is the Messenger of Allah?" When they informed her that her husband died, she replied, "And how is the Messenger of Allah?" Finally, when she saw the Prophet ﷺ alive, she said in relief, "May my father and mother be sacrificed for you, O Messenger of Allah! Any calamity after you is bearable."[646]

Silver Linings

Uḥud was widely considered a loss, especially when considering the number of Muslim deaths as well as the notable deaths of Ḥamzah, Muṣʿab, and their like. It was indeed a major blow. However, the goal of the Quraysh was to eliminate the Muslims, which they decidedly did not, and the goal of the Muslims was to defend Medina, which they did. Moreover, the Battle of Uḥud provided the Muslims with invaluable lessons.

The Battle of Badr distinguished the Muslims from the Pagans. Allah ﷻ said, "...so Allah may separate the evil from the good."[647] Likewise, the Battle of Uḥud distinguished the Muslims from the Hypocrites. Allah ﷻ said, "Allah would not leave the believers in the condition you were in until He distinguished the good from the evil."[648] Until Uḥud, the Muslims greatly underestimated the danger and evil intent of the Hypocrites, as they still viewed them as sincere Muslims. Allah states regarding Badr, "It was Allah's Will to establish the truth by His Words and uproot the disbelievers."[649] Regarding Uḥud, He ﷻ states, "So what you suffered on that day the two armies met was by Allah's Will so that He might distinguish the believers and expose the Hypocrites."[650]

After Uḥud, the Prophet ﷺ had a dream and narrated it to the Companions, "I saw a dream where I struck with my sword, but my sword broke. And this is what afflicted the Muslims at Uḥud. Then I hit it again and it reformed as strong as it ever was, and this was the victory Allah gave to the Muslims and the coming together of the believers."[651] The mentality of the Muslims at Badr was worlds apart from the mentality of some of the Muslims at Uḥud, and the consequences were made clear. The overarching symbolisms of the consequences of Uḥud are twofold: first, those who compromise the Hereafter for the this life enjoy neither; and second, disobeying Allah and His Messenger never yields success.

The Prophet's Marriage to Umm Salamah رضي الله عنها

Hind bint Ḥudhayfah ibn al-Mughīrah, famously known as Umm Salamah رضي الله عنها, was of the first people to emigrate to Abyssinia. She, alongside her husband Abū Salamah رضي الله عنه, also emigrated to Medina, and they were known as "The People of Two Emigrations". Abū Salamah suffered a serious injury in the Battle of Uḥud, dying from his wounds six months later in Jumādā al-Ākhirah 4 AH. Umm Salamah was thus widowed with four children. As a noblewoman with prestigious lineage, she was extremely sought after for marriage. The culture of the time desired noble lineage in a partner just as much as modern society desires beauty and wealth. Abū Bakr al-Ṣiddīq رضي الله عنه, ʿUmar al-Fārūq رضي الله عنه,

and many more Companions all proposed but she rejected them all, as she held Abū Salamah in such high regard that she did not think anyone could compete.

Eventually, the Prophet ﷺ himself proposed, and in the rarest of events, she did not immediately accept his proposal. She replied, "O Messenger of Allah, I have three issues: I am a jealous woman; I am no longer young; and I have children." The Prophet ﷺ responded beautifully, "As for your jealousy, I will make *du'ā'* to Allah to remove it for you; as for your age, then I am suffering from the same ailment; and as for your family, then they will be my family."[652]

Abū Salamah once narrated to Umm Salamah that the Prophet ﷺ said, "Whenever a person is afflicted with a calamity and makes the following *du'ā'*, Allah ﷻ will replace it with something better, 'To Allah we belong and to Him we shall return. O Allah, recompense me [for my patience] in my calamity and replace it with that which is better.'"[653] When Abū Salamah ؓ died, the first thing Umm Salamah uttered was the above *du'ā'*. She later recalled, "When I made the *du'ā'*, I said to myself: who can be better than Abū Salamah? Then Allah ﷻ did grant me someone better."[654]

External and Internal Threats 17

Following Uḥud, the Muslims suffered further back-to-back blows in the form of treacherous massacres and dissent from within. The setback of Uḥud led to some Bedouin tribes around Medina feeling greedy, wanting to capitalise on the Ummah's moment of weakness.

The Massacre of Bi'r Maʿūnah (The Well of Maʿūnah)

A famous Chieftain of the Najd (northern Arabia), Abū al-Barā' ʿĀmir ibn Mālik, visited Medina, and the Prophet ﷺ made great effort to give him *daʿwah*. The province of Najd was a far greater area in land mass than Mecca and Medina combined, and although most of its inhabitants were Bedouins, they were also greater in number. Abū al-Barā' was very impressed with the Prophet ﷺ and the Message of Islam but was hesitant to convert. He requested time to consider the proposition but encouraged the Prophet ﷺ to send a delegation to the Najd to preach Islam, guaranteeing their protection. This was a vital opportunity to spread Islam, so the Prophet ﷺ chose 70 learned Companions, most of whom were Ahl al-Ṣuffah, to give *daʿwah*. This was the biggest number of delegates the Prophet ﷺ ever sent, and choosing the cream of the crop of Ahl al-Ṣuffah was a clear statement of intent.

When they arrived at Bi'r Maʿūnah they sent a letter to a local Chieftain by the name of ʿĀmir ibn Ṭufayl. The Prophet ﷺ previously gave *daʿwah* to ʿĀmir ibn Ṭufayl but he only offered to convert in exchange for worldly benefit; his condition was that he control the Bedouin areas while the Prophet ﷺ controls the cities. Alternatively, he would consider accepting Islam if he were chosen as the Prophet's successor after his death. The Prophet ﷺ of course declined both offers, as Islam only ever promises its followers riches in the Hereafter. ʿĀmir ibn Ṭufayl then grew in arrogance and animosity towards Islam and used this opportunity to exact his revenge.

The group of Companions sent Ḥarām ibn Milḥān ؓ to deliver the letter, and when ʿĀmir ibn Ṭufayl realised who he was, he signalled to his guard to immediately execute him. The reprehensibility of this act cannot be understated—not only is killing messengers universally condemned in every society across the world, but Ḥarām ibn Milḥān was explicitly granted amnesty according to tribal law. The guard stabbed Ḥarām ibn Milḥān ؓ through his back with his spear, exiting through his chest. In his last waking moment, Ḥarām ؓ exclaimed, "I won, by the Lord of the Kaʿbah!"[655] He died instantly. One of the guards was so astonished by Ḥarām's delight at facing martyrdom that he began enquiring about Islam and later became a Muslim.

ʿĀmir ibn Ṭufayl acted quickly, sending messages to nearby tribes suggesting that they join forces and kill the remaining 69 delegates. Most of the Chieftains refused because Abū al-Barā' gave the Muslims his protection, and contravening tribal law was a grave offence. Eventually, three subtribes agreed: ʿAṣiyyah, Ruʿl, and Dhakwān.[656] At least 400–500 of them marched to Bi'r Maʿūnah and surrounded the Companions. Vastly outnumbered, unarmed, and unprepared for battle, the Companions ؓ were all slaughtered except for three. Kaʿb ibn Zayd ؓ was injured and trapped under the pile of bodies. He was assumed dead but eventually escaped. The two remaining survivors were ʿAmr ibn Umayyah and al-Mundhir ibn Muhammad ؓ, who had left to run an errand shortly before the massacre. As they returned, they saw vultures in the air circling, and they knew that their companions had been killed. ʿAmr suggested that they return to the Prophet ﷺ and inform him of what happened, but al-Mundhir responded, "As for me, I will not be reduced to a messenger that lives to tell their story."[657] They agreed to march back in and were eventually captured. As per their initial intentions, al-Mundhir was killed and ʿAmr was held hostage, perhaps to send a message to the Prophet ﷺ.

As ʿAmr returned to Medina, he met two people from the tribe of ʿĀmir ibn Ṭufayl. Unbeknownst to him, they had been given protection from the Prophet ﷺ, and they had no knowledge of the massacre that had just occurred. ʿAmr killed them both, assuming them to be complicit in the crime. He then found a letter of protection from the Prophet ﷺ in their belongings and grew extremely anxious. He returned to Medina and informed the Prophet ﷺ of the massacre as well as his mistaken judgement in killing the two tribesmen.[658] The Prophet ﷺ then paid the blood money to the families of the two men from the public treasury, as they were protected by his word.

The Massacre of al-Rajīʿ

On the very same day, the Prophet ﷺ was brought news of the massacre of al-Rajīʿ. The tribe of Hudhayl orchestrated a plot to kill a group of Muslims. They paid the tribes of ʿAḍal and al-Qārrah to pretend to accept Islam and then beg the Prophet ﷺ to send as many Companions as he could to teach them about Islam. Ten learned Companions volunteered and travelled under the leadership of ʿĀṣim ibn Thābit ﷺ. As they reached the well of al-Rajīʿ, 100 people ambushed them. The Companions took shelter in a nearby hill and began launching arrows from afar. However, as they were vastly outnumbered, they were killed.

In the Battle of Uḥud, ʿĀṣim ibn Thābit ﷺ killed the husband of a lady named Sulāfah. In her extreme resentment, she offered 100 camels to anyone who would retrieve ʿĀṣim's head so she may drink wine out of his skull. ʿĀṣim ﷺ knew there was animosity and that he would be tortured if captured, so he committed to fight to the death. He then made *duʿā'*, "O Allah, inform our Prophet that we were sincere."[659] He continued, "O Allah, as I protected your religion in the day, protect my body at night."[660] He fought with bow and arrow until he ran out of arrows, then he fought with his sword until his sword broke, and he was killed after fighting a brave fight. After the battle ended, everyone rushed to retrieve his body to claim the reward until suddenly a giant swarm of wasps surrounded his body and stung anyone who approached. They waited until sunset, but as soon as the wasps left, a river suddenly appeared—despite there being no rain—and swept his body away. Allah certainly answered his *duʿā*.

Three out of the ten Companions survived the onslaught: Khubayb, Zayd, and ʿAbdullāh ibn Ṭāriq ﷺ. The attackers urged them to surrender, promising their safety, but as soon as they did, they captured and shackled them. ʿAbdullāh ibn Ṭāriq ﷺ refused to comply with any of their commands and was killed on the spot. Khubayb ﷺ was sold to the Banū Ḥārith because he killed one of their tribesmen in the Battle of Badr, and they wanted to exact revenge. Likewise, Zayd ﷺ was sold to Ṣafwān ibn Umayyah because Zayd helped kill his father, Umayyah ibn Khalaf.

Khubayb was informed that he was to be executed, and his final request was for a blade and some water so that he may shave his pubic hair and bathe in order to meet Allah ﷻ in a state of purity. As he was sitting with the blade in his hand, a baby crawled towards him. The baby's mother began to scream, as she was scared that Khubayb would kill him. Facing certain death and with nothing to lose, she assumed he may snatch the baby as ploy to escape. Disgusted by the insinuation, Khubayb ﷺ said, "Are you scared that I would kill this child? By Allah I would never do such a thing." The same mother later remarked, "I have never seen a prisoner nobler or more well-mannered than him." Before his execution, he asked to pray two units of prayer. Upon completion, he said, "By Allah, were it not for the fact that you'd think I was being cowardly, I would have lengthened my prayer."[661] Khubayb had the honour of initiating the Sunnah of praying two units of prayer before execution. It was his own *ijtihād* (independent judgement), but the Prophet ﷺ later approved, and it became a Sunnah.

As for Zayd ﷺ, he was paraded around Mecca and the entire city joined in torturing and abusing him. Moments before his execution, Abū Sufyān said, "I ask you by Allah to answer honestly, don't you wish that Muhammad was in your place, and you were with your family and children?" Zayd, with nothing to gain by lying, replied unwaveringly, "By Allah, I would rather die like this than the Messenger of Allah ﷺ be pricked by a thorn."[662] Abū Sufyān later said, "I have never seen a leader more beloved to his people than Muhammad is to his Companions."[663]

Both these devastating events were conveyed to the Prophet ﷺ on the same day. 70 deaths in a single event outside battle constituted an unprecedented massacre, and being informed of 80 deaths in the same day was deeply hurtful to the Prophet ﷺ. He prayed every single prayer for an entire month with *qunūt al-nāzilah*[i]. He ﷺ made specific *duʿā'* for the martyrs of both massacres and asked Allah ﷻ to deal with the treacherous perpetrators. ʿĀmir ibn Ṭufayl eventually died a slow, painful death after he contracted leprosy. His tribe and family abandoned him due to his illness and he died alone and in pain.

These events demonstrate that sacrifice and loss are an inherent part of Islam, as sacrificing in this life is inextricably linked to reward in the Hereafter. The Prophet ﷺ once said, "If Allah wills good for a person, He afflicts them with trials."[664] Most of the martyred were from Ahl al-Ṣuffah, and they were known for their devotion to the Qur'an and the night prayer (*tahajjud*). While these devastating events were a loss for the Ummah, they were a victory for the martyrs.

The Expulsion of the Banū Naḍīr

The blood money of the two protected tribesmen of the Banū ʿĀmir ibn Ṭufayl was paid from the public treasury. Ordinarily, the perpetrator

i *Qunūt* is an optional component of the prayer whereby one remains standing in the last unit of the prayer before prostrating in order to make *duʿā'*. In times of dire need, the Prophet ﷺ utilised a form of the *qunūt* prayer known specifically as *qunūt al-nāzilah*—"standing [in times] of catastrophe".

of murder pays the entirety of the blood money, but in the case of involuntary manslaughter (i.e., accidentally killing someone), the blood money is distributed amongst the entire tribe. The Prophet ﷺ then collected blood money from every tribe. He ﷺ did so from the Muslim tribes and then headed to the Jewish tribes.

Tensions were already brewing between the Muslims and the Banū Naḍīr, as discussed; the Banū Naḍīr were complicit in assisting the Quraysh's plots against the Muslims on a number of occasions, and their provocation and aggravation of the Prophet ﷺ and Muslims led to a few tense moments. The killing of Kaʿb ibn al-Ashraf further heightened the tensions, and the relationship between the two groups was very fragile.

Nevertheless, the Prophet ﷺ personally walked to the Banū Naḍīr alongside Abū Bakr and ʿUmar ﷻ. They arrived at the gate of their fortresses and were received with smiles and hospitality. The Banū Naḍīr requested that the Prophet ﷺ wait outside while they prepare, but after deliberating, they decided to kill the Prophet ﷺ by throwing a boulder off the wall directly onto him ﷺ. This was a common method of defending fortresses, and so the boulder was already in place. As the Muslims waited, unaware of their imminent danger, the Prophet ﷺ suddenly stood up and walked back to Medina without uttering a word. The Muslims did not understand why, but upon arriving in Medina the Prophet ﷺ told them that Jibrīl ﷺ had informed him of the imminent danger and instructed him to leave urgently. Years later, Allah ﷻ revealed, "O believers! Remember Allah's favour upon you: when a people sought to harm you, but He held their hands back from you. Be mindful of Allah. And in Allah let the believers put their trust."[665]

The Prophet ﷺ then sent a messenger back to the Banū Naḍīr explaining in detail their own plot and that the Prophet ﷺ was aware of their intentions. He ﷺ informed them that they have ten days to leave Medina, and whoever remains will be executed. The Banū Naḍīr were shocked at the Prophet's knowledge of their plan, and they were not able to retort. They tried to bargain with the messenger,

Muhammad ibn Maslamah ﷺ, who was their ally in Jāhiliyyah, but Muhammad ibn Maslamah explained that the advent of Islam changed his allegiance to Allah and His Messenger.

News spread in Medina, and ʿAbdullāh ibn Ubayy ibn Salūl was incensed. He sent the Banū Naḍīr a letter with the utmost support. He exclaimed in no uncertain terms that they will not leave Medina under any circumstance; he will take care of them and guarantee their protection; he will not obey anyone that expels them; he will fight with them with the support of external allies; and if all else fails, he will exile himself in a show of unity.[666] Allah ﷻ rejected his claims, "Have you not seen the Hypocrites who say to their fellow disbelievers from the People of the Book, 'If you are expelled, we will certainly leave with you, and we will never obey anyone against you, and if you are fought against, we will surely help you.'? But Allah bears witness that they are truly liars. Indeed, if they are expelled, they will never leave with them. And if they are fought against, they will never help them. And even if they did, they would certainly flee, then they (i.e., the disbelievers) would be left with no help."[667] The Banū Naḍīr of course did not follow the Qur'an and thus did not take heed.

Ḥuyayy ibn Akhṭab, a Chieftain from the Banū Naḍīr, took a stand. Most of the Jewish subtribes wanted to leave, but after ʿAbdullāh ibn Ubayy's show of support, Ḥuyayy ibn Akhṭab rallied them up and convinced them to remain and stand their ground. They were eventually convinced and sent a messenger back to the Prophet ﷺ, "We will not leave, so do as you please."[668] The Prophet ﷺ simply declared, "*Allāhu Akbar*! (God is the Greatest!)" Within hours, the Muslims mobilised and marched towards the Banū Naḍīr, armed to the hilt. The Banū Naḍīr locked themselves in their fortresses and waited for support from ʿAbdullāh ibn Ubayy and his external backing, but nothing came. ʿAbdullāh ibn Ubayy did not lift a finger, nor did he call for any support—just as Allah ﷻ proclaimed.

The Prophet ﷺ then took most of the Muslim army and marched towards the Banū Qurayẓah—the third and final Jewish tribe in Medina—to renew their pledge to the Treaty of Medina. The Prophet ﷺ gave them the choice of opting out, but if they were to stick to the treaty, there must be no betrayal. The Banū Qurayẓah retook their oaths, reaffirming their allegiance, and the Prophet ﷺ marched back to the Banū Naḍīr once more. Days passed and the Banū Naḍīr were still surrounded. The Prophet ﷺ then began burning down the date palm farms, which were an invaluable asset. Some of the Companions wondered if it were the right thing to do because they would inherit these valuable fields, but Allah ﷻ revealed, "Whatever date palm trees you cut down or left standing intact, it was [all] by Allah's Will, so that He might disgrace the rebellious."[669]

The Banū Naḍīr could not withstand any longer, and after seven to ten days they unconditionally surrendered. Despite their Chieftains attempting to assassinate the Prophet ﷺ, their lives were spared, and they could take as much wealth as their camels could carry. A handful of them converted to Islam and remained in their abodes, but the majority of them destroyed their own houses in spite and left with as much as they could.

As for the fields, Allah ﷻ said, "As for gains granted by Allah to His Messenger from the people of [other lands], they are for Allah and the Messenger, his close relatives, orphans, the poor, and [needy] travellers, so that wealth may not merely circulate among your rich."[670] This is one of the most explicit verses pertaining to Islamic finance, and the Islamic ethos of finance is clearly underpinned by the distribution of wealth amongst society. Allah ﷻ continued, "Whatever the Messenger gives you, take it. And whatever he forbids you from, leave it. And fear Allah. Surely Allah is severe in punishment. [Some of the gains will be] for poor Emigrants who were driven out of their homes and wealth, seeking Allah's bounty and pleasure, and standing up for Allah and His Messenger. They are the ones true in faith."[671] Based on this verse, the Prophet ﷺ distributed much of the land to those who did not have property, most of whom were from the Muhājirūn, and a handful were from the Anṣār.

Before the Anṣār could feel any bitterness or ill-will, Allah ﷻ revealed the next verse with the most lavish praise for the Anṣār, "As for those who had settled in the City and [embraced] the faith before the arrival of the Emigrants, they love whoever emigrates to them, never having a desire in their hearts for whatever is given to the Emigrants. They give them preference over themselves even though they may be in need. And whoever is saved from the selfishness of their own souls, it is they who are truly successful."[672] The Anṣār were overjoyed with this praise, and it sufficed them. The next verse encompassed all Muslims that follow the blessed Companions, "And those who come after them will say, 'Our Lord! Forgive us and our fellow believers who preceded us in faith, and do not allow bitterness into our hearts towards those who believe. Our Lord! Indeed, You are Ever Generous, Most Merciful."[673]

A Beacon of Joy

As a source of light amidst a sea of trials, the Prophet's first grandson, Ḥasan ibn ʿAlī ﷺ, was born. He was born in Shaʿbān 5 AH, and his brother, Ḥusayn ibn ʿAlī ﷺ, was born ten months later.[674] When Ḥasan was born, the Prophet ﷺ said, "Bring me my son!" He then asked for his name, and ʿAlī said, "His name is Ḥarb (War)." The Prophet ﷺ replied, "No, he is not War; he is Beauty (Ḥasan)."[675] Ḥusayn is a variation of Ḥasan, which means "The little Ḥasan". Upon Ḥasan's birth, the Prophet ﷺ gave the *adhān* in his right ear. This practice, as well as most rulings of the *ʿaqīqah*[ii], are narrated from Ḥasan's birth.

The Prophet ﷺ loved Ḥasan and Ḥusayn immeasurably, and there are numerous Hadiths of him displaying his affection. The Prophet ﷺ was once leading the prayer, and one of the two toddlers climbed on his head while he was prostrating. The Prophet ﷺ remained in prostration for a prolonged period so as not to disturb him.[676] In another narration, he ﷺ was giving the Friday Sermon, and when he saw them both walk in with their beautiful red garments, tripping over each other, he could not help himself but to pause the sermon to pick them both up. He then said, "Indeed, what Allah said is true,

ii The rituals pertaining to a newborn, such as sacrificing an animal and giving charity.

'Your wealth and children are a test.'[677]"[678] The Prophet ﷺ also said, "Ḥasan and Ḥusayn are the leaders of the youth in Paradise, and their father is [even] better than them."[679]

The Prophet's Marriage to Zaynab bint Jaḥsh

The Prophet's marriage to Zaynab is one of two[iii] marriages commanded by Allah. Zaynab was initially married to Zayd ibn Ḥārithah after she was sent a proposal by the Prophet ﷺ on Zayd's behalf. She initially thought and hoped it was from the Prophet ﷺ himself, but when she realised it was for Zayd, she was disappointed and refused. She was the Prophet's cousin and a noblewoman whereas Zayd was a freed slave, and she did not believe it was a match. The Prophet ﷺ insisted, and some scholars of Qur'an state that the following verse was revealed about this matter, "It is not for a believing man or woman—when Allah and His Messenger decree a matter—to have any other choice in that matter. Indeed, whoever disobeys Allah and His Messenger has clearly gone astray."[680] Zaynab acquiesced and accepted the Prophet's suggestion.

Unfortunately, the marriage was riddled with conflict from the start, and Zaynab's initial reservations rang true. Eventually, Zayd approached the Prophet ﷺ and expressed his wish to divorce Zaynab. The Prophet ﷺ said, "Keep your wife and fear Allah."[681] Zayd tried to follow the Prophet's instruction, but the relationship continued to deteriorate, and Zayd eventually divorced her. After the divorce was formalised, Allah revealed, "And remember when you said to the one for whom Allah has favoured and you too have favoured (i.e., Zayd), 'Keep your wife and fear Allah' while concealing within yourself what Allah was going to reveal. You were considering the people, whereas Allah was more worthy of your consideration. So when Zayd totally lost interest in [keeping] his wife, We gave her to you in marriage so that there would be no blame on the believers for marrying the ex-wives of their adopted sons after their divorce. And Allah's command is totally binding."[682]

---

iii The other being that of 'Ā'ishah.

Prior to this, the Prophet ﷺ saw Zaynab ؓ one day and some feelings entered his heart. His loyalties, however, remained with Zayd ؓ and when Zayd expressed his desire to divorce Zaynab, the Prophet ﷺ urged him to reconcile. Allah ﷻ then gently reprimanded the Prophet ﷺ for concerning himself with what the people may think rather than what Allah ﷻ thinks i.e., that which is halal. The earliest scholars explain the statement, "...while concealing within yourself what Allah was going to reveal..." as the Prophet's feelings for Zaynab.[683] Some later scholars, however, have argued that it refers to the eventual command that the Prophet ﷺ must marry Zaynab.[684] While the second view is a valid interpretation, the first view is perhaps more in line with the Qur'anic narrative.

As for the statement of Allah ﷻ, "...We gave her to you in marriage...", it is a command from Allah ﷻ and the completion of the marriage contract.[685] The Prophet ﷺ was therefore wed to Zaynab ؓ by Allah ﷻ without a dowry, witnesses, or any other contractual requirement as per the Shariah because it was ordained by Allah ﷻ Himself. ʿĀ'ishah ؓ and Anas ibn Mālik ؓ both stated, "If the Prophet ﷺ were to ever conceal a verse of the Qur'an, it would have been this one."[686] This is because Allah ﷻ references the Prophet's feelings directly and the potential public murmurs, but as a Messenger of God, the Prophet ﷺ was obliged to convey the commands of Allah ﷻ and His Revelation.

The Expedition of Dhāt al-Riqāʿ

The Ghaṭafān were a tribe in northern Arabia comprised of Bedouins that would primarily raid caravans as their main form of sustenance. They wanted to raid Muslim caravans, and the Prophet ﷺ led a group of 700 Companions as a show of strength and self-determination. The Muslims camped outside their land in visual distance for a week or two, but the Ghaṭafān did not engage, and the Muslims returned, successful in their goal.

As they journeyed back home, the Muslims found an area to rest, as was custom during the scorching midday heat. The Prophet ﷺ

took a siesta under the shade of a tree when a lone Bedouin from the Ghaṭafān by the name of Ghawrath sneaked upon the Prophet ﷺ with the intention to assassinate him. As the Companions all slept, Ghawrath took the Prophet's sword, unsheathed it, and waved it in the face of the Prophet ﷺ who then woke up. Ghawrath sneered, "Are you scared of me?" The Prophet ﷺ flatly responded, "No. Why would I be scared of you?" Ghawrath, taken aback, responded, "Are you not scared of me? Who will protect you from me?" The Prophet ﷺ responded, "Allah!" Ghawrath then began to tremble and dropped the sword. The Prophet ﷺ instantly picked it up and stood up, saying, "And who will protect *you* from me?" Ghawrath then pleaded, "Be the better of the two!" The Prophet ﷺ asked, "Do you testify that there is no god but Allah and that I am His Messenger?" Ghawrath replied honestly, "I testify and promise that I will never fight you again." The Prophet ﷺ then forgave Ghawrath and let him go. When Ghawrath reached Ghaṭafān, he said, "I have come from the best of mankind." [687]

Another notable incident en route home from Ghaṭafān is detailed in the Hadith of Jābir ibn ʿAbdillāh ؓ. Imam al-Nawawī ؒ states, "The Hadith of Jābir is replete with numerous benefits." [688] Jābir narrated that he was struggling behind everyone else, as his camel was the oldest and weakest. He was also depressed, as his father had died in the Battle of Uḥud leaving behind seven daughters and a massive debt, which Jābir would inherit. He recalled, "All of my worries were piling on me." He then heard a voice asking, "Who is that in the back?" It was none other than the Prophet's soothing call.

The Prophet ﷺ asked, "Why do I see you so gloomy?" Jābir explained his situation, and the Prophet ﷺ asked if he were married, as he was a teenager at the time. He replied in the affirmative, and the Prophet ﷺ asked if he married a young girl or an older woman. Jābir replied that he married an older widow, and the Prophet ﷺ said, "Why did you not marry a young girl so that you may play with her and she may play with you, and that you may make her laugh and that she may make you laugh?" Jābir explained that he wanted to marry someone who may help take care of his sisters rather than be another dependent. The Prophet ﷺ smiled and responded, "You have done the right thing."

Jābir explained that the only possession he had was his decrepit camel. The Prophet ﷺ instructed him to stop his camel. He ﷺ then rode his camel and said "In the Name of Allah! (*Bismillāh!*)" Jābir commented that it suddenly became the fastest camel he had ever seen, as it raced past him. The Prophet ﷺ then asked to buy the camel, and Jābir, in his youthful zeal, declined the request. He thought of his sisters and that he needed the camel to provide for them, so despite rejecting the request of the Messenger of Allah, it was a noble decision. The Prophet ﷺ persisted, so Jābir offered it as a gift. The Prophet ﷺ then declined and insisted that it be bought, so Jābir asked for the price. The Prophet ﷺ proposed a price of one dirham (a very small amount), to which Jābir—once again in his teenage zeal—declined. The Prophet ﷺ then offered two dirhams and Jābir declined, and this continued until they agreed on a fair market price of 40 dirhams.[689]

Jābir requested that he ride the camel until they reach Medina, and the Prophet ﷺ agreed. Jābir raced ahead, eager to return as a newlywed. The Prophet ﷺ then advised him to stay calm and allow her to prepare herself for him by bathing, combing, and shaving. The next morning, Jābir entered the Prophet's Mosque and the Prophet ﷺ instructed him to pray two units of prayer before discussing business. The Prophet ﷺ then told Bilāl ؓ to weigh the money and round it up. He then handed the money to Jābir, and as he began walking away, the Prophet ﷺ said, O Jābir, did you think I would cheat you out of your camel? Take the money and keep your camel."[690]

The benefits of this narration are innumerable. The Prophet ﷺ played this extended trick on Jābir solely so that he did not feel like he was being given charity. He ﷺ teased him and bartered playfully to cheer up a gloomy teenager. As he cheered him up, he continued to teach him about Islam, such as the etiquette of returning home to one's family, the Sunnah of praying in the mosque before engaging in worldly affairs, and general marital advice. Moreover, the Prophet ﷺ was the first to notice that a Companion was lagging behind, and he was the first to console him. He ﷺ spent time personally mentoring a teenager, displaying once again his attention to detail in taking care of his Ummah—just as he did as a shepherd with his sheep.

The Expedition of al-Muraysīʿ

The Banū al-Muṣṭaliq lived by a pond called al-Muraysīʿ, south of Medina. They had a historical alliance with ʿAbd al-Muṭṭalib and thus sided with the Quraysh at the Battle of Uḥud, despite the war being against the very grandson ﷺ of ʿAbd al-Muṭṭalib. Conveniently situated between Mecca and Medina, they served as useful allies for the Quraysh. Their Chieftain, al-Ḥārith ibn Abī Ḍirār, was keen to re-open the trade routes compromised by the Muslims, so he planned an attack on Medina. The Prophet ﷺ—not one to act on rumours—sent a Companion by the name of Buraydah ibn al-Ḥaṣīb ؓ to Muraysīʿ posing as a Bedouin. Buraydah asked al-Ḥārith to join this potential attack to acquire some war booty, and al-Ḥārith happily agreed, thereby confirming the rumour.

Buraydah surreptitiously returned and informed the Prophet ﷺ who then immediately mobilised 700 Companions. As a pre-emptive attack, it was expected to be a guaranteed success. As a result, many of the Hypocrites—including ʿAbdullāh ibn Ubayy ibn Salūl—joined the caravan despite missing previous battles due to cowardice. The Muslims arrived immediately after Fajr and the Banū al-Muṣṭaliq were so unprepared that there was barely any fighting, resulting in a mere handful of casualties. Over 200 entire households were taken as prisoners of war alongside 2,000 camels and 5,000 sheep.[691]

As for the Muslims, the only casualty was via friendly fire at the hands of a fellow Muslim. An Anṣārī mistook Hishām ibn Ṣubābah ؓ for an enemy fighter and mistakenly killed him. Upon hearing the news, Hishām's brother, Miqyas ibn Ṣubābah, a non-Muslim, pretended to convert to Islam and travelled to Medina to claim the blood money. The Prophet ﷺ paid 100 camels from the public treasury as per the Shariah, and in the dead of the night Miqyas murdered the Anṣārī who accidentally killed his brother and fled back to Mecca with the 100 camels. The Prophet ﷺ made sure to remember his name at the Conquest of Mecca.

The Prophet's Marriage to Juwayriyyah ﷺ

Juwayriyyah bint al-Ḥārith, daughter of the Chieftain of the Banū al-Muṣṭaliq, was captured as a prisoner of war. She agreed with her captor to purchase her freedom, as per her right in Shariah. ʿĀ'ishah ﷺ narrates that she was stunningly beautiful, and that no-one saw her except that they were captivated. Juwayriyyah approached the Prophet ﷺ and asked for a monetary loan to buy her freedom. The Prophet ﷺ offered her something greater: a hand in marriage. She agreed, and her dowry was her freedom. News spread amongst the Anṣār that the Prophet ﷺ married Juwayriyyah ﷺ, and they felt uneasy with owning the Prophet's relatives, "How can we have the Prophet's in-laws as captives?"[692] Every single captive was thus freed and returned to al-Muraysīʿ as a free person.

Unaware of the abovementioned events, al-Ḥārith asked to ransom his daughter. The Prophet ﷺ deferred to Juwayriyyah and gave her the option of leaving or staying according to her preference. Juwayriyyah chose to remain with the Prophet ﷺ, and her choice left her father in so much awe that he embraced Islam. After al-Ḥārith embraced Islam, his entire tribe followed suit and accepted Islam. The Prophet ﷺ then reinstated al-Ḥārith as their leader, returned the gold, sheep, and camels, and encouraged them to return home. In short, everything returned to the status quo except that the entire tribe of the Banū al-Muṣṭaliq were now Muslim, and Juwayriyyah was the Mother of the Believers. ʿĀ'ishah ﷺ commented, "I do not know of any lady that brought more blessings to her tribe than Juwayriyyah."[693]

Juwayriyyah was known for her piety and abundant worship. Once, the Prophet ﷺ left the house for Fajr prayer and she was supplicating to Allah ﷻ. He returned many hours later and found her in the same spot continuing to supplicate. The Prophet ﷺ asked if she remained in the same place the whole time, to which she replied in the affirmative. The Prophet ﷺ then said, "Should I not tell you of a supplication that equates to all that you have done? Say, 'Glory be to Allah by the multitude of His creation, by His Pleasure, by the weight of His Throne, and by the extent of His Words.'"[694]

Stoking the Flames of Tribal Ignorance

As the Companions travelled back to Medina, two youths began to quarrel regarding a trivial matter, and it devolved into a fist fight. One of them said, "O Muhājirūn, come and help me!" The other in turn said, "O Anṣār, help me!" Two groups began to form, and things began to escalate; tempers flared, and weapons were almost drawn. The Prophet ﷺ heard the commotion and rushed out. He severely reprimanded them, "What is this call to [Pre-Islamic] Ignorance? Leave it, for it is rotten!"[695] The Prophet ﷺ immediately and emphatically quashed the conflict, as it was fuelled by tribalism. It was permissible to identify as a Muhājir or Anṣārī, but because these identities were being used for un-Islamic aims, it was rejected. The Prophet ﷺ was even harsher on divisions based on tribe, ethnicity, or race. He ﷺ said, "He is not one of us who calls to tribalism. He is not one of us who fights for the sake of tribalism. He is not one of us who dies following the way of tribalism."[696]

When ʿAbdullāh ibn Ubayy ibn Salūl heard about the rift, he was pleased, but he was disappointed that it was quelled so soon. He was quick to stoke the fires of tribal Ignorance, saying to his friends, "They (i.e., the Muhājirūn) have competed with us in both their quality and quantity. This is exactly like fattening your dog, only for it to come and eat you! By Allah, if we return to Medina, the honourable will expel the inferior. You (i.e., the Anṣār) have brought this on yourselves; you have allowed them to come onto your land and have given them your wealth. If only you withheld all of this, they would have been forced to go back to their homes."[697]

A young Companion by the name of Zayd ibn Arqam ؓ was present, and he could not believe the *kufr* he heard being uttered so brazenly. Zayd rushed back to the Prophet ﷺ and relayed exactly what he heard. The Prophet ﷺ called ʿAbdullāh ibn Ubayy and asked him directly if it were true. ʿAbdullāh ibn Ubayy vehemently denied all claims, making oath after oath, swearing by his innocence. The Prophet ﷺ accepted his claims, as he was still an outward Muslim swearing by Allah. Seeing right through his blatant lies, ʿUmar ؓ turned to the

Prophet ﷺ and said, "O Messenger of Allah, allow me to execute him!" The Prophet ﷺ replied, "Leave him. I do not want the people to say, 'Muhammad kills his own companions.'"[698] The Prophet ﷺ then ordered everyone to pack their things and march straight for Medina. They marched, without stopping, for 20 straight hours. The Prophet ﷺ wanted to exhaust them such that no-one had any energy left for gossip. As planned, when they camped just outside Medina, they spent the whole day sleeping and recuperating.

Zayd was deeply disheartened, as his testimony was effectively rejected and his honour was bruised. However, the next morning, Allah ﷻ revealed the entirety of Sūrah al-Munāfiqūn (The Hypocrites),

> "When the hypocrites come to you, they say, 'We bear witness that you are certainly the Messenger of Allah'—and surely Allah knows that you are His Messenger—but Allah bears witness that the Hypocrites are truly liars. They have made their [false] oaths as a shield, hindering [others] from the Way of Allah. Evil indeed is what they do! This is because they believed and then abandoned faith. Therefore, their hearts have been sealed, so they do not comprehend. When you see them, their appearance impresses you. And when they speak, you listen to their speech. But they are just like [worthless] planks of wood leaned [against a wall]. They think every cry is against them. They are the enemy, so beware of them. May Allah condemn them! How can they be deluded [from the truth]? When it is said to them, 'Come! The Messenger of Allah will pray for you to be forgiven', they turn their heads [in disgust], and you see them turn away in arrogance.
>
> It is the same whether you pray for their forgiveness or not, Allah will not forgive them. Surely Allah does not guide the rebellious people. They are the ones who say [to one another], 'Do not spend anything on those [Emigrants] with the Messenger of Allah so that they

will break away.' But to Allah [alone] belong the treasuries of the Heavens and the Earth, yet the Hypocrites do not comprehend.

They say, 'If we return to Medina, the honourable will expel the inferior.' But all honour and power belongs to Allah, His Messenger, and the believers, yet the Hypocrites do not know. O believers! Do not let your wealth or your children divert you from the remembrance of Allah. For whoever does so, it is they who are the [true] losers. And donate from what We have provided for you before death comes to one of you, and you cry, 'My Lord! If only You delayed me for a short while, I would give in charity and be one of the righteous.' But Allah never delays a soul when its appointed time comes. And Allah is All-Aware of what you do." [699]

Allah provided a thorough and precise refutation, quoting ʿAbdullāh ibn Ubayy directly. The Prophet ﷺ called Zayd ibn Arqam ؓ and held him by his ear, saying, "Allah has confirmed that you have spoken the truth!" [700] Meanwhile, those in Medina heard about what occurred, and ʿAbdullāh ibn Ubayy's son—who was a Muslim and was also called ʿAbdullāh—grew increasingly anxious. He approached the Prophet ﷺ and said, "O Messenger of Allah, it has reached me that you are considering executing my father. If you command anyone to execute him, I do not know if I can bear to watch another man roaming the streets of Medina, knowing that he has killed my father, without wanting to exact revenge and kill him. And if I kill an innocent Muslim I will go to the Hellfire. So, I think the only solution is for you to command me to execute him." [701]

ʿAbdullāh's astonishing comments here are a product of a pious man grappling with his tribal upbringing and innate feelings towards his family. However, his piety and love for Allah and His Messenger overcame his embedded feelings of tribalism. The Prophet ﷺ reassured him that his father would not be executed, replying, "No, your duty is to be a good companion to him."[702] 'Abdullāh 🌸 felt huge relief but was still angry at his father. As his father approached the border of Medina, he said, "You were the one who said, 'If we return to Medina, the honourable will expel the inferior.' But By Allah, I will not allow you to enter Medina until the Prophet 🌸 has granted you permission." They then waited until the Prophet 🌸 granted explicit permission for him to enter.[703]

Prior to this event, the Muslims had underestimated 'Abdullāh ibn Ubayy's true nature, assuming some goodness—as is expected of a believer—but this event exposed him and the Hypocrites and the true extent of their evil. The revealing of Sūrah al-Munāfiqūn led many of 'Abdullāh ibn Ubayy's companions to leave him and disassociate from the Hypocrites. The Prophet 🌸 later remarked to 'Umar ibn al-Khaṭṭāb 🌸, "What do you think, O 'Umar, if I executed 'Abdullāh ibn Ubayy the day you requested it? Indeed, I would have turned away many people. But if I ask those same people to kill 'Abdullāh ibn Ubayy today, they would do it." 'Umar simply replied, "By Allah, I know that the opinion of the Messenger of Allah 🌸 is always more blessed than mine."[704]

18 A Heinous Slander

Seething from his divinely ordained humiliation, ʿAbdullāh ibn Ubayy was desperate for revenge. When the opportunity presented itself to besmirch the Prophet's honour, he took it with both hands, directing his malice towards the Prophet's own family and personal life. He targeted the Prophet's most innocent wife, Mother of the Believers ʿĀ'ishah bint Abī Bakr ﷺ.

ʿĀ'ishah narrated the entire story first-hand and in great detail. She described the events as the Companions were returning to Medina from al-Muraysīʿ. The Verses of Hijab[i] had already been revealed, so ʿĀ'ishah ﷺ was travelling in her own private carriage. As they prepared to leave, ʿĀ'ishah excused herself to a secluded area to relieve herself. When she returned, she realised that her prized necklace was missing.

i In modern vernacular, "hijab" refers to the headscarf worn by Muslim women which covers one's hair and chest. However, in classical Qur'anic Arabic, the word "*khimār* (khimar)" is used in this regard. The word "*ḥijāb* (hijab)" in classical Arabic meant "barrier" and it referred to rules specific to the Mothers of the Believers (i.e., the wives of the Prophet ﷺ). While Muslim women are required to cover their bodies, the Mothers of the Believers were further required to conceal their private spaces. Allah ﷻ states, "And when you ask his wives for something, ask them from behind a barrier." (*al-Aḥzāb*, 53).

As it had so much sentimental value, she was deeply worried and spent a lengthy time looking for it. Meanwhile, the guards responsible for carrying her carriage did not notice her absence. As she narrated the story, she excused them, "I did not weigh much, so they did not notice my absence."[705] Their respect and veneration for her was so much that they did not engage her in conversation even to confirm her presence. Consequently, they left while 'Ā'ishah was still looking around. When she finally returned, the entire camp had disappeared, and she was alone in an empty desert. Lo and behold, the necklace was in plain sight, as it was underneath her camel the whole time.

As it was so dangerous travelling alone in the desert, 'Ā'ishah stayed put and waited under the shade of a tree. She fell asleep under the tree—an illustration of her blissful reliance on Allah. Eventually, the Companion Ṣafwān ibn Muʿaṭṭal al-Sulamī ☙, who had overslept and was catching up, passed by and saw her. While narrating, she remarked, "He had seen me before the Verses of Hijab so he recognised me."[706] To wake her up, Ṣafwān recited loudly, "*Innā lillāhi wa innā ilayhi rājiʿūn* (To Allah we belong and to Him we shall return)." 'Ā'ishah woke up and covered her face with her jilbab[ii]. Ṣafwān then lowered his camel, walked away and turned his back so that he does not see her embarking, and guided the camel with his hands while in front. 'Ā'ishah stated, "By Allah, we did not converse with one another nor did he say one word to me the whole way to Medina."[707] They eventually caught up to the group and at the back of the group was none other than 'Abdullāh ibn Ubayy ibn Salūl.

As soon as 'Ā'ishah ☙ arrived in Medina she fell sick with a severe fever and was bed ridden for an entire month. She remained completely oblivious as the rumours began to circulate and grow, and her absence only fuelled the fire for those perverted individuals. It is a testament to the integrity of Hadith narrators and historians that the specifics of the slander are never explicitly mentioned. Nevertheless, the implication

267

A HEINOUS SLANDER

THE MEDINANERA

---

ii   An outer garment worn by Muslim women comprising the overall command of hijab. It is referenced in the Qur'an, "O Prophet! Ask your wives, daughters, and believing women to draw their jilbabs over their bodies..." (*al-Aḥzāb*, 59).

is clear, and the shamelessness of the perpetrators knew no bounds. ʿĀ'ishah stated that she had no knowledge whatsoever about what was being said, and the only indication that something was awry was that the Prophet ﷺ was slightly aloof. ʿĀ'ishah was sick, and the Prophet ﷺ was trying to deal with the matter privately.

The Perils of Gossip

Those who fabricated the lies and were most active in spreading them were solely from ʿAbdullāh ibn Ubayy's group of Hypocrites. They were mostly comprised of the Khazraj but only because ʿAbdullāh ibn Ubayy was a leader of the Khazraj. However, three believing Companions succumbed and engaged in gossip (e.g., "Have you heard what they are saying about So-and-so?"). They were Misṭaḥ ibn Uthāthah, Ḥassān ibn Thābit, and Ḥamnah bint Jaḥsh. While they did not lie about ʿĀ'ishah ؓ or even accuse her, merely gossiping about the topic was a grave blunder.

ʿĀ'ishah remarked, "Zaynab was the only other wife of the Prophet ﷺ who rivalled me, but Allah protected her tongue due to her religiosity."[708] Ḥamnah intended to raise Zaynab's rank by lowering ʿĀ'ishah's, but Zaynab's piety prevented her from joining in the gossip. Zaynab said to the Prophet ﷺ, "O Messenger of Allah, I will not cause my eyes and my ears to fall into sin; by Allah I only know good of ʿĀ'ishah."[709] Once again, ʿĀ'ishah's decorum and dignity is unparalleled in describing the events; she provided excuses for the gossipers while praising her co-wife for her piety despite having previous tensions. Likewise, Zaynab ؓ maintained her integrity and remained honest rather than utilising the opportunity for her own gain.

After a month, ʿĀ'ishah recovered enough to leave the house. She went with Umm Misṭaḥ (Misṭaḥ's mother and Abū Bakr's cousin) to the outdoor bathroom area. As they walked, Umm Misṭaḥ tripped and blurted, "May Misṭaḥ be cursed!" ʿĀ'ishah was shocked and immediately reprimanded her, "Woe to you! How can you curse your own son when he attended [the Battle of] Badr?"[710] Badr was such a blessed and historic event that the attendees were held in extremely high esteem. It is also worth noting the honourable nature of the Mother of the Believers, who was so quick to defend someone behind their back. Umm Misṭaḥ replied, "Don't you know what he said?" ʿĀ'ishah of course had no idea, so Umm Misṭaḥ told her and ʿĀ'ishah fainted on the spot. She was so innocent and pure that she could not imagine that people could possibly say such things.

ʿĀ'ishah immediately returned home. She narrated, "I felt worse than my initial sickness." The Prophet ﷺ entered upon her, not knowing that she now knew. ʿĀ'ishah ؓ asked for permission to stay at her parents' house, and the Prophet ﷺ granted it. She asked her mother, "My dear mother, what are the people saying about me? And why didn't you tell me?" Her mother, Umm Rūmān ؓ, replied, "My daughter, be easy on yourself. By Allah, never does a good man love his wife as much as your husband loves you except that people talk about her." Despite trying to console her, her response effectively confirmed that people were indeed slandering her. ʿĀ'ishah responded, "*SubḥānAllāh* (Glory be to Allah), have the people really said this?" Once again, her innocent mind could not comprehend how—or why—people would stoop so low. Narrating the story, ʿĀ'ishah said, "That night I cried and cried, and the tears would not stop. I cried until the break of dawn without tasting the sweetness of sleep. I continued to cry during the day and my tears would not stop flowing until I thought that my liver would burst open from the pain. A lady from the Anṣār then asked for permission to enter, and she sat beside me and cried with me."[711]

ʿĀ'ishah's family home was on the outskirts of Medina, so the Prophet ﷺ now had some space to investigate. He called his closest and most trusted family members: ʿAlī ibn Abī Ṭālib and Usāmah ibn Zayd ؓ. ʿAlī was the Prophet's cousin and son-in-law, interacting with his family on a daily basis. Usāmah was born in the Prophet's own house, son of the famous Zayd ibn Ḥārithah ؓ. His mother was Umm Ayman ؓ, the Prophet's own nanny. He was thus nicknamed "The Prophet's beloved, son of the Prophet's beloved".[712] Usāmah strongly defended ʿĀ'ishah and rejected the accusations in the most emphatic terms. ʿAlī said, "O Messenger of Allah, Allah has not restricted you, and there are plenty of women to choose from. But if you want to ask about her character then why not ask her maid servant, Barīrah." ʿAlī's relatively neutral response displeased ʿĀ'ishah but he did not accuse her or imply her guilt.

The Prophet ﷺ called Barīrah forward for questioning. Barīrah was a former slave whom ʿĀ'ishah purchased in order to free. In her appreciation and loyalty, she remained close to ʿĀ'ishah and served her as a free woman. The Prophet ﷺ asked Barīrah, "O Barīrah, have you seen anything in ʿĀ'ishah that has caused you any doubt?" Barīrah grew increasingly nervous—she wanted to remain loyal to ʿĀ'ishah but would not dare lie to the Prophet ﷺ. She reluctantly disclosed, "By Allah, O Messenger of Allah, I have not seen anything [doubtful] from her, but sometimes when she is supposed to knead dough, she falls asleep, and the goat eats the dough."[713] Barīrah's supposed confession comically highlights ʿĀ'ishah's purity and innocence, as her falling asleep when doing chores was considered her biggest shortcoming.

The Stench of Ignorance

The Prophet ﷺ then called a general assembly in the mosque. He ﷺ called out, "O believers! Who will excuse me against a person who has hurt me even regarding my own family? By Allah, I know nothing but good from my wives. And I know nothing but good from this man they mention (i.e., Ṣafwān ibn Muʿaṭṭal)."[714] Ṣafwān had the honour of being personally praised by the Prophet ﷺ. Ṣafwān was a chaste bachelor who later said, "By He in Whose Hand is my soul, I have never even lifted the veil of a woman."[715] Allah blessed him with martyrdom during the reign of ʿUmar ibn al-Khaṭṭāb ﷺ.

The Prophet ﷺ was addressing the Companions directly, defending ʿĀ'ishah publicly and putting pressure on ʿAbdullāh ibn Ubayy without explicitly mentioning him. The famous Saʿd ibn Muʿādh ﷺ stood up and said, "O Messenger of Allah, as for me, I excuse you to do whatever you wish. If this man is from the Aws, I will execute him myself, but if he is from the Khazraj, then you must command me and then I will execute him." Saʿd was a leader of the Aws and was cognisant of the tribal implications, as ʿAbdullāh ibn Ubayy was the foremost leader of the Khazraj.

Saʿd ibn ʿUbādah ﷺ, a young leader of the Khazraj, immediately stood up and exclaimed, "By Allah you have lied! You would not dare to kill him, and you cannot kill him! Had he been from your tribe, you would never kill him!" Narrating the story, ʿĀ'ishah ﷺ excused Saʿd ibn ʿUbādah, saying, "Saʿd was a righteous man, but the pride of [Pre-Islamic] Ignorance momentarily overcame him."[716] After Saʿd's outburst, someone else from the Aws stood up and blurted, "Rather, *you* are the liar! We *will* kill him, and you are just a Hypocrite fighting on behalf of the other Hypocrites!"

The gathering devolved and the ignorant pride of tribalism overtook the Anṣār; tribal politics distracted the Companions from the important purpose of the meeting. The Companions were the best generation but were nonetheless inherently human and thus inherently flawed. The Prophet ﷺ once said, "Four things from [the era of] Ignorance will remain in my Ummah: pride over tribalism, discrediting lineages, astrology, and wailing over the dead."[717] The Prophet ﷺ calmed the Companions down and immediately quashed the argument before leaving to visit ʿĀ'ishah.

A Divine Vindication

The Prophet ﷺ entered upon ʿĀ'ishah to discuss the matter. He began by praising Allah—as was his custom before speaking—then continued, "I have heard about you such-and-such. If you are innocent then Allah will clear you of this charge, and if you have slipped into a sin then seek Allah's forgiveness and repent to Him, for indeed when a servant of Allah commits a sin and repents, Allah ﷻ forgives the sin."[718] Narrating the story, ʿĀ'ishah commented, "Suddenly my tears came to a halt, and I began to feel anger." She responded, "O dear mother, respond to him on my behalf." Her mother replied, "O my dear daughter, I don't know what to say." ʿĀ'ishah then turned to her father, Abū Bakr ﷺ,

and said, "O dear father, respond to him on my behalf." Abū Bakr ﷺ replied, "O my dear daughter, I do not know what to say." Stuck between a rock and a hard place, her parents were at a loss.

ʿĀ'ishah ﷺ was then left to fend for herself. As she narrated the story, she recalled, "I was still a young lady at the time so I had not memorised much Qur'an. I could not recall the name of [Prophet] Yaʿqūb ﷺ so I said, 'All I can say to you is what Abū Yūsuf (i.e., the father of Prophet Yūsuf ﷺ) said, "So [I can only endure with] beautiful patience! It is Allah's help that I seek to bear your claims."[719]' I then turned around and faced the wall."

ʿĀ'ishah felt entirely alone, so she placed her unwavering trust and reliance on Allah ﷻ alone, the Creator of the Heavens and Earth. Suddenly, the Prophet's head lowered and he began to receive Revelation via Jibrīl ﷺ. Eventually, he regained consciousness with a huge smile and a laugh. His first words were, "O ʿĀ'ishah, indeed Allah has revealed your innocence!"[720] Allah ﷻ revealed a lengthy section of Sūrah al-Nūr,

> "Indeed, those who came up with that slander are a group of you. Do not think this is bad for you. Rather, it is good for you. They will be punished, each according to their share of the sin. As for their mastermind, he will suffer a tremendous punishment. If only the believing men and women had thought well of one another, when you heard this [rumour], and said, 'This is clearly an outrageous slander!' Why did they not produce four witnesses? Now, since they have failed to produce witnesses, they are truly liars in the sight of Allah. Had it not been for Allah's Grace and Mercy upon you in this world and the Hereafter, you would have certainly been touched with a tremendous punishment for what you plunged into—when you passed it from one tongue to the other and said with your mouths what you had no knowledge of, taking it lightly while it is extremely serious in the sight of Allah. If only you had said upon hearing it, 'How can we speak about such a thing!

> Glory be to You [O Lord]! This is a heinous slander!' Allah forbids you from ever doing something like this again if you are true believers. And Allah makes [His] commandments clear to you, for Allah is All-Knowing, All-Wise. Indeed, those who love to see indecency spread among the believers will suffer a painful punishment in this life and the Hereafter. Allah knows and you do not know. [You would have suffered] had it not been for Allah's Grace and Mercy upon you, and had Allah not been Ever Gracious, Most Merciful."[721]

ʿĀ'ishah later recalled, "I knew that Allah ﷻ would reveal my chastity but I never, in my wildest imagination, envisaged that Allah would reveal Qur'an about me." She thought that perhaps the Prophet ﷺ would experience a Prophetic dream, but she did not even anticipate timeless Revelation in her honour. When the verses were revealed, her mother said, "O ʿĀ'ishah, stand up (to thank the Prophet ﷺ)." ʿĀ'ishah, still reeling from a rollercoaster of emotions, replied, "By Allah I will not stand, and I will not thank anyone except Allah, for He is the One Who vindicated me."

Abū Bakr ؓ would regularly pay for Misṭaḥ's living expenses. After hearing these verses, Abū Bakr said, "By Allah I will never spend on Misṭaḥ again after what he said regarding ʿĀ'ishah." Allah ﷻ then revealed, "Do not let the people of virtue and affluence among you swear to suspend donations to their relatives, the needy, and the Emigrants in the cause of Allah. Let them pardon and forgive. Do you not love to be forgiven by Allah? And Allah is All-Forgiving, Most Merciful."[722] Abū Bakr then said, "By Allah I would like to be forgiven by Allah." He then continued his stipend to Misṭaḥ and vowed never to stop spending on him. The divine standards of justice are simply unparalleled. Despite Misṭaḥ gossiping about the daughter of his financial supporter, Abū Bakr ؓ, he continued to spend on him, seeking Allah's Mercy.

Before the verses were revealed, the wife of Abū Ayyūb al-Anṣārī entered upon him and uttered the words, "Have you heard…?" Abū Ayyūb ؓ immediately responded, "How can we speak about such a thing! Glory be to You [O Lord]! This is a heinous slander!" His response was so noble that Allah ﷻ quoted him directly despite it being said in a private conversation. Abū Ayyūb's honouring demonstrates the loftiness of rejecting gossip and slander as well as the perils of falling into such a sin. The three Muslims who joined in the gossip were lashed 80 times according to the Qur'anic punishment whereas the Hypocrites who fabricated the lies were left unpunished. Scholars comment that worldly punishment absolves one's punishment in the Hereafter, and Allah ﷻ did not want to diminish the forthcoming punishment of the Hypocrites for their heinous crimes.[723] As for the Muslims who slipped in their fallibility, they repented and were forgiven.

The whole ordeal was a testament to the veracity of the Qur'an and the Prophethood of Muhammad ﷺ. Even the Prophet—a slave of God—experienced a month of anguish and unease, tolerating public slander and disparaging remarks until Allah ﷻ sent Revelation and vindicated his wife. As emphasised throughout this book, Allah ﷻ tests His servants according to their status and level of piety. He ﷻ promises both hardship and ease, "So surely with hardship comes ease."[724] The Prophet ﷺ himself was no exception to this divine rule.

The Battle of the Trench (Khandaq) 19

After their expulsion from Medina, the Banū Naḍīr relocated to Khaybar, an oasis roughly 150 km north of Medina. However, they remained discontent with their newfound humble lifestyle and yearned to return to their riches in Medina. They sent an official delegation to Mecca comprised of the elite of their nobility in a bid to form an alliance against the Muslims. They promised the Quraysh riches as well as reminding them of their common goal of eradicating Islam. The Quraysh historically had an inferiority complex towards the Jews, as they were an illiterate nation whereas the Jews had a history of literature and Prophethood.

The Quraysh said, "You are people of the book and are aware of our differences with Muhammad. So, is our religion better or his?"[725] Indeed, Judaism is the closest religion to Islam in both theology and laws, and the Quraysh were correct in their assessment. Despite this, the Banū Naḍīr replied, "You are more rightly guided, and you are closer to the truth than Muhammad and his companions." Allah ﷻ exposed their hypocrisy, "Have you not seen those who were given a portion of the Scriptures yet believe in idols and false gods and reassure the disbelievers that they are better guided than the believers?"[726] Nevertheless, the Quraysh accepted their offer, and an alliance was formed.

The Banū Naḍīr then sent a delegation to the Ghaṭafān. As aforementioned, the Ghaṭafān were uncouth raiders, and they were apathetic to the Banū Naḍīr's struggles. Instead, the Banū Naḍīr offered them half of the produce from Khaybar for a whole year, which was a tremendous fortune. The Ghaṭafān therefore joined as mercenaries. After securing an agreement with the Quraysh from the south and the Ghaṭafān from the north, the Banū Naḍīr approached every small tribe whose income was affected by the halted trade route, such as the Banū Asad, the Banū Sulaym, the Banū Murrah, the Banū Ashjaʿ, the Banū Kinānah, and so on. Each tribe contributed either by sending fighters, weapons, or supplies. The battle was therefore also called "The Battle of the Confederates (Ghazwah al-Aḥzāb)", referring to the various tribes fighting together. Ibn Isḥāq estimates around 10,000 fighting men—over four times the available Muslim fighters.[727]

Word reached the Prophet ﷺ who then convened a gathering in his mosque and sought counsel from his Companions, as per his Sunnah. The Companions were hard pressed for ideas until Salmān al-Fārisī (The Persian) ؓ suggested that they dig a trench, as was common in Persia. The exact dimensions of the trench are not known, but it is estimated to have been 2 km long and 13 ft wide. Medina was naturally protected by volcanic plains on one side and large date palm farms on the other, both of which were impossible for large armies to cross. The Muslims therefore planned to have their backs towards Mount Sela (Silaʿ) and face the trench.

They had less than ten days to dig this trench, so every single Companion, rich and poor, young and old, contributed. The Prophet ﷺ physically participated to the extent that al-Barāʾ ibn ʿĀzib ؓ said, "The Prophet ﷺ was carrying dirt for so long that his chest hair was completely covered with dust, and he was a man with a lot of hair."[728] It was a hugely motivating factor which rallied the Companions to work harder and faster. The Prophet ﷺ would further rally them by reciting, "By Allah, without Allah we would not have been guided, neither would we have given in charity, nor would we have prayed. So please send tranquillity upon us and make our feet firm if we meet the enemy, as the enemy have rebelled against us. And if they intended affliction, we would refuse! We would refuse!" The Companions would then chant alongside him ﷺ, "We would refuse! We would refuse! (Abaynā! Abaynā!)"[729] He ﷺ make duʿāʾ, "O Allah, there is no good except the good of the Hereafter, so have mercy on the Anṣār and the Muhājirah!"[730]

Divine Blessings

It is reported that there were food shortages from the beginning of the siege.[731] While no explicit reason has been recorded, it is likely due to a combination of the siege taking place in winter and it being a complete surprise. As a result, the Muslims did not have any food stockpiled, and the ten days they had to prepare for the battle were spent entirely on digging the trench. The Companions were reported to have sufficed themselves on the simplest of foods such as dried barley mixed with oil, or even mere date pits.[732] Jābir ؓ narrated that he saw the Prophet ﷺ digging, and when his shirt was raised, Jābir saw a large rock tied to his stomach, a method of subduing one's hunger. Jābir ؓ returned to his wife and said, "I just saw something that I do not have the strength to bear. What do we have in the house [to eat]?" His wife replied, "I only have a small amount of bread and a small goat." Infant goats would not typically be slaughtered, as they do not produce enough meat. Nevertheless, Jābir needed to take action, so he slaughtered the goat while his wife kneaded the dough.

Jābir ⸎ returned to the Prophet ﷺ and whispered, "O Messenger of Allah, my wife has prepared some food. Why don't you, with one or two people, come to eat?" To Jābir's great concern, the Prophet ﷺ stood up and announced to everyone, "O People of the Trench! Jābir and his wife have prepared a meal for us. All of you, welcome!" Jābir rushed back in distress, as he clearly did not have enough food for more than a handful of people. His wife asked, "Did the Prophet ﷺ invite them, or did you?" When Jābir confirmed that it was the Prophet's instruction, she replied calmly, "Then it will be fine." The Prophet ﷺ said, "Do not open the pot until I come." He ﷺ then arrived while the pot was still on the stove. He made *duʿā'* and gently spat in the food—as his saliva was blessed—then invited the Companions in ten at a time. Each group of ten ate their fill, one after the other, until every single person was sufficed. Jābir counted around 1,000 Companions.[733]

The Companions were tirelessly digging the trench, and they came across a boulder that was too difficult to break. Some of them suggested that they dig around the boulder, but other Companions refused because the Prophet ﷺ physically delineated the lines of where the trench would be dug, and they would not dare deviate from his instruction without receiving his express permission. The Prophet ﷺ was called, and he took the axe and descended into the trench. He ﷺ said, "*Bismillāh, wa Allāhu Akbar*!" and he hit the boulder. One third of the boulder crumbled, and he said, "*Allāhu Akbar*! Allah has given me the keys to al-Shām (Greater Syria). By Allah I can see the red castles in al-Shām." He ﷺ said "*Bismillāh, wa Allāhu Akbar*!" and hit the boulder again, and another third crumbled. He said, "I have been given the keys to Persia! By Allah I can see the white pillars of al-Madā'in (Ctesiphon)." He ﷺ said "*Bismillāh, wa Allāhu Akbar*!" for a third time and hit the boulder again, breaking the final third. He then said, "*Allāhu Akbar*! I have been given the keys to Yemen. By Allah, I can see the doors of Sanaa."[734] As prophesised, the first land conquered after the Prophet's passing was Syria. In an inexplicable turn of events immediately following the death of the Prophet ﷺ, Muslim forces brought both Persian (Sassanid) and Roman (Byzantine) Empires to their knees.

Preparing for Battle

The Prophet ﷺ organised the Muslim army, and a group of the Companions were designated as patrol. They were instructed to shout "*Allāhu Akbar*!" at intervals as they patrolled in order to give the impression that every area of the trench was protected and guarded. Umm Salamah ؓ narrated, "I witnessed many battles with the Prophet ﷺ in which there was fighting and fear—al-Muraysīʿ, Khaybar, Ḥudaybiyyah, The Conquest of Mecca, and Ḥunayn—but none of them was more tiring or fearful than [the Battle of] Khandaq. The Muslims were in a very precarious situation, and we were worried about our children. Medina was patrolled all night and you could hear the *takbīr* (chants of "*Allāhu Akbar*!") all night until Fajr."[735] The Muslims were fatigued, hungry, and cold, and the worst was yet to come.

Danger from Within

Before the battle began, the Prophet ﷺ instructed the Companions to gather the women of Medina and take them to al-Fāriʿ, the fortress of the Banū Ḥārithah. As previously explained, the Jews were distinct in their architectural ability. The Arabs did not acquire such skills, but the Banū Ḥārithah attempted to emulate them. While it was not to the same standards, it was the biggest fortress from amongst the Arabs. Every able-bodied Muslim man would be protecting Medina from external forces, and so the women and children within Medina would be unprotected. Usually that would not be an issue, but the Prophet ﷺ was wary of the Banū Qurayẓah and was suspicious of their true loyalties.

The Prophet's suspicions were vindicated, as the Banū Qurayẓah had reneged on their oaths. Ḥuyayy ibn Akhṭab, leader of the Banū Naḍīr, sneaked into Medina and rendezvoused with Kaʿb ibn Asad, the Chieftain of the Banū Qurayẓah. Kaʿb ibn Asad initially refused, as he swore his oath with the Prophet ﷺ on three separate occasions. Ḥuyayy continued to implore him and promise his protection until Kaʿb buckled. As the Prophet's suspicions grew, he called on his Companions for a volunteer to enter upon the Banū Qurayẓah and investigate. Zubayr ibn al-ʿAwwām ﷺ came forth, to which the Prophet ﷺ uttered his famous praise, "Every Prophet has his disciples, and my disciple is Zubayr ibn al-ʿAwwām."[736]

Zubayr ﷺ sneaked in on the Banū Qurayẓah and witnessed preparations for battle. He returned to the Prophet ﷺ and said, "O Messenger of Allah, I found them fortifying their fortresses and clearing their roads (to facilitate the easy movement of their troops towards the Muslims). They have also gathered all their livestock."[737] This confirmed that the treaty was indeed broken. The Prophet ﷺ did not want to take deeply consequential actions without verifying, so he sent four of the most senior members of the Anṣār who had close ties with the Banū Qurayẓah before Islam: Saʿd ibn Muʿādh, Saʿd ibn ʿUbādah, ʿAbdullāh ibn Rawāḥah, and Khawwāt ibn Jubayr ﷺ. They spoke to the Banū Qurayẓah directly and it quickly became clear to them that they had no intention of upholding any agreement with the Muslims. They were received with arrogance and provocation; the Banū Qurayẓah mocked them and even denied the existence of the treaty. Saʿd ibn Muʿādh ﷺ was so enraged that he began swearing and cursing at them, and the Banū Qurayẓah returned his insults in kind. Saʿd ibn ʿUbādah ﷺ held Saʿd ibn Muʿādh back and said, "Leave off cursing them, for the matter between us and them is now more than that."[738] In other words, they now have a lot more to worry about.

When the Prophet ﷺ sent the delegation, he instructed them to return and relay the information discretely. He ﷺ was camped in public amongst the Muslims and did not want to dishearten the Muslims or cause them to panic. When the delegation returned, they greeted the Prophet ﷺ and said, "ʿAḍal and al-Qārrah". They were the names of the two tribes that betrayed the Muslims in the Massacre of al-Rajīʿ, so the Prophet ﷺ clearly understood the implication. The Prophet ﷺ responded, "*Allāhu Akbar*! This is good news and glad tidings."[739] He ﷺ had utmost faith in Allah ﷻ to deliver success in this dire moment, and the treachery of the Banū Qurayẓah would, in time, prove to be a grave blunder.

Eventually, news broke of Banū Qurayẓah's betrayal. Many Companions described that night as the worst night of their lives; as they faced a 10,000-man external army, their wives and children were left unprotected from internal enemies. Allah ﷻ states, "[Remember] when they came at you from above (the Confederates) and from below (the Banū Qurayẓah), when your eyes grew wild [in horror] and your hearts jumped into your throats, and you entertained [conflicting] thoughts about Allah. There and then the believers were put to the test and were violently shaken."[740] The Companions did not disbelieve nor lose all hope, but facing disaster in all directions shook some of their hearts. Adding salt to their wounds, the Hypocrites began causing strife, demanding to go back to Medina under the guise of protecting their families. One of them uttered, "Here was Muhammad promising us the treasures of Kisrā and Qayṣar (Khosrow and Caesar), and now we cannot even go home and defecate!"[741]

A Misguided Federation

The Ghaṭafān, joining the battle as mercenaries, did not have strong loyalties. They sent an emissary to the Prophet ﷺ with a proposal. As the Banū Naḍīr offered them half of the produce of Khaybar, they promised to refrain from fighting if the Prophet ﷺ offered a third of the produce of Medina. The Ghaṭafān comprised the second largest group amongst the confederates, and the Muslims were in a dire situation behind the trench, so the Prophet ﷺ considered their proposal and sought counsel from his Companions. He gathered with Saʿd ibn Muʿādh and Saʿd ibn ʿUbādah ؓ, the leaders of the Aws and Khazraj respectively. They both asked, "Is this something that Allah ﷻ has commanded you to do? If it is Revelation, then we listen and obey; but if it is a matter of *ijtihād* (independent judgement), then we have never humiliated ourselves in [the era of Pre-Islamic] Ignorance, so why should we humiliate ourselves in [the era of] Islam?"[742] Neither the Aws nor the Khazraj had ever been conquered, so they retained their elite mentality of independence. The Prophet ﷺ thus rejected the Ghaṭafān's proposal and continued to plan.

A small group of the Aḥzāb (Confederates) managed to cross the trench and encroach onto Muslim territory. They were led by ʿAmr ibn ʿAbd Wudd, famous for his ferocity in battle. He donned his red "Turban of Death" similar to that of Abū Dujānah ﷺ at Uḥud. He declared, "Who will fight me?!" ʿAlī ibn Abī Ṭālib ﷺ—the brave warrior that he was—volunteered himself yet again. The Prophet ﷺ stopped him and said, "Sit down ʿAlī, that is ʿAmr." ʿAlī ﷺ was a young man in his twenties while ʿAmr ibn ʿAbd Wudd was in the prime of his fighting life with years of experience and insight, so the Prophet ﷺ feared for his safety. ʿAmr yelled again, "Who will fight me?!" ʿAlī ﷺ volunteered himself again, and the Prophet ﷺ again said, "Sit down." ʿAmr asked a third time, and ʿAlī stood up a third time, and the Prophet ﷺ repeated, "Sit down, that is ʿAmr." But this time ʿAlī responded, "Even if it were ʿAmr!" The Prophet ﷺ was impressed with his valour and allowed ʿAlī to fight.

ʿAmr asked ʿAlī to identify himself then said, "Go back my nephew and bring one of your uncles, for I do not wish to spill your blood." ʿAlī responded defiantly, "But I *do* wish to spill *your* blood!" Enraged, ʿAmr charged forward ferociously, as did ʿAlī, and the dust from their galloping horses enveloped them completely, so much so that no-one knew who won until they heard a cheer of *"Allāhu Akbar!"* from within the dust.[743] Nawfal ibn ʿAbdillāh also crossed the trench, and Zubayr ibn al-ʿAwwām ﷺ charged and struck him with so much force that Nawfal's body split in half from head to toe. Someone remarked, "What an amazing sword!" to which Zubayr responded, "It is not the sword, it is the arm!"[744]

Khālid ibn al-Walīd ﷺ—not yet Muslim—also crossed over. He engaged in a sword fight but crossed back without inflicting any casualties. Likewise, ʿIkrimah ibn Abī Jahl crossed and returned. In total, two or three of the Aḥzāb died while five or six Muslims were martyred, primarily from arrows from afar. Despite having the largest number of fighters against the Muslims, the Battle of the Trench produced the lowest number of Muslim casualties.

Despite the low number of deaths, the barrage of arrows and threats was severe. At one point, defending the trench was so intense that the Muslims could not even pray ʿAṣr until after the Sun had set. The Prophet ﷺ said, "They busied us from the Middle Prayer (i.e., ʿAṣr) until the Sun had set. May Allah fill their graves and houses with the Fire [of Hell]."[745] The Prophet ﷺ never cursed his enemies for trying to kill him, but being forced to miss the prayer infuriated him ﷺ.

The tragedy of the Battle of the Trench was the death of the great Saʿd ibn Muʿādh ﷺ. Ḥibbān ibn al-ʿAriqah shot him afar with an arrow and yelled, "This is a gift from Ibn al-ʿAriqah!" "*ʿAraq*" means "sweat", so Saʿd yelled back, "Allah will cause your face to sweat in the Hellfire!"[746] Allah and His Messenger both loved Saʿd ibn Muʿādh. The Prophet ﷺ said, "The Throne of the Most Gracious shook at the death of Saʿd ibn Muʿādh."[747] There simply cannot be any greater praise for a man. Years later, the Prophet ﷺ received a luxurious Roman robe as a gift, and the Companions were awestruck at its magnificence. The Prophet ﷺ was in turn surprised at their awe, and he ﷺ said, "Are you impressed by this? By Allah the handkerchief of Saʿd ibn Muʿādh in Paradise is more luxurious than this!"[748]

A Gift from Allah ﷻ

The Muslims were fending off attacks successfully, but the trench was merely a temporary solution. With food supplies empty and a dastardly threat from the Banū Qurayẓah looming, the situation was dire and there was no respite in sight. Other than through unwavering trust in Allah, one could not foresee from where a solution would appear. Allah ﷻ then used a man from the Ghaṭafān by the name of Nuʿaym ibn Masʿūd ﷺ to turn the tides. Nuʿaym sneaked into Muslim territory and crept into the Prophet's own tent. He said, "O Messenger of Allah, I have accepted Islam, but my people are unaware, so command me as you wish—I am at your service."[749] Nuʿaym ﷺ later remarked, "Allah threw Islam into my heart that day."[750] Nuʿaym was one man, so he would not be of much help on the Muslim side, so the Prophet ﷺ instructed him to return to his base and try to make an impact as a spy. Nuʿaym asked if he was allowed to lie, to which the Prophet ﷺ replied, "War is deception."[751] While deception or trickery (*khadʿah*) is permitted in Islam during times of war, treachery or betrayal (*khiyānah*) is categorically forbidden in Islam at all times.

Nuʿaym ⬥ returned with a meticulous plan in mind. He approached the Banū Qurayẓah, with whom he had close ties, and planted seeds of doubt in their minds regarding their alliance with the Quraysh. He urged them to be wary and suggested that the Quraysh were wavering. Finally, he advised them to demand hostages from the Quraysh to ensure their loyalty. The next morning, he approached the Quraysh and planted seeds of doubt regarding the loyalty of the Banū Qurayẓah, suggesting that they were buckling under pressure. He disclosed that the Banū Qurayẓah made a deal with the Muslims to capture and execute 70 of the Quraysh in exchange for forgiveness for reneging on their treaty. He made it clear: if the Banū Qurayẓah ask for hostages, be wary. Finally, he returned to his own tribe, the Ghaṭafān, and likewise commented on the wavering resolve of both the Quraysh and the Jewish tribes.

A short while later, an emissary from the Banū Qurayẓah indeed arrived, asking Abū Sufyān for assurances in the form of 70 of their nobility. Alarm bells rang for Abū Sufyān, as Nuʿaym's warning was coming to effect. Each group sent their emissaries asking for assurances, but each group insisted that they be sent their hostages first to no avail. The three groups were thus left in a deadlock of mistrust, and Nuʿaym's plan was working to perfection. The Banū Qurayẓah understood the Quraysh's refusal as a clear sign of their wavering loyalty, and they began to panic. Kaʿb ibn Asad, the Chieftain, began to wail, "Woe to me! I knew this would happen! By Allah, this man (i.e., Ḥuyayy ibn Akhṭab) brings nothing but bad luck!" Another senior member, Zubayr ibn Baṭṭā, cried, "The Quraysh has now left us and Muhammad will surround us." [752] The Banū Qurayẓah were aware of the grave consequences of their actions when they took them but foolishly did so anyway.

Abū Sufyān grew agitated and distrustful, so he demanded an ultimatum: we all attack tomorrow morning or leave. He sent ʿIkrimah to the Banū Qurayẓah and demanded that they attack from within as the Quraysh and the Ghaṭafān attack the trench. However, Allah ⬥ willed that he approached the Banū Qurayẓah on Friday, and the following day was Saturday—the Sabbath. According to the Halakha (Jewish law), it is strictly forbidden to engage in any form of work or fighting on Saturday. The Banū Qurayẓah requested an extra day so that they may participate on Sunday. The Quraysh were not familiar with Jewish laws and customs, and the idea of the Sabbath was extremely alien to them. The request was so strange to them that it intensified their suspicions. ʿIkrimah returned to Abū Sufyān and declared, "They have betrayed us."

The Tide Officially Turns

Abū Sufyān was furious. He called Ḥuyayy ibn Akhṭab, leader of the Banū Naḍīr, and demanded an explanation. Ḥuyayy explained the concept of the Sabbath, and Abū Sufyān was left perplexed and unsatisfied, shouting, "By al-Lāt and al-ʿUzzā, this is your treachery!" [753] Ḥuyayy was so panicked that he sneaked back into the Banū Qurayẓah and pleaded with them to break the Sabbath despite being a Jew himself. As a devout Jew, Kaʿb ibn Asad was insulted at the very notion and flatly refused. Ḥuyayy was so fearful of the consequences that he chose to remain within the fortress of the Banū Qurayẓah and did not return to the Quraysh.

Meanwhile, the Muslims were unaware of the collapsing allegiances of the Confederates. A fierce storm began to brew, and by the evening it was described as the worst storm some of the Companions ever experienced. The Prophet ﷺ asked for a volunteer to enter enemy territory and gather information. Ḥudhayfah ibn al-Yamān ؓ narrated the story in the first person: one day, decades later, some young Successors were discussing the Battle of Khandaq, and they began waxing lyrical about their own bravery and how they would have fought valiantly for the Prophet ﷺ. One young Successor exclaimed, "I would not have let the Prophet ﷺ walk on his own feet! I would have carried him on my back!" [754] Ḥudhayfah ؓ was incensed at their disrespect of the Companions, and he narrated,

> "I will tell you of that night! We were with the Prophet ﷺ and a fierce storm was gathering all around us. The Quraysh were above us and the Banū Qurayẓah were

below us (quoting Sūrah al-Aḥzāb, 10), and we were scared for our own families. No night had come upon us darker and colder than that night. The wind itself sounded like thunder, and it was so dark that we could not see our fingertips if we extended our hands. The Prophet ﷺ then stood up and said, 'Who will bring me news of the enemy, and I shall be his companion on the Day of Judgement?' Not a single soul replied. The Prophet ﷺ asked again, 'Who will bring me news of the enemy, and I shall be his companion on the Day of Judgement?' Once again, no-one responded. The Prophet ﷺ asked for a third time, 'Who will bring me news of the enemy, and I shall be his companion on the Day of Judgement?' And no-one stood up. The Prophet ﷺ finally said, 'O Ḥudhayfah! You go and bring me news of the enemy.' The Prophet ﷺ named me, so I had no choice but to comply."[755]

Ḥudhayfah ؓ humbly depicted the desperation amongst the Companions and their depleted energy levels after weeks of malnutrition and a harsh environment. No-one had the energy to be the hero, but when called upon, Ḥudhayfah ؓ did not hesitate to obey the command.

Ḥudhayfah stood up, shivering and trembling from the fear and freezing cold, and the Prophet ﷺ made du'ā' for him, "O Allah, preserve and protect him from in front, from behind, from his right, from his left, from above, and from below."[756] Ḥudhayfah commented, "After that du'ā', every fear that I felt disappeared from my heart." He walked through the unforgiving darkness and howling winds and finally made it to the Quraysh's camp. Ḥudhayfah was chosen due to his bravery but also because he was an Anṣārī, and the Quraysh did not recognise him. He said, "I saw someone that I figured must be Abū Sufyān. I had a clear shot, and I was about to reach for my arrow until I remembered that the Prophet ﷺ instructed me to remain anonymous."

Abū Sufyān announced, "I am about to speak [confidentially] so each of you verify the identity of the person next to you." In his quick-wittedness,

Ḥudhayfah grabbed the person to his right aggressively and demanded, "Who are you?!" He then grabbed the person to the left and demanded, "Who are you?!" They both identified themselves, and due to his projected aura of confidence and authority, they did not think to ask him. Abū Sufyān continued, "My people! We are away from our homes, and we cannot remain here forever. Our animals have perished, our horses are tired, and the Banū Qurayẓah have betrayed us. The winds are harming us so much that we cannot light a fire nor keep our pots closed. I advise you to all leave; as for me, I have decided." He then marched straight to his camel and left.

Ḥudhayfah ﷺ returned to base and found the Prophet ﷺ praying. He narrated, "Whenever the Prophet ﷺ was disturbed, he would turn to prayer."[757] The Prophet ﷺ prayed, "O Allah, Revealer of the Book, swift to account—destroy the Confederates, destroy them and shake [the ground beneath] them."[758] The Prophet ﷺ was so cold that he was praying with a blanket wrapped around him. He noticed Ḥudhayfah shivering and motioned to him to join him inside the blanket as he ﷺ prayed. Ḥudhayfah then sat beside the Prophet's feet and the Prophet ﷺ prayed until he finished. Ḥudhayfah then informed the Prophet ﷺ of the good news, and Allah ﷻ revealed, "O believers! Remember Allah's favour upon you when enemy forces came to [besiege] you, so We sent against them a [bitter] wind and forces you could not see. And Allah is All-Seeing of what you do."[759] Humiliated and disgraced, the Quraysh left, never to return again. The tide had officially turned.

The Banū Qurayẓah

After the Confederates left—defeated and disgraced—the Prophet ﷺ returned home. As soon as he ﷺ put down his sword, Jibrīl ﷺ arrived, asking, "Have you put down your weapon?" The Prophet ﷺ answered, "Yes." Jibrīl ﷺ replied, "As for the Angels, they have not put theirs down yet, and I have arrived with a new battalion. O Muhammad, Allah is commanding you to go to the Banū Qurayẓah. I am heading to them now, and I will shake the ground beneath them!"[760] After a month of fatigue, hardship, and forbearance, the Prophet ﷺ

was ordered to march once more before he could enjoy a moment of respite.

The Prophet ﷺ immediately sent out criers throughout Medina, "Whoever listens must obey! No-one is to pray ʿAṣr except at the Banū Qurayẓah."[761] The instruction was direct and non-negotiable, so much so that as the Sun began to set, the Companions were conflicted: should they pray ʿAṣr before the time for Maghrib entered, or follow the command literally and withhold until they arrived? A group of the Companions prayed ʿAṣr en route and continued forth, as missing the prayer is of the gravest of sins, while the other group feared disobeying the Prophet's literal command and thus withheld until they reached the Banū Qurayẓah. Upon their arrival, they informed the Prophet ﷺ of their dispute to which he remained silent.[762] This has been explained by the scholars of Islam as tacit approval of both stances.[763]

The betrayal of the Banū Qurayẓah could not be ignored. They took and re-took their oaths of allegiance three times, vowing to honour the Treaty of Medina only to turn against the Muslims at their most crucial time of need. Had the Quraysh not retreated, the Muslim women and children would have been massacred from within. Allah ﷻ thus demanded from the Prophet ﷺ that action be taken. The Prophet ﷺ arrived at their fortress and instructed them to surrender. They refused, so the Prophet ﷺ laid siege for 25 days, which meant that the Muslims had left their homes for almost two continuous months.

The Banū Qurayẓah began to deliberate amongst themselves. Kaʿb ibn Asad suggested, "We have three options: we accept this man's religion; by Allah we all know that he is the Prophet predicted in our Books." They replied, "By Allah, we will never leave our laws and religion." Kaʿb continued, "Or we kill our own families and charge outside with our swords." They refused, so he continued, "The final option is to launch a surprise attack, and the best surprise would be to attack on the Sabbath, as they would not expect us to do so." They replied, "We will never violate the Sabbath! Allah will send a punishment upon us." Kaʿb blurted, "By Allah, since the day your mothers have given birth to you, none of you have ever made a decision!"[764]

They then sent a messenger to the Prophet ﷺ to plead, "Grant us what you granted the Banū Naḍīr (i.e., exile)." The Prophet ﷺ refused, and they returned and offered to relinquish all their property and wealth, and the Prophet ﷺ again refused. They then requested that Abū Lubābah be sent in, a Companion from the Aws who had close ties with the Banū Qurayẓah in the days of Ignorance, and the Prophet ﷺ agreed. Abū Lubābah entered upon them, and they asked him whether they should surrender. Abū Lubābah looked around and saw the destitute men, wailing women, and crying children, and his heart softened towards them. He was overwhelmed with sympathy, and in a moment of weakness, he replied, "Yes, you should..." However, he then gestured with his thumb across his throat, as if to say "...but you will be executed." Abū Lubābah narrated, "As soon as I said this, I immediately realised that I had been treacherous to Allah and His Messenger." [765]

Abū Lubābah left the fortress surreptitiously, sneaked past the Muslims, marched straight to the Prophet's Mosque, tied himself to a pillar, and said, "By Allah, I will remain tied to his pillar until Allah accepts my repentance, and I shall never return to the Banū Qurayẓah again, for I will never be in an area where I disobeyed Allah and His Messenger." The Prophet ﷺ eventually asked about Abū Lubābah and was informed about what occurred. He ﷺ then said, "If he had come to me, I would have asked Allah to forgive him, but now that he has made an oath to Allah, I cannot intervene." [766]

One day, the Prophet ﷺ woke up laughing, and Umm Salamah ؓ asked, "What has made you laugh, O Messenger of Allah? May Allah keep you ever laughing!" The Prophet ﷺ replied, "Allah has accepted the repentance of Abū Lubābah." Allah ﷻ revealed, "Some others have confessed their wrongdoing: they have mixed goodness with evil. [It is right to] hope that Allah will turn to them in Mercy. Surely Allah is All-Forgiving, Most Merciful." [767] Imam Abū ʿUthmān al-Nahdī ؓ commented, "This verse is the most optimistic verse for the Ummah in the whole Qur'an." [768] Umm Salamah ؓ said to Abū Lubābah, "Rejoice! Allah has accepted your repentance." The Companions tried to untie him, but he resisted, saying, "No! I will remain until the Prophet ﷺ comes and unties me himself." The Prophet ﷺ then personally untied him and informed him of Allah's verdict.

As for the Banū Qurayẓah, some guards noticed a man escaping the fortress. The man was ʿAmr ibn Saʿdā, one of the only members of the Banū Qurayẓah who vocally opposed their decision to betray the Prophet ﷺ. Muhammad ibn Maslamah ؓ seized him but knew that he was against their treachery. He let him go and said, "O Allah, overlook my overlooking of him." ʿAmr ibn Saʿdā fled to Medina, and the next morning disappeared, never to be heard from again. The Prophet ﷺ commented, "That was a man whom Allah saved due to his integrity."[769]

The next morning, the Banū Qurayẓah finally surrendered. The Prophet ﷺ had not yet declared the punishment, but the Aws began pleading with him ﷺ to be lenient in his verdict, as they were sympathetic due to their previous ties. The Prophet ﷺ finally relented and said, "Would you be happy if one of your own decided their fate?" They said, "Of course, O Messenger of Allah!" He ﷺ replied, "I have thus chosen Saʿd ibn Muʿādh."[770] The Prophet ﷺ knew that he would be unconditionally followed, but he treated the Aws with kindness. Saʿd, their revered leader, was on his deathbed from the blow he suffered in the Battle of the Trench a month prior. The Aws continued to plead with Saʿd to rule with clemency, reminding him of his previous ties with the Banū Qurayẓah, to which he replied, "Now is the time for Saʿd to disregard the criticism of any critic on matters relating to Allah and His Messenger." In other words, Saʿd was moments from death, so pleasing Allah was his only concern.

As Saʿd was carried to the Muslims, the Prophet ﷺ said, "Stand up to greet your leader."[771] There is no other person in the entire *sīrah* for whom the Prophet ﷺ instructed others to stand up to greet, and the Prophet ﷺ even forbade the Companions from standing up to greet himself ﷺ.[i] The Prophet ﷺ truly held Saʿd ibn Muʿādh in the highest regard. He ﷺ then said, "Your people have accepted you as a judge to

---

i The Prophet ﷺ said, "Whoever loves that people stand up for him, let him be prepared to sit down in the fire of Hell." (Abū Dāwūd al-Sijistānī, *Sunan Abī Dāwūd*, vol. 7, p. 516). These Hadiths can be reconciled by clarifying that the threat of Hell is for those who are pleased that people stand up for them and expect it, whereas it is permissible to stand up for someone on a special occasion.

rule over these people." Saʿd 🙼 then turned to the Aws and demanded, "I ask you by Allah! Will you obey my verdict?" The Aws replied in the affirmative, then Saʿd turned to the Prophet 🙼—lowering his head out of humility and respect—and asked coyly, "And you, O Messenger of Allah?" The Prophet 🙼 also agreed.

Saʿd 🙼 then immediately ruled, "My judgement is that their men be executed, their property distributed, and their women and children taken captive." The Prophet 🙼 replied, "By Allah, O Saʿd, you have decreed upon them the verdict of Allah 🙼 from above the Seven Heavens."[772] The ruling was also consistent with the Banū Qurayẓah's own laws; as per the Torah, "When the Lord, your God, delivers it (i.e., victory) in your hand, put to the sword all the men in it. And as for the women children, livestock, and everything else in the city, you may take it as plunder for yourselves, and you may use the plunder your Lord has given you from your enemies."[773]

Ḥuyayy ibn Akhṭab, leader of the Banū Naḍīr, inadvertently trapped himself with the Banū Qurayẓah when he was too scared to return to the Quraysh. As he was being marched away, he turned to the Prophet 🙼 and said, "By Allah, I do not regret my animosity towards you, but whomever Allah humiliates is truly humiliated."[774] As Kaʿb ibn Asad, leader of the Banū Qurayẓah, was marched away, the Prophet 🙼 said, "O Kaʿb, why didn't you benefit from Ibn Kharrāsh, for he believed in me and commanded you to follow me." Ibn Kharrāsh was a Rabbi who predicted the coming of a Prophet before the time of the Prophet 🙼. Kaʿb replied, "I swear by Allah, O Abū al-Qāsim, that is true. Were it not for the fact that the Jews would criticise me and accuse me of cowardice and fear of death, I would follow you now. But I die upon the faith of my people."[775] The adult males were thus executed as per divine judgment. No women or children were killed except for one woman who had killed a Companion during the siege by pushing a boulder over the wall and crushing him.

The Companion Thābit ibn Qays ibn Shammās 🙼 was once saved in the Battle of Buʿāth by a man from the Banū Qurayẓah by the name of Zubayr ibn Baṭṭā'. Thābit approached Zubayr and offered to repay the favour by facilitating his freedom. Thābit requested Zubayr's freedom and the Prophet ﷺ accepted. Zubayr remarked, "What use is life without family?" Thābit then requested the Prophet ﷺ to free his family, and the Prophet ﷺ again accepted. Zubayr then said, "What use is life without possessions?" Thābit once more asked the Prophet ﷺ and it was approved. Zubayr then asked about the whereabouts of his friend and was informed that he had been killed. He continued to ask about his colleagues, who had all been killed, until he finally said, "What is the purpose of life without companions?" He then resigned himself to death and requested not to be saved. A few other people were spared following similar requests from the Companions, and a few others accepted Islam, but the majority were executed.

Critics describe this event as a "massacre" in a bid to besmirch the honour of the Prophet ﷺ. It was not a massacre, but a punishment for the crime of treason. Tribal politics of 7th century Arabia, as already discussed, qualify every male adult to be of fighting status. It is also essential not to interpret the event in isolation, but rather understand the verdict within the context of ongoing betrayal and treason. The Banū Qaynuqāʿ were expelled due to their aggression and effrontery in breaking the treaty. The Banū Naḍīr, in addition to conspiring with the Quraysh against the Muslims in the Battle of Sawīq, attempted to assassinate the Prophet ﷺ. Instead of replying in kind, the Prophet ﷺ spared them and instead ruled to exile, only for them to return with a 10,000-man strong army. The Banū Qurayẓah, having witnessed these events, affirmed their oath of allegiance and pledged their loyalty. Nevertheless, they conspired and betrayed the Muslims at their most vulnerable point whereby they had no-one to protect them except the Mercy of Allah ﷻ.

The Banū Qurayẓah were fully aware that their actions constituted treason—as per their Torah as well as the Shariah—but consciously took the risk in a bid to capitalise on the Ummah's weakness. They were unsuccessful and ultimately paid the price. The fact that specific people were spared and forgiven because of their past good deeds clearly demonstrates that the punishment was due to their actions, not their identity, ethnicity, or religion.

Capturing Thumāmah ibn Uthāl

A short while after the Battle of the Trench, travelling back from a short expedition, Muhammad ibn Maslamah ﷺ encountered a small, visibly prestigious entourage. Unaware of their intentions, he captured them and brought them to the Prophet ﷺ. The Prophet ﷺ asked, "Don't you know who your captive is? You have captured Thumāmah ibn Uthāl, the Chieftain of the Banū Ḥanīfah."[776] Leader of one of the largest tribes of the whole of Arabia, he rivalled the likes of Abū Ṭālib in prestige. Thumāmah was a supporter of the Quraysh against Islam, and at one point publicly threatened to kill the Prophet ﷺ if he was given the chance.[777] Nevertheless, the Prophet ﷺ ordered the Companions to treat him well, and he was held in the Prophet's Mosque. He was fed the same meal as the Prophet ﷺ, and while the Prophet's food did not differ from the rest of the Companions, it was a symbolic honour to be fed the same food as the leader.

The next morning, the Prophet ﷺ asked, "What do you have to say, O Thumāmah?" As a man of prestige, Thumāmah did not beg for his life. He replied, "O Muhammad, if you kill me, you will kill a man whose blood is of worth; if you are generous, you are generous to a man who knows how to show gratitude; and if you want money, then name your price."[778] Put plainly, Thumāmah expressed that his death would lead to a war but freeing him would be mutually beneficial. The Prophet ﷺ then left without responding. Thumāmah continued to be held in the mosque, which was a calculated decision by the Prophet ﷺ. Thumāmah observed the Muslim lifestyle for the entire day, including five daily prayers, reminders by the Prophet ﷺ, and the overarching atmosphere of brotherhood.

The Prophet ﷺ approached him again the following morning, asked the same question, and received the same reply. He ﷺ returned the third day, asked the same question, and received the same response. This time, the Prophet ﷺ instructed the Companions to set him free without a ransom. Thumāmah was released, and he immediately took a bath then declared, "I bear witness that there is no god but Allah, and I bear witness that Muhammad is the Messenger of Allah."

He then said, "O Muhammad, I swear by Allah that there was no face in this world more despised to me than yours, but now, by Allah, it is the most beautiful face to me. And I swear by Allah that there was no religion more despised to me than your religion, but now, by Allah, it is the most beautiful religion to me. And I swear by Allah that there was no city more despised to me than your city, but now, by Allah, it is the most beautiful city to me."[779] Within three days of observing the Prophet ﷺ and the Companions ﵁, Thumāmah's heart flipped, and Islam entered it entirely.

Thumāmah then explained to the Prophet ﷺ that he was en route to perform 'Umrah when he was captured, which also explains why he was relatively unarmed. He asked the Prophet ﷺ if he should continue to perform 'Umrah, and the Prophet ﷺ agreed. Thumāmah thus embarked on his 'Umrah and became the first Muslim to perform 'Umrah with a monotheistic *talbiyah*[ii]. The Quraysh were shocked at hearing this *talbiyah* and asked, "Are you a Sabian, O Thumāmah?" Thumāmah replied, "No, I have become a Muslim!" The Quraysh were enraged and began to surround him and unsheathe their swords. Eventually, they backed down, as they realised that killing a man of his status would have extreme repercussions. Thumāmah, in turn, was furious, and threatened, "By Allah, not a single grain will reach Mecca until the Prophet ﷺ explicitly commands me to do so!"[780] Most of the produce in Mecca was brought through routes controlled by Thumāmah, and so the Quraysh were wholly dependent on his co-operation.

Thumāmah fulfilled his threat, and all forms of sustenance transported from the Najd were cut off entirely. Supplies in Mecca dwindled for months until they reached a point of famine, eating the most destitute meals, such as *'ilhiz*, a combination of camel blood, camel hair, and

---

ii   *"Talbiyah"* is from the word *"labbayk"* which means "At your service". It refers to the supplication chanted during Hajj and 'Umrah, which is, "At your service, O Allah, at your service. At your service—You have no partner—at your service. Certainly, [all] Praise and Blessings are Yours, as is the Dominion. You have no partner." After the phrase "You have no partner...", the Quraysh, as Pagans, would add "...except for a partner You control and who has no control [over You]." This of course constitutes *shirk*, so the Prophet ﷺ taught Thumāmah the correct *talbiyah*.

other undesirable ingredients. The Quraysh were on the brink of death, and Abū Sufyān was forced to humiliate himself and approach the Prophet ﷺ. Despite being faced with famine, his animosity was still present in his tone, "I ask you by Allah, and by our ties of kinship, do you not claim that Allah sent you as a mercy to the worlds?" The Prophet replied, "Yes." Abū Sufyān then stated, "By Allah, I have seen you do nothing but kill fathers with swords and kill their sons with hunger."[781] They were in a literal state of war, but the Prophet ﷺ retained his compassion and wrote to Thumāmah instructing him to lift the boycott.

The Treaty of Ḥudaybiyyah

20

In 6 AH, the Prophet ﷺ dreamt that he was performing *ṭawāf* in *iḥrām*. As already explained, the dreams of the Prophet ﷺ constitute Revelation, and the Prophet ﷺ interpreted the dream as a command from Allah ﷻ to perform ʿUmrah. The Qur'an corroborates, "Indeed, Allah will fulfil His Messenger's vision in all truth: Allah willing, you will surely enter the Sacred Mosque, in security—[some with] shaved heads and [others with] hair shortened—without fear. He knew what you did not know, so He first granted you the triumph at hand."[782]

The Prophet ﷺ announced his intention to perform ʿUmrah and urged everyone to join. The Companions were elated, as they had not seen Mecca in six years. They were overwhelmed with excitement and began preparing immediately. However, some Bedouins around Medina refused to participate, citing family or work obligations. Allah ﷻ states, "The Bedouins who stayed behind will say to you, 'We were preoccupied with our wealth and families, so ask forgiveness for us.' They say with their tongues what is not in their hearts. Say, 'Who then can stand between you and Allah in any way, if He intends harm or benefit for you? In fact, Allah is All-Aware of what you do. The truth is: you thought that the Messenger and the believers would never return to their families again. And that was made appealing in your hearts. You harboured evil thoughts [about Allah], and so became a doomed people.'"[783]

The Bedouins' laziness and fear prevented them from upgrading their honour and status in the eyes of Allah and His Messenger. There are levels of prestige amongst the Companions. The highest rank amongst the Companions is the "Ten Promised Paradise", namely: Abū Bakr al-Ṣiddīq, ʿUmar ibn al-Khaṭṭāb, ʿUthmān ibn ʿAffān, ʿAlī ibn Abī Ṭālib, Ṭalḥah ibn ʿUbaydillāh, Zubayr ibn al-ʿAwwām, ʿAbdurraḥmān ibn ʿAwf, Saʿd ibn Abī Waqqāṣ, Saʿīd ibn Zayd, and Abū ʿUbaydah ibn al-Jarrāḥ ﵃. The second level is the attendees of the Battle of Badr, and the third level is the attendees of Ḥudaybiyyah. After these three levels, those who accepted Islam before the Conquest of Mecca are considered to be better than those who accepted Islam after. These Bedouins therefore deprived themselves of being included within the highest three ranks of the Companions due to their arrogance and negligence.

On the 1st of Dhū al-Qaʿdah, 1,400 Companions left Medina with the intention of performing ʿUmrah. The scholars differ as to whether they were armed for battle, but the opinions are easily reconciled by explaining that they were not carrying their arms due to being in *iḥrām*, but their arms were in their caravans ready to be used if needed. However, the Prophet ﷺ waited until the 1st of Dhū al-Qaʿdah, which is the first day of the Four Sacred Months wherein fighting is forbidden, as he was sending a clear message that war was not intended. He ﷺ also did not cover his tracks and embarked straight to Mecca via the main routes rather than hiding his tracks, as would typically be done when intending battle.

The Prophet ﷺ sent Busr ibn Sufyān al-Khuzāʿī ﵁ to Mecca to observe the Quraysh and report back. He specifically sent someone from the Banū Khuzāʿah, as they were a neutral tribe, and the Quraysh would not suspect them of being Muslim. The Prophet ﷺ once again demonstrated wisdom and caution despite retaining complete *tawakkul* in Allah. The Prophet ﷺ reached ʿUsfān, an area around the half-way mark between Mecca and Medina. Busr returned and informed the Prophet ﷺ that the Quraysh have armed themselves and have worn their leopard skins, which was a symbol of war. Abū Sufyān sent Khālid ibn al-Walīd to camp at Ghumaym, which was an area towards the entrance of Mecca.

The Prophet ﷺ remarked, "Woe to the Quraysh, they are consumed by war. Why must they involve themselves in my affairs? What would they lose by letting the other Arabs deal with me? If the other Arabs attack me and win, they will get their desired result; and if I win over the other Arabs, the honour will be with them too (as he ﷺ is a Qurashī). By Allah I will continue to fight them with that which Allah has sent me until Allah grants me victory or this neck of mine is cut off."[784] The Prophet ﷺ lamented the Quraysh's desire for war, especially with their own people, but never abandoned Allah's command.

The Prophet ﷺ then addressed his Companions. As always, he began by praising Allah ﷻ then he explained the situation. The Prophet ﷺ suggested that they attack the surrounding tribes that have sent men alongside the Quraysh, which will draw out the Quraysh. He ﷺ then asked what the Companions thought, and Abū Bakr ؓ said, "O Messenger of Allah, you left your house intending only the House of Allah (i.e., to perform ʿUmrah, not engage in battle), so let us go where we initially intended, and we will only fight if they fight us." The Prophet ﷺ agreed and said, "Let us go forth in the Name of Allah, Most High."[785]

Khālid ibn al-Walīd had blocked the main entrance to Mecca, so the Muslims searched for an alternative route. They were forced to pass by an extended area of thorns as well as volcanic plains, which was extremely arduous. The Prophet ﷺ said to the Companions, "This valley for you is like the door was for the Children of Israel." He ﷺ then recited the verse, "And [Remember] when We said, 'Enter this city and eat wherever you please; enter the door with humility, saying, "Absolve us." We will forgive your sins and multiply the reward for the good-doers.'"[786] The Prophet ﷺ then said, "No-one shall pass through this valley except that all of their sins shall be forgiven."[787]

As night fell, they reached the plain of Ḥudaybiyyah. The Prophet's camel, called al-Qaswā', then suddenly sat down and refused to move. The Companions tried to move her but could not, and they commented frustratingly, "Al-Qaswā' has become stubborn!" The Prophet ﷺ replied, "Al-Qaswā' has not become stubborn, nor is that in her nature. Rather, she is being prevented by the One Who prevented the elephant[i]."[788] They also ran out of drinking water, as their trip was extended by the detour. The well of Ḥudaybiyyah was also almost empty, and the Companions were beginning to worry. The Prophet ﷺ instructed some Companions to enter the well and retrieve a bucket of water. He ﷺ gargled some water and placed the water back in the bucket and back into the well. Water then suddenly began to gush out of the well, which was enough for the entire 1,400-man group for the entire time they were camped at Ḥudaybiyyah.[789]

Insistence on Peace

The Prophet ﷺ then announced to the Companions, "I swear by the One in Whose Hand is my soul that the Quraysh will not stipulate any condition to respect the signs of Allah (i.e., the Sacred Months) except that I will accept those conditions."[790] In other words, the Prophet ﷺ will do whatever it takes to ensure that battle does not take place in order not to violate the sanctity of the Sacred Months. Despite the Prophet ﷺ insisting on peace, the Quraysh were planning a surprise attack. 80 of the Quraysh attacked the Muslims at Ḥudaybiyyah before Fajr, but the Muslim scouts intercepted their movements, and the Muslims surrounded them. Following the Prophet's strict instructions, they forced all 80 fighters to surrender without causing any bloodshed. The Prophet ﷺ forgave all 80 of them and sent them back to Mecca. The Prophet ﷺ clearly demonstrated, once more, his intention for peace. Allah ﷻ revealed, "He is the One Who held back their hands from you and your hands from them in the valley of [Ḥudaybiyyah, near] Mecca, after giving you the upper hand over [a group of] them. And Allah is All-Seeing of what you do."[791]

The first man to act as a mediator was Budayl ibn Warqā', the Chieftain of the Banū Khuzā'ah, who were neutral. They were sympathetic to Islam but had not yet converted at this point. He approached the Prophet ﷺ and said, "O Muhammad, I have just returned from

i In reference to Abraha's attempt to destroy the Holy Ka'bah using African elephants.

the other side of Ḥudaybiyyah, and I have left the sons of Kaʿb and ʿAmr ibn Luʾayy armed to the teeth." Kaʿb and ʿAmr ibn Luʾayy were of the ancestors of the Quraysh, and Budayl's choice of describing the Quraysh in this manner was a form of respect. He continued, "They are armed and are waiting to fight you to prevent you from entering the Ḥaram."[792]

The Prophet ﷺ responded, "We did not come to fight. Rather, we have come to show honour to the House of Allah (i.e., to perform ʿUmrah). Indeed, war has hurt the Quraysh, and if they wish, we can negotiate peace. But if they wish, I swear by the One in Whose Hand is my soul that I will show them what we are capable of, and we will fight until my head is separated from my neck and Allah decides the matter (an Arabic expression to mean 'we will fight to the death')."[793] The Prophet ﷺ then offered to wait if the Quraysh preferred to vacate the city while the Muslims performed ʿUmrah so as not to create tension within the Ḥaram.

Budayl approached the Quraysh to relay what the Prophet ﷺ said, but he was not officially chosen as a mediator, so he sought permission first. Ibn Isḥāq ؒ commented, "The foolish amongst them said, 'We have no reason to listen to you; you have nothing new to tell us.' But the people of intelligence said, 'Let him speak and tell us what he has to say.'"[794] Wisdom prevailed, and Budayl relayed the Prophet's preference of peace but readiness to fight. He then added, "O Quraysh, you are being hasty with this man. He has not come to fight, he has come to visit this House, honouring its sanctity." The Quraysh responded, "By Allah we will never allow him to enter Mecca while the Arabs say that he had the better hand over us."[795]

The Quraysh's crime in this regard cannot be understated: the Kaʿbah was a Ḥaram for all, and the act of barring someone from venerating its sanctity was truly unprecedented. The Arabs would say, "A man would see his father's killer performing *ṭawāf* and he could not touch him."[796] The Quraysh, and every custodian of the Kaʿbah before the Quraysh, had never prevented anyone from visiting the Kaʿbah, especially to perform ʿUmrah. Nevertheless, the pride and ego of the Quraysh could not tolerate the Muslims entering, as it may result in neighbouring Arab tribes gossiping about their supposed weakness.

ʿUrwah ibn Masʿūd al-Thaqafī then volunteered to mediate. He belonged to the tribe of Thaqīf in Ṭā'if and thus enjoyed a brotherly relationship with the Quraysh. ʿUrwah stood up and attempted to cajole the Quraysh, "Am I not a father to you? Am I not a son to you?" In other words, are we not still relatives? He continued, also reminding them of his history of helping and supporting them. The Quraysh finally caved and allowed him to represent them in the mediation.

ʿUrwah approached the Muslims, and the Prophet ﷺ repeated the same sentence emphasising peace. ʿUrwah, as if he did not register anything the Prophet ﷺ said, replied, "O Muhammad, you say you are calling to Allah, but then you come with a group of unknown people. You break the ties of kinship, violate the sanctity of the Ḥaram, and intend to spill blood." The Prophet ﷺ refuted his claims, "I have only come to fulfil the ties of kinship. I have come to change their religion for the better and make their lives better."[797]

ʿUrwah said, "O Muhammad, [if you attack them,] have you heard of anyone destroying their own tribe before you? [And if they attack you,] then by Allah I do not see dignified men around you. They seem to be a medley of different bandits, and they will flee at the earliest opportunity." Suddenly, Abū Bakr al-Ṣiddīq ؓ—the softest, kindest, noblest Companion—yelled from afar the vilest, most abhorrent curse[ii] he could conjure. ʿUrwah demanded, "Who is that?!" Abū Bakr

ii Disclaimer: graphic content. The curse was "Suck the clitoris of al-Lāt!" The exact Arabic wording is *"Umṣuṣ baẓr al-Lāt"* and it can be found in Ṣaḥīḥ al-Bukhārī, the most authentic book of Hadith. (Bukhārī, *Ṣaḥīḥ al-Bukhārī*, p. 670). Such indecent words may shock the audience, especially from the noble likes of Abū Bakr al-Ṣiddīq ؓ. It is important to note, however, that it was an extreme exception. When Abū Bakr ؓ would be insulted, he would often reply with the verse, "The servants of the Most Compassionate are those who walk on the Earth humbly, and when the foolish address them [improperly], they only respond with peace." (*al-Furqān*, 63). However, in this instance, Abū Bakr ؓ was enraged on behalf of the Prophet's honour and thus chose the vilest disparage he could conjure in the moment. Even in such cases, it is the only recorded instance of such language being used.

then shouted defiantly, "The son of Abū Quḥāfah!" ʿUrwah then said, "By Allah if I did not still owe you for a favour, I would have responded in kind." Abū Bakr never resorted to bad language when cursed or abused, but he could not tolerate the Prophet ﷺ being insulted and his Companions being accused of treachery. ʿUrwah attempted to help, but due to not understanding the true essence of Islam, inadvertently aggravated the situation. He viewed the situation from a tribal lens, and the vast majority of the Companions were not Qurashī; rather, they comprised mainly of the Aws and Khazraj as well as converts from various other tribes. He did not understand the overriding power of Islam in creating an unparalleled bond of brotherhood.

It was the custom of the Arab Chieftains to gently grab the beards of their counterparts as a gesture of tenderness and brotherhood. Whenever ʿUrwah would touch the Prophet's beard, a Companion guarding the Prophet ﷺ would smack ʿUrwah's hand with the pommel of his sword. The blows would be harder each time until finally the guard said, "Get your hand away from the Prophet ﷺ before it is cut off from its owner." The Companion's face was covered, so ʿUrwah asked, "Who is this man?!" It turned out to be his own nephew, al-Mughīrah ibn Shuʿbah al-Thaqafī ؓ. ʿUrwah continued to try and persuade the Prophet ﷺ but to no avail, eventually returning to the Quraysh.

ʿUrwah narrated his experience to the Quraysh,

> "O people, I have visited kings and have entered the palaces of Caesar in Rome, Khosrow in Persia, and the Negus in Abyssinia. By Allah, I have never seen any king shown more respect than the Companions of Muhammad show Muhammad. By Allah, he did not even spit except that one of them would catch it before it reaches the ground and rub it over their body. He did not perform ablution except that they would fight each other to catch the droplets. If he commanded them to do something, he would simply raise his face and they would race to be the one chosen to fulfil the command. When he spoke, they lowered their faces before him,

and none of them would even look at his face directly out of shyness and veneration."[798]

ʿUrwah's comprehensive transformation in a single hour is nothing short of miraculous; after initially accusing the Companions of wavering in their belief and support, he began showering them with lavish praise of commitment and veneration. He continued, "If you wish the sword, then they will give you what you wish. I have seen a group that do not care what happens to them if their companion (i.e., the Prophet ﷺ) is harmed. By Allah, even the women amongst them will never hand him over, no matter the cost. Take my advice: I fear that you will not be able to win over him, and besides, he is a man who has come to this House wishing to honour it, bringing sacrificial animals, but is being denied and prevented."[799] Blinded by their arrogance, the Quraysh dismissed all that ʿUrwah had to say. ʿUrwah then left and took the tribe of Thaqīf with him.

The Prophet ﷺ then sent Khirāsh ibn Umayyah ؓ from the tribe of Khuzāʿah, as he was neither from the Anṣār nor the Muhājirūn. Though he was a Muslim, he had a degree of tribal neutrality. To further emphasise his intent for peace, he sent Khirāsh on al-Thaʿlab, one of the Prophet's own camels. However, the Quraysh took badly to this and began attacking him, injuring al-Thaʿlab and nearly killing Khirāsh. Another Khuzāʿī eventually stopped the brawl and reminded the Quraysh not to spark tribal tensions with the Banū Khuzāʿah. Khirāsh rushed back, and the ball was in the court of the Quraysh to send their own emissary. Eventually, they sent al-Ḥulays ibn ʿAlqamah from the tribe of Kinānah, the largest tribe surrounding Mecca.

As al-Ḥulays approached from a distance, the Prophet ﷺ said to the Companions, "This is al-Ḥulays ibn ʿAlqamah from the tribe of Kinānah. They respect sacrificial animals, so bring out the camels." The Prophet ﷺ himself had 70 camels to sacrifice for the poor of Mecca. Altogether, there were hundreds of camels ready to be sacrificed, and they were all brought out. Al-Ḥulays approached, seeing all these animals ready to be sacrificed for the sake of Allah, as well as the Muslims in *iḥrām* chanting the *talbiyah*, and he did not even enter the Muslim camp; he turned straight back to the Quraysh and said, "O people of Quraysh! We never allied with you to support such actions. Is it right to block the passage of those who intend to come and honour the House of Allah?"[800] The Quraysh again replied arrogantly, calling al-Ḥulays an ignorant Bedouin. Al-Ḥulays then left and took the Kinānah with him.

The Prophet ﷺ then chose ʿUmar ibn al-Khaṭṭāb ؓ. After numerous attempts of mediation, he chose an elite member of the Quraysh. However, ʿUmar said, "O Messenger of Allah, my animosity towards the Quraysh is well known, and I fear that the Quraysh will kill me, as I do not have anyone from my subtribe to protect me. If you want me to go, I will go; but ʿUthmān ibn ʿAffān is more noble in their eyes than me."[801] Nobody can ever accuse the famously brave ʿUmar of cowardice, so it is clear that ʿUmar is suggesting this as a strategic manoeuvre. ʿUthmān was the son of Abū Sufyān's cousin, so there was a familial link, and he was thus sent to the Quraysh to mediate.

ʿUthmān ؓ embarked to Mecca but was blocked at the entrance by a group of the Quraysh. They denied him entry and told him to return, but amongst them was his cousin, Abān ibn al-Saʿīd ibn al-ʿĀṣ. Abān's heart softened towards his younger cousin, and so he promised ʿUthmān protection in Mecca and allowed him to enter the city on Abān's horse. As he left, the Prophet ﷺ instructed ʿUthmān to visit all the struggling Muslim converts and inform them that Allah ﷻ is aware of their situation and that He will make a way out for them soon.

The Pledge of Divine Acceptance

ʿUthmān began to negotiate with the Quraysh, but the Muslims began to worry about the length of time he was in Mecca. Rumours began to spread that ʿUthmān was hurt, and those rumours grew and eventually it was said that he was killed. The Prophet ﷺ was told definitively that ʿUthmān had been killed, so he said, "By Allah, we will not leave until he is avenged." A crier was sent out to the Muslims, notifying them that Jibrīl ؑ descended, calling them to pledge an oath to the Prophet ﷺ. Allah ﷻ of course knew that ʿUthmān was alive, but it was a test for the Muslims: the pledge was to fight the Quraysh until the death, with no option to retreat.

This oath would be known as "The Pledge of Divine Acceptance" (Bayʿah al-Riḍwān[iii]), as Allah ﷻ revealed, "Indeed, Allah was pleased with the believers when they pledged their allegiance to you under the tree. He knew what was in their hearts, so He sent down serenity upon them and rewarded them with a victory at hand."[802] He ﷻ also revealed, "Surely those who pledge allegiance to you are actually pledging allegiance to Allah. Allah's Hand is over theirs. Whoever breaks their pledge, it will only be to their own loss. And whoever fulfils their pledge to Allah, He will grant them a great reward."[803]

The Muslims were outnumbered by three to one, fatigued from their travel with minimal resources, and were not prepared for battle, but Allah ﷻ demanded a pledge of allegiance. This is why the attendees of the Pledge of Divine Acceptance hold the highest station after the attendees of the Battle of Badr. The Prophet ﷺ took an oath from every single attendee except for one Hypocrite who was hiding behind his camel. Demonstrating his undying love and respect for ʿUthmān ؓ, the Prophet ﷺ took his left hand and clasped it in his right and said, "This is for ʿUthmān!" i.e., this is ʿUthmān's pledge. He ﷺ then said to his Companions, "You are the best people on Earth right now."[804] After he returned to Medina, he ﷺ said, "None who gave the Pledge of Divine Acceptance under the tree will enter the Fire of Hell."[805]

Word reached the Quraysh that the Muslims had pledged to avenge ʿUthmān, so they quickly sent him back alive and well. As ʿUthmān returned, some of the Muslims remarked that ʿUthmān must have enjoyed himself and performed *ṭawāf*, to which the Prophet ﷺ said, "I do not think he would while we are confined." The Prophet ﷺ knew ʿUthmān intimately and knew that he would not perform *ṭawāf* while the Muslims were deprived. ʿUthmān ؓ finally arrived, and someone jokingly remarked, "Have you satisfied yourself?" to which ʿUthmān ؓ

---

iii *"Riḍwān"* can be translated as "pleasure" but in this context is more accurately described as "Divine Acceptance".

replied, "What an evil thought you had of me! Did you think I would perform *ṭawāf* while the Prophet ﷺ was out here? By Allah, if I stayed in Mecca for one year, I would not perform *ṭawāf* until the Prophet ﷺ did so first."[806] This chapter is usually titled "The Treaty of Ḥudaybiyyah" but most of the Companions referred to it as "The Battle (Ghazwah) of Ḥudaybiyyah" despite no actual fighting taking place. The fact that they did not fight but still counted it amongst their battles provides a useful insight into the mentality of the Companions. As the Prophet ﷺ said, "Actions are judged by their intentions."[807]

The Treaty

The rumours regarding ʿUthmān ‎ؓ inadvertently accelerated the negotiation process, as the Quraysh became acutely aware of what the Muslims, fuelled by *īmān*, were willing to do. They first sent Mikraz ibn Ḥafṣ to no avail but then finally sent a senior delegate, Suhayl ibn ʿAmr. Suhayl ‎ؓ would later accept Islam and cement himself as a man of piety and honour, but at this moment in time was still against Islam. The Quraysh instructed Suhayl that he may compromise on any clause except that the Muslims were not to perform ʿUmrah this year, as it would seem like a defeat for the Quraysh in the eyes of the neighbouring Arabs.

Suhayl sat with the Prophet ﷺ to draw up a treaty, and the Prophet ﷺ chose ʿAlī ‎ؓ as his scribe. The Prophet ﷺ dictated, "In the Name of Allah, the Most Compassionate, Most Merciful..." Suhayl interrupted the Prophet ﷺ and said, "As for this phrase, I have never heard it, and I do not know this 'Most Compassionate (al-Raḥmān)'. Instead, write, 'In the Name of Allah' as we are accustomed." The Prophet ﷺ agreed then dictated, "This is an agreement between Muhammad, the Messenger of Allah, and Suhayl ibn ʿAmr..." As ʿAlī ‎ؓ wrote "Messenger of Allah..." Suhayl interrupted again, "As for you being the Messenger of Allah, had we believed this to be true, we would not prevent you from the Kaʿbah nor would we have fought you. Instead, write, 'Muhammad ibn ʿAbdillāh'." The Prophet ﷺ said, "By Allah, I am the Messenger of Allah even if you deny it." He ﷺ then instructed ʿAlī to write "Muḥammad ibn ʿAbdillāh". Angered and defiant, ʿAlī ؓ refused to erase "Messenger of Allah", so the Prophet ﷺ scratched it out with his own blessed hand.

The Prophet ﷺ then stipulated that the Quraysh must allow the Muslims to perform ʿUmrah. Suhayl said, "As for this year, then no; rather, that will be next year." Suhayl then added extra conditions, "Any man that renegades from the Quraysh must be handed back to Mecca." Suhayl's own children were locked up in Mecca for attempting to leave and join the Prophet ﷺ, so Suhayl personally benefited from this stipulation. The Muslims were outraged at such a suggestion, as most Muslims were Emigrants. They remarked, "How can we return a Muslim to the Polytheists after they come to us as a Muslim?" ʿAlī ؓ also argued against this stipulation, refusing to write it down.

Suddenly, in an extraordinary turn of events, the clanging of chains was heard from afar, and it was none other than Abū Jandal ؓ, the son of Suhayl ibn ʿAmr. He had escaped from his dungeon after years of imprisonment; previously, escape was futile, as there was no way to travel to Medina, but he must have heard of the Muslims' presence, and seized the opportunity to escape. Not realising his father was present, he began screaming, "Help, O Muslims!" Unbeknownst to Abū Jandal, he was a live embodiment of the very stipulation being debated. Suhayl pointed to his son and said, "O Muhammad, this is the first person upon whom the stipulation will be applied." [808]

The Prophet ﷺ remarked that the stipulation had not even been written yet, but Suhayl was so emotionally invested that he threatened to abandon the entire treaty if the condition was not accepted. The Prophet ﷺ then negotiated, "Gift him to me." In other words: let Abū Jandal stay, and the stipulation will be enforced thereafter. Suhayl refused, and the Prophet ﷺ continued to request, "Just do it!" [809] It is the only time in the entire *sīrah* where the Prophet ﷺ insisted on a matter to such an extent, but Suhayl would not acquiesce. Eventually, Mikraz suggested that Abū Jandal remain but that his safety and good treatment would be guaranteed, and the Prophet ﷺ reluctantly accepted.

Abū Jandal cried in despair, "O Muslims! Will you return me to the Pagans after I have come to you as a Muslim? Don't you see what they have done to me?" For years, Abū Jandal was counting the days until he joined the Muslims, and when his moment finally came, he was being turned back at the final moment. The marks of torture were visible on his body from years of brutal treatment. The Prophet ﷺ turned and addressed him directly, "Be patient and await the rewards of the Hereafter, O Abū Jandal, for Allah will make a way out for you all."[810] Truly enraged, ʿUmar ؓ stood up and approached Abū Jandal, "Be patient, O Abū Jandal." He then gestured to his sword with his eyes and said, "Their blood is not worth anything." The implication was clear, but Abū Jandal did not act on ʿUmar's suggestion.

The condition of returning renegades only applied to the Muslims. Conversely, it was demanded that any Muslim who apostates and flees to Mecca is not to be sent back to Medina. The treaty also stipulated that there would be no fighting between the two sides for ten years. Moreover, both groups may engage in treaties with any tribe, and the same conditions must apply to said tribe. It was finally decided that the Muslims may perform ʿUmrah next year, and the Quraysh would vacate the city for three days while the Muslims completed their pilgrimage.

ʿUmar could not contain himself, asking the Prophet ﷺ rhetorically, "Are you not the Messenger of Allah?" The Prophet ﷺ said, "Yes." ʿUmar asked, "Are we not upon the Truth, and our enemies upon misguidance?" The Prophet ﷺ said, "Yes." ʿUmar then asked, "Then how can we accept the lower hand [of humiliation] and be disgraced in our religion?" The Prophet ﷺ replied resolvedly, "I am the Messenger of Allah, and I will not disobey Allah—He will help me." ʿUmar then attempted a new line of reasoning, asking, "O Messenger of Allah, didn't you tell me that we would be performing *ṭawāf* around the House of Allah?" The Prophet ﷺ replied, "Indeed, I did. But did I tell you it was this year?" ʿUmar replied, "No." The Prophet ﷺ thus said, "Then you will indeed come and perform *ṭawāf* around it."[811] ʿUmar ؓ was angered for the sake of Allah, not himself, as he could not bear the religion of Islam being harmed. Nevertheless, the Prophet ﷺ was more aligned with

Allah's commands than 'Umar, and the Prophet ﷺ insisted on peace, relying on the help of Allah ﷻ.

'Umar could not quell his frustration. He approached Abū Bakr ؓ—undoubtedly the Prophet's second in command—and asked the same rhetorical questions. However, Abū Bakr replied angrily, "O man! He is the Messenger of Allah, and he will not disobey his Lord! So hang on to the stirrup of his saddle, otherwise there will be no hope for you!"[812] Abū Bakr sternly warned 'Umar to know his place and stand firm alongside Allah's Messenger lest he be led astray. 'Umar later remarked, "After this, I continued to perform good deeds in the hope that Allah would forgive me for what I had done."[813] 'Umar was reported to have freed many slaves, prayed through many nights, and fasted many days to atone for his remarks. Although this emotional outburst was for the sake of Allah and His Religion, it was not befitting to address the Prophet ﷺ in that manner.

The Muslims were forced to humble themselves to an extent they would not have tolerated had it been commanded by anyone other than Allah's Messenger ﷺ. However, even the Prophet's commands that day required the strongest of *īmān* to implement. After the representatives from the Quraysh left, the Prophet ﷺ ordered the Muslims to shave their heads, slaughter their animals, and take off their *iḥrām*, despite not performing their intended 'Umrah. The Muslims were extremely demoralised after such an anticlimactic conclusion, and no-one moved. The Prophet ﷺ repeated his command again, and in an unprecedented moment in the *sīrah*, the Companions did not immediately adhere to the Prophet's command. He ﷺ repeated his command a third time, and perhaps due to the "diffusion of responsibility" phenomenon whereby a person is less likely to take responsibility when addressed in a group, once again no-one stood up.

The Prophet ﷺ retreated to his tent, and Mother of the Believers Umm Salamah ؓ noticed his visible agitation. She asked, "Do you wish that they follow you, O Messenger of Allah?" The Prophet ﷺ replied in the affirmative, so she suggested, "Why don't you do it first? When they see you do it, they will follow suit."[814] The Prophet ﷺ then began shaving his hair in public, and the Companions rushed to follow suit; despite their low morale, their hearts were always with the Messenger of Allah ﷺ. The Muslims sent their sacrificed meat to the poor of Mecca despite not being allowed in, and they left for Medina.

"A Clear Triumph"

As they returned home, ʿUmar began feeling guilty about questioning the Prophet ﷺ, so he approached him ﷺ and conveyed his *salām*, but the Prophet ﷺ did not respond. ʿUmar tried three times and the Prophet ﷺ did not respond. ʿUmar then left, fearing the worst. He bemoaned, "Let ʿUmar's mother mourn the loss of her son!"[815] A Companion then approached ʿUmar and informed him that the Prophet ﷺ had called for him, and it seemed that ʿUmar's nightmare was proving to be true. However, he saw that the Prophet's face was beaming with joy. The Prophet ﷺ began reciting from Sūrah al-Fatḥ, "Indeed, We have granted you a clear triumph…"[816] and the entirety of Sūrah al-Fatḥ was revealed.

Sūrah al-Fatḥ is commonly thought to be in reference to the Conquest of Mecca, but it was actually revealed at the Treaty of Ḥudaybiyyah. ʿUmar ؓ excitedly enquired, "Is it [really] a victory, O Messenger of Allah?" The Prophet ﷺ replied, "Yes, by Allah, it is a victory." ʿUmar yelled, "*Allāhu Akbar*!" and began racing along the Muslims, reciting, "Indeed, We have granted you a clear triumph!"[817] The Prophet ﷺ then said, "Allah has sent down a *sūrah* that is more beloved to me than everything on this Earth."[818]

Despite strong reservations at the time, it turned out to be one of the biggest successes in the entire *sīrah*. The Battle of Khaybar—the biggest financial victory to date—would soon come to pass, followed by the Conquest of Mecca. The extent to which the Treaty of Ḥudaybiyyah was a victory will only become clear through the events that follow. Allah ﷻ revealed, "Indeed, Allah was pleased with the believers when they pledged allegiance to you under the tree. He knew what was in their hearts, so He sent down serenity upon them and rewarded them with a victory at hand, and many spoils of war they will gain. For Allah is Almighty, All-Wise."[819] Scholars note that "a victory at hand" refers to the Conquest of Mecca, and "many spoils of war" refers to the Battle of Khaybar.

The Treaty of Ḥudaybiyyah, despite its drawbacks, marked the first instance wherein the Quraysh recognised the Muslims as an independent entity. It was a turning point in the *sīrah,* and the Quraysh had accepted that the Muslims were here to stay. It was also a crossroads for many of the Quraysh who realised that Islam was the Truth, leading to the last batch of converts before the Conquest of Mecca. Allah ﷻ states, "[...We would have let you march through Mecca] had there not been believing men and women, unknown to you. You might have trampled them underfoot, incurring guilt for [what you did to] them unknowingly. That was so Allah may admit into his Mercy whoever He wills. Had those [unknown] believers stood apart, We would have certainly inflicted a painful punishment on the disbelievers."[820]

Until Ḥudaybiyyah, the Muslims had been living under a constant threat, which had officially ended. The Battle of the Trench showed that even their safe haven of Medina could be attacked, but the Treaty of Ḥudaybiyyah guaranteed at least ten years of safety and security. This newfound security allowed the Prophet ﷺ to finally spread the Message of Islam globally, writing to international leaders. Ibn Shihāb al-Zuhrī ؒ, one of the greatest scholars of the Successors, comments, "There was no greater victory given to Islam before Ḥudaybiyyah that was bigger than Ḥudaybiyyah. Not a single intelligent person heard about Islam except that he accepted it. Within two years of Ḥudaybiyyah, the number of Muslims doubled, or more."[821] Ibn Hishām comments on al-Zuhrī's statement, adding, "There were 1,400 people in the Pledge of Divine Acceptance, and two years later in the Conquest of Mecca, there were 10,000 people."[822] The whole saga provides invaluable insight and timeless guidance into topics of compromise, foresight, patience, and *tawakkul.*

Abū Baṣīr's Camp

Abū Baṣīr was the first Muslim to emigrate to Medina after the Treaty of Ḥudaybiyyah. Soon after, two emissaries from the Quraysh arrived, demanding his return. The Prophet ﷺ called Abū Baṣīr and said, "These two men have come to take you, and you came while knowing the treaty we signed. I will not be treacherous, so return to your people."

Abū Baṣīr responded as Abū Jandal did, "Will you return me to the Pagans after I have come as a Muslim?" The Prophet ﷺ likewise responded as he did to Abū Jandal, "Be patient and await the rewards of the Hereafter, for Allah will make a way out for you all."[823]

As Abū Baṣīr left with the two emissaries, he began building rapport with them through lighthearted conversation until he eventually caught them off guard. He snatched their sword, killed one of them, and the other fled to Medina. The man reached Medina, panting and dishevelled, yelling, "My companion has been killed, so protect me!" Abū Baṣīr also returned and said to the Prophet ﷺ, "O Messenger of Allah, you fulfilled your responsibility by returning me to them, but Allah allowed me to escape." The Prophet ﷺ did not respond to him directly and instead turned away, responding in the third person, "Woe to his mother, what a great warrior he is!"—a classical Arabic expression describing a doomed man, i.e., "a dead man walking". He ﷺ then said, "If only he had someone to help him." Abū Baṣīr clearly understood that the Prophet ﷺ would be handing him back to the Quraysh so as not to violate the treaty, so he immediately escaped.

Abū Baṣīr then set up camp in a remote area on the outskirts of Mecca. Word reached Abū Jandal, and he fled once more to join him. News spread, and Muslim converts continued to join them until 80 Muslims had formed a settlement. They began intercepting the Quraysh's caravans as they entered and exited Mecca, and 80 fighters engaging in guerrilla warfare were almost impossible to stop. The Muslims did not violate the treaty, as Abū Baṣīr's camp did not form an allegiance with the Muslim state in Medina. They continued to raid the Quraysh relentlessly for 18 months until Abū Sufyān wrote a letter to the Prophet ﷺ, invoking ties of kinship and imploring him to integrate the 80 men into Medina.

The Prophet ﷺ sent a letter to Abū Baṣīr inviting them all to Medina. Abū Baṣīr received the letter but was very ill and Allah ﷻ decreed that he pass away before reaching Medina with the Prophet's letter in his hand. Abū Jandal therefore marched the settlement into Medina, completing a divine turn of events which began with his emotional failed escape in shackles and ended with him leading a 79-man strong army into Medina at the request of the Quraysh. As Allah ﷻ states regarding those against Jesus Christ, "They planned and Allah planned—and Allah is the best of planners."[824] This story is also a testament to the impenetrable faith of Abū Jandal; after years of torture at the hands of his own family, he finally escaped only to be sent back to his dungeon. Nevertheless, he persevered, escaped once more to a new settlement, and eventually marched—dignified and vindicated—back to the Prophet ﷺ.

After this saga, Umm Kulthūm, daughter of ʿUqbah ibn Abī Muʿayṭ, accepted Islam and escaped Mecca, somehow making it to Medina. The Prophet ﷺ faced a tough dilemma, as returning a woman back to her abusers is far more sensitive than returning a fighting man. Allah ﷻ then revealed, "O believers! When the believing women come to you as Emigrants, test their intentions—their faith is best known to Allah—and if you find them to be believers, then do not send them back to the disbelievers. These women are not lawful [wives] for the disbelievers, nor are the disbelievers lawful [husbands] for them. But repay the disbelievers whatever [dowries] they had paid. And there is no blame on you if you marry these women as long as you pay them their dowries. And do not hold on to marriage with polytheistic women. But demand repayment of whatever [dowries] you had paid, and let the disbelievers do the same. That is the judgement of Allah—He judges between you. And Allah is All Knowing, All-Wise."[825] Allah ﷻ decreed that it was not acceptable to return a Muslim woman to be abused. The treaty specified men, so the letter of the law was not violated. While the spirit of the law may have dictated that it should encompass all people, protecting the honour of Muslim women was deemed a greater priority.

The Battle of Khaybar

21

After the Prophet ﷺ secured peace with the Quraysh, he could finally turn his attention inwards once more. A group of the previously expelled Banū Qaynuqāʿ and Banū Naḍīr still posed a constant and immediate threat that the Prophet ﷺ could not address until now. After their expulsion, they relocated to Khaybar and organised the biggest army Medina ever faced in the Battle of the Trench. The Treaty of Ḥudaybiyyah allowed the Prophet ﷺ to organise his efforts towards these belligerent tribes.

Immediately after Ḥudaybiyyah, the Prophet ﷺ launched a preemptive attack on Khaybar before they had a chance to organise another attack on Medina. The Muslims marched continuously from Medina to Khaybar and camped overnight out of sight. They marched towards Khaybar after Fajr, catching them completely off-guard. Khaybar was comprised of a number of fortresses even more magnificent and imposing in stature than those of Medina. The vast fortresses were spread across acres of lush farmland. As they approached the first fortress, the inhabitants were leaving with their farming tools, preparing for the day's work. When they saw the Muslim army, they scrambled back inside the fortress, yelling, "Muhammad and his army have arrived!" [826]

Despite launching a surprise attack, their response clearly indicates a level of expectation; a retaliation for their prior aggressions was foreseen.

The Prophet ﷺ yelled out, "*Allāhu Akbar*! Khaybar has been destroyed! Whenever we arrive at the border of a land, then what an evil morning it is for those who have been warned!"[827] The Muslims then began attacking the first fortress. The inhabitants of Khaybar were now all hiding within their own fortresses, and the ingenuity of the fortresses being isolated from one another served as their downfall, as each tribe could not assist the other. The entirety of the Muslim army could therefore attack each fortress individually and move onto the next.

Nonetheless, the fortresses were notoriously difficult to penetrate; their walls were tall and strong, and they would shoot arrows from above as well as throwing down boulders. The first fortress held off the Muslims for over ten days; a notable Anṣārī, Maḥmūd ibn Maslamah ؓ, was martyred after a large log was thrown over the wall. The Muslims were demoralised by his gruesome death, so the Prophet ﷺ announced after the 'Ishā' prayer, "Tomorrow, I will hand the banner to someone whom Allah and His Messenger love, and Allah will grant us victory through him." 'Umar ibn al-Khaṭṭāb ؓ narrated, "Never in my life did I wish to become a leader more than on that day."[828]

The next morning, the Prophet ﷺ prayed Fajr then asked, "Where is 'Alī ibn Abī Ṭālib?" 'Alī ؓ was afflicted with an eye-infection whereby he could not open his eye, so the Prophet ﷺ gently spat in his eye, curing him instantly. He ﷺ then handed 'Alī the banner and said, "Go forth! In the Name of Allah, go forth and do not turn back!"[829] 'Alī took the banner, marched forward, then paused. He wanted to ask the Prophet ﷺ a question but did not want to turn around lest he disobey the Prophet ﷺ by "turning back". Instead, he yelled, while facing forwards, "O Messenger of Allah! What conditions shall I give them?" The Prophet ﷺ replied, "Fight them until they testify that there is no god but Allah and that Muhammad is the Messenger of Allah. If they do so, then their wealth and properties are protected, and their affair is with Allah ﷻ. By Allah, if Allah guides even one person through you then it is better for you than a herd of camels (i.e., a vast amount of wealth)."[830]

A warrior within Khaybar by the name of Mirḥab challenged the Muslims to a duel. ʿĀmir ibn al-Akwaʿ ؓ accepted his challenge but was martyred. ʿAlī ؓ then challenged Mirḥab despite being the leader of the battalion. Being the formidable force that he was, ʿAlī defeated Mirḥab decisively, causing a detrimental blow in morale to the opposition. The inhabitants then charged out of the fortress and engaged in a severe battle which the Muslims eventually won. The Muslims moved on to the next fortress and conquered it in three days. They continued forth and conquered one after the other. Eventually, half of Khaybar was conquered, and the Muslims began attacking the second half until the survivors of all the remaining fortresses congregated in one big fortress. The Muslims camped outside for two weeks until the inhabitants of the fortress realised they had no choice but to surrender.

The survivors of Khaybar pleaded with the Prophet ﷺ to compromise and allow them to remain. They said, "O Abū al-Qāsim, your people are not familiar with these lands, and our people can maximise its benefit. Why don't we agree to share a percentage of its profits?"[831] The Prophet ﷺ agreed and allowed them to remain in Khaybar in exchange for half of all profits while the Jews were responsible for all costs and labour. The Muslims also reserved the right to cancel the treaty at any point. The treaty remained in effect until the Caliphate of ʿUmar ibn al-Khaṭṭāb many years later. Khaybar comprised many acres of rich farms, and 50% of all produce was an unfathomable amount of wealth. ʿAbdullāh ibn ʿUmar ؓ narrates, "We never ate to our fill until after Khaybar."[832] After two decades of sacrifice, the Muslims were being showered with worldly gains as well as that of the Hereafter.

The Attempted Poisoning

After the treaty was finalised, the Prophet ﷺ and the Muslims were offered a banquet, as was custom when greeting a new leader.

The widow of a Jewish leader cooked the meal and asked for the Prophet's favourite meat, which was lamb shoulder. She poisoned the entire lamb but concentrated the poison in the shoulder. The Prophet ﷺ placed a piece in his mouth, and as soon as he tasted it, he stopped and instructed everyone to immediately stop eating. He ﷺ said, "The shoulder of the lamb has told me that it has been poisoned."[833] Those who spat out the meat before swallowing felt ill and needed to be treated, but unfortunately a Companion by the name of Bishr ibn al-Barrā' ؓ took a bite and swallowed before the Prophet ﷺ instructed them all to stop. He fell severely ill and eventually died from the poison.

The Prophet ﷺ interrogated the tribe and they admitted their crime. They justified their actions by saying, "If you are a liar, we would be free of your rule; and if you are truthful, then we knew it would not have harmed you."[834] Despite the Prophet ﷺ surviving and proving their theory of his truthfulness, their arrogance prevented them from accepting the Truth. The cook also admitted her crime and explained that she wanted to exact revenge on the Prophet ﷺ. There are conflicting reports as to whether the Prophet ﷺ forgave her or whether she was punished, but Imam Ibn al-Qayyim reconciles the reports by explaining that the Prophet ﷺ forgave her for what she did to him ﷺ, but when Bishr ؓ died, she had to be punished for murder as per the divine mandate of *qiṣāṣ* (equal retaliation).[835]

The Muslims in Abyssinia Return

The immense spoils of war were distributed, and the attendees of the Pledge of Divine Acceptance were given a generous share as a result of the promise of Allah ﷻ, "...And many spoils of war they will gain. For Allah is Almighty, All-Wise."[836] As the spoils were being distributed, the Prophet's cousin, Jaʿfar ibn Abī Ṭālib ؓ, along with the rest of the Muslims who emigrated to Abyssinia, had returned after over a decade. Jaʿfar ؓ was the Prophet's family and close friend, and the Prophet ﷺ stood up and greeted him with glee. He ﷺ kissed him on the forehead and said, "I don't know which pleases me more: conquering Khaybar or the return of Jaʿfar!"[837] Despite arriving after the war, the returnees from Abyssinia were also given a share of the spoils of Khaybar. Allah ﷻ rewarded their immense sacrifice for over a decade, living in a foreign land in turbulent times.

When Asmā' bint 'Umays ؓ, one of the emigrants to Abyssinia, visited Medina for the first time, she reunited with her friend Ḥafṣah ؓ. 'Umar ibn al-Khaṭṭāb ؓ joked, "We have more right to the Prophet ﷺ than you because we emigrated to Medina with him!" Asmā' snapped back, "No, by Allah! You do not have more right to the Prophet ﷺ than us! You were at least with him all these years; he would console you at times of grief, feed you when you were hungry, and guide you when you were mistaken. Meanwhile, we suffered and toiled in a strange land. By Allah, I will not eat or drink until I tell the Prophet ﷺ exactly what you said!" She immediately stormed off to the Prophet ﷺ and relayed the story. The Prophet ﷺ replied, "He does not have any more right to me than you. Go back and tell him that he made one hijrah and you made two!"[838] The news spread like wildfire, and all the emigrants to Abyssinia approached Asmā', asking her to repeat the story.

The Prophet's Marriage to Ṣafiyyah ؓ

Ṣafiyyah bint Ḥuyayy ؓ was the daughter of Ḥuyayy ibn Akhṭab, a Chieftain from the Banū Naḍīr who relocated to Khaybar. Ṣafiyyah was captured as a prisoner of war and was allocated to Diḥyah al-Kalbī ؓ. However, a Companion approached the Prophet ﷺ and said, "O Messenger of Allah, that lady is the daughter of Ḥuyayy. It is not appropriate for anyone to have her except for you." The Prophet ﷺ called Ṣafiyyah and said, "I will give you two choices: accept Islam and stay with me or stay upon your faith and I will likely free you and grant you a way back to your people."[839] Ṣafiyyah immediately responded, "O Messenger of Allah, I desired to accept Islam and believed in you before you even called me to Islam. I love Allah and His Messenger more than I love my freedom and more than returning to my people." Upon seeing her sincerity and conviction, the Prophet ﷺ immediately freed her and offered a hand in marriage.

Some people were sceptical about her faith due to her sudden transition from a captive to a devout Muslim. However, her journey towards Islam began much earlier. She narrated that her father was initially excited about the arrival of the Prophet ﷺ in Medina, as the Jews were expecting a new Messenger. However, he was bitterly disappointed when the Prophet ﷺ came with a new religion. When asked by his peers if the Prophet ﷺ was "The One" i.e., the awaited Messenger, Ḥuyayy replied in the affirmative, but when asked about what he would do, he responded, "I will be his enemy for as long as I live." [840] Pride prevented him from ever accepting Islam, but Ṣafiyyah, as a child, overheard the conversation, and it planted the seed of *īmān* in her heart. She realised that they knew the truth but refused to accept it.

The Prophet's Marriage to Umm Ḥabībah

A year prior, the Prophet ﷺ married Ramlah bint Abī Sufyān, more commonly known as Umm Ḥabībah. Umm Ḥabībah was the daughter of Abū Sufyān, and while she accepted Islam and emigrated to Abyssinia early on, Abū Sufyān was not yet Muslim. The Prophet ﷺ was so keen to secure her hand in marriage that he sent an envoy to Abyssinia, proposed to marry her, and suggested the Negus to be her guardian, as she had no male Muslim family member. The Negus was overjoyed on behalf of the Prophet ﷺ, throwing a lavish party for the Muslims in Abyssinia and giving Umm Ḥabībah a variety of royal gifts. However, as she was in Abyssinia and the Prophet ﷺ was in Medina, they did not meet after their marriage for a full year until the Muslims of Abyssinia returned to Medina.

A Prophetic Invitation

22

As the Muslim state solidified its security and international recognition, the Prophet ﷺ began approaching international leaders, inviting them to Islam. Letters were sent over a period of time, but they began after the Treaty of Ḥudaybiyyah, continuing up until the death of the Prophet ﷺ.

A Letter to the Negus

The Prophet ﷺ sent an official letter to the Negus. As discussed, the Negus died a Muslim, but the exact moment of his conversion is not confirmed. Some scholars state that he accepted Islam when the Muslims emigrated to Abyssinia over a decade prior. However, if that were the case, one would question why the Prophet ﷺ still sent an official invitation to Islam a decade later. It may therefore be the case that while the Negus' heart was inclined towards Islam, he officially converted after the Prophet's letter. Alternatively, Imam Ibn Ḥajar 🙞 opines that they were two different rulers; the first Negus accepted Islam earlier, and the Prophet ﷺ sent a letter to his successor.

As "The Negus" is a title given to all rulers of Abyssinia, this may be the most plausible theory.

The letter read as follows:

> "In the Name of Allah—the Most Compassionate, Most Merciful. From Muhammad, the Messenger of Allah, to the Negus, King of Abyssinia. Embrace Islam, for I am conveying to you my praise of Allah and gratitude to Him; there is no deity worthy of worship other than Him, '...the King, the Most Holy, the All-Perfect, the Source of Serenity, the Watcher [of all]...'[841] I bear witness that ʿĪsā is the son of Maryam, the Spirit of Allah, and 'the fulfilment of His Word through Maryam'[842], the chaste one. She conceived him, and He created him from a Spirit into which He breathed, just like He created Adam by His own Hand. I call you to [worship] Allah, alone and without partners, and to stick to His obedience, and I call you to follow me and believe [in the Revelation] that has come to me, for I am certainly the Messenger of Allah. I call you and your soldiers to [worship] Allah. I have conveyed and advised, so accept my advice. 'Salvation will be for whoever follows the guidance.'[843]"[844]

A Letter to the Caesar

The Caesar—Emperor of Rome—was Heraclius, who gained fame for his military success after the Roman Empire was on the brink of extinction. His success was predicted in Sūrah al-Rūm, *"Alif-Lām-Mīm. The Romans have been defeated in a nearby land. Yet following their defeat, they will triumph within a few years."*[845] At the time of Revelation, the Romans were nearly destroyed by the Persians, and such a prediction was unfathomable. Surely enough, Roman victory transpired soon after, as divinely ordained.

The Prophet ﷺ sent a letter via Diḥyah al-Kalbī ؓ to the governor of Bosra [i], Syria. Abū Sufyān, who was trading in Syria—still non-Muslim at the time—narrates that he was called to the Caesar's palace for questioning. The Caesar wanted to enquire about the Prophet ﷺ but knew Abū Sufyān was his adversary, so he orchestrated a setting to ensure he would tell the truth. The Caesar instructed Abū Sufyān to stand ahead of his companions, and instructed his companions to make a gesture if Abū Sufyān lied, presumably incentivising their compliance. Abū Sufyān remarked, "By Allah, if I had not been afraid that my companions would have accused me of lying, I would not have spoken the truth." [846]

The Caesar asked, "Has anyone in your society claimed to be a Prophet before him?" Abū Sufyān replied, "No, he was the first." The Caesar asked, "Were any of his ancestors kings?" Abū Sufyān replied, "No." The Caesar asked, "Are his followers the rich and noble, or the poor and downtrodden?" Abū Sufyān replied, "The poor and downtrodden." The Caesar asked, "Are their numbers increasing or decreasing?" Abū Sufyān replied, "They are increasing." The Caesar asked, "Do the converts give up and leave, or remain in the faith?" Abū Sufyān replied, "They remain in the faith." The Caesar asked, "Have you ever previously accused him of lying?" Abū Sufyān replied, "No, we know him to be an honest man." The Caesar asked, "Does he break his promises?" Abū Sufyān replied, "No, he has not broken any promises, but at the moment we have a treaty, and we are not sure whether he will break it or not." The Caesar asked, "Have you ever warred with him?" Abū Sufyān replied, "Yes." The Caesar asked, "What was the outcome?" Abū Sufyān replied, "Sometimes they win, and sometimes we win." The Caesar asked, "What does he command you to do?" Abū Sufyān replied, "He commands us to worship Allah alone and not worship anything our forefathers used to worship. He ordered us to pray, be chaste, speak the truth, and retain good ties with our relatives." [847]

The Caesar then explained his questions. He said, "I asked you if anyone claimed to be a Prophet before him and you said no; if the answer had

i Not to be confused with Basra, a city in Southeastern Iraq.

been yes, it may have been a fad. I asked you if his ancestors were kings and you said no; if the answer had been yes, I would have said that it was a tactic to regain his kingdom. I asked you if he had been accused of lying and you said no; if a person never lied about money, how could he lie about God? I asked you if his followers were rich or poor and you said poor; this is the way of all the Prophets of God. I asked whether his followers were increasing or decreasing, and you said they were increasing; this is also a sign of truth. I asked you if anyone left his religion and you said no; whence faith enters the heart, it can never leave the heart thereafter. I asked if he ever betrayed you and you said no; the Prophets of God can never betray or break a promise. I asked you what he ordered you to do, and your answers are all the marks of a Prophet. If what you have said is true, then he will very soon occupy this space under my feet. We knew that God would send somebody, but we did not expect it to be from your race."[848] He then called for the Prophet's letter to be opened.

The Prophet's letter read as follows:

> "In the Name of Allah—the Most Compassionate, Most Merciful. From Muhammad ibn 'Abdillāh, the Messenger of Allah, to Heraclius, Might of the Romans. 'Salvation will be for whoever follows the guidance.'[849] To proceed: I call you with the call of Islam. If you embrace Islam, Allah will give you a double reward, but if you turn away, then you will bear responsibility for the sins of the Byzantines.
>
> 'Say, "O People of the Book! Let us come to common terms: that we will worship none but Allah, associate none with Him, nor take one another as lords instead of Allah." But if they turn away, then say, "Bear witness that we have submitted [to Allah alone]."'[850]"

Abū Sufyān muttered to his companions, "This matter has become so big that the ruler of the Romans is scared of him." As he narrated, he remarked, "That was when I realised that this matter (i.e.,

Islam) would eventually prevail, and Islam entered my heart for the first time."[851]

A Letter to Khosrow

Khosrow—Emperor of Persia—was Aparwez, the last main king of the Sassanid Dynasty. The Prophet ﷺ sent a letter via 'Abdullāh ibn Ḥudhāfah ؓ to the ruler of Bahrain to pass onto Khosrow, which read as follows:

> "In the Name of Allah—the Most Compassionate, Most Merciful. From Muhammad, the Messenger of Allah, to Khosrow, leader of the Persians. 'Salvation will be for whoever follows the guidance'[852], believes in Allah and His Messenger, and bears witness that there is no deity worthy of worship except Allah, alone and without partners, and that Muhammad is His slave and Messenger. I call you with the call of Allah, for I am, without doubt, the Messenger of Allah to all humankind, 'to warn whoever is [truly] alive and fulfil the decree [of torment] against the disbelievers.'[853] If you embrace Islam, then you will be safe and secure, but if you turn away, then you will bear responsibility for the sins of the Magians."[854]

Khosrow, known for his arrogance, scoffed and tore up the letter. When news reached the Prophet ﷺ that his letter was torn, he said, "Allah will thoroughly tear up his kingdom."[855] Shortly after, Khosrow's son killed his father and launched a *coup d'état* to become Emperor. Within a few short years, all Persian lands would fall under Islamic rule.

A Letter to Muqawqis

Muqawqis—Governor of Egypt—was Jurayj ibn Mīnā, also known as Cyrus of Alexandria. Egypt was under Byzantine rule, and Jurayj served as the final Byzantine prefect over Egypt before it fell under Islamic rule. Muqawqis received the Prophet's letter well and sent back a polite response alongside a collection of gifts including gold, cloth, and more. The Prophet ﷺ commented, "He has protected his kingdom [for now] through his politeness, but Allah will not allow his kingdom to last."[856]

Overall, the Prophet ﷺ was reported to have sent over 20 letters to different rulers and Chieftains. The letters were direct and concise but were tailored to each ruler; the letter to the Caesar included the verse in Sūrah Āl 'Imrān, as they were from The People of the Book, whereas Khosrow was not. The letter to the Negus did not mention any consequences of not accepting Islam unlike the letters to the Caesar or Khosrow. This is most likely due to the Prophet ﷺ recognising that the Negus was already inclined to Islam, only needing a slight push to accept.

There was no immediate political impact resulting from these letters, but the Prophet's intention was to ensure that the Message of Islam was spread globally. Within a decade, every single land that received a letter was under Islamic rule.

PART IV • THE MEDINAN ERA

Fulfilling the Treaty 23

ʿUmrah al-Qaḍāʾ

The Prophet ﷺ and his Companions ﷺ were rewarded for their ʿUmrah at Ḥudaybiyyah as if they had completed it due to their intention and resolve. Nevertheless, the Prophet ﷺ was keen to fulfil his initial plans, so he set off to perform ʿUmrah in Dhū al-Qaʿdah, 7 AH. *Qaḍāʾ* is the act of compensating a previously unfulfilled act of worship. A *qaḍāʾ* prayer, for example, is compensating a previously missed prayer. This ʿUmrah was thus called ʿUmrah al-Qaḍāʾ.

2,000 Muslims embarked with the Prophet ﷺ, armed to the hilt. The Quraysh were alarmed at this news, sending a delegation led by Mikraz ibn Ḥafṣ. He said, "O Muhammad, we have never known you to be treacherous, so why have you brought weapons when we agreed that you will enter without weapons except for swords inside their scabbards?" The Prophet ﷺ said, "We shall not enter Mecca except as we agreed."[857] The Prophet ﷺ intended to fulfil his pledge—as he always did—but he did not trust the Quraysh, so he ensured there was a contingency in place. 200 Muslims guarded the weapons outside the Ḥaram while the remaining 1,800 Muslims performed *ṭawāf* and then they alternated.

Some of the Quraysh left Mecca for three days, some congregated in the Dār al-Nadwah, and others remained in their houses. It was the first time that the Muslims had returned to Mecca after seven long years, and they missed it dearly. Rumours spread amongst the women of the Quraysh that the Muslims were harmed by the plagues of Medina and were now weak and emaciated. The Prophet ﷺ commanded the Muslims to showcase their strength by raising their voices in *talbiyah* as well as uncovering their right shoulders and briskly walking (*raml*) for a section of the *ṭawāf*. The Quraysh were surprised at the Muslims' energy and vigour and realised that they were not weakened at all.

The Prophet's Marriage to Maymūnah ﵂

As the Muslims reunited with their kin in Mecca, al-ʿAbbās ﵁ suggested that the Prophet ﷺ marry his sister-in-law, Maymūnah bint al-Ḥārith ﵂, who was a widow. Time and again we note the inclusive culture of the Companions and a distinct absence of taboo regarding a person's previous marital status. The Prophet ﷺ agreed and wed Maymūnah, and al-ʿAbbās ﵁ served as her *walī* (guardian). There is a difference of opinion as to whether the Prophet ﷺ married Maymūnah in the state of *iḥrām*; Ibn ʿAbbās narrates that he ﷺ did,[858] but Maymūnah herself narrates that she married the Prophet after his ʿUmrah was complete.[859] In any case, there is a consensus that the marriage was consummated after the ʿUmrah and outside Mecca.[860]

The Prophet ﷺ requested the Quraysh to extend his time in Mecca, citing his marriage. Using the opportunity to ease tensions, he ﷺ invited them to a celebratory feast, but the Quraysh replied sternly, "We have no need for your food."[861] The Prophet ﷺ therefore honoured the treaty and left, camping outside Mecca to consummate the marriage.

Competing in Chivalry

As the Muslims marched out of Mecca, a young girl ran towards them, calling, "O uncle! O uncle! Take me! Don't leave me in Mecca!"

She was ʿUmārah, the daughter of Ḥamzah ibn ʿAbd al-Muṭṭalib ﷺ. As her cousin, ʿAlī ibn Abī Ṭālib ﷺ immediately took her by the hand. Zayd ibn Ḥārithah ﷺ then came and said, "The Prophet ﷺ made me brothers with Ḥamzah, which makes her my niece. Therefore, we should take care of her." Jaʿfar ﷺ also approached and said, "I have the same rank as ʿAlī (i.e., I am her cousin too), but my wife is also her maternal aunt."[862] A dispute ensued, and the three noble men began arguing about who will care for the young girl.

Less than two decades ago, the Arabs would bury their daughters alive out of shame and disappointment, yearning for a son. Allah ﷻ even revealed, "...and when baby girls, buried alive, are asked for what crime they were put to death..."[863] Now, after the guidance of Islam, tensions were rising over who would have the honour of caring for a young girl. The Prophet ﷺ inevitably intervened. He began by praising all three men, saying to ʿAlī ﷺ, "You are from me, and I am from you." He said to Zayd ﷺ, "You are my brother and protector." And he said to Jaʿfar ﷺ, "You resemble me most in both looks and manners." He ﷺ then decided, "Jaʿfar, she is yours because the maternal aunt takes the status of the mother."[864]

Final Conversions before the Conquest

For the first time in history, a congregation of 2,000 people were performing ʿUmrah in *iḥrām*, which would have been a truly daunting sight for the Quraysh. It was a defining moment which showcased the changing tide between the Quraysh and the Muslims. This sight indeed caused a ripple effect amongst the Quraysh, as it led to three notable conversions.

After the Battle of Khandaq, ʿAmr ﷺ professed, "By Allah, Muhammad will certainly prevail over the Quraysh."[865] He approached a group of friends that looked up to him and said, "I have been telling you that the affairs of this man (i.e., the Prophet ﷺ) shall reign supreme very quickly. So let us emigrate to the Negus and live under his rule. If Muhammad is successful, we shall live under the Negus, and if the

Quraysh is successful, we can always return."[866] ʿAmr and his entourage thus left Mecca for Abyssinia along with many gifts. Upon his arrival, he noticed a Muslim envoy, and he devised a plan to retain the respect of the Quraysh: he asked the Negus if he could kill the Muslim envoy.

Unbeknownst to ʿAmr, the Negus was already Muslim. He was so angry at ʿAmr's request that he smacked his own nose—an expression of utmost disgust. ʿAmr narrated, "I felt so terrified at his anger that I wished that the Earth would swallow me." Before the Negus even spoke, ʿAmr fell down and apologised profusely. The Negus remarked, "Do you ask me to hand over the envoy of the one upon whom the Great Spirit descends?"[867] The Negus and ʿAmr were already familiar with one another, so the Negus said, "Woe to you, O ʿAmr! Obey me in this regard and follow this man. By Allah, he is upon the Truth, and he will be victorious over his enemies just as Mūsā ﷺ was victorious over the Pharoah."[868]

ʿAmr left Mecca to escape the Prophet's Message only to face it once more in Abyssinia. Allah ﷻ willed that it was the Negus who finally convinced ʿAmr to see the Truth, and ʿAmr accepted Islam at the Negus' hand. ʿAmr did not disclose his conversion to his colleagues but instead excused himself and returned to Mecca. As he approached Mecca, he came across Khālid ibn al-Walīd and ʿUthmān ibn Ṭalḥah, who were leaving. He asked them where they were going, and they both disclosed that they were heading to the Prophet ﷺ to convert, as the matter had now become clear to them. They said, "For how long will we deny it?" ʿAmr replied, "By Allah, that is the exact reason why I have returned."[869]

As for Khālid ibn al-Walīd ﷺ, he narrated,

> "When Allah wanted good for me, He thrust Islam into my heart. I participated in battles against the Prophet ﷺ, and every time I engaged, I sensed that I was being turned away and that the Prophet ﷺ would be victorious. The final straw was at Ḥudaybiyyah when I was prepared to charge but even when he was praying, he was protected. I then thought to myself: where

should I go? My first thought was to go to Abyssinia, but his followers are also there. Then I thought about Rome, but I would have to become a Christian and live as a stranger in a new land and culture. I continued to remain in a state of confusion until ʿUmrah al-Qaḍāʾ took place. The Prophet ﷺ entered Mecca and asked about me through my brother (al-Walīd ibn al-Walīd, who accepted Islam at Badr). My brother wrote to me,

'In the Name of Allah, the Most Compassionate, Most Merciful. I have not seen anything stranger than you running away from Islam while you are as smart as you are. For how long will you oppose Islam? The Prophet ﷺ asked about you when he entered Mecca. He ﷺ asked, "Where is Khālid?" And I responded, "Allah will bring him." The Prophet ﷺ said, "It is not befitting for someone like him to neglect Islam. If he were to use his talents with us against the polytheists, it would be better for him, and he would be honoured over others." So, my dear brother, make up what you have already lost because many opportunities have already passed you by. Peace.'

After reading his letter, Islam entered my heart. And I was pleased that the Prophet ﷺ asked about me. I then thought about who I should take with me. I approached Ṣafwān ibn Umayyah and said, 'Can't you see our state? It has become clear that Muhammad has prevailed. If we follow him, his honour will also be ours!' But he rejected in the sternest manner, saying, 'If I were the last person on Earth, I would still not follow him.' I thought to myself, 'This is a person whose brother and father were killed at Badr.' I then went to ʿIkrimah ibn Abī Jahl and I told him the same thing I told Ṣafwān, but he responded as Ṣafwān did. I then saw ʿUthmān ibn Ṭalḥah and we walked out until we saw ʿAmr ibn al-ʿĀṣ."[870]

'Amr, Khālid, and Ṭalḥah ⬢ travelled to the Prophet ⬢ and declared their Islam. When the Prophet ⬢ stretched his hand out to 'Amr to accept his conversion, 'Amr pulled his hand back. The Prophet ⬢ asked, "What's wrong, O 'Amr?" 'Amr replied, "Before I embrace Islam, I have one condition: that all my past sins be forgiven." The Prophet ⬢ responded with glad tidings, "O 'Amr, don't you know that Islam erases everything before it? And that the Emigration erases everything before it? And that Hajj erases everything before it?"[871]

'Uthmān ibn Ṭalḥah ⬢ held the keys to the Ka'bah, representing the religiosity of the Quraysh. As a senior statesman and shrewd politician, 'Amr ibn al-'Āṣ ⬢ represented the political elite of the Quraysh. And Khālid ibn al-Walīd ⬢, the master tactician, represented the military prowess of the Quraysh. The three of them emigrated together, becoming the last converts to Islam before the Conquest of Mecca. As Allah ⬢ said, "Those of you who donated and fought before the Conquest [of Mecca] are unparalleled. They are far greater in rank than those who donated and fought afterwards."[872]

The Battle of Mu'tah

24

"Mu'tah" is the name of a small village in modern-day Jordan which was part of the Roman province of Syria. Most early scholars refer to this event as a *ghazwah* despite the Prophet ﷺ not attending. This is most likely due to the size and significance of the battle, with over 3,000 Companions in attendance. Facing the Romans, it is also the only time the Muslims fought a non-Arab enemy in the lifetime of the Prophet ﷺ. Nevertheless, a *ghazwah* is defined by the Prophet's participation, so later scholars refer to this event as a *sariyyah*. The Companions, on the other hand, referred to it as "Expedition of the Army of the Leaders" because it was the only instance where the Prophet ﷺ named three leaders. As a sobering indication of the task at hand, the Prophet ﷺ appointed Zayd ibn Ḥārithah ﷺ as the leader then said, "If Zayd is killed, then Jaʿfar, and if Jaʿfar is killed, then ʿAbdullāh ibn Rawāḥah."[873]

It is not mentioned in reports why the Prophet ﷺ did not attend despite attending forthcoming expeditions such as the Expedition of Tabūk. The purpose of the battle is also not entirely clear. Al-Wāqidī posits that the battle was revenge for the killing of al-Ḥārith ibn ʿUmayr al-Azdī ﷺ, the Prophet's messenger.[874] He was sent to the Romans, which entailed passing through Arab Christian lands, the largest of which was the

Banū Ghassān (The Ghassanids), a vassal state to the Roman Empire. Al-Ḥārith ﷺ was captured by the Ghassanids led by Shuraḥbīl ibn ʿAmr. Despite being a messenger—and thus universally protected—Shuraḥbīl tied him up, tortured him, and personally killed him.[875]

In Jumādā al-Ūlā 8 AH, the Prophet ﷺ instructed the Companions to head to the Ghassanids. He encouraged them to volunteer, and 3,000 Companions signed up. They left on Friday morning, and ʿAbdullāh ibn Rawāḥah ﷺ was deliberating as to whether he should leave with the army or pray the Friday Prayer and catch up with them. He decided to pray the Friday Prayer first, but when the Prophet ﷺ saw him, he ﷺ asked why he did not leave with the army. ʿAbdullāh ibn Rawāḥah ﷺ explained that he wanted the extra reward of praying the Friday Prayer, but the Prophet ﷺ, highlighting the status of jihad, replied, "If you were to give *ṣadaqah* (charity) equivalent to all the money in this world, you would not be able to make up the reward (i.e., if you had left early with the army)."[876]

As the Companions bade farewell to their loved ones, ʿAbdullāh ibn Rawāḥah ﷺ began crying. Someone asked him why he was crying, to which he said, "I am not crying due to a love for this world, nor am I crying because I am inclined towards it. I am crying thinking of the verse of the Qur'an where Allah ﷻ said, 'There is none of you who will not pass over it (i.e., the Hellfire). This is a decree your Lord must fulfil.'[877] How will I fare in that crossing?"[878] ʿAbdullāh ibn Rawāḥah ﷺ was a formidable poet and fighter, an elite of the Anṣār, and beloved by the Prophet ﷺ.

The Muslims travelled for over a month, and as they approached, the Ghassanids panicked and sent emissaries to every one of their allies. They called upon the Romans as well as a number of Christian Arab tribes such as Lukham, Judhām, and Alqīn. The Arab Christian tribes alongside a small Roman contingent gathered before the Muslims arrived in Mu'tah. Classical sources cite over 100,000 fighters,[879] but that is extremely unlikely, as the Arab tribes in totality did not even comprise 100,000 people, and it is a common psychological phenomenon for large crowds to be overestimated. A more reasonable figure would be up to 10,000 fighters, which was still triple that of the Muslim army.

The Muslims camped outside Mu'tah for two days, debating their next move. They expected to fight the Ghassanids alone but were now faced with over double their amount. The Romans were also far more advanced in weaponry and training, and the task at hand was now vastly different to that which was initially anticipated. A group of Companions suggested that they remain camped while they send a message to the Prophet ﷺ and await instruction. However, it would take two weeks for the fastest rider to travel to Medina and back. Another group suggested that they turn back, as the reality did not reflect their initial intention.

Zayd ibn Ḥārithah asked ʿAbdullāh ibn Rawāḥah for his advice. Zayd knew what he would say but wanted to utilise Ibn Rawāḥah for his unmatched eloquence. Ibn Rawāḥah gave a fiery speech, "O my people! That which you fear (i.e., martyrdom) is exactly what you desire! What is the matter with us? Allah will bless us with one of two beautiful things: victory or martyrdom. We know that Allah does not help us through our quantity or weapons, but rather through the Islam with which Allah has blessed us. So let us go forth and face one of the two inevitable realities."[880] Zayd's tactic succeeded, as the troops—galvanised and resolved—marched forward.

Abū Hurayrah's eyes widened as he saw the mammoth army ahead of him. Another Companion chided him, "What is the matter, O Abū Hurayrah? Are you surprised at how large the army is?" Abū Hurayrah ؓ replied in the affirmative, and the Companion said, "But you were not with us at Badr. We did not win due to the size of our army!"[881] Zayd ؓ then commanded the Muslims to charge, and he held the flag himself. As the Prophet ﷺ handed the flag to Zayd personally, he refused to give it to anyone else despite being the commander. He raised the flag and charged from the front until he was surrounded on all sides and was martyred. The status of Zayd ibn Ḥārithah ؓ cannot be understated. He is the only Companion mentioned by name in the Qur'an.[i] ʿĀ'ishah ؓ said, "Never did the Prophet ﷺ send Zayd on an expedition except that he was the leader." She went as far as to say,

i In reference to *al-Aḥzāb*, "...so when Zayd totally lost interest in [keeping] his wife, We gave her to you in marriage..."

"If Zayd had been alive when the Prophet ﷺ died, he would have been chosen [as Caliph]."[882]

After Zayd was martyred, Jaʿfar ؓ took the flag and fought one of the most vicious fights ever recorded in Islamic history. He fought valiantly until his horse's legs were cut off. He then fought standing, swinging with his left hand as he held the flag with his right. Eventually, someone chopped off his entire right arm, and he grabbed the flag with his left hand before it touched the ground. His left arm was then sliced off, and he grabbed the flag with his two stumps before an enemy soldier cleaved him apart from behind.

Ibn ʿUmar ؓ narrated, "After the battle, we began searching for Jaʿfar's body and found it under a huge pile of enemy corpses. We counted over 90 wounds across his entire body." The Prophet ﷺ said, "I saw Jaʿfar in Paradise—Allah had given him two wings to replace his two arms." Whenever Ibn ʿUmar ؓ would pass by Jaʿfar's son, he would say, "Peace be upon you, O son of the one with two wings."[883]

Ibn Rawāḥah ؓ then took the flag and took charge. Before he plunged in, he hesitated. He then rebuked his soul, "O my soul! I see you hold Paradise in disdain! I swear by Allah, there you will remain! Residing willingly or compelled to its shade!"[884] He then leaped into battle and met his desire. Ibn Rawāḥah's hesitation beautifully epitomised the Companions' humanity; he hesitated despite yearning for martyrdom for so long. His greatness was in challenging his shortcomings, as he rebuked his soul and charged forward in spite of its doubts.

Thābit ibn Arqam ؓ then grabbed the flag and ran away from the melee. Turning one's back to the enemy in battle is forbidden in Islam as per the Qur'anic command, "O believers! When you face the disbelievers in battle, never turn your backs to them."[885] However, the following verse stipulates an exception to the rule, "...unless it is a manoeuvre or to join their own troops..."[886] He shouted, "O Muslims, appoint a leader!"[887] Some Companions regrouped and immediately suggested that Thābit himself be the leader, but he swiftly refused. They began to scan the group, and all eyes fell on the newest convert amongst them—Khālid ibn al-Walīd ؓ.

When Khālid saw everyone turn to him, he said, "How could I lead?" We view Khālid as the undefeatable "Sword of Allah"[888], as per the Prophet's description. However, at the time, Khālid had been Muslim for less than a month, and despite his military prowess, his reputation amongst the Muslims was yet to be earned. Nevertheless, the Companions recognised his military strength and nominated him as the leader. Khālid took the flag and quickly devised a plan. He realised that preservation of life was the priority, so he formulated a two-pronged tactic. The first stage was to organise the Muslim army to attack in a quick burst for maximum short-term impact. The method was effective, and Khālid ﵁ narrated himself that he broke through nine swords until he was left with a shield.[889] He utilised archers to stop the Roman onslaught and cause their temporary retreat such that by nightfall, the two armies were separated. The following morning, the Muslims managed to retreat entirely and leave the battlefield.

A Victory or Loss?

Scholars differ as to whether the Battle of Mu'tah was a victory or loss. A group of scholars view Mu'tah as a victory, as the Prophet ﷺ described it as such. He ﷺ received news from Jibrīl ﵇ of events in real-time, narrating it to the Companions in Medina. The Prophet ﷺ described the events, "Zayd took the flag and was killed, then Jaʿfar took it and was killed, then Ibn Rawāḥah took it and was killed." The narrator added, "The Prophet's eyes began to tear" and ʿĀ'ishah ﵂ commented that the Prophet ﷺ was forced to sit down out of emotion. The Prophet ﷺ continued, "Until a sword from amongst the swords of Allah (i.e., Khālid) took the flag and Allah granted them victory."[890] Moreover, out of 3,000 combatants, less than 1% of the Muslim army died, which is a positive outcome by any means. This is the view of Mūsā ibn ʿUqbah ﵀, a *sīrah* expert and contemporary of Ibn Isḥāq, as well as the likes of al-Bayhaqī and Ibn Kathīr.

Others describe the battle as a loss. Simply put, the Muslims retreated, which is not typically the characteristic of the victor. Moreover, the Muslims lost their three leaders consecutively, all of whom were highly influential figures. The Companions deeply mourned their loss and they suffered emotionally for a while following the battle. This is the view of al-Wāqidī and Ibn Saʿd as well as most non-Muslim historians. Ibn Isḥāq, Ibn ʿAbd al-Barr, Ibn al-Qayyim, and many other scholars view the Battle of Mu'tah as a neutral outcome i.e., a draw. They argue that both armies suffered similar casualties, neither army captured any prisoners of war, and there was no definitive victory on either side.

There is a case to be made that all three opinions hold weight: militarily, the Muslims retreated; however, the Prophet ﷺ described it as a victory, which is a theological perspective. Similarly, the Prophet ﷺ described Ḥudaybiyyah as a victory despite the short-term loss; it transpired to be a resounding success in the long term, as promised. Following the Battle of Mu'tah, the Roman Empire would be brought down to its knees, and this battle can be viewed as the first meeting within a greater war. Therefore, it could be said that the battle was lost while paving the way for the war to be won. Moreover, the Battle of Mu'tah made it clear to the international powers that the Muslim state was an international force to be reckoned with. The Roman and Persian Empires viewed the Arabs as backward desert-dwelling Bedouins, hence the brazen disrespect shown by the Ghassanid Chieftain, but Mu'tah categorically dispelled that notion. In short, the Muslims did not defeat the enemy on the battlefield, but many successes were achieved.

A few days after their return to Medina, a smear campaign of sorts was being spread, perhaps by some Hypocrites, against the participants of Mu'tah. The Prophet ﷺ saw the wife of Salamah ibn Hishām ؓ and asked, "Is there something wrong with Salamah? I haven't seen him in the mosque."[891] His wife replied, "No, by Allah, but he has not left his house because every time he leaves, people mock him, saying, 'O you who fled! Have you fled from the path of Allah?'"[892] The Prophet ﷺ then addressed the congregation, "They are not those who flee (*furrār*), they are those who regroup to fight again (*kurrār*)."[893]

The Prophet ﷺ found a group of the Companions sitting together, crying. The Prophet ﷺ asked why they were crying, and they replied, "Why should we not cry, O Messenger of Allah, when the best and most noble of us has left?" They were of course referring to the three martyred leaders. Indeed, the Prophet ﷺ was narrated to have teared up when he saw Usāmah ibn Zayd ؓ who closely resembled his noble father.[894] The Prophet ﷺ replied to them, "But do not cry, for the example of my Ummah is a garden whose owner has cut its leaves and branches such that each year gives a better crop than the last." He ﷺ added, "The Dajjāl will meet this Ummah and there will be a group that he meets that are like you or even better. And Allah ﷻ will not humiliate an Ummah in which I am the first and the Messiah is the last."[895]

The Rights of a Leader

A Companion killed a Roman soldier with luxurious weapons and armour, including a golden coat of armour and a prestigious horse. As per Shariah, he was entitled to it all even though it was worth far more than the average amount. Khālid ibn al-Walīd ؓ, perhaps yet to be acquainted with the details of the Shariah regarding the distribution of war booty, said it was too much for one man and ordered him to give it to the general treasury. As they returned to Medina, the man immediately complained to the Prophet ﷺ. After confirming the events, the Prophet ﷺ instructed Khālid to return it all back to the man.

The man scoffed and began to mock Khālid, boasting that the verdict was given in his favour. The Prophet ﷺ was so angry at the man's insolence that he instructed Khālid ؓ not to hand anything over, saying to the man, "Will you not leave my commanders for me? Take the good from them and leave the bad."[896] The Prophet ﷺ sent a clear message to his people: do not treat your commanders with disrespect. Khālid ؓ was wrong in his judgement but was not chastised, as he made his own sincere *ijtihād*, whereas the man was right but still chastised due to his poor attitude.

Dhāt al-Salāsil

Not to be confused with the Battle of Dhāt al-Salāsil in the reign of 'Umar ibn al-Khaṭṭāb ؓ, this expedition was a much smaller affair, but one through which we derive much benefit. A few weeks after the Battle of Mu'tah, the Muslims attacked the Banū Quḍāʿah, who assisted the Banū Ghassān in battle. ʿAmr ibn al-ʿĀṣ ‎ narrated that the Prophet ‎ called him and said, "I wish to appoint you as the leader of an army, and Allah will protect you and grant you many spoils of war." ʿAmr, slightly hurt, replied, "O Messenger of Allah, I did not accept Islam to become wealthy; rather, I accepted Islam to be a Muslim and to be with you, O Messenger of Allah." The Prophet ‎ in turn responded, "O ʿAmr, how beautiful is pure money for a righteous man?"[897] The Prophet ‎ clarified that acquiring wealth is completely permissible in Islam as long as the person is righteous, and the money is acquired in a halal manner.

The Prophet ‎ sent 300 men to ambush the Banū Quḍāʿah, and ʿAmr ‎ was appointed the leader despite being the newest Muslim. It was perhaps a test from the Prophet ‎ to judge ʿAmr's potential as a Muslim leader just as he was a tribal leader in [The Era of] Ignorance. They travelled clandestinely, and ʿAmr refused to even light a fire so as not to attract attention. The Companions complained of the piercing cold nights, but ʿAmr refused, threatening that anyone who lights a fire would be pushed into it. When they approached the outskirts of the Banū Quḍāʿah, he realised that they were vastly outnumbered, and that 300 men were not enough. He then sent a message to the Prophet ‎ requesting reinforcements.

The Prophet ‎ sent 200 men—including the likes of Abū Bakr al-Ṣiddīq and ʿUmar ibn al-Khaṭṭāb ‎—under the leadership of Abū ʿUbaydah ibn al-Jarrāḥ ‎. The Prophet ‎ instructed Abū ʿUbaydah, "When you reach your companion (i.e., ʿAmr), make sure that you agree and do not quarrel."[898] The reinforcements arrived, and it was time for prayer. As they lined up to pray, an awkward moment transpired whereby both ʿAmr and Abū ʿUbaydah stepped forward to lead the prayer. Abū ʿUbaydah was senior to ʿAmr in every regard: he accepted Islam earlier; he was more knowledgeable; he memorised more Qur'an and with better recitation; he was the elite of the Companions and was even amongst the ten promised paradise. However, traditionally, the leader of the army was also the Imam in prayer.

ʿAmr instructed Abū ʿUbaydah to step back, as he was still the leader of the army whereas Abū ʿUbaydah was only leading the reinforcements. Tensions were beginning to rise until Abū ʿUbaydah stepped down, saying, "O ʿAmr, the last thing the Prophet ﷺ said to me was 'make sure that you agree and do not quarrel'. So, even if you disobey me, I will not disobey you."[899] Abū ʿUbaydah ؓ then stepped back and ʿAmr led the prayer and thenceforth the army. This small dispute once again demonstrated the humanity of the Companions as they differed over leadership. It also, however, revealed the true nature of leadership; two decades of tutelage under the Prophet ﷺ taught Abū ʿUbaydah how to lead from behind, compromising in the right moment, and relinquishing power despite being more qualified. Abū ʿUbaydah understood that unity took precedence over his own opinion—an invaluable and timeless lesson for us all.

The Banū Quḍāʿah were caught off guard and immediately fled. The Muslims acquired many spoils of war, as promised by the Prophet ﷺ. More importantly, they sent a much-needed message to the Banū Quḍāʿah and their neighbouring tribes.

The Conquest of Mecca

25

The Conquest of Mecca, in many respects, was the climax of the *sīrah*. Every decision the Prophet ﷺ made after leaving Mecca was geared towards an eventual return to his beloved hometown.

The Raid on the Banū Khuzāʿah

The Treaty of Ḥudaybiyyah stipulated that both sides were free to create alliances but that the rules of the treaty would apply to those tribes too. Members from amongst the Banū Khuzāʿah accepted Islam, and the tribe made an official alliance with the Prophet ﷺ. The Quraysh also made an alliance with the Banū Bakr, one of the few remaining Pagan tribes in the vicinity. The Khuzāʿah and the Banū Bakr were historically engaged in intermittent conflict similar to that of the Aws and Khazraj before the advent of Islam. This conflict was subdued after they joined the Treaty of Ḥudaybiyyah, but the Banū Bakr eventually raided a caravan from the Khuzāʿah. Before they did so, they sought permission from the Quraysh, explaining that they desired revenge for historic deaths. The Quraysh not only gave permission, but actively participated, as high-ranking tribesmen such as

Suhayl ibn ʿAmr and Ṣafwān ibn Umayyah supplied the Banū Bakr with weapons.

The Banū Bakr then set off to launch a surprise attack against the Khuzāʿah on the outskirts of Mecca. However, some of the Khuzāʿah were awake, and the raid did not go according to plan. A typical raid would target livestock and wealth, and one or two deaths may occur through collateral damage. Women and children were always off-limits as per tribal honour. However, as the Khuzāʿah were awake and ready to defend themselves, carnage ensued, and over 20 people amongst the Khuzāʿah were killed, including women and children. This was a very significant loss in the context of a single tribe. Moreover, one member of the Khuzāʿah fled and was pursued until he reached the confines of the Ḥaram. He then turned around and said, "I am in the Ḥaram! Fear your god! Fear your god!" The assailant replied, "There is no god today!"[900] He then killed him inside the sacred land.

News spread rapidly, and the Chieftain of the Banū Khuzāʿah arrived in Medina with 40 delegates, requesting assistance from the Prophet ﷺ. The Chieftain, ʿAmr ibn Sālim, recited a page-long monologue of the most eloquent poetry urging the Prophet ﷺ to help. He cited his common ancestry with the Prophet ﷺ as well as the treaty of Ḥudaybiyyah. He then referred to historic treaties between the two tribes. The Banū Khuzāʿah were the ruling tribe of Mecca for 300 years before Quṣayy wrestled power back into the lineage of the Quraysh. The two tribes remained on amicable terms, but ʿAbd al-Muṭṭalib eventually codified an alliance between them, pledging their allegiance to one another indefinitely. ʿAmr ibn Sālim continued to implore the Prophet ﷺ, "...they slaughtered us while we were bowing [in prayer] and in prostration!" The Prophet ﷺ was moved by his speech and replied, "You shall be helped, O ʿAmr ibn Sālim."[901]

The raid on the Banū Khuzāʿah was a direct violation of the Treaty of Ḥudaybiyyah. Most scholars of Islamic history explain that the Prophet ﷺ marched into Mecca as a direct result of this raid,[902] but the likes of Ibn Ḥajar comment that the Prophet ﷺ first tried to negotiate with the Quraysh, who refused, thus leading to the Conquest.

In a narration reported from a Successor, the Prophet ﷺ wrote a letter to the Quraysh, demanding that they cut off ties with the Banū Bakr and pay blood money for the deceased.[903] The Quraysh refused both demands, but in an unprecedented move, Abū Sufyān travelled to Medina to negotiate.

A Mighty Fall from Grace

Abū Sufyān approached the Prophet ﷺ but did not even receive a response. Worried, he then went to Abū Bakr, who replied flatly, "I cannot help you at all." He then tried speaking to ʿUmar, who went further and even mocked him, "Do you think I will ask the Prophet for you?!" Finally, he approached ʿAlī, desperately adding, "O ʿAlī, you are the closest person to me [in lineage] in this whole city, and I need your help. Can you please go to Muhammad and intercede on my behalf? Do not let me return to my people embarrassed and humiliated." ʿAlī was half his age, which in 7th century Arabia was the equivalent of a modern middle-aged man begging a small child for help. ʿAlī responded, "Woe to you, O Abū Sufyān! By Allah, when the Prophet ﷺ decides a matter, we will not persuade him otherwise."

Astonishingly, Abū Sufyān turned to Fāṭimah ؓ and said, "O daughter of Muhammad! Can you ask this little boy of yours (five-year-old Ḥasan) to go and seek protection on our behalf? If he does so, he shall be respected amongst the Arabs until the Day of Judgement!" Fāṭimah ؓ responded, "My son has not even reached the age to be able to grant security, and no-one can offer protection against the Prophet ﷺ." Abū Sufyān turned once more to ʿAlī, pleading, "O Abū al-Ḥasan! O Abū al-Ḥasan! You see my desperate situation—give me counsel. What should I do?" ʿAlī responded, "I do not know anything that can help you now, but you are the leader of the Banū Kinānah (i.e., the Quraysh), so why don't you go to the mosque and just announce your plea for protection." Indeed, Abū Sufyān went to the mosque and publicly begged for protection, "O people! I am Abū Sufyān! Is there *anyone* who will grant me protection?" The Companions of course did not dare betray the judgement of the Prophet ﷺ, and Abū Sufyān did not receive a single response.

Before he left Medina, he paid one more visit to his own daughter, Mother of the Believers, Umm Ḥabībah bint Abī Sufyān ﷺ, whom he had not seen for over a decade. As he entered and sat down on her bed, Umm Ḥabībah removed the blanket from the ground, leaving him to sit on the hard frame. He turned to her and asked, "Are you protecting me from the mattress, or protecting the mattress from me?" Umm Ḥabībah replied, "This is the blanket of the Prophet ﷺ, and you are an impure polytheist!"[904] Abū Sufyān returned to Mecca, humiliated and degraded. He relayed the entire story to the Quraysh who in turn called him a fool.

A few weeks later, the Prophet ﷺ announced to the Companions that he is to lead a very large expedition somewhere, and that everyone *must* attend. Every single male of fighting age was called upon, but he ﷺ did not even disclose the details to his closest confidant, Abū Bakr al-Ṣiddīq ﷺ or even his wife, ʿĀ'ishah ﷺ or daughter, Fāṭimah ﷺ. The Prophet ﷺ was exercising exceptional caution, not even confiding in his most trusted supporters, lest the news accidentally leak. The Prophet ﷺ even sent a small scouting party to the north—the opposite direction—to give the impression that an army would be deployed in that direction. The day before they embarked, the Prophet ﷺ disclosed that they were headed to Mecca. Over 10,000 Companions marched with the Prophet ﷺ to liberate Mecca less than a decade after they left.

A Grave Mistake

A Companion by the name of Ḥāṭib ibn Abī Baltaʿah made a grave error in judgement and tried to warn the Quraysh about the Muslim army. Ḥāṭib was a Muslim but was worried about the safety of his family in Mecca. He was a *mawlā* so he did not enjoy prestigious status in Meccan society. He feared for his wife and children and erroneously thought that if he were to help the Quraysh, they would protect his family. He wrote a letter and paid an anonymous woman to smuggle it into Mecca. He ordered her not to read the contents and deliver the message with utmost secrecy, so she hid the letter in the braids of her hair.

Were it not for divine intervention, no-one could have exposed his plan, but Jibrīl ﷺ informed the Prophet ﷺ who then instructed ʿAlī ibn Abī Ṭālib and Zubayr ibn al-ʿAwwām ﷺ to intercept the letter. He ﷺ informed them exactly where she was and how to identify her, and they found her as per the Prophet's description. They demanded that she hand over the letter, and she expectedly denied any knowledge of the matter. After they did not find anything in her belongings, ʿAlī snapped, "By Allah, the Messenger of Allah has not been lied to, and neither have we. You will either hand over the letter or we will strip-search you."[905] After she realised how serious they were, she asked them to turn around and she retrieved the letter from her braids.

They returned her to the Prophet ﷺ and she revealed that Ḥāṭib paid her to deliver a letter anonymously. The history books do not mention her again, and it can be assumed that she was forgiven, as she was not privy to the crime she was facilitating. Ḥāṭib confessed, and ʿUmar ibn al-Khaṭṭāb ﷺ immediately said, "O Messenger of Allah, allow me to strike his neck, as he has revealed his Hypocrisy."[906] The Prophet ﷺ instead asked Ḥāṭib why he would do such a thing, to which Ḥāṭib replied, "O Messenger of Allah, why would I abandon my belief in Allah and His Messenger? I did not do it to abandon my faith, nor do I prefer *kufr* over Islam. I did not do this for a love of *kufr*, and I have not changed who I am (i.e., I am still a Muslim). I did not intend to betray Islam, nor did I want to become a Hypocrite. I knew that Allah would fulfil His promise and execute His command (i.e., liberate Mecca), but I wanted to establish a favour with the Quraysh so that my family and property would be protected. All your other Companions have family to protect their relatives, and I have no-one in Mecca to protect my family."[907]

The Prophet ﷺ said, "Ḥāṭib has spoken the truth, so do not speak of him except with goodness."[908] ʿUmar, still fuming, said, "O Messenger of Allah, he has betrayed Allah and His Messenger, so allow me to kill him." He changed his justification from apostasy to treason, but still requested to enact capital punishment. The Prophet ﷺ replied profoundly, "O ʿUmar, perhaps Allah has looked upon all the attendees of Badr and said, 'Do as you please, for I have forgiven you.'"[909]

ʿUmar ‎ began to cry, saying, "Allah and His Messenger know best." It is unclear as to whether ʿUmar cried because he was also an attendee of Badr and was overwhelmed with Allah's Mercy, or whether he felt guilty about accusing Ḥāṭib, but it once again demonstrates ʿUmar's soft core underneath his harsh exterior.

Allah ‎ then revealed Sūrah al-Mumtaḥanah, "O believers! Do not take My enemies and yours as trusted allies, showing them affection even though they deny what has come to you of the Truth. They drove the Messenger and yourselves out [of Mecca] simply for your belief in Allah, your Lord. If you [truly] emigrated to struggle in My cause and seek My pleasure, [then do not take them as allies,] disclosing secrets to the Pagans out of affection for them, when I know best whatever you conceal and whatever you reveal. And whoever of you does this has truly strayed from the Right Way."[910] Allah ‎ said he "...strayed from the Right Way" but he remained a Muslim. Scholars differ as to whether Ḥāṭib was forgiven due to his intention or solely because he attended the Battle of Badr, but he was indeed forgiven, and no-one spoke ill of him thereafter.

The Final Emigrant

The Muslims embarked, and as they passed by the valley of Juḥfah, less than a quarter of the way, they encountered the uncle of the Prophet ‎, al-ʿAbbās ibn ʿAbd al-Muṭṭalib. He was completely unaware of the expedition and was Emigrating to Medina as a Muslim. Allah ‎ honoured him as the last human being to be counted amongst the Emigrants. As the Prophet ‎ said, "There is no Emigration after the Conquest."[911] The Prophet ‎ rejoiced immensely then instructed al-ʿAbbās ‎ to take his family to Medina and join the army.

There are various opinions as to when exactly al-ʿAbbās ‎ accepted Islam. Ibn ʿAbd al-Barr argues that he accepted Islam just before Khaybar,[912] Ibn Ḥajar believes that he accepted Islam at this point i.e., just before the Conquest,[913] and Ibn Kathīr maintains that he was living in Mecca as a Muslim but concealed his faith outwardly at the behest of the Prophet ﷺ. The evidence is not entirely clear, but it can be definitively said that his heart softened towards Islam at the Battle of Badr, though the exact time of conversion may be ambiguous.

The Companions respected al-'Abbās ؓ immensely and held him in the highest regard, as did the Prophet ﷺ. When someone irritated al-'Abbās ؓ, the Prophet ﷺ gave an entire sermon, "O people! Do not irritate my uncle! For indeed, the uncle of a man is like his father."[914] Whenever senior Companions such as 'Umar and 'Uthmān ؓ encountered al-'Abbās, they would dismount and greet him.[915] When the Muslims suffered in the Year of the Drought in 18 AH, 'Umar gathered all the Companions to pray for rain, including early Muslims and attendees of Badr, then chose al-'Abbās ؓ to make *du'ā'* on everyone's behalf.[916]

As the Muslim army neared Mecca, rumours began to spread that the Prophet ﷺ was coming. Two of the Prophet's cousins—and staunch adversaries in Mecca—panicked and waited for the Prophet ﷺ on the outskirts of Mecca before he entered the city. His paternal cousin, Abū Sufyān[i] ibn al-Ḥārith ibn 'Abd al-Muṭṭalib, and his maternal cousin, 'Abdullāh ibn Abī Umayyah ibn al-Mughīrah, intercepted the Prophet ﷺ before the army entered Mecca, pleading for mercy. Both of them were of the most brazen mockers of Islam in Mecca; Abū Sufyān ibn al-Ḥārith wrote the most scathing poems against the Prophet ﷺ, and 'Abdullāh ibn Abī Umayyah would challenge the Prophet ﷺ publicly, so much so that Allah ﷻ quoted him directly, "They challenge [the Prophet], 'We will never believe in you until...you ascend into Heaven. And even then we will not believe in your ascension until you bring down a book that we can read.'"[917]

'Abdullāh ibn Abī Umayyah was also the half-brother of Mother of the Believers, Umm Salamah ؓ. He begged her to intercede to the Prophet ﷺ on their behalf, and she felt pity on her brother. She approached the Prophet ﷺ and asked, "O Messenger of Allah, your

---

i   Not to be confused with the famous Abū Sufyān ibn Ḥarb ibn Umayyah, the leader of the Quraysh who will accept Islam after the Conquest.

cousins are here. Do you need anything from them?" In other words: can you help them? The Prophet ﷺ replied, "I have no need for either of them."[918] They mocked and abused the Prophet ﷺ for an entire decade in Mecca, and the pain was all the more potent as they were his own cousins with whom he ﷺ was raised. While the Prophet ﷺ was known for his mercy and compassion, those who cross the line must bear the consequences. Moreover, the Prophet's rejection would be a test for them: was their request sincere, or would they reply arrogantly?

When Umm Salamah returned with bad news, Abū Sufyān began begging the Prophet ﷺ from afar, raising his voice. He raised his son's hand—the Prophet's nephew—and pleaded, "O Messenger of Allah! I swear by Allah that if you do not let us in, my son and I will traverse the desert alone and die a miserable death!"[919] The Prophet's heart—gentle as it was—softened, and he ﷺ let them all in. Abū Sufyān then recited a lengthy poem of the utmost eloquence. As he recited the line, "...A guide other than myself guided me to Allah—A guide whom I repelled at every turn, but he continued to guide me to Allah." The Prophet ﷺ struck him on the chest and said, "Yes, by Allah, you repelled me at every turn."[920] The Prophet ﷺ clearly felt profound pain at his cousins' treatment, and his forgiveness was nothing short of Prophetic. The Prophet ﷺ accepted their Islam, and they both became pious Muslims, serving Islam for the remainder of their lives.

A Reluctant Conversion

The Muslim army camped at Marr al-Ẓahrān, less than 20 km from Mecca, and the Prophet ﷺ instructed the Companions to light their campfires. In other words: let the Quraysh know that we are here. Newly converted, al-ʿAbbās ؓ felt sympathy for the Quraysh; he requested the Prophet ﷺ to allow him to enter Mecca and negotiate a surrender one last time. The Prophet ﷺ gave al-ʿAbbās ؓ his own mule and instructed him to go forth in the Name of Allah. Al-ʿAbbās ؓ entered Mecca and encountered Abū Sufyān ibn Ḥarb, Budayl ibn Warqāʾ, and Ḥakīm ibn Ḥizām, three of the most senior leaders of the Quraysh. They stood in shock and awe as they saw the entire plain of Marr al-Ẓahrān occupied by 10,000 men. Budayl rejoiced, "This must be the Banū Khuzāʿah burning with the rage of war!" But Abū Sufyān quickly quelled his enthusiasm, "They neither have the courage nor the quantity [to support us]." [921]

Al-ʿAbbās ﷺ recognised Abū Sufyān's voice and called out, "O Abū al-Ḥanẓalah (i.e., Abū Sufyān)...woe to you! This is the army of Muhammad! If he conquers you tomorrow, know that you shall be executed." [922] Abū Sufyān desperately asked al-ʿAbbās for advice, and al-ʿAbbās suggested that he accompany him to the Prophet ﷺ to beg for forgiveness. Al-ʿAbbās then placed Abū Sufyān on the Prophet's mule and marched into the Muslim camp in the dead of the night. Whenever anyone would approach them or ask who they were from afar, he would respond, "It is al-ʿAbbās with the mule of the Prophet!" and they would be given safe passage. As they drew closer to the Prophet ﷺ, they encountered ʿUmar who immediately recognised Abū Sufyān. He exclaimed, "Abū Sufyān, enemy of Allah! Praise be to Allah for granting you to me without any covenant or treaty!" Al-ʿAbbās intervened, "He is under my protection!" [923]

They were granted an audience with the Prophet ﷺ, and ʿUmar began requesting his execution, imploring the Prophet ﷺ to punish his enemy. Al-ʿAbbās then interjected sternly, "Be quiet, O ʿUmar! By Allah, if he were from the Banū ʿAdiyy, you would never want to kill him, but because he is from the Banū ʿAbd Manāf, you wish to do so." Al-ʿAbbās was a recent convert and was still processing events through a partially tribal lens. ʿUmar, stopped in his tracks, replied, "Be careful, O ʿAbbās! For by Allah, your acceptance of Islam was more beloved to me than if al-Khaṭṭāb (i.e., his own father) had accepted Islam—because the Prophet ﷺ was happier at your Islam than he would have been at my father's Islam." [924] ʿUmar showed al-ʿAbbās the kind of love Islam instils, and how the bonds of tribalism pale in comparison.

The Prophet ﷺ instructed everyone to return to their tents to reconvene the following morning. Al-ʿAbbās spent the entire night in discussion with Abū Sufyān, trying to convert him, until they met the Prophet ﷺ the following morning. The Prophet ﷺ finally asked,

"O Abū Sufyān! Isn't it time for you to finally acknowledge that there is no god but Allah?" Abū Sufyān replied with the Arabs' highest praise, "May my mother and father be ransomed for you—how gentle are you? How merciful are you? How fulfilling [of ties of kinship] are you?" Abū Sufyān was stunned at the Prophet's willingness to accept him despite decades of fierce rivalry. He then said, "Had there been any other gods besides Allah, they would have helped me by now." In other words, yes, indeed, there is no god but Allah.

The Prophet ﷺ then said, "Woe to you, O Abū Sufyān! Isn't it time for you to finally acknowledge that I am the Messenger of Allah?" Abū Sufyān replied again, "May my mother and father be ransomed for you—how gentle are you? How merciful are you? How fulfilling [of ties of kinship] are you?" He then added coyly, "As for this matter, there is still some [hesitancy] in my heart."[925] Al-ʿAbbās became fed up and turned to Abū Sufyān, "Either accept or you will be executed!" The Prophet ﷺ did not make the threat, as one cannot compel another to convert, but al-ʿAbbās was Abū Sufyān's friend and he grew tired of his reluctance in accepting that which was best for him. Abū Sufyān then finally uttered the *shahādah*. After Abū Sufyān converted, al-ʿAbbās said, "O Messenger of Allah, you know that Abū Sufyān is a man of pride and honour. Can you give him something to make him feel proud?" The Prophet ﷺ then said, "We are entering Mecca tomorrow. Whoever enters the Ḥaram is safe; whoever remains in their home is safe; and whoever enters the house of Abū Sufyān is safe."[926]

Abū Sufyān then toured the Muslim army, dazzled by the numerous camps and their banners. Eight years ago, the Prophet ﷺ fled Mecca for his life. Three years ago, in the Battle of Aḥzāb, the largest army Arabia had ever seen surrounded Medina to destroy it. Now, 10,000 Muslims march in unison to liberate Mecca. Abū Sufyān asked about each banner, as they were all converts across Arabia whom he had never encountered. He then finally gazed upon the most prestigious convoy, and Abū Sufyān asked, "Who is *this* convoy?" Al-ʿAbbās ؓ replied, "That is the Messenger of Allah with the Emigrants and the Helpers." Abū Sufyān, amazed, declared, "O ʿAbbās, your nephew's kingdom has indeed become great." Al-ʿAbbās responded, "Woe to you! It is not a kingdom—it is Prophethood."[927]

Returning Home

The Prophet ﷺ divided the Muslim army into three primary contingents, which were in turn split into many smaller groups. The Emigrants were on one side led by Khālid ibn al-Walīd ؓ, the Helpers were on the other side led by Saʿd ibn ʿUbādah ؓ, and the Prophet ﷺ led the third group in the middle comprising of a mix of both Emigrants and Helpers alongside other converts. Altogether, there were 700 Emigrants, 4,000 Helpers, and the remaining 5,300 were an amalgamation of external tribes.[928]

As Saʿd marched, he chanted, "Today is the Armageddon! Today the Kaʿbah will be made halal (i.e., lose its sanctity)!" Abū Sufyān heard this and complained to the Prophet ﷺ, to which the Prophet ﷺ replied, "Saʿd is mistaken." He even ordered that the banner be taken from Saʿd and given to Zubayr ibn al-ʿAwwām ؓ.[929] The middle group's banner was held by Abū ʿUbaydah ibn al-Jarrāḥ ؓ, meaning that all three banners were held by those who were Qurashī. This was clearly an intentional move by the Prophet ﷺ, as it was more psychologically befitting that Meccans lead the way in liberating Mecca.

Al-ʿAbbās ؓ advised Abū Sufyān to rush into Mecca and urge the people not to fight in order to avoid bloodshed. Abū Sufyān bolted into Mecca, yelling, "O people of the Quraysh! Here is Muhammad! He has come to you with an army that you simply cannot fight. Come to my house and you will be safe!"[930] Al-ʿAbbās ؓ clearly understood Abū Sufyān's psychology when he wisely asked the Prophet ﷺ to grant him a token. As expected, Abū Sufyān used this token to urge the Meccans to yield. Abū Sufyān continued to call everyone to surrender until his own wife, Hind, darted through the crowd and smacked him in the face. She twisted his beard and hurled the harshest insults she could conjure, demanding that he be killed for his cowardice and treachery for even suggesting a surrender.[931]

Abū Sufyān continued to address the crowd, "Woe to you! Do not let her cause you to act irrationally; I am telling you that an army has come which you cannot fight. Whoever enters the house of Abū Sufyān will be safe!" Someone replied, "Of what use is your house to all of us?" Abū Sufyān then replied with the Prophet's full instruction, "Whoever enters the Ḥaram is safe; whoever remains at home is safe; whoever enters my house is safe." The people thus began scurrying into their houses, and those without houses fled into the Ḥaram.

Two of the contingents entered Mecca from the east and west sides, and the Prophet ﷺ strictly instructed them not to fight anyone unless they are attacked.[932] A small group of the Quraysh led by ʿIkrimah ibn Abī Jahl alongside Ṣafwān ibn Umayyah and Suhayl ibn ʿAmr banded together to fight back. They attacked, and Khālid ibn Walīd's convoy fought back, killing around a dozen people, with two or three Muslim deaths.[933] The remainder of the Meccans yielded, and there was no further resistance.

Enacting Justice

The Prophet ﷺ would shortly forgive the inhabitants of Mecca and grant them amnesty. However, a handful of individuals were singled out as criminals who could not evade punishment. They were: ʿIkrimah ibn Abī Jahl, ʿAbdullāh ibn Khaṭal, Miqyas ibn Ṣubābah, al-Ḥuwayrith ibn al-Nuqaydh, Habbār ibn al-Aswad, ʿAbdullāh ibn Saʿd ibn Abī Sarḥ, Waḥshī ibn Ḥarb, and Fartānah and Sārah.

ʿAbdullāh ibn Khaṭal was a Muslim who emigrated to Medina. He was sent by the Prophet ﷺ on an expedition, but he apostated, killed the Companion with him, stole his belongings, and returned to Mecca. He then bought two slave girls and ordered them to write poetry insulting the Muslims and the Prophet ﷺ. At the Conquest, he ran towards the Kaʿbah and grabbed the door, begging for clemency. He cloaked himself with the curtain of the Kaʿbah, calling on its sanctity for protection. The Companions did not know how to navigate this dilemma, so they sent a message back to the Prophet ﷺ

requesting instruction, and the Prophet ﷺ ordered that he be killed.[934] Fartānah and Sārah were the two slave girls he hired to propagandise about the Prophet ﷺ. Fartānah was killed but Sārah managed to flee, later returning and seeking forgiveness, which was granted. Miqyas ibn Ṣubābah also committed a similar act of treason. As explained in the Expedition of al-Muraysīʿ, Miqyas pretended to embrace Islam in order to kill a Companion, and the Prophet ﷺ remembered his name at the Conquest.

ʿAbdullāh ibn Saʿd ibn Abī Sarḥ accepted Islam and emigrated to Medina. He was a scribe for the Prophet ﷺ but eventually apostated and returned to Mecca where he began slandering the Prophet ﷺ and spreading lies about Islam. At the Conquest, he sought refuge in ʿUthmān ibn ʿAffān's house, who shared the same foster mother. Eventually, ʿUthmān ؓ brought him to the Prophet ﷺ and sought his forgiveness. The Prophet ﷺ remained silent, and the Companions all waited; the deafening silence continued, growing in tension until the Prophet ﷺ finally accepted his plea. After he left, the Prophet ﷺ turned to the Companions and said, "Weren't any of you wise enough to understand? The command was to execute him." One of the Companions asked, "O Messenger of Allah, why didn't you motion with your eyes?" The Prophet ﷺ replied, "It is not befitting for a Prophet of Allah to order a killing by motioning with his eyes."[935] Allah ﷻ therefore willed that ʿAbdullāh ibn Saʿd ibn Abī Sarḥ survive, and through His decree, his status in Islam grew, living a righteous life and eventually becoming the governor of Egypt.[936]

When ʿIkrimah ibn Abī Jahl lost the skirmish at the Conquest, he quickly fled, taking a ship to Abyssinia. En route to Abyssinia, a fierce storm overwhelmed the ship, and they all resigned themselves to their inevitable deaths. The captain remarked, "Now is the time to make *duʿā'* to Allah, for by Allah, we all know that our [other] gods cannot help us now." They miraculously survived, and ʿIkrimah recalled, "It suddenly struck me that if our gods cannot help us when we need them most, why should we worship them when we don't need them?" After two decades of opposition, ʿIkrimah internalised the truth of monotheism. He said, "O Allah, if You save me, I will accept Islam, and I will go to Your Messenger and put my hand in his, and I will find him to be forgiving and merciful."[937] He then travelled right back to Mecca and concealed himself, traversing through the crowds until he stood in front of the Prophet ﷺ, unveiled himself, and quickly declared, "I bear witness that there is no god but Allah, and I bear witness that you are the Messenger of Allah." 'Ikrimah lived the remainder of his life as a Muslim, eventually dying as a martyr fighting the Romans.

Ḥabbār ibn al-Aswad caused the miscarriage of the grandson of the Prophet ﷺ when he caused Zaynab ؓ to fall off her camel. Zaynab was attempting to emigrate, and Ḥabbār attacked her camel, causing her to fall and lose her baby. Al-Ḥuwayrith ibn al-Nuqaydh similarly caused two of the Prophet's daughters harm as they tried to emigrate, threatening them and causing them to fall off their horse. Al-Ḥuwayrith was killed but Ḥabbār somehow managed to negotiate his forgiveness.[938] Waḥshī ibn Ḥarb, the final name on the list, famously killed Ḥamzah ؓ, as already explained in detail. He fled to Ṭā'if and eventually accepted Islam when the people of Ṭā'if converted. Of all the people in Mecca, only nine people were on the kill-list, and of those people, only four were eventually executed.

The Conquest of Mecca occurred because the Treaty of Ḥudaybiyyah was violated when the Banū Bakr, with the assistance of the Quraysh, attacked the Banū Khuzāʿah. The Prophet ﷺ therefore allowed the Banū Khuzāʿah to attack the Banū Bakr by way of qiṣāṣ. However, the Prophet ﷺ instructed that they must end their attack and quash their rivalry at ʿAṣr, which was a few short hours away. After the ʿAṣr prayer, the Prophet ﷺ strictly forbade all forms of fighting, and the sanctity of the Ḥaram returned to its default position.

The following day, a member of the Banū Khuzāʿah killed someone from the Banū Bakr to which the Prophet ﷺ grew extremely angry. He ﷺ gave a fiery sermon condemning anyone who violates the sanctity of Mecca, threatening that the families of those killed will be allowed to enact qiṣāṣ on anyone who spills blood. The Prophet ﷺ said, "The Ḥaram has returned to its sanctity the way that Allah ﷻ created it. And if anyone tells you that the Prophet fought and shed blood in it, then say to them, 'Allah allowed the Prophet, and He did not allow you! And Allah only allowed him for a brief hour in the day.'"[939] Mecca remained sacred, and thus no war booty was taken, and no land was seized.

Liberating Mecca

Mecca was finally liberated from the shackles of Paganism. After 21 years of struggle, the Prophet ﷺ returned as the undisputed leader of his city of birth. The Prophet ﷺ entered Mecca on his camel, lowering his blessed head so much that his forehead was almost touching the back of his camel. He ﷺ praised Allah, glorified Him, and recited from Sūrah al-Fatḥ, "Indeed, We have granted you a clear triumph."[940] The Prophet ﷺ arrived at the Kaʿbah and began performing *ṭawāf* on his camel, and every time he passed by one of the idols, of which there were over 360, he would point to it with his staff and it would be knocked over.[941] He ﷺ would repeat the verse, "And declare, 'The Truth has come and falsehood has vanished; indeed, falsehood is bound to vanish.'"[942]

The people of Mecca congregated around the Kaʿbah, watching the Prophet's every move. He ﷺ called for the keys to the Kaʿbah and personally destroyed all the idols, ornaments, and pictures inside. As he threw out pictures of what the Pagans supposed was Prophet Ibrāhīm ﷺ, the Prophet ﷺ proclaimed, "May Allah curse them! What has Ibrāhīm got to do with this Paganism?"[943] He then recited the verse, "Ibrāhīm was neither a Jew nor a Christian; he submitted in all uprightness and was not a polytheist."[944]

After purifying the House of Allah from all forms of polytheism, the Prophet ﷺ turned and addressed the people of Mecca as he stood on the steps of the Kaʿbah. He ﷺ gave a short sermon, "There is no god but Allah, alone; He fulfilled His promise; He aided His servants; He destroyed all the armies alone; there is no god but Allah. Indeed, every aspect of Ignorance has been abolished except for two: custodianship of the Kaʿbah and feeding the pilgrims." He ﷺ then ended his sermon by stating, "O people of the Quraysh, indeed, Allah has abolished the arrogance of [the tribal orders of] Ignorance; every one of you is from Adam, and Adam is [created] from dirt. 'O people! Indeed, We created you from a male and a female, and made you into peoples and tribes so that you may know one another. Surely, the most noble of you in the sight of Allah is the most righteous among you. Allah is truly All-Knowing, All-Aware.'[945]"[946]

The Prophet ﷺ then asked the people, "How do you think I will deal with you?" The people called out, "[With] goodness! [You are] a noble brother, son of a noble brother." The Prophet ﷺ then replied profoundly, quoting Prophet Yūsuf ﷺ, "Go forth, for you are free. 'There is no blame on you today. May Allah forgive you! He is the Most Merciful of the merciful.'[947]"[948] Allah ﷻ revealed this verse when the Prophet ﷺ was suffering in Mecca, as if Allah ﷻ was instructing: a day will come when you are in command—just as Prophet Yūsuf ﷺ was on the throne—so you must follow the footsteps of Yūsuf ﷺ.

The Prophet ﷺ then instructed Bilāl ؓ to climb onto the roof of the Kaʿbah and give the *adhān*. The same voice that roared "One; One!" in the face of torture and abuse was now standing on the Kaʿbah above thousands of people, calling the inhabitants of Mecca to Allah. While others relented, Bilāl ؓ persevered in proclaiming the Oneness of Allah, and Allah ﷻ allowed him to proclaim His Oneness five times a day. As Allah ﷻ states, "Is there any reward for goodness except goodness?"[949]

It was unprecedented in Arabia that a freed slave with no recognised lineage occupy such a prestigious role, being raised—literally and figuratively—above the noblemen of the land. ʿAttāb ibn Asīd bemoaned, "Allah honoured my father [by allowing him] to be dead right now and not witness the humiliation of this black man being chosen above us." Al-Ḥārith ibn Hishām, Abū Jahl's brother, added, "By Allah, if I thought this man (i.e., the Prophet ﷺ) was upon the truth, I would have followed him." Abū Sufyān, who had accepted Islam moments prior, narrated, "As for me, I could not say anything, for even the rocks would notify the Prophet ﷺ of what I would say."[950] Abū Sufyān would need time for *īmān* to settle in his heart. His faith was not yet strong enough to refute their ignorant statements, and even sympathised to an extent with their sentiments, yet he believed in the Prophet's miracles and did not want to speak against him.

Later, the Prophet ﷺ approached the three of them and disclosed their own conversation to them word by word. Al-Ḥārith immediately said, "By Allah, you must be a Prophet because no-one was listening to our conversation. I bear witness that there is no god but Allah, and I bear witness that you are the Messenger of Allah."[951] Al-Ḥārith immediately accepted Islam, and ʿAttāb later followed. They grew into practicing Muslims, and al-Ḥārith in particular grew in piety and would try to learn from the Prophet ﷺ, eventually dying as a martyr in the Battle of Yarmūk.

The Prophet ﷺ then headed to Mount Safa where he took the pledge of allegiance from all those who embraced Islam. The people queued up to pledge their allegiance on the same mountain that he ﷺ announced his Prophethood to the people of Mecca, fulfilling the verse, "And you see the people embracing Allah's Way in crowds."[952] After the Prophet ﷺ took the pledge from the men, the women of Mecca all gathered. Amongst them was Hind bint ʿUtbah, the wife of Abū Sufyān, veiled to conceal her identity. The Prophet ﷺ instructed them to pledge their allegiance, quoting the verse, "O Prophet! When the believing women come to you, pledging to you that they will neither associate anything with Allah [in worship], nor steal, nor fornicate, nor kill their children, nor falsely attribute [illegitimate] children to their husbands, nor disobey you in what is right, then accept their pledge, and ask Allah to forgive them. Surely Allah is All-Forgiving, Most Merciful."[953]

When the Prophet ﷺ said, "...they will neither associate anything with Allah..." Hind called out, "You are asking of us something you did not ask the men!" The Prophet ﷺ corrected her and continued. When he ﷺ said, "...nor steal..." she called out, "I used to take from the money of Abū Sufyān without his knowledge." In a bid to avoid any controversy, Abū Sufyān added, "I have forgiven it all!" This dialogue clearly exposed Hind's identity, and the Prophet ﷺ asked, "Are you Hind?" Exposed, Hind responded, "Yes, I am. Forgive the past, may Allah forgive you!"[954] The Prophet ﷺ did not respond, and instead continued with the verse. The memories of Ḥamzah's gruesome death were always raw, and the Prophet ﷺ accepted her Islam, but he did not need to continue the conversation.

The Prophet ﷺ continued, "...nor fornicate..." and Hind once again retorted, "Would a free lady fornicate?!" Hind's statement demonstrated society's attitude towards indecency even though they were steeped in Paganism. Nevertheless, the Prophet ﷺ continued, "...nor kill their children..." Hind once again spoke out, and quick-wittedly retorted, "As for this, by Allah we took care of them as children and you killed them as adults at the Battle of Badr!" ʿUmar ibn al-Khaṭṭāb ؓ was so taken aback at her response that he burst out laughing, falling backwards in his laughter.[955] The Prophet ﷺ once again ignored her response, and after he completed the verse, he took their pledges but without shaking their hands directly.

Protective Jealousy

The Anṣār observed as the Prophet ﷺ was emotionally reunited with his kith and kin as well as his beloved hometown. Some of them felt deflated, and one remarked, "Now that he has returned home, softness has overtaken him for his people." The Anṣār were deeply in love with the Prophet ﷺ and feared that he may now neglect them. Jibrīl ؑ notified the Prophet ﷺ directly as to what the Anṣār were saying, and he ﷺ then called them over. The Prophet ﷺ called out, "O Anṣār, did you say that the love of my family has overtaken me?" The Anṣār immediately admitted their guilt, and the Prophet ﷺ asked, "Who am I? I am the slave of Allah and His Messenger! I emigrated to you, with you, and for you! My life is your life, and my death is your death!"[956]

At the Covenant of ʿAqabah, the Anṣār asked the Prophet ﷺ if he would leave them once he gained victory and reunited with his people, and the Prophet ﷺ replied resolutely, "My blood is your blood, and my destruction is your destruction (i.e., we are now one)."[957] Here, the Prophet ﷺ is reiterating his promise as well as his integrity as a slave and Messenger of God. The Anṣār began to cry, begging for forgiveness. The Prophet ﷺ then consoled them, "Allah and His Messenger believe you and excuse you."[958]

Converts after the Conquest

The Prophet ﷺ remained in Mecca to teach the people of Mecca the tenets of Islam. He gave a sermon, "O people! Indeed, Allah has made Mecca sacred the day that He created the Heavens and the Earth, and it shall remain sacred until the Day of Judgement. It is not allowed for any believer who believes in Allah and the Last Day to shed any blood (human or animal). Mecca was never halal (i.e., not sacred) before me, nor shall it be halal after me; and even for me it was made halal for a brief hour in the day (i.e., during the Conquest of Mecca). So if someone says, 'The Prophet made Mecca halal', you respond to them, 'Allah made it halal for the Prophet and He did not make it halal for you!'"[959] Some of the Companions took this instruction so seriously that if a pigeon were to land on their belongings, they would not shoo it away out of respect for the sanctity of the City.

The Prophet ﷺ remained for 19 days, and a handful of notable conversions took place in that time. Fuḍālah ibn ʿUbayd was a young man of the Quraysh who could not bear the new status quo so he decided to take matters into his own hands. He planned to assassinate the Prophet ﷺ and waited until he ﷺ performed *ṭawāf*, which would provide ample opportunity. Fuḍālah concealed his dagger and approached the Prophet ﷺ; as soon as he reached to pull out his dagger, the Prophet ﷺ turned to him and asked, "Are you Fuḍālah?" Fuḍālah replied in the affirmative and the Prophet ﷺ asked, "What were you about to do, O Fuḍālah?" Startled, Fuḍālah claimed he was just supplicating and performing *ṭawāf*. The Prophet ﷺ laughed and placed his blessed hand on Fuḍālah's chest. Narrating the story, Fuḍālah commented, "As soon as he placed his hand on my chest, no-one became more beloved to me in the whole world than him." Fuḍālah then immediately accepted Islam.[960]

Ṣafwān ibn Umayyah, son of Umayyah ibn Khalaf, was amongst those who tried to fight back at the Conquest. After they failed, he fled, vowing to commit suicide as he could not tolerate the humiliation. Ṣafwān was the one that urged 'Umayr ibn Wahb ☙ to assassinate the Prophet ﷺ, assuring him that he would take care of his family. After 'Umayr embraced Islam, Ṣafwān was left disgruntled in Mecca. After the Conquest, 'Umayr searched for his old-time friend and heard that he fled Mecca vowing to commit suicide. 'Umayr rushed to the Prophet ﷺ and begged him to grant Ṣafwān clemency. The Prophet ﷺ promised protection and even gave 'Umayr his turban as a sign of trust.

'Umayr tracked Ṣafwān down in Jeddah. Assuming he was being hunted, Ṣafwān was enraged, accusing 'Umayr of treachery. 'Umayr assured Ṣafwān that he was safe, "O Ṣafwān, I have come to you from the best of mankind! He is your cousin, and he is most merciful and kind. His honour is your honour; his kingdom is your kingdom; and his glory is your glory! Here is his turban—he sent it to you promising your safety." [961] Ṣafwān was hesitant, but the gesture stunned him, and he eventually returned. As he entered Mecca, he was too scared to dismount, so he called out to the Prophet ﷺ, "O Muhammad! 'Umayr told me that you granted me protection. Is this true?" The Prophet ﷺ called him over, and Ṣafwān, still terrified, refused until the Prophet ﷺ publicly and explicitly confirmed his protection. Ṣafwān requested two months of protection, and the Prophet ﷺ replied, "We shall give you four months!" Ṣafwān finally dismounted.[962] He did not convert immediately but accepted Islam after the Battle of Ḥunayn, eventually dying as a martyr.[963]

Suhayl ibn 'Amr was not on the kill-list and was therefore already forgiven, but he remained in his house in fear. He remarked to his son, "I do not know anyone still alive that has done more wrong to this man (i.e., the Prophet ﷺ) than me. I fought him at Badr, Uḥud, and Khandaq, and I showed him harshness at Ḥudaybiyyah. I do not know what he will do to me, so go and beg him for forgiveness."[964] His son, ʿAbdullāh, asked the Prophet ﷺ for protection, and the Prophet ﷺ replied, "Yes, he is protected by the protection of Allah." ʿAbdullāh rejoiced and informed his father, Suhayl, who proclaimed, "Truly this man has been righteous as a young man and as an adult."[965] The Prophet ﷺ then instructed the Companions, "When Suhayl comes, show him respect and do not stare at him sternly, for he is a man of intelligence and honour. He is too intelligent to be ignorant of Islam, and if he sees benefit, he will embrace Islam."[966] Suhayl then approached the Prophet ﷺ and engaged in conversation but did not accept Islam immediately. He eventually accepted Islam after the Battle of Ḥunayn.[967]

Abū Quḥāfah, the father of Abū Bakr al-Ṣiddīq ؓ, was the oldest person in Mecca. He was a stern adversary in Mecca, mocking the Prophet ﷺ as well as his own son, Abū Bakr ؓ, for accepting Islam. At the Conquest, however, he had softened and was willing to pledge his allegiance and accept Islam. However, he was too old, blind, and decrepit to physically attend the pledge. His granddaughter, Asmāʾ ؓ, brought him by the hand to the Prophet ﷺ and the Prophet ﷺ said, "Why didn't you leave the old gentleman for us to come to his house?" Abū Bakr ؓ replied, "No, O Messenger of Allah, by Allah it is more befitting for us to come to you."[968]

Despite Abū Quḥāfah's history of contempt, the Prophet ﷺ respected his elder, leading his Ummah by example. As Abū Quḥāfah placed his hand in the Prophet's to pledge his allegiance, Abū Bakr ؓ began to cry, saying, "O Messenger of Allah, how I wish that this hand was the hand of your uncle, Abū Ṭālib, rather than the hand of my own father."[969] Abū Bakr's love for the Prophet ﷺ is truly inexplicable, as his first thought when experiencing the long-awaited conversion of his father was to think of the Prophet ﷺ and his family.

The Conquest of Mecca served as a conquest of the hearts and minds of the people of Arabia. The numerous neutral tribes and provinces were awaiting the outcome of this final showdown, and after the Muslims were victorious, they all accepted Islam in droves. One by one, the tribes of Arabia pledged their allegiance to the grandson of

ʿAbd al-Muṭṭalib, Muhammad ﷺ. Hundreds of thousands of Arabs then presented themselves to the Prophet ﷺ to accept Islam, and Paganism was eliminated from the entire Arabian Peninsula.

A Deadly Blunder

The Prophet ﷺ sent a number of small expeditions to neighbouring tribes to invite them to Islam as well as to destroy the communal centres of idolatry. All the personal idols were destroyed in Mecca, but there remained some communal temples, and the Prophet ﷺ sought to eradicate them all. The famous idols such as al-ʿUzzā, Manāt, and Suwā were to be destroyed once and for all.

The Prophet ﷺ sent Khālid ibn al-Walīd ؓ to several tribes to invite them to Islam. One such tribe was the Banū Jadhīmah with whom Khālid had historical tensions; blood was spilled, and his uncle was killed. When Khālid approached them from a distance, they assumed that he returned for revenge, and so they took up arms. Some of them attacked Khālid and he defended himself, which was justified. However, Khālid made a grave blunder and attacked the whole tribe in retaliation—even those who did not take up arms. This was the standard according to tribal norms but was strictly forbidden in Islam. As a new Muslim, Khālid acted on his tribal instincts, but the senior Companions with him refused, as they knew better.

Khālid ordered them to attack but the likes of ʿAbdullāh ibn ʿUmar ؓ and ʿAbdurraḥmān ibn ʿAwf ؓ flatly refused, as they knew this action was strictly forbidden. Khālid was furious at their dissent, as he was still their military commander; he spewed vile curses at them but they held their ground.[970] The remainder of the Banū Jadhīmah yielded, proclaiming, "We are Sabian! We are Sabian!" The senior Companions knew that they intended to say, "We have accepted Islam!" but that they were not aware of the correct vernacular. Khālid was not as well acquainted and made the dreadful error of killing them despite their pleas.

As soon as news reached the Prophet ﷺ, he stood up, faced the Ka'bah, and raised his hands, saying, "O Allah, I free myself of Khālid's actions!" [971] The Prophet ﷺ then sent 'Alī ibn Abī Ṭālib ؓ with a large amount of blood money and instructed him to profusely apologise on the Prophet's behalf and explain the error. Amongst those killed was a young man engaged to be married. As he was dying, he recited lines of poetry to his betrothed, and she returned beautiful couplets, and he died in her arms. When the Prophet ﷺ heard this story, he grew even more enraged, demanding from the Companions, "Wasn't there amongst you a man of mercy [to put a stop to this]?!" [972] The Prophet ﷺ had a soft spot for tenderness, and this injustice wounded him deeply.

When 'Abdurraḥmān ibn 'Awf ؓ returned to the Prophet ﷺ, he also complained about Khālid's insults, and the Prophet ﷺ scolded Khālid, "Do not abuse my Companions! By Allah, if one of you were to give [the weight of] Mount Uḥud in gold to charity it would not equate to them giving a handful or even half a handful." [973] The Prophet ﷺ was addressing the Companions, but there was indeed a hierarchy amongst the Companions, and the senior Companions held a dear place in the Prophet's heart.

The Battle of Ḥunayn

26

After the Conquest of Mecca, news reached the Prophet ﷺ that a large army gathered from Ṭā'if to fight the Muslims. The primary tribe in Ṭā'if was the Banū Thaqīf, who had been the Quraysh's main rival and contemporary for centuries prior. They were superior to the Quraysh in many aspects such as finances and military prowess, but the Quraysh was home to the Kaʿbah, which was the epitome of prestige and nobility. After the Muslims liberated Mecca, the Banū Thaqīf became the bastion of Paganism, and they felt obliged to defend their beliefs. Their aims were twofold: to preserve Paganism, and to finally gain custodianship of the Kaʿbah.

The Banū Thaqīf began sending emissaries to every remaining Pagan tribe, urging them to unite and bear arms. Every battle in the *sīrah* thus far has witnessed larger and larger armies as the lines were drawn between monotheism and polytheism; the Battle of Ḥunayn comprised over 20,000 Pagans united against the Muslims in a truly unprecedented event. Thaqīf was the main tribe within the city of Ṭā'if, and Hawāzin was the largest Bedouin tribe surrounding Ṭā'if, and they comprised the bulk of the army, but numerous smaller tribes joined the fight under one banner.

After verifying the mammoth task at hand, the Prophet ﷺ called on all the new Muslims of Mecca and the surrounding areas to join the battle, and even non-Muslims such as the likes of Ṣafwān ibn Umayyah joined the battle and provided support. The Prophet ﷺ left Mecca with 12,000 people on the 6th of Shawwāl—10,000 from Medina and 2,000 new recruits from Mecca—arriving in the valley of Ḥunayn on the 10th of Shawwāl.[974]

Experience vs. Zeal

The Chieftain of Ṭā'if was a newly appointed young man by the name of Mālik ibn ʿAwf al-Naṣrī. At 30 years of age, he was leading his first major battle. He ordered the army to camp at Ḥunayn before the Muslims arrived, and he ordered that the women, children, and livestock be brought to the battlefield as a declaration of confidence and commitment. Durayd ibn al-Ṣimah was a famous warrior of Hawāzin who had grown blind and frail in his old age but still possessed his wits and foresight. He was brought to the battlefield to grant his blessing and impart his wisdom but immediately noticed the women and livestock. He demanded, "Why is it that I can hear the babies crying, the goats bleating, and the mules braying?" Mālik responded, "I brought them because I want every man to have his family and property behind him so that he fights the best fight possible." Durayd severely rebuked him, calling the move risky and foolish, asserting that it would not help win the war.

Durayd then enquired about specific subtribes whom he respected the most, and he was told that they did not show up. He then said, "They have done the right thing; had this truly been a day of honour and glory, then these people would never have abandoned this plain. I advise you and your men to return home." He continued, "If you will not listen to me in this regard, then at least take the precious eggs of Thaqīf (i.e., the women and children) back to their fortress, for their presence on this battlefield will not assist you. If you win, you may return and enjoy their company, and if you lose, they will be safe back home." The people of Thaqīf began contemplating his sound advice, but in a bid to assert himself, Mālik mocked Durayd and accused him of being senile. He then turned to his people and proclaimed, "By Allah, if you do not obey me as your leader, I will take my sword and kill myself in front of you all." His people urged him to calm down and assured him that they would follow him as their Chieftain, and the women and children remained on the battlefield.[975]

The Drawbacks of New Faith

Throughout the *sīrah*, the Muslims would enter battles as the underdogs, relying on Allah's assistance and blessings. As they marched to Ḥunayn—12,000 strong—some Muslims grew overconfident. One of them remarked, "How could we possibly be destroyed when we are 12,000?" News reached the Prophet ﷺ who immediately reprimanded them, saying, "Indeed, there was a Prophet before you that looked upon his nation with pride such that he said, 'Nothing will be able to overcome us!'...Within three days, 70,000 people among them perished."[976]

As the Muslims marched to Ḥunayn, they passed by Dhāt Anwāṭ (The Hanging Tree), a magnificent tree of grandiose stature and presence. The Quraysh would pass by yearly and sacrifice their animals as they hung their weapons on the tree for additional blessings, effectively turning the tree into an idol. Abū Wāqid al-Laythī, who had accepted Islam less than a week ago, requested, "O Messenger of Allah, can you make another Hanging Tree for us, just as they have one?" The Prophet ﷺ proclaimed, "Glory be to Allah! I swear by the One in Whose Hand is my soul, you have said exactly what the Children of Israel said to Mūsā, 'Make for us a god like their gods.' He (i.e., Mūsā ﷺ) replied, 'Indeed you are a people acting ignorantly!'[977] By Allah, it is decreed that you (i.e., the Ummah) will follow the pathways of those before you!"[978] Abū Wāqid did not ask for an idol, but the Prophet ﷺ went so far as to swear by Allah that his request equated to the Children of Israel asking for a god. The Prophet's emphatic response showcases the sensitivity of theology and the delicate nature of monotheism, as Shayṭān leads humankind down the path of deviancy in gradual steps.

The Muslims arrived at the valley of Ḥunayn and prayed ʿIshāʾ. Some Companions volunteered to scope the Pagan army, and they reported their vast livestock and property, even citing the presence of all their women and children. Murmurs began amongst the Muslims, and Mālik ibn ʿAwf's plan of showcasing their confidence was working, but the Prophet ﷺ simply smiled and said, "It will be the Muslims' war booty tomorrow, *inshāAllāh* (if Allah wills)[i]."[979] The Sunnah of the Prophet ﷺ was to be optimistic. The Prophet ﷺ once said, "If a person says, 'All the people are destroyed', then they are the worst of them."[980] This underscores the perils of pessimism and exhibiting a self-defeating mentality. It also demands an optimistic outlook alongside faith and trust in Allah ﷻ.

"I am the Messenger, No Lie!"

The Banū Thaqīf were well-acquainted with the plains of Ḥunayn, and they planned according to their unique insight. They stationed a small contingent of the Hawāzin at the end of a valley that the Muslims must cross, and they awaited the Muslim attack. However, they stationed several archers throughout the hidden crevices to the left and right, perfectly situated to ambush an oncoming army. The Muslims were lured into the valley, and the small contingent of the Hawāzin fled, encouraging more Muslims into the valley. Once all the Muslims inadvertently boxed themselves inside, the archers let loose a flurry from above followed by a devastating blow of a cascading 20,000-strong army.

The Muslim army fell into disarray, and thousands of fighters began to flee in all directions. Utter chaos ensued, and the entire army began to capitulate. The turmoil was compounded by a number of factors: first, the Muslims were taken aback, as the attack was completely unexpected; second, the new Muslims within the army had not been trained in fortitude as the senior Companions were; third, the unique nature of an

i Allah ﷻ states in the Qur'an, "And never say of anything, 'I will definitely do this tomorrow' without adding, 'if Allah wills'." (*al-Kahf*, 23–24). It is therefore imperative to say *inshāAllāh* whenever intending something in the future, as it affirms Allah's control of all affairs.

onslaught of arrows from above is particularly terrifying, as one cannot gauge the direction of attack nor does one have the ability to anticipate them; and fourth, due to the sheer quantity of the Muslim army, the bulk of them did not have helmets nor armour and were therefore defenceless.

The Prophet ﷺ quickly assessed the situation then stood up on his mount and began to call out, "Where are you going, O people? Come to me! I am the Messenger of Allah! I am Muhammad ibn ʿAbdillāh!"[981] The Prophet ﷺ was with the senior Companions, so he turned to al-ʿAbbās, who was famous for his loud voice, and said, "O uncle, call out to So-and-so!" The Prophet ﷺ then began listing specific groups and names, "Call out to the people of Divine Acceptance! (i.e., those who pledged at Ḥudaybiyyah)...call out to the people of Badr...call out to the Anṣār!" The Prophet ﷺ then began listing specific subtribes, "Call out to the Banū Sulaym! Call out to So-and-so!" As each tribe was called by name, it was as if they awoke from a slumber.[982] They all began rushing to the Prophet ﷺ, yelling, "Here I am, O Messenger of Allah! Here I am!" The Prophet ﷺ continued to yell out, "I am the Messenger, no lie! I am the son of ʿAbd al-Muṭṭalib!"[983] As the Muslims reassembled, the Prophet ﷺ proclaimed, "Now the real battle has begun!"

The Prophet ﷺ appealed to both religious and tribal loyalties in a critical moment; the senior Companions fled to "I am the Messenger, no lie!" and the newly converted Arabs perhaps fled to "I am Muhammad, son of ʿAbd al-Muṭṭalib!" This instance demonstrates the permissibility of appealing to tribal tendencies as long as they do not contradict Islamic values. Alongside the Prophet ﷺ was his cousin, Abū Sufyān ibn al-Ḥārith ibn ʿAbd al-Muṭṭalib. The Prophet ﷺ looked to his side and asked, "Who is this?" and Abū Sufyān responded, "I am the son of your mother (i.e., your close relative)."[984] After a decade of opposing the Prophet ﷺ, Abū Sufyān vindicated himself and proved his sincere conversion to Islam as he remained and called the Quraysh back while others fled.

The Banū Thaqīf and Hawāzin over-relied on their initial plan, and when the Muslims withstood their onslaught and fought back, the Pagans panicked and fled. The Prophet ﷺ instructed the Companions to pursue them as far as they could down every valley so that they could not regroup and attack. This vital instruction prevented the Pagans from recuperating, forcing them to disperse. The Prophet ﷺ then sent dozens of small contingents in each direction to conquer each subtribe and ensure a comprehensive victory.

In the aftermath of the battle, the Prophet ﷺ was upset at the sight of a dead woman on the battlefield. He asked, "It was not right for her to have been killed. Who did this?" The Companions informed him that it was Khālid ibn al-Walīd to which the Prophet ﷺ said, "Intercept Khālid and instruct him that he is not to kill any women, children, or servants."[985] As explained throughout the *sīrah*, the notion of civilians *vis-à-vis* combatants did not exist in 7th century Arabia—every male of fighting age was considered a combatant unless specified otherwise. Furthermore, in times of battle, there was no concept of protected status regardless of age or gender. Here, the Prophet ﷺ was codifying the underlying rule of warfare: no civilians may be harmed.

The Siege of Ṭā'if

Some historians consider the Siege of Ṭā'if to be a separate battle to the Battle of Ḥunayn, as it was a distinct event that occurred at the fortress of Ṭā'if. However, many historians refer to them both in the same chapter, as one occurred immediately after the other. As soon as the Muslims were victorious at Ḥunayn, they marched straight to Ṭā'if. When the Pagans dispersed and fled, the Banū Thaqīf fled to their fortresses in Ṭā'if. Unlike the fortresses of Medina, Ṭā'if was located on a luscious mountainous plateau surrounded by beautiful greenery and plentiful vegetation. It was therefore extremely difficult to penetrate, and due to their natural resources, they had fresh water and enough stock to last over a year. The people of Ṭā'if were planning to attack the Muslims for months prior so they made sure to stock up on supplies in case of a siege.

The Prophet ﷺ likewise prepared in advance; as the Muslims marched to Ḥunayn, he sent ʿUrwah ibn Masʿūd and Ghaylān ibn Salamah ﷺ on a special expedition to the Roman tribe of Jurash to learn about special instruments of war. They learned how to build and use a catapult[ii]; how to attack a fortress using the testudo[iii] formation; and how to build and use a battering ram.[iv] All these devices and techniques were completely foreign to the Arabs, but the Prophet ﷺ was proactive in enhancing techniques in warfare.

ii A device that uses a long arm to hurl projectiles over a large distance, most commonly used to attack fortresses in sieges.

iii "Testudo" is Latin for "tortoise", and the "testudo formation" is when soldiers group together to form a communal shield to protect themselves from attacks from all directions. They were most commonly used by Roman legions, particularly in sieges.

iv A device that uses a large wooden beam to break down large walls during a siege.

Despite their best efforts in utilising these advanced techniques and devices, the Muslims struggled to penetrate the imposing walls. The people of Ṭā'if threw boulders, poured boiling oil, and showered the Muslim army with arrows, inflicting many casualties. The Muslims were struggling to maintain the attack, and the Prophet ﷺ suggested that they leave and return at a later date. Some Companions, in their unrestrained zeal, were adamant in their desire to remain. After tasting the victories of Mecca and Ḥunayn, they pleaded with the Prophet ﷺ to continue, to which he agreed.

The Companions then resorted to an unfavourable tactic of burning the crops, which would destroy their agricultural produce for decades to come. The people of Ṭā'if began to wail and plead from the rooftops for the Muslims to stop, "We ask you by Allah and by our blood relation!" The Prophet's heart softened upon hearing their pleading, and he ﷺ forbade the Companions from burning any agriculture. The Prophet ﷺ then announced to the people of Ṭā'if, "Anyone who joins us will be protected! And any slave who joins us will be freed!"[986] Many people then escaped in the night and joined the ranks of the Muslims, but the state of affairs remained as it was. The Companions tried once more to penetrate the walls and again were faced with major casualties. The Prophet ﷺ then suggested for a second time that they return home, and the Companions quietly agreed.

After almost two weeks of an unsuccessful siege, the Muslims left, and the Companions asked the Prophet ﷺ to make *duʿāʾ* against the Banū Thaqīf. Not only did they expel the Prophet ﷺ years prior and cause him the most emotional distress he ever faced, but they now caused many Muslim deaths and rejected the call to Allah once more. The Prophet ﷺ raised his hands and all the Companions raised their hands, and the Prophet ﷺ prayed, "O Allah, guide Thaqīf! O Allah, bring the people of Thaqīf [to us]!"[987] The Prophet ﷺ prayed for them when they brutally expelled him, and now he prayed for them again, as his priority was always their guidance.

The unsuccessful siege of Ṭā'if demonstrates the limitations of this world—even the Messenger of Allah ﷺ could not guarantee automatic victory at every stage. Allah ﷻ could have easily handed the Prophet ﷺ another victory following Mecca and Ḥunayn, but the siege of Ṭā'if provides the believer with an invaluable lesson in patience and acceptance. Victory and loss do not necessarily represent Allah's pleasure or anger; rather, victories and losses are both tests from Allah ﷻ—the former tests one's gratitude and ego, and the latter tests one's patience and acceptance. Above all, the believer's trust is in Allah ﷻ, not in their own actions.

Unprecedented Spoils

The Battle of Ḥunayn produced the most spoils of war in the history of the *sīrah*, far exceeding the spoils gained in Khaybar. The young Chieftain's bold move of bringing everyone's property onto the battlefield proved to be a fatal error, and the old warrior's stern warning was justified. It is estimated that 6,000 prisoners of war were captured as well as over 24,000 camels and 40,000 goats.[988] These figures equate to tens of millions of dollars in modern-day currency—riches that the Companions could never previously fathom.

As the prisoners of war were being taken, a lady began to yell, "What do you think you are doing with me! Don't you know that I am the sister of your own companion?!" The Companions were taken aback as she explained that she was the Prophet's milk-sister, Shaymā'—Ḥalīmah's daughter. The Prophet ﷺ called her over and asked how he could be sure that she was Shaymā', as he had not seen her for 56 years. Shaymā' responded, "I still have the mark on my back from when you bit me!"[989] The Prophet ﷺ laughed and realised it was indeed Shaymā'. He ﷺ freed her and gave her two options: remain with the Muslims and be treated with honour and love, or return to your people with gifts. Shaymā' opted to take the gifts and return to her people, and it is not clear whether or not she accepted Islam.

The Prophet ﷺ waited for almost a month before distributing the spoils of war because if the Hawāzin returned and accepted Islam, he would return it all to them as he did with previous tribes such as the Banū al-Muṣṭaliq. The Prophet ﷺ never questioned their intention while doing so, as the priority was the communal blessing of Islam. Even if some of them were insincere in their faith, the sincere amongst them would be Muslim, including their own offspring. Moreover, as evidenced throughout the *sīrah*, even many of those who convert with ulterior motives develop a sincere love for Islam over time.

The Hawāzin did not arrive in time so the Prophet ﷺ began distributing the spoils of war. Every warrior received their share according to Shariah, but the commander chooses how to allocate the surplus. In this instance, the Prophet ﷺ chose to gift certain people and tribes with exorbitant amounts of wealth. The Prophet ﷺ gave Abū Sufyān 100 camels; he gave Ṣafwān ibn Umayyah—yet to embrace Islam—100 camels; he gave ʿUyaynah ibn Ḥiṣn—the uncouth leader of the Ghaṭafān—100 camels; he gave al- Aqraʿ ibn Ḥābis—a leader from the Banū Tamīm—100 camels. The Prophet ﷺ continued to gift senior noblemen such as Abū Jahl's brother, al-Ḥārith ibn Hishām, and Abū Sufyān's son, Muʿāwiyah. While they did not have the strongest faith, they had the most to gain from the Prophet's magnanimity. These tribes were of the last to convert, and the Prophet ﷺ allocated extra reward for them as a tactical manoeuvre to soften their hearts.

The only group left without receiving anything from these surplus riches was the Anṣār. Some of the young members of the Anṣār, in their humanness, felt disheartened after doing so much more and receiving so much less. One muttered, "When there is war, we are told to come, but when there is war booty, we are nowhere to be found." Another even remarked, "May Allah forgive the Messenger of Allah; he gives to the Quraysh and leaves us while our swords are still dripping with their blood."[990] The youngsters continued to murmur until Saʿd ibn ʿUbādah ﷺ realised that he must inform the Prophet ﷺ. Saʿd politely expressed the growing sentiment and the Prophet ﷺ asked whether Saʿd agreed. Saʿd replied coyly, "O Messenger of Allah, I am one of my people."[991] Saʿd empathised with the youngsters but his resolute *īmān* and love for the Prophet ﷺ did not allow him to voice his own complaints.

The Prophet ﷺ then called a private meeting with the Anṣār and instructed that no-one other than the Anṣār could attend. He began asking them, "O Anṣār, did I not leave my people for you? Did I not choose you above all people?" He continued to praise them, saying, "Were it not for the Hijrah (i.e., were I not from Mecca), I would have been an Anṣārī. And if the Anṣār went in one direction, and all of mankind went in another direction, I will go with the Anṣār."[992] He made *duʿā'* for them, "O Allah, forgive the Anṣār and the sons of the Anṣār."[993] He ﷺ said, "I give to some people because I fear for their greed and desires, and I don't give to others because I trust that what Allah has given them in their hearts is more than what I can give them." The Prophet ﷺ then asked the most beautiful question, "O Anṣār, are you not happy that these people go back with sheep and money, and you go back with the Prophet?" The Anṣār began to weep until their beards were soaked, and they never expressed such sentiments again. They said, "We are pleased with Allah as our Lord, and with Islam as our religion, and with Muhammad ﷺ as our Prophet."[994]

Indeed, the Prophet ﷺ truly loved the Anṣār from the bottom of his heart. He ﷺ also said, "Love for the Anṣār is a sign of *īmān* and hating the Anṣār is a part of hypocrisy."[995] Of course, the Prophet's wisdom was indeed vindicated, as one of these tribal leaders who received so much returned to his people and said, "O my people, embrace Islam! For Muhammad freely gives and does not fear poverty (i.e., he must be a Prophet)."[996] The leader was shown how a Prophet acts compared to a warlord or an imperial conqueror.

The Perils of Greed

Ḥakīm ibn Ḥizām was also given large amounts of wealth. As the Prophet ﷺ gave, he asked for more, and each time he asked for more, the Prophet ﷺ continued to give. After the third time of asking for more, the Prophet ﷺ said, "O Ḥakīm, this money is sweet and luscious; whoever takes it with an open and generous heart will be granted many blessings, but whoever takes it with desire and greed will continue to consume without ever reaching his fill."[997] The Prophet's statement shook Ḥakīm, and he replied, "O Messenger of Allah, I will never ask anyone for anything again after this." Ḥakīm lived a long life, and he truly did not ask others again.

The people began queuing for money. An uncouth Bedouin went as far as to grab the Prophet's collar and demand, "Give me some of the wealth of Allah that is at your disposal!" The Prophet ﷺ smiled and instructed the Companions to give him some money.[998] The Prophet ﷺ continued to hand out the money—not taking a penny for himself—until it completely ran out. Some Bedouins continued to surround the Prophet ﷺ, crowding him until his shirt was stuck on a thorny bush. The Prophet ﷺ finally retorted, "Return my garment to me! For by Allah, if I had as many camels as the thorns in the shrubs around us, you would have found me giving the last one to you."[999]

Worse yet, a man approached the Prophet ﷺ and demanded, "Be just!" The Prophet ﷺ responded angrily, "Woe to you! And who is more just than me?" The man continued his effrontery, "This distribution is not for the sake of Allah!" The Prophet ﷺ responded once more, "Will you not trust me when the One in the Heavens trusts me?!"[1000] The man stormed away in arrogance, and ʿUmar ؓ urged the Prophet to allow him to execute him for his blatant apostasy. The Prophet ﷺ replied,

"Woe to me if the people start to say that I kill my own companions." The Prophet ﷺ then uttered the famous premonition, "From his ilk[v] will come a group of people who will recite the Qur'an, but their recitation will not pass their throats (i.e., they will not comprehend it), and they will leave Islam just as an arrow leaves its bow."[1001]

The Prophet ﷺ smiled in the face of the uncultured Bedouin but responded adamantly to the arrogant man who questioned his integrity. A Bedouin may be excused as they are not acquainted with appropriate etiquette, but arrogance is the deadliest of sins. The man effectively proclaimed to be holier than the Prophet ﷺ, and the Prophet ﷺ only prevented 'Umar from taking action due to his concern for the greater good of the community. Allah ﷻ revealed, "There are some of them who are critical of your distribution of alms. If they are given some of it, they are pleased, but if not, they are enraged. If only they had been content with what Allah and His Messenger had given them and said, 'Allah is sufficient for us! Allah will grant us out of His bounty, and so will His Messenger. To Allah we turn with hope.'"[1002]

After the spoils of war were distributed and nothing remained, the Hawāzin eventually arrived, requesting to accept Islam. The Prophet ﷺ accepted their Islam but explained that their property had already been distributed. The Prophet ﷺ nevertheless sympathised with them, as their families had been captured as prisoners of war, so he ﷺ suggested that they rely on the Muslims' generosity to return them. After the prayer, the Prophet ﷺ encouraged the Hawāzin to ask for their families back and cite the Prophet ﷺ as an intercessor. The Prophet ﷺ then stood up and announced, "As for the prisoners with the Banū 'Abd al-Muṭṭalib, they are all yours." Each tribe leader then followed suit and returned the prisoners of war to their families. The only exception was a handful of recently converted Bedouin tribes; they did not gift the

v The scholars of Islam point to this event as the birth of the first sect in Islam. The Kharijites (Khawārij) are a group of Muslims that appear outwardly pious and increase in acts of worship but are quick to spill the blood of fellow Muslims and excommunicate people from the religion. This man is considered a proto-Kharijite, as the Prophet ﷺ explained that the Khawārij will spread from his ilk. The Prophet ﷺ explained that this sect will remain until the Day of Judgement.

prisoners of war but instead offered to sell them. The Prophet ﷺ could not force them otherwise, so he ﷺ offered to buy them on behalf of the Hawāzin and pay from the spoils of war of the next battle.

The Battle of Ḥunayn signified the end of Paganism in the Arabian Peninsula. With the exception of the fortress of Ṭā'if, which would accept Islam shortly, Paganism would cease to exist in Arabia. The land of idolatry was cleansed of idol worship, and the Prophet ﷺ turned his attention towards the Roman Empire.

PART IV • THE MEDINAN ERA

The Expedition of Tabūk

27

The Expedition of Tabūk took place in Rajab 9 AH and was the last expedition in the *sīrah* of the Prophet ﷺ. It was also the furthest the Prophet ﷺ ever travelled with an army. The purpose of the expedition is not entirely clear, but scholars offer their theories. Some explain that the Romans were preparing a large army to attack the Muslims after the Chieftain of the Ghassanids sent a letter to Rome urging their support.[1003] However, it may be far-fetched for the Roman Empire to send thousands of troops to the Arabs. Another theory explains that the Ghassanids themselves were the target of the attack,[1004] which is perhaps more plausible. However, it would not explain why the Prophet ﷺ would embark in the hottest month of the year, which—as will be explained below—caused extreme hardship. The most conceivable explanation, therefore, is that it was a command from Allah ﷻ to test the believers. The subtext of the expedition, in any case, was a pre-emptive attack on Roman forces, and the Muslims were expecting a formidable foe.

The Expedition of Tabūk comprised the biggest army in the whole *sīrah*, with sources claiming over 30,000 attendees.[1005] This may be an overestimation due to the enormous crowds and the impossible task of counting them, but it was still the largest army that ever accompanied the Prophet ﷺ. The expedition took place in the scorching heat of summer, which is particularly severe in Arabia. The desert climate further exacerbated the heat, which grew almost unbearable. The Companions endured this for an entire month, as they travelled for over 1,000 miles. Moreover, the Prophet ﷺ embarked just before the harvest season. Most people did not enjoy a regular salary; rather, they earned their income on a yearly basis according to their harvest. The army left before the harvest and returned after the harvest, effectively forgoing an entire year's income.

Most of the Companions would refer to The Expedition of Tabūk as "The Army of Hardship" due to the extreme difficulties suffered despite no actual fighting taking place. Allah ﷻ also references this, "Allah has certainly turned in mercy to the Prophet as well as the Emigrants and the Helpers who stood by him in the time of hardship, after the hearts of a group of them had almost faltered. He then accepted their repentance. Surely He is Ever Gracious and Most Merciful to them."[1006] Due to the unprecedented number of attendees coupled with the blistering heat, the Companions ran out of both food and water.

Qatādah, the student of Ibn ʿAbbās ؓ, commented, "This verse refers to the Expedition of Tabūk. They left towards Syria in the blazing summer and were tested severely, so much so that it is mentioned that two or more people rationed one date per day. They would split that date amongst themselves and then suck on the date pits."[1007] Ibn ʿAbbās ؓ once asked ʿUmar ibn al-Khaṭṭāb ؓ about the Army of Hardship, to which ʿUmar said, "We left with the Prophet ﷺ to Tabūk in extremely hot weather, and we were so thirsty that we thought our throats would collapse. People went out in search for water but returned even more tired and thirsty. Some people sacrificed their camels in order to squeeze water out of the camel..."[1008]

The Expedition of Tabūk was a personal obligation (*farḍ ʿayn*)[i] on every Muslim, as the Prophet ﷺ explicitly commanded every capable adult male to attend. Moreover, the entirety of Sūrah al-Tawbah was revealed, which is the most direct *sūrah* in urging jihad. Allah ﷻ states, "O believers! What is the matter with you that when you are asked to march forth in the cause of Allah, you cling firmly to [your] land? Do you prefer the life of this world over the Hereafter? The enjoyment of this worldly life is insignificant compared to that of the Hereafter. If you do not march forth, He will afflict you with a painful torment and replace you with other people. You are not harming Him in the least. And Allah is Most Capable of everything."[1009]

These strong commands corroborate the theory that the Expedition of Tabūk was a test from Allah ﷻ, as the same type of language is not used in any other *sūrah* when encouraging jihad. It was the final expedition with the Prophet ﷺ, and Allah ﷻ wanted to test the believers' sincerity to the cause. The fact that no fighting took place but the expedition itself was extremely testing further adds to the notion that it was all a test.

The Prophet ﷺ raised funds by calling on the Companions to support the cause. Despite gaining vast riches at Ḥunayn, nothing remained, as the Prophet ﷺ gave it all away for the sake of Allah ﷻ. The Prophet ﷺ rallied the Companions to give whatever they could, promising, "Whoever finances the expedition will be granted Paradise!" Most of the Companions gave whatever they could but the lion's share of the funds came from ʿUthmān ibn ʿAffān ؓ. As the Prophet ﷺ continued to rally the Companions on the pulpit, asking, "Who will give? Who will give?" ʿUthmān ؓ stood up and declared, "I will give 100 camels

i Islamic obligations are categorised into two: personal obligations (*farḍ ʿayn*) and communal obligations (*farḍ kifāyah*). Personal obligations, such as prayer and fasting, are mandated upon every single Muslim as long as they meet the requirements of the obligation. Communal obligations are required of a community, and once the obligation is fulfilled, the community is absolved of the responsibility. Examples include the Friday Sermon and the funeral prayer—if no-one performs these obligations, the whole community is deemed sinful, but if someone does, the community is absolved.

and all that is on them!" The Prophet ﷺ continued to ask, "Who will give?" and ʿUthmān ؓ stood up again and said, "I will give 200 camels and all that is on them!" The Prophet ﷺ again asked and ʿUthmān ؓ again stood up and said, "I will give 300 camels and all that is on them!" The Prophet ﷺ then said, "ʿUthmān has no sin after what he has done today!"[1010] ʿUthmān's trade caravan had just returned from Syria, and he gave it all for the sake of Allah. As the Prophet ﷺ spread his hand through the pile of gold coins, he said, "By Allah, nothing can harm ʿUthmān after what he has done today.[ii]"[1011]

After hearing the Prophet's promise of Paradise, ʿUmar ؓ went home and gathered half his entire wealth for the sake of Allah ﷻ. The Prophet ﷺ asked, "O ʿUmar, what did you leave for your family?" ʿUmar replied that he left an equal amount for them. Abū Bakr ؓ then arrived with the entirety of his wealth. The Prophet ﷺ asked, "O Abū Bakr, what did you leave for your family?" Abū Bakr ؓ replied resiliently, "I left them Allah and His Messenger." ʿUmar ؓ then professed, "I will never compete with you again."[1012]

The Hypocrites accused those who gave in abundance of showing off, and they mocked those who gave small amounts; meanwhile, they gave nothing themselves. A poor man did not have a single possession to donate, so he worked tirelessly through the night pulling water out of a well to earn a few dates. He donated half of them for the sake of Allah and kept the other half to feed his family. ʿAbdullāh ibn Ubayy ibn Salūl began laughing with his cronies, ridiculing his feeble attempt. One of them said, "Do you think Allah needs these dates?" Another mocked, "You are in more need of these dates than anyone else!"[1013] The Companion felt embarrassed after his tireless effort to produce these mere dates for Allah's sake, but Allah ﷻ revealed, "There are those who slander the believers for donating freely and mock others for giving only the little they can afford. Allah will throw their mockery back at them, and they will suffer a painful punishment."[1014]

ii Decades later, ʿUthmān ؓ and Ibn ʿAbbās ؓ both cited this Hadith when the Kharijites attacked ʿUthmān ؓ and called for his overthrow as the Caliph.

The Hypocrites also gave pitiful excuses not to attend the expedition both before and after. The Prophet ﷺ asked al-Jadd ibn Qays, a notable Hypocrite and friend of ʿAbdullāh ibn Ubayy, why he was not attending, to which he said, "O Messenger of Allah, can you not excuse me? By Allah, my people know that I have a weakness for women, and I am afraid that if I see the Roman women that I would not be able to control myself." [1015] Allah ﷻ revealed, "There are some of them who say, 'Exempt me and do not expose me to temptation.' They have already fallen into temptation. And Hell will surely engulf the disbelievers." [1016]

Allah ﷻ further revealed, "Those [Hypocrites] who remained behind rejoiced for doing so in defiance of the Messenger of Allah and hated [the prospect of] striving with their wealth and their lives in the cause of Allah. They said, 'Do not march forth in the heat.' Say, 'The Fire of Hell is far hotter!' If only they could comprehend! So let them laugh a little—they will weep much as a reward for what they have committed." [1017] And, "Had the gain been within reach and the journey shorter, they would have followed you, but the distance seemed too long for them. And they will swear by Allah, 'Had we been able, we would have certainly joined you.' They are ruining themselves. And Allah knows that they are surely lying." [1018]

In contrast, a small group of Companions were termed "The Criers (al-Bakkā'ūn)" because they were so grieved at not being able to afford a camel to join the Prophet ﷺ. On the day of departure, the Prophet ﷺ announced regrettably, "I have no mounts to give you." They were distraught, but Allah ﷻ referenced them, "Nor [is there any blame on] those who came to you for mounts, then when you said, 'I can find no mounts for you', they left with eyes overflowing with tears out of grief that they had nothing to contribute." [1019] The Criers are perfectly juxtaposed with the Hypocrites; one group is obliged to attend but makes woeful excuses while the other is excused but cries in regret.

Allah ﷻ also excused anyone else who could not attend for a valid reason, "There is no blame on the weak, the sick, or those lacking the means [if they stay behind], as long as they are true to Allah and His Messenger. There is no blame on the good-doers. And Allah is All-Forgiving, Most Merciful."[1020] The Prophet ﷺ said to the Companions at Tabūk after they suffered extreme hardship, "You left people behind in Medina who have not taken a step, spent any wealth, or crossed a valley, yet they are still with you." The Companions asked, "O Messenger of Allah, how can they be with us while they are in Medina?" The Prophet ﷺ replied, "They were held back due to a legitimate excuse."[1021] This Hadith is truly a glad tiding for any Muslim that has intention to carry out good even if they could not.

A Lesson in Repentance

Kaʿb ibn Mālik ﷺ was a senior Companion of the Anṣār from the tribe of the Banū Salamah. He was one of the few Helpers that accepted Islam before the Hijrah, as he attended the Covenant of ʿAqabah. Kaʿb is therefore considered to be of the elite of the Anṣār. Nevertheless, he was fallible and susceptible to error, as all humans are, and he made a grave error in the Expedition of Tabūk by failing to attend.

Kaʿb's story offers a masterclass in repentance and a guide for every Muslim on how to react to a sin. Kaʿb narrated the whole story in the first person, describing to his son, "I never remained behind in any expedition that the Prophet ﷺ attended except Tabūk and Badr—but Badr was not intended as a war. I witnessed the Covenant of ʿAqabah, and that is more precious to me than Badr. I would not substitute it for Badr even though Badr is more popular amongst the people than the Covenant of ʿAqabah."[1022]

Kaʿb set the scene of his story by outlining his accomplishments. This follows a pattern of the senior Companions showing pride in their service to Islam. A distinction must be made between pride and arrogance, as the Companions were proud of their actions—hoping that Allah ﷻ accepted them—but were not arrogant by attributing their positive actions to themselves. Instead, they linked their success to Allah's mercy and blessing. It is also worth noting that the Hadith is narrated by his own son, ʿAbdullāh. While most people hide their faults from their children, Kaʿb laid all to bare in explicit detail, demonstrating his sincerity and transparency. This candour offers an excellent insight into raising righteous children, as it teaches them humility and accountability to Allah ﷻ.

Kaʿb ؓ continued, "As for the Expedition of Tabūk, I had never been physically stronger or better prepared financially than I was when I missed that expedition." The valid excuses for not attending were a lack of health or wealth. Each fighter would finance their own travel and food, so the extremely poor were excused, as were those in poor health. Kaʿb clarified that he could not, in good conscience, rely on either excuse. He added, "Whenever the Messenger ﷺ intended an expedition, he would never reveal the location until it was time to leave, but in this case—due to the severe heat, the long journey, crossing the desert, and facing a great number of enemies—he announced it in advance to give us time to prepare."

Kaʿb continued, "The number of attendees was so great that it could not be listed in any register or book. Any man who intended to be absent assumed that his absence would be hidden (due to the large crowds) unless Allah exposed him through Revelation. The Prophet ﷺ embarked on this expedition when the fruits were ripe and the shade was sweet, and I was more eager for those two than the expedition." Kaʿb's frank admission is truly humbling, as he succumbed to his humanness.

He continued, "The Prophet ﷺ and the Companions continued to prepare for the battle, and I also sought to begin preparing, but each day would pass and I would return home without having prepared anything. Each day I would say, 'I can prepare tomorrow.' But I kept delaying until one day the Prophet ﷺ left with the army after Fajr while I had not yet started my preparation. I said to myself, 'I will do it today and catch up with the army.' That day went by, as did the next, and once again I did not prepare anything. O how I wish I had acted. After the Prophet ﷺ departed, whenever I walked outside it grieved me to see no-one left in the city except those known for their Hypocrisy or the weak and excused."[1023]

Kaʿb's narration truly highlights the perils of procrastination. Imam Ibn al-Jawzī ؒ states, "Beware of procrastination, for it is the most important weapon of Iblīs."[1024] Imam Ibn al-Qayyim ؒ adds, "How often does a virtuous deed run towards you only to be stopped at the door by the guards of 'perhaps', 'soon', and 'maybe'."[1025] Allah ﷻ continually encourages taking action with an emphasis on hastening to avoid procrastination and delay, "And hasten towards forgiveness from your Lord and a Paradise as vast as the Heavens and Earth, prepared for those mindful [of Allah]."[1026]

When the Prophet ﷺ arrived in Tabūk, he noticed Kaʿb's absence and asked about his whereabouts. Kaʿb narrated, "A man from the Banū Salamah said, 'O Messenger of Allah, his fine clothes and luxuries kept him back!' Muʿādh ibn Jabal retorted, 'Woe to you! By Allah, O Messenger of Allah, I only know Kaʿb to be a good man.'" Kaʿb's own tribesman spoke ill of him but Muʿādh ibn Jabal ؓ defended him without hesitation. The Prophet ﷺ once said, "The most knowledgeable person in my Ummah of matters of halal and haram is Muʿādh ibn Jabal."[1027] We clearly see in this instance Muʿādh's understanding of the Shariah. As the Prophet ﷺ said, "Whoever defends the honour of his brother in his absence, Allah ﷻ will defend him from the Fire of Hell."[1028] In the same vein, Kaʿb specifies Muʿādh's name when relaying the story but says "A man from the Banū Salamah" when referring to his critic. Not wanting to expose his companion, Kaʿb embodied the true nature of brotherhood that we observe throughout the *sīrah* whenever a Companion narrates a story hiding the identities of their critics. It is also worth noting—once again—that the Prophet ﷺ noticed the absence of a single Companion within tens of thousands.

Eventually, the Muslim army returned, and Kaʿb narrated, "When I heard that the Prophet ﷺ was returning, my concerns deepened, and my mind was racing through every excuse I could think of, saying to myself, 'What can I say to avoid the anger of the Prophet ﷺ when he returns?' When the Prophet ﷺ had returned, all the excuses disappeared, and I knew that I could never escape this problem with a lie. I was then resolved to tell the truth and confess." Kaʿb outlining the intricate details of his thought process is a frank yet beautiful demonstration of a righteous person's battle with their soul; he considered fabricating an excuse to escape punishment but eventually defeated his soul and surrendered his cause to Allah and His Messenger. Nothing can save one from a sin except genuine sincerity. The Prophet ﷺ once said, "Regret is [the essence of] repentance."[1029]

Kaʿb continued, "When the Prophet ﷺ would return, he would always pray two units of prayer in the mosque and then welcome the people. The next day, the stragglers who failed to attend queued up and gave their excuses to the Prophet ﷺ, and we were around 80 people." The Prophet ﷺ accepted everyone's excuse without question but Allah ﷻ gently reprimanded him, "May Allah pardon you! Why did you give them permission [to stay behind] before those who told the truth were distinguished from those who were lying?"[1030] He ﷻ also said, "Had they really intended to march forth, they would have prepared for it. But Allah disliked that they should go, so He let them lag behind, and it was said [to them], 'Stay with those [helpless] who remain behind.'"[1031]

Kaʿb narrated in beautiful detail, "Then it was my turn. When I approached him, he smiled to me the way that an angry person smiles." An angry person's smile is distinct from that of a joyful person, and the Prophet ﷺ was deeply disappointed with Kaʿb, but he ﷺ still forced a smile as per his tender nature. The Prophet's disappointment was indeed a mercy for Kaʿb, as it demonstrates his expectation of a righteous man, whereas he ﷺ did not bother with the Hypocrites. The Prophet ﷺ then asked, "What is your excuse, O Kaʿb? Were you not of good health? Did you not recently buy a second camel?" Kaʿb responded, "By Allah, O Messenger of Allah, if I were in front of anyone else in this world, I would have talked my way out of this situation, for I have been granted eloquent speech. But if I were to lie to you today to placate you, Allah would expose me and make you angry at me tomorrow; and if I tell you the truth and anger you today, I can hope that Allah will forgive me. O Messenger of Allah, I swear by Allah that I have no excuse." The Prophet ﷺ responded, "This man has spoken the truth."[1032]

Kaʿb continued his narration, "As I walked away, my tribesmen surrounded me, saying, 'O Kaʿb, you were a good man! We have never seen any evil from you. You are well-known in the community. Why didn't you join the others by making an excuse? Why did you embarrass yourself—and us—by sticking out like this? Go back and try again!' They continued to hound me until I almost caved in. But then I asked, 'Was there anyone else in the queue that did not have an excuse?' They said, 'Yes, there were two men: Murārah ibn al-Rabīʿ al-ʿAmrī and Hilāl ibn Umayyah al-Wāqifī.' By Allah, they mentioned two men of *īmān* and piety, both of whom attended Badr. Their company is a blessing, so I stuck to my position." Indeed, Allah ﷻ revealed, "Those who believe in Allah and the Last Day do not ask for exemption from striving with their wealth and their lives. And Allah has perfect knowledge of those who are mindful [of Him]. No-one would ask for exemption except those who have no faith in Allah or the Last Day, and whose hearts are in doubt, so they are torn by their doubts."[1033]

Allah ﷻ decreed that those without an excuse be punished. The Prophet ﷺ forbade all Muslims from interacting with the three of them in any capacity. Once again, the Hypocrites did not suffer a worldly punishment while the pious believers were cleansed of their sin in this life in order to meet Allah ﷻ in the Hereafter with a clean slate. However, as they committed a major sin, the punishment was severe, and the three men suffered greatly.

Kaʿb narrated, "The people's attitude towards us changed so much that I felt like a foreigner in my own land. The world, despite its vastness, became a constricted place. The other two (i.e., Murārah and Hilāl) locked themselves in their houses and did not interact with the people, as it was too painful. Instead, they remained at home and wept. As for me, I was the youngest and most sociable of the three, so I would intentionally walk in the marketplace and pray in the mosque, but no-one would talk to me or even look at me. I would greet the Prophet ﷺ publicly every day, wondering if his lips would move in response, but they did not. When I prayed, I noticed the Prophet ﷺ looking at me, but when I looked back, he turned away." Kaʿb's heart-breaking description shows that the Prophet ﷺ cared for Kaʿb and was concerned but he ﷺ did not dare disobey Allah ﷻ.

As the anguish continued, Kaʿb grew desperate. He narrated, "I felt so exasperated that I went to my best friend and cousin, Abū Qatādah. I jumped over his wall into his garden and greeted him but by Allah he did not even return my *salām*. I then said, 'O Abū Qatādah! I ask you by Allah! Don't you know me to be a Muslim who loves Allah and His Messenger?' But he did not even look at me. I asked again, and he ignored me. I begged for a third time, and he declared towards the sky, 'Allah and His Messenger know best.' The tears began bursting forth from me and I rushed home to cry."

Kaʿb's test was then compounded, as a Christian from Syria approached him and handed him a letter from the king of the Ghassanids. There was clearly a spy in Medina—perhaps from amongst the Hypocrites—reporting to the Ghassanids. The letter read, "I have been informed that your friend has treated you coldly. Allah would not allow you to live in a place where you are inferior and your rights are lost, so join us and we will console you and please you."[1034] Kaʿb stated, "As soon as I read it, I said to myself, 'This is part of the test.' I then immediately burned the letter in my furnace." Kaʿb's plight showcases the necessity of having both knowledge and piety—piety is required to pass the test, but knowledge is necessary to identify whether something is even a test.

Kaʿb's test continued to intensify, and he continued to persevere. On the 50th morning of the boycott, a messenger approached Kaʿb and said, "O Kaʿb, the Messenger of Allah is commanding you to leave your wife." Unfazed, Kaʿb responded immediately, "Should I divorce her, or just send her to her parents?" The messenger replied, "No, don't divorce her. Just send her back so as not to have any relations." Kaʿb then sent his wife to her parent's house, and the same command was given to Murārah and Hilāl. Hilāl's wife then approached the Prophet ﷺ and said, "O Messenger of Allah, Hilāl is too old to take care of himself. May I stay with him to prepare his food?" The Prophet ﷺ replied, "Yes, but do not sleep in the same bed (i.e., do not have relations)." Hilāl's wife then said, "O Messenger of Allah, ever since your command, Hilāl has had no need of me—he has been facing the wall, crying, for 50 days."[1035]

Ten more days passed, and Kaʿb narrated, "As I was sitting in my state as Allah described me (referring to Sūrah al-Tawbah, '…the Earth, despite its vastness, seemed to close in on them, and their souls were in anguish.'[1036]), and I prayed Fajr on my rooftop, I heard someone yell from Mount Sela, 'O Kaʿb ibn Mālik! Rejoice!' As soon as I heard this, I fell in prostration, realising that Allah's help had arrived. The Prophet ﷺ had announced after Fajr that Allah ﷻ had forgiven us, and the people came to congratulate us. I was so happy that I gifted the first person to congratulate me the shirt on my back, as it was the only thing I owned. I did not have another garment, so I knocked on my neighbour's door and borrowed a shirt to go and see the Prophet ﷺ." Kaʿb previously mentioned that he was in a healthy financial situation but now states that he had no wealth except the clothes on his back, indicating that he gave all his wealth away in repentance during those 60 days.

Kaʿb went straight to the mosque, and he narrated, "The people began receiving me in batches everywhere I went, congratulating me and giving me glad tidings of Allah's repentance. I saw the Prophet ﷺ surrounded by the Companions, and Ṭalḥah ibn ʿUbaydillāh stood up, shook my hand, and congratulated me. By Allah, he was the only one of the Muhājirūn to do that, and by Allah I will never forget his gesture. I then greeted the Prophet ﷺ and his face was bright with joy like the full Moon. Whenever the Prophet ﷺ was happy, it was like the full Moon. The Prophet ﷺ said, 'Rejoice, O Kaʿb! [This is] the best news you have ever heard since the day your mother gave birth to you.' I then said, 'O Messenger of Allah, is this from you, or from Allah?' And the Prophet ﷺ said, 'It is from Allah!'"

The Companions' jubilation is a beautiful demonstration of community and brotherhood, as they were all ecstatic at hearing that the three men were forgiven. Even when they shunned them for 60 days, it was simply out of firm obedience to Allah and His Messenger. Moreover, the fact that Kaʿb was narrating this decades later and still remembered Ṭalḥah's gesture with great fondness is a testament to the effect we have on others through our kindness in their times of need.

Kaʿb then said to the Prophet ﷺ, "O Messenger of Allah, because Allah has accepted my repentance, I will give all of my possessions for the sake of Allah." Kaʿb already donated his money but he still owned property acquired from the Battle of Khaybar. However, the Prophet ﷺ replied, "Keep some of your wealth, as that is better for you." [1037] Kaʿb's selflessness and sincerity was admirable, but the Prophet ﷺ was keen to ensure that the Companions remained self-sufficient. One may question why the Prophet ﷺ did not give Abū Bakr ؓ the same response when he donated all his belongings, and the answer is that Abū Bakr ؓ is simply unmatched in his status, and no-one—not even the senior Companions—can be expected to maintain Abū Bakr's level of piety and trust in Allah ﷻ.

Kaʿb declared, "By Allah, Allah has never bestowed upon me a greater blessing—other than Islam—than the fact that I did not lie to the Prophet ﷺ that day. If I lied, I would have been destroyed like the Hypocrites were destroyed, because Allah described the Hypocrites with the worst descriptions that He ever used for anyone. He ﷻ says, 'When you return, they will swear to you by Allah so that you may leave them alone. So leave them alone—they are truly evil. Hell will be their home as a reward for what they have committed.' [1038] We (i.e., the three that had no excuse) were turned away by the Prophet ﷺ while he gave the Hypocrites outward forgiveness and left their affair to Allah ﷻ. As for us, he told the people to leave us. And this is the reference[iii] in the Qur'an." [1039]

A Companion by the name of Abū Khaythamah ؓ was moments away from suffering the same fate as the aforementioned three Companions. He also procrastinated and found himself lagging in preparation, so much so that the Prophet ﷺ left with the army and he was still at home.

iii Kaʿb ؓ is referring to the verse, "And [Allah has also turned in Mercy to] the three who had been turned away until the Earth, despite its vastness, seemed to close in on them, and their souls were in anguish. They knew there was no refuge from Allah except in Him. Then He turned to them in Mercy so they might repent. Surely Allah is the Accepter of Repentance, Most Merciful." (*al-Tawbah*, 118). Many explanations of the Qur'an translate *"wa ʿalā al-thalāthah al-ladhīna khullifū"* as "the three who had remained behind", but Kaʿb is clarifying that it means "the three who had been turned away" in reference to their judgement being deferred until Allah ﷻ accepted their repentance.

He entered his garden and saw that his two wives had prepared food under the shade of a tree. As he saw the blissful state, he suddenly said to himself, "What am I doing here? I am here in this pleasure while the Prophet ﷺ is in the heat of the desert? By Allah I will not enter any of your gardens until I join the Messenger of Allah, so prepare my provisions for travel."[1040] He immediately rushed out to catch up with the army. The following day, the Prophet ﷺ saw a lone rider racing in the distance, and he ﷺ said, "May it be Abū Khaythamah!" Indeed it was, and the Prophet ﷺ asked why he was so late. Abū Khaythamah bared all, and the Prophet ﷺ replied endearingly, "Woe to you, O Abū Khaythamah!" Abū Khaythamah saved himself in the last moment, and the Prophet ﷺ knew it.

Masjid al-Ḍirār (The Harmful Mosque)

So many verses of the Qur'an were revealed chastising the Hypocrites that they became irritated, and tensions grew. Not only did they refuse to help finance the Expedition of Tabūk but they had the audacity to raise funds to build their own mosque so that they could gather in peace without being corrected or criticised. To add insult to injury, their mosque was in walking distance from Masjid Qubā', which clearly demonstrates its superfluous and disingenuous purpose.

In a clear expression of their misguided priority, the Hypocrites completed the construction of their mosque before the Muslim army even left for the Expedition of Tabūk. In a blatant show of disrespect, ʿAbdullāh ibn Ubayy ibn Salūl went as far as to ask the Prophet ﷺ to "bless" the mosque by praying in it. The Prophet ﷺ asked why they even needed a mosque to which they responded with a lacklustre excuse such as catering to the weak and needy who could not walk to another mosque. The Prophet ﷺ felt uneasy but his gentle nature prevented him from denying them explicitly. Instead, he replied, "We are busy now preparing for travel. When I return—if Allah wills."[1041]

As the Muslims were returning from Tabūk, Allah ﷻ revealed, "There are those who set up a mosque to cause harm, promote disbelief, divide the believers, and as a base for those who had previously fought against Allah and His Messenger. They will swear, 'We intended nothing but good', but Allah bears witness that they are surely liars. Do not ever pray in it. Certainly, a mosque founded on righteousness from the first day is more worthy of your prayers. In it are men who love to be purified. And Allah loves those who purify themselves. Which is better: those who laid the foundation of their building on the fear and pleasure of Allah, or those who did so on the edge of a crumbling cliff that tumbled down with them into the Fire of Hell? And Allah does not guide the wrongdoing people. The building which they erected will never cease to fuel hypocrisy in their hearts until their hearts are torn apart. And Allah is All-Knowing, All-Wise."[1042]

As soon as Allah ﷻ revealed these verses, the Prophet ﷺ ordered ʿAmmār ibn Yāsir رضي الله عنه with a group of Companions to destroy the mosque and burn it down entirely. The Prophet ﷺ thus never entered Masjid al-Ḍirār nor did he ever come close to it. As for "a mosque founded on righteousness from the first day", there are three opinions: some scholars state that it refers to Masjid Qubā',[1043] others maintain that it refers to the Prophet's Mosque,[1044] and a third opinion is that it is a general reference to all mosques built on righteousness.[1045]

Some reports state that the mastermind behind Masjid al-Ḍirār was Abū ʿĀmir al-Rāhib. After his embarrassment at Uḥud, he fled to Rome and sought refuge in the Roman Empire. As a respected Christian, he quickly rose through the ranks and gained influence with the Caesar. According to these reports, Abū ʿĀmir sent a letter to the Hypocrites suggesting that they create a base, and once their position in Medina strengthened, he would return alongside Roman troops.[1046] In any case, the mosque was swiftly destroyed, and their momentum was crushed.

The Expedition

Before the army left, the Prophet ﷺ appointed Muhammad ibn Maslamah رضي الله عنه in charge of Medina. He ﷺ also requested ʿAlī ibn Abī Ṭālib رضي الله عنه to stay behind and care for his family. The Hypocrites mocked

ʿAlī ﷺ relentlessly, accusing him of being unworthy of fighting and unwanted by the Prophet ﷺ. As a fierce warrior and a young man full of vigour, ʿAlī was deeply embarrassed, and the taunts affected him. Eventually, he grabbed his mount and sword and caught up with the Prophet ﷺ, pleading, "O Messenger of Allah, are you leaving me with the women and children while the Hypocrites mock me? They claim that you left me behind because I am not qualified to fight!" The Prophet ﷺ reassured him, "Are you not content to be to me as Hārūn was to Mūsā, except that there is no Prophet after me? They are liars, for I have only left you behind to take care of my family." [1047] ʿAlī ﷺ returned as instructed, and the Prophet ﷺ marched on.

As there was no battle, the narrations on the Expedition of Tabūk largely relate to miscellaneous events to and from Tabūk. One such event was narrated by Muʿādh ibn Jabal ﷺ,

> "After the Fajr prayer, everyone resumed their travels, and as the Sun began to rise, people began falling asleep on their mounts. As the people fell asleep, their camels began wandering. I tried to keep up with the Prophet ﷺ, but I too was falling asleep, and my camel veered towards the Prophet ﷺ. I jerked the camel back and it stood on its hind legs, scaring the Prophet's camel, which ran forward. The Prophet ﷺ turned around to see who scared his camel, and he saw me. He ﷺ said, 'O Muʿādh!' And I responded, 'Here I am, O Prophet of Allah!' He asked me to come closer, so I came so close that our saddles were touching. I then said, 'O Messenger of Allah, the people became sleepy and their camels wandered in different directions.' The Prophet ﷺ replied, 'And I too was sleeping.'
>
> When I realised that I was so close to the Prophet ﷺ and there was no-one else in sight, I said, 'O Messenger of Allah, may I have permission to ask something? I have pondered this question for so long that I have been sick just thinking about it.' The Prophet ﷺ replied,

'Ask whatever you wish.' I said, 'O Prophet of Allah, tell me something that will admit me into Paradise which I cannot ask anyone else.'

The Prophet ﷺ replied,

'Bravo! You have asked about a truly great matter! You have asked about a truly great matter! You have asked about a truly great matter! And it is easy for the one whom Allah wants good! It is easy for the one whom Allah wants good! It is easy for the one whom Allah wants good! Believe in Allah and the Last Day, establish the prayer, worship Allah alone, and do this until you die upon it. If you want, O Muʿādh, I will tell you about the head of this matter, its backbone, and its pinnacle.'

I replied, 'Yes of course! May my mother and father be ransomed for you.'

The Prophet ﷺ then said,

'The head of this matter is to declare that there is no god except Allah alone without partners, and that Muhammad is His slave and Messenger; its backbone is establishing the prayer and giving *zakāh*; and its pinnacle is jihad for the sake of Allah. I have been commanded to fight the people until they establish the prayer, pay *zakāh*, and declare that there is no god but Allah and that Muhammad is the Messenger of Allah. If they do so, their rights and properties are protected by Allah. I swear by the One in Whose Hand is my soul, no face becomes tired and no foot becomes dusty in any deed that will raise him higher in Paradise after the obligatory prayers except jihad in the path of Allah ﷻ. And nothing makes the Scales [of deeds on the Day of Judgement] heavier than spending money on an animal (i.e., for travel and sustenance) in the path of Allah.'" [1048]

This profound Hadith provides a plethora of insights into the essence of Islam as well as the beautiful relationship between the Prophet ﷺ and his Companions. It should also be understood in the context of the Companions embarking upon the toughest expedition of their lives. Tens of thousands of Muslims marched on towards a formidable foe, and Allah ﷻ was testing the believers, setting apart the devout believers from the insincere who only intend to join Islam in its time of glory for its worldly benefit.

The Muslims finally arrived at Tabūk, parched and dishevelled. They came across an almost empty well, and the Prophet ﷺ instructed that no-one drink before he arrived. He ﷺ then placed his hand in the little water that remained, made *duʿā'*, gargled the water, and spat it inside the well. The well suddenly erupted, and the water filled to the very top; the entire army drank until their fill and the well sufficed them for their entire stay in Tabūk.[1049] As soon as they settled in Tabūk, the Prophet ﷺ gave a sermon. ʿUqbah ibn ʿĀmir al-Juhanī narrated, "The Messenger of Allah ﷺ praised and glorified Allah Exalted as He deserves, and then said:

> 'O people! To proceed: the most truthful speech is the Book of Allah, the firmest handhold is the statement of righteousness, the best way is the way of Ibrāhīm, and the greatest Sunnah is the Sunnah of Muhammad. The most honourable speech is the remembrance of Allah, and the most beautiful stories are [found in] this Qur'an. The best matters are those performed with the most devotion and resolve, and the worst are those which are innovated. The greatest guidance is the guidance of the Prophets, and the most honourable death is the death of a martyr. The blindest person is the one who follows misguidance after being guided. The best actions are those which benefit, and the greatest guidance is that which is put into practice. The worst blindness is the blindness of the heart. The giving hand is better than the receiving hand, and a little which suffices is more desirable than an abundance

which distracts. The worst apology is when death arrives, and the worst regret is on the Day of Judgement. There are some people who only attend the Friday prayer on rare occasions, and some who only remember Allah reluctantly.

The gravest sin is a tongue that continuously lies. The greatest wealth is the wealth of the soul, and the greatest provision is piety. The pinnacle of wisdom is to fear Allah ﷻ, and the best thing that can settle in the heart is certainty and conviction, for suspicion is a part of disbelief. Deception leads to Hell, drunkenness is a burning from the Fire, [malicious] poetry is from Iblīs, intoxicants are the mother of all evil, and [for men,] women are the lure of Shayṭān. Youth is a type of insanity. The most wretched profits are the profits of interest, and the worst thing to consume is the wealth of an orphan. The joyful one is the person who learns from [the mistakes of] others, and the miserable one was already that way in his mother's stomach. Each one of you will end up in a place of four cubits (i.e., the grave) and your affairs will be decided in the Hereafter. The most important of your actions are the last. The worst dream is a false dream, and everything that is destined is close.

Insulting a believer is evil, killing a believer is disbelief, to eat his flesh (i.e., to backbite him) is to disobey Allah, and the sanctity of his wealth is like the sanctity of his blood. Whoever swears [falsely] by Allah has lied about Allah. Whoever forgives will be forgiven [by Allah], and whoever overlooks the faults of others will have his faults overlooked. Allah will reward whoever suppresses his anger and compensate whoever shows patience in the face of affliction. Allah will debase whoever chases fame and reputation, multiply the rewards of those who remain steadfast, and punish whoever disobeys Him.

> Allah forgive me and my nation, Allah forgive me and my nation, Allah forgive me and my nation.
>
> I seek the forgiveness of Allah for myself and for you.'"[1050]

As always, the Prophet's sermon was concise, profound, impactful, and practical, perfectly blending the tenets of Islam and spiritual admonition with practical guidance. The Prophet ﷺ remained in Tabūk for 20 days until it became clear that the enemy would not appear. Scholars differ as to whether the enemy—whether the Ghassanids or the Roman Empire itself—had backed out or never even intended to fight.

During those 20 days, the Prophet ﷺ sent Khālid ibn al-Walīd ؓ with a small contingency to the tribe of Kindah. Khālid swiftly captured their king, Ukaydir, and brought him to the Prophet ﷺ. Ukaydir did not convert but agreed to break off ties with the Roman Empire, instead serving the Prophet ﷺ as a vassal state. Similar agreements occurred with a handful of tribes across the northern border, and a barrier between the Muslims and the Romans was created, which proved to be crucial in the expeditions following the *sīrah*. Ukaydir sent the Prophet ﷺ a series of gifts, including an opulent gold-threaded garment—the same garment that the Companions were in awe of and to which the Prophet ﷺ remarked, "Are you impressed by this? By Allah, the handkerchief of Saʿd ibn Muʿādh in Paradise is more luxurious than this!"[1051]

One morning, the Companions were waiting for the Prophet ﷺ to lead the Fajr prayer as he ﷺ went out to answer the call of nature and perform ablution. The Prophet's absence was prolonged, and sunrise was nearing. Fearing that they may miss the prayer, the Companions began the prayer and ʿAbdurraḥmān ibn ʿAwf ؓ was appointed as the Imam. The Prophet ﷺ returned and joined them in prayer as they were in the second unit (*rakʿah*). ʿAbdurraḥmān ibn ʿAwf ؓ noticed and stepped back for the Prophet ﷺ to lead but the Prophet ﷺ motioned forward for ʿAbdurraḥmān to remain as the Imam. ʿAbdurraḥmān ibn

ʿAwf ﷺ thus had the honour of being the only[iv] person ever to have led the Prophet ﷺ in prayer.[1052]

Exposing the Insincere

On their way back to Medina, a number of incidents occurred which exposed certain people as Hypocrites. Most of the Hypocrites remained behind out of cowardice and laziness, but some of them attended but were exposed, which was the purpose of the expedition—to differentiate the true believers from the insincere. On the way back to Medina, the army ran out of water again. The Prophet ﷺ made *duʿā'* for rain, and it rained throughout the night. Some of the Hypocrites denied the miracle, instead attributing the rain to the blessings of a particular star. The next morning, the Prophet ﷺ announced to the people, quoting Allah ﷻ, "Allah ﷻ said, 'Some of My servants woke up this morning believing in Me, and some of My servants rejected Me. As for those who said that rain has fallen because of My Mercy and Grace, they are believers in Me and rejecters in the stars; and as for those who said that rain has fallen because of the stars, then they are believers in the stars and rejectors of Me.'"[1053] This incident highlights the perils of believing in omens unrelated to Islam, as the Prophet ﷺ identified it as disbelief.

As they camped for rest, the Prophet's camel wandered and was lost, and a Hypocrite blasphemed, "This is a man who thinks he is a Prophet and tells you that Revelation comes from the Heavens, and he doesn't even know where his camel is!"[1054] A Companion from the same regiment as the Hypocrite was with the Prophet ﷺ when he ﷺ said, "Some of

iv A similar incident occurred with Abū Bakr al-Ṣiddīq ﷺ, however he refused to lead the Prophet ﷺ. Towards the end of the Prophet's life, he ﷺ was sick for a week, and Abū Bakr ﷺ led the Muslims in prayer. One day, the Prophet ﷺ felt well enough to join the prayer, so he ﷺ began praying behind Abū Bakr. As soon as Abū Bakr noticed, he stepped back for the Prophet ﷺ to lead, and the Prophet ﷺ motioned forward, but Abū Bakr persisted and stepped back again, forcing the Prophet ﷺ to lead. After the prayer, the Prophet ﷺ asked, "What caused you to disobey me?" Abū Bakr ﷺ replied, "It does not befit the son of Abū Quḥāfah to lead the Messenger of Allah in prayer." (Bukhārī, *Ṣaḥīḥ al-Bukhārī*, p. 294.)

you have said such-and-such, and by Allah I am a human, and I only know what Allah tells me. Allah has just told me that my camel is stuck in such-and-such valley, and its harness was caught in a tree."[1055] The Companions retrieved the camel, which was in the exact location described, and the Companion next to the Prophet ﷺ returned to his tent on the other side of the army and relayed the story. He realised that the Hypocrite in question was in his own tent so he expelled him, declaring him an enemy of Allah.

On yet another occasion, some Hypocrites were laughing and jesting, and one remarked, "This man (i.e., the Prophet ﷺ) actually thinks that he will conquer Rome and Persia with all of their fortresses! How will that happen?" Another even said, "These people around us recite the Qur'an but are cowardly, dishonest, and fat!"[1056] Indeed, the forthcoming capitulation of the Persian Empire and the dissection of the Roman Empire at the hands of the Muslims in such a short space of time was nothing short of a miracle by every definition of the word. Historians struggle to explain the turn of events that followed the death of the Prophet ﷺ, particularly the rapid expansion of the Islamic world. One would therefore require true *īmān* to have believed the Prophet's predictions.

A Companion overheard these remarks, and he scolded them, "You have lied, O enemy of Allah! I will tell the Prophet of what you have said!" He then raced towards the Prophet ﷺ to relay their blasphemous jokes. As he raced forward, the Prophet ﷺ was already receiving Revelation. The Hypocrite in question also grew worried and began galloping towards the Prophet ﷺ. As the Companion reached the Prophet ﷺ, he ﷺ was already reciting the Qur'an that had just been revealed, "The Hypocrites fear that a *sūrah* should be revealed about them, exposing what is in their hearts. Say, 'Keep mocking! Allah will bring to light what you fear.'"[1057]

The Hypocrite reached the Prophet ﷺ and jumped off his horse. As he tried to blurt out his excuse, the Qur'an already quoted him before he managed to vocalise his excuses, "If you question them, they will certainly say, 'We were only talking idly and joking around.'

Say, 'Was it Allah, His Revelations, and His Messenger that you ridiculed?' Make no excuses! You have disbelieved after your belief."[1058] The Companion narrated, "I saw the Hypocrite running behind the Prophet's camel, holding onto its stirrup as he was dragged behind it, and the Prophet ﷺ would not even look at him. He ﷺ just repeated the verse, 'Make no excuses! You have disbelieved after your belief.'[1059]"[1060]

A short while later, some Hypocrites also scoffed, "If Islam is really true, then we are more misguided than donkeys!" When the news reached the Prophet ﷺ, and they were questioned, they vehemently rejected the accusation and even swore by Allah. These events culminated in a bizarre assassination attempt. The Prophet's camel wandered towards a cliff, and over a dozen masked men charged towards the Prophet ﷺ on horseback. The Prophet ﷺ swiftly evaded them and navigated down the valley. He ﷺ then said to ʿAmmār ibn Yāsir رضي الله عنه, "Do you know who they were? They were of the Hypocrites, and they wanted to push me off the cliff."[1061] The Hypocrites quickly fled, and they were never identified.

Allah ﷻ then addressed both events, "They swear by Allah that they never said anything [blasphemous], while they did in fact utter blasphemy, lost their faith after accepting Islam, and plotted what they could not carry out. It is only through resentment that they pay Allah and His Messenger back for enriching them out of His bounty! If they repent, it will be better for them. But if they turn away, Allah will torment them with a painful punishment in this world and the Hereafter, and they will have no-one on Earth to protect or help them."[1062]

A Worthy Reception

The army finally neared Medina, and the Muslims of Medina gathered at Thaniyyāt al-Wadāʿ (The Farewell Mount)—termed as such because people would accompany their travellers out of Medina and bid farewell at Thaniyyāt al-Wadāʿ. As the Prophet ﷺ and the Muslim army arrived, the people of Medina sang,

Ṭalaʿa al-badru ʿalaynā	The full Moon rose over us
Min Thaniyyāt al-Wadāʿ	From the Farewell Mount.
Wajaba al-shukru ʿalaynā	It is incumbent upon us to show gratitude
Mā daʿā lillāhi dāʿ	For as long as he calls us to Allah.
Ayyuhā al-mabʿūthu fīnā	O you who were sent from amongst us
Ji'ta bi al-amri al-muṭāʿ	Coming with that which is to be obeyed,
Ji'ta sharrafta al-Madīnah	You have brought to this city nobility
Marḥaban yā khayra dāʿ	Welcome, O caller to a good way.[1063]

It is commonly believed that the people of Medina sang this famous song when the Prophet ﷺ performed Hijrah. However, this is not possible, as Thaniyyāt al-Wadāʿ is north of Medina, and the Prophet ﷺ arrived from the south when performing the Hijrah. Furthermore, most people in Medina were not yet Muslim when the Prophet ﷺ performed the Hijrah, whereas they were all Muslim and eagerly anticipating the Prophet's return after the month-long journey of Tabūk.

A Hypocrite's Demise

Within a month of the Prophet's return to Medina, ʿAbdullāh ibn Ubayy ibn Salūl fell sick and was nearing his death. The head of the Hypocrites consistently opposed the Prophet ﷺ and was a constant thorn in his side. As the most senior tribesman in Medina when the Prophet ﷺ emigrated, he had the most to lose in the creation of an Islamic state, and his resentment never subdued. His offences were numerous: he abandoned the Muslims at Uḥud, returning home with over one third of the army; he supported the Banū Naḍīr against the Muslims; he threatened to expel the Muslims from Medina;

and worst of all, he spread the egregious slander against the Mother of the Believers, ʿĀʾishah ☙. The Companions urged the Prophet ﷺ to execute him for his crimes on more than one occasion, but the Prophet responded, "I do not want the people to say, 'Muhammad kills his own companions.'" [1064]

On his deathbed, ʿAbdullāh ibn Ubayy begged the Prophet ﷺ to visit him and pray for his salvation. In a twisted understanding of faith, he believed that the Prophet's prayers could benefit him, yet that did not prevent him from treating the Prophet ﷺ with contempt and disrespect throughout his time in Medina. An uncanny parallel can be made with Iblīs: an element of belief was present in both, but their kufr is derived from their disobedience and arrogance. As already mentioned, Iblīs believed in Allah ﷻ but was labelled a disbeliever because he "refused and acted arrogantly" [1065]. Similarly, Allah ﷻ declares the Hypocrites to be the lowest of all humankind, "Surely the Hypocrites will be in the lowest depths of the Fire, and you will never find for them any helper." [1066]

As per his gentle nature, the Prophet ﷺ was willing to visit ʿAbdullāh ibn Ubayy and pray for him. ʿUmar ibn al-Khaṭṭāb ☙ protested, "O Messenger of Allah, will you visit him when he is an enemy of Allah?" The Prophet ﷺ replied, "I hope that through him Allah will cause 1,000 [v] more to embrace Islam." [1067] The Prophet ﷺ did not defend ʿAbdullāh ibn Ubayy but rather had daʿwah in mind. ʿAbdullāh ibn Ubayy even asked to use the Prophet's shirt as a kafan (cloth for shrouding), and the Prophet ﷺ obliged.

ʿAbdullāh ibn Ubayy's son—also called ʿAbdullāh—then asked the Prophet ﷺ to lead his funeral prayer, and the Prophet ﷺ again obliged. ʿUmar ☙ once again protested, this time holding onto the Prophet's shirt, "O Messenger of Allah, will you pray for him after he has done such-and-such..." ʿUmar ☙ began listing ʿAbdullāh ibn Ubayy's long

---

v   ʿAbdullāh ibn Ubayy did not have 1,000 followers, but the Prophet's statement was a figure of speech expressing his intent of swaying the hearts and minds of those with weak faith who may look up to ʿAbdullāh ibn Ubayy.

list of crimes, then continued, "…and even when Allah has prohibited you from praying for the Hypocrites?"[1068] ʿUmar ﷺ was referring to the verse, "[It does not matter whether you] pray for their forgiveness or do not pray for their forgiveness. Even if you pray for their forgiveness 70 times, Allah will never forgive them. That is because they have lost faith in Allah and His Messenger. And Allah does not guide the rebellious people."[1069] The Prophet ﷺ replied, "Rather, Allah has given me a choice, and I have chosen to ask." The Prophet ﷺ then repeated the abovementioned verse, "…pray for their forgiveness or do not pray for their forgiveness…" The Prophet ﷺ then said, "If I knew that asking for forgiveness more than 70 times would have forgiven them, I would have done so."[1070]

This event showcases the Companions' confidence to question the Prophet ﷺ, which was a direct result of their nearness to him ﷺ. More importantly, it demonstrates the Prophet's proclivity for forgiveness, as evidenced throughout the *sīrah*. The Prophet ﷺ was cognisant of the reality of Hell, and he did not wish it upon anyone who did not outwardly oppose Allah ﷻ. The Prophet ﷺ did not only lead ʿAbdullāh ibn Ubayy's funeral prayer, he ﷺ climbed into the grave and placed his corpse into its place and then made a long *duʿā'* as per his custom. However, Allah ﷻ then revealed, "And do not ever offer [funeral] prayers for any of their dead, nor stand by their grave, for they have lost faith in Allah and His Messenger and died rebellious."[1071]

The Year of Delegations

28

Delegations began after the Battle of Khandaq in 5 AH and continued until the end of the *sīrah*. However, 9 AH is known as The Year of Delegations due to the vast number of delegations that arrived in Medina, with a new group arriving every few days. Many of them pledged their allegiance and accepted Islam, others discussed with the Prophet ﷺ and requested time to deliberate, some were Hypocrites who only outwardly accepted Islam, and some were tribes who did not accept Islam but requested a peace treaty. Every delegation and tribe name is recorded in the books of *sīrah*, but they are too vast to list here. Instead, a number of incidents will be mentioned to derive benefit.

The First Delegate

The tribe of ʿAbd al-Qays were the first tribe to send a delegation in 5 AH. They accepted Islam without ever receiving a messenger from the Prophet ﷺ; they heard of the Message of Islam and came to the Prophet ﷺ of their own accord, and the Prophet ﷺ praised them abundantly. They arrived during the sacred months and explained to the Prophet ﷺ that they were warring with a nearby Pagan tribe and could only return the following year when the sacred months recommence. They said, "O Messenger of Allah, tell us something that can cause us to enter Paradise so we can teach our people when we return." The Prophet ﷺ replied, "I command you to have *īmān* (faith) in Allah. And do you know what *īmān* in Allah is? It is to testify that there is no god but Allah and that Muhammad is the Messenger of Allah; to establish the prayer; to fast Ramadan; and to pay *zakāh*."[1072] The Prophet ﷺ listed the pillars of Islam except for Hajj, which was yet to be revealed as a pillar. The Banū ʿAbd al-Qays returned and became the first tribe to build a mosque outside the Hijaz, and the first to perform the Friday Prayer outside Medina.

Unrefined Sincerity

In 9 AH, the Banū Saʿd ibn Bakr, a subtribe within the Hawāzin, sent a delegation. After the Battle of Ḥunayn, they dispersed and fled but did not accept Islam. They arrived to negotiate a treaty with the Prophet ﷺ but not to accept Islam. They sent one of their elders, Ḍimām ibn Thaʿlabah, to negotiate with the Prophet ﷺ. As Bedouins, they were abrasive and uncouth, and Ḍimām epitomised that image. He stomped his way into Medina, dismounted his camel right outside the entrance of the mosque, and demanded, "Who is the son of ʿAbd al-Muṭṭalib?"

The Prophet ﷺ identified himself and Ḍimām announced, "I will ask you, and I will be tough with you, so don't be upset with me!" The Prophet ﷺ encouraged him to continue, and he said, "Your messenger reached us and said that you are the Messenger of Allah." The Prophet ﷺ replied, "He has spoken the truth." Ḍimām continued, "So who created the Heavens?" The Prophet ﷺ replied, "Allah." Ḍimām asked, "And who created the Earth?" The Prophet ﷺ replied, "Allah." Ḍimām asked, "Who created the mountains?" The Prophet ﷺ replied, "Allah." Ḍimām asked, "Who placed everything around us?" The Prophet ﷺ replied, "Allah." Ḍimām then continued to dramatise his questioning, "So I ask you by the One Who created the Heavens; by the One Who created the Earth; by the One Who created the mountains;

by the One Who placed everything around us; I ask you by Allah! Are you swearing that Allah has sent you to us?" The Prophet ﷺ replied defiantly, "I swear by Allah that He sent me."

Ḍimām continued, "Your messenger also said that you command us to pray five times a day. I ask you by the One Who has sent you: did Allah command you to tell us to pray five times a day?" The Prophet ﷺ replied in the affirmative, and Ḍimām asked the same question about *zakāh*, fasting, and Hajj, and the Prophet ﷺ replied in the affirmative to all his questions. Ḍimām then declared, "I swear by the One Who has sent you that I will follow this instruction without increasing or decreasing one bit!" Ḍimām then stormed out and the Prophet ﷺ said to his Companions, "If he is truthful (about following the instruction without increasing or decreasing), he will enter Paradise."[1073]

Ḍimām's story showcases the pillars of Islam as the foundation of the religion. Ḍimām declared that he would not exceed the bare minimum one iota and the Prophet ﷺ promised him Paradise. It also demonstrates the Prophet's patience; Ḍimām was not acquainted with proper etiquettes but the Prophet ﷺ was patient with him and accepted his questioning as sincere. When Ḍimām returned to his tribe, he began preaching Islam, and he was so respected that his entire tribe accepted Islam on the same day.

The Banū Asad ibn Khuzaymah arrived and declared to the Prophet ﷺ, "O Messenger of Allah, we testify that there is no god but Allah and that you are His slave and Messenger. We would like you to know that we have come to you without you sending a messenger, and we have come to you without you needing to fight us!"[1074] They continued to brag about their efforts until Allah ﷻ revealed, "They regard their acceptance of Islam as a favour to you. Tell them, 'Do not regard your Islam as a favour to me. Rather, it is Allah Who has done you a favour by guiding you to the faith, if indeed you are faithful.'"[1075] As more people accept Islam with varying intentions, Allah ﷻ emphasised that humility in worshipping Him is integral, as Islam is a blessing bestowed by Him.

A Never-Ending Reward

The Chieftain of Daws, Ṭufayl ibn ʿAmr al-Dawsī ☙, accepted Islam in the Meccan era when he came to perform ʿUmrah. At the time, the likes of Abū Jahl were warning visitors of a "magician" leading people astray—referring to the Prophet ☙. Ṭufayl tried his best to avoid the Prophet ☙ but one day found himself next to the Prophet ☙ as he prayed. Upon hearing the Qur'an, Ṭufayl was captivated and realised that his fears were irrational. He spoke to the Prophet ☙ and accepted Islam after the Truth became clear to him. He even invited the Prophet ☙ to emigrate to Yemen, but Allah ☙ had willed otherwise.

In 8 AH, Ṭufayl ☙ headed to Medina not only as a delegate but as an emigrant. Despite his stature and prestige in Yemen, he preferred the companionship of the Prophet ☙. This decision may not be appreciated in a globalised modern world, but in medieval society, uprooting yourself from your hometown—especially from a position of status and prestige—is the pinnacle of sacrifice. Alongside him was a man who would become one of the greatest assets of the Ummah. He would eventually be known as "The Preserver of the Sunnah" [1076], ʿAbd al-Raḥmān ibn Ṣakhr al-Dawsī—famously known as Abū Hurayrah ☙. Despite only accompanying the Prophet ☙ for around two years, Abū Hurayrah narrated the most Hadiths of all the Companions. Critically, every single one of those good deeds—as well as the good deeds of anyone who acted on those Hadiths—is credited to Ṭufayl ibn ʿAmr ☙, as Abū Hurayrah ☙ accepted Islam at his hand.

"Like the Companion of Yā-Sīn"

During the negotiations at Ḥudaybiyyah, ʿUrwah ibn Masʿūd al-Tha qafī ☙ was sympathetic to Islam and exerted himself in trying to mediate a truce. Years later, when the Muslim army left Ṭāʾif after failing to penetrate its walls, ʿUrwah caught up with the Prophet ☙ and officially accepted Islam as the Muslim army was returning to Medina. The Prophet ☙ encouraged ʿUrwah to emigrate and join the army, but ʿUrwah ﵁ suggested to the Prophet ﷺ that he return to his people and spread the Message of Islam. The people of Ṭā'if were besieged a mere few moments ago, and emotions were still raw. The Prophet ﷺ said, "I fear that that they may kill you [if you return a Muslim]."

ʿUrwah replied, "O Messenger of Allah, they love me more than they love their own daughters! If they found me asleep, they would not even wake me up [out of respect]." Indeed, ʿUrwah enjoyed a position of great prestige. Even the Quraysh recognised him as elite, and the Qur'an referenced him indirectly, "And they (i.e., the Quraysh) exclaimed, 'If only this Qur'an was revealed to a great man from one of the two cities!'"[1077] The two cities were Mecca and Ṭā'if, and the two men in question were al-Walīd ibn al-Mughīrah and ʿUrwah ibn Masʿūd.

The Prophet ﷺ eventually agreed, and ʿUrwah returned home and announced his conversion. As the Prophet ﷺ expected, they emphatically rejected him, hurling curses and insults. ʿUrwah was deflated but ultimately chose to remain. The next morning, he rose to pray Fajr. He climbed onto his rooftop, which overlooked the entire city of Ṭā'if, and began calling the *adhān*. As he reached the phrase, "I bear witness that there is no god but Allah; I bear witness that Muhammad is the Messenger of Allah", an arrow struck him from afar and killed him, just as the Prophet ﷺ warned. As he breathed his last breaths, his family asked him how they should avenge him, to which he said, "This is a gift from Allah. He has honoured me with martyrdom, so bury me with the martyrs who fought with the Messenger of Allah."[1078]

When the Prophet ﷺ heard, he said, "This man was to his people as the companion of [Sūrah] Yā-Sīn was to his"[1079], referring to the verses, "Then from the farthest end of the city a man came, rushing. He advised, 'O my people! Follow the Messengers! Follow those who ask no reward of you and are rightly guided. And why should I not worship the One Who has originated me, and to Whom you will be returned? How could I take besides Him other gods whose intercession would not be of any benefit to me, nor could they save me if the Most Compassionate intended to harm me? Indeed, I would then be clearly astray. I do believe in your Lord, so listen to me.' [But they killed him, and] he was told [by the Angels], 'Enter Paradise!' He said, 'If only my people knew of how my Lord has forgiven me and made me of the honourable.'" [1080]

A Guilty Conscience and a Grudging Heart

The crimes of the people of Ṭā'if continued to stack up—not only did they expel the Prophet ﷺ in the vilest of manners when he sought protection, and reject his call at the Siege of Ṭā'if, they killed their own Chieftain, which was a horrendous act according to their own tribal laws and norms. By 9 AH, when it became increasingly clear that Islam would dominate the Peninsula, the people of Ṭā'if were terrified that they would be called to task for their actions. Each tribe leader refused to go to the Prophet ﷺ as a delegate lest they be captured and punished—an incorrect assumption borne of their guilty consciences. Eventually, the tribe leaders agreed to all travel together and share the burden.

As they arrived in Medina, they met with al-Mughīrah ibn Shuʿbah ؓ, who belonged to the Thaqīf. Overjoyed with the prospect that the Thaqīf may accept Islam, al-Mughīrah sprinted towards the Prophet ﷺ. Abū Bakr ؓ asked why he was running to which he explained that he wanted to give the Prophet ﷺ glad tidings of the news. Desperate to bring joy to the Prophet ﷺ, Abū Bakr ؓ said, "I ask you by Allah! Allow me to give the Prophet ﷺ the glad tidings." Out of respect for his seniority, al-Mughīrah yielded and Abū Bakr ؓ informed the Prophet ﷺ, who was indeed overjoyed.

Abū Bakr ؓ explained the relevant protocols to the Chieftains, such as initiating a conversation with the *salām* and addressing the Prophet ﷺ as the Messenger of Allah. The Chieftains entered upon the Prophet ﷺ and ignored all Abū Bakr's instructions, greeting the Prophet ﷺ with the pre-Islamic greeting of "*Anʿim ṣabāhā* (good morning)" and referring to him ﷺ as "Muhammad". The Prophet ﷺ ignored their insolence and welcomed them. He ﷺ treated them most generously and honourably, ordering that a special tent be erected for them inside the mosque.

Khālid ibn Saʿīd ibn al-ʿĀṣ ﷺ had ties to both the Quraysh and the Thaqīf and was therefore chosen as a mediator in the negotiations. The Thaqīf had such a guilty conscience that they were worried about their food being poisoned so they insisted that Khālid ibn Saʿīd eat with them at every meal. Apprehensive, they asked whether they were allowed to make a treaty. The Prophet ﷺ replied that a treaty was available if they accepted Islam, otherwise they were to return home. The Thaqīf had committed too many crimes to co-exist peacefully without accepting Islam. The Prophet ﷺ did not force them to accept Islam, but he ﷺ did not allow them to negotiate a peace treaty if they did not.

The Thaqīf realised that their only recourse was to accept Islam. They began enquiring about Islamic rulings: they asked about usury (*ribā*), and the Prophet ﷺ replied by quoting one of the many verses of the Qur'an prohibiting usury; they asked about fornication (*zinā*), and the Prophet ﷺ similarly explained its prohibition; they asked about drinking alcohol, and the Prophet ﷺ once more quoted the Qur'an outlining why it is prohibited. The Thaqīf conferred internally but were still resistant. One Chieftain protested, "We will never comply with such demands!" Indeed, without the driving force of faith, forsaking such acts is a tall order. Another Chieftain responded frankly, "What choice do we have?" A third person added, "If they can all do it, so can we."[1081]

The Thaqīf then asked about the most important matter of all—idolatry. They were home to the second most prestigious and central idols of Arabia, al-Lāt (after Hubal). The Prophet ﷺ answered definitively that it is to be destroyed. They requested a three-year buffer period, and the Prophet ﷺ rejected; they then asked for two years, and the Prophet ﷺ rejected; they continued to suggest shorter time frames and the Prophet ﷺ continued to categorically reject their offers. Eventually, they agreed but requested that the Muslims destroy the idol, as they could not bring themselves to do so.

The Prophet ﷺ then taught them the pillars of Islam, and they even attempted to negotiate their obligations. They complained of poor physical health and requested a concession from the prayer to which the Prophet ﷺ said, "There is no goodness in a religion without prayer."[1082] They even requested a concession from *wuḍū'*, and the Prophet ﷺ likewise rejected their request. Interestingly, when they requested a concession for *zakāh* and jihad, the Prophet ﷺ accepted their request. However, when they left, the Prophet ﷺ remarked to his Companions, "They shall give *zakāh* and they shall perform jihad."[1083] Some scholars explain that the Prophet ﷺ made this statement as he ﷺ knew that once faith entered their hearts, they would fulfil all the tenets of faith. They add that this authority to provide such a concession was specific to the Prophet ﷺ.[1084] Other scholars argue that the leader has the authority to accept temporarily reduced obligations for new Muslims.

The reality is that the Thaqīf did not accept Islam with great enthusiasm and sincerity; they dragged their feet with great reluctance and accepted Islam grudgingly. Islamic authorities are not required to check the hearts of each person to gauge sincerity—communal benefit outweighs individual sincerity, and Islamic authorities are not tasked with testing one's intention. Moreover, the offspring of the Thaqīf were practicing Muslims, and they still are over 1,400 years later, further demonstrating the wisdom of prioritising communal welfare over individual sincerity.

The Wretched Liar

The leader of the Christian tribe of the Banū Ḥanīfah was Musaylamah ibn al-Ḥabīb. He travelled in his younger years to Jerusalem to study Christianity. He learned Latin and adopted Roman customs and upon his return became a highly respected tribal leader. By the advent of Islam, he was the undisputed Chieftain of Yamāmah. The Banū Ḥanīfah were divided in their acceptance of Islam; Musaylamah was far too arrogant and drunk on power to willingly submit himself to another leader, but notable Chieftains of subtribes within the Banū Ḥanīfah accepted Islam along with their subtribes. Examples include Thumāmah ibn Uthāl ؓ, who accepted Islam after being intercepted and hosted in Medina, as previously discussed.

Musaylamah arrived in Medina to negotiate with the Prophet ﷺ, and his entourage surrounded him in a show of opulence and reverence akin to the customs of the Roman kings. He then made the Prophet ﷺ an offer, "If you grant me power after your death, I will follow you." The Prophet ﷺ picked up a twig and said, "By Allah, if you asked me for this twig, I would not have given it to you."[1085]

When Musaylamah returned to Yamāmah, he wrote a letter to the Prophet ﷺ stating, "From Musaylamah, the Messenger of Allah, to Muhammad, the Messenger of Allah, peace be upon you. Know that I have been placed in this matter (i.e., Prophethood) alongside you. The Quraysh have half, and I have the other half, but the Quraysh are a people that transgress their bounds." The letter was delivered to the Prophet ﷺ, and the Prophet ﷺ asked the messengers, "What do you say about Musaylamah?" The messengers replied, "We agree with the letter: we believe him to be the Messenger of Allah." The Prophet ﷺ replied, "Were it not for the fact that messengers are not killed, I would have executed you."[1086] Musaylamah was the first to ever claim to be a Prophet after Prophet Muhammad ﷺ. The Prophet ﷺ once said, "The Hour (i.e., the Day of Judgement) will not be established until 30 deceptive liars (i.e., false prophets) appear, with every one of them claiming to be a messenger of Allah."[1087]

After the death of the Prophet ﷺ, a number of outlying tribes apostated and Abū Bakr ؓ, as Caliph, embarked on a number of Apostasy Wars, the most significant of which was against Musaylamah the Liar. Allah ﷻ decreed that he be famously killed by none other than Waḥshī. He said, "When I heard about Musaylamah the Liar, I made *duʿāʾ* to Allah ﷻ to allow me to kill Musaylamah to atone for [killing] Ḥamzah. I took the same spear with which I killed Ḥamzah, and I targeted and killed Musaylamah as I did Ḥamzah."[1088]

A Thirst for Knowledge and Blessings

A number of tribes travelled to Medina as delegates solely to seek knowledge from the Prophet ﷺ. A particularly noteworthy incident was when the tribe of Ḥimyar asked the Prophet ﷺ, "We have come all the way from Yemen to ask you about this creation: how did Allah create the world, and how did it all begin?" The Prophet ﷺ replied, "There was Allah, and there was nothing before Him. He then created the Heavens and the Earth while His Throne was on the Water.[i]" The narrator of the Hadith, ʿImrān ibn Ḥusayn, then remarked, "As I was listening to the Prophet ﷺ, someone yelled, 'O ʿImrān, your camel has fled!' I saw my camel fleeing into the desert, and I rushed after it. I did not catch the camel nor did I hear the rest of the Hadith. O how I wish I let the camel go and finished the Hadith." [1089] The people of Ḥimyar asked the question but did not pass on the Hadith, as they returned to Yemen. ʿImrān ibn Ḥusayn narrated the Hadith to the Companions, but Allah ﷻ decreed that only this portion of the Hadith be preserved.

A delegate from the Banū Kulfah arrived in Medina, and their representative, al-Ḥakam ibn Ḥazn, narrated, "We were around nine people and we entered upon the Prophet ﷺ and said, 'We have come to you, O Messenger of Allah, so that you may pray for us.' The Prophet ﷺ made *duʿā'* for us, took care of us, fed us, and was hospitable. We stayed in Medina for a few days and even managed to attend the Friday Prayer with the Prophet ﷺ. I remember one phrase from the sermon, which was, 'O people! Do what you can, and know that you will never be able to do everything you are commanded, but come [as] close [as you can] and fill in the gap.'" [1090]

The Verse of God's Curse (Āyah al-Mubāhalah)

The Prophet ﷺ wrote a letter to the Christians of Najrān, which began, "In the Name of the God of Ibrāhīm, Isḥāq, and Yaʿqūb..." The Prophet ﷺ then invited them to worship Allah ﷻ and advised that accepting Islam was better for them, but also gave the option of paying jizyah (tax). Should they refuse both options, the last resort was war.[1091]

---

i This Hadith indicates that the world as we know it is not the only creation to exist. Allah's Throne and the Water were already in existence, and there is no implication that humans (alongside jinns and Angels) are the only creation.

The people of Najrān convened to discuss their options. One of them said, "We know that there is a Prophet predicted from amongst the people of Ismāʿīl, perhaps it is him." They eventually agreed, sending a large delegation of 60 people to Medina.

They arrived at The Prophet's Mosque and were received by the Prophet ﷺ. It was time for their own prayer so they asked permission to pray. The Companions hesitated to allow them to pray in the mosque, but the Prophet ﷺ granted them permission. The Christians then turned towards the east and prayed their own prayers inside The Prophet's Mosque.[1092] Afterwards, they began their discussions with the Prophet ﷺ, asking many questions about Jesus Christ ﷺ. After a lengthy discussion, they asked, "If you agree with us that ʿĪsā ﷺ was born of a virgin, then who was his father?" The Prophet ﷺ replied that he did not have an answer for them but would wait until Allah ﷻ revealed the answer. The next day, Allah ﷻ revealed the first 60 verses of Sūrah Āl ʿImrān, most notably, "Indeed, the example of ʿĪsā in the sight of Allah is like that of Adam. He created him from dust then said to him, 'Be!' and he was!"[1093] They also asked about the religion of Ibrāhīm ﷺ, claiming that he was a Christian. Allah ﷻ revealed, "Ibrāhīm was neither a Jew nor a Christian; he submitted in all uprightness and was not a polytheist."[1094]

After two full days of discussions, Allah ﷻ revealed, "Now, whoever disputes with you concerning ʿĪsā after full knowledge has come to you, say, 'Come! Let us gather our children and your children, our women and your women, ourselves and yourselves—then let us sincerely invoke Allah's curse upon the liars.'"[1095] This verse is termed "The Verse of God's Curse (Āyah al-Mubāhalah)" and is used as a tool of *daʿwah* but is reserved as a last resort. Each group is claiming that the other is telling a lie about Allah ﷻ, and each group is claiming sincerity, so Mubāhalah puts that sincerity to the test. Not only were they to invoke Allah's curse on themselves, they were to damn their entire families. In a family-orientated, tribal society, that is the biggest declaration one could make. The Christians took Mubāhalah seriously, and after conferring, they decided that it was too risky to invoke such a curse. They instead decided to accept the option of paying jizyah.

On the way back, the younger brother of a senior leader cursed the Prophet ﷺ. The leader said, "Do not curse him!" The younger brother asked why, and the leader replied, "Because he is the foretold Prophet." Perplexed, the younger brother asked why they did not accept Islam if he was a true Prophet, and the leader responded, "Do you want us to give up all of the honour, wealth, and ties given to us by the Caesar?" The younger brother was stunned by their insincerity, and upon learning the truth, he defected and returned to Medina to accept Islam.

Delegates continued to pour in to meet the Prophet ﷺ. Some delegates describe their life-changing encounter with the Prophet ﷺ. ʿAbdur-raḥmān ibn ʿAqīl ؓ narrated, "I was one of the delegates to the Prophet ﷺ. When we arrived, there was no-one on Earth more despised to us than the one we were sent to meet, but when we left, there was no-one on Earth more beloved to us than the one from whom we departed. One of our youngsters said to the Prophet ﷺ, 'O Messenger of Allah, why don't you ask your Lord to grant you a kingdom like that of [Prophet] Sulaymān?' The Prophet ﷺ laughed and replied, 'Perhaps your companion (i.e., himself) has been given a kingdom better than that of Sulaymān. Allah ﷻ has never sent a Prophet except that He grants them one request. Some of those Prophets requested something of this world, others requested a punishment for their people, but as for me, I have kept that request between me and my Lord. It shall be my intercession for my Ummah on the Day of Judgement.'"[1096]

The Death of Ibrāhīm

Ibrāhīm was born in Dhū al-Ḥijjah 8 AH. His mother was Māriyyah bint Shamʿūn, famously known as Māriyyah al-Qibṭiyyah (The Copt), a Christian servant. Jurayj ibn Mīnā, the Muqawqis of Egypt, gifted the Prophet ﷺ two servant sisters: Māriyyah and Sīrīn. It was a custom amongst the Christians to gift children of noble families to serve the Church, and the Muqawqis in turn gifted them to the Prophet ﷺ alongside vast amounts of gold and luxurious items. The Prophet ﷺ

gifted Sīrīn to Ḥassān ibn Thābit and kept Māriyyah for himself.[ii] The Prophet ﷺ was overjoyed with the birth of Ibrāhīm. He ﷺ entered the mosque with a beaming smile, stating, "Last night a baby boy was born to me, and I shall call him the name of my father, [Prophet] Ibrāhīm."[1097]

Less than a year and a half into his short life—the most tender age of a child—Ibrāhīm fell deathly sick. As he was on his deathbed, the Prophet ﷺ kissed him, smelled him, and began to cry. ʿAbdurraḥmān

---

ii The topic of slavery in Islam is an intricate topic which requires a detailed explanation, the extent of which falls outside the scope of this book. For an in-depth and comprehensive analysis, see: Jonathan Brown, *Slavery and Islam*, Oneworld Academic (2019).

In short, the institution of slavery has been practiced for tens of thousands of years in every society since the dawn of humankind. Perhaps the cruellest manifestation of this practice was the institutionalisation of the transatlantic slave trade, which was distinct for its extreme brutality and racism. This transatlantic trade was a unique phenomenon predicated on the enslavement of a particular race and their characterisation as sub-humans.

Slavery in Islam had no relation to race or ethnicity. In fact, the institution as practiced in Muslim lands was so different that it is simply inaccurate to use the shared term of "slavery". "Bondage by virtue of circumstance" would be a more accurate description. Such people in Islamic society experienced a different status to the Western notion of a slave, so much so that they were regularly appointed to positions of power in government. The "Mamluk Empire", translated as "The Slave Empire", was a state ruled by "slaves" for over 250 years.

Slavery—or servitude—was deeply ingrained in society, and its abolishment would be akin to a society in the 21st century attempting to abolish poverty: a noble, yet impossible, goal. Instead, Islam facilitated the gradual abolishment of slavery through a number of mechanisms, including the freeing of individual slaves to be reintegrated into society. The expiation of breaking many rules in Islam, such as breaking one's fast in Ramadan, was to free a slave. Islam also limited the ways in which a person can become a slave. Kidnapping and enslaving free people was strictly forbidden by Islam, and the only avenue into slavery in Islam was by being captured as a prisoner of war.

In a medieval society which pre-dates the notion of imprisonment (which, ironically, was deemed too inhumane), prisoners of war were faced with two choices: mass execution or bondage. The latter was deemed a more humane option, and Islam ensured that such bondage was merely a stepping-stone to their eventual reintegration into society. As a result, no group of people remained slaves beyond their own generation, as the majority of each batch gained full freedom and were completely reintegrated into society.

ibn ʿAwf ‎ remarked, "O Messenger of Allah, even you are weeping!" The Prophet ‎ replied, "O Ibn ʿAwf, this is mercy." He continued to weep and said, "Indeed the eyes shed tears and the heart grieves, but we will not say except what pleases our Lord. And were it not for the decree of Allah, and that the latter amongst us shall meet the former (i.e., we will be reunited), we would have been much more grieved at your departure. O Ibrāhīm! We are indeed grieved by your separation."[1098] The Prophet ‎ outlived his parents, his first wife Khadījah ‎, and six out of seven of his children, once more fulfilling his role as our leader and role model. Time and again, he ‎ demonstrated the Prophetic method of handling loss and placing one's trust in Allah ‎.

Within a few hours of Ibrāhīm's death, there was a solar eclipse, and the people began to say, "The Sun is grieving at the sorrow of the Prophet!" The Prophet ‎ immediately gathered the Companions and gave a sermon, "The Sun and the Moon are two of the signs of Allah—they do not eclipse for anyone's birth or death. When you see an eclipse, hasten towards the prayer and the remembrance of Allah."[1099] This is yet another event that showcases the integrity and sincerity of the Prophet ‎ as a Messenger of Allah; he could have utilised this coincidence to "prove" his Prophethood but was quick to correct the Companions and instead used it as a teachable moment.

Anas ibn Mālik ‎ once said, "Had Ibrāhīm lived, he would have been a righteous Prophet."[1100] The Prophet Muhammad ‎ being the final Messenger in Islam is a fundamental tenet of our faith, and Allah ‎ ensured the finality of his Prophethood ‎. This was a mercy from Allah ‎, as Islamic history has since devolved into sectarian chaos surrounding the Prophet's grandchildren ‎ through his daughter, Fāṭimah ‎. A direct male descendant would have perhaps been a source of confusion and chaos on a grander scale.

The Marital Dispute

The Prophet ‎ lived an extremely humble life. Born an orphan, he was raised with nothing. As a shepherd, he worked "for pennies"[1101], and he continued to live humbly throughout his life. After the Battle of Khaybar in 7 AH—almost 20 years into his Prophethood—the Prophet ﷺ was gifted the plantations of Fadak, which he used to provide for his family. The Battle of Ḥunayn provided an abundance of riches, and the leader is entitled to a portion as per the Shariah, but the Prophet ﷺ donated the entirety of his share, which amounted to millions of dollars in modern currency. Despite the Ummah's increasing fortunes and ever-improving financial state, the Prophet's lifestyle did not change nor did his worldly possessions increase.

The Prophet ﷺ once sat with Jibrīl, and another Angel appeared. Jibrīl said, "Allah has allowed this Angel to descend for the first time since the beginning of time in order to meet you." The Angel then spoke, "O Muhammad, may peace be upon you. Your Lord has sent me to ask you a question: do you want to be a Prophet King or a Slave Messenger?" The highest position on Earth is that of a king, and the lowest position is that of a slave. However, a Messenger holds a higher rank than a Prophet in the sight of Allah. Jibrīl made a motion suggesting the lower position i.e., the Slave Messenger. The Prophet ﷺ replied, "I choose to be a Slave Messenger." It was narrated, "After this incident, the Prophet ﷺ was never seen even eating with his back resting against a wall until he met his Lord."[1102]

As the communal wealth of the Ummah increased, many Companions' lifestyles visibly improved. Meanwhile, the Prophet's lifestyle remained as it was during the difficulties of the Meccan era as per his covenant with Allah. The Prophet's wives—in their humanness—felt this disparity and began requesting more from the Prophet ﷺ. It is worth noting that their requests were halal, and that they did not request extravagance. However, as explained, the Prophet ﷺ deferred his comfort for the Hereafter, and this extended to his family. The wives' efforts were spearheaded by ʿĀ'ishah and Ḥafṣah and the remaining wives united in their requests.

'Umar ibn al-Khaṭṭāb ⬢, Ḥafṣah's father, narrated the entire incident,

"We were a people from the Quraysh that would dominate our women but when we came to Medina, we found that the women of Medina dominate their men. When we moved to Medina, our women were influenced by the Anṣārī women. One day, I became angry with my wife and reprimanded her, and she answered back! I rebuked her, 'How dare you answer back?' She responded, 'You're rebuking me for responding back, but don't you know that the wives of the Prophet ⬢ respond back to him so much so that sometimes they leave him in their anger for the whole day?!' Her statement petrified me, and I said to myself, 'Whoever amongst them does such a thing has suffered an immense loss.'

I immediately went to Ḥafṣah and asked, 'My daughter, do you argue and respond back to the Messenger of Allah such that you remain angry for the whole day?" She said, 'Yes, we do.' I rebuked her, 'Whoever does this has lost everything! Are you not scared of the anger of Allah upon you if the Messenger of Allah is angry with you?! Never respond back to the Prophet! And never ask him for any of your extra needs—come to me and do not irritate him. Don't let the status of your companion (i.e., 'Ā'ishah ⬢) deceive you about your status! For indeed, she is dearer to the Prophet ⬢ than you are!'

I had a companion from the Anṣār, and we would take turns in accompanying the Prophet ⬢; one of us would attend to our work and the other would visit the Prophet ⬢ for the day. One day, I went to sleep after 'Ishā' and my neighbour came running, banging on my door. I rushed out and asked, 'What is the matter? Have the Ghassanids attacked?' My neighbour replied, 'No, something worse has happened! The Prophet ⬢

has divorced his wives!' As soon as we prayed Fajr, the Prophet ﷺ secluded himself in his private room. I went to Ḥafṣah and she was weeping. I said, 'Didn't I tell you this would happen? Has the Prophet ﷺ divorced you all?' She replied, 'I don't know. He left us and went to his private room.'

There was a servant standing outside the room, and I said, 'Ask the Prophet ﷺ for permission for me to enter.' The servant went in and returned, saying, 'I mentioned that you were outside but the Prophet ﷺ did not respond.' I went to the mosque and waited by the pulpit, and I saw everyone crying and distressed on behalf of the Prophet ﷺ. Eventually, I returned and asked the servant again, and he gave the same response. I left again and returned a third time. This time, I said loudly (so the Prophet ﷺ could hear), 'I think that the Prophet ﷺ thinks I am coming for Ḥafṣah's sake (i.e., as a father-in-law). No, by Allah, that is not the case! For if Allah and His Messenger command me to execute Ḥafṣah, I would obey the command.' I was given permission and entered the room.

In the room I found a handful of dried barley, a tanned leather bag for water, and a chamber pot. I began to cry looking at this state. The Prophet ﷺ was lying down and when he turned to face me, I saw the marks on his back (from the bed made of date palm branches). I asked him immediately, 'Have you divorced your wives?' The Prophet ﷺ replied that he did not. I then said, 'O Messenger of Allah, don't you remember how we (i.e., the Quraysh) would dominate our women? But then we came to Medina and saw that the women of Medina dominate their men, and our women have learned from them! I became angry at my wife, and lo and behold, she responded back to me! I did not approve but she said, "Who are you to not approve when the wives of the Prophet ﷺ respond back to him?"' ('Umar then narrated his story to the Prophet ﷺ.) Finally, the Prophet ﷺ smiled.

I then asked the Prophet ﷺ if I could take a seat. The Prophet ﷺ granted permission. I looked around and by Allah I could not see anything else in the room, and I said, 'O Messenger of Allah, why don't you make *duʿā'* to Allah to grant you sustenance just as He has given the Caesar and Khosrow even though they don't worship Allah?' I began to cry, and the Messenger of Allah ﷺ said, 'O son of Khaṭṭāb, why are you crying?' I replied, 'O Messenger of Allah, the Caesar and Khosrow are indulging in their riches while you are Allah's Messenger!' The Prophet ﷺ then sat up and said, 'O son of Khaṭṭāb! Are you in doubt? Are you not content that Allah has chosen us over them in the next world and has given them this world for their pleasure?' I replied, 'O Messenger of Allah, ask Allah to forgive me!'"[1103]

The Prophet ﷺ informed ʿUmar that he made an oath to Allah that he would not approach his wives for one month. After an entire month, the Prophet ﷺ went to ʿĀ'ishah's house and said, "O ʿĀ'ishah, I am going to talk to you about a matter but don't be hasty in your decision; go and consult your parents before you decide." The Prophet ﷺ then recited from Sūrah al-Aḥzāb, "O Prophet! Say to your wives, 'If you desire the life of this world and its luxury, then come, I will give you compensation and let you go graciously. But if you desire Allah and His Messenger and the [everlasting] Home of the Hereafter, then surely Allah has prepared a great reward for those of you who do good.'"[1104] ʿĀ'ishah ﷺ responded immediately, "What is there to consult, O Messenger of Allah? I have chosen Allah and His Messenger and the Home of the Hereafter!"[1105] Every single wife followed suit and chose the Messenger of Allah, turning down luxury in this world for the Hereafter.

The benefits derived from this incident are innumerable. Allah ﷻ could have willed that the Prophet's private life was pristine, but the Prophet's role on Earth was to guide and teach the Ummah, and these incidents allow us to learn from the Prophet's patience and forbearance. In a society where physically abusing one's wife was completely normal, the Prophet ﷺ never once harmed his wives. ʿĀ'ishah ؓ narrated, "I swear by Allah, never was the Prophet's hand lifted against any woman or servant."[1106] The incident also demonstrated the Companions' love for the Prophet ﷺ, as they mourned his struggles more than their own. ʿUmar's neighbour described the Prophet ﷺ divorcing his wives (as per the rumour) as worse than a military attack, and ʿUmar scolded his own daughter for inconveniencing the Prophet ﷺ.

29 The Farewell Hajj

Mecca was liberated in 8 AH but the Ummah did not collectively perform Hajj as the political climate was not stable enough. Ṭā'if, Tabūk, and Najrān were not yet Muslim, and Medina would be left exposed. A small group of Muslims did perform Hajj led by the governor of Mecca, ʿAttāb ibn Asīd ﷺ. The Prophet ﷺ appointed him as governor despite only accepting Islam at the Conquest of Mecca because the senior Companions all pledged their loyalties to the Anṣār and promised that they would remain in Medina after their Emigration. 8 AH therefore marked the first time that Hajj was performed according to the Islamic methodology.

The Hajj of Abū Bakr ﷺ

In 9 AH, the people of Ṭā'if accept Islam and the Expedition of Tabūk subdued any threat from the north. The political climate was now stable, and the Muslims were firmly in control. The Prophet ﷺ then sent Abū Bakr ﷺ to lead a group of 300 Muslims on Hajj but did not join them. He ﷺ said, "The polytheists perform *ṭawāf* around the Kaʿbah naked, and I do not wish to perform Hajj until that is abolished."[1107]

It is noteworthy that the Prophet ﷺ did not forbid Abū Bakr ؓ from attending but just highlighted that it was not befitting for a Prophet.

The polytheists claimed that their nakedness represented piety just as Adam and Eve were naked. Allah ﷻ revealed, "Whenever they commit a shameful deed, they say, 'We found our forefathers doing it and Allah had commanded us to do it.' Say, 'No! Allah never commands shamefulness. How can you attribute to Allah what you do not know?'"[1108] He ﷻ also said, "O children of Adam! We have provided for you clothing to cover your nakedness and as an adornment. But the best clothing is righteousness. This is one of Allah's bounties, so perhaps you will be mindful. O children of Adam! Do not let Shayṭān deceive you as he tempted your parents (i.e., Adam and Eve) out of Paradise and caused their cover to be removed in order to expose their nakedness. Surely he and his soldiers watch you from where you cannot see them. We have made the devils allies of those who disbelieve."[1109]

The Prophet ﷺ sent Abū Bakr ؓ to ensure that the non-Islamic rituals were abolished, and that Hajj was to be performed according to the Shariah. Within hours of Abū Bakr's arrival, Allah ﷻ revealed the first section of Sūrah al-Tawbah directed at the Pagans of Arabia. Sūrah al-Tawbah is the only *sūrah* in the Qur'an that does not start with the *basmalah* i.e., "In the Name of Allah, the Most Compassionate, Most Merciful." When ʿAlī ؓ was asked why, he replied, "The *basmalah* is issued as a contract of protection and mercy. Sūrah Barā'ah[i] was revealed with the sword and provides no such protection."[1110]

> "[This is] a discharge from all obligations, by Allah and His Messenger, to the polytheists you have entered into treaties with: 'You [polytheists] may travel freely through the land for four months but know that you will have no escape from Allah, and that Allah will disgrace the disbelievers.' A declaration from Allah and His Messenger to all people on the day of the Greater

i Sūrah Barā'ah is another name for Sūrah al-Tawbah, taken from the first word of the *sūrah*, which means "disassociation" or "a discharge from all obligations".

Hajj that Allah and His Messenger are free of the polytheists. So if you repent, it will be better for you. But if you turn away, then know that you will have no escape from Allah. And give good news to the disbelievers of a painful punishment.

As for the polytheists who have honoured every term of their treaty with you and have not supported an enemy against you, honour your treaty with them until the end of its term. Surely Allah loves those who are mindful [of Him]. But once the Sacred Months have passed, kill the polytheists [who violated their treaties] wherever you find them, capture them, besiege them, and lie in wait for them on every way. But if they repent, perform prayers, and pay *zakāh*, then set them free. Indeed, Allah is All-Forgiving, Most Merciful. And if anyone from the polytheists asks for your protection [O Prophet], grant it to them so they may hear the Word of Allah, then escort them to a place of safety, for they are a people who have no knowledge. How can such polytheists have a treaty with Allah and His Messenger, except those you have made a treaty with at the Sacred Mosque? So, as long as they are true to you, be true to them. Indeed Allah loves those who are mindful [of Him].

How [can they have a treaty]? If they were to have the upper hand over you, they would have no respect for kinship or treaty. They only flatter you with their tongues, but their hearts are in denial, and most of them are rebellious. They chose a fleeting gain over Allah's Revelations, hindering [others] from His Way. Evil indeed is what they have done! They do not honour the bonds of kinship or treaties with the believers. It is they who are the transgressors. But if they repent, perform the prayer, and pay *zakāh*, then they are your brothers in faith. This is how We make the Revelations clear for people of knowledge. But if they break their oaths after making a pledge and attack your faith, then fight the champions of disbelief—who never honour their oaths—so perhaps they will desist. Will you not fight those who have broken their oaths, conspired to expel the Messenger [from Mecca], and attacked you first? Do you fear them? Allah is more deserving of your fear if you are believers. [So] fight them and Allah will punish them at your hands, put them to shame, help you overcome them, and soothe the hearts of the believers—removing rage from their hearts. And Allah pardons whoever He wills, for Allah is All-Knowing, All-Wise.

Do you [believers] think that you will be left without Allah proving who among you [truly] struggles [in His cause] and never takes trusted allies other than Allah, His Messenger, or the believers? And Allah is All-Aware of what you do. It is not for the polytheists to maintain the mosques of Allah while they openly profess disbelief. Their deeds are void, and they will be in the Fire forever. The mosques of Allah should only be maintained by those who believe in Allah and the Last Day, establish the prayer, pay *zakāh*, and fear none but Allah. It is right to hope that they will be among the [truly] guided. Do you [Pagans] consider providing the pilgrims with water and maintaining the Sacred Mosque as equal to believing in Allah and the Last Day and struggling in the cause of Allah? They are not equal in Allah's sight. And Allah does not guide the wrongdoing people." [1111]

The Prophet ﷺ sent ʿAlī ibn Abī Ṭālib ؓ to catch up with Abū Bakr ؓ, as he ﷺ said, "No-one shall convey these verses except someone from my household." [1112] The Prophet ﷺ understood that the Pagans of Arabia still held lineage as the primary authority, and ʿAlī was an extension of himself ﷺ. When Abū Bakr ؓ saw ʿAlī ؓ riding on the Prophet's camel, he immediately asked, "Are you being sent as a commander over me or am I still the commander?" ʿAlī responded that Abū Bakr was still the commander.[1113]

It is against the Shariah to terminate a contract without prior notice. Allah ﷻ thus notified all Pagans in Arabia that they had four months of safety and freedom before they must disperse. However, if the treaty stipulated a length of time, then the Prophet ﷺ was commanded to uphold that time clause even if it continued beyond the four months. Abū Bakr ؓ then made four major announcements: no-one shall enter Paradise except a Believer; no-one shall perform *ṭawāf* naked; no polytheist shall perform *ṭawāf*; and any treaty between the Believers and the Pagans will expire after four months except if it stipulated a specific timeframe.

As for "the verse of the sword", i.e., "But once the Sacred Months have passed, kill the polytheists [who violated their treaties] wherever you find them, capture them, besiege them, and lie in wait for them on every way. But if they repent, perform prayers, and pay *zakāh*, then set them free. Indeed, Allah is All-Forgiving, Most Merciful." [1114], it was revealed in the specific context of idol-worshipping in the Ḥaram. Paganism in the Sacred Mosque was no longer tolerated, and this verse was a strong deterrent to ensure its sanctity is upheld. No-one was killed as a result of this verse, and it is not a free licence to kill disbelievers—this is evidenced by the fact that no Muslim leader, including the Caliphs, ever killed and expelled their non-Muslim residents.

The Prophet's Hajj ﷺ

By 10 AH, the Ḥaram was finally free from non-Islamic practices, and Allah ﷻ revealed, "Surely the first House [of worship] established for humanity is the one at Mecca—a blessed sanctuary and a guide for all people. In it are clear signs and the standing-place of [Prophet] Ibrāhīm. Whoever enters it should be safe. And Pilgrimage to this House is an obligation by Allah upon whoever is able amongst the people. And whoever disbelieves, then surely Allah is not in need of [His] creation." [1115] The Prophet ﷺ then announced that he is to perform

Hajj, and tens of thousands of Muslims flocked to join him. He ﷺ left Medina on the 25th of Dhū al-Qaʿdah 10 AH and tens of thousands more joined them as they travelled. The Companions narrated that the crowds were as far as the eyes could see. Sources state 100,000 attendees, and while it would have been impossible to accurately count, there were at least tens of thousands of pilgrims.[1116]

The Prophet ﷺ referred to this Hajj as the Farewell Hajj but the Companions did not understand that it was the Prophet's farewell to humanity. Ibn ʿUmar ؓ said, "We called it the Farewell Hajj while the Prophet was with us, but we did not understand the implication."[1117] It may seem obvious to the reader that the Prophet ﷺ was bidding farewell to his Ummah but the Companions did not truly comprehend that the Prophet would ever leave them. He ﷺ was so integral to their lives that they could not possibly imagine a life without him ﷺ. They would follow the Prophet ﷺ unquestioningly so when he referred to it as the Farewell Hajj, they did too.

All the rules pertaining to Hajj are derived from the Farewell Hajj. The Prophet ﷺ clarified the Islamic methodology of Hajj and outlined the different ways of completing Hajj as well as the expiations attached to mistakes made while performing Hajj. There are hundreds of Hadiths narrated during the Farewell Hajj, the most comprehensive of them being the Hadith of Jābir ؓ. ʿAlī ibn Abī Ṭālib's great grandson—Muhammad ibn ʿAlī ibn Ḥusayn ibn ʿAlī—narrated,

> "We went to Jābir ibn ʿAbdillāh and he asked who was present (he was blind) until he came to me. I said, 'I am Muhammad ibn ʿAlī ibn Ḥusayn. He placed his hand on my head, unfastened my top, and put his hand on my chest.[ii] He said, 'Welcome, nephew. Ask about whatever you wish'…I said, 'Tell us about the Hajj of the Messenger of Allah ﷺ.' He indicated nine with his hand,

ii It was very common for the Companions to show extra reverence to the household of the Prophet ﷺ. They represented the Prophet's presence on Earth, and they reminded them of him ﷺ.

and then he replied, 'For nine years, the Messenger of Allah ﷺ did not perform the pilgrimage. Then, in the tenth year, he announced to the people that he would be performing Hajj. Many people came to Medina, eager to join the Messenger of Allah ﷺ and to follow his actions, and we travelled alongside him until we arrived at Dhū al-Khulayfah.

There, Asmā' bint 'Umays gave birth to Muhammad ibn Abī Bakr, and she sent an envoy to the Messenger of Allah ﷺ, asking how she should proceed. The Messenger ﷺ said, "Wash and cover yourself with a cloth, and put on the *iḥrām*." The Messenger of Allah ﷺ prayed in the mosque, then he mounted al-Qaṣwā' (his camel), and she carried him to al-Bayḍā'. The people riding and walking in front of me stretched as far as my eyes could see, and the same went for the crowds to my right, to my left, and behind me. The Messenger of Allah ﷺ was present amongst us and he was the one who received the Revelation of the Qur'an and understood its meaning, so whenever he did something we would follow. He proclaimed the Oneness of Allah out loud, saying, "At your service, O Allah, at your service. At your service—You have no partner—at your service. Certainly, [all] Praise and Excellence are Yours, as is the Dominion. You have no partner."

We only had the intention of performing Hajj and we were unaware of [the possibility of] performing 'Umrah [at the same time], but when we arrived at the House alongside the Messenger ﷺ, he touched the Corner (i.e., the Black Stone), and then moved briskly (*raml*) for three [circuits of the Ka'bah] and walked for four. Next, he proceeded to the Station of Ibrāhīm and recited, "[You may] take the standing-place of Ibrāhīm as a site of prayer"[1118] He stood with the Station between himself and the House [and offered two units of prayer]. My father used to say that the Prophet ﷺ recited "Say, 'He is Allah—One'" (i.e., Sūrah al-Ikhlāṣ) and "Say, 'O you disbelievers!'" (i.e., Sūrah al-Kāfirūn) in the two units of prayer. He then returned to the Corner and touched it before leaving from the gate towards Safa.

When he approached Safa, he recited "Indeed, [the hills of] Safa and Marwah are among the symbols of Allah" [1119] and said, "I will begin with that which Allah began." So, he started with Safa, ascended until he could see the House, and then turned to face the qiblah, declared the Oneness and the Greatness of Allah, and said, "There is no deity worthy of worship except Allah, alone and without partners. The kingdom is His, and all praise and gratitude are for Him, for He is Most Capable of everything. There is no deity worthy of worship except Allah alone, [the One Who] fulfilled his promise, aided His slave, and defeated the combined forces alone." The Messenger ﷺ repeated this supplication three times and then descended towards Marwah. When he reached the centre of the valley he moved briskly, and when he began to ascend, he walked [at a normal pace] until he reached Marwah. At the top of Marwah, he did just as he had upon Safa [and continued to repeat in this manner].

When he reached Marwah for the final time, the Messenger ﷺ said, "If I had known before what I know now, I would not have brought the sacrificial animals and I would have made this an 'Umrah. So, whoever amongst you does not have a sacrificial animal with them should take off their *iḥrām* and make this an 'Umrah." Surāqah ibn Mālik stood up and asked, "O Messenger of Allah, does this [instruction] apply for this year only, or forever?" The Messenger of Allah ﷺ intertwined two of his fingers together and said,

"'Umrah has been joined with Hajj' twice, before adding, 'Rather, [it applies] forever."

ʿAlī arrived from Yemen with the sacrificial animals of the Prophet ﷺ, and he found that Fāṭimah had replaced her *iḥrām* with dyed clothes and applied kohl [to her eyes], and he expressed his disapproval. Fāṭimah informed him, "My father instructed me to do this." When he was in Iraq, ʿAlī used to say, "I went to the Messenger of Allah ﷺ, feeling annoyed at what Fāṭimah had done and seeking his verdict on what she had related from him. The Messenger of Allah ﷺ said, 'She has told the truth. She has told the truth.' Then, he asked me, 'What did you say when you undertook to perform the pilgrimage?' I said, 'O Allah, I embark [on this pilgrimage] with the same [intention] as Your Messenger.' The Messenger of Allah ﷺ said, 'I have the sacrificial animals with me, so do not remove your *iḥrām*.'"

The total number of sacrificial animals, between those brought by ʿAlī from Yemen and those the Prophet ﷺ brought himself, came to one hundred. Everyone removed their *iḥrām* and had their hair clipped except for the Prophet ﷺ and whoever had a sacrificial animal with them. On the Day of al-Tarwiyah (i.e., the 8th day of Dhū al-Ḥijjah), they went to Mina and put on the *iḥrām* for Hajj. The Messenger of Allah ﷺ rode out and led the Ẓuhr, ʿAṣr, Maghrib, ʿIshāʾ, and Fajr prayers, then he waited a while until the Sun had risen. He instructed for a tent made of animal hair to be erected for him at Namirah. The Messenger of Allah ﷺ continued on his way, and the Quraysh were certain that he would stop at the sacred site just as they used to do in [the era of] Ignorance, but he passed it and continued until he reached Arafat. He found the tent that had been pitched for him at Namirah and stopped off there until the Sun began to decline. Then, he called for al-Qaṣwā', and she was saddled and prepared for him.

When he got down to the heart of the valley, the Messenger ﷺ addressed the people and said, "Certainly, your blood and your wealth are sacred, just like this [sacred] day of yours in this [sacred] month of yours in this [sacred] town of yours. All the matters of Jāhiliyyah are abolished beneath my feet. The blood [revenge] of Ignorance is abolished, and the first blood [revenge] I will abolish is Ibn Rabīʿah ibn al-Ḥārith, who was breastfed by the Banū Saʿd tribe and was killed by Hudhayl. The usury of Ignorance is abolished, and the first usury I will abolish is that of ʿAbbās ibn ʿAbd al-Muṭṭalib. It is completely wiped out. Be conscious of Allah regarding your women, for you have taken them with the Trust of Allah, they have been made permissible to you by the Word of Allah, and you have the right [to demand] that they do not allow anyone you dislike to sit on your mattress. If they do that, then reprimand them without hurting them. They have the right to provision and clothing in a wholesome manner. I have left amongst you that which, if you hold fast to it, you will never go astray: the Book of Allah. [When] you are asked about me on the Day of Judgement, what will you say?" The people replied, "We bear witness that you have conveyed [the Message of Islam], fulfilled [your mission], and sincerely advised. The Messenger ﷺ raised his forefinger towards the sky and pointed at the people, saying "O Allah, bear witness. O Allah, bear witness. O Allah, bear witness."

The *adhān* and the *iqāmah* were called, and the Messenger ﷺ led the Ẓuhr prayer. Then, the *iqāmah* was called again, and the Messenger ﷺ led ʿAṣr, without praying anything between the two. Then, the Messenger ﷺ rode [his camel] until he came to the stopping point. He made al-Qaṣwā' face the rocks, with the path of those travelling on foot in front of him, and turned towards the qiblah. He remained standing there until the Sun set, the yellow light diminished a little, and the disc [of the Sun] had disappeared. With Usāmah riding behind him, the Messenger ﷺ pulled tightly on the reins of al-Qaṣwā' until her head touched the saddle, and he indicated with his right hand for the people to move with tranquillity. Every time he came to a hill, he would loosen the reins a little for his camel to ascend, until we arrived at al-Muzdalifah.

There, he prayed Maghrib and ʿIshā' with one *adhān* and two *iqāmahs*, without any voluntary prayers between the two, and then lay down until dawn. When the morning became clear, he prayed Fajr, preceded by an *adhan* and *iqāmah*. He then mounted al-Qaṣwā' and rode until he reached the sacred site. The Messenger ﷺ turned to face the qiblah, supplicated Allah, glorified Him, and declared His Uniqueness and Oneness (i.e., uttered the *shahādah*), and he continued standing there until the morning was very bright. Before the Sun rose, the Messenger ﷺ quickly left, with al-Faḍl ibn ʿAbbās riding behind him. Al-Faḍl was a handsome man with beautiful hair. As the Messenger of Allah ﷺ continued on his way, there were a group of women travelling alongside them, and al-Faḍl started looking at them. The Messenger ﷺ placed his hand on the face of al-Faḍl, but al-Faḍl turned to the other side and continued looking, until they arrived at the heart of Muḥassir. The Messenger ﷺ steered and prompted [al-Qaṣwā'] a little until she took the middle path which comes out at the largest *jamrah* (stoning pillars). When he came to the *jamrah* by the tree, he threw seven small pebbles like the pebbles found at the bottom of a wadi, saying "*Allāhu Akbar*" with each throw. He then proceeded to the place of sacrifice and slaughtered sixty-three [camels] himself before handing over to ʿAlī, who slaughtered the remaining animals and shared in the sacrifice. The Messenger ﷺ instructed for a piece of each animal to be cooked in a pot, and they both ate from the meat and drank from the broth.

The Messenger of Allah ﷺ rode his animal again and returned to the House, praying Ẓuhr in Mecca. He then went to the Banū ʿAbd al-Muṭṭalib tribe, who were responsible for providing people with Zamzam water, and said, "Draw water for me, O Banū ʿAbd al-Muṭṭalib. If it was not for [fear of] the people usurping your responsibility, I would have drawn with you." So, they gave him a bucket, and he drank from it.'"[1120]

The Prophet ﷺ had an audience of up to 100,000 Muslims, most of whom were meeting him for the first time. He utilised this auspicious occasion to obliterate the notion of tribalism and unite the Ummah. The Prophet ﷺ refused to accept the blood money owed to him and nullified the usury owed to his uncle, al-ʿAbbās ؓ, making it clear that he ﷺ is starting with himself and that no-one is above the Shariah. In a society where women had no rights and were trampled on and abused, the Prophet ﷺ specified in front of the largest audience he ever faced that they are to fear Allah in the treatment of their womenfolk.

On the 9th of Dhū al-Ḥijjah while the Prophet ﷺ was at Arafat, Allah ﷻ revealed the famous verse, "Today I have perfected your faith for you, completed My favour upon you, and chosen Islam as your way."[1121] During the Caliphate of ʿUmar ؓ, a Jewish man approached him and said, "O Commander of the Believers, you have a verse in your Qur'an that if we had the equivalent, we would have taken it as a day of celebration." ʿUmar ؓ replied, "I know exactly when this verse was revealed. The Prophet ﷺ was standing on the plains of Arafat on Friday during the Greater Hajj and Allah ﷻ revealed this verse (i.e., it was already a celebration in the form of Eid)."[1122]

On the 10th of Dhū al-Ḥijjah, the Prophet ﷺ said, "Certainly, your blood, wealth, and honour are as sacred as this day of yours, in this city of yours, in this month of yours. You will meet your Lord and you will be asked about your actions, so do not return to disbelief or misguidance after my departure, with some of you striking the necks of others. Let whoever is present convey what I have said to whoever is absent, for perhaps some of those to whom it is conveyed will comprehend more than those who heard it directly." Then, he proclaimed, "Indeed, have I not conveyed?!" [1123]

The Incident of Ghadīr Khumm

As ʿAlī ؓ returned from Yemen, he left his entourage to greet the Prophet ﷺ. The person he left in charge in his stead decided to distribute new clothes intended for charity to the entire group, as they felt that they deserved a reward. Incensed, ʿAlī commanded them to return it all to the treasury. They were disgruntled and begrudgingly complied, but as soon as they returned, they complained to the Prophet ﷺ. However, instead of siding with them, the Prophet ﷺ rebuked them and passionately defended ʿAlī ؓ. He ﷺ gathered people at Ghadīr Khumm (The Well of Khumm) and said, "If I am a person's protector, then ʿAlī is their protector!" And, "I am leaving behind me two weighty matters: the first is the Book of Allah, which contains light and guidance, so hold firmly on to it and uphold its teachings. The second is my household: I remind you of my household, I remind you of my household, I remind you of my household!" [1124]

The Greatest Calamity

30

After the Prophet ﷺ performed Hajj, he returned to Medina for the very last time. Two months later, in Ṣafar 10 AH, he sent an army to the Byzantine Empire to liberate Jerusalem. The Prophet ﷺ sent many senior Companions including Abū Bakr, ʿUmar, and the like ؓ, but he ﷺ chose 18-year-old Usāmah ibn Zayd ؓ as the leader. Murmurs began to spread in Medina as to why such a young, non-Qurashī man was leading such a great army. The Prophet ﷺ did not tolerate these murmurs, and he gathered the Companions and said, "If you dislike his leadership then remember that you also criticised the leadership of his father before him. By Allah, he is worthy of being a leader, and this man is the most beloved to me after his father." [1125]

Appointing Usāmah was a wise choice indeed, as the Prophet ﷺ wanted him to avenge the death of his father. The Prophet ﷺ said to Usāmah, "Go to where your father was killed." [1126] Usāmah was not heading directly to Muʾtah, but the Prophet ﷺ wanted Usāmah to remember his father's death and use that hurt as motivation. The symbolism of the Prophet ﷺ commanding the Muslim army to liberate Jerusalem as his final command is clear: Islam is not confined to the Arabian Peninsula. The Prophet ﷺ may pass but the Message lives on.

As the army left Medina, a messenger came galloping, notifying Usāmah that the Prophet ﷺ had fallen ill. Usāmah camped outside Medina awaiting further news. The Prophet ﷺ continued to alternate his visits between his wives until he felt so weak that he asked their permission to stay in ʿĀ'ishah's house while he rests. His health continued to deteriorate and he fell deathly ill. The Prophet ﷺ had a severe fever, and at the time there was no medication for fevers; people would sometimes die from the pain of a fever alone. The Prophet ﷺ once said, "Fevers are from the heat of Hell." [1127]

ʿĀ'ishah ؓ continued to care for the Prophet ﷺ, and one day she felt a severe headache. She joined the Prophet ﷺ in bed and cried, "O my head! O my head!" The Prophet ﷺ smiled and said, "No, O ʿĀ'ishah. Rather, O *my* head!" He ﷺ then said, "O ʿĀ'ishah, what would you lose if you were to die right now and I wash your body, place you in your shroud, and pray over you?" ʿĀ'ishah, quick-witted as ever, replied, "I'm sure you are waiting for that, O Messenger of Allah, so no-one else will stop you going to your other wives!" [1128] In his weakest moment, the Prophet ﷺ still teased his wife while reminding her about every person's inevitable fate.

The truth is that the Companions did not expect the Prophet ﷺ to ever pass away. The indications were clear in both the Qur'an and the Prophet's own speech, but their hearts could not comprehend it. The Qur'an states, "You [O Prophet] will certainly die, and they will die too." [1129]; "Muhammad is no more than a Messenger; other Messengers have gone before him. If he were to die or be killed, would you regress into disbelief?" [1130]; and "We have not granted immortality to any human before you [O Prophet], so if you die, will they live forever?" [1131] The Qur'an was explicit, but it is human nature to avoid thinking about that which is too difficult to bear.

One day, when the Prophet ﷺ appointed Muʿādh ibn Jabal ؓ as the Governor of Yemen, they walked out of Medina together, and the Prophet ﷺ insisted that he walk while Muʿādh ride the donkey. The Prophet ﷺ said, "O Muʿādh, I certainly love you. Perhaps you shall not see me after this year, and perhaps when you return to Medina you will find my mosque and my grave."[1132] In his Caliphate, ʿUmar ibn al-Khaṭṭāb ﷺ quizzed the senior Companions about the meaning of Sūrah al-Naṣr, "When Allah's help comes and the victory [is achieved], and you see the people embracing Allah's Way in crowds, then glorify the praises of your Lord and seek His Forgiveness, for certainly He is ever Accepting of Repentance."[1133] No-one knew the answer except the young man, ʿAbdullāh ibn ʿAbbās ﷺ, who explained that it was Allah ﷻ indicating to the Prophet ﷺ that his time on Earth was coming to an end.[1134]

The health of the Prophet ﷺ continued to deteriorate, and his family would pour buckets of water over him to cool him down. His closest relatives, ʿAlī and al-ʿAbbās ﷺ, carried him on their shoulders to the mosque. The Companions' concern began to grow, and the senior Companions camped inside the Prophet's Mosque on stand-by, as the Prophet ﷺ had never been this ill before. He could not even stand on the pulpit, so he sat down and said, "May Allah's curse be upon the Jews and Christians because they took the graves of their Prophets as mosques[i]."[1135] He then said, "If anyone has a debt that I have not paid, then here is my wealth to take."[1136] He also said, "If I have hit anyone in my whole life, then here is my back."[1137]

The Prophet ﷺ continued to make these statements until the Companions feared that if they did not step forward, they might be sinful. One Companion then said, "O Messenger of Allah, you owe me three dinars. O Messenger of Allah, I would not have said so, but you repeated it so many times that I thought I would be sinful [if I did not disclose it]. One day, there was a beggar passing, and you said, 'Who will give him money on my behalf?' I gave him three dinars and you did not pay me back. And by Allah had you not kept on asking us to come forward, I would not have said anything."[1138] The Prophet ﷺ then ordered for the Companion to be paid his three dinars.

i The grave of the Prophet ﷺ is currently located inside the Prophet's Mosque, but this Hadith does not apply to it, as the grave is not being worshipped. The Mosque was expanded numerous times which inevitably encompassed his house and therefore his grave ﷺ.

The Prophet ﷺ said, "There is a servant from amongst the servants of Allah, and Allah asked him to choose between the glories of this world and his Lord, and he has chosen his Lord."[1139] As he described the situation generically, the Companions still did not realise that he was referring to himself ﷺ. Only one man understood, and that man began sobbing hysterically—Abū Bakr al-Ṣiddīq ؓ. The Prophet ﷺ then said, "Do not cry, O Abū Bakr, for you are the one I trust the most in my companionship and with my family. Were I able to take a *khalīl* (close friend) in this world, my *khalīl* would be Abū Bakr, but I cannot take a *khalīl* because Allah has chosen me as His *khalīl*. But, O Abū Bakr, between you and I is the brotherhood of Islam." The Prophet ﷺ then announced, "All the doors of the Mosque [that connect to the private houses] are to be closed except Abū Bakr's door."[1140]

The final prayer that the Prophet ﷺ led was Maghrib on the Friday before his death, and he recited Sūrah al-Mursalāt. For ʿIshā', the Prophet ﷺ stood up to lead the people in prayer but fainted on his bed. When he awoke, he stood up again and fainted again for an even longer period of time. He asked, "Have the people prayed yet?" Someone replied, "No, they are waiting for you, O Messenger of Allah." He then stood up again and fainted once more, and this occurred several times.

When he realised that he cannot pray, he said to ʿĀ'ishah ؓ, "Go command Abū Bakr to lead the people in prayer."[1141] ʿĀ'ishah ؓ was reluctant for her father to lead the prayer, as she did not want people to associate Abū Bakr leading the prayer with the Prophet's illness or death. She said, "O Messenger of Allah, my father is a soft-hearted man; when he stands in prayer, he cries, and people won't like it." The Prophet ﷺ insisted, "Go command Abū Bakr to lead the people in prayer." ʿĀ'ishah ؓ then urged Ḥafṣah ؓ to ask the Prophet ﷺ to allow ʿUmar to lead instead, and the Prophet ﷺ repeated—even more emphatically—"Go and find Abū Bakr to lead! You are acting like the women around [Prophet] Yūsuf (i.e., you are conspiring)."[1142]

Abū Bakr ؓ therefore led the prayers, and the following day, the Prophet ﷺ gained enough energy to walk into the mosque while the Companions were praying Ẓuhr. Abū Bakr ؓ realised and stepped back to allow the Prophet ﷺ to lead. The Prophet ﷺ motioned to Abū Bakr for him to stay in his place but Abū Bakr—out of respect and reverence—did not follow the Prophet's command, stepping back once more and in turn forcing the Prophet ﷺ to lead. After the prayer, the Prophet ﷺ asked, "O Abū Bakr! What caused you to disobey me?" Abū Bakr ؓ replied, "It does not befit the son of Abū Quḥāfah to lead the Messenger of Allah in prayer." [1143]

After Ẓuhr, the Prophet ﷺ was lifted onto the pulpit and he gave the last sermon of his life. He ﷺ said, "I command you to take care of the Anṣār, as they have been my best advisors, and they have fulfilled the duties obliged upon them." [1144] This was a subtle indication that the Prophet ﷺ wanted the Muhājirūn to rule because taking care of someone implies authority over them. He also commanded that the Arabian Peninsula be purified of all forms of Paganism. He then instructed that the future delegates and future converts be treated with the same hospitality that the Prophet ﷺ offered them. One of his final phrases was, "None of you should die except with good thoughts of Allah." [1145] And last thing he said publicly was, "[Guard] the prayer! [Guard] the prayer! And fear Allah with those under your authority." [1146]

The day before his death, the Prophet ﷺ asked ʿĀ'ishah ؓ how much money he had, and ʿĀ'ishah collected seven coins, which was a meagre amount. He ﷺ then held the seven coins and said, "What will I say to Allah if I meet Allah with these coins?" [1147] He then commanded ʿĀ'ishah to give the money to the poor, and he fell unconscious. When he awoke, he asked her if she gave it to the poor. ʿĀ'ishah promised to do so, and the Prophet ﷺ fainted once more. When he awoke, he again asked her, and he continued to ask until ʿĀ'ishah donated every item in the house. When the Prophet ﷺ returned to his Lord, he was penniless.

The next day, the Prophet ﷺ was in bed as Abū Bakr ؓ led the Muslims in prayer. He ﷺ asked to be sat up in his bed, and he lifted the curtain to observe his Companions in prayer. Anas ibn Mālik ؓ said, "We diverted our attention and almost invalidated our prayers out of happiness." [1148] Anas ؓ recalled that this was the last time that they saw the blessed face of the Prophet ﷺ. During the day, the Prophet ﷺ lost and gained consciousness intermittently as his fever intensified. His beloved daughter, Fāṭimah ؓ, cried, "How painful is the suffering of my father!" The Prophet ﷺ replied, "O Fāṭimah, your father will not suffer after today."[1149]

As the Prophet ﷺ wiped sweat from his forehead, he said, "Indeed, death has its pangs! There is no god but Allah. Indeed, death has its pangs!"[1150] The fever intensified so much that the Prophet ﷺ was no longer able to speak. At this point, Usāmah ibn Zayd ؓ could not wait any longer, and he returned to Medina to visit the Prophet ﷺ. The Prophet ﷺ was too weak to speak so instead pointed to Usāmah then pointed to the sky. In other words, "Go, and Allah is with you!"

ʿĀ'ishah ؓ placed the Prophet's head on her lap and cradled him ﷺ. The Prophet ﷺ then looked over to ʿAbdurraḥman ibn Abī Bakr's miswak and motioned. ʿĀ'ishah loosened the miswak and the Prophet ﷺ mustered enough energy to clean his teeth before meeting his Lord. The Prophet ﷺ then raised his eyes upwards and began whispering. ʿĀ'ishah lowered her head to hear what he was saying, and she heard, "With the Prophets, the truthful, the martyrs, and the righteous. O Allah, forgive me, have mercy on me, and allow me to be with al-Rafīq al-Aʿlā (The Loftiest Company)." His final words were "al-Rafīq al-Aʿlā".[1151] Scholars explain that al-Rafīq al-Aʿlā is Allah ﷻ Himself i.e., the loftiest company. Fāṭimah ؓ cried out, "O my father! You have answered the call of your Lord! O my father! You will enter the Highest Paradise! O my father! We give the news of your death to Jibrīl!"[1152]

ʿĀ'ishah ؓ later recalled, "The Messenger of Allah once told me, 'No soul of a Prophet is taken except that they are presented their location in Paradise and are offered the choice [between this life and the next].' He then lost consciousness as his head was resting on my thigh. When he awoke, he stared above and said, 'O Allah, al-Rafīq al-Aʿlā!', and I knew that he had chosen Allah over us."[1153] She then said, "Of the greatest blessings that Allah gave me was that the Prophet ﷺ died in my house, on my day, between my neck and my chest, with my saliva in his mouth (from the miswak)."[1154]

News spread, and the Companions did not know how to react. ʿUmar ibn al-Khaṭṭāb ﷺ was hysterical, refusing to believe it. He grew enraged, shouting, "The Hypocrites have spread these lies! Whoever says that the Prophet ﷺ has passed away will be executed! He is going to Allah just as [Prophet] Mūsā went to Allah for 40 days! Anyone who says otherwise will face my sword!"[1155] The Companions were petrified as ʿUmar continued to scream until Abū Bakr ﷺ finally galloped in. He immediately entered upon the Prophet ﷺ to verify, and he saw the body of the Prophet ﷺ covered. He lifted the cover and began to cry. He kissed the Prophet ﷺ on the forehead and said, "O how I would give my mother and father for you, O Messenger of Allah. You shall taste death but once, and this is your death. How beautiful you are in life and in death, O Messenger of Allah."[1156]

Meanwhile in the mosque, ʿUmar's hysteria continued, and Abū Bakr ﷺ—the one man courageous enough to scold ʿUmar—yelled, "Sit down, O ʿUmar!" ʿUmar could not register Abū Bakr's command, and he refused to sit down. Abū Bakr ﷺ then climbed the pulpit but did not dare stand on the highest step—the step of the Prophet ﷺ—to address the Companions. He began by praising Allah ﷻ then uttered the famous statement, "Whoever used to worship Muhammad ﷺ then know that Muhammad ﷺ has died, and whoever used to worship Allah ﷻ then know that Allah ﷻ is alive and never dies." He then recited the verse, "Muhammad is no more than a Messenger; other Messengers have gone before him. If he were to die or be killed, would you regress into disbelief? Those who do so will not harm Allah whatsoever. And Allah will reward those who are grateful."[1157] ʿUmar ﷺ suddenly collapsed to his knees. The fearless warrior could not hold his own weight at the realisation that his beloved was gone. He later said, "It was as if I heard the verse for the very first time."[1158]

The Companions mourned like they never mourned before. Anas ibn Mālik ﷺ said, "The day the Prophet ﷺ entered Medina was the brightest day of our lives, and the day he left was the darkest day of our lives."[1159] The Companions began reciting poetry, the most eloquent of which was composed by Ḥassān ibn Thābit ﷺ,

What ails these eyes of mine? They fail to sleep,
Their corners grooved and singed as dark as kohl
By rivulets of tears of aching grief
Upon your passing to the next abode.

O Best of all who ever trod the Earth ﷺ,
Don't go so far away from me, I beg.
Alas! Alas, to shield you from the dirt,
If only I could give my flank instead!

Would I were hid from view before this date,
In *al-Baqī'* amongst the boxthorn trees.
Whose death did I behold upon this day?
I wish instead my parents' lives had ceased!

You've passed away, while I remain forlorn
And linger still, bewildered and confused.
O how I wish that I were never born!
How now to live amongst this multitude?

The blackest poison, were it but at hand,
I'd drink my fill of it. Or better still,
Tomorrow or today, let God's command
Come fast to pass on us. And by His will,

The Hour shall come, and we shall meet once more
The Purest One ﷺ, most noble of his line.
With gladdest tidings he was chastely born,
Āminah's firstborn ﷺ—blessedness enshrined,

A light illuminating all creation,
The one who's steered towards which has been guided.
O Lord, unite the Prophet ﷺ and his nation
In Gardens that leave Envy's eyes unsighted,

In Paradise. And such for us decree,
O Lord, Majestic, Glorious, Exalted.

By God, so long as I abide, I'll weep
And weep upon the passing of the Prophet ﷺ.

Woe be to both the Helpers and his tribe,
The Prophet's passed while we remain alive!

The land constricts upon us Helpers now,
Our faces etched in *ithmid's* [ii] hues of grey
As we recount the blessings he endowed.
We birthed him.[iii] Now, among us is his grave.

How oft the Helpers did receive sublime
Counsel with which to carry ever onward;
And more, at every moment seen in time,
By God's Apostle's presence they were honoured.

The Lord of All and those around His throne
And all the pure do send their blessings on
The person worthy of such praise alone:
Allah's belov'd, Aḥmad ﷺ the Blessed One ﷺ.[1160]

The Era of Caliphs

Before the Prophet ﷺ was even buried, the Companions convened and discussed the appointment of a new leader. They were in mourning but still understood the urgency of unifying the Ummah. A few hours after the death of the Prophet ﷺ, the Anṣār gathered at their usual gathering place. It is important to note that the Anṣār did not premeditate a meeting about the Prophet's succession; rather, they met to discuss the Prophet ﷺ and the conversation inevitably turned to the topic of leadership. The obvious choice for the Anṣār was Saʿd ibn ʿUbādah ؓ, the most senior leader of the Anṣār after Saʿd ibn Muʿādh ؓ was martyred.

ii Antimony

iii This a reference to the fact that the great-great-grandmother of the Prophet ﷺ was from Medina (Yathrib).

As the Anṣār were gathering, Abū Bakr and ʿUmar ﵄ were in the mosque. They were notified about the gathering, and ʿUmar said, "Let's go and discuss the matter with our brothers from the Anṣār." [1161] Abū Bakr and ʿUmar then left with a group of the Muhājirūn to discuss the matter with the Anṣār. Meanwhile, the Prophet's closest family, such as ʿAlī ibn Abī Ṭālib, al-ʿAbbās, and Zubayr ibn al-ʿAwwām ﵃, were taking care of the Prophet's personal matters such as washing his blessed body and organising internal family matters.

After Abū Bakr and ʿUmar arrived and exchanged pleasantries, a member of the Anṣār stood up and said, "We are the Helpers of Allah, and we are the vanguard of Islam. You, O Emigrants, are a group amongst us. You came to us gradually and joined us." [1162] In the politest manner, the Anṣār expressed their reasoning as to why they should lead. The Anṣār were in the thousands while the Muhājirūn were in the hundreds, and the Anṣār provided the Prophet ﷺ with the base he needed to thrive.

ʿUmar ﵁ then narrated,

> "As he was speaking, I was thinking to myself: what should I say in response? When he finished, I had my response ready—and I knew it was a little harsh—but before I was able to stand up, Abū Bakr pulled me down and said, 'Stay put, O ʿUmar!' I obeyed him as I was scared to make him angry. Abū Bakr then stood up, praised Allah, and gave a lecture. By Allah, he was wiser and gentler than I would have been, and there was not a single point I wanted to make except that he made it, and more. He said, 'I know that the Prophet ﷺ said, "If the Anṣār went in one direction, and all of mankind went in another direction, I would go with the Anṣār."' He then recalled every Hadith we know about praise of the Anṣār. He then moved on and said, 'O Saʿd, I know that you were sitting right in front of the Prophet ﷺ when he said, "It is the Quraysh who shall lead this matter of ours. The righteous amongst them

shall lead the righteous of mankind, and the impious
shall lead the impious of mankind.'" Sa'd responded,
'You have spoken the truth: you are the leaders, and we
are the helpers.'" [1163]

Abū Bakr ◉ then held onto the hands of 'Umar and Abū 'Ubaydah ◉
and said, "I have nominated these two: choose whichever you like."
Another member of the Anṣār then stood up and said, "I have a solution:
why don't we have two leaders? One from you and one from us."
More people began adding their input and voices began to raise over
each other. 'Umar ◉ then raised his voice above everyone else's and said,
"O Abū Bakr, stretch forth your hand! We shall pledge our allegiance to
you!" 'Umar placed his hand in Abū Bakr's hand and officially pledged
his allegiance to him. The Muhājirūn quickly followed suit and the
Anṣār did too. Abū Bakr ◉ was thus nominated as the first Caliph in
Islam and successor of the Prophet ◉.

The following morning—24 hours after the passing of the
Prophet ◉—the Companions all gathered in the Prophet's Mosque.
'Umar ◉ announced, "O people! What I said yesterday (about the
Prophet ◉ not being dead) was from myself. I did not find it in
the Book of Allah nor did the Prophet ◉ tell me. I thought that the
Prophet ◉ would not leave us until life on Earth ended and he would
be the last of us to go. But Allah has left you with His Book, and in
it is the Sunnah of the Prophet ◉, so hold on to it and you shall be
guided. Allah has gathered your affairs and has chosen the Companion
of the Prophet; 'one of two while they were both in the cave'[iv], [1164]
so stand up and pledge your allegiance to him!" [1164] The Companions
then formed a queue and pledged their allegiance to Abū Bakr one
by one.

The Ummah is unified in recognising Abū Bakr al-Ṣiddīq ◉ as the
best of the Companions and the closest to the Prophet ◉. There is

---

iv   'Umar ◉ is quoting *al-Tawbah*, 40, where Allah ◉ describes Abū Bakr ◉ as the
      Prophet's Companion, "[When] he was only one of two while they were both in the
      cave, he reassured his companion, 'Do not worry, for Allah is certainly with us.'"

a difference, however, as to whether the Prophet ﷺ explicitly chose him as the leader. Some scholars state that the Prophet ﷺ did not choose anyone for leadership, and that the Companions themselves decided.[1165] They explain that the Companions recognised Abū Bakr's status as the best, and saw it appropriate for him to therefore lead the Ummah politically. Other scholars argue that the Prophet ﷺ not only identified Abū Bakr ؓ as the best Companion but also indicated that he ought to lead.[1166] They explain that the Prophet ﷺ did not explicitly name his successor, as he may not have wanted to establish a precedent of kings and rulers naming their successors. Instead, he commanded that Abū Bakr ؓ lead the prayer in his stead; this is a strong indication that he approved his Caliphate, as the Imam in Islam represents authority.

A third minority group of scholars claim that the Prophet ﷺ explicitly commanded for Abū Bakr ؓ to rule after him, but there are no authentic reports in this regard.[1167] In short, the first two opinions can be merged to state that the Prophet ﷺ did not explicitly appoint his successor but that his instruction that Abū Bakr ؓ lead the prayer in his stead serves as a strong indication that he is to be the leader. Allah ﷻ referring to Abū Bakr as the Prophet's Companion further bolsters this argument, as do the plethora of Hadiths in praise of Abū Bakr's faith.

After the Companions all pledged their allegiance, Abū Bakr ؓ stood up and gave a short yet impactful speech, "O people! I have been put in charge of you even though I am not the best of you. If I do good, help me; and if I do bad, correct me. Being truthful is the essence of trustworthiness and lying is treachery. The weak amongst you is strong in my eyes until I return his right to him (i.e., the weakest are closest to me), and the strongest amongst you is the weakest in my eyes. Never does a group leave striving for the sake of Allah except that Allah strikes them with humiliation, and never does lewdness spread except that Allah envelopes them with His punishment. Obey me as long as I obey Allah and His Messenger, but if I disobey Allah and His Messenger then I have no right that you should obey me. Stand up and pray, may Allah have mercy on you."[1168]

The Greatest Legacy

The Qur'an is a timeless miracle whose miraculous nature can be observed today—over 1,400 years later. However, it is often overlooked that the life of the Prophet ﷺ was a miracle in its own right. Within 23 years, the Message of an unlettered man engulfed the entirety of Arabia, and after a further 20 years, the seemingly impenetrable Roman and Persian Empires were brought to their knees. The Prophet's legacy, however, transcends military success; the Message of worshipping Allah ﷻ alone has spread throughout the globe, and Allah ﷻ is glorified by His creation every second of every day.

Each and every Muslim's duty is to honour the Prophet ﷺ for spreading God's Message on Earth. Drawing closer to His Messenger ﷺ draws us closer to Him ﷻ. Allah ﷻ instructs the Prophet ﷺ to address the Ummah, "Say [O Prophet], 'If you sincerely love Allah, then follow me; Allah will love you and forgive your sins. For Allah is All-Forgiving, Most Merciful.'"[1169] Following the Prophet ﷺ therefore leads us to the Mercy and Forgiveness of Allah ﷻ. The Prophet ﷺ said, "Whoever sends blessings upon me, Allah will send blessings upon them tenfold."[1170] Allah ﷻ Himself states, "Indeed, Allah showers His blessings upon the Prophet, and His Angels pray for him. O Believers! Invoke Allah's blessings upon him, and salute him with worthy greetings of peace."[1171] Any effort made to honour the Prophet ﷺ is time well spent, as he is God's steward on Earth.

Following the teachings and example of the Prophet ﷺ is the greatest form of reverence. This book outlined the character of the Prophet ﷺ, demonstrating time and time again the exemplary conduct of the Prophet ﷺ and the Prophetic model of dealing with one another. The book also displayed the Prophet's humanness, which perfectly situates him as the ideal role model for us all. Allah ﷻ states, "Say [O Prophet], 'Had there been Angels walking on Earth, well settled, We would have surely sent down for them an Angel from Heaven as a Messenger.'"[1172] Allah ﷻ could have sent an Angel as a Messenger but instead sent a human to walk amongst us. While we can never reach the heights of nobility set by the Prophet ﷺ, the fact that he is human serves as motivation to follow his teachings to the best of our ability.

Endnotes

1 *al-Inshirāḥ*, 4.

2 Abū ʿAbdillāh Muhammad al-Qurṭubī, *al-Jāmiʿ li Aḥkām al-Qur'ān*, Mu'assasah al-Risālah, Beirut (1427/2006), vol. 22, p. 357.

3 Referring to *al-Anbiyā'*, 107.

4 Abū ʿĪsā al-Tirmidhī, *al-Shamā'il al-Muḥammadiyyah*, Dār al-Ḥadīth, Beirut (1408/1988), p. 178.

5 Abū ʿAbdillāh Muhammad al-Qurṭubī, *al-Tadhkirah fī Aḥwal al-Mawtā wa Umūr al-Ākhirah*, Dār al-Minhāj, Riyadh (1425/2004), vol. 3, p. 1219.

6 *Āl ʿImrān*, 144; *al-Aḥzāb*, 40; *Muhammad*, 2; *al-Fatḥ*, 29.

7 *al-Ṣaf*, 6.

8 Muhammad ibn Ismāʿīl al-Bukhārī, *Ṣaḥīḥ al-Bukhārī*, Dār Ibn Kathīr, Beirut (1423/2002), 1169; Muslim ibn al-Ḥajjāj al-Naysābūrī, *Ṣaḥīḥ Muslim*, Dār Ṭaybah, Riyadh (1427/2006), p. 107.

9 Bukhārī, *Ṣaḥīḥ al-Bukhārī*, pp. 1169-1170; Muslim, *Ṣaḥīḥ Muslim*, p. 107.

10 *al-Aḥzāb*, 40.

11 Muslim, *Ṣaḥīḥ Muslim*, p. 86.

12 Ibn Qayyim al-Jawziyyah, *Badā'iʿ al-Fawā'id*, Majmaʿ al-Fiqh al-Islāmī, Jeddah (1425/2004), vol. 3, p. 1167.

13 Muhammad ibn ʿAbdullāh ibn ʿAbdurraḥmān al-Dārimī, *Musnad al-Dārimī*, Dār al-Mughnī, Riyadh (1421/2000), vol. 1, p. 204.

14 Bukhārī, *Ṣaḥīḥ al-Bukhārī*, p. 876.

15 Tirmidhī, *al-Shamā'il al-Muḥammadiyyah*, p. 14.

16 Muslim, *Ṣaḥīḥ Muslim*, p. 66.

17 Tirmidhī, *al-Shamā'il al-Muḥammadiyyah*, p. 7.

18 Tirmidhī, *al-Shamā'il al-Muḥammadiyyah*, p. 9.

19 Muslim, *Ṣaḥīḥ Muslim*, pp. 684-685.

20 Tirmidhī, *al-Shamā'il al-Muḥammadiyyah*, p. 156-157.

21 Bukhārī, *Ṣaḥīḥ al-Bukhārī*, p. 623.

22 Tirmidhī, *al-Shamā'il al-Muḥammadiyyah*, pp. 70-71.

23 Tirmidhī, *al-Shamā'il al-Muḥammadiyyah*, pp. 65-67.

24 *al-Takāthur*, 8.

25 Bukhārī, *Ṣaḥīḥ al-Bukhārī*, p. 1709.

26 Muslim, *Ṣaḥīḥ Muslim*, pp. 1092-1093.

27 Bukhārī, *Ṣaḥīḥ al-Bukhārī*, pp. 1561-1562.

28 Bukhārī, *Ṣaḥīḥ al-Bukhārī*, p. 1520.

29 Tirmidhī, *al-Shamā'il al-Muḥammadiyyah*, pp. 113-114.

30 *al-Aḥzāb*, 21.

31 *al-Mu'minūn*, 24.

32 *Hūd*, 120.

33 Ibn Ḥazm, *al-Faṣl fī al-Milal wa al-Ahwā' wa al-Niḥal*, Dār al-Jīl, Beirut (1416/1996), vol. 2, p. 231.

34 Al-Khaṭīb al-Baghdādī, *al-Jāmiʿ li Akhlāq al-Rāwī wa Ādāb al-Sāmiʿ*, Dār al-Risālah, Beirut (1416/1996), vol. 2, p. 288.

35 This occurs in many places throughout the Qur'an, such as *al-Tawbah*, 70; *Ibrāhīm*, 9; *Ghāfir*, 30; and so on.

36 ʿAbdurraḥmān ibn Muhammad ibn Khaldūn, *Muqaddimah Ibn Khaldūn*, Dār al-Fikr, Beirut (1431/2000), vol. 2, p. 21.

37 Ibn Ḥajar al-ʿAsqalānī, *Fatḥ al-Bārī: Sharḥ Ṣaḥīḥ al-Bukhārī*, Maktabah al-Malik Fahd al-Waṭaniyyah, Riyadh (1421/2001), vol. 6, p. 621.

38 Ibn Ḥajar al-ʿAsqalānī, *Fatḥ al-Bārī: Sharḥ Ṣaḥīḥ al-Bukhārī*, vol. 6, p. 621.

39 Ibn ʿAsākir, *Tārīkh Madīnah Dimashq*, Dār al-Fikr, Beirut (1415/1995), vol. 74, p. 81.

40 Ṣalāḥ ad-Dīn al-Ṣafadī, *al-Wāfī bi al-Wafayāt*, Dār Iḥyā al-Turāth al-ʿArabī, Beirut (1421/2000), vol. 1, p. 62.

41 *Fāṭir*, 24.

42 Bukhārī, *Ṣaḥīḥ al-Bukhārī*, p. 870.

43 Ibn Qayyim al-Jawziyyah, *Ighāthah al-Lahfān min Maṣāyid al-Shayṭān*, Dār al-Kutub al-ʿIlmiyyah, Beirut (1432/2011), p. 178.

44 Bukhārī, *Ṣaḥīḥ al-Bukhārī*, p. 1172.

45 *al-ʿAnkabūt*, 61.

46 *Ṣād*, 3.

47 *Yūnus*, 18.

48 Tirmidhī, *Sunan al-Tirmidhī*, Dār al-Gharb al-Islāmī, Beirut (1996), vol. 5, p. 382.

49 Muslim, *Ṣaḥīḥ Muslim*, p. 1080.

50 *Quraysh*, 1-4.

51 ʿAbd al-Malik Ibn Hishām, *al-Sīrah al-Nabawiyyah*, Dār al-Kitāb al-ʿArabī, Beirut (1410/1990), pp. 163-165.

52 Ibn Kathīr, *al-Bidāyah wa al-Nihāyah*, vol.2, pp. 248-249.

53 *al-Baqarah*, 129.

54 Ibn Isḥāq, *al-Sīrah al-Nabawiyyah*, p.28

55 Abū al-Faraj Ibn al-Jawzī, *al-Wafā fī Aḥwāl al-Muṣṭafā*, al-Mu'assasah al-Saʿīdiyyah, Riyadh (1396/1976), vol. 1, pp. 154-155.

56 Muslim, *Ṣaḥīḥ Muslim*, pp. 519-520.

57 ʿAbd al-Raḥmān al-Suhaylī, *al-Rawḍ al-Unuf fī Sharḥ al-Sīrah al-Nabawiyyah li Ibn Hishām*, Dār al-Kutub al-ʿIlmiyyah, Cairo (1430/2009), vol. 1, p. 283.

58 Ibn Saʿd, *al-Ṭabaqāt al-Kabīr*, Maktabah al-Khānjī, Cairo (1421/2001), vol. 1, p. 81.

59 Ibn Kathīr, *al-Bidāyah wa al-Nihāyah*, Maktabah al-Maʿārif, Beirut (1410/1990), vol. 2, p. 260.

60 Al-Bayhaqī, *Dalā'il al-Nubuwwah*, Dār al-Kutub al-ʿIlmiyyah, Beirut (1408/1988), vol. 1, p. 113.

61 Ibn Isḥāq, *al-Sīrah al-Nabawiyyah*, pp. 26-27.

62 Muslim, *Ṣaḥīḥ Muslim*, p. 87.

63 Muslim, *Ṣaḥīḥ Muslim*, p. 87.

64 al-*Inshirāḥ*, 1.

65 Muslim, *Ṣaḥīḥ Muslim*, p. 950.

66 Muslim, *Ṣaḥīḥ Muslim*, pp. 433-434.

67 *Ṭā Hā*, 41.

68 Muslim, *Ṣaḥīḥ Muslim*, p. 1360.

69 Bukhārī, *Ṣaḥīḥ al-Bukhārī*, p. 539.

70 Ibn Hishām, *al-Sīrah al-Nabawiyyah*, vol. 1, p. 210.

71 Ibn Kathīr, *al-Bidāyah wa al-Nihāyah*, vol. 2, pp. 291-292.

72 Ibn Hishām, *al-Sīrah al-Nabawiyyah*, vol. 1, pp. 154-155.

73 Ṭabarānī, *al-Muʿjam al-Kabīr*, Maktabah Ibn Taymiyyah, Cairo (2008), vol. 2, pp. 209-210.

74 Ibn Sa'd, *al-Ṭabaqāt al-Kabīr,* vol. 1, p. 109.

75 Al-Mu'āfā ibn Zakariyyā al-Nahrawānī, *al-Jalīs al-Ṣāliḥ al-Kāfī wa al-Anīs al-Nāṣiḥ al-Shāfī,* 'Ālam al-Kutub, Beirut (1413/1993), vol. 4, pp. 32-33.

76 Muḥibb al-Dīn Aḥmad ibn 'Abdullāh al-Ṭabarī, *al-Simṭ al-Thamīn fī Manāqib Ummuhāt al-Mu'minīn,* al-Maktabah al-Tijāriyyah, Mecca (1408/1988), p. 28.

77 Ibn Sa'd, *al-Ṭabaqāt al-Kabīr,* vol. 1, p. 109.

78 Ibn Ḥajar al-'Asqalānī, *al-Iṣābah fī Tamyīz al-Ṣaḥābah,* Dār al-Kutub al-'Ilmiyyah, Beirut (1415/1995), vol. 8, p. 103.

79 Ibn Kathīr, *al-Bidāyah wa al-Nihāyah,* vol. 2, p. 294.

80 Ibn Sa'd, *al-Ṭabaqāt al-Kabīr,* vol. 10, p. 18.

81 Al-Ḥākim al-Naysābūrī, *al-Mustadrak 'alā al-Ṣaḥīḥayn,* Dār al-Kutub al-'Ilmiyyah, Cairo (1422/2002), vol. 3, pp. 200-201.

82 Ibn Hishām, *al-Sīrah al-Nabawiyyah,* vol. 1, p. 275.

83 Al-Qurṭubī, *al-Jāmi' li-Aḥkām al-Qur'ān,* vol. 22, p. 529.

84 *al-Kawthar,* 1-3.

85 Bukhārī, *Ṣaḥīḥ al-Bukhārī,* pp. 44-45.

86 Bukhārī, *Ṣaḥīḥ al-Bukhārī,* p. 45.

87 Ibn Ḥajar al-'Aṣqalānī, *Fatḥ al-Bārī: Sharḥ Ṣaḥīḥ al-Bukhārī,* vol. 3, p. 524.

88 Ibn al-Athīr, *Usd al-Ghābah fī Ma'rifah al-Ṣaḥābah,* Dār al-Kutub al-'Ilmiyyah, Beirut (1415/1994), vol. 2, p. 352.

89 Ibn al-Athīr, *Usd al-Ghābah,* vol. 2, p. 352.

90 Bukhārī, *Ṣaḥīḥ al-Bukhārī,* p. 1201.

91 *al-Aḥzāb,* 5.

92 'Alī ibn 'Alī al-Ghazzī, *al-Kawākib al-Durriyyah bi Sharḥ al-Barzakhiyyah,* Dār al-Kutub al-'Ilmiyyah, Beirut (1441/2020), p. 137.

93 Tirmidhī, *Sunan al-Tirmidhī,* vol. 6, p. 142.

94 Aḥmad ibn Ḥanbal, *Musnad al-Imām Aḥmad,* vol. 43, p. 74.

95 Muslim, *Ṣaḥīḥ Muslim,* p. 1080.

96 *al-Qadr,* 1.

97 Muslim, *Ṣaḥīḥ Muslim,* p. 519.

98 *al-'Alaq,* 1-5.

99 Yūsuf Effendī Zādah, *Najāḥ al-Qārī li Ṣaḥīḥ al-Bukhārī,* Dār al-Kutub al-'Ilmiyyah, Beirut (1442/2021), vol. 23, p. 617.

100 Ibn Ḥajar al-'Asqalānī, *Fatḥ al-Bārī: Sharḥ Ṣaḥīḥ al-Bukhārī,* vol. 8, p. 602.

101 *al-Muzzammil,* 5.

102 Ibn Ḥajar al-'Asqalānī, *Fatḥ al-Bārī: Sharḥ Ṣaḥīḥ al-Bukhārī,* vol. 8, p. 602.

103 Muhammad ibn Ḥamzah al-Kirmānī, *Asrār al-Takrar fī al-Qur'ān,* Dār al-Faḍīlah, Riyadh (1397/1977), p. 252.

104 *al-ʿAlaq*, 4-5.

105 Bukhārī, *Ṣaḥīḥ al-Bukhārī*, pp. 7-8.

106 Bukhārī, *Ṣaḥīḥ al-Bukhārī*, pp. 7-8.

107 Tirmidhī, *Sunan al-Tirmidhī*, vol. 4, p. 127.

108 Bukhārī, *Ṣaḥīḥ al-Bukhārī*, p. 8.

109 *al-Muddaththir*, 1-7.

110 Ibn Kathīr, *al-Bidāyah wa al-Nihāyah*, vol. 3, p. 17.

111 *al-Ḥajj*, 52.

112 Abū al-Qāsim ʿAlī ibn Balbān, *al-Iḥsān fī Taqrīb Ṣaḥīḥ Ibn Ḥibbān*, Dār al-Tāʾṣīl, Cairo (1435/2004), vol. 1, pp. 452-455.

113 Ibn Qayyim al-Jawziyyah, *Zād al-Maʿād fī Hadī Khayr al-ʿIbād*, Muʾassasah al-Risālah, Beirut (1418/1998), vol. 1, p. 77.

114 *al-Qaṣaṣ*, 7.

115 Muslim, *Ṣaḥīḥ Muslim*, pp. 23-24.

116 Bukhārī, *Ṣaḥīḥ al-Bukhārī*, p. 7.

117 Bukhārī, *Ṣaḥīḥ al-Bukhārī*, p. 7.

118 Ibn Qayyim al-Jawziyyah, *Zād al-Maʿād fī Hadī Khayr al-ʿIbād*, Muʾassasah al-Risālah, Beirut (1418/1998), vol. 1, p. 79.

119 *al-Muddaththir*, 2.

120 Muslim, *Ṣaḥīḥ Muslim*, p. 240.

121 Bukhārī, *Ṣaḥīḥ al-Bukhārī*, p. 990.

122 Abū Manṣūr al-Daylamī, *al-Firdaws bi Maʾthūr al-Khiṭāb*, Dār al-Kutub al-ʿIlmiyyah, Beirut (1406/1986), vol. 4, p. 92.

123 *al-Tawbah*, 40.

124 *al-Tawbah*, 40.

125 Ibn al-Athīr, *Usd al-Ghābah*, vol. 2, p. 455.

126 *Luqmān*, 15.

127 Ṭabarānī, *al-Muʿjam al-Awsaṭ*, Dār al-Ḥaramayn, Cairo (1415/1995), vol. 8, pp. 268-269.

128 Bukhārī, *Ṣaḥīḥ al-Bukhārī*, p. 704.

129 Bukhārī, *Ṣaḥīḥ al-Bukhārī*, pp. 493-494.

130 Aḥmad ibn Ḥanbal, *Musnad al-Imām Aḥmad*, vol. 6, p. 82.

131 Muhammad Yazīd Ibn Mājah, *Sunan Ibn Mājah*, Dār Iḥyāʾ al-Kutub al-ʿArabiyyah, Cairo, p. 49.

132 Aḥmad ibn Ḥanbal, *Musnad al-Imām Aḥmad*, vol. 6, p. 398.

133 Bukhārī, *Ṣaḥīḥ al-Bukhārī*, pp. 9-10.

134 Muslim, *Ṣaḥīḥ Muslim*, pp. 371-372.

135 Muslim, *Ṣaḥīḥ Muslim*, pp. 371-372.

136 *al-Fatḥ*, 1.

137 *al-Ḥijr*, 94.

138 *al-Shuʿarā'*, 214.

139 ʿAbdurraḥmān ibn Abī Bakr al-Suyūṭī, *al-Durr al-Manthūr fī al-Tafsīr bi al-Ma'thūr*, Dār al-Fikr, Beirut (1432/2011), vol. 6, pp. 328-329.

140 Ibn Jarīr al-Ṭabarī, *Tārīkh al-Rusul wa al-Mulūk*, vol. 2, pp. 319-321.

141 Muhammad ibn Yūsuf al-Ṣāliḥī, *Subul al-Hudā wa al-Rashād fī Sīrah Khayr al-ʿIbād*, al-Majlis al-Aʿlā li al-Shu'ūn al-Islāmiyyah, Cairo (1418/1997), vol. 2, p. 432.

142 *al-Masad*, 1-5.

143 *al-Shuʿarā'*, 214.

144 Ibn Hishām, *al-Sīrah al-Nabawiyyah*, p. 299.

145 al-Ḥākim al-Naysābūrī, *al-Mustadrak*, vol. 3, p. 668.

146 Ibn Hishām, *al-Sīrah al-Nabawiyyah*, p. 299.

147 Ibn Jarīr al-Ṭabarī, *Tārīkh al-Rusul wa al-Mulūk*, vol. 2, pp. 326-327.

148 Ibn Jarīr al-Ṭabarī, *Tārīkh al-Rusul wa al-Mulūk*, vol. 2, p. 327.

149 Ibn Ḥajar al-ʿAsqalānī, *al-Iṣābah fī Tamyīz al-Ṣaḥābah*, vol. 7, p. 199.

150 Bukhārī, *Ṣaḥīḥ al-Bukhārī*, p. 1172.

151 *al-Isrā'*, 110.

152 Ibn Hishām, *al-Sīrah al-Nabawiyyah*, vol. 1, p. 341.

153 Ibn Hishām, *al-Sīrah al-Nabawiyyah*, vol. 1, pp. 341-342.

154 Ibn Hishām, *al-Sīrah al-Nabawiyyah*, vol. 1, pp. 342-343.

155 Ibn Hishām, *al-Sīrah al-Nabawiyyah*, vol. 1, p. 343.

156 Bukhārī, *Ṣaḥīḥ al-Bukhārī*, p. 1273.

157 *al-Ḍuḥā*, 1-11.

158 Aḥmad ibn Ḥanbal, *Musnad al-Imām Aḥmad*, vol. 6, p. 376.

159 Muhammad ibn Isḥāq, *al-Sīrah al-Nabawiyyah*, Dār al-Kutub al-ʿIlmiyyah, Beirut (1424/2004), pp. 232-233.

160 Muhammad ibn Isḥāq, *al-Sīrah al-Nabawiyyah*, p. 233.

161 Aḥmad ibn Ḥanbal, *Musnad al-Imām Aḥmad*, vol. 25, pp. 401-402.

162 Muslim, *Ṣaḥīḥ Muslim*, pp. 385-386.

163 *al-ʿAnkabūt*, 48.

164 Al-Ḥākim al-Naysābūrī, *al-Mustadrak*, vol. 2, pp. 550-551.

165 Al-Ḥākim al-Naysābūrī, *al-Mustadrak*, vol. 2, pp. 550-551.

166 *al-Muddaththir*, 11-29.

167 *al-Anʿām*, 111.

168 *al-Isrā'*, 59.

169 *al-Kāfirūn*, 1-6.

170 Abū al-Faraj Ibn al-Jawzī, *al-Muntaẓam fī Tārīkh al-Mulūk wa al-Umam*, Dār al-Kutub al-ʿIlmiyyah, Beirut (1415/1995), vol. 2, p. 369.

171 *Ṣād*, 5.

172 Ibn Hishām, *al-Sīrah al-Nabawiyyah*, vol. 1, pp. 322-323.

173 Ibn Hishām, al-Sīrah al-Nabawiyyah, vol. 1, p.323

174 *Fuṣṣilat*, 1-12.

175 *Fuṣṣilat*, 12.

176 Ibn Hishām, *al-Sīrah al-Nabawiyyah*, vol. 1, pp. 323-324.

177 Ibn Isḥāq, *al-Sīrah al-Nabawiyyah*, pp. 238-239.

178 Ibn Isḥāq, *al-Sīrah al-Nabawiyyah*, p. 239.

179 Ibn Kathīr, *Tafsīr al-Qur'ān al-ʿAẓīm*, vol. 5, p. 124.

180 *al-Jinn*, 19.

181 *al-Isrā'*, 1.

182 *al-Furqān*, 1.

183 *al-Kahf*, 1.

184 *al-Ḥadīd*, 9.

185 *al-Isrā'*, 85.

186 Ibn Hishām, *al-Sīrah al-Nabawiyyah*, vol. 1, p. 347.

187 Ibn Mājah, *Sunan Ibn Mājah*, p. 53.

188 Ibn Hishām, *al-Sīrah al-Nabawiyyah*, vol. 1, p. 344.

189 Aḥmad ibn Yaḥyā al-Balādhurī, *Jumal min Ansāb al-Ashrāf*, Dār al-Fikr, Beirut (1417/1997), vol. 1, pp. 209-210.

190 Al-Balādhurī, *Jumal min Ansāb al-Ashrāf*, vol. 1, p. 210.

191 *al-Raḥmān*, 60.

192 Bukhārī, *Ṣaḥīḥ al-Bukhārī*, p. 811.

193 Bukhārī, *Ṣaḥīḥ al-Bukhārī*, p. 729.

194 Abū Nuʿaym al-Iṣfahānī, *Ḥilyah al-Awliyā' wa-Ṭabaqāt al-Aṣfiyā'*, Dār al-Fikr, Cairo (1416/1996), vol. 1, p. 144.

195 Abū Nuʿaym al-Iṣfahānī, *Ḥilyah al-Awliyā'*, vol. 1, p. 145.

196 Al-Ḥākim al-Naysābūrī, *al-Mustadrak*, vol. 3, p. 432.

197 *al-Naḥl*, 106.

198 Ibn Mājah, *Sunan Ibn Mājah*, p. 52.

199 Al-Ḥākim al-Naysābūrī, *al-Mustadrak*, vol. 3, p. 438.

200 Al-Ḥākim al-Naysābūrī, *al-Mustadrak*, vol. 3, p. 450.

201 Al-Ḥākim al-Naysābūrī, *al-Mustadrak*, vol. 3, p. 452.

202 *al-Baqarah*, 207.

203 Al-Qurṭubī, *al-Jāmiʿ li-Aḥkām al-Qur'ān*, vol. 8, p. 390.

204 *al-Anʿām*, 52.

205 Muslim, *Ṣaḥīḥ Muslim*, pp. 1287-1288.

206 Muslim, *Ṣaḥīḥ Muslim*, p. 1288.

207 *al-ʿAlaq*, 6-19.

208 Ibn Isḥāq, *al-Sīrah al-Nabawiyyah*, pp. 261-262.

209 *Ghāfir*, 28.

210 Aḥmad ibn Ḥanbal, *Musnad al-Imām Aḥmad*, vol. 5, p. 442.

211 *Hūd*, 7.

212 *al-ʿAnkabūt*, 1-3.

213 *Āl ʿImrān*, 142.

214 *al-Baqarah*, 214.

215 Bukhārī, *Ṣaḥīḥ al-Bukhārī*, p. 1719.

216 *al-Ḥujurāt*, 13.

217 *al-Ḥadīd*, 10.

218 Ibn Isḥāq, *al-Sīrah al-Nabawiyyah*, pp. 247-248.

219 Bukhārī, *Ṣaḥīḥ al-Bukhārī*, p. 550.

220 Abū Nuʿaym al-Iṣfahānī, *Ḥilyah al-Awliyā'*, pp. 29-30.

221 Bukhārī, *Ṣaḥīḥ al-Bukhārī*, p. 550.

222 Bukhārī, *Ṣaḥīḥ al-Bukhārī*, p. 551.

223 Aḥmad ibn Ḥanbal, *Musnad al-Imām Aḥmad*, vol. 3, p. 267.

224 *al-Najm*, 62.

225 Bukhārī, *Ṣaḥīḥ al-Bukhārī*, p. 261.

226 *al-Najm*, 20-21.

227 Ibn Saʿd, *al-Ṭabaqāt al-Kabīr*, vol. 1, p. 174.

228 Ibn Jarīr al-Ṭabarī, *Jāmiʿ al-Bayān ʿan Ta'wīl Āy al-Qur'ān*, Dār Hijr, Cairo (1422/2001), vol. 16, pp. 603-609.

229 Bukhārī, *Ṣaḥīḥ al-Bukhārī*, p. 940.

230 Abū Nuʿaym al-Iṣfahānī, *Ḥilyah al-Awliyā'*, vol. 1, p. 103.

231 Abū Nuʿaym al-Iṣfahānī, *Ḥilyah al-Awliyā'*, vol. 1, p. 104.

232 *Quraysh*, 3-4.

233 Ibn Kathīr, *al-Bidāyah wa al-Nihāyah*, vol. 3, p. 72.

234 Ibn Isḥāq, *al-Sīrah al-Nabawiyyah*, p. 248.

235 Abū Nuʿaym al-Iṣfahānī, *Ḥilyah al-Awliyā'*, vol. 1, p. 114.

236 Aḥmad ibn Ḥanbal, *Musnad al-Imām Aḥmad*, vol. 3, p. 266.

237 Aḥmad ibn Ḥanbal, *Musnad al-Imām Aḥmad*, vol. 3, p. 267.

238 Aḥmad ibn Ḥanbal, *Musnad al-Imām Aḥmad*, vol. 3, p. 267.

239 Al-Bayhaqī, *Dalā'il al-Nubuwwah,* vol. 2, p. 310.

240 Ibn Hishām, *al-Sīrah al-Nabawiyyah,* vol. 1, p. 366.

241 Ibn Isḥāq, *al-Sīrah al-Nabawiyyah,* p. 250.

242 Muhammad ibn ʿAbd al-Bāqī al-Zurqānī, *Sharḥ al-Zurqānī ʿalā Muwaṭṭa' al-Imām Mālik,* Dār al-Kutub al-ʿIlmiyyah, Beirut (1432/2011), vol. 2, p. 80.

243 Ibn Isḥāq, *al-Sīrah al-Nabawiyyah,* p. 212.

244 Ibn Isḥāq, *al-Sīrah al-Nabawiyyah,* pp. 212-213.

245 Ibn Isḥāq, *al-Sīrah al-Nabawiyyah,* p. 213.

246 Ibn Isḥāq, *al-Sīrah al-Nabawiyyah,* p. 212.

247 Ibn al-Athīr, *al-Kāmil fī al-Tārīkh,* Dār al-Kutub al-ʿIlmiyyah, Beirut (1407/1987), vol. 1, p. 602

248 Ibn al-Athīr, *al-Kāmil fī al-Tārīkh,* vol. 1, p. 602.

249 Tirmidhī, *Sunan al-Tirmidhī,* vol. 6, pp. 56-57.

250 *al-Ḥāqqah,* 41.

251 *al-Ḥāqqah,* 42.

252 *al-Ḥāqqah,* 43.

253 *al-Ḥāqqah,* 44-46.

254 Aḥmad ibn Ḥanbal, *Musnad al-Imām Aḥmad,* vol. 1, pp. 262-263.

255 Al-Muttaqī al-Hindī, *Kanz al-ʿUmmāl fī Sunan al-Aqwāl wa al-Afʿāl,* Mu'assasah al-Risālah, Beirut (1405/1985), vol. 12, p. 552.

256 Ibn al-Athīr, *al-Kāmil fī al-Tārīkh,* vol. 1, p. 602.

257 Ibn al-Athīr, *al-Kāmil fī al-Tārīkh,* vol. 1, p. 602.

258 Ibn al-Athīr, *al-Kāmil fī al-Tārīkh,* vol. 1, p. 602.

259 Ibn al-Athīr, *al-Kāmil fī al-Tārīkh,* vol. 1, p. 602.

260 Bukhārī, *Ṣaḥīḥ al-Bukhārī,* p. 906.

261 Abū Nuʿaym al-Iṣfahānī, *Ḥilyah al-Awliyā',* vol. 1, p. 40.

262 Ibn al-Athīr, *al-Kāmil fī al-Tārīkh,* vol. 1, p. 604.

263 Ibn Balbān, *al-Iḥsān fī Taqrīb Ṣaḥīḥ Ibn Ḥibbān,* vol. 7, pp. 501-502.

264 Al-Suhaylī, *al-Rawḍ al-Unuf,* vol. 2, p. 160.

265 Al-Suhaylī, *al-Rawḍ al-Unuf,* vol. 2, p. 161.

266 Bukhārī, *Ṣaḥīḥ al-Bukhārī,* pp. 1216-1217.

267 Ibn al-Athīr, *al-Kāmil fī al-Tārīkh,* vol. 1, p. 605.

268 Ibn al-Athīr, *al-Kāmil fī al-Tārīkh,* vol. 1, p. 606.

269 Bukhārī, *Ṣaḥīḥ al-Bukhārī,* p. 328.

270 Bukhārī, *Ṣaḥīḥ al-Bukhārī,* p. 328.

271 *al-Tawbah,* 113.

272 Bukhārī, *Ṣaḥīḥ al-Bukhārī,* p. 950.

273 *al-Anbiyā'*, 23.

274 *al-Qaṣaṣ*, 56.

275 *al-Mujādilah*, 22.

276 *al-Baqarah*, 34.

277 Bukhārī, *Ṣaḥīḥ al-Bukhārī*, p. 935.

278 Aḥmad ibn Ḥanbal, *Musnad al-Imām Aḥmad*, vol. 41, p. 356.

279 Ibn al-Athīr, *Usd al-Ghābah*, vol. 7, p. 86.

280 Ibn Isḥāq, *al-Sīrah al-Nabawiyyah*, p. 246.

281 Ibn Kathīr, *al-Bidāyah wa al-Nihāyah*, vol. 3, p. 134.

282 Ibn Kathīr, *al-Bidāyah wa al-Nihāyah*, vol. 3, p. 134.

283 Ibn Hishām, *al-Sīrah al-Nabawiyyah*, vol. 2, pp. 67-68.

284 *ʿAbasa*, 1-7.

285 Bukhārī, *Ṣaḥīḥ al-Bukhārī*, p. 798.

286 Al-Khaṭīb al-Baghdādī, *al-Jāmiʿ li Akhlāq al-Rāwī wa Ādāb al-Sāmiʿ*, vol. 2, p. 414.

287 *Yūsuf*, 86.

288 *al-Ḥijr*, 39.

289 Ibn Hishām, *al-Sīrah al-Nabawiyyah*, vol. 2, pp. 68-69.

290 Bukhārī, *Ṣaḥīḥ al-Bukhārī*, pp. 798-799.

291 *al-Anbiyā'*, 107.

292 *al-Aḥqāf*, 29.

293 *al-Aḥqāf*, 30-31.

294 Ibn Qayyim al-Jawziyyah, *Zād al-Maʿād*, vol. 3, p. 30.

295 Ibn Qayyim al-Jawziyyah, *Zād al-Maʿād*, vol. 3, p. 30.

296 Ibn Kathīr, *al-Bidāyah wa al-Nihāyah*, vol. 3, pp. 131-132.

297 Bukhārī, *Ṣaḥīḥ al-Bukhārī*, p. 954.

298 Bukhārī, *Ṣaḥīḥ al-Bukhārī*, p. 1296.

299 *al-Inshirāḥ*, 5-6.

300 *al-Mulk*, 3.

301 *Fuṣṣilat*, 12.

302 Ibn al-Athīr, *Usd al-Ghābah*, vol. 7, p. 86.

303 *al-Isrā'*, 1.

304 *al-Dhāriyāt*, 56.

305 Muslim, *Ṣaḥīḥ Muslim*, p. 87.

306 *al-Najm*, 18.

307 ʿAṭīyyah Ṣaqr, *Mawsūʿah Aḥsan al-Kalām fī al-Fatāwā wa al-Aḥkām*, Maktabah Wahbah, Cairo (1431/2010), p. 38.

308 Ibn Hishām, *al-Sīrah al-Nabawiyyah*, vol. 2, p. 49.

309 Aḥmad ibn Abī Bakr Ismāʿīl al-Būṣīrī, *Itḥāf al-Khayrah al-Maharah bi Zawā'id al-Masānīd al-ʿAsharah,* Maktabah al-Rushd, Riyadh (1419/1998), vol. 9, p. 59.

310 Muslim, *Ṣaḥīḥ Muslim,* p. 86.

311 *al-Najm,* 11-18.

312 Muslim, *Ṣaḥīḥ Muslim,* p. 86.

313 *Yūsuf,* 92.

314 *Maryam,* 57.

315 Bukhārī, *Ṣaḥīḥ al-Bukhārī,* p. 777.

316 Tirmidhī, *Sunan al-Tirmidhī,* vol. 5, p. 455.

317 *al-Zukhruf,* 77.

318 Ibn Hishām, *al-Sīrah al-Nabawiyyah,* vol. 2, p. 54.

319 Bukhārī, *Ṣaḥīḥ al-Bukhārī,* p. 822

320 Ibn Ḥajar al-ʿAsqalānī, *Fatḥ al-Bārī: Sharḥ Ṣaḥīḥ al-Bukhārī,* vol. 7, p. 253.

321 Muslim, *Ṣaḥīḥ Muslim,* p. 86.

322 *Fāṭir,* 1.

323 *al-Najm,* 18.

324 Ibn Kathīr, *al-Bidāyah wa al-Nihāyah,* vol. 1, pp. 8-9.

325 Muslim, *Ṣaḥīḥ Muslim,* p. 95.

326 *al-Najm,* 13.

327 *al-Takwīr,* 23.

328 *al-Najm,* 9.

329 *al-Anʿām,* 103.

330 *al-Shūrā,* 51.

331 Muslim, *Ṣaḥīḥ Muslim,* p. 96.

332 Muslim, *Ṣaḥīḥ Muslim,* p. 96.

333 Referenced in *al-Aʿrāf,* 143.

334 *al-Baqarah,* 285-286.

335 Bukhārī, *Ṣaḥīḥ al-Bukhārī,* p. 983.

336 Bukhārī, *Ṣaḥīḥ al-Bukhārī,* p. 1856.

337 Bukhārī, *Ṣaḥīḥ al-Bukhārī,* p. 1857.

338 This is referenced in *al-Nisā',* 164.

339 *al-Dhāriyāt,* 56.

340 *al-Nisā',* 28.

341 *al-Anbiyā',* 20.

342 *Ṭā-Hā,* 14.

343 *Hūd,* 114.

344 Examples include *al-Isrā'*, 78; *al-ʿAnkabūt*, 45; *Luqmān*, 17, and more.

345 *al-Najm*, 1-18.

346 Ibn Kathīr, *al-Bidāyah wa al-Nihāyah*, vol. 3, p. 113.

347 Al-Ḥākim al-Naysābūrī, *al-Mustadrak*, vol. 3, p. 65.

348 Aḥmad ibn Ḥanbal, *Musnad al-Imām Aḥmad*, vol. 25, pp. 401-409.

349 Ibn Hishām, *al-Sīrah al-Nabawiyyah*, vol. 2, p. 73.

350 Ibn Kathīr, *al-Bidāyah wa al-Nihāyah*, vol. 3, p. 143.

351 *al-An'am*, 151.

352 *al-Naḥl*, 90.

353 Ibn Kathīr, *al-Bidāyah wa al-Nihāyah*, vol. 3, p. 144.

354 *al-Baqarah*, 208.

355 *al-Kāfirūn*, 1-6.

356 Bukhārī, *Ṣaḥīḥ al-Bukhārī*, p. 941.

357 Ibn Kathīr, *al-Bidāyah wa al-Nihāyah*, vol. 3, p. 147.

358 Ṭabarānī, *al-Muʿjam al-Kabīr*, vol. 1, p. 276.

359 *al-Baqarah*, 89.

360 *al-Mumtaḥanah*, 12.

361 Ibn Hishām, *al-Sīrah al-Nabawiyyah*, vol. 2, p. 81.

362 Bukhārī, *Ṣaḥīḥ al-Bukhārī*, p. 953.

363 Ibn Hishām, *al-Sīrah al-Nabawiyyah*, vol. 2, pp. 83-84.

364 Al-Ḥākim al-Naysābūrī, *al-Mustadrak*, vol. 2, pp. 681-682.

365 Al-Bayhaqī, *Dalā'il al-Nubuwwah*, vol. 2, p. 444.

366 Ibn Hishām, *al-Sīrah al-Nabawiyyah*, vol. 2, p. 89.

367 Ibn Hishām, *al-Sīrah al-Nabawiyyah*, vol. 2, p. 89.

368 Al-Dhahabī, *Siyar Aʿlām al-Nubalā'*, vol. 2, p. 278.

369 Ibn Jarīr al-Ṭabarī, *Tārīkh al-Rusul wa al-Mulūk*, vol. 2, p. 364.

370 Ibn Jarīr al-Ṭabarī, *Tārīkh al-Rusul wa al-Mulūk*, vol. 2, pp. 364-365.

371 Ibn Hishām, *al-Sīrah al-Nabawiyyah*, vol. 2, p. 94.

372 Bukhārī, *Ṣaḥīḥ al-Bukhārī*, p. 1059.

373 Bukhārī, *Ṣaḥīḥ al-Bukhārī*, p. 928.

374 Aḥmad ibn Ḥanbal, *Musnad al-Imām Aḥmad*, vol. 18, p. 255.

375 Ibn Hishām, *al-Sīrah al-Nabawiyyah*, vol. 2, p. 110.

376 Ibn Hishām, *al-Sīrah al-Nabawiyyah*, vol. 2, p. 111.

377 *al-Ḥadīd*, 10.

378 *al-Nisā'*, 58.

379 ʿAlī ibn Aḥmad al-Wāḥidī, *Asbāb Nuzūl al-Qur'ān*, Dār al-Kutub al-ʿIlmiyyah, Beirut (1411/1991), p. 162.

380 Ibn al-Athīr, *Usd al-Ghābah*, vol. 4, p. 144.

381 Muhammad Sulaymān Salmān al-Manṣūr Fawrī, *Raḥmah li al-ʿĀlamīn*, Dār al-Salām, Riyadh (1418/1998), vol. 1, p. 78.

382 Ibn Hishām, *al-Sīrah al-Nabawiyyah*, vol. 2, p. 126.

383 Al-Balādhurī, *Jumal min Ansāb al-Ashrāf*, vol. 1, p. 308.

384 Aḥmad ibn Ḥanbal, *Musnad al-Imām Aḥmad*, vol. 44, p. 520.

385 *al-Anfāl*, 30.

386 Ibn Jarīr al-Ṭabarī, *Tārīkh al-Rusul wa al-Mulūk*, vol. 2, pp. 370-372.

387 Ibn Mājah, *Sunan Ibn Mājah*, p. 1037.

388 Bukhārī, *Ṣaḥīḥ al-Bukhārī*, p. 898.

389 Ibn Kathīr, *al-Bidāyah wa al-Nihāyah*, vol. 3, p. 186.

390 Ibn Ḥajar al-ʿAsqalānī, *al-Iṣābah fī Tamyīz al-Ṣaḥābah*, vol.3, pp. 35-36.

391 *al-Ḥajj*, 58.

392 *al-Nisā'*, 97.

393 *al-Baqarah*, 219.

394 *al-Nisā'*, 43.

395 *al-Mā'idah*, 90.

396 Ibn Jarīr al-Ṭabarī, *Jāmiʿ al-Bayān ʿan Ta'wīl Āy al-Qur'ān*, vol. 7, p. 382.

397 *al-ʿAnkabūt*, 10.

398 Ibn Jarīr al-Ṭabarī, *Jāmiʿ al-Bayān ʿan Ta'wīl Āy al-Qur'ān*, vol. 7, pp. 393-396.

399 *al-Nisā'*, 98-99.

400 Muslim, *Ṣaḥīḥ Muslim*, p. 903.

401 Ibn Balbān, *al-Iḥsān fī Taqrīb Ṣaḥīḥ Ibn Ḥibbān*, vol. 5, p. 551.

402 Aḥmad ibn Ḥanbal, *Musnad al-Imām Aḥmad*, vol. 30, p. 483.

403 Bukhārī, *Ṣaḥīḥ al-Bukhārī*, p. 831.

404 Ṭabarānī, *al-Muʿjam al-Kabīr*, vol. 17, p. 18.

405 Bukhārī, *Ṣaḥīḥ al-Bukhārī*, p. 452.

406 Bukhārī, *Ṣaḥīḥ al-Bukhārī*, p. 452.

407 Bukhārī, *Ṣaḥīḥ al-Bukhārī*, p. 452.

408 Muslim, *Ṣaḥīḥ Muslim*, p. 620.

409 Bukhārī, *Ṣaḥīḥ al-Bukhārī*, p. 452.

410 Muslim, *Ṣaḥīḥ Muslim*, p. 623.

411 Aḥmad ibn Ḥanbal, *Musnad al-Imām Aḥmad*, vol. 9, pp. 319-320.

412 Bukhārī, *Ṣaḥīḥ al-Bukhārī*, p. 1440.

413 Ibn Mājah, *Sunan Ibn Mājah*, p. 453.

414 *al-Tawbah*, 108.

415 Muslim, *Ṣaḥīḥ Muslim*, p. 386.

416 *Āl ʿImrān*, 30.

417 *Qāf*, 29.

418 *al-Ṭalāq*, 5.

419 *al-Aḥzāb*, 71.

420 *al-ʿAnkabūt*, 3.

421 *al-Ḥajj*, 78.

422 *al-Anfāl*, 42.

423 Ibn Kathīr, *al-Bidāyah wa al-Nihāyah*, vol. 3, p. 213.

424 Ibn Kathīr, *al-Bidāyah wa al-Nihāyah*, vol. 3, p. 214.

425 Ibn Kathīr, *al-Bidāyah wa al-Nihāyah*, vol. 3, p. 214.

426 Ibn Kathīr, *al-Bidāyah wa al-Nihāyah*, vol. 3, p. 214.

427 Al-Bayhaqī, *Dalā'il al-Nubuwwah*, vol. 2, p. 505.

428 Aḥmad ibn Ḥanbal, *Musnad al-Imām Aḥmad*, vol. 21, p. 41.

429 Ibn Mājah, *Sunan Ibn Mājah*, p. 1083.

430 Ibn Saʿd, *al-Ṭabaqāt al-Kabīr*, vol. 1, p. 203.

431 Al-Ḥākim al-Naysābūrī, *al-Mustadrak*, vol. 3, p. 521.

432 Muslim, *Ṣaḥīḥ Muslim*, p. 986.

433 Bukhārī, *Ṣaḥīḥ al-Bukhārī*, p. 959.

434 Bukhārī, *Ṣaḥīḥ al-Bukhārī*, p. 167.

435 Ibn Hishām, *al-Sīrah al-Nabawiyyah*, vol. 2, p. 138.

436 Bukhārī, *Ṣaḥīḥ al-Bukhārī*, p. 956.

437 Yūsuf ibn ʿAbdullāh ibn ʿAbd al-Barr, *al-Tamhīd li-mā fī al-Muwaṭṭa' min al-Maʿānī wa al-Asānīd*, Dār al-Kutub al-ʿIlmiyyah, Beirut (1431/2010), vol. 6, p. 421.

438 Muslim, *Ṣaḥīḥ Muslim*, p. 1016.

439 Tirmidhī, *Sunan al-Tirmidhī*, vol. 1, pp. 231-232.

440 *al-Ḥashr*, 9.

441 Muslim, *Ṣaḥīḥ Muslim*, p. 848.

442 Bukhārī, *Ṣaḥīḥ al-Bukhārī*, p. 927.

443 Tirmidhī, *Sunan al-Tirmidhī*, vol. 4, p. 265.

444 *al-Anfāl*, 75.

445 Ibn Hishām, *al-Sīrah al-Nabawiyyah*, vol. 2, p. 143.

446 Aḥmad ibn Ḥanbal, *Musnad al-Imām Aḥmad*, vol. 4, p. 258.

447 Ibn Hishām, *al-Sīrah al-Nabawiyyah*, vol. 2, p. 143.

448 Ibn Hishām, *al-Sīrah al-Nabawiyyah*, vol. 2, p. 144.

449 Ibn Hishām, *al-Sīrah al-Nabawiyyah*, vol. 2, p. 144.

450 Ibn Hishām, *al-Sīrah al-Nabawiyyah*, vol. 2, p. 145.

451 Ibn Hishām, *al-Sīrah al-Nabawiyyah*, vol. 2, p. 144.

452 *al-Ḥujurāt*, 13.

453 *al-Ḥujurāt*, 13.

454 Al-Suyūṭī, *al-Durr al-Manthūr fī al-Tafsīr bi al-Ma'thūr*, vol. 1, pp. 343-344.

455 *al-Baqarah*, 144.

456 *al-Baqarah*, 144.

457 *al-Baqarah*, 142.

458 Ibn Qayyim al-Jawziyyah, *Zād al-Maʿād*, vol. 3, p. 60.

459 *al-Baqarah*, 177.

460 *al-Baqarah*, 145.

461 Bukhārī, *Ṣaḥīḥ al-Bukhārī*, p. 1052.

462 Aḥmad ibn Ḥanbal, *Musnad al-Imām Aḥmad*, vol. 2, p. 203.

463 Bukhārī, *Ṣaḥīḥ al-Bukhārī*, pp. 1382-1383.

464 Ḍiyā al-Raḥmān al-Aʿẓamī, *Abū Hurayrah fī Ḍaw' Marwiyyātih* (Mecca: M.A. Thesis, Shariah College), p. 7; Muhammad ʿAjāj al-Khaṭīb, *Abū Hurayrah: Rāwiyah al-Islām*, Maktabah al-Wahbah, Cairo (1402/1982), pp. 136-138.

465 Bukhārī, *Ṣaḥīḥ al-Bukhārī*, p. 493.

466 Bukhārī, *Ṣaḥīḥ al-Bukhārī*, pp. 1507-1508.

467 Bukhārī, *Ṣaḥīḥ al-Bukhārī*, pp. 471-472.

468 *al-Baqarah*, 185.

469 Ibn Mājah, *Sunan Ibn Mājah*, p. 751.

470 Muslim, *Ṣaḥīḥ Muslim*, p. 58.

471 *al-Nisā'*, 77.

472 *al-Ḥajj*, 39.

473 Ibn Jarīr al-Ṭabarī, *Jāmiʿ al-Bayān ʿan Ta'wīl Āy al-Qur'ān*, vol. 16, p. 574.

474 Muslim, *Ṣaḥīḥ Muslim*, p. 880.

475 Ibn Ḥajar al-ʿAsqalānī, *Fatḥ al-Bārī fī Sharḥ Ṣaḥīḥ al-Bukhārī*, vol. 7, pp. 326-328.

476 Ibn Jarīr al-Ṭabarī, *Tārīkh al-Rusul wa al-Mulūk*, vol. 2, p. 411.

477 Ibn Jarīr al-Ṭabarī, *Tārīkh al-Rusul wa al-Mulūk*, vol. 2, p. 412.

478 *al-Baqarah*, 217.

479 Muslim, *Ṣaḥīḥ Muslim*, p. 917.

480 Ibn Hishām, *al-Sīrah al-Nabawiyyah*, vol. 2, pp. 249-250.

481 Muhammad al-Qurṭubī, *al-Jāmiʿ li Aḥkām al-Qur'ān*, vol. 5, p. 293.

482 Abū al-Qāsim ʿAlī ibn Balbān, *al-Iḥsān fī Taqrīb Ṣaḥīḥ Ibn Ḥibbān*, Dār al-Ta'ṣīl, Cairo (1435/2004), vol. 1, pp. 452-455.

483 Abū al-Ḥasan Muqātil ibn Sulaymān, *Tafsīr Muqātil ibn Sulaymān*, Dār al-Kutub al-ʿIlmiyyah, Beirut (1441/2020), vol. 1, p. 132.

484 Aḥmad ibn Ḥanbal, *Musnad al-Imām Aḥmad*, vol. 7, pp. 75-76.

485 Ibn Hishām, *al-Sīrah al-Nabawiyyah*, vol. 2, pp. 250-251.

486 Ibn Hishām, *al-Sīrah al-Nabawiyyah*, vol. 2, p. 251.

487 Ibn al-Athīr, *al-Kāmil fī al-Tārīkh*, vol. 2, p. 15.

488 Al-Suyūṭī, *al-Durr al-Manthūr fī al-Tafsīr bi al-Ma'thūr*, vol. 6, pp. 250-251.

489 Ibn Hishām, *al-Sīrah al-Nabawiyyah*, vol. 2, p. 253.

490 Abū al-Fiḍā' Ismāʿīl ibn Kathīr, *Tafsīr al-Qur'ān al-ʿAẓīm*, Dār al-Kutub al-ʿIlmiyyah, Beirut (1419/1998), vol. 4, p. 28.

491 *al-Anfāl*, 19.

492 *al-Anfāl*, 47.

493 Ibn Jarīr al-Ṭabarī, *Jāmiʿ al-Bayān ʿan Ta'wīl Āy al-Qur'ān*, vol. 11, pp. 217-218.

494 *al-Anfāl*, 5-8.

495 Ibn Jarīr al-Ṭabarī, *Tārīkh al-Rusul wa al-Mulūk*, vol. 2, p. 436.

496 *al-Anbiyā'*, 30.

497 Muslim, *Ṣaḥīḥ Muslim*, p. 855.

498 *al-Anfāl*, 7.

499 Muslim, *Ṣaḥīḥ Muslim*, p. 1314.

500 A quote from *al-Mā'idah*, 24.

501 Ibn Hishām, *al-Sīrah al-Nabawiyyah*, vol. 2, pp. 257-258.

502 Ibn Hishām, *al-Sīrah al-Nabawiyyah*, vol. 2, p. 258.

503 *al-Ḥujurāt*, 13.

504 Al-Ḥākim al-Naysābūrī, *al-Mustadrak*, vol. 3, pp. 482-483.

505 Muslim, *Ṣaḥīḥ Muslim*, p. 843.

506 Ṭabarānī, *al-Muʿjam al-Kabīr*, vol. 10, p. 181.

507 Aḥmad ibn Ḥanbal, *Musnad al-Imām Aḥmad*, vol. 2, p. 299.

508 *al-Anfāl*, 11.

509 Ibn Kathīr, *Tafsīr al-Qur'ān al-ʿAẓīm*, vol. 2, p. 128.

510 *al-Anfāl*, 43.

511 *al-Mumtaḥanah*, 4.

512 Ibn Hishām, *al-Sīrah al-Nabawiyyah*, vol. 2, pp. 268-269.

513 Muslim, *Ṣaḥīḥ Muslim*, pp. 843-844.

514 *al-Anfāl*, 9.

515 *al-Qamar*, 45.

516 Ibn Kathīr, *Tafsīr al-Qur'an al-ʿAẓīm*, vol. 7, p. 446.

517 Al-Dhahabī, *Siyar Aʿlām al-Nubalā'*, vol. 1, p. 304.

518 Ibn Hishām, *al-Sīrah al-Nabawiyyah*, vol. 2, p. 265.

519 Ibn Jarīr al-Ṭabarī, *Tārīkh al-Rusul wa al-Mulūk*, vol. 2, p. 411.

520 Aḥmad ibn Ḥanbal, *Musnad al-Imām Aḥmad,* vol. 2, p. 260.

521 Ibn ʿAsākir, *Tārīkh Madīnah Dimashq,* vol. 38, p. 254.

522 Ibn Hishām, *al-Sīrah al-Nabawiyyah,* vol. 2, pp. 267-268.

523 Muslim, *Ṣaḥīḥ Muslim,* p. 917.

524 Muslim, *Ṣaḥīḥ Muslim,* pp. 917-918.

525 Aḥmad ibn Ḥanbal, *Musnad al-Imām Aḥmad,* vol. 2, p. 81.

526 Abū Bakr Aḥmad al-Bazzār, *al-Baḥr al-Zakhkhār,* Maktabah al-ʿUlūm wa al-Ḥikam, Medina (1409/1988), vol. 7, p. 254.

527 *al-Anfāl,* 9.

528 Bukhārī, *Ṣaḥīḥ al-Bukhārī,* p. 980.

529 Ibn Ḥajar al-ʿAsqalānī, *Fatḥ al-Bārī fī Sharḥ Ṣaḥīḥ al-Bukhārī,* vol. 6, p. 478.

530 *Maryam,* 25.

531 Muslim, *Ṣaḥīḥ Muslim,* p. 844.

532 Aḥmad ibn Ḥanbal, *Musnad al-Imām Aḥmad,* vol. 2, pp. 260-261.

533 Bukhārī, *Ṣaḥīḥ al-Bukhārī,* p. 774.

534 Bukhārī, *Ṣaḥīḥ al-Bukhārī,* pp. 774-775.

535 Ibn Hishām, *al-Sīrah al-Nabawiyyah,* vol. 2, pp. 277-278.

536 Aḥmad ibn Ḥanbal, *Musnad al-Imām Aḥmad,* vol. 6, p. 375.

537 Ibn Hishām, *al-Sīrah al-Nabawiyyah,* vol. 2, p. 273.

538 Ibn Hishām, *al-Sīrah al-Nabawiyyah,* vol. 2, p. 274.

539 *al-Mujādilah,* 22.

540 Bukhārī, *Ṣaḥīḥ al-Bukhārī,* p. 331.

541 Bukhārī, *Ṣaḥīḥ al-Bukhārī,* p. 976.

542 *al-Anfāl,* 1.

543 *al-Anfāl,* 41.

544 Bukhārī, *Ṣaḥīḥ al-Bukhārī,* p. 774.

545 Tirmidhī, *Sunan al-Tirmidhī,* vol. 6, p. 56.

546 Muslim, *Ṣaḥīḥ Muslim,* p. 844.

547 *Ibrāhīm,* 36.

548 *al-Mā'idah,* 118.

549 *Nūḥ,* 26.

550 *Yūnus,* 88.

551 Aḥmad ibn Ḥanbal, *Musnad al-Imām Aḥmad,* vol. 6, pp. 138-140.

552 Muslim, *Ṣaḥīḥ Muslim,* p. 844.

553 *al-Anfāl,* 67-69.

554 Ibn Jarīr al-Ṭabarī, *Jāmiʿ al-Bayān ʿan Ta'wīl Āy al-Qur'ān,* vol. 17, p. 400.

555 Al-Ḥākim al-Naysābūrī, *al-Mustadrak,* vol. 3, pp. 24-25.

556 Ibn Hishām, *al-Sīrah al-Nabawiyyah*, vol. 2, p. 287.

557 Ibn Hishām, *al-Sīrah al-Nabawiyyah*, vol. 2, p. 287.

558 Bukhārī, *Ṣaḥīḥ al-Bukhārī*, p. 614.

559 Al-Ḥākim al-Naysābūrī, *al-Mustadrak*, vol. 3, p. 367.

560 Al-Ḥākim al-Naysābūrī, *al-Mustadrak*, vol. 3, p. 367.

561 *al-Anfāl*, 70.

562 Abū Nuʿaym al-Iṣfahānī, *Dalā'il al-Nubuwwah*, Dār al-Nafā'is, Beirut (1406/1986), p. 477.

563 Ibn Hishām, *al-Sīrah al-Nabawiyyah*, vol. 2, p. 292.

564 Muslim, *Ṣaḥīḥ Muslim*, p. 866.

565 Bukhārī, *Ṣaḥīḥ al-Bukhārī*, p. 1121.

566 Ṭabarānī, *al-Muʿjam al-Kabīr*, vol. 17, p. 56.

567 Ibn Hishām, *al-Sīrah al-Nabawiyyah*, vol. 2, p. 302.

568 Ibn Hishām, *al-Sīrah al-Nabawiyyah*, vol. 2, p. 303.

569 Ṭabarānī, *al-Muʿjam al-Kabīr*, vol. 17, p. 57.

570 Ibn Hishām, *al-Sīrah al-Nabawiyyah*, vol. 2, p. 303.

571 Ṭabarānī, *al-Muʿjam al-Kabīr*, vol. 17, p. 57.

572 Ibn Hishām, *al-Sīrah al-Nabawiyyah*, vol. 2, p. 303.

573 Ibn Hishām, *al-Sīrah al-Nabawiyyah*, vol. 2, p. 303.

574 Ṭabarānī, *al-Muʿjam al-Kabīr*, vol. 17, p. 57.

575 Abū Dāwūd al-Sijistānī, *Sunan Abī Dāwūd*, Dār al-Risālah, Beirut (1430/2009), vol. 4, p. 616.

576 *al-Anfāl*, 58.

577 Ibn Hishām, *al-Sīrah al-Nabawiyyah*, vol. 3, p. 11.

578 ʿAbd al-ʿAzīz al-Ḥumaydī, *al-Tārīkh al-Islāmī: Mawāqif wa ʿIbar*, Dār al-Andalus, Riyadh (1418/1998), vol. 5, p. 32.

579 *al-Nūr*, 63.

580 Ibn Hishām, *al-Sīrah al-Nabawiyyah*, vol. 3, p. 10.

581 *al-Mā'idah*, 51.

582 *al-Mā'idah*, 52.

583 ʿAbd al-ʿAzīz al-Ḥumaydī, *al-Tārīkh al-Islāmī: Mawāqif wa ʿIbar*, vol. 5, p. 42.

584 *al-Baqarah*, 142.

585 Ibn Jarīr al-Ṭabarī, *Jāmiʿ al-Bayān ʿan Ta'wīl Āy al-Qur'ān*, vol. 7, p. 24.

586 *al-Nisā'*, 36-37.

587 Ibn Hishām, *al-Sīrah al-Nabawiyyah*, vol. 3, pp. 12-13.

588 Bukhārī, *Ṣaḥīḥ al-Bukhārī*, p. 990.

589 Bukhārī, *Ṣaḥīḥ al-Bukhārī*, p. 990.

590 Ibn Ḥajar al-ʿAsqalānī, *al-Iṣābah fī Tamyīz al-Ṣaḥābah*, vol. 8, p. 85.

591 Bukhārī, *Ṣaḥīḥ al-Bukhārī*, p. 1305.

592 *al-Anfāl*, 36.

593 Ibn Hishām, *al-Sīrah al-Nabawiyyah*, vol. 3, pp. 26-27.

594 Ibn Hishām, *al-Sīrah al-Nabawiyyah*, vol. 3, p. 26.

595 Ibn Hishām, *al-Sīrah al-Nabawiyyah*, vol. 3, p. 27.

596 Bukhārī, *Ṣaḥīḥ al-Bukhārī*, p. 1818.

597 Ibn Hishām, *al-Sīrah al-Nabawiyyah*, vol. 3, p. 27.

598 *Āl ʿImrān*, 166-167.

599 *al-Anfāl*, 37.

600 *al-Nisā'*, 88.

601 *Āl ʿImrān*, 122.

602 Ibn Jarīr al-Ṭabarī, *Tārīkh al-Rusul wa al-Mulūk*, vol. 2, p. 506.

603 Ibn ʿAsākir, *Tārīkh Madīnah Dimashq*, vol. 19, pp. 263-264.

604 Ibn Hishām, *al-Sīrah al-Nabawiyyah*, vol. 3, p. 29.

605 Bukhārī, *Ṣaḥīḥ al-Bukhārī*, p. 747.

606 Ibn Hishām, *al-Sīrah al-Nabawiyyah*, vol. 3, p. 30.

607 Ibn Jarīr al-Ṭabarī, *Tārīkh al-Rusul wa al-Mulūk*, vol. 2, p. 511.

608 Ibn Jarīr al-Ṭabarī, *Tārīkh al-Rusul wa al-Mulūk*, vol. 2, p. 511.

609 Ibn Hishām, *al-Sīrah al-Nabawiyyah*, vol. 3, p. 30.

610 Bukhārī, *Ṣaḥīḥ al-Bukhārī*, p. 993.

611 Ibn Hishām, *al-Sīrah al-Nabawiyyah*, vol. 3, p. 31.

612 Ibn Hishām, *al-Sīrah al-Nabawiyyah*, vol. 3, p. 47.

613 Bukhārī, *Ṣaḥīḥ al-Bukhārī*, p. 1000.

614 Ibn Jarīr al-Ṭabarī, *Jāmiʿ al-Bayān ʿan Ta'wīl Āy al-Qur'ān*, vol. 6, p. 130.

615 *Āl ʿImrān*, 152.

616 Ibn Jarīr al-Ṭabarī, *Jāmiʿ al-Bayān ʿan Ta'wīl Āy al-Qur'ān*, vol. 6, p. 147.

617 *Āl ʿImrān*, 153.

618 Ibn Jarīr al-Ṭabarī, *Tārīkh al-Rusul wa al-Mulūk*, vol. 2, p. 530.

619 Bukhārī, *Ṣaḥīḥ al-Bukhārī*, p. 810.

620 *Yūsuf*, 92.

621 Bukhārī, *Ṣaḥīḥ al-Bukhārī*, pp. 999-1000.

622 Abū ʿAbdullāh Muhammad al-Wāqidī, *Kitāb al-Maghāzī*, ʿĀlam al-Kutub, Beirut (1404/1988), vol. 1, p. 286.

623 Ibn Hishām, *al-Sīrah al-Nabawiyyah*, vol. 3, pp. 34-35.

624 Bukhārī, *Ṣaḥīḥ al-Bukhārī*, p. 1000.

625 Ibn Hishām, *al-Sīrah al-Nabawiyyah*, vol. 3, p. 36.

626 Ibn Hishām, *al-Sīrah al-Nabawiyyah*, vol. 3, pp. 35-36.

627 Al-Muttaqī al-Hindī, *Kanz al-ʿUmmāl fī Sunan al-Aqwāl wa al-Afʿāl*, Mu'assasah al-Risālah, Beirut (1405/1985), vol. 12, p. 377.

628 Bukhārī, *Ṣaḥīḥ al-Bukhārī*, p. 996.

629 Muslim, *Ṣaḥīḥ Muslim*, p. 862.

630 *Āl ʿImrān*, 128.

631 Bukhārī, *Ṣaḥīḥ al-Bukhārī*, p. 861.

632 Bukhārī, *Ṣaḥīḥ al-Bukhārī*, p. 922.

633 Ibn Jarīr al-Ṭabarī, *Tārīkh al-Rusul wa al-Mulūk*, vol. 2, p. 517.

634 Bukhārī, *Ṣaḥīḥ al-Bukhārī*, p. 994.

635 *al-Aḥzāb*, 23.

636 Al-Ḥākim al-Naysābūrī, *al-Mustadrak*, vol. 3, p. 298.

637 Bukhārī, *Ṣaḥīḥ al-Bukhārī*, pp. 993-994.

638 Ibn Jarīr al-Ṭabarī, *Tārīkh al-Rusul wa al-Mulūk*, vol. 2, pp. 524-525.

639 Ibn Hishām, *al-Sīrah al-Nabawiyyah*, vol. 3, p. 58.

640 *al-Naḥl*, 126.

641 Bukhārī, *Ṣaḥīḥ al-Bukhārī*, p. 1001.

642 *al-Raḥmān*, 3.

643 Aḥmad ibn Ḥanbal, *Musnad al-Imām Aḥmad*, vol. 24, pp. 246-247.

644 Bukhārī, *Ṣaḥīḥ al-Bukhārī*, p. 978.

645 Ibn Hishām, *al-Sīrah al-Nabawiyyah*, vol. 3, p. 62.

646 Ṭabarānī, *al-Muʿjam al-Awsaṭ*, vol. 7, p. 280.

647 *al-Anfāl*, 37.

648 *Āl ʿImrān*, 179.

649 *al-Anfāl*, 7.

650 *Āl ʿImrān*, 166-167.

651 Bukhārī, *Ṣaḥīḥ al-Bukhārī*, p. 1002.

652 Al-Dhahabī, *Siyar Aʿlām al-Nubalā'*, vol. 2, p. 205.

653 Muslim, *Ṣaḥīḥ Muslim*, p. 408.

654 Muslim, *Ṣaḥīḥ Muslim*, p. 408.

655 Bukhārī, *Ṣaḥīḥ al-Bukhārī*, p. 1005.

656 Bukhārī, *Ṣaḥīḥ al-Bukhārī*, p. 1004.

657 Ibn Hishām, *al-Sīrah al-Nabawiyyah*, vol. 3, p. 139.

658 Ibn Jarīr al-Ṭabarī, *Tārīkh al-Rusul wa al-Mulūk*, vol. 2, p. 547.

659 Bukhārī, *Ṣaḥīḥ al-Bukhārī*, p. 1003.

660 Abū al-Layth al-Samarqandī, *Baḥr al-ʿUlūm*, Dār al-Kutub al-ʿIlmiyyah, Beirut (1413/1993), vol. 3, p. 341.

661 Bukhārī, *Ṣaḥīḥ al-Bukhārī*, p. 1003.

662 Ibn Hishām, *al-Sīrah al-Nabawiyyah*, vol. 3, pp. 126-127.

663 Ibn Hishām, *al-Sīrah al-Nabawiyyah*, vol. 3, p. 127.

664 Bukhārī, *Ṣaḥīḥ al-Bukhārī*, p. 1431.

665 *al-Mā'idah*, 11.

666 Ibn Jarīr al-Ṭabarī, *Jāmiʿ al-Bayān ʿan Ta'wīl Āy al-Qur'ān*, vol. 22, p. 500.

667 *al-Ḥashr*, 11-12.

668 Ibn Saʿd, *al-Ṭabaqāt al-Kabīr*, vol. 2, p. 54.

669 *al-Ḥashr*, 5.

670 *al-Ḥashr*, 7.

671 *al-Ḥashr*, 7-8.

672 *al-Ḥashr*, 9.

673 *al-Ḥashr*, 10.

674 Ibn ʿAbd al-Barr, *al-Istiʿāb fī Maʿrifah al-Aṣḥāb*, Dār Hijr, Cairo (1440/2019), vol. 2, p. 431.

675 Al-Ḥākim al-Naysābūrī, *al-Mustadrak*, vol. 3, p. 180.

676 Al-Ḥākim al-Naysābūrī, *al-Mustadrak*, vol. 3, p. 181.

677 *al-Taghābun*, 15.

678 Abū Dāwūd al-Sijistānī, *Sunan Abī Dāwūd*, vol. 2, pp. 326-327.

679 Al-Ḥākim al-Naysābūrī, *al-Mustadrak*, vol. 3, p. 182.

680 *al-Aḥzāb*, 36.

681 Bukhārī, *Ṣaḥīḥ al-Bukhārī*, p. 1831.

682 *al-Aḥzāb*, 37.

683 Ibn Jarīr al-Ṭabarī, *Jāmiʿ al-Bayān ʿan Ta'wīl Āy al-Qur'ān*, vol. 19, pp. 115-116.

684 Muhammad ibn Aḥmad ibn Juzayy al-Kalbī, *al-Tashīl li ʿUlūm al-Tanzīl*, Dār al-Kutub al-ʿIlmiyyah, Beirut (1415/1995), vol. 2, p. 190.

685 Al-Qurṭubī, *al-Jāmiʿ li-Aḥkām al-Qur'ān*, vol. 17, p. 160.

686 Bukhārī, *Ṣaḥīḥ al-Bukhārī*, p. 1831; Tirmidhī, *Sunan al-Tirmidhī*, vol. 5, p. 264.

687 Al-Bayhaqī, *Dalā'il al-Nubuwwah*, vol. 3, pp. 375-376.

688 Yaḥyā ibn Sharaf al-Nawawī, *al-Minhāj bi Sharḥ Ṣaḥīḥ Muslim*, al-Maṭbaʿah al-Miṣriyyah, Cairo (1349/1930), vol. 11, p. 35.

689 Aḥmad ibn Ḥanbal, *Musnad al-Imām Aḥmad*, vol. 23, p. 271.

690 Bukhārī, *Ṣaḥīḥ al-Bukhārī*, pp. 579; 731-732; Aḥmad ibn Shuʿayb al-Nasā'ī, *Sunan al-Nasā'ī*, Dār al-Ḥaḍārah, Riyadh (1436/2015), p. 625.

691 Ibn Saʿd, *al-Ṭabaqāt al-Kabīr*, vol. 2, p. 60.

692 Abū Dāwūd al-Sijistānī, *Sunan Abī Dāwūd*, vol. 6, p. 75.

693 Abū Dāwūd al-Sijistānī, *Sunan Abī Dāwūd*, vol. 6, p. 75.

694 Muslim, *Ṣaḥīḥ Muslim*, pp. 1251-1252.

695 Muslim, *Ṣaḥīḥ Muslim*, p. 1200.

696 Abū Dāwūd al-Sijistānī, *Sunan Abī Dāwūd*, vol. 7, p. 441.

697 Ibn Jarīr al-Ṭabarī, *Tārīkh al-Rusul wa al-Mulūk*, vol. 2, p. 605.

698 Muslim, *Ṣaḥīḥ Muslim*, p. 1201.

699 *al-Munāfiqūn*, 1-11.

700 Tirmidhī, *Sunan al-Tirmidhī*, vol. 5, pp. 338-339.

701 Ibn Kathīr, *al-Bidāyah wa al-Nihāyah*, vol. 3, p. 158.

702 Ibn Kathīr, *al-Bidāyah wa al-Nihāyah*, vol. 3, p. 158.

703 Ibn Jarīr al-Ṭabarī, *Jāmiʿ al-Bayān ʿan Taʾwīl Āy al-Qurʾān*, vol. 22, p. 663.

704 Ibn Hishām, *al-Sīrah al-Nabawiyyah*, vol. 3, p. 239.

705 Bukhārī, *Ṣaḥīḥ al-Bukhārī*, p. 1016.

706 Bukhārī, *Ṣaḥīḥ al-Bukhārī*, p. 1017.

707 Bukhārī, *Ṣaḥīḥ al-Bukhārī*, p. 1017.

708 Bukhārī, *Ṣaḥīḥ al-Bukhārī*, p. 1019.

709 Bukhārī, *Ṣaḥīḥ al-Bukhārī*, p. 1019.

710 Bukhārī, *Ṣaḥīḥ al-Bukhārī*, p. 1017.

711 Bukhārī, *Ṣaḥīḥ al-Bukhārī*, p. 1189.

712 ʿAlī ibn ʿAlī al-Ghazzī, *al-Kawākib al-Durriyyah bi Sharḥ al-Barzakhiyyah*, Dār al-Kutub al-ʿIlmiyyah, Beirut (1441/2020), p. 137.

713 Bukhārī, *Ṣaḥīḥ al-Bukhārī*, p. 1188.

714 Bukhārī, *Ṣaḥīḥ al-Bukhārī*, p. 1188.

715 Bukhārī, *Ṣaḥīḥ al-Bukhārī*, p. 1019.

716 Bukhārī, *Ṣaḥīḥ al-Bukhārī*, p. 1018.

717 Muslim, *Ṣaḥīḥ Muslim*, p. 415.

718 Bukhārī, *Ṣaḥīḥ al-Bukhārī*, p. 1018.

719 *Yūsuf*, 18.

720 Bukhārī, *Ṣaḥīḥ al-Bukhārī*, p. 1019.

721 *al-Nūr*, 11-20.

722 *al-Nūr*, 22.

723 Ibn Qayyim al-Jawziyyah, *Zād al-Maʿād*, vol. 3, pp. 235-236.

724 *al-Layl*, 5.

725 Ibn Hishām, *al-Sīrah al-Nabawiyyah*, vol. 3, p. 166.

726 *al-Nisāʾ*, 51.

727 Ibn Hishām, *al-Sīrah al-Nabawiyyah*, vol. 3, pp. 171-172.

728 Bukhārī, *Ṣaḥīḥ al-Bukhārī*, p. 1006.

729 Bukhārī, *Ṣaḥīḥ al-Bukhārī*, p. 1006.

730 Bukhārī, *Ṣaḥīḥ al-Bukhārī*, pp. 701-702.

731 Al-Bayhaqī, *Dalā'il al-Nubuwwah*, vol. 3, p. 422.

732 Ibn Hishām, *al-Sīrah al-Nabawiyyah*, vol. 3, p. 170.

733 Bukhārī, *Ṣaḥīḥ al-Bukhārī*, p. 1008.

734 Al-Bayhaqī, *Dalā'il al-Nubuwwah*, p. 421.

735 Taqī al-Dīn Aḥmad al-Maqrīzī, *Imtāʿ al-Asmāʿ*, Dār al-Kutub al-ʿIlmiyyah, Beirut (1420/1999), vol. 1, p. 235.

736 Bukhārī, *Ṣaḥīḥ al-Bukhārī*, p. 704.

737 Al-Wāqidī, *Kitāb al-Maghāzī*, vol. 2, p. 457.

738 Ibn Hishām, *al-Sīrah al-Nabawiyyah*, vol. 3, p. 173.

739 Ibn Hishām, *al-Sīrah al-Nabawiyyah*, vol. 3, p. 173.

740 *al-Aḥzāb*, 10-11.

741 Ibn Hishām, *al-Sīrah al-Nabawiyyah*, vol. 3, pp. 173-174.

742 Al-Bayhaqī, *Dalā'il al-Nubuwwah*, vol. 3, pp. 430-431.

743 Ibn Hishām, *al-Sīrah al-Nabawiyyah*, vol. 3, p. 176.

744 Al-Maqrīzī, *Imtāʿ al-Asmāʿ*, vol. 6, p. 243.

745 Bukhārī, *Ṣaḥīḥ al-Bukhārī*, p. 1593.

746 Ibn Hishām, *al-Sīrah al-Nabawiyyah*, vol. 3, pp. 177-178.

747 Bukhārī, *Ṣaḥīḥ al-Bukhārī*, p. 931.

748 Bukhārī, *Ṣaḥīḥ al-Bukhārī*, pp. 1645-1646.

749 Ibn Hishām, *al-Sīrah al-Nabawiyyah*, vol. 3, p. 179.

750 Ibn al-Jawzī, *al-Muntaẓam fī Tārīkh al-Mulūk wa al-Umam*, vol. 3, p. 235.

751 Ibn Hishām, *al-Sīrah al-Nabawiyyah*, vol. 3, p. 179.

752 Al-Wāqidī, *Kitāb al-Maghāzī*, vol. 2, p. 497.

753 Al-Wāqidī, *Kitāb al-Maghāzī*, vol. 2, p. 485.

754 Muslim, *Ṣaḥīḥ Muslim*, p. 861.

755 Muslim, *Ṣaḥīḥ Muslim*, p. 861.

756 Al-Qurṭubī, *al-Jāmiʿ li Aḥkām al-Qur'ān*, vol. 17, p. 110.

757 Abū Dāwūd al-Sijistānī, *Sunan Abī Dāwūd*, vol. 2, p. 485.

758 Bukhārī, *Ṣaḥīḥ al-Bukhārī*, p. 723.

759 *al-Aḥzāb*, 9.

760 Ibn Jarīr al-Ṭabarī, *Tārīkh al-Rusul wa al-Mulūk*, vol. 2, p. 581.

761 Ibn Hishām, *al-Sīrah al-Nabawiyyah*, vol. 3, p. 184.

762 Muslim, *Ṣaḥīḥ Muslim*, p. 848.

763 Al-Suhaylī, *al-Rawḍ al-Unuf*, vol. 3, pp. 438-439.

764 Ibn Hishām, *al-Sīrah al-Nabawiyyah*, vol. 3, p. 186.

765 Ibn Jarīr al-Ṭabarī, *Tārīkh al-Rusul wa al-Mulūk*, vol. 2, p. 584.

766 Ibn Jarīr al-Ṭabarī, *Tārīkh al-Rusul wa al-Mulūk*, vol. 2, p. 585.
767 *al-Tawbah*, 102.
768 Al-Suyūṭī, *al-Durr al-Manthūr fī al-Tafsīr bi al-Ma'thūr*, vol. 4, p. 278.
769 Ibn Jarīr al-Ṭabarī, *Tārīkh al-Rusul wa al-Mulūk*, vol. 2, p. 586.
770 Ibn Hishām, *al-Sīrah al-Nabawiyyah*, vol. 3, p. 189.
771 Bukhārī, *Ṣaḥīḥ al-Bukhārī*, pp. 931-932.
772 Ibn Jarīr al-Ṭabarī, *Tārīkh al-Rusul wa al-Mulūk*, vol. 2, p. 588.
773 *Deuteronomy*, 20: 13-14.
774 Ibn Hishām, *al-Sīrah al-Nabawiyyah*, vol. 3, p. 191.
775 Al-Wāqidī, *Kitāb al-Maghāzī*, vol. 2, p. 516.
776 ʿAlī ibn Burhān al-Dīn al-Ḥalabī, *al-Sīrah al-Ḥalabiyyah*, Dār al-Kutub al-ʿIlmiyyah, Beirut (1432/2011), vol. 3, p. 245.
777 Ibn Ḥajar al-ʿAsqalānī, *al-Iṣābah fī Tamyīz al-Ṣaḥābah*, vol. 1, p. 526.
778 Bukhārī, *Ṣaḥīḥ al-Bukhārī*, p. 1070.
779 Bukhārī, *Ṣaḥīḥ al-Bukhārī*, pp. 1070-1071.
780 Bukhārī, *Ṣaḥīḥ al-Bukhārī*, p. 1071.
781 Al-Qurṭubī, *al-Jāmiʿ li Aḥkām al-Qur'ān*, vol. 15, p. 76.
782 *al-Fatḥ*, 27.
783 *al-Fatḥ*, 11-12.
784 Aḥmad ibn Ḥanbal, *Musnad al-Imām Aḥmad*, vol. 31, p. 212.
785 Bukhārī, *Ṣaḥīḥ al-Bukhārī*, p. 1026.
786 *al-Baqarah*, 58.
787 Ibn Saʿd, *al-Ṭabaqāt al-Kabīr*, vol. 5, p. 223.
788 Ibn Hishām, *al-Sīrah al-Nabawiyyah*, vol. 3, p. 257.
789 Bukhārī, *Ṣaḥīḥ al-Bukhārī*, p. 881.
790 Abū Dāwūd al-Sijistānī, *Sunan Abī Dāwūd*, vol. 4, p. 393.
791 *al-Fatḥ*, 24.
792 Ibn Jarīr al-Ṭabarī, *Tārīkh al-Rusul wa al-Mulūk*, vol. 2, p. 625.
793 Ibn Jarīr al-Ṭabarī, *Tārīkh al-Rusul wa al-Mulūk*, vol. 2, pp. 625-626.
794 Ibn Jarīr al-Ṭabarī, *Tārīkh al-Rusul wa al-Mulūk*, vol. 2, p. 626.
795 Ibn Hishām, *al-Sīrah al-Nabawiyyah*, vol. 3, pp. 258-259.
796 Ibn Jarīr al-Ṭabarī, *Jāmiʿ al-Bayān ʿan Ta'wīl Āy al-Qur'ān*, vol. 2, p. 521.
797 Al-Muttaqī al-Hindī, *Kanz al-ʿUmmāl fī Sunan al-Aqwāl wa al-Afʿāl*, vol. 1, p. 331.
798 Bukhārī, *Ṣaḥīḥ al-Bukhārī*, p. 671.
799 Al-Wāqidī, *Kitāb al-Maghāzī*, vol. 2, pp. 598-599.
800 Ibn Hishām, *al-Sīrah al-Nabawiyyah*, vol. 3, p. 259.
801 Ibn Hishām, *al-Sīrah al-Nabawiyyah*, vol. 3, p. 261.

802 *al-Fatḥ*, 18.

803 *al-Fatḥ*, 10.

804 Bukhārī, *Ṣaḥīḥ al-Bukhārī*, p. 1022.

805 Muslim, *Ṣaḥīḥ Muslim*, p. 1166.

806 Al-Muttaqī al-Hindī, *Kanz al-ʿUmmāl fī Sunan al-Aqwāl wa al-Afʿāl*, vol. 10, p. 483.

807 Bukhārī, *Ṣaḥīḥ al-Bukhārī*, p. 7.

808 Bukhārī, *Ṣaḥīḥ al-Bukhārī*, p. 672.

809 Bukhārī, *Ṣaḥīḥ al-Bukhārī*, p. 672.

810 Aḥmad ibn Ḥanbal, *Musnad al-Imām Aḥmad*, vol. 31, p. 219.

811 Bukhārī, *Ṣaḥīḥ al-Bukhārī*, p. 672.

812 Bukhārī, *Ṣaḥīḥ al-Bukhārī*, p. 672.

813 Ibn Hishām, *al-Sīrah al-Nabawiyyah*, vol. 3, p. 263.

814 Bukhārī, *Ṣaḥīḥ al-Bukhārī*, p. 672.

815 Bukhārī, *Ṣaḥīḥ al-Bukhārī*, pp. 1025-1026.

816 *al-Fatḥ*, 1.

817 *al-Fatḥ*, 1.

818 Aḥmad ibn Ḥanbal, *Musnad al-Imām Aḥmad*, vol. 1, pp. 336-337.

819 *al-Fatḥ*, 18-19.

820 *al-Fatḥ*, 25.

821 Ibn Hishām, *al-Sīrah al-Nabawiyyah*, vol. 3, pp. 268-269.

822 Ibn Hishām, *al-Sīrah al-Nabawiyyah*, vol. 3, p. 269.

823 Aḥmad ibn Ḥusayn al-Bayhaqī, *al-Sunan al-Kubrā*, Dār al-Kutub al-ʿIlmiyyah, Beirut (1424/2003), vol. 9, p. 381.

824 *Āl ʿImrān*, 54.

825 *al-Mumtaḥanah*, 10.

826 Ibn Hishām, *al-Sīrah al-Nabawiyyah*, vol. 3, p. 277.

827 Bukhārī, *Ṣaḥīḥ al-Bukhārī*, p. 104.

828 Ibn Saʿd, *al-Ṭabaqāt al-Kabīr*, vol. 2, p. 104.

829 Muslim, *Ṣaḥīḥ Muslim*, p. 1130.

830 Ibn Kathīr, *al-Bidāyah wa al-Nihāyah*, vol. 4, p. 185.

831 Ibn Saʿd, *al-Ṭabaqāt al-Kabīr*, vol. 2, p. 104.

832 Bukhārī, *Ṣaḥīḥ al-Bukhārī*, p. 1043.

833 Ibn Hishām, *al-Sīrah al-Nabawiyyah*, vol. 3, p. 287.

834 Ibn Kathīr, *al-Bidāyah wa al-Nihāyah*, vol. 4, p. 209.

835 Ibn Qayyim al-Jawziyyah, *Zād al-Maʿād*, vol. 3, p. 298.

836 *al-Fatḥ*, 19.

837 Ibn Hishām, *al-Sīrah al-Nabawiyyah*, vol. 3, p. 307.

838 Ibn Kathīr, *al-Bidāyah wa al-Nihāyah*, vol. 4, pp. 205-206.

839 Ibn Saʿd, *al-Ṭabaqāt al-Kabīr*, vol. 10, p. 119.

840 Abū Nuʿaym al-Iṣfahānī, *Dalā'il al-Nubuwwah*, p. 78.

841 *al-Ḥashr*, 23.

842 *al-Nisā'*, 171.

843 *Ṭā-Hā*, 47.

844 Al-Bayhaqī, *Dalā'il al-Nubuwwah*, vol. 2, p. 309.

845 *al-Rūm*, 1-3.

846 Muslim, *Ṣaḥīḥ Muslim*, p. 850.

847 Muslim, *Ṣaḥīḥ Muslim*, p. 851.

848 Muslim, *Ṣaḥīḥ Muslim*, p. 851.

849 *Ṭā-Hā*, 47.

850 *Āl ʿImrān*, 64.

851 Muslim, *Ṣaḥīḥ Muslim*, p. 851.

852 *Ṭā-Hā*, 47.

853 *Yā-Sīn*, 70.

854 Ibn Jarīr al-Ṭabarī, *Tārīkh al-Rusul wa al-Mulūk*, vol. 2, p. 654.

855 Ibn Jarīr al-Ṭabarī, *Tārīkh al-Rusul wa al-Mulūk*, vol. 2, p. 654.

856 Ibn Saʿd, *al-Ṭabaqāt al-Kabīr*, vol. 1, p. 224.

857 Ibn Kathīr, *al-Bidāyah wa al-Nihāyah*, vol. 4, p. 231.

858 Bukhārī, *Ṣaḥīḥ al-Bukhārī*, p. 444.

859 Muslim, *Ṣaḥīḥ Muslim*, p. 638.

860 Ibn Ḥajar al-ʿAsqalānī, *Fatḥ al-Bārī: Sharḥ Ṣaḥīḥ al-Bukhārī*, vol. 9, pp. 70-71.

861 Ibn Hishām, *al-Sīrah al-Nabawiyyah*, vol. 4, p. 8.

862 Ibn Kathīr, *al-Bidāyah wa al-Nihāyah*, vol. 4, pp. 234-235.

863 *al-Takwīr*, 8-9.

864 Ibn Kathīr, *al-Bidāyah wa al-Nihāyah*, vol. 4, p. 235.

865 Al-Wāqidī, *Kitāb al-Maghāzī*, vol. 2, p. 742.

866 Ibn Jarīr al-Ṭabarī, *Tārīkh al-Rusul wa al-Mulūk*, vol. 3, p. 30.

867 Ibn Jarīr al-Ṭabarī, *Tārīkh al-Rusul wa al-Mulūk*, vol. 3, p. 30.

868 Ibn Jarīr al-Ṭabarī, *Tārīkh al-Rusul wa al-Mulūk*, vol. 3, p. 31.

869 Ibn Jarīr al-Ṭabarī, *Tārīkh al-Rusul wa al-Mulūk*, vol. 3, p. 31.

870 Al-Bayhaqī, *Dalā'il al-Nubuwwah*, vol. 4, pp. 349-352.

871 Muslim, *Ṣaḥīḥ Muslim*, p. 66.

872 *al-Ḥadīd*, 10.

873 Bukhārī, *Ṣaḥīḥ al-Bukhārī*, p. 1044.

874 Ibn Saʿd, *al-Ṭabaqāt al-Kabīr,* vol. 2, p. 119

875 Ibn Saʿd, *al-Ṭabaqāt al-Kabīr,* vol. 2, p. 119

876 Aḥmad ibn Ḥanbal, *Musnad al-Imām Aḥmad,* vol. 3, pp. 431-432.

877 *Maryam,* 71.

878 Ibn Hishām, *al-Sīrah al-Nabawiyyah,* vol. 4, p. 12.

879 Ibn Jarīr al-Ṭabarī, *Tārīkh al-Rusul wa al-Mulūk,* vol. 3, p. 37.

880 Ibn Jarīr al-Ṭabarī, *Tārīkh al-Rusul wa al-Mulūk,* vol. 3, pp. 37-38.

881 Ibn Kathīr, *al-Bidāyah wa al-Nihāyah,* vol. 4, p. 244.

882 Aḥmad ibn Ḥanbal, *Musnad al-Imām Aḥmad,* vol. 43, p. 74.

883 Bukhārī, *Ṣaḥīḥ al-Bukhārī,* p. 1044.

884 Ibn Hishām, *al-Sīrah al-Nabawiyyah,* vol. 4, p. 18.

885 *al-Anfāl,* 15.

886 *al-Anfāl,* 16.

887 Ibn Kathīr, *al-Bidāyah wa al-Nihāyah,* vol. 4, p. 245.

888 Bukhārī, *Ṣaḥīḥ al-Bukhārī,* p. 922.

889 Bukhārī, *Ṣaḥīḥ al-Bukhārī,* p. 1044.

890 Bukhārī, *Ṣaḥīḥ al-Bukhārī,* p. 1044.

891 Aḥmad ibn Manẓūr al-Anṣārī, *Mukhtaṣar Tārīkh Dimashq,* Dār al-Fikr, Beirut (1404/1984), vol. 10, p. 95.

892 Aḥmad ibn Manẓūr al-Anṣārī, *Mukhtaṣar Tārīkh Dimashq,* vol. 10, p. 95.

893 Ibn Jarīr al-Ṭabarī, *Tārīkh al-Rusul wa al-Mulūk,* vol. 3, p. 45.

894 Ibn Kathīr, *al-Bidāyah wa al-Nihāyah,* vol. 4, p. 255.

895 Al-Suyūṭī, *al-Durr al-Manthūr fī al-Tafsīr bi al-Maʾthūr,* vol. 2, p. 742.

896 Muslim, *Ṣaḥīḥ Muslim,* pp. 837-838.

897 Aḥmad ibn Ḥanbal, *Musnad al-Imām Aḥmad ibn Ḥanbal,* vol. 29, pp. 298-299.

898 Al-Maqrīzī, *Imtāʿ al-Asmāʿ,* vol. 1, p. 345.

899 Ibn Kathīr, *al-Bidāyah wa al-Nihāyah,* vol. 4, p. 274.

900 Ibn Kathīr, *al-Bidāyah wa al-Nihāyah,* vol. 4, p. 279.

901 Ibn Hishām, *al-Sīrah al-Nabawiyyah,* vol. 4, p. 35.

902 Jaʿfar Abū al-Qāsim al-ʿAzāwī al-Ikīslī, *Mutʿah al-Anẓār fī Sharḥ Masraḥ al-Afkār ī Sīrah al-Nabī al-Mukhtār,* Dār al-Kutub al-ʿIlmiyyah, Beirut (1439/2018), vol. 2, p. 195.

903 Ibn Ḥajar al-ʿAsqalānī, *al-Maṭālib al-ʿĀliyyah bi Zawāʾid al-Masānīd al-Thamāniyyah,* Dar al-ʿĀṣimah, Riyadh, (1419/1998), vol. 17, p. 458.

904 Ibn Hishām, *al-Sīrah al-Nabawiyyah,* vol. 4, p. 36.

905 Ibn Hishām, *al-Sīrah al-Nabawiyyah,* vol. 4, p. 39.

906 Bukhārī, *Ṣaḥīḥ al-Bukhārī,* p. 1046.

907 Bukhārī, *Ṣaḥīḥ al-Bukhārī*, p. 1046.

908 Al-Muttaqī al-Hindī, *Kanz al-ʿUmmāl fī Sunan al-Aqwāl wa al-Afʿāl*, vol. 10, p. 524.

909 Bukhārī, *Ṣaḥīḥ al-Bukhārī*, p. 1046.

910 al-*Mumtaḥanah*, 1.

911 Muslim, *Ṣaḥīḥ Muslim*, p. 903.

912 Ibn ʿAbd al-Barr, *al-Istiʿāb fī Maʿrifah al-Aṣḥāb*, vol. 5, p. 439.

913 Ibn Ḥajar al-ʿAsqalānī, *Fatḥ al-Bārī fī Sharḥ Ṣaḥīḥ al-Bukhārī*, vol. 7, p. 95.

914 Tirmidhī, *Sunan al-Tirmidhī*, vol. 6, p. 108.

915 Ibn ʿAsākir, *Tārīkh Madīnah Dimashq*, vol. 26, p. 354.

916 Bukhārī, *Ṣaḥīḥ al-Bukhārī*, p. 245.

917 *al-Isrā'*, 90-93.

918 Al-Ḥākim al-Naysābūrī, *al-Mustadrak*, vol. 3, p. 46.

919 Al-Ḥākim al-Naysābūrī, *al-Mustadrak*, vol. 3, p. 46.

920 Al-Ḥākim al-Naysābūrī, *al-Mustadrak*, vol. 3, p. 47.

921 Ibn Hishām, *al-Sīrah al-Nabawiyyah*, vol. 4, p. 43.

922 Ibn Kathīr, *al-Bidāyah wa al-Nihāyah*, vol. 4, p. 289.

923 Ibn Hishām, *al-Sīrah al-Nabawiyyah*, vol. 4, p. 43.

924 Ibn Hishām, *al-Sīrah al-Nabawiyyah*, vol. 4, pp. 43-44.

925 Ibn Hishām, *al-Sīrah al-Nabawiyyah*, vol. 4, p. 44.

926 Abū Dāwūd al-Sijistānī, *Sunan Abī Dāwūd*, vol. 4, pp. 633-634.

927 Ibn Hishām, *al-Sīrah al-Nabawiyyah*, vol. 4, p. 45.

928 Al-Wāqidī, *Kitāb al-Maghāzī*, vol. 2, pp. 800-801.

929 Bukhārī, *Ṣaḥīḥ al-Bukhārī*, pp. 1047-1048.

930 Ṭabarānī, *al-Muʿjam al-Kabīr*, vol. 8, p. 14.

931 Ṭabarānī, *al-Muʿjam al-Kabīr*, vol. 8, p. 14.

932 Ibn Hishām, *al-Sīrah al-Nabawiyyah*, vol. 4, p. 51.

933 Ibn Jarīr al-Ṭabarī, *Tārīkh al-Rusul wa al-Mulūk*, vol. 3, pp. 57-58.

934 Bukhārī, *Ṣaḥīḥ al-Bukhārī*, p. 846.

935 Ibn Kathīr, *al-Bidāyah wa al-Nihāyah*, vol. 4, pp. 297-299.

936 Al-Dhahabī, *Siyar Aʿlām al-Nubalā'*, vol. 3, pp. 33-34.

937 Ibn Kathīr, *al-Bidāyah wa al-Nihāyah*, vol. 4, p. 298.

938 Al-Maqrīzī, *Imtāʿ al-Asmāʿ*, vol. 2, pp. 238-239.

939 Bukhārī, *Ṣaḥīḥ al-Bukhārī*, p. 39.

940 *al-Fatḥ*, 1.

941 Ibn Kathīr, *al-Bidāyah wa al-Nihāyah*, vol. 4, pp. 301-302.

942 *al-Isrā'*, 81.

943 Bukhārī, *Ṣaḥīḥ al-Bukhārī*, p. 825.

944 *Āl ʿImrān*, 67.

945 *Ḥujurāt*, 13.

946 Ibn Hishām, *al-Sīrah al-Nabawiyyah*, vol. 4, p. 54.

947 *Yūsuf*, 92.

948 Ibn Hishām, *al-Sīrah al-Nabawiyyah*, vol. 4, pp. 54-55.

949 *al-Raḥmān*, 60.

950 Ibn Hishām, *al-Sīrah al-Nabawiyyah*, vol. 4, p. 56.

951 Ibn Hishām, *al-Sīrah al-Nabawiyyah*, vol. 4, p. 56.

952 *al-Naṣr*, 2.

953 *al-Mumtaḥanah*, 12.

954 Ibn Jarīr al-Ṭabarī, *Tārīkh al-Rusul wa al-Mulūk*, vol. 3, p. 62.

955 Ibn Jarīr al-Ṭabarī, *Tārīkh al-Rusul wa al-Mulūk*, vol. 3, p. 62.

956 Muslim, *Ṣaḥīḥ Muslim*, p. 856.

957 Ibn Hishām, *al-Sīrah al-Nabawiyyah*, vol. 2, p. 89.

958 Muslim, *Ṣaḥīḥ Muslim*, p. 856.

959 Tirmidhī, *Sunan al-Tirmidhī*, vol. 3, p. 76.

960 Ibn Hishām, *al-Sīrah al-Nabawiyyah*, vol. 4, pp. 59-60.

961 Ibn Jarīr al-Ṭabarī, *Tārīkh al-Rusul wa al-Mulūk*, vol. 3, p. 63.

962 Ibn Jarīr al-Ṭabarī, *Tārīkh al-Rusul wa al-Mulūk*, vol. 3, p. 63.

963 Al-Dhahabī, *Siyar Aʿlām al-Nubalā'*, vol. 2, p. 565.

964 Al-Wāqidī, *Kitāb al-Maghāzī*, vol. 2, pp. 846-847.

965 Al-Wāqidī, *Kitāb al-Maghāzī*, vol. 2, p. 847.

966 Al-Wāqidī, *Kitāb al-Maghāzī*, vol. 2, p. 847.

967 Al-Wāqidī, *Kitāb al-Maghāzī*, vol. 2, p. 847.

968 Al-Ḥākim al-Naysābūrī, *al-Mustadrak*, vol. 3, p. 49.

969 Ibn ʿAsākir, *Tārīkh Madīnah Dimashq*, vol. 66, p. 327.

970 Ibn Hishām, *al-Sīrah al-Nabawiyyah*, vol. 4, pp. 73-74.

971 Bukhārī, *Ṣaḥīḥ al-Bukhārī*, p. 1061.

972 Ibn Kathīr, *al-Bidāyah wa al-Nihāyah*, vol. 4, pp. 315-316.

973 Bukhārī, *Ṣaḥīḥ al-Bukhārī*, p. 903.

974 Ibn Hishām, *al-Sīrah al-Nabawiyyah*, vol. 4, p. 84.

975 Ibn Hishām, *al-Sīrah al-Nabawiyyah*, vol. 4, pp. 82-83.

976 Ṭabarānī, *al-Muʿjam al-Kabīr*, vol. 8, p. 48.

977 *al-Aʿrāf*, 138.

978 Tirmidhī, *Sunan al-Tirmidhī*, vol. 4, pp. 49-50.

979 Abū Dāwūd al-Sijistānī, *Sunan Abī Dāwūd*, vol. 4, p. 156.

980 Muslim, *Ṣaḥīḥ Muslim*, pp. 1213-1214.
981 Ibn Hishām, *al-Sīrah al-Nabawiyyah*, vol. 4, p. 86.
982 Ibn Hishām, *al-Sīrah al-Nabawiyyah*, vol. 4, p. 89.
983 Bukhārī, *Ṣaḥīḥ al-Bukhārī*, p. 708.
984 Ibn Hishām, *al-Sīrah al-Nabawiyyah*, vol. 4, p. 89.
985 Ibn Kathīr, *al-Bidāyah wa al-Nihāyah*, vol. 4, p. 337.
986 Ibn Saʿd, *al-Ṭabaqāt al-Kabīr*, vol. 9, p. 15.
987 Al-Maqrīzī, *Imtāʿ al-Asmāʿ*, vol. 14, p. 24.
988 Ibn Saʿd, *al-Ṭabaqāt al-Kabīr*, vol. 2, p. 141.
989 Ibn Hishām, *al-Sīrah al-Nabawiyyah*, vol. 4, p. 101.
990 Bukhārī, *Ṣaḥīḥ al-Bukhārī*, p. 776.
991 Ibn Hishām, *al-Sīrah al-Nabawiyyah*, vol. 4, p. 138.
992 Bukhārī, *Ṣaḥīḥ al-Bukhārī*, p. 1059.
993 Aḥmad ibn Ḥanbal, *Musnad al-Imām Aḥmad*, vol. 18, p. 255.
994 Ṭabarānī, *al-Muʿjam al-Kabīr*, vol. 7, p. 180.
995 Bukhārī, *Ṣaḥīḥ al-Bukhārī*, p. 928.
996 Muslim, *Ṣaḥīḥ Muslim*, p. 1093.
997 Bukhārī, *Ṣaḥīḥ al-Bukhārī*, p. 679.
998 Bukhārī, *Ṣaḥīḥ al-Bukhārī*, p. 1524.
999 Aḥmad ibn Ḥanbal, *Musnad al-Imām Aḥmad*, vol. 11, p. 340.
1000 Bukhārī, *Ṣaḥīḥ al-Bukhārī*, pp. 888, 1064-1065.
1001 Bukhārī, *Ṣaḥīḥ al-Bukhārī*, p. 1065.
1002 *al-Tawbah*, 58-59.
1003 Al-Muttaqī al-Hindī, *Kanz al-ʿUmmāl fī Sunan al-Aqwāl wa al-Afʿāl*, vol. 13, p. 37.
1004 Muhammad Suhayl Ṭaqūsh, *Tārīkh al-Khulafāʾ al-Rāshidīn: al-Futūḥāt wa al-Injāzāt al-Siyāsiyyah*, Dār al-Nafāʾis, Beirut (1432/2011), p. 114.
1005 Al-Wāqidī, *Kitāb al-Maghāzī*, vol. 3, p. 1002.
1006 *al-Tawbah*, 117.
1007 Ibn Jarīr al-Ṭabarī, *Tārīkh al-Rusul wa al-Mulūk*, vol. 17, p. 51.
1008 Ibn Kathīr, *al-Bidāyah wa al-Nihāyah*, vol. 5, p. 9.
1009 *al-Tawbah*, 38-39.
1010 Tirmidhī, *Sunan al-Tirmidhī*, vol. 6, p. 69.
1011 Al-Ḥākim al-Naysābūrī, *al-Mustadrak*, vol. 2, p. 110.
1012 Abū Dāwūd al-Sijistānī, *Sunan Abī Dāwūd*, vol. 3, p. 108.
1013 Ibn Jarīr al-Ṭabarī, *Jāmiʿ al-Bayān ʿan Taʾwīl Āy al-Qurʾān*, vol. 11, pp. 589-596.
1014 *al-Tawbah*, 79.

1015 Muhammad al-Ṭāhir ibn ʿĀshūr, *Tafsīr al-Taḥrīr wa al-Tanwīr,* al-Dār al-Tūnisiyyah, Tunis (1429/2008), vol. 10, pp. 220-221.

1016 *al-Tawbah,* 49.

1017 *al-Tawbah,* 81-82.

1018 *al-Tawbah,* 42.

1019 *al-Tawbah,* 92.

1020 *al-Tawbah,* 91.

1021 Abū Dāwūd al-Sijistānī, *Sunan Abī Dāwūd,* vol. 4, p. 162.

1022 Bukhārī, *Ṣaḥīḥ al-Bukhārī,* p. 1081.

1023 Bukhārī, *Ṣaḥīḥ al-Bukhārī,* pp. 1081-1082.

1024 Abū al-Faraj ʿAbd al-Raḥmān ibn al-Jawzī, *Ṣayd al-Khāṭir,* Dār al-Qalam, Beirut (1441/2020), p. 148.

1025 Ibn Qayyim al-Jawziyyah, *al-Fawā'id,* Dār al-Kutub al-ʿIlmiyyah, Beirut (1434/2013), p. 74.

1026 *Āl ʿImrān,* 133.

1027 Aḥmad ibn Ḥanbal, *Musnad al-Imām Aḥmad,* vol. 20, p. 252.

1028 Tirmidhī, *Sunan al-Tirmidhī,* vol. 3, p. 488.

1029 Ibn Mājah, *Sunan Ibn Mājah,* p. 1420.

1030 *al-Tawbah,* 43.

1031 *al-Tawbah,* 46.

1032 Bukhārī, *Ṣaḥīḥ al-Bukhārī,* p. 1082.

1033 *al-Tawbah,* 44-45.

1034 Bukhārī, *Ṣaḥīḥ al-Bukhārī,* p. 1083.

1035 Bukhārī, *Ṣaḥīḥ al-Bukhārī,* p. 1083.

1036 *al-Tawbah,* 118.

1037 Bukhārī, *Ṣaḥīḥ al-Bukhārī,* p. 1083.

1038 *al-Tawbah,* 95.

1039 Bukhārī, *Ṣaḥīḥ al-Bukhārī,* p. 1084.

1040 Ibn Kathīr, *al-Bidāyah wa al-Nihāyah,* vol. 5, pp. 7-8.

1041 Ibn Hishām, *al-Sīrah al-Nabawiyyah,* vol. 4, p. 171.

1042 *al-Tawbah,* 107-110.

1043 Ibn Kathīr, *Tafsīr al-Qur'an al-ʿAẓīm,* vol. 4, pp. 186-187.

1044 Ibn Jarīr al-Ṭabarī, *Jāmiʿ al-Bayān ʿan Ta'wīl Āy al-Qur'ān,* vol. 14, p. 479.

1045 Ibn Taymiyyah, *al-Tafsīr al-Kabīr,* Dār al-Kutub al-ʿIlmiyyah, Beirut (1433/2012), vol. 7, p. 532.

1046 Ibn Kathīr, *Tafsīr al-Qur'ān al-ʿAẓīm,* vol. 4, p. 185.

1047 Ibn Kathīr, *al-Bidāyah wa al-Nihāyah,* vol. 5, p. 7.

1048 Al-Bazzār, *al-Baḥr al-Zakhkhār*, vol. 7, pp. 111-113.

1049 Ibn Hishām, *al-Sīrah al-Nabawiyyah*, vol. 4, pp. 167-168.

1050 Al-Bayhaqī, *Dalā'il al-Nubuwwah*, vol. 5, pp. 241-242.

1051 Bukhārī, *Ṣaḥīḥ al-Bukhārī*, pp. 1645-1646.

1052 Abū Dāwūd al-Sijistānī, *Sunan Abī Dāwūd*, vol. 1, p. 105.

1053 Bukhārī, *Ṣaḥīḥ al-Bukhārī*, p. 207.

1054 Ibn Hishām, *al-Sīrah al-Nabawiyyah*, vol. 4, p. 163.

1055 Ibn Hishām, *al-Sīrah al-Nabawiyyah*, vol. 4, p. 163.

1056 Ibn Jarīr al-Ṭabarī, *Jāmiʿ al-Bayān ʿan Ta'wīl Āy al-Qur'ān*, vol. 11, p. 545.

1057 *al-Tawbah*, 64.

1058 *al-Tawbah*, 65-66.

1059 *al-Tawbah*, 66.

1060 Ibn Jarīr al-Ṭabarī, *Jāmiʿ al-Bayān ʿan Ta'wīl Āy al-Qur'ān*, vol. 11, p. 545.

1061 Al-Bayhaqī, *Dalā'il al-Nubuwwah*, vol. 5, pp. 257-258.

1062 *al-Tawbah*, 74.

1063 Abū al-Ḥasan al-Khilaʿī, *al-Fawā'id*, Mu'assasah al-Rayyān, Beirut (1431/2010), p. 458.

1064 Bukhārī, *Ṣaḥīḥ al-Bukhārī*, p. 1241.

1065 *al-Baqarah*, 34.

1066 *al-Nisā'*, 145.

1067 Al-Qurṭubī, *al-Jāmiʿ li-Aḥkām al-Qur'ān*, vol. 10, p. 323.

1068 Al-Bayhaqī, *al-Sunan al-Kubrā*, vol. 8, p. 346.

1069 *al-Tawbah*, 80.

1070 Al-Bayhaqī, *al-Sunan al-Kubrā*, vol. 8, p. 347.

1071 *al-Tawbah*, 84.

1072 Bukhārī, *Ṣaḥīḥ al-Bukhārī*, p. 24.

1073 Ibn Hishām, *al-Sīrah al-Nabawiyyah*, vol. 4, p. 216.

1074 Al-Suyūṭī, *al-Durr al-Manthūr fī al-Tafsīr bi al-Ma'thūr*, vol. 7, p. 585.

1075 *al-Ḥujurāt*, 17.

1076 Muhammad ʿAjāj al-Khaṭīb, *Abū Hurayrah: Rāwiyah al-Islām*, p. 126.

1077 *al-Zukhruf*, 31.

1078 Ibn Saʿd, *al-Ṭabaqāt al-Kabīr*, vol. 1, p. 270.

1079 Ibn Saʿd, *al-Ṭabaqāt al-Kabīr*, vol. 1, p. 270.

1080 *Yā-Sīn*, 20-27.

1081 Ibn Kathīr, *al-Bidāyah wa al-Nihāyah*, vol. 5, p. 33.

1082 Ibn Hishām, *al-Sīrah al-Nabawiyyah*, vol. 4, p. 183.

1083 Abū Dāwūd al-Sijistānī, *Sunan Abī Dāwūd*, vol. 4, p. 637.

1084 Ibn Rajab al-Ḥanbalī, *Jāmiʿ al-ʿUlūm wa al-Ḥikam*, Dār Ibn Kathīr, Beirut (1429/2008), pp. 207-209.

1085 Bukhārī, *Ṣaḥīḥ al-Bukhārī*, p. 1072.

1086 Abū Dāwūd al-Sijistānī, *Sunan Abī Dāwūd*, vol. 4, p. 389.

1087 Bukhārī, *Ṣaḥīḥ al-Bukhārī*, p. 888.

1088 Bukhārī, *Ṣaḥīḥ al-Bukhārī*, p. 789.

1089 Bukhārī, *Ṣaḥīḥ al-Bukhārī*, p. 789.

1090 Aḥmad ibn Ḥanbal, *Musnad al-Imām Aḥmad*, vol. 29, p. 399.

1091 Al-Bayhaqī, *Dalā'il al-Nubuwwah*, vol. 5, p. 385.

1092 Ibn Jarīr al-Ṭabarī, *Jāmiʿ al-Bayān ʿan Ta'wīl Āy al-Qur'ān*, vol. 5, p. 172.

1093 *Āl ʿImrān*, 59.

1094 *Āl ʿImrān*, 67.

1095 *Āl ʿImrān*, 61.

1096 Ibn Ḥajar al-ʿAsqalānī, *al-Maṭālib al-ʿĀliyyah bi Zawā'id al-Masānīd al-Thamāniyyah*, vol. 18, p. 583.

1097 Muslim, *Ṣaḥīḥ Muslim*, p. 1094.

1098 Bukhārī, *Ṣaḥīḥ al-Bukhārī*, p. 315.

1099 Bukhārī, *Ṣaḥīḥ al-Bukhārī*, p. 792.

1100 Aḥmad ibn Ḥanbal, *Musnad al-Imām Aḥmad*, vol. 19, p. 359.

1101 Bukhārī, *Ṣaḥīḥ al-Bukhārī*, p. 539.

1102 Ṭabarānī, *al-Muʿjam al-Kabīr*, vol. 10, pp. 349-350.

1103 Bukhārī, *Ṣaḥīḥ al-Bukhārī*, pp. 597-598; pp. 1244-1245.

1104 *al-Aḥzāb*, 28-29.

1105 Muslim, *Ṣaḥīḥ Muslim*, p. 679.

1106 Muslim, *Ṣaḥīḥ Muslim*, p. 1098.

1107 Ibn Abī Ḥātim al-Rāzī, *Tafsīr al-Qur'an al-ʿAẓīm*, Maktabah Nizār Muṣṭafā al-Bāz, Riyadh (1417/1997), p. 1746.

1108 *al-Aʿrāf*, 28.

1109 *al-Aʿrāf*, 26-27.

1110 Al-Ḥākim al-Naysābūrī, *al-Mustadrak*, vol. 2, p. 361.

1111 *al-Tawbah*, 1-19.

1112 Ibn Jarīr al-Ṭabarī, *Jāmiʿ al-Bayān ʿan Ta'wīl Āy al-Qur'ān*, vol. 11, p. 316.

1113 Ibn Jarīr al-Ṭabarī, *Jāmiʿ al-Bayān ʿan Ta'wīl Āy al-Qur'ān*, vol. 11, p. 316.

1114 *al-Tawbah*, 5.

1115 *Āl ʿImrān*, 96-97.

1116 Muhammad Zakarīyyā Kāndhlawī, *Ḥajjah al-Widāʿ wa Juz' ʿUmrāt al-Nabī Ṣallā Allāh ʿAlayhi wa Sallam*, Dār al-Arqam, Beirut (1418/1997), p. 32.

1117 Bukhārī, *Ṣaḥīḥ al-Bukhārī*, p. 1077.
1118 *al-Baqarah*, 125.
1119 *al-Baqarah*, 158.
1120 Muslim, *Ṣaḥīḥ Muslim*, pp. 556-558.
1121 *al-Mā'idah*, 3.
1122 Bukhārī, *Ṣaḥīḥ al-Bukhārī*, p. 21.
1123 Bukhārī, *Ṣaḥīḥ al-Bukhārī*, pp. 419-420.
1124 Muslim, *Ṣaḥīḥ Muslim*, p. 1130.
1125 Bukhārī, *Ṣaḥīḥ al-Bukhārī*, pp. 1041-1042.
1126 Al-Wāqidī, *Kitāb al-Maghāzī*, vol. 3, p. 1117.
1127 Bukhārī, *Ṣaḥīḥ al-Bukhārī*, p. 805.
1128 Ibn Hishām, *al-Sīrah al-Nabawiyyah*, vol. 4, p. 290.
1129 *al-Zumar*, 30.
1130 *Āl ʿImrān*, 144.
1131 *al-Anbiyā'*, 34.
1132 Aḥmad ibn Ḥanbal, *Musnad al-Imām Aḥmad*, vol. 36, p. 376.
1133 *al-Naṣr*, 1-3.
1134 Bukhārī, *Ṣaḥīḥ al-Bukhārī*, p. 892.
1135 Bukhārī, *Ṣaḥīḥ al-Bukhārī*, p. 336.
1136 Al-Bayhaqī, *al-Sunan al-Kubrā*, vol. 6, p. 123.
1137 Ṭabarānī, *al-Muʿjam al-Kabīr*, vol. 18, p. 280.
1138 Ṭabarānī, *al-Muʿjam al-Kabīr*, vol. 18, p. 281.
1139 Bukhārī, *Ṣaḥīḥ al-Bukhārī*, p. 125.
1140 Bukhārī, *Ṣaḥīḥ al-Bukhārī*, p. 125.
1141 Bukhārī, *Ṣaḥīḥ al-Bukhārī*, p. 169.
1142 Bukhārī, *Ṣaḥīḥ al-Bukhārī*, p. 169.
1143 Bukhārī, *Ṣaḥīḥ al-Bukhārī*, p. 294.
1144 Bukhārī, *Ṣaḥīḥ al-Bukhārī*, p. 931.
1145 Muslim, *Ṣaḥīḥ Muslim*, p. 1316.
1146 Abū Dāwūd al-Sijistānī, *Sunan Abī Dāwūd*, vol. 7, pp. 464-465.
1147 Ibn Saʿd, *al-Ṭabaqāt al-Kabīr*, vol. 1, pp. 210-211.
1148 Bukhārī, *Ṣaḥīḥ al-Bukhārī*, p. 169.
1149 Bukhārī, *Ṣaḥīḥ al-Bukhārī*, p. 1092.
1150 Bukhārī, *Ṣaḥīḥ al-Bukhārī*, p. 1619.
1151 Bukhārī, *Ṣaḥīḥ al-Bukhārī*, pp. 1087-1088.
1152 Bukhārī, *Ṣaḥīḥ al-Bukhārī*, p. 1092.
1153 Bukhārī, *Ṣaḥīḥ al-Bukhārī*, p. 1088.

1154 Bukhārī, *Ṣaḥīḥ al-Bukhārī*, p. 1090.

1155 Ibn Jarīr al-Ṭabarī, *Tārīkh al-Rusul wa al-Mulūk*, vol. 3, p. 200.

1156 Bukhārī, *Ṣaḥīḥ al-Bukhārī*, p. 1091.

1157 *Āl ʿImrān*, 144.

1158 Ibn Mājah, *Sunan Ibn Mājah*, p. 520.

1159 Ibn Mājah, *Sunan Ibn Mājah*, p. 522.

1160 Ibn Saʿd, *al-Ṭabaqāt al-Kabīr*, vol. 2, pp. 280-281.

1161 Ibn Hishām, *al-Sīrah al-Nabawiyyah*, vol. 4, p. 308.

1162 Ibn Hishām, *al-Sīrah al-Nabawiyyah*, vol. 4, p. 310.

1163 Aḥmad ibn Ḥanbal, *Musnad al-Imām Aḥmad*, vol. 1, 199.

1164 Ibn Hishām, *al-Sīrah al-Nabawiyyah*, vol. 4, pp. 311-312.

1165 Ibn Abī al-ʿIzz, *Sharḥ al-ʿAqīdah al-Ṭaḥāwīyyah*, Mu'assasah al-Risālah, Beirut (1411/1990), vol. 2, p. 699.

1166 Ibn Kathīr, *al-Bidāyah wa al-Nihāyah*, vol. 5, p. 250.

1167 Ibn Taymiyyah, *Minhāj al-Sunnah al-Nabawiyyah*, Jāmiʿah al-Imām Muhammad ibn Saʿūd, Riyadh (1406/1986), vol. 1, pp. 486-493.

1168 Ibn Hishām, *al-Sīrah al-Nabawiyyah*, vol. 4, p. 312.

1169 *Āl ʿImrān*, 31.

1170 Muslim, *Ṣaḥīḥ Muslim*, p. 193.

1171 *al-Aḥzāb*, 56.

1172 *al-Isrā'*, 95.

Index

ʿAbdullāh ibn Ubayy ibn Salūl, 137, 214, 218–9, 227–9, 232, 253, 260, 262, 267, 381, 391, 401
ʿAbdullāh ibn ʿUmar, 45, 187, 230, 316, 362
ʿAbdullāh ibn Zayd, 169–70
ʿAbdullāh ibn al-Zubayr, 43
ʿAbdurraḥmān ibn ʿAqīl, 415
ʿAbdurraḥmān ibn ʿAwf, 10, 57–8, 88, 171, 202–4, 297, 362–3, 397
Abū ʿĀmir al-Fāsiq, 232
Abū ʿĀmir al-Rāhib, 232, 392
Abū Ayyūb al-Anṣārī, 167, 273
Abū Bakr al-Ṣiddīq, xiv, 15, 56, 119, 132, 168, 178, 245, 297, 301, 339, 344, 361, 398, 439, 446
Abū al-Barāʾ ʿĀmir ibn Mālik, 247
Abū Baṣīr, 311–2
Abū al-Bukhtarī, 198
Abū Dharr, 128
Abū Dujānah, 231–3, 282
Abū Hālah ibn Zurārah, 36
Abū al-Haytham ibn Tayyahān, 144
Abū Ḥudhayfah ibn ʿUtbah, 88
Abū Hurayrah, 178–9, 334, 407, 463, 480
Abū Jahl, 40–1, 68–72, 74, 81–5, 98–106, 110–1, 131, 151–3, 188–91, 198–206, 215–6, 356, 373, 407
Abū Jandal ibn Suhayl, 307–12
Abū Khaythamah, 390–91
Abū Lahab, 62–4, 70, 85, 104, 111–2, 134, 151, 189, 215
Abū Lubābah ibn ʿAbd al-Mundhir, 187, 289
Abū Quḥāfah, 67, 150, 242, 302, 361, 398, 440
Abū Rajāʾ al-ʿUṭāridī, 19
Abū Saʿīd al-Khudrī, 168, 230
Abū Salamah ibn ʿAbd al-Asad, 147
Abū Sufyān ibn Ḥarb ibn Umayyah, 347
Abū Sufyān ibn al-Ḥārith ibn ʿAbd al-Muṭṭalib, 368
Abū Ṭālib, 31, 37–8, 65–7, 72, 99, 104–11, 137, 293, 361
Abū ʿUbaydah ibn al-Jarrāḥ, 205, 241, 297, 339, 351
Abū Umayyah ibn al-Mughīrah, 42
Abū ʿUthmān al-Nahdī, 289
ʿĀd, 17, 73, 76

ʿAddās, 51, 115–6
Adhān, 80, 170, 255, 356, 408, 432–3
ʿAdnān, 17–21
Ahl al-Ṣuffah, 177–8, 247–51
Aḥmad, 4, 6, 444
Aḥzāb (Confederates), 282, 350
ʿĀ'ishah bint Abī Bakr, 39, 150, 266
Ākhirah, xiv, 10
Al-Akhnas ibn Shurayq, 118
Alḥamdulillāh, 5, 125, 138
ʿAlī ibn Abī Ṭālib, xiv, 9, 56, 62, 149, 162, 187, 195–6, 232, 269, 282, 297, 315, 328, 345, 363, 392, 426, 445
ʿAlī ibn al-Ḥusayn, 14
Allāhu Akbar, 102, 125, 138, 154, 210, 253, 278–82, 310, 315, 433
Al-Amīn, 161
Āminah bint Wahb, 23
ʿĀmir ibn al-Akwaʿ, 316
ʿĀmir ibn Fuhayrah, 152
ʿĀmir ibn Lu'ayy, 36
ʿĀmir ibn Rabīʿah, 88
ʿĀmir ibn Ṭufayl, 248–51
ʿAmmār ibn Yāsir, 59, 392, 400
ʿAmr ibn ʿAbasa, 59
ʿAmr ibn ʿAbd Wudd, 282
ʿAmr ibn al-ʿĀṣ, 8, 79, 85, 93, 330–31, 339
ʿAmr ibn Luḥayy al-Khuzāʿī, 18
ʿAmr ibn Sālim, 342
Anas ibn Mālik, 9, 11, 30, 241, 257, 417, 440, 442
Anas ibn al-Naḍr, 241
Al-Anṣār, 137
Apostasy Wars, 178, 238, 412
ʿAqabah, 113, 138–42, 145, 194, 358, 383
Al-ʿĀqib, name of the Prophet, 4
Al-Aqsa Mosque, 122–4, 131–2
Al-ʿArab al-ʿĀribah, 17
Al-ʿArab al-Bā'idah, 17
Al-ʿArab al-Bāqiyah, 17

Banū Najjār, 167
Banū Nawfal, 118
Banū Qaynuqāʿ, 217–8, 222, 292, 314
Banū Quḍāʿah, 339–40
Banū Qurayẓah, 253–4, 279–92
Banū Saʿd ibn Bakr, 29, 405
Banū Salamah, 162, 177, 229, 383, 385
Banū Shaybān, 135, 137
Banū Sulaym, 276, 368
Banū Thaqīf, 364, 367–9, 372
Al-Barā' ibn ʿĀzib, 187, 233, 277
Basmalah, 75, 424
Battle of Badr, 86, 111, 116, 155, 171, 183, 186, 194, 196, 205, 207, 210, 215, 224–5, 237, 245, 250, 268, 297, 305, 346–7, 358
Battle of Buʿāth, 137–8, 140, 143, 291
Battle of Dhāt al-Salāsil, 338
Battle of Ḥunayn, 153, 360–1, 364, 369, 372, 377, 405, 418
Battle of Khaybar, 207, 310, 314, 390, 418
Battle of Mu'tah, 46, 332, 336–7, 339
Battle of Qādisiyyah, 154
Battle of Sawīq, 220, 223, 292
Battle of the Trench (Khandaq), viii, 275, 282–3, 290, 293, 311, 314
Battle of Uḥud, viii, 50, 114, 142, 145, 209, 221, 225–6, 237, 244–6, 249, 258, 260
Battle of Yarmūk, 145, 357
Al-Bayhaqī, 336, 451, 457, 460, 462, 469, 471, 473–4, 480–2
Al-Bayt al-Maʿmūr, 127
Bishr ibn al-Barrā', 317
Bilal ibn Rabāḥ, 59, 79, 204
Bosra, 322
Boycott of Banū Hāshim, 208, 226
Buʿayd ibn ʿĀmir, 104
Budayl ibn Warqā', 299, 348
Al-Burāq, 123, 131
Buraydah ibn al-Ḥaṣīb, 260
Busr ibn Sufyān al-Khuzāʿī, 297

Ḥamnah bint Jaḥsh, 244, 268
Ḥamzah ibn ʿAbd al-Muṭṭalib, 63, 98, 237, 328
Ḥanīf, 20, 293, 411
Haram, 18, 33–4, 100, 165, 173–4, 190, 213, 228, 248, 300–1, 326, 342, 350, 352, 354, 385, 427
Ḥarām ibn Milḥān, 248
Al-Ḥārith ibn Hishām, 54, 356, 373
Al-Ḥārith ibn ʿUmayr al-Azdī, 332
Hārūn, 125, 393
Ḥasan ibn ʿAlī, 255
Ḥassān ibn Thābit, 79, 268, 416, 442
Hāshim, 21–3, 62–6, 98, 104–6, 111, 133, 143, 151, 188, 198, 208, 226
Ḥāṭib ibn Abī Baltaʿah, 344
Hawāzin, 33, 224, 364–8, 373–7, 405
Ḥawḍ, 7
Heraclius, 59, 321, 323
Hijaz, 139, 405
Ḥijr, 34, 216, 456, 469
Hijrah, 16, 50, 61, 82, 84, 88–9, 112, 146–56, 168, 178–9, 183, 220, 318, 374, 383, 401
Ḥilf al-Fuḍūl, 35
Hind bint ʿUtbah, 357
Hishām al-Kalbī, 38
Al-Ḥubāb ibn al-Mundhir, 195, 228
Hubal, 18–9, 242, 410
Ḥudhayfah ibn al-Yamān, 235, 285
Ḥulays ibn ʿAlqamah, 303
Ḥusayl ibn Jābir al-Yamān, 235
Ḥusayn ibn ʿAlī, 255, 428
Al-Ḥuwayrith ibn al-Nuqaydh, 352, 354
Ḥuyayy ibn Akhṭab, 253, 279, 284–5, 291, 318

ʿIbādah, 122
Iblīs, 109, 115, 385, 396, 402
Ibn al-Daghinah, 88–9
Ibn Ḥazm, 14, 28, 450
Ibn Hishām, vii, 16, 27, 54, 91, 111, 206, 311, 337, 356, 373, 451–83

Ibn Kathīr, 28, 196, 336, 346, 449–83
Ibn Khaldūn, 17
Ibn al-Qayyim, 242, 317, 337, 385
Ibn Saʿd, ix, 27, 337, 451–6, 462, 469, 472–83
Ibn Shihāb al-Zuhrī, 16, 311
Ibn Taymiyyah, 53, 451, 479, 483
Ibrāhīm, 6, 17–20, 23–4, 34, 39, 43–4, 76, 123–5, 129, 159, 184, 192, 208, 355, 395, 413–7, 427–9, 450, 465
Idrīs, 125
Iḥrām, 34, 296–7, 303, 309, 327–8, 429–31
Ijtihād, 250, 281, 338
ʿIkrimah ibn Abī Jahl, 8, 225–6, 282, 330, 352–3
Ilhām, 54
ʿIlhiz, 294
Īmān, 14, 82, 108, 123, 141, 144–6, 159, 171, 200, 226, 232, 243, 306, 309, 319, 357, 374, 387, 399, 405
ʿImrān ibn Ḥusayn, 413
InshāAllāh, 77, 367
Iqra', 50–1
ʿIshā', vii, 60, 169, 315, 367, 419, 431, 433, 439
Isḥāq, 24, 77, 413
Ismāʿīl, 17–24, 34, 414
Isnād, 16
Al-Isrā' wa al-Miʿrāj, 7, 55, 121–2, 169
Istinjā', 179

Jabal ʿAynayn, 230–1
Jābir ibn ʿAbdillāh, 142, 258, 428
Jābir ibn Samurah, 8
Jaʿfar ibn Abī Ṭālib, 88, 93–4, 317
Jāhiliyyah, 18, 36, 44–5, 236, 253, 432
Jaḥsh ibn Ri'āb, 88
Jamrah, 433
Jamīl ibn Maʿmar, 103
Janāzah, 243
Jesus Christ, 4, 95–6, 313, 414

People of the Book, 76, 176, 253, 275, 323, 325
Persian Empire, 137, 154, 337, 399, 448
Pledge of Divine Acceptance, 304–05, 311, 317

Qaḍā', 326, 330
Qahṭān, 17, 44
Qāri', 68, 452
Qasam, 7
al-Qaswā', 210, 298–9, 429, 433
Qatādah, 206, 239, 379, 388
Qays ibn Abī Ṣaʿṣaʿah, 195
Qiblah, 175–7, 430, 433
Qiṣāṣ, 317, 354
Qubā', 83, 161–2, 188, 227, 391–2
Qunūt al-nāzilah, 251
Quraysh, 8, 19, 21–3, 29, 33–41, 60–2, 65–70, 73–9, 82–5, 88–95, 99–100, 103–5, 108–12, 118, 131–8, 143–55, 161, 172–3, 181–3, 186–93, 195–8, 200–1, 204–7, 210–1, 213, 215, 220–1, 225–6, 229–36, 240–4, 252, 260, 275–6, 284–8, 291–314, 326–9, 331, 341–8, 351–9, 364–8, 374, 408, 410, 412, 419–20, 431, 445, 451, 456
Quṣayy ibn Kilāb, 21
Quss ibn Sāʿidah al-Iyādī, 20

Rabīʿah ibn ʿAbbād, 133
Rāfiʿ ibn Khadīj, 230
Rakʿāt, 60, 123, 169
Rasūl, 159
Ribā, 181, 410
Roman Empire, 61, 137, 321, 333, 337, 377–8, 392, 397–9
Al-Rubayyiʿ bint Muʿawwidh, 8
Rūḥ, 5, 7, 77–8
Ruqayyah bint Muhammad, 39, 88, 207, 210

Sabian, 103, 111, 145, 362
Ṣafiyyah bint ʿAbd al-Muṭṭalib, 58, 63
Ṣafiyyah bint Ḥuyayy, 39, 318
Ṣaḥābah, 10, 14, 452–4, 461, 467, 472

Notes

صلى
الله
عليه
وسلم

May the peace and
blessings of Allah
be upon him.